all the Young dudes

THE HOOPLE and IAN HUNTER

THE OFFICIAL BIOGRAPHY

by Campbell Devine

Forewords by
BRIAN MAY and JOE ELLIOTT

CHERRY
RED BOOKS

THE RED OAK PRESS LIMITED

For the musicians mentioned herein,
and all the people and new-found friends
I have met through their music.
Also in memory of Michael Ronson.

First published in 1998 by

CHERRY RED BOOKS
a division of Cherry Red Records Ltd
Unit 17, Elysium Gate West,
126–8 New King's Road
London sw6 3jh

E-mail: infonet@cred.demon.co.uk

in association with The Red Oak Press Ltd

A catalogue record for this book is available from the British Library.

ISBN 1 901447 05 7

Typeset in Adobe Garamond by Strathmore Publishing Services, London n7

Printed in Great Britain by Biddles Ltd, Guildford and King's Lynn

Ah, Mott The Hoople! Precursors of punk. Barons of Britrock. Quite simply one of popular music's most valuable and influential bands. Yes, Mott The Hoople! The first ever rock group to sell out a week of Broadway concerts in New York's theatreland and instigators of scenes likened to Beatlemania at the Royal Albert Hall, which caused rock music to be banned from that venue for some considerable time. Creators of *Mott* (number 2 in a recent retrospective chart), 'All the Young Dudes' (voted number 33 on Mojo magazine's All-Time Top 100 singles chart in 1997) and 1971's *Brain Capers*, the primer for punk rock six years later. Forget ye not 'Violence' and 'Crash Street Kidds' which brilliantly predicted and posted warning of a rising tide of social unrest in the UK.

'It's a mighty long way down rock 'n' roll!' Thus spake Ian Hunter in his classic 'All the Way from Memphis', and he was right. Herein lies the ballad of Mott The Hoople spanning over thirty years of musical accomplishment and covering all the players' backgrounds in unprecedented depth; the history of various Sixties pre-Mott groups, Hunter's early days in Hamburg alongside Tony Sheridan and Ritchie Blackmore and Mick Ronson's wizardry with David Bowie, through the heady days of Ziggy Stardust. The book traces Mott The Hoople's formation, their work with Bowie on *All the Young Dudes*, their rise to international stardom and beyond, including offshoots such as Mick Ralphs' Bad Company, Mott, British Lions plus Hunter and Ronson's solo careers and collaborations with Van Morrison, Bob Dylan and Morrissey.

Devoid of borrowed information and the usual re-cycled press clippings, this official biography contains new, sensational and humorous inside stories, controversial quotes and an array of private and previously unpublished views from the band, embellished with comprehensive appendices including discographies and session listings.

The author has collaborated with vocalist Ian Hunter and all of Mott's founder members – drummer Dale Griffin, bass player Overend Watts, organist Verden Allen and original lead guitarist Mick Ralphs – who have provided their own anecdotes, photographs and memorabilia to illustrate and enhance the project. There are further personal contributions from Luther Grosvenor, Morgan Fisher, Stan Tippins, Diane Stevens, Muff Winwood, Ray Major, John Fiddler, Blue Weaver, Miller Anderson, Sixties' rocker Freddie 'Fingers' Lee and many other sources close to Hunter and the group.

Queen, theClash, Kiss, Def Leppard, Motley Crue, REM, Primal Scream and Oasis have all cited Mott and Hunter as important influences. It is fitting, therefore, that Hoople fans Joe Elliott and Brian May, have provided their own forewords, paying long overdue and worthy tributes on behalf of the music industry.

Already described as the 'definitive tome' on their careers, this unique and fascinating biography is by far the most scrupulously researched written work ever produced on Mott the Hoople, Hunter and Ronson. It will be welcomed by both the committed and casual rock reader, and by all Dudes, young and post-young!

Contents

List of Illustrations

The illustrations are placed between pages 334 and 335

viii ALL THE YOUNG DUDES

Foreword

Brian May

Hey!

Mott The Hoople were the first Rock 'n' Roll band we ever knew. I don't mean ever heard, or heard *of* – because we'd heard loads, by the time we precocious young boys of 'Queen' started out into the world. I mean this was the first Real Band we ever were close enough to touch, smell and share our lives with. I vividly remember the first day we turned up to the rehearsal theatre for the tour we were about to embark on, as support group to Mott (the only time Queen *ever* supported anyone). We were pretty full of ourselves, and probably already felt we knew it all – we knew the theory, we had made our first album and we were fast discovering our own style in music, ethos, clothes and staging. But as we surveyed the excitingly huge amount of gear on the Mott stage, up strolled the Band. They looked 'The Business' – they were obviously It, seemingly without trying. They appeared as an agglomeration of bright colours, bizarre shapes, scarves, leather, sunglasses, velvet, huge boots, strange felt hats, blending seamlessly into the masses of hair, beer bottles, fags, battered guitar cases covered with stickers and *swagger*. They looked lived-in; they exuded Attitude and easy humour and the utter confidence born of 'Knowing you are Good'. They were.

They were friendly to us and courteously treated their warm-up group as equals from the start, but in the following months, as we toured Britain and the USA with them, I was always conscious that we were in the presence of something great, something highly evolved, close to the centre of the Spirit of Rock and Roll, something to breathe in and learn from.

Travelling a lot together, we soon learned the Mott language as we shared countless buses ('It was *open*, Stan I'm starving!!!'), planes (Esheven Lags this tour, Rog ...), hotel bars ('Raging Pits'), shopping expeditions (to the Shawn Pops!) and philosophical discussions. I vividly remember Ian's advice to me, late one night, realising I was missing my home comforts, ('If you need your things around you, Brian, you're in the wrong business' – he was right....). I remember Ariel Bender and Morgan Fisher crashing through my hotel door as one body, with a bevy of beauties in tow, with the cry 'looking for a bit of head, Bri?!' (I was too shy). I remember the whole world of rock and roll girls Mott attracted and felt so at home with – they became a big part of our world too. I remember standing around back-of-stage in an arena in Memphis, seeing the place erupt to the first chords of 'All the Way from Memphis', truly a great moment of re-connection to the original capital city of White Rock. I remember the night-long party afterwards in a Holiday Inn on the banks of the steamy Mississippi, a scene comparable with the Pirates of the Caribbean ride in Disneyland, with a seamingly endless traffic of revellers in and out of everybody's rooms ... and a lady who said, 'I'm going to make you a Rock Star.' And so much more.

Oh, and there was the Music! We worked our butts off on the tour, with great success; luckily for us most of the Mott fans took to our style. But there was never any doubt who was the Headline Act. Mott would swing relentlessly and unstoppably into their show every night, like a marauding band of outlaws and every night there was something close to a riot – the kids couldn't get close enough to the stage – they simply couldn't get enough. Every night the legendary Silver-Cross-Painted-on-Chest Overend Watts would be winched on stage in his impossibly high boots, to thunder deafeningly, and menace the audience from on high. Ian Hunter (the unwritten Boss) would plant himself centre stage behind his shades and *dare* anyone to remain seated, pianos would be pushed off stage, amps would be thrashed, dedicated roadies would scuttle tensely across the stage, always aware of the possibility that the strong and silent Buffin would suddenly lose his rag and trash the drum kit over their heads. Ariel Bender played – screamed – on guitar, with his whole body and spirit, rushing around the entire stage, on his feet, on his back, guitar behind head, or held aloft or however the mood took him – an inspiration.

And it *rocked.* It was raw, fun, angry, glorious, jagged. It was everything except normal or predictable.

All things must pass. Mott The Hoople passed away much too soon. But it all lives on in our heads. And in the surviving recordings there are hints, echoes of those days of Danger and Wonder.

God bless 'em!

BRIAN MAY
London, 1998

Foreword

Joe Elliott

The memory, as time goes by, plays tricks on us, which is why it's difficult for me to pinpoint the exact moment when I realised Mott The Hoople was the greatest rock 'n' roll band ever.

It was either hearing 'The Original Mixed Up Kid' on a friend's compilation album (*El Pea*) or sneaking a listen to 'Record of the Week' ('Downtown') on Radio Luxembourg when I was supposed to be asleep! I think I was ten years old then, but it was some time after the event that I really got hooked. Yes, I'd heard the singles, yes, I'd seen the band on *Top of the Pops*, but it wasn't until 1975 (after they'd split!), whilst queueing for lunch at Shannington College, Sheffield, that the familiar rings of an 'unknown' song caught my ear. A kid a year above me was stood five feet behind me singing 'Drivin' Sister'. 'I know that song!' – 'Well, you should,' he said, 'it's Mott The Hoople. Best band ever!'

You see, for years I'd had a battered vinyl copy of *Mott* with *no* labels and scratched to hell to the point where 'Drivin' Sister' and 'Violence' were the only two playable tracks. I had no idea who the band was! It has to be one of the strangest re-introductions to a group ever.

Since then of course, things got a lot better. I spent years freaking out as all the original albums were finally released on CD. I abused my 'celebrity status' to the maximum listening to unreleased Mott The Hoople material courtesy of Peter Overend Watts. I followed the band's splintered careers with a passion. I really dug the 'Nigel Benjamin' Mott (sorry Ian!). I saw British Lions, Hunter Ronson and Ian Hunter live so many times I've lost count. I joined Ian on stage on numerous occasions and shared the honour of Def Leppard performing 'All the Young Dudes' with Hunter. I guess you could call me the ultimate male groupie!

But it's music that counts and *Mott the Hoople made music!* Some songs just breeze past you, others make the hairs on the back of your neck stand up. I can't think of many Mott songs that don't do the latter. From the crashing guitars of 'Rock And Roll Queen' to the haunting 'Through The Looking Glass', from the autobiographical 'Ballad of Mott The Hoople' to the sad lament of 'Saturday Gigs', which still brings a tear to my eye.

My biggest regret is that I never saw Mott The Hoople live. I witnessed every other incarnation but not the original. Still, regrets are few when it comes to Mott because the pleasure that they have given me and countless thousands of others, outweighs all. Anyone who knows me knows I was weaned on Bowie and Bolan but the best was always, and will always be, Mott The Hoople.

Having had the opportunity to read sections of this official biography prior to publication, I was amazed but also thrilled to discover things I didn't know about Mott and Hunter on almost every page, so I know you are in for a damn good read. This book is the perfect companion for some of the best music *ever* to come out of rock 'n' roll.

Nice one, Mott The Hoople! Shame you weren't around for a little longer.

JOE ELLIOTT
Los Angeles, 1998

Acknowledgements

The author and publishers would like to give sincere thanks to the following, who gave assistance and contributed personally to this project:

Verden Allen, Miller Anderson, Richie Anderson, Hugh Attwooll, Ariel Bender, Jet Black, Tony Brainsby, Patrick Brooke, Buffin, Mel Bush, Fred Cheeseman, Tim Clarke, Jeff Dexter, Richard Digby-Smith, Joe Elliott, John Fiddler, Morgan Fisher, Pete Frame, Dale Griffin, Luther Grosvenor, Ian Hunter, Trudi Hunter, Steve Hyams, Paul Jeffery, Ray Laidlaw, Alec Leslie, Ray Major, Willard Manus, Benny Marshall, Brian May, Les Norman, Mick Ralphs, Mick Rock, Mick Ronson, Maggi Ronson, Peter Sanders, Johnny Smack, Diane Stevens, Dave Tedstone, Billy Thunder, Stan Tippins, Lord Peter Overend Watts, Blue Weaver, Muff Winwood, Roy Wood, Trevor Wyatt.

They also thank and acknowledge the following:

BBC Radio One, Andy Basire, Kevin Cann, Deb and Little H for undying patience, Martin Colley, Andrew Darlington, Steve Davis & Chrysalis Records, Ray Fox Cumming, Kris Gray, Sven Gusevik, Mark Hagen, Bob Harris, Martin Hayman, Bill Henderson, Island Records, George Jamieson & Gary Jones, Jo Murphy and Brian O'Reilly, Norsk Plateproduksjon, Paul O'Mahony, John McDermott, Mojo, Alan Price & Demon Records, Justin Purington, Q, Record Collector, Martin Roach, Carlton Sandercock, Charles Shaar Murray, Sony Music, Windsong Records, Ray Zell, Zig Zag.

The publishers acknowledge the following for permission to reproduce lyrics in the text:

Blue Mountain Music, Island Music Ltd, EMI Songs Ltd, April Music Inc., Spiv Music, PRI Music Inc. / Jesse John Music Inc., News Music BMI, Mick Ronson Music Inc., Kehr Bros. BMI, Necessary/Maxwood/Maxwood, Jesse John Music and Island Music Inc. / Warner Tamerelane Publishing Corp. BMI.

Every effort has been made to contact copyright holders: if any have been inadvertently omitted, the publishers will be pleased to make the proper acknowledgement at the earliest opportunity.

* * *

In 1991, I was urged to compile a 'new' article on Mott The Hoople. Eventually, I surrendered and interviewed the elusive Verden Allen and that November 1992 evening in Hereford became the launchpad for this project, a personal 'journey' that I had wanted to attempt for years. The road has been interesting, to say the least, confirming that the outside world is permitted to see one aspect of the music business – the positive side. Fans and record-buying public alike are sheltered from the darker, negative elements and so, whilst I have tried to document 'stories told and untold', I have also respected the 'code of the road'. Some of the Ballad of Mott The Hoople and Ian Hunter therefore remains unsung, and it will remain that way. I have far too much respect and affection for the players and participants to do otherwise. In any case, there are differing recollections and some interesting contradictions in this complex tale, so it will be fun to read between the lines.

This project is meant to appeal to 'students' of Mott The Hoople and Ian Hunter and to the casual music fan; hopefully that dual mission has been achieved. The biography is a companion to Sony Music's new Mott the Hoople CD set: *All the Young Dudes – The Anthology.*

It has been a privilege to have such a close and unprecedented first-hand view of the musicians, their music and history. I extend extra special thanks to Ian Hunter, Dale Griffin (for flying the Mott flag – always), the incredible Pete Watts, Verden Allen, Mick Ralphs, Stan Tippins, Luther Grosvenor, Morgan Fisher, Ray Major, John Fiddler, Steve Hyams, Richard Digby-Smith, Miller Anderson, Freddie 'Fingers' Lee, Richie Anderson and Benny Marshall – who aided and abetted me, beyond the call of duty, to make this biography possible. Hunter, Watts, Griffin and Allen deserve special mention for their unyielding support. My gratitude to Brian May and Joe Elliott, for writing such stunning forewords, is also immeasurable.

I would also like to thank Carlton Sandercock (who paved the way to Cherry Red Books), Iain McNay and Ian Carlile of Cherry Red for their faith, Nicholas Jones of Strathmore, who took care with type and photographs, and Hugh Attwooll of Sony Music, who helped me down the home straight on this project.

I could not have completed this biography without the unbelievable patience of my family. I am indebted to them, and now promise to make up for lost time.

By no means least, thank you to one of the nicest individuals I ever met, Mick Ronson.

CAMPBELL DEVINE
London, August 1998

Introduction

Mott the Hoople was one of the world's most exciting and innovative rock groups, from their formation in June 1969 to their demise in December 1974, when Hunter Ronson departed to form their own band and Watts, Griffin and Fisher re-grouped as Mott.

The band originated in Herefordshire where guitarist Peter Watts and drummer Terry Griffin met at school and played in various groups throughout the sixties, before linking up with guitarist Mick Ralphs and organist Terry Allen to form Silence. They auditioned for legendary producer Guy Stevens and, via a music paper advertisement, secured the services of pianist and lead vocalist Ian Hunter Patterson.

Taking their name from a Willard Manus novel, Mott The Hoople signed to Guy Stevens and Island Records, recording four crazed but crucial albums between 1969 and 1971. Their material varied considerably in style, between the writing of Hunter and Ralphs and the harder edge of LPs such as *Mad Shadows* and *Brain Capers*, to the softer, 'country' tone of *Wildlife*. These early records received wide critical acclaim and, although they failed to sell in quantity, Mott The Hoople became one of Britain's most successful live acts. As Mott's career progressed, the red-maned and shaded Hunter was recognised as one of rock music's most distinctive vocalists and impressive songwriters, and visually, to many, the embodiment of rock and roll. Combining the swagger of The Rolling Stones with the poetic fervour of Bob Dylan, delivered with Hunter's anglicised vocals, Mott The Hoople mixed tenderness and toughness with irony and compassion.

An inexplicable lack of record sales eventually meant that the group struggled to maintain a viable cashflow and they split during a European tour in March 1972. However, David Bowie, who was a secret fan of the band and admirer of Hunter's on-stage persona, wrote a classic single for them, 'All the Young Dudes', and produced an album. Armed with their first ever hit and a stronger belief in their abilities, Mott The Hoople were rejuvenated and went on to produce a total of seven hit singles and four chart albums for CBS/Columbia Records. *Mott,* issued in 1973, is still regarded as one of the classic rock albums of the seventies. Encouraged by Bowie, Ian Hunter assumed leadership of Mott The Hoople, which eventually was to cost them the services of Verden Allen and Mick Ralphs. For the second half of their first headlining tour of the USA in September 1973, Hunter recruited Ariel Bender, formerly Luther Grosvenor of Spooky Tooth, to replace Ralphs on lead guitar and subsequently engaged Morgan Fisher, ex-Love Affair, on keyboards.

This line-up achieved increased commercial success and, in 1974, Mott the Hoople became the first-ever rock act to appear on Broadway playing a week of sell out concerts in New York's theatreland. However, the Ariel Bender association did not work out and the band was considering splitting again, until Mick Ronson joined in late 1974. On paper, the combined potential of Mott The Hoople and Ronson was awesome but, during their first European concert dates, a split started to develop in the ranks and, within a month, Mott The Hoople had ceased to exist when Ian and Mick, decided to leave the group.

Post-Hoople, Watts, Griffin and Fisher formed Mott, recorded two CBS albums and then re-grouped as British Lions in 1977 for a further two LPs before largely disappearing from the music scene. Ian Hunter has released ten commercially intriguing and stylistically varied solo albums since 1975 and is still recording and touring. Many of his projects featured Ronson, with whom Hunter worked regularly until Mick's tragic death from cancer in 1993.

Mott The Hoople remain astonishingly influential almost thirty years after their birth. For over two decades, they have been cited as a major inspiration by a host of contemporary music's biggest and most successful names – Queen, Kiss, The Clash, Motley Crue, Def Leppard, REM, Primal Scream to name but a few. Many recent Britpop bands, Oasis and Blur included, also bear more than a passing resemblance to Mott The Hoople. Several of Hunter's compositions have been covered by artists as diverse as Barry Manilow, Willie Nelson, Status Quo, Brian May, The Pointer Sisters and Great White and charted as significant hits. The quality of Ian's writing throughout his career has been honest and uncompromising and today he remains one of very few creditable rock artists, both in terms of studio and live performance.

Precursors of punk, Mott The Hoople's impact on late seventies music was enormous and probably greater than any other band preceding that era. 'The Moon Upstairs', from their 1971 *Brain Capers* album, set the musical tone for the 'New Wave' six years later and 'Crash Street Kidds', from 1974's *The Hoople* LP, predicted the onslaught, all with a style and attack that rendered the new movement tame, clumsy and lacking in real lyrical substance or musical credit. Ian Hunter's percipience and lyrical foresight was unmatched by any other early seventies rock composer.

Whilst many will claim that Mott The Hoople were not the world's greatest band in technical terms, they were, without question, one of the most innovative and valuable. They strived to capture their true spirit on tape, but, in hindsight, were ahead of their time, and perhaps so different musically that they were virtually unrecordable using seventies technology and the dead studio sounds of that period. 'We never learned much about Mott The Hoople,' says Ian Hunter. 'Part of the charm of Mott The Hoople was that nobody within it knew anything about it. The sound came because we really didn't know that much.'

The beginnings of Mott The Hoople go back to the early sixties, when a guitarist and drummer first met in Ross-on-Wye, near Hereford, and subsequently formed a series of bands including Silence, The Buddies, The Doc Thomas Group and The Shakedown Sound. This early period, and some of the Mott The Hoople story is sketchy. Drummer and founder member, Dale Griffin, regards the history of the band as impenetrably complex and subject to personal memory and bias. Numerous events and external influences worked on the group – wives, girlfriends, families, friends, managers and record company people.

This biography, with personal input from all the players, traces the story of Mott The Hoople and Ian Hunter from their early days, through their rise to international stardom and beyond. Peppered with previously untold tales from all the group members, it's a story of determination versus adversity, triumph and tribulation, rapture and rupture, strut and stumble. It's a unique and exciting musical journey. It's a mighty long way down rock and roll!

1
It's a mighty long way
down rock and roll

'All the Way from Memphis' – Ian Hunter

The early sixties were an interesting and crucial watershed for society and popular music in Britain. Car ownership, a relative luxury in the 1950s, weekly earnings and the number of students in higher education were all increasing rapidly. The Conservative Prime Minister, Harold Macmillan, resigned in 1963, the year of the Great Train Robbery, after the notorious Profumo sex scandal and, by 1964, Harold Wilson led the Labour Party to victory, promising increased social change.

Music was changing, too. The wilder fifties rock and roll vocalists like Jerry Lee Lewis and Little Richard were on the wane, and while the British album charts were led by an assortment of film soundtracks, Cliff Richard and the Everly Brothers began to hog the singles charts, along with a much-tamed Elvis Presley. 1963 saw Beatlemania spread like wildfire and 'The Fab Four' flattened all before them in their helter-skelter ride to glory. The Rolling Stones, The Kinks and The Who aided and abetted this new musical direction and, of course, other important and influential groups were to follow including David Bowie, Roxy Music and Mott The Hoople.

To students of Mott, 1963 was an important year for another reason, as it brought together, for the first time, two youngsters who formed a school band. This meshing of musical wills was common during a period that marked the early development of numerous late sixties and early seventies rock groups, but, without this particular catalyst, at Ross Grammar School, the long and winding road to Hoopledom would never have begun. However there was to be an important distinguishing factor in this particular case. The group that would be formed six years later, as the zenith of various Herefordshire bands, would never seek to be an obvious or direct derivative of its more illustrious predecessors. It would be unique.

In 1969, groups became progressive, often devoid of personality and were reverentially scrutinised by press and fans alike. Mott The Hoople were unlike other 'rival' bands and perceived this state of affairs to be ludicrous. Believing there must be a more unconventional approach to making music, Mott would thrive on struggle and adversity, generate unprecedented energy and occasional anarchy, and unwittingly leave behind musical and lyrical influences which would continue to inspire new artists nearly thirty years later.

Sleepy, some would say comatose, Ross-on-Wye, in the county of Herefordshire, all but ignored the Rock 'n' Roll revolution of the mid-1950s, since Skiffle and Trad[itional] Jazz were more to the liking of most 'hip' Rossians. One hundred and twenty miles from London, Herefordshire was one of England's smaller and more rural counties, sandwiched between Gloucester, Worcester and Shropshire to the East and the neighbouring Welsh border counties of Monmouth, Brecknock and Radnor to the West.

Born in Ross, on 24 October 1948, Terence Dale Griffin became Mott The Hoople's drummer. He was the first-born child of the late Joyce Addis and Fred Griffin, a local farmer, and he has four siblings, Bill, Christine, Bob and Anna. Educated at Walford County Primary and Ross Grammar Schools, Dale subsequently worked briefly as a Kleenezee brush salesman and then as a public relations officer for an electrical firm, while his drumming and part-time musical career developed. Inspired initially by his parents' records (Frankie Laine, Doris Day and Johnny Ray), and subsequently fuelled by influences such as The Beatles and The Who, his intermediate interests had been the big bands including The Ted Heath Band, Count Basie and Duke Ellington, then singers like Little Richard, Eddie Cochran and Buddy Holly. Dale's boyhood hero was John Leyton, a British TV actor who scored a number-one hit with the Joe-Meek-produced single 'Johnny Remember Me', and starred in the films *Krakatoa, East of Java!* and *The Great Escape.* 'Leyton had long hair, wore great "togs" and drove an Austin Healey sports car, complete with gorgeous female passenger. I was keen to emulate him!' says Griffin.

'I had a happy childhood. Great Britain was still in the grip of post-war austerity when I was born, but I got my National Health orange juice and, when I started school, the regulation one-third pint of milk per day in the classroom. Despite coming from a farming family with a large dairy herd, I loathed milk, especially when unchilled, always seeking to gift it to a willing classmate, which regularly resulted in my being punished for snubbing the State's great gift to me. My parents were young and the house was full of music, mostly middle-of-the-road stuff, until my father 'got' rock 'n' roll in the mid-fifties, when blue-labelled HMV (His Master's Voice) 78 rpm discs by the oddly-named Elvis Presley began to appear in the living room.'

Fred Griffin was a keen musician who could play piano, guitar and mouth organ but young Terry was only ever interested in drumming. Beginning with knitting needles as sticks, and any hard surface and metal fruit servers as his 'kit', he swiftly graduated to his first instrument, an Eric Delaney snare and 8-inch cymbal, which was closely followed by a red sparkle Gigster snare, tom-tom and bass drum. Questioned about his musical education, Dale once commented, 'You must be joking. As Carl Palmer once said, "As a drummer he's got natural talent as a road-sweeper!"'

Terry met Peter Overend Watts, Mott's bass player, in 1961, when Watts first attended Ross Grammar School, having moved to Ross-on-Wye from Worthing, near Brighton, at the age of thirteen. Pete was a Midlander, born in Yardley, Birmingham, on 13 May 1947. His father, Ronald Overend Watts, originally from the Lake District, married Joan Aylwin Lineker, a distant relative of England footballer Gary Lineker's family. Ronald was a college lecturer in metallurgy and applied mathematics and became a headmaster in Ross. Pete has one younger sister, Jane.

'In the early fifties, I remember my Dad saying that computers were the thing of the future and they would take over the world,' says Pete. 'I didn't know what he was on about. I kept imagining these little blokes with funny eyes. He also delved into our family history, hence the Lineker connection, and found that the Christian name Overend was probably the family surname at one time.'

Pete's middle name was traditionally given to the eldest son of the Watts family and apparently originated several hundred years before in Westmorland. Overend was to develop considerable dexterity at corrupting names and generating amusing spoonerisms and was responsible for the derivation of Dale's nickname, Buffin – 'Sniffin' Griff Griffin' (a name adopted for drumming purposes) became 'that little bugger Sniffin' and later 'that little Snigger Buffin!' He did the same with Terry Allen, Mott's keyboard player, and devised group names such as The Natalie Tokered Band, Shane Cleaven and the Clean Shaven and working titles ('Why King Turtles') for group songs.

Pete attended Church Road and Eastbourne House schools in Birmingham, followed by Worthing High, after he moved with his family to Sussex on the south coast of England. The Watts finally ended up at Bridstow in Ross-on-Wye and, like Dale, Pete studied at Ross Grammar School. Overend claims his early musical interests were singing along, at three years of age, with 78 rpm records on his Mother's wind-up gramophone – Italian opera, Mario Lanza and show soundtracks like *Oklahoma!* were big favourites – but young Watts also started playing his father's cello guitar when he was four, which his dad traded for a clarinet and hid under his bed.

'I wasn't allowed to touch Dad's guitar, but when he was at work, I used to go and open the case and pluck the strings. At that time I knew how to tune the guitar, because I remembered what it sounded like. Lucky for me that it was in tune in the first place, or else I'd have learned wrongly!

'I listened to the radio a lot as a tiny kid, all the standard pop tunes of the day or easy listening, semi-classical music which they used to play. I still look out for fifties light music records now and try and collect them. I always liked music and my favourite song was "The Runaway Train". I used to mispronounce the title and even sang "glory to the Newport King" in "Hark! The Herald Angels Sing" at Christmas. I once asked my parents if we could go to Newport to see the King.

'What really blew me away was when I saw Tommy Steele on television doing "Singing the Blues", round about 1956. I flipped when I saw him, but my parents didn't like that type of music and said it was a bad influence, so, of course, I did everything I could to go and hear him at other people's houses. Then he did 'Little White Bull" and I instantly went off him, but Mum and Dad suddenly thought he was nice. I also saw an Elvis film poster at the cinema with Dad once and, although he wouldn't take me to see it and yanked me out of the foyer, I was intrigued. Then, there was Little Richard, Chuck Berry and Jerry Lee who were incredible, not just the music, but their attitude as well. By the time I was ten or eleven, I was really hooked. I used to grip the arms of my chair with excitement and anticipation when *Drumbeat* was coming on the telly. I was even smitten by the trombone and sax players with Bob Miller and the Millermen. Dad was a radio ham and he went out and spent 43 guineas on a new innovation, a Capitol stereo system, which was lucky for me, because he could play classical records and I could play The Everly Brothers. My father was something of a musician and he'd written a song called "I've Got a Cow That's Got Three Legs", which was brilliant. It could still be a hit today!'

When Pete moved to Ross with his family in 1960, he heard The Shadows' record, 'Apache', and the effect upon him, of that guitar sound, meant there was no turning back. 'Hank Marvin started me playing, just as people like Brian May will admit. From there on in, I guess we all had the same influences. Lonnie Donegan was highly influential to all of us and was probably the most under-rated person in the history of British pop music. I still think The Beatles are the greatest band of all time and can never ever be surpassed by anybody. It's a joke to compare Oasis with them and Oasis would be the first people to admit that. The recent *Anthology* CDs were an incredible insight into how The Beatles' material was recorded and were exciting releases for musicians like me. The Who were also influential and were the greatest live band I've ever seen. They were aggressive and exciting. Townshend is still a hero to me.' Watts' other musical influences include Neil Young and David Bowie *(Man Who Sold the World / Hunky Dory* era), and he remains fanatical over Nils Lofgren and Grin, Warren Zevon, and sixties groups such as The West Coast Pop Art Experimental Band, The Monks, Buffalo Springfield and Love.

'When I'd heard the Shadows and then saw a 1960 Hofner V3 electric guitar in a shop window, that's what finally did it for me,' enthuses Watts. 'It was the poor man's Fender Stratocaster, sunburst finish, with three chrome pick ups and a tremolo arm. There was also a Junior Futurama 2 and a Rosetti Bass in Hickey's shop in Gloucester that day and my father had to drag me away from the window. I kept saying to Dad I wanted an electric guitar and he said if I learned to play his, he'd buy me one. That was April 1961, and by Christmas I'd learned and he bought me a Hofner Colorama, two-pick-up, six-string, for 32 guineas – four weeks wages!'

Pete's non-musical jobs were later to include Christmas relief postman and a year spent as a trainee architect with R. J. Wilson & Partners in Hereford, but by the age of fifteen he was already playing 'wild guitar' with Rory Haisley and a 55 year-old drummer, Ronald Rudge, who appeared resplendent in RAF handle-bar moustache, fancy waistcoat and bow tie. Ron Rudge and his Ploughman Band played local village halls and Young Farmers' Club Dances, but when Rudge couldn't appear at some gigs, the remaining line up performed, minus drums, as The Hawaian Airs. Watts' next band was an unnamed group, some-times embarrassingly billed as The Crystals, who were formed to play at Ross Grammar School's Hobbies Exhibition and Women's Institute concerts in 1962.

In the same year, Pete joined the former Camp Road Cats – Paul Jeffery (rhythm), Lionel Jeffery (high bass guitar) and Robert Fisher (snare drum and cymbal) – in a new instrumental group. Now named The Sandstorms, after the B-side of a Johnny and The Hurricanes single, the Boy Watts played his Hofner and was always deafening and continually required to 'turn it down'. At one concert, a particularly exasperated member of the public gave him 1s 6d to 'go and have an orange juice and give my bloody ears a rest!'

One lunchtime at Ross Grammar School, Dale Griffin heard the Jeffery brothers and Pete playing blues and instrumentals on three guitars in a Form

Room and, as they had no drummer, he set to work on his Dad to upgrade his Gigster kit which was not considered 'rock 'n' roll'. Blessed with a new four-piece blue sparkle Premier set, acquired from a Cheltenham music store, Dale made sure his latest acquistion became known to Pete.

'I'd always seen Buffin around the school and he seemed like an odd sort of kid,' says Watts. 'Then one day I saw a big group of twenty or thirty kids laughing in the playground and I went over and Buffin was doing a silly walk and crashing into posts. Then he'd fall into a great big puddle on the floor and roll around and everyone would be laughing. And I thought, "What's wrong with him, what's the matter with that kid?" He had a happy-go-lucky attitude and I took to him, I liked him. I used to call him "my friend" because I didn't even know his name. He was known as "my friend" for about six months. We'd walk around Ross, lounge around the cafes and tea shops and he'd ponce money from me.

'There were three of us on guitars doing old numbers at school one day and Buffin came up to me with a ticket in his hand with Premier written on it. I thought, "What's this, a new pair of shoes?" I didn't know what Premier was. He said it was a drumkit so I said we needed a drummer. We had a bit of a drummer by this time in Patrick 'Softee' Brooke, but he'd only just got his kit and we arranged to have a secret practice with Buffin. The next Sunday afternoon Dale and his Dad turned up at my house in a Jag. His father looked like a film star, like John Leyton, and Buff had this incredible looking blue sparkle drumkit with him. It was a professional kit and he was only thirteen. I suddenly felt inadequate with my Watkins Westminster amp and Colorama. Buffin was amazing and Softee was out. It was so good that Pat O'Donnell, one of the vocalists, said we had to play that night. He phoned around all the pubs in Ross and asked if we could perform that Sunday evening, which we did, at the Hope and Anchor.'

Thus began a summer residency for the hurriedly named Anchors, which was a big mistake according to Dale, ('Just add a "W" at the front and what do you get?'). With a repertoire that embraced Beatles, Kingston Trio, Shadows, Ventures and old rock 'n' roll songs, Watts and Griffin, with Bob Davies (rhythm guitar and vocals), Patrick O'Donnell (vocals and percussion) and John Sutton (double bass) played at The Cabin Bar adjoining the pub through June and July. In 1963, The Hope and Anchor on the edge of the River Wye in Ross was a regular date for the group, and although they were under age, they were paid £2 a week plus two pints of beer each night by Harry Thomas, the landlord.

John Sutton soon departed to play bass with the National Youth Orchestra of Great Britain, whilst Bob Davies and Pat O'Donnell went to the south of France – troubadours to the stars, they performed for Brigitte Bardot and Sylvie Varten amongst others. Later, Bob went to teaching college in Birmingham, then formed successful bands called The Vacant Lot and Cinnamon Quill, who cut several cult singles in the late sixties. Davies and Sutton later became headmasters and O'Donnell a senior Art lecturer in Hereford. Bob eventually taught Ben Tippins, future Silence singer and Mott tour manager Stan Tippins' son.

The second incarnation of The Anchors had Paul 'Twiddlefries' Jeffery (rhythm guitar and vocals), Fred Fishpool, aka Robert Fisher (rock 'n' blues bawling) and Patrick Brooke (lead vocals) with Peter 'Dog' Watts on lead guitar, and 'That Little Snigger' Buffin on drums, but no bass player. There were various local guest singers including John 'Screw' Farr, Tommy 'Knucky' Hall, John 'Bomber' Dean and Mike 'Jeambers' Chambers (brother of Pretenders drummer, Martin Chambers). Brooke also became the clean-cut 'teen idol' vocalist in contrast to Fisher, the 'down and dirty' rock 'n' roller.

The Anchors Mark II played from July to September, and they were learning – their new *modus operandi* was to 'lure women'! Due to the exigencies of scholastic duties however, they were forced to end their tenure at the Hope and Anchor. Next in a line of Ross Grammar School groups was Wild Dog's Hell Hounds, led by Pete 'Wild Dog' Watts and raucous singer Moanin' Cass Brown (Robert Fisher). The Hell Hounds lasted from September 1963 to February 1964 and had the same line up as The Anchors Mark II. Pete confesses that the band did not have a particularly auspicious career.

'We were really wild, although all we ever used to play was school dances. I had a gold lame waistcoat made out of curtain material and used to wear Marks & Spencer's see-through shirts, with string vests borrowed from my father underneath and Beatle wigs. We used to leap about the stage playing rhythm and blues. Everybody would request "Twenty-Four Hours from Tulsa" and we would give them "Lucille". The school hall we used to play had a little trap door in the stage and I used to hide a rubber bone down there before the start. The group would come on and start playing "Lucille" but I'd be off the stage and I'd come on on my own like the big star with the gold waistcoat and wig. I'd go down on all fours, open up the trap and take out the bone and start biting it, then I'd drink water from a bowl that said "Dog" on the side. I also had "the hat of many horns" – a big bowler hat pushed over a smaller bowler hat, with two horns wedged out of the side. Then I used to pick up the guitar and all the band would stop, I'd play a great big BEEENNND on the guitar and then we'd go berserk and that was the first number in the act!

'Fishpool would do wild songs like "Some Other Guy" and blues numbers, and Patrick was the pop idol of the group singing the commercial hits of the day, that girls liked, such as "Travelling Light" and "Do You Want to Know a Secret". Fishpool's sex appeal was non-existent at that stage. He'd had some of his front teeth punched out in various fights and he'd get pissed, remove his false teeth and put them on the end of his nose. We've always done strange things. Wild Dogs wasn't really a group though, more a name that was hanging around for about a year I suppose, and we probably only did three or four school dances. The headmaster didn't like us very much!'

Two days in January 1964 changed the lives of the Hell Hounds forever. First the group spied a Vox AC30 six input guitar amplifier in a local electrical store, and, although priced at £115 10s, they acquired it on hire purchase, signed for by Fred Griffin. This bona fide professional gear soon fuelled the ambitions of the group to get gigs outside of the Ross area. Then, three weeks later, Mersey band The Undertakers played at the New Inn in Ross and Fred Fishpool, seeing their bassist and singer Jackie Lomax, knew instantly that his future lay in being a bass player with a sleazy, slurring vocal style. Two days later he was bassman with the newly named The Soulents, having taken up Pat Brooke's Harmony Bass at a group practice. He never put it down again.

'We were named The Soulents because we played "with soul", and because, unlike The Anchors, this wasn't a name that could be turned into something rude – unless prefaced with an "Ar", which we failed to notice,' says Dale.

In 1964, The Soulents 'became semi-pro' and secured frequent good gigs in Wales and the Hereford area at venues such as Aubrey Street's 1600 Club and the Hillside Ballroom in Redhill, playing for between eight and thirteen pounds a night. Whilst The Anchors' sets had been high in instrumental content, The Soulents adopted a tougher stance. The band grew in confidence as the equipment, musicianship and gigs improved and they became more focused. They also became determined, such as the evening they walked out of a gig at the Top Spot Ballroom in Ross following a row with the owner over sound levels and played free instead at the Ross Rhythm Club, previously the local jazz club.

The Soulents ran into difficulty in October 1964 when Paul 'Bunglefries' Jeffery left to enter University in Coventry, but they now had Paul Davies, former manager/agent of rival band The Beatniks, taking care of business, and high profile support slots materialised with The Zombies and The Yardbirds.

'The Soulents was going really well,' recalls Watts. 'Bunglefries Jeffery, as a rhythm guitarist, was a very stabilising influence on the group. He wasn't that important musically, although he was a good singer and played good rhythm, but when he left, although the four-piece became tighter musically, it never seemed the same without Bunglefries to me. I always liked him there.'

By this time, The Who had arrived on the British music scene and showed everybody that drums, bass and one guitar could work, so The Soulents battled on. They utilised Arbour Hill Farm in Ross-on-Wye, the Griffin's house, as their rehearsal base, a location they would use up to and including their late sixties bands such as The Shakedown Sound and Silence. Fred Griffin gave the boys great encouragement and acquired a £30 van for the group.

'We were presented with a van by Buff's father and, since I was the only member with a driving licence, it fell to me to be chauffeur,' recalls Paul Jeffery. 'We were certainly privileged at that time to have our own transport – with the band's name emblazoned on the side panels and a large "S" on each hubcap – and we drove around like lords, oblivious, in our youthful mix of naivety and arrogance, to the fact that many of our contemporaries nursed within them a gnawing desire to drag us from its sanctuary and beat us to pulp.'

One evening during a group practice, the band received a phone call to rush to a gig at Hereford's hippest venue – the 1600 Club. Throwing all their equipment into the vehicle desperate to seize their big break, the Bedford van was driven at great speed by Jeffery, who got lost.

'In the panic, I swerved round a corner in Hereford's back streets, on the wrong side of the road, with a barrage of contradictory directional advice (coupled with torrents of foul, personal abuse) being bawled at me by my idiot companions. In a split second I found the club and crashed into it, much to the bemusement of the waiting throng of clubsters and howls of pain from the other Soulents, who were being bombarded by flying Vox AC30s.'

The Soulents developed a large local following and Paul recalls their van soon became covered with lipstick and eyebrow pencil from girl fans. 'The van's paintwork was eventually covered with countless, shamelessly lascivious messages from young girls, affording us all great comfort, solace and succour through the long journeys of the night. Ah yes! Sweet, well-spent youth.'

In October and November 1964, The Soulents breezed through the preliminary rounds of the Malvern Beat Contest cheered on by coach loads of supporters. In the final of the contest, held at Malvern Winter Gardens on 3 December 1964, they came up against The Ravons, an all female outfit from Pershore, Worcestershire. Like the entire audience, The Soulents were transfixed with the girls' compelling version of '(Remember) Walking In The Sand', George 'Shadow' Morton's song and record production for The Shangri-Las. Even the boys could not complain about coming second. Brooke sang on crutches having damaged his knee in a rugby match and Watts had to play on a Harmony Rocket six string borrowed from Buffin's brother, which he didn't give back to Bill for a year.

Herefordshire produced a number of other good rock groups at this time and The Soulents enjoyed intense but friendly rivalry with them. The Tyrants, who now featured Pat O'Donnell on vocals and harmonica, played electric versions of Bob Dylan songs before Dylan got himself a band, and The Ups 'n' Downs (formerly Johnny Rio And The Ricardos) were a wild R'n'B outfit who could easily have made it to the top.

While Watts and Griffin had been honing their musical abilities, two other key players who would be central to Mott The Hoople, had been doing the same. A good group that The Soulents often saw playing at gigs was The Buddies from Bromyard, with Mick Ralphs on lead guitar and vocalist Stan Tippins, who was regarded as something of a local heart throb. In March 1965, The Buddies turned professional and The Soulents continued to build, supporting several major national bands including The Zombies at venues like The Top Spot in Ross, and The Yardbirds, when Jeff Beck played his debut gig at Hereford's Hillside Ballroom. Overend remembers these formative years.

'When I left school, I was originally a trainee architect from August 1964 to October 1965, but I was playing semi-professionally with The Soulents. Each night, after work, I went out to see The Yardbirds or The Who, or simply to play gigs. At work, I constantly fell asleep with my head on the drawing board. Nobody seemed to mind the snoozing, but they kept telling me to get my hair cut.'

In July 1965, it was decided that the surviving quartet should change the group name from The Soulents to The Silence, and they began to take on more of the 'Pop Art' feel of the time, securing an increasingly sizeable fan base. They supported The Merseybeats at The 1600 Club. 'We were Merseybeat fans. We went down a storm and they died. Embarrassing,' remarks Griffin, 'and unjust.'

The Silence also supported The Who at the Blue Moon Club in Cheltenham that same month, as Dale remembers. 'This time *we* died! We'd all been to see The Who and loved 'em, so we started to perform many of their stage numbers.

We became so full of ourselves that we accepted a date supporting The Who. Big mistake – the stage was so tiny we had to use all their equipment *and* play their songs, much to Keith Moon's annoyance. He came and glared at me for a while. Then, disaster: Wattsy couldn't get the feedback from Townshend's amps – both guitar and bass amps blew and the audience was patently unimpressed. We slunk off, but worse was to come. Whilst waiting for the club to clear, Fooshers sat on the neck of one of Townshend's Rickenbackers and snapped it. We panicked and disappeared into the night, in shame and fear.'

A young Peter Watts was featured in the local press in October when he received a gift of a fifty-year-old French harmonium! Whilst he was surveying, during his day job, Watts had noticed the harmonium lying idle in a vicarage coach house at Kington and thought it would make a good sound for the group. He asked his boss if he could speak to the vicar about buying it and was given the instrument for nothing. The harmonium wasn't used on many bookings, except those nearer home, because of transportation and amplification difficulties.

Suddenly, in November 1965, unsuspected and unwelcome, the bubble burst. Watts left The Silence to turn professional with local rivals The Buddies, excited by the prospect of following in The Beatles' footsteps to Germany. 'I liked The Silence but had to leave,' admits Pete. 'I could see no future and was saying to them, "Look at The Buddies, going off to Europe." Buff was sixteen and still at school so he couldn't do anything, but the singer, Patrick Brooke, was the main problem, because his mother and father were very strict. He was a trainee accountant, working near me in Hereford and there was no way they were going to let him leave. He was going to be an accountant and that was it. Fred Fishpool was on the dole so he was professional for all intents and purposes.

'I always respected The Buddies, although they weren't quite as wild as The Silence, and when they asked me to join, whilst I didn't want to let the guys down, people were saying I had to think of myself. It stood to reason that they should have taken our bass player Fred Fishpool, but, because he was more scruffy and I had a job as a trainee architect and didn't look too wild, I fitted in nicely with The Buddies' clean cut image.

'I remember the first time I saw Ralpher in The Buddies at the Hostel in Hereford. He looked about fifteen and had a Rickenbacker and long hair at the front with a short back and sides. I got on with Ralpher straight away and struck up a friendship, because we both loved guitars. He came to see our group at Percival Hall and said we sounded like The Big Three which was an amazing compliment. We were always bumping into one another in the music shop in Hereford. Mick had a couple of other guitars as well as his Rickenbacker. He was well-off compared to me because he had a job that paid good money whereas I had one that didn't pay good money, and he kindly lent me things, including a Danelectro 12-string, which I used on gigs. By the time I joined Ralpher, eighteen months later, he had switched to a standard Fender Telecaster, which were quite hard to get at the time, and played that until he swapped it for a red Gibson SG Standard in 1968.'

When Watts linked up with Ralphs and Tippins, this soon lead to the demise of his former group. The Silence cast around for a string-strangler and played a trio of gigs with singer/guitarist Ricky Welch, formerly of legendary Gloucester band The Beatniks. However they only survived for a further month when they decided to disband during December in great dismay, parted company with Welch and invited Paul Jeffery to complete their final gigs.

'The Silence split shortly after Pete left because we could not find a suitable replacement,' says Dale. 'Fisher and Brooke joined another local band, The Uncertain Kind, and did a stint in Germany. I'd love to have gone there at that time. Everyone who did go has great stories to tell of their experiences.'

Dale was now lured to a 'proper job' in Gloucester and played in bands in the evening, including The Charles Kingsley Creation with whom he performed his first gig at the Pontypridd Mineworkers' Club in Wales. Griffin also got involved in his first studio work, session drumming at Future Sound, owned by Kingsley and Charles Ward. The studio, equipped with two mono tape decks and a mixing desk, was a converted potato loft above a barn at the brothers' family farm near Monmouth. Dale appeared on two 1966 singles, 'Is It Really What You Want?' by The Interns, on Parlophone, and 'Black Is The Night', backed with 'Do Blondes Really Have More Fun?' by (Bryn) Yemm and the Yemen on Columbia. In fact, it was The Charles Kingsley Creation who provided the instrumental backing to the Bryn Yemm single and Dale made a live promotional appearance with the group on Television Wales and West's *TWW Reports* at their studios in Bristol.

Meanwhile, Watts switched from six-string Rickenbacker to Fender Precision bass, joining Bob Hall, Ralphs and Tippins in Herefordshire's only professional beat group. The Buddies were older than The Silence and Pete actually thought they were a bit old fashioned, although musically tight. He wasn't sure if he could play bass, but believed it couldn't be that difficult! 'I was happy to switch from six-string to bass. The only thing I'd never have considered being was a drummer, because you get all the hard work and none of the glory. Bass was much easier because you didn't have to look at what you were doing and could do whatever you wanted on stage, including moving freely, eyeing girls and looking cool.'

Like Dale, Stan and Mick both hailed from rural Herefordshire. Stanley William Tippins was born on 14 May 1945 in Sarnesfield, the son of Ernest Albert Tippins and Florence Rhoda Matthews. His father was a farm worker, wagoner and cowman and Stan lived in Sarnesfield for twenty years, until the family moved into Hereford in October 1965. Stan, his brother Les, who died of a heart attack in 1989, and his sister Ruth were educated at Weobley School near Sarnesfield. He was interested in football and played centre half for the school team but also enjoyed English and History. Leaving school at 15, he joined Henry Wiggins' factory in Hereford for five years and, although he had no musical education, he became a professional musician in 1965. Tippins has been married twice, the first lasting three years and his second marriage to Jenny spanning more than twenty, resulting in four children and two grandchildren.

Stan was influenced musically by artists like P. J. Proby, Cliff Bennett and the Rebel Rousers, Stuart James (Mojos) and, particularly, the image-laden rockers Johnny Kidd and the Pirates who, with their 1959 debut hit, 'Please Don't Touch', made the first authentic rock and roll record originated by a UK artist. Kidd was

Britain's first 'rock' singer in Stan's eyes. 'I saw them eight times altogether and they were fabulous. Johnny Kidd had such a great stage show and was probably the best mover I've ever seen, and the best rock and roll singer of all time in my opinion, both British and American. My other interests were Jerry Lee Lewis, Sam Cooke, Little Richard, Gene Vincent, Buddy Holly and Brenda Lee. In those days, there were hardly any albums around – it was all singles. I remember listening to Radio Luxembourg very quietly in my bedroom late at night and that's really all there was back then. I was keen on music and used to do some singing at school at about ten or eleven years of age. My specialities were "The Man From Laramie" and "Davy Crockett", which the teacher would let me sing for the class.'

Tippins formed his first group, Jet Black and the Stormraisers, in 1963. Stan became a good vocalist and dynamic front man and would come on stage in black leather under the name of Jet Black and subsequently Billy Thunder. The group line up included Ed Barnett on guitar, Mick Jaguar on bass and Dave Scudder on drums.

'The Stormraisers really came about because my friend, Ed Barnet, who lived two miles away, was a keen footballer like me and used to play in a field near my place. One day it rained very heavily and he asked me to come round to his house and listen to some of his records. I didn't know he liked music too. Ed fancied himself as a lead guitarist so he started playing and I started singing. It took months and months to learn all these Johnny Kidd and Jerry Lee Lewis songs and then we got our first gig at the Unicorn Village Hall, Weobley on 6 December 1963. It cost three shillings to get in, was absolutely packed and we got six pounds for the night. I would wear black leather trousers and a black and white shirt on stage and we went round putting up posters in shops and started playing all the local halls and youth clubs.'

After a while Jet Black was 'laid to rest' and Stan became Billy Thunder, at the suggestion of the group's new manager. Billy Thunder and the Stormraisers played the Herefordshire circuit for a while, but the band fell apart when Ed found a girlfriend. He was replaced by guitarist Alan Lovell and Taffy Jones took over on drums.

'I couldn't believe it because Ed was the keenest of all of us and couldn't think of anything but music,' says Stan 'One night we were doing a gig near Monmouth, and he should have been playing a guitar solo and we looked across to find him holding his girlfriend's hand. It wasn't the same without Ed, and eventually The Stormraisers came to an end. I turned down a few offers to go with other local groups until I was approached by The Buddies. Les Norman, their singer/guitarist, was leaving to go to college away from Hereford. The Buddies were a very bluesy five-piece and Les was an excellent vocalist. I joined and changed them a bit because I felt uncomfortable with some of their material and was more of a pop–rock singer.'

Stan was described by his fellow band members as a forceful character with the sheer brute power to make others do what was necessary. Dale recalls an example of this a year or two later when Pete Watts would not play one of the numbers in their live act.

'In those early days you didn't play an hour or a two-hour set, you played for eight or ten hours in total, which meant that you couldn't possibly have enough different songs to play throughout that time, so you would have to repeat things. On this particular evening Stan was introducing the song "My Girl" for about the third or fourth time and Pete just refused to play it, which made life difficult, because the song opens with a bass riff and it relied on Watts to start it. Stan glared at Pete and went back to the microphone and said, "Right, now we're going to do a number called 'My Girl', and looked very meaningfully at Pete who still wouldn't play. And this happened another couple of times. Stan and Pete stood their ground, they're both Taureans and very stubborn. After introducing the song again, Tippins turned to Pete and said, "If you don't start this fucking song now, I'm going to break your fucking nose." Lo and behold, Wattsy played the riff instantly. If push comes to shove you don't say "no" to Stanley; you do what you're told!'

Fellow Buddies member, Michael Geoffrey Ralphs was born in Hereford on 31 March 1944 and was brought up in Lower House, Stoke Lacey, a village near Bromyard in Herefordshire. His late father, Geoffrey Henry Ralphs, worked for the Army in a clerical post with the SAS at Bradbury Lines near Hereford and married Florence Kathleen Grace. Mick is an only child, but his cousin, Sue, lived with the family from the age of three until she was seventeen. His parents managed the village post office in Stoke Lacey and his father subsequently ran a bookshop in Bromyard. Mr Ralphs was a keen writer and poet and, in addition to preparing articles on The Buddies for the local press, he had one of his short stories read on BBC radio.

Mick was educated at junior school in Hereford and then Bromyard Grammar School. He describes his principal educational interest as 'leaving', although he later attended Hereford Technical College and, finally, Keele University, where he studied electrical engineering. 'I used to work for the Midlands Electricity Board in Bromyard, as an apprentice electrician, and that entailed cleaning the showroom windows and making tea, which was *very* electrical!'

Ralphs was to marry and divorce three times. He has three children, Ben and James with his third wife Krista whom he married in 1989, and Jessica by American Debbie Roden, after divorcing his first wife Nina. 'I suppose it comes with the musical territory,' remarks Ralphs. 'It's difficult to keep it all together.'

Mick's range of musical influences included Chuck Berry, Eddie Cochran, Buddy Holly, Ricky Nelson ('mainly for the guitar playing of James Burton'), Buffalo Springfield and Mountain guitarist Leslie West. But Ralphs had not been a lover of rock music initially and actually started his musical career quite late, not as a young teenager like Watts and Griffin. 'I was self-taught and only started playing when I was about eighteen. Before that I couldn't afford a guitar. My first instrument was a horrible Rosetti Lucky Seven guitar and an amp that looked like a radio. I never really liked the pop music of the day that much, it was Cliff Richard and the like, all very soft stuff, which didn't do much for me. Then, when I was about eighteen, I heard "Green Onions" by Booker T and the MGs and that really grabbed me, so I took an interest in the guitar. Chuck Berry was one of my main heroes, both as a writer and a performer. I also like records such as The Righteous Brothers' "You've Lost That Loving Feeling", "My Baby Left Me" by Elvis Presley and Don McLean's "Vincent" – anything with feeling, really.'

Ralphs' first group was The Mighty Atom Dance Band, which featured Mick's aunt on accordion! He then played in another dance group, The Melody Makers, for twelve months, before joining The Buddies. Les Norman had formed a school band, The Hi Fi's in 1957. The group became The Renegades, who backed Paul Raven (later Gary Glitter) at one Herefordshire gig, before changing their name to The Buddies. The bass player, Des Grubb, who always caused great concern in the band by wearing a woolly hat, lived in a caravan in the Ralphs' orchard. The early drummers who worked with Les Norman were Brian Bailey and Paul Stratton. Ralphs had seen The Buddies play and made an effort to speak to Les and the group, eventually performing his audition for lead singer Norman on the fire escape stairs outside the Hereford YMCA building, during a Buddies gig. Les was impressed and Mick was in!

'In those days, whoever had the reddest guitar was the leader,' says Ralphs. 'I never differentiated between rhythm and lead, it was just guitar, so I guess I was a guitarist at that time. There were lots of good local bands around Hereford, but the stand out for me was The Ups 'n' Downs. Of all the groups in the area, they should have made it, because they were really very good and had an amazing wild image, almost a cross between The Stones, The Doors and The Pretty Things. They would go down to London and check out what was going on there, and come back and incorporate some of the ideas into their stuff, and of course most of the bands locally were quite timid and provincial.'

The Ups 'n' Downs featured Phil Tippins, Stan's cousin on drums, and Richard 'Dicky' Weaver on bass and Hohner electric piano. Weaver was later to direct Mott The Hoople's promotional videos for CBS Records.

With Ralphs in tow, The Buddies recorded four songs in 1964 at Hollick and Taylor's, a former BBC studio in Handsworth, Birmingham, including a cover version of 'House of the Rising Sun'. Two of the session tracks were pressed up as a single on the Hollick and Taylor label, Jimmy Reed's 'I Ain't Got You' and a Norman/Ralphs composition 'It's Goodbye', and 100 copies distributed by the group's Worcester management company. The studio, where Gerry Anderson's *Thunderbirds* soundtracks were recorded, was linked to Pye, but a possible release of The Buddies single on the Pye record label never materialised.

Stan Tippins joined The Buddies shortly after Mick, when Les Norman departed to pursue his career in architecture. The group now comprised Ralphs on lead guitar, Roger Brinn on rhythm guitar, drummer Taffy Jones and Cyril Townsend, from Leominster, on bass, whom Tippins thought looked great and could have blended in with The Stones or The Pretty Things. Guitarist Brinn soon quit and a new drummer, Bob Hall, joined, making the group a four-piece. Ralphs was regarded by some members as the proverbial cuckoo in the group's nest, getting individuals in and out of the band at various times. Stan recalls how The Buddies played numerous halls and pubs throughout Herefordshire with some success. 'The Buddies got a lot of work and it was unbelievable that a small

county like Herefordshire could provide us with three gigs a week. We also played
in Worcestershire and Wales and found a female manager in Worcester, who got
us an agent in London with a lot of contacts in Germany.'

By October 1965, The Buddies, comprising Ralphs, Tippins, Hall and
Townsend, were styled on James Brown and Cliff Bennett. Described on a promotional card as 'The Buddies – The Entertainers You'll Like', their agent, Guy
Williams, set up a German tour for the band to play in West Berlin and at the
Obere Sonne in Konstanz near Stuttgart. 'We spent a month in Germany at a
place called Konstanz near the Swiss border,' remembers Stan. 'Initially we
thought it was heaven and that we were made for life, because we were the first
British band to go there and there was a lot of interest in us. We had a lovely little hotel, rooms to ourselves, free breakfast and free dinner at night before we
went on stage.'

Just before Watts' arrival, The Buddies taped four more songs for a possible
single including 'Young Blood' and 'Something You Got', at Decca Records'
Studio in Hamburg. These tracks were never released.

The work in Konstanz was only a month's residency, so the group then came
home to play the usual local village halls, at which point Cyril Townsend decided he would leave. Stan already had a new bass player in his sights. 'When replacements were discussed I said, "That lead guitarist in The Silence, he's got a
good image, let's make him play bass," so we approached Pete Watts. He was a
bit hesitant and his Dad was reluctant because of his trainee architectural job, so
I decided with Mick that I'd have to go down and see Pete's father.'

Pete will never forget Tippins' visit and the masterful technique he used to
charm his parents. 'Stan put his suit and tie on and came to my Mum and Dad's
house. He was like a bank manager saying, "Now listen Mr and Mrs Watts, it will
all be all right – Peter will earn £30 a week," and they were very impressed with
it all. Mum and Dad thought he was amazing and that's why they let me go, because they thought Stan was great. He was 20 and I was 17, but in those days that
was a big difference. It's like David Gilmour once said about Pink Floyd, the
playground hierarchy when you're that age really exists. To my parents I was a
boy, but Stan was a man.'

Watts couldn't see The Silence going anywhere in terms of career, gigs or
recording, whilst The Buddies, whose musical identity seemed vague and rather
tepid to Pete, at least offered the chance of work in Germany, Italy ... the world!
Having played his last gig with The Silence in November 1965, Watts joined The
Buddies in December full of anticipation after Tippins' heavenly tales of
Konstanz. After frantic rehearsals with Pete, the group headed back to Germany,
but the first dates in Hagen were hell and this time, a horrible time was had by
all playing 'low-or-no-pay' gigs for long, long hours.

'We were in for a shock because we had been the first British group to have
played in Konstanz and were treated like royalty, like The Beatles arriving,' says
Stan. 'Then, when we went to industrial cities like Hamburg and Hagen it was,
"The Buddies? Who the hell are The Buddies?" They'd had hundreds of bands
by then and the novelty had gone. The hotels and flats were awful, with no
furniture or bedding – nothing but burnt-out mattresses on the floor – and it was

hard to actually get money from promoters, even after playing four or five hours a night. I was losing weight and my voice was going. It was terrible and very hard to do.'

Playing at the Pferdestall (Horse Stable) in Hagen, near Essen and Dortmund, from 1 to 20 December 1965, was a nightmare for the group. 'It was really tough,' admits Watts. 'The Horse Stable was full of prostitutes and gangsters and we played eight hours a night, six in the evening until six in the morning, 45 minutes on and 15 off, all night. In that time you were allowed two free drinks. There were some horrible fights in there. We just used to play, as quietly as we could, looking at the floor, so as not to attract attention. We couldn't afford to come home for Christmas as they used to rob us right, left and centre.

'One night in the Horse Stable, a guy wearing a camel hair coat walked in. He had two other blokes with him. Suddenly, he whipped this sword stick out and ripped the Turkish owner's white shirt wide open. There was blood everywhere, but the intruders were too slow and the owner's staff were on to them straight away and almost murdered them with bottles. We thought they'd killed this bloke, because the camel hair coat was completely covered in blood. A few days later, we were sitting in a cafe along the road, when somebody nudged me. I looked up and this same bloke was hobbling in the door in *another* camel hair coat. I thought, Christ, he's still alive. He looked like the Invisible Man. He had bandages all round his face and head, all over his hands and he must have had slits in the bandages, because he had dark glasses on. He still had a walking stick with a sword in it. He sat down not far away from us and then got up and went to the jukebox and put on Jim Reeves' "He'll Have to Go!".

'We moved to Marburg and played Club Europa, but got chased out of there at the point of a gun. In the German clubs, the type of music requested by audiences would change several times in the course of each evening. I remember one demand was, "Play jazz or die". The owners would always be screaming at us from in front of the stage, shouting, "Make show, make show!"

The Buddies spent only four nights in Marburg, a medieval town, seventy miles from Frankfurt, before travelling 1,300 miles in their Ford Thames wagon via Brenner, Innsbruck and the Austrian Tyrol to the luxury ski resort of Cortina d'Ampezzo, in northern Italy, where they became the resident band at Club Canadian. They returned to Cafe Giovani and Club Europa at Marburg in January and made the long trip back to Cortina once again in February to play during the bobsleigh championships. Their Italian highlights were a marathon eight-hour New Year session and a one night stand at a party thrown by an Italian Count at a 'James Bond' style residence high in the Dolomites. During their trip, Watts fell ill and was replaced, temporarily, by Dave Mason, lead guitarist with Worcester's The Hellions. February and March saw The Buddies playing The Big Apple and Crazy Horse Clubs in Hamburg, a happier location for the group. 'Hamburg was good fun,' recalls Ralphs. 'We used to go down to The Top Ten Club and saw people there like Elton John with Long John Baldry in Bluesology. Elton was playing a Vox Continental organ, but all the really famous bands had been and gone by this time.'

The Buddies had came home in February, 1966, but their manager, Guy

Williams, told them that a friend of his in Hamburg had been let down by another group, and they had to go back to Germany straight away. 'Most of the club owners were gangsters, frightening blokes,' says Pete. 'In Hamburg, there were bottles and broken glass in a great big pile up to the ceiling in one corner of our room, and I went out and bought a mop and cleaned a space to lay my mattress. It was absolute hell, hard to communicate, and we didn't get paid properly.'

The months of dates in Hagen, Marburg and Hamburg were wild and crazy days for the group, with gangsters and guns, prostitutes and pimps and hard drink and hard drugs at every turn. Our boys however, emerged shaken but un-scarred. Staying in Germany until April 1966, The Buddies played with several cult bands including The Sorrows, The VIPs (who would later work with Guy Stevens), Mal Ryder and The Primitives and The Rokes, who, Pete recalls, had suits and ties like The Beatles, but with long hair to their waists. The groups were also quirky, like The Monks, ex-American GIs who wore habits, ropes round their necks and short hair with the top shaved out. Watts still raves about The Monks and how they used feedback to overdrive their amps before anyone else ever did.

Returning home, yet again, to play village halls around Herefordshire and the Welsh borders, The Buddies found the local press (Ralphs' dad) describing them as 'The Ambassadors of Beat'. Three months of working six nights a week, three hours a night, had made a vast difference to the group and on a revisit to The 1600 Club in Hereford, one journalist described them as 'smooth professional musicians'. But the English gigs were not a particularly happy memory for Mick Ralphs. 'From April until June, we played in England, during which time we lost the group van, due to a serious crash, in which our road manager, Vivian Phillips, was injured. We also lost a lot of money.'

Vivian Phillips was a farming family boy, an eccentric's eccentric and the band all say they could not do him justice in words alone. A legend in his teens, he would leave future outfit The Doc Thomas Group to work with the budding Traffic and, in time, became Island Record's boss Chris Blackwell's personal pilot. Phillips now manages Steve Winwood. 'Viv was our pyrotechnics bloke,' says Watts. 'In other words, he got sugar and weedkiller and made bombs, but he knew what he was doing. We used to blow TVs up on stage. If we were on a long journey somewhere and caught in traffic, for a happening we would get our tele-visions out of the van and set them up at the side of the road and sit and pretend we were watching them. Then we'd blow them up and people in cars nearby would flip. Ralpher and Viv would always get these old clapped out tellies and sometimes we took dozens of them with us from England for continental gigs.

'Viv used to chain smoke and we were so poor in those days, he got an allowance of around one thousand lira a day for food, about 1s 6d. Of course, he was buying fags and wasn't eating and in the end he collapsed and had to be taken to hospital suffering from malnutrition.'

Ralphs, Watts and Tippins believed that The Buddies was no longer a suitable name for a professional outfit. After Phillips' road accident, a local newpaper had described the incident with the headline – 'Problem for The Buddies'. The

Problem was born and by now group names were starting to become flags of convenience. 'Problem was just one of those names that we had when we used to go back and forth to Germany and Italy for a month at a time,' says Ralphs. 'We'd always have to leave under dodgy circumstances and we'd reappear a week later under a different guise. We also traded as Silence and The Shakedown Sound.'

British gigs were now uninspiring after the thrill of Europe and the group could not get excited about playing venues in Nantwich, Cheshire with Kenny Ball and his Jazzmen! In spite of losing their van, in June The Buddies drove via Luxembourg and Switzerland to play the Gabiano Night Club, the Pepper Club and the Woodpecker Night Club in Milano Marittima, Italy, thanks to the intervention of Dave Tedstone, previously with The Astrals, who agreed to provide transport if he could be road manager. 'Dave came with us because he had loaned us some money to buy a van, and he didn't think we'd ever pay him back, so we said he could accompany us if he didn't trust us and play along, which he did,' reveals Ralphs.

In the summer of 1966, The Problem changed name again. Dave Mason of future Traffic fame, lived in Worcester, played with Jim Capaldi in The Hellions and was a friend of Ralphs. Mason had already deputised for The Buddies in Germany when Watts was taken ill and he mentioned he would like to form a band. Ralphs admits they used to enjoy each other's playing, but The Hellions worked the Midlands circuit while The Buddies worked predominantly in Herefordshire, Wales and Europe. Mason seemed eager to work with Mick and Pete.

'Dave Mason didn't want to form a band with me because obviously he sang too,' says Stan. 'He was talking to Mick and Pete because we were going through a difficult patch with these horrible German shows that we'd got involved in. I think everybody got a bit disillusioned at some point, so I guess that's why they were speaking to him.'

Watts recalls, 'Dave used to leap up and jam with us. He was good. He tried to get us to form a group with him but we thought he was a bit pushy and that he'd try to take over.'

Declining Mason's offer to form a band, Problem adopted his idea for a new name instead, The Doc Thomas Group. Back in Germany for another month of gigs, the band met a young Italian waiter named Rinaldo Ricci, who said his father was an agent in Italy and could get them gigs there. The guys were sceptical, but gave Rinaldo their names and addresses and returned to Hereford. 'We took all this with a pinch of salt,' says Watts, 'but a contract arrived in the summer of '66 and we went out to the Adriatic Coast, and ended up going there every summer until 1968. We even went over there with Mott The Hoople in 1969 to get some performance experience, out of the way of the English music press. Rinaldo was instrumental in getting us to Italy and his father became our manager.'

David Woolley also became their manager for a while and they secured plenty of work in Italy, where British bands were very popular at the time. Based at Riccione, just South of Rimini, on the eastern Adriatic coast, the Doc Thomas

Group first performed at Milano Marittima playing one hour sets at The Woodpecker Club each afternoon, for teenagers as they came off the beach. In the evening, the group had nothing to do at first, other than watch the Italian bands. They got on well with the agent, Signor Ricci, and he introduced them to Gian Stellari, a record producer. In double quick time the Doc Thomas Group was offered a recording contract by a company called Interrecord and the band travelled to Milan to record with Stellari.

'I thought we'd gone into the studio to do demos, but we recorded twenty tracks in two evenings, all cover versions, and it was hard work,' says Stan. 'We were even dragging people in off the streets to sing on the choruses of songs like Sam Cooke's "Shake". We went back to England again briefly and I couldn't believe it when, a few weeks later, our album came through the post.'

In spite of the strain, Tippins' vocals were very good on the recordings. Ralphs now played a Telecaster through a Vox AC30, while Tedstone used a Les Paul with Fender Bassman amp. 'I played some lead on "Steal Your Heart Away", "I'll Be Doggone", "Rescue Me" and "Just Can't Go To Sleep",' remarks Dave Tedstone.

Twelve tracks were selected for *The Doc Thomas Group*, released in January 1967 on the Dischi Interrecord label. The album was based on their stage act repertoire and recorded 'as live' in the studio. According to Ralphs and Watts, the tracks which remain unreleased include 'Happy Together', 'First I Look At The Purse', 'My Girl' and 'Cool Jerk'. A single from the LP, 'Just Can't Go To Sleep' coupled with 'Harlem Shuffle', was issued in a picture sleeve similar to the album cover, featuring the band draped over their Commer van. 'Rescue Me' was also pressed as an Italian promotional jukebox single.

Bob Hall and Dave Tedstone suddenly departed, allowing Buffin to join Watts, Ralphs and Tippins in the Doc Thomas Group in late 1966. 'I never really got on with Bob from day one in The Buddies,' says Pete. 'He was a bit older than the others and looked on me as a bit of an upstart. I remember we all had hammocks in the same room one night and Stan and Mick asked me what I thought we could do to make the group better. So I said we needed to update the band more, it was too old fashioned, and 'The Heel', Bob Hall, went mad at me screaming, "What the hell do you know?"'

Buffin now joined the group, with his eyes already on a new champagne sparkle Ludwig drum kit, soon acquired in London with assistance from his Dad, Ralphs and Watts. 'The three of us drove to London one Saturday and parked at White City to take the underground into town,' says Pete. 'It was difficult lugging these old drums down the escalators. At one point we lost control and they crashed down to the bottom causing an almighty racket and much fear and chaos amongst the public. We bumped into Pete Townsend in Orange Music shop and he was great as always. He didn't know us but he was always very polite and friendly, although I'm sure he couldn't remember us each time he saw us. He explained how he had switched from Rickenbacker guitars to Fender Strats simply because they 'bounced' a lot better.'

After frantic rehearsals with Buffin, (attended by Steve Winwood and Jim Capaldi) in Bullingham School opposite Tippins's family home, followed by a slew of local gigs, the 'new' Doc Thomas Group set off for Milan to record two shows for RAI-TV promoting their album and single. One of the programmes, broadcast on 22 April, was called *Diamoci del Tu* and the group played 'My Baby' and 'Shake'. On the other TV show, *Bandiera Gialla* (*Yellow Flag*), featuring 'Just Can't Go to Sleep', critic James Paine coined the term 'Sinatra of Beat' to describe Tippins. Caterina Caselli, Francoise Hardy and Giorgio Gaber were the 'names' involved with both programmes.

Manager Mr Ricci now insisted there must be five members in the group, so Tippins was obliged to return to the UK and recruit former Advocats' bassist, Geoff Peacey from Gloucester as Doc Thomas Group organist. Stan and Viv Phillips collected Peacey, his Lowrey organ gear and his huge Commer diesel van, returning in convoy with the Tippins Mini to Italy. The band had all known Geoff for some time and regarded him as a first rate player and a great chap who fitted in perfectly. The 'Geoff Peacey' Doc Thomas Group played a month long residency at The Whiskey Club, Bologna but were deported due to an outrageous incident involving a member of their 'touring party' who had accompanied the band with quite devastating results according to Watts.

'A "friend" of ours had come along as a sort of mechanic-roadie-helper. He was a lot older than the rest of us, and was a hard man from Bromyard who gradually got into bad drinking ways over there. He became a bit of a tyrant, and started to bully the group, drinking whisky in the clubs we played, quicker than we could earn the money to pay for it. I suspect we were on about twenty quid a night, and he'd be drinking thirty pounds worth of whisky and charging it at the bar. We couldn't tell him to stop because he was a heavy geezer. He was extremely strong, and would pull lamp posts over at a forty-five degree angle into the road, and Stan would run along behind him trying to twist them back. He terrorised the owner of the hotel where we stayed, forcing wine down his throat.'

Another friend of the group, Robert Jones, known as 'Joner', also accompanied the group to Italy for the 1967 season. He was a darkly-deep mysterious character, from the darkest, deepest depths of Bromyard. Of farming stock, he had interests ranging from ancient magycke and Aleister Crowley, to the latest in the shaggy-chic fashions of the day. He became a 'style guru' to the band, providing piles of clothing and stage props, as Watts recalls. 'Joner helped us a lot. He used to get American catalogues sent over and he could order wild clothes like strange fringed jackets, really peculiar ones. You couldn't get much of that stuff over here in the mid-sixties.'

Tiptoeing back to Italy, and a four week engagement at The Titan Club in Rome, the group stayed in a hotel owned by 'Madam Julia' and staffed by transsexual and transvestite 'maids' – an arrangement unknown in Hereford! The whole band was soon arrested, after Tippins got into a 'strada rage' incident with a huge American, Stan flooring the fellow with one blow. Put into a room to cool their heels, the strip light dropped from the ceiling and a picture fell from the wall, untouched by the group, but the police were incandescent with rage. The name of 'Madam Julia' soon provoked a change in police tone and the band were suddenly freed upon her arrival and waved on their way. And sleaze is a new phenomenon?

The group attracted considerable attention at The Titan, when they smashed their stock of televisions on stage (*à la* Move) and set off smoke bombs. One of their shows created press headlines back in England – 'Hereford Style Roman Candle A Big Success' – the article describing the Club being taken by surprise with an end of set 'freak out'. Mick's father, Geoff Ralphs continued to pen these reviews. While Tippins and Watts smashed TV sets under dozens of coloured flashing lights, exploding smoke bombs sent four foot high flames into the air, which caused a shocked crowd of dancers to retreat a cautious twenty feet from the stage during the finale, to watch a spectacle unknown to Italy's beat scene.

'The whole place filled with smoke and panic followed,' recalls Dale. 'Huge, monumental, epic, Italian panic – there is none finer. The manager of The Titan thundered at us, "Imbeciles, bastards, you've ruined my club. Never do this again." The next night, no smoke bombs, no smashed TVs. After the tame show the manager raged at us, "Are you trying to make a monkey out of me? Why no smoke? Why no spectacle? The whole of Rome is here to see this. You must do it every night!" We moved to Milano Marittima and set off a special Gaz container during a beach gig. The container had been rattling around in our van for months and had been converted into a bomb by Gaza, a member of a Liverpool group stranded in Rome. It blew a HUGE hole in the sand, triggered burglar alarms and set the Carabinieri into action. We ran for it in all directions thinking – "We could have been *sitting* on that thing!" .'

The Doc Thomas Group's TV smashing was carried out by Tippins armed with an axe and Watts using his beloved bass guitar. 'My Fender Precision sunburst was an early sixties' model which I bought for £45 in a shop in Hereford. It had belonged to a guy in The Vagabonds, but they were out of fashion then, as people like John Entwhistle were playing Danelectros. I used the Fender all through Germany and Italy and started smashing it up on the televisions. Geoff Peacey had to come in and glue the bass up each morning before the next gig. I eventually painted it matt black and it looked great. I would use the Precision on the first two Mott The Hoople albums.'

After Rome, Milano Marittima, Forli and Riccione were regular venues for the 1967 summer season. The group would perform La Panoramica and The Bat Caverna Club at Riccione, but were largely based in Milano Marittima where they played at The Pepper Club, and on occasion, free guest spots at an outdoor cafe in the afternoons using borrowed equipment. Evening concerts were at The Pineta Club, where the group gear was based, and comprised two forty-five minute sets at low volume.

'We also played at an Italian ski resort once and the rule was that you performed for six or seven hours a night, until the last customer had gone,' says Stan, 'I used to try and get them out early by wearing a hat and coat on stage. When we did these tours abroad, we would play for four or six weeks at a club and then come back to England for a while. We were always hungry in Italy and in the summer, as we travelled, we'd stop and stuff ourselves with cherries up on the hillsides and come through villages very early in the morning to pinch milk from doorsteps. When we came home, people would be amazed at how thin we were.'

'The gigs in Italy lasted on and off for a couple of years and gave us a great deal of experience,' says Ralphs. 'We used to get 1,000 lira a day which was about seven and a half new pence! The food there was cheap, Spaghetti Bollocknose for about 80 lira. Good English groups were very popular over there at the time but we got sick of pandering to the pop crowd with numbers like "Release Me". We really wanted to play our own type of music.'

Dale recalls, 'If we ever played "Release Me", it was but once, as a spoof, at a Panoramica night club gig. We used to swap instruments and play incredibly quiet, awful "jazz", which the audience preferred to our proper repertoire. We also played pop and soul material including "Sergeant Pepper's Lonely Hearts Club Band", "With a Little Help from My Friends", "A Whiter Shade of Pale", Sam and Dave's "Hold on, I'm Coming", James Brown's "I Got You" and "Get Ready" by The Temptations. Mick Ralphs' ambition was to join Tony Rivers (later a backing vocalist to Cliff Richard) and The Castaways who did loads of Beach Boys and similar harmony songs, whilst Watts and I continually tried to get The Doc Thomas Group to adopt a more powerful sound and image.'

The band returned home after the summer season in Italy, when, to their distress, Geoff Peacey's father insisted that he quit forthwith. Geoff was a mere 17 years of age and had been reduced to paupery by The Doc Thomas Group. They kept his truck though! Peacey subsequently joined a progressive German band called Lake in the 1970s.

The group now began doing gigs as a four-piece but there was unrest in the camp. Mick Ralphs was still showing signs of wishing to work with other bands and said he would audition for Tony Rivers and the Castaways. However, he was offered the chance to join The Shakedown Sound, a backing band for Jamaican singing star, Jimmy Cliff during his 'soul man' days pre-reggae.

The future Mott The Hoople began to take real shape at this juncture with the entrance of organist, Terence (Verden) Allen, who played in The Shakedown Sound. Allen was eventually persuaded to join The Doc Thomas Group in early 1968 thus providing the final link with Tippins, Ralphs, Watts and Griffin in the group that would sign for Island Records. Known simply as Terry at this time, the name Verden was based on his father's middle name and adopted later by Mott's first manager, Guy Stevens. Verden was subsequently nicknamed Phally by Mott, a unique and interesting title for an organ player and another infamous Watts corruption; Terry Allen became Hairy Talon, then Hairy Phallus and finally Phally!

Terry Allen was born in Woodland Road, Crynant, a small village near Swansea in South Wales on 26 May 1944. He was an only child to the late Philip Verdun Allen and Rose Preddy, his father working first as a coalminer and then for alloys manufacturer Henry Wiggins.

Verden was educated at Crynant Infants, Crynant Junior and Cadoxton Secondary Modern Schools. He then went on to Neath Technical College 'for further education' and, as he describes it, Mott The Hoople 'for even further education.' As a youngster, Verden received classical piano tuition, firstly from Mr James Hugh, who was the organist in Crynant Church and also his godfather, and then from Miss Gwyneth James. Verden passed one music examination at the Victoria College of Music and five grades through the Royal Schools of Music.

The Allen family moved from Wales to St Weonards in the Herefordshire countryside and then to Tupsley in the suburbs of Hereford. Influenced by Liberace, jazz albums, organ players like Jimmy Smith, and ultimately R'n'B/soul artists like Booker T and the MGs and The Animals, Verden expanded his musical interests, while, in the daytime, he trained and worked as a car bodywork repairer at Belmont Road garage in Hereford.

'After leaving South Wales with my parents to live in Hereford in 1959, I was re-attracted to the piano by my uncle, Colin Thornton, who was a pub pianist. He took me away from the classical approach of my previous tutors to an un-inhibited ad-lib style of playing.'

During his time with The Anchors in 1963, Dale Griffin recalls that they were glared at during some of their gigs by two threatening looking 'teddy boy' types who turned out to be Terry Allen and his cousin John. Verden was to play in a rival Hereford group and had simply been watching The Anchors to pick up hints. Switching from piano to organ, Allen joined The Inmates in 1964 with Brian Pilling (vocals), Tony Breen (guitar), Gerry Broad (bass) and Dave Scudder (drums). Later that year, Verden switched to The Astrals who had lead singer Lee Starr (real name Jon Best), bass player Percy Francis and drummer Rob Harris.

The original Shakedown Sound, featuring guitarist Kevin Gammond, vocalist Jess Roden and keyboard player Gus Eadon, had been formed in Worcester. Roden went on to join The Alan Bown Set, The Butts Band with members of The Doors, and Bronco, before forming The Jess Roden Band. Gus Eadon, who once sought stardom via the television talent show 'Opportunity Knocks', would later work with future Mott The Hoople pianist Morgan Fisher in sixties teen band The Love Affair. In 1967, when Gammond left the original group, he agreed to link up with Verden Allen, Jon Best (also known as Johnny Lee) now on bass and drummer Sean Jenkins, who played with Gus Eadon in The Elastic Band. They decided to re-use the name Shakedown Sound, but then Verden was approached to join the Doc Thomas Group and accompany them to Italy. He declined the Doc Thomas offer, and kept his day job, until the Shakedown Sound got the chance to back Jimmy Cliff.

'While Doc Thomas were in Italy, the Shakedown Sound went to London,' says Allen. 'There had been an advert in *Melody Maker* for Jimmy Cliff, who wanted a backing band, so we went down and auditioned. Three days later, I was in Paris and packed my day job in. I thought things were going to happen musically, and they did.'

Jimmy Cliff had been persuaded to come to the UK by Island Records' boss Chris Blackwell during a US tour in 1964. After several singles, Cliff recorded an album, *Hard Road To Travel*, for Island in 1967, with American producer Jimmy Miller, and Verden made his recording debut on one track, 'A Whiter Shade Of Pale'. The remaining material featured members of Spooky Tooth as session players, brought in by Miller. Allen and the band accompanied Cliff to France, playing venues such as The Voom Voom Club in St Tropez, The Psychedelic Club in Nice, and gigs in Lens, Courcheval and Paris, where they performed at a fashion show one evening. The panel of judges included Bill Haley. Shortly afterwards,

Mick Ralphs joined Verden in The Shakedown Sound for about six months, after Kevin Gammond left the group to join The Band of Joy, precursor to Led Zeppelin.

'I said to Pete and Buffin that I was going to join this band and try and get a foot in the door in London and if I did, I'd come back and hopefully we'd have a few contacts,' says Ralphs. 'So I came to live in London in 1967 and shared a flat with Verden and Jon Best the bass player. I later left Jimmy Cliff and the Shakedown Sound and took Verden with me.'

Watts, Griffin and Tippins attempted to find a new guitarist as Ralphs and Allen started spending most of their time in Jimmy Cliff's backing band. Nobody of any use came along although Pete remembers they did audition guitarist Len Tuckey, (Suzi Quatro's husband to be), but didn't employ him. Watts was to have a brief liaison with Suzi, after an early seventies US festival that Mott played in Cinncinatti, but no bass playing offspring resulted!

Pete soon made contact with Ralphs again. 'Mick was now living in London and kept ringing me up, telling me how useless most of the groups were that he'd seen. He said that we ought to get back together after Jimmy Cliff. When Ralphs eventually left Jimmy, he took Verden Allen and brought him to us.'

Meanwhile, in early 1968, Terry Griffin auditioned for Love Sculpture with Dave Edmunds and his bassist John David Williams at Future Sound Studios and was offered the job. Dale felt he would have to think things over and Edmunds was far from pleased. When Griffin left he found his car battery was flat and Edmunds and John David refused to help push start the vehicle, before Kingsley and Charles Ward came to the rescue. Dale opted instead to work with Ralphs and Allen for the final three weeks of the Shakedown's Jimmy Cliff contract. Cliff went on to record two top ten hit singles, including a cover of Cat Stevens' 'Wild World', and starred in the 1972 cult hit film *The Harder They Come*.

Ralphs and Griffin went off and held discussions with Tippins and Watts and it was decided to invite Allen to form a band with them, thus completing 'the merging of the Motts'. The 'new' Shakedown Sound was managed by Norman Dickens and the Norsan Agency. After three weeks of rehearsal at Arbour Hill Farm, the quintet began doing gigs as the Shakedown Sound, because that group was well known in the Midlands and the North of England and had a reasonable following. The name was also a useful key to considerable live work over a wider area and the participants needed the money!

As Verden's musical knowledge developed in these early groups, he was already starting to devise a playing style and sound that would later distinguish Mott The Hoople's material. Allen was one of the first rock musicians in Britain to own a Leslie tone cabinet and he subsequently developed a totally unique sound for Mott, much admired by rival bands, using an American Acoustic amp and speaker with fuzz facility.

'My first keyboard was a Hohner Pianet which I exchanged for a Vox Continental as I was influenced by The Animals,' recalls Verden. 'I parted with the Vox and bought a Hammond M100 and became aware of people like Jimmy Smith, Jimmy McGriff and Richard 'Groove' Holmes, all great jazz organ players.

I also liked the way Booker T used the Hammond. The first pro-gig that I did using my Hammond M100 was with Jimmy Cliff in Paris. I had only just bought the organ, and didn't have any amplification, so I shared a Selmer Goliath bass system and speaker with Jon Best. It sounded like a distorted fart. After that I used Jimmy Cliff's Wallace P.A. system. Returning to Hereford, I purchased one of the first Leslie speaker cabinets imported into the UK. I later used a direct sound from the Hammond through a Marshall system and then switched to a HiWatt Head and Marshall cabinet, combining it with the Leslie.'

Watts observed how Verden always kept his instruments in pristine condition. 'The M100 was quite a medium sized Hammond, wooden, and it was immaculate. The Leslie tone cabinet was cubic, french polished with slats in it, very posh. When Phally wasn't on the road, his mother would polish these, and put mats and flowers on them using them as furniture around the house. Everybody else's Hammonds were either beaten up looking or painted matt black – not Phally's. This organ didn't split into two sections to assist handling and transportation, so it was extremely heavy. Taking it up and down flights of stairs was hell and Verden used to suggest we should throw ourselves under the organ to protect it if it started to slip. We manhandled this bloody thing for years until one day in Olympic Studios, in 1970, we were halfway up the stairs with it, when it slid sideways and pinned Ian Hunter's head against the wall, snapping his shades with a sharp crack. His skull was saved by the rest of us, but the incident caused much argument, especially in the group car on the way to gigs, as it kept coming up again and again – as things did with Mott. Verden never paid Ian the 3s 11d for the glasses, so he refused to carry the Hammond anymore, as I did, subsequently, when my fingers got badly trapped.'

The Shakedowns continued to do gigs in England and made some demo recordings at Future Sound Studios. As the summer of '68 approached, the band was offered Italian dates as the Doc Thomas Group, at The Bat Caverna Club, Riccione and The Pineta Club in Milano Marittima. Prior to these concerts, however, they were booked to play at a nightclub on the outskirts of Milan, where they performed outdoors, facing a turkey farm which stank. Needless to say, very few patrons were tempted to attend these soirées and there was great relief when the contract ended, but, as usual, very little money!

On arrival in Milano Marittima, the group found that their 'manager', Willy, had disappeared and was rumoured to be in jail. They never saw him again and life was far less fun without him. Willy had become the Doc Thomas Group's image manager, because he hated their dowdy clothing and lacklustre stage act. The Italians thought the group were the sons of eccentric English aristocrats, playing in bands for fun, rather than their daily bread and gruel. Willy was great manic company, a ribald raconteur, outrageous womaniser and supremely raffish, rogueish, Rabelaisian hellraiser, bullshitter and friend, as Watts recalls. 'Willy was very arty. He was a friend who hung around with us and he became influential in terms of ideas, though not musically.'

The Pineta Club dates were not a great success, it was a rather older crowd, not used to British bands, but The Bat Caverna was fun-filled at least. During this time Pete Watts had become engaged to a beautiful young Italian artist called

Maria Jannelli and was also in discussions to join a major Italian rock band, who had several hits to their credit, as Dale recalls. 'The summer had seen the end of The Doc Thomas Group and the Italian campaign. Our final days there found us minus our truck, which had gone to that great service station in the sky, and too poor to replace it. We were also minus our bass player, as Watts had decided to stay in Italy with Maria and to join major stars I Giganti (The Giants), having been lured away by their leader, Checco (the cad) with promises of money, fast cars, villas and fame. I Giganti were a well-known band, but Checco wanted to form a 'supergroup', as was becoming the fashion, with selected musicians.'

In September 1968, the rest of the band were forced to take a taxi and caravan back to the UK, with the group equipment. It was not a happy journey, as they pondered the future, bass-less. Back in Britain, the remaining members of the Doc Thomas Group auditioned various bass guitarists (unsuccessfully) and played some 'disastrous' gigs. They couldn't find a replacement for Pete. This grim period was reminiscent of the final days of The Silence, when Watts left to join The Buddies. Surprise, surprise, Pete returned to the UK within four weeks, because Checco's great promises and the supergroup had failed to materialise. Watts had written his first song though, 'Shades Of Life', which Silence would later play on stage.

As Allen had originally joined The Shakedown Sound via bass player Jon Best, Mick, Verden, Pete and Dale backed Best on two demo recordings at Marquee Studios, 'Good Morning' and 'I've Found Something Better'. The songs, described by Griffin as 'priceless, sub-psychedelic rubbish', were to fulfil Best's quest for solo stardom, but they achieved nothing and he soon joined progressive band, Titus Groan, instead. Best nearly joined Silence a short time afterwards as a second bassist; while he played deep bass, Pete would play high bass, Ralphs having been inspired by The Marmalade who tried a similar approach, likewise Alex Harvey.

In late 1968, Ralphs, Watts, Griffin, Tippins and Allen decided to resurrect the name Silence, but there the similarities ended. This time new and important changes lay ahead.

2
The Loner

In May 1969, Ian Hunter Patterson was to audition successfully for Guy Stevens and Silence, and one of Britain's most influential rock groups, Mott The Hoople, was formed. Hunter was Born in Oswestry near Shrewsbury, in Shropshire on 3 June 1939. Oswestry is situated only forty-five miles north of Hereford, but Ian was not to encounter his future Mott colleagues until thirty years later in London.

Ian's father, Walter Walker Patterson, was a Scot from Hamilton, near Glasgow, who married Freda Potts, from Wellington, Shropshire. They had two sons, Ian and Bob, who was eight years younger and went on to work in computing. In true Scottish tradition, Ian was christened with Hunter as his middle name, a late substitute for Jarvie.

When the Second War World started Ian's family was soon evacuated from Shropshire. 'At that time, England was obviously in chaos,' says Hunter. 'My mother was standing on the station platform leaving home and she'd never even been on a train before. We had to go Scotland, because all the families were being taken out of the towns in England and my father had a sister, Nettie, there. She lived in Wellhall Road near Peacock Cross in Hamilton, in a tenement building. It had a communal backyard, where they did the washing, and a little green for the kids to play on. It's still there, in fact one of my early best mates, Jim Feeney, still lives in the apartment opposite ours.'

Ian stayed in Hamilton until 1945 and his mother worked for the war effort in Glasgow, while Aunt Nettie looked after him and his brother. Towards the end of the war, Ian and his family moved back south, to Wellington in Shropshire. 'I think my mother wanted to be near her father, who owned a boot and shoe store in Walker Street and we had the flat above it, number eight. I recall D-Day in Wellington and being scared of the fireworks. I even remember the rationing well and "Anchor" cigarettes.'

Ian's father came back from the war, having been an Army Captain in Sicily and re-joined the family in Shropshire, taking a job in the police force. 'We stayed in Wellington for a little while, but I don't think my Dad got on well with my Mum's father, Percy Potts, so he joined the police force and we moved to Ellesmere in Shropshire, where I went to school for the first time. Schools weren't really schools at that time, they were just places to send kids after the war.'

A few months later, the Pattersons moved to Market Drayton, but only for a further year. Ian went to two more educational establishments in a relatively short space of time and his life was becoming chaotic and unsettled. The family relocated again, to Widchurch in Shropshire, where Ian attended Claypit Street School. 'I fell in love there for the first time, with this teacher, Miss Ashley. I was about ten years old and I passed my eleven plus examination, because I fell madly in love with her and because my old man said he'd buy me a bike. I imagined it would be a Raleigh three-speed; it was, in fact, a Hercules safety model, no gears, no lights! Not quite so glamorous.'

Ian went to Widchurch Grammar, a school with large grounds, which he enjoyed, but his father was again transferred to another station, and Ian was forced to change to Shrewsbury Priory Grammar School for Boys. 'I hated every minute of it and they didn't like me either. I got comments like 'hostile' on my school reports. My brother joined just after I left and they had him in on the first day and said, "Look, if you think you're going to be anything like him you can forget it." Apparently I was a bit of a lad there. The Priory was terrible, bloody awful.'

Hunter hated the whole concept of enforced learning, and, realising he could not find another soulmate like himself, he soon became a truant and a loner, and used to go into fits of depression at school. 'I was a loner because I had to be, because I couldn't find anyone else who was on my wavelength. I moved to Northampton later on and I made a few friends there, but I found people who were like me were, in the main, villains. With most people, there was a line they wouldn't go past. They lived "by the book", observed the rules. With the villains there were no lines, you could be really broad. It was loose, it was easy. I never got involved in crime, although, my old man was, more than once, advised by the Northampton Constabulary to get me to go home because I was in the wrong company. But I knew what I was doing. I enjoyed their company because I played a couple of chords on guitar and they'd get me to sing them a few songs.

'I thought I was crazy or ill. My parents were talking about having me committed at one time and that was only because I couldn't mix with all these complete idiots. I thought they were idiots at the time. It took another fifteen years to find out they actually *were* idiots. My parents *did* think there was something seriously wrong with me at one point, but you must understand Britain was in upheaval at that time. The youth had rebelled and it was a bit of a shock to the older generation. "What's the matter with my child? He's out of control. I thought he was going to have a proper job." I didn't know what was going on. I was just this tearaway and my Dad was a cop, which made it even worse because when I got into trouble it reflected on him.'

Ian had major confrontations with his father who wouldn't even let him have a guitar in the house and his school days were unsettled and unhappy. Hunter hated the non-creativity and total emulation of the educational system, so truancy became a frequent pastime. 'I was up in the snooker hall most of the time, which was halfway between where we lived and the school. I had an amazing amount of trouble getting past the snooker hall and more often than not failed. There used to be guys in there with skin-tight drainpipe trousers and I would stand there, trying to pull my baggy trousers tight to look like everybody else, a slave to fashion! If my old man had caught me, he'd have killed me, because he had a position in society to protect. I didn't have many mates who seemed to understand. I think I was a city kid and I was brought up in the country so I was at odds. I was in the wrong place.'

The only thing Ian learned at school was how to cheat at exams, but, these darker academic moments aside, he did have a degree of sporting success at

Shrewsbury Priory. 'The other guys let me cheat, because most of them were smaller than me and too scared to say anything. I remember being captain of the middle school for athletics and I'm still in the records I think for the high jump, which, of course, I did my way. I was still doing the Splits, while they wanted you to do the Fosbury Flop or the Western Roll.'

Hunter's first employment was with the *Wellington Evening Journal* based in Shrewsbury, before he went into labouring. His home town could not fuel his personal or musical ambitions which he still ruefully acknowledges today. 'Shrewsbury never has been a haven for rock 'n' roll. Even when Mott got big, we never played round there. I think the nearest we ever got was Birmingham. I never had anything there and the whole Patterson clan never seemed to make friends easily. I don't really have friends in the music business today, because I don't seem to be in tune with most people.'

Ian soon got into trouble in Shrewsbury and decided to leave home at seventeen. 'I went to Butlins Holiday Camp, which was the biggest legalised brothel in Britain. One day I went past a chalet and I heard someone playing guitars. I knew how to play the chords C, F and G, so I just banged on the door and there were these two lads from Northampton, Colen Yorke and Colin Broome, who were in a band called The Apex. We entered a Butlins talent competition, and we sang "Blue Moon" with Spanish guitars. Colin Broome and I did the "ooohs", while Colen Yorke sang the song. We won it and got a free week's holiday at the end with the Titbits competition winners. It was all tying in. It looked like the beginning of the end with this particular girl I was going out with, Margaret Oliver, I was in a bit of trouble, so my Dad and me were falling out and things were not good at home. I decided to make a move and went to Northampton.'

Initially, Ian stayed with Colin Broome and his parents, who had a newsagents' shop. Having been an apprentice at Sentinel / Rolls Royce in Shrewsbury, Hunter transferred to British Timpkin in Northampton to continue an engineering apprenticeship. It was then that his involvement with groups first began. Ian joined the jazz-influenced Apex, a band who had originally formed in the late fifties. Run by vocalist Frank Short, with Broome and Yorke in tow, Ian played rhythm guitar, and the group were regular performers around Northamptonshire.

'The Apex was composed, at that time, of enthusiasts more than an actual group. They were guys who were all older than me, so I just played rhythm and didn't sing, but I used to jump around like a total lunatic. Later on, when I saw the punks doing it, I realised what I had been doing. Music affected me so much. The rest of them just stood there. It was funny, because I had kids who came just to watch me do this and I can't imagine what it looked like; they just stared at me. I think I was doing what a lot of people did later on, jumping up and down like a maniac and playing C, F and G which was the basic punk thrash.'

The Apex recruited a new drummer named Johnny Lever, the owner of a local record store, who arranged some demos for the band. Hunter does not remember if he played on these but he did make his first recording in 1963 – The Apex Rhythm & Blues All-Stars EP containing four rock and roll standards – 'Tall Girl', Chuck Berry's 'Reeling And A' Rocking', 'Down The Road Apiece' performed by Berry and The Rolling Stones, and 'Sugar Shack' by Jimmy Gilmer & The Fireballs. The EP was released on John Lever Records, a small company formed by Johnny to press up private copies of discs. Lever's shop had a record-making facility based in Gold Street, Northampton and the session was record-ed at NSRS (Northampton Sound Recording Service), also home to a label called Studio 36. Unsurprisingly, the single failed to attract the attention of any estab-lished record companies.

Playing middle-class rhythm and blues, The Apex performed mainly in the officers' clubs of the garrisons and air bases around Northampton. Freddie Lee, Hunter's future musical partner in the sixties, saw The Apex and thought they were a great band, with a fine vocalist in Frank Short. Hunter, however, was not so keen. 'Frank was a very clever businessman and he had the American base circuit all tied up. They paid an awful lot more than the English gigs. In fact, he caught me trying to get shows, some time later, for my first band, and put me up against a wall. We had to wear jackets in The Apex, and one night I refused, and again, it was up the wall, no messing. I put the jacket on! The Apex were an R&B style band whereas I was a Jerry Lee Lewis fanatic and a Little Richard and Screaming Lord Sutch fan. Also, I didn't like hanging out with the guys in The Apex and some of their friends who they'd introduced me to, so I naturally grav-itated back down towards the bottom of the barrel and started hanging out with the rogues in Northampton; great guys and some of the best mates I ever had.'

It wasn't long therefore before Ian got into trouble again. 'I wasn't making my hire purchase payments and "little jobs" were getting done and people were get-ting smacked, and I was never in the middle of it, but I was always somewhere in the area. My old man came over to see me and said, "You've got to come back, you're in trouble and you've got to pay these bills off." I'd been buying clothes and hadn't been paying for them. I was a total whacko. I didn't wear any kind of underwear whatsoever and my clothes would stay on me for about a year, so I must have reeked a bit. I never noticed and I had no shortage of willing ladies, but I must have been a bit of a mess. I couldn't really look after myself. I found that impossible. All I wanted to do was go completely mad the whole time.'

Hunter returned to Shrewsbury, found a new girlfriend, Diane Coles, and took a job with McGowans fruit and vegetable company, travelling occasionally to places like Liverpool, buying produce to sell to retailers. In Shrewsbury, he also formed a harmonica duo with a friend called Tony Wardle, inspired by The Morton Fraser Harmonica Gang, a well known quartet on stage and television variety bills around this time. Ian was an excellent harmonica player, according to Freddie Lee, who remembers him working solo at this point, under the name Rusty Hunter.

'I stuck it out in Shrewsbury until I'd paid off the hire purchase debts and got myself out of this mess and then went straight back to Northampton. Diane followed soon after and we were married there. Somebody got me a house in St James's End in Northampton and we rented it for three quid a week. My eldest son, Stephen, was born there in 1962. I was young when I got married the first time and the kids came when I was young too. It just wasn't meant to be. Diane was a really nice girl and the kids grew up great, but she married an average working bloke and then I turned into this other thing and it didn't work. A lot was going on; there were a lot of US servicemen around and I was buying and selling American cigarettes and cars and I didn't even have a licence. My mates were wide boys too, people like Alan Manship, Jimmy Taylor, Barry Parkes and Tony Perrett, who went on to become a successful scrap metal merchant.'

Freddie Lee recalls Hunter's friends attending many of his gigs 'guarding' the front of the stage with sledgehammers. Ian was still playing in The Apex at this point but it was turning into a band who were far too safe and unadventurous for his liking. 'When skiffle stopped, we started doing stuff like "Kansas City" and conservative R&B, but I'd seen Screaming Lord Sutch at a gig, and Nero and the Gladiators and Johnny Kidd and the Pirates and I was thinking more in terms of that style of music, performance and presentation.'

Believing that he was not a good singer, but desperately wanting to front a band, Ian formed his own group, in 1963. Hurricane Henry and the Shriekers aimed to play out and out rock 'n' roll. Tony Marriott, who became a good friend of Hunter, and subsequently died as a result of alcoholism, was on drums, and Julian Coulter, who went on to replace Jimmy Page in Nero and the Gladiators, played lead guitar. 'Julian was amazing,' says Ian. 'He was the best guitar player in Northampton. There was another kid, Roger Green, who was good too, but Julian was better. His Dad owned a fruit and vegetable stall on Northampton outdoor market though and music came to an end for Julian when he took over his father's business.'

Hunter was still performing with The Apex in American bases and getting good money but had formed Hurricane Henry as direct competition with them. However, His musical pursuits became difficult with a day job, wife and child and a second infant on the way. 'It was mad. We were wearing sacks and Viking horns on our heads and there was many a crazy situation with the Hurricane Henry band. It was fabulous and a lot of people came to see us, so Frank Short was getting a bit fed up and I may actually have been fired from The Apex. I kept working, getting little jobs all over the place. I was also hanging about with all these low-lifes, as high-lifes are called by average-lifes, so I was pretty busy and out most nights. I did have a small amount of time to spend with my family though and so Tracey came along in 1964, when we were living in Alcombe Road, which is not far off Abington Square in central Northampton.'

Ian became hooked on mad ferocious rock and roll when he first heard Jerry Lee Lewis's 'Whole Lotta Shakin' ' and Elvis Presley's 'Heartbreak Hotel'. The American rock 'n' roll of the fifties was his inspiration and Jerry Lee and Little Richard were to be major lifelong influences on Hunter, although The Rolling Stones, Leon Russell, Bob Dylan and Jesse Winchester would also kindle his musical ambition. Hunter rated Jerry Lee even higher than Elvis. 'I thought when Jerry Lee Lewis first came out it was the comedian, who'd just put Lee in the middle of his name. It's hard to imagine but America was a million miles away then, not 3,000 miles for me. It always had to be the heavy ones, like Gene Vincent, Little Richard and Jerry Lee Lewis. It was really how kids were at that time. The pimply ones loved The Shadows and the rebels liked Sutch and Johnny Kidd.

They were the only bands you could see that played loud, fast and heavy. It was a great time for rock 'n' roll.'

Jerry Lee Lewis and Little Richard (Richard Penniman), were born in the American South in the early to mid 1930s and epitomised the wild arrogant musical assault that became fifties rock 'n' roll. Both singers influenced a host of American and British teenagers and artists. If Presley was the sex symbol of the time, Lewis was the craziest, howling, white performer playing piano with a sustained boogie attack, and Penniman the most bizarre and flamboyant black star with irrepressible raucous vocals and heavy make up. Their music affected Ian, his first musical partner Freddie Lee and Mott's future mentor Guy Stevens very deeply. Several Lewis and Penniman songs were later performed live by Mott and Hunter over the years including 'What'd I Say', 'Whole Lotta Shakin' Goin' On', 'The Girl Can't Help It', 'Keep A-Knockin' ' and 'Don't Wanna Discuss It'.

The UK equivalents, meanwhile, included Johnny Kidd and the Pirates and Screaming Lord Sutch, both influential figures in the birth of British rock during the late fifties. Kidd's 'Please Don't Touch' single was one of very few authentic home-based rock 'n' roll performances and 'Shakin' All Over' with its radical stop-start tempo was equally remarkable, and Kidd wrote them too. Sutch rose to prominence in 1960 with long flowing hair and the most accomplished of live acts, based on the US performer, Screaming Jay Hawkins. Although his Lordship's Joe-Meek-produced singles like 'Jack The Ripper' and 'I'm A Hog For You Baby' failed to chart, Sutch was able to recruit the likes of Ritchie Blackmore, Paul Nicholas and Nicky Hopkins for his group The Savages.

As rock 'n' roll music captivated Ian and his life became more and more frantic, he is the first to confess that he neglected his marriage. Furthermore, he lost his job at British Timpkin, because he was supposed to attend technical college one day a week to learn theory as an apprentice, but played truant for a year and was duly fired. 'They could have done me for fraud, because technically they paid me for five days a week and I actually only ever did four.' Hunter had numerous jobs over the years – capstan operator, Rolls Royce employee, driver – although he had no licence, so he would take work for a couple of weeks, saying his licence was in the post. But all his jobs he found dismal. 'It was frightening. They give you a green card and map out fifty years of your life in about a minute. If I knew what I'd be doing five years from now I'd be suicidal. I worked day jobs until 1968 and had over forty jobs. I used to go back to the same places over and over. They always thought they could make a good man of me, that I could have been a foreman. Semi-skilled, capstan, grinding, drilling – I did anything to do with engineering, having done a three and a half year apprenticeship.'

Ironically, it was another pianist, Freddie 'Fingers' Lee, who helped Hunter decide that his future was in rock 'n' roll, Ian had first seen Fred playing piano with Screaming Lord Sutch's The Savages in 1963, the group comprising drummer Carlo Little, bass player Rick Fenton, and Ritchie Blackmore on guitar.

Frederick Cheeseman was born in Chopwell, near Newcastle, on 24 November 1937. He attended school in Consett, County Durham, after his family moved there when Fred was three years of age. The Cheeseman's were very musical; Dad played the drums, Mum piano and Grandfather the violin, "Irish jig style", so Freddie got his first guitar when he was twelve. 'In those days there was nobody to teach you, so we all bought "How to play in a day", but you never could. It was always in tune as far as we were concerned, even when it wasn't. That was how I learned and then I went on to play piano, bass, harmonica, banjo and drums, almost anything I could turn my hand to. I was fortunate because there was always music in our house, but all the popular music we had was Radio Luxembourg's Top 20 and it used to be on when I was in bed. Because it was late, my mother wouldn't let me come down again, so my Dad used to turn up the volume so I could hear it upstairs.'

Fred was raised on Frankie Laine records, his first idol, and then he heard the skiffle music of Lonnie Donegan. 'From day one I was a guitarist before I ever thought of piano. Lonnie Donegan literally changed my life, I idolised the bloke. That's all I played for a couple of years. I went professional when I was a kid with a band in Scunthorpe called The Hillbilly Skiffle Group. I sounded like Donegan and I played like Donegan. We toured the Star Cinema circuit in the fifties playing between films. That was my start in those days; no money, but it was big time.'

Lee also played guitar in a band that appeared on a Newcastle TV show called *The Golden Disc* but when Jerry Lee Lewis released 'Whole Lotta Shakin' Goin' On' in 1957, Fred stopped dead in his tracks. 'I heard "Whole Lotta Shakin'" and I didn't believe that a man alive could play a piano like that. It was just unbelievable. But it was another two years before I began to learn to play like him.'

Freddie's non-musical jobs included steel erector, scaffolder and fitter welder. Wearing a glass eye since an industrial injury, Lee became known as 'The One-Eyed Boogie Boy' and later even released a solo album which he titled *Ol' One-Eye's Back*. He was to marry three times, and have a son and two daughters.

While he served an apprenticeship as a rigger and steel erector, Fred continued to play music. In 1958 he returned to Consett and joined The Saints Skiffle Group, followed by The Olympics, and also played the part of a savage in a local pantomime – *Robinson Crusoe*. However, Jerry Lee Lewis had made a huge impression on Fred and he went to London in 1959 and took up piano, learning Jerry Lee songs in his landlady's house. Fred joined a group called Lee Lynch and The Heartbreakers on guitar, playing Buddy Holly, Chuck Berry and Eddie Cochran material, before linking up with Screaming Lord Sutch. David Sutch had been gigging since 1960, his mainstays being ex-Cyril Davies and The All Star Band and ex-Rolling Stone drummer Carlo Little with Tony Dangerfield on bass, who both formed the nucleus of the group up to their demise in April 1967. 'Tony Dangerfield I knew on and off,' says Ian. 'I saw him play with Sutch. He was a good bass player. He worked with Pete Philips a lot so I probably worked with him at some point too.'

Freddie spent two periods working with Screaming Lord Sutch. 'He advertised for a guitarist and I applied. When I got there the job had gone, but he also wanted a piano player – "Jerry Lee Lewis style" – and I said I could do it. I couldn't. I could only play six numbers, so they sussed out what I was doing and, in the end, I got the sack.' Lee moved on to join The Citizens and worked at the Top Ten Club in Hamburg, sitting in on piano with as many bands as possible.

Eventually, he was good enough to re-join Sutch's group as pianist, in the Ritchie Blackmore – Carlo Little line up. Blackmore, who, in pre-Deep Purple days and during his time with The Savages was a respected session musician, went on to join The Condors and then Neil Christian and the Crusaders, before playing in Mandrake Root and Roundabout, prior to the formation of Deep Purple in 1968.

Fred went back to Hamburg with Sutch playing the infamous Star Club, rubbing shoulders with the likes of Chuck Berry, Jerry Lee, Little Richard, Johnny Burnette and Gene Vincent. The name Freddie Lee was adopted by Cheeseman as a tribute to Jerry Lee Lewis, courtesy of David Sutch. 'He wanted a name for me and used to call me Humping Jerry Lee. At the time, Tom Littlewood managed Lord Sutch and they put an advert in the paper which was misprinted as Freddie "Fingers" Lee. The name just stuck.'

Screaming Lord Sutch was sensational in concert and he and Fred contrived some amazing on-stage antics. 'We had this routine where I'd run round the theatre dressed in a leopard skin and he was chasing me as Jack the Ripper. There was a sloping stage at this particular theatre in Sheffield and I'd put wedges under the piano. When I ran back on stage and jumped on to the piano, the wedges came out and the instrument rolled off into the orchestra pit with me on top of it. Sutch ran to get me out but shouted to the roadies, "Quick, quick, phone the papers, phone the papers – after you've done that, phone for an ambulance!"'

Freddie also adopted a crazed approach in his own stage act. Concert promoters usually provided a special piano for Fred to take apart with a large axe at the end of his set, after he once began the demolition of a rare concert Steinway at Birmingham Town Hall. A bag of loose piano keys were kept in the lid of the instrument for Freddie to launch into the audience at strategic points in the set. Buzz saws and paint rollers were also utilised on stage, and Lee would often set fire to his headgear, on some occasions leading to partial destruction of ceilings and curtains.

Ian Hunter chanced upon wild rocker Freddie in a Northamptonshire public house one day in 1963, and it was probably this meeting and collaboration, more than any other, that cemented Ian's future in music. Hunter vowed that one day he'd be a leader and not a follower and that he would swap the factory floor for the stage. 'The Hurricane Henry band was moving forward at full throttle,' recalls Ian. 'We were working five or six nights a week and I used to go out and get gigs for the following month. I was about twelve miles from Northampton one day and there was a guy in this pub leaning against the jukebox dressed in steel erector clothes, covered in dust, with hammers and things hanging down from his leather belt. I knew the face. It was Freddie "Fingers" Lee, who I'd seen with Sutch, so I went up and asked, "Excuse me, are you Freddie Lee?" and he said, "Yeah, why?" It turned out he thought I was going to hit him, because he looked distinctly nervous when I spoke to him. I said, "I'm a big fan of yours. What are you doing here?" Apparently he'd taken a lot of speed and had been in hospital. When he came out, Sutch had picked up Paul Nicholas, the guy who later went on to fame and fortune as a stage, TV and film actor and singer. Now Fred was out of work, so he'd gone back to his old trade, which was steel erecting and here he was, doing a job in this town near Northampton.

'So I said, "Fred you can't do this, you've got to come back to Northampton and be a local star. Why don't you join my band?" He said, "Great" and moved in at Alcombe Road with Diane, Stephen, Tracey and me. I remember Tracey used to poke his glass eye out every morning!'

Fred stayed with Ian and his family until he found his own flat, and Lee remains grateful. 'I owe him a lot in that respect, because I'd had a bad drugs scene in London. I was busy getting out of that and had gone back to work to pull myself back to reality when I met Ian. I had a very, very soft spot for his son Stephen, I loved the little kid and used to take him everywhere with me and Diane was a really beautiful girl with a heart of gold.'

Lee joined The Shriekers in March 1964. The line-up still comprised Hunter, Marriott and Coulter, but their bass player, Bob, decided to quit at this point and left his Burns bass with Ian, who learned the instrument, so Fred could take over on piano and lead vocals. Assisted by the Eric Easton Agency, which co-managed The Rolling Stones with Andrew Oldham, and personal manager Vic Merrick, Freddie 'Fingers' Lee & The Shriekers gigged frantically. Guitarist Roger Green soon joined the band, replacing Julian Coulter. Hunter now contemplated song-writing for the first time, admitting later that Fred was a star in his eyes and he had never thought of composing until he met him. 'I did encourage Ian, because I used to write a lot and actually worked as a songwriter for Southern Music at one time,' says Lee. 'It wasn't that I saw things hidden in Ian, it was just his burn-ing ambition. He always wanted to be famous and be recognised. It would take some time but he got his wish.'

Hunter had played rhythm guitar at first, which he only ever picked up to relieve monotony, and was now proficient on bass, although *he* felt he couldn't play properly. 'I was just in love with the idea of show business. I wanted to go pro, and with Fred it was possible, because he had contacts in Germany. I went there with him a couple of times as a bass player. Fred always played rock 'n' roll and always will. In hindsight, his big trouble was that he was Jerry Lee Lewis' double; he played like him, sang like him and he had a passion for country music which I didn't particularly like at the time.'

Freddie says that he was attracted musically to Hurricane Henry and the Shriekers. 'They were a very rough and ready band which suited me down to the bloody ground, because I was just about the same and they had a reputation for doing wild shows, so, naturally I was interested. The group went down a storm in Germany. There was one problem though – we didn't get paid. The inevitable happened; we were stranded on the docks in Hamburg without our fares home, and if it hadn't been for the sympathy of various frauleins, we probably wouldn't have got back to England. I didn't actually rename the band Freddie "Fingers" Lee & The Shriekers, it just happened, probably because I sang all the lead vocals, while Ian and Julian did the backing.'

At Freddie's suggestion, The Shriekers played in northern Germany at the Starpalast in Kiel, Bremen Beat Club and various Hamburg locations, including the Star Club. Hamburg's Reeperbahn, with its seedy night clubs and sordid drugs and prostitution, developed into a leading centre for rock and roll, particu-larly with British bands, and it became synonymous with the rise of The Beatles.

Of the two main venues, the Top Ten Club was 'elite', if such a description could exist in that part of the city, while the Star Club was rough and ready, but its bands played real rock 'n' roll. Fred opines that there will never be anything like it again in popular music. Germany inspired Ian now, as he and Freddie met artists such as Tony Sheridan, Roy Young, Howie Casey, Alex Harvey and The Searchers.

'The first time the bug really hit me was when I went to Germany playing bass with Freddie. That's when music became the obsession which took over my life,' recalls Hunter. 'Fred had enthused, "We'll go to Hamburg, we'll go to Kiel, Rendsburg, Duisburg, all these places in Germany." When you played a gig there, it was packed and people stood and stared at you, but sometimes you got paid by the club owners and sometimes you didn't. One minute you were stars and the next minute you were back in Northampton working in a factory. I sometimes had jobs for only one or two weeks, steel erecting or selling clothes in Milletts.'

'We went to Germany as professional musicians,' says Lee. 'Pro and semi-pro meant nothing really; we called ourselves pro or semi-pro depending on whether we had a job or not I suppose. All I can really say of the days in Germany and the early sixties is, it truly was sex, drugs and rock and roll and we made a meal of the whole bloody lot while we were there too.'

'Hamburg, in those days, was fantastic, it really was totally unbelievable,' enthuses Hunter. 'I never went to bed more than once every three days and then for about four hours. Things were going on twenty-four hours a day. There were often seven bands on the bill and sometimes you'd play at five in the afternoon and five the following morning. The best slots were at eleven and one – the place was always full. You could always tell if you were playing well, because all the lanterns on the bar at the back of the Star Club would start swaying. I even remember one show in Rendsburg where we played for nine hours non-stop.

'In Hamburg, Ritchie Blackmore, who had been playing with Sutch, asked Fred if he could join our band as the guitar player, but Fred said no because he thought Ritchie was disruptive and would wreck any group he ever joined. I sub-sequently played with Ritchie one night in the Speakeasy. He came over and asked if I wanted to get up so I did. I've never been a major fan of Blackmore because I don't think he plays with feeling, but, boy, can he play. When you stand next to him it's breathtaking.

'I was also Tony Sheridan's "gofer" for a while in Hamburg, running up and down the strip with five mark pieces for wine out of the automats. Tony was a maniac. You really didn't want to get on the wrong side of him. There were holes at the side of the stage in the Star Club where he'd butted the wall with his head.'

Ian points out that the bands never made much money and were regularly cheated by promoters. 'At one club in Kiel, our van broke down and the guy who ran the club knew we were stuck and wouldn't pay us. You never went to the British Embassy, because you hadn't the brains and if you did, they'd send you home, but take your passport away and you wouldn't be able to come back again. As bad as it was, you always wanted to return because it was what you were made to do. The little I got, I spent on food and drink, but half the time they wouldn't pay you at all. I used to get very depressed at the time. You'd go to Germany for four weeks work, get ripped off, come back home and do six to eight weeks at regular jobs until you got the next gig.'

In Kiel, Ian got increasingly desperate, as Diane and his children were with his mother in Blackpool, and they had no money. Neither did Hunter. 'I went into the club owner's office with a knife one day and threatened him saying: "You've got to give me some cash." He went white and said, "I'll go up to the flat and get you some money." When he came back, he brought Bob Xavier with him, this black guy, his number one heavy, who was a mate of mine, but if he said to Bob, "Shoot him," Bob would shoot me. The owner gave me ten pfennigs and said, 'This is for the stamp, to put on the card, to send to your wife, to tell her you send her nothing!'

Revenge was taken on the owner before the band departed, however. One Good Friday, when the club was closed and the group had nowhere to go, the phone rang and Lee answered it. 'There was a guy who wanted Freddie "Fingers" Lee, of all people, down in Duisburg,' explains Hunter. 'A band from Stockport on the same bill as us in Kiel offered to take us. I couldn't believe they'd drive us all the way from Kiel to Duisburg. We had no money and I don't know how we got the petrol. I remember a tyre blew on the way down there and I don't recall how we got round that one, either. But they were getting paid, and we weren't. I don't know who that band were, but I thank them to this day.'

'The Kiel club owner was Adolf Palfi, a former Yugoslavian boxing champion,' recalls Lee. 'He was a big gangster and was later charged with murder for killing a Yugoslavian ambassador, his wife and daughter. I used to see the "Wanted" posters in Hamburg. We took out our revenge for non-payment, not on the club owner, but his pets. He had a parrot and a cat which he loved dearly. Before we left we put a gas gun through the owner's office keyhole to kill the bird, and I killed his cat and nailed it to the office door. I'm very sad to say that now, but we were young, angry and stupid.'

In Duisburg, Freddie, Ian and the band played in a club called the New York City. 'The owner was a very nice guy, but if people of a certain nationality went into his club he would go mad,' says Hunter. 'He had a nice place but nobody would go there, so he would pay us in watches after two sets and seven hours a night. We would then go round restaurants exchanging the watches for food and that was how we lived.'

'Whilst we were in Duisburg, we had no money, as usual,' recalls Freddie. 'Ian and Roger smoked, Tony and I didn't, so Tony and I opted to put our money together and buy a loaf of bread and a jar of jam and Ian and Roger bought ten cigarettes. But when they'd had a smoke, they were hungry and we had the food, so a fight ensued between Ian and me over this food, with him adamant he was going to get it and me adamant he wasn't. We began brawling, the loaf of bread ended up as crumbs all over the room and nobody had anything to eat.'

Another English band on their way back from Holland passed by the New York City Club and helped The Shriekers home, packing their 15-cwt van with both sets of equipment. 'Only two of our group travelled,' says Freddie. 'Ian and I stayed behind in Germany and that's when we lived off the kindness of two young frauleins in return for certain favours exchanged. It took us a week to con the money out of them to get home, and we got as far as London and couldn't get any further. So we rang our so-called manager, Vic Merrick, and at quarter to two in the morning, he came down to the station, picked us up, and took us back to Northampton. That was the end of our German tour.'

The band did return to Germany, playing at the Star Club. 'We'd earn forty pounds a week,' says Hunter. 'They used to get you out there on contracts, but somehow the document was always lost and you were so enthusiastic and keen to go that you just went anyway, and then you'd be there at their mercy, especially if the van broke down, which ours had done. Bands used to buy vans for fifteen pounds and just hope that they would last the journey there and back.'

'The group carried on for a while and we went back to the Star Club, but split in 1965,' says Lee. 'Ian left and we got another bass player, but it wasn't the same without Hunter. We had a cameraderie that I've never really found in any another band. We were always fighting like hell, Ian and me, and arguing like shit, so because one of us just had to leave and that was the end of it. Unfortunately, Hunter moved on.'

After the demise of The Shriekers, Ian joined The Homelanders, a band that Freddie regarded as Northampton's 'gentlemen', playing all the 'society do's' while the other groups played rock 'n' roll venues. One of the local rival acts was Ian's old friend Colen Yorke, who ironically went out under the name of Dane Hunter and did fairly well. 'I joined The Homelanders around this period, because some of my mates went into jail, and others were in trouble, but I soon wanted to be in a band,' says Ian. 'The groups around this period would play gigs at both ends of the spectrum including St Mary's Hall on a Saturday night for eight pounds and working men's clubs midweek for five pounds. Twelve pounds was good remuneration for the evening.'

Things were changing for Hunter both musically and domestically. His wife Diane had started to tire of the oscillating employment situation and the musical rolling stone that Ian had become. 'She thought she'd married a normal guy who was going to get a job and have kids and settle down and then, I start turning in to this other person altogether, because music was really getting to me. I was also thinking I had to get out of Northampton because we'd taken things as far as they could go. I'd been in three of the biggest bands they'd ever seen there and I'd still got no record deal and we were not getting nationwide work. I decided to sell up and move down to London.'

Around this time, Freddie Fingers Lee secured a recording contract through Joe Brown's drummer, Howie Conder. Dale Griffin recollects that he sold Howie a drum kit some years later. 'This has to be Howie Conder, the bastard who gave me £140 part exchange for an amazing Ludwig champagne sparkle super classic drum kit. The swine! I'd never realised he'd been Joe's drummer. I always think of the great Bobbie Graham as the Bruvvers' drummer. It was only recently that I found the original receipt pertaining to this foul transaction. Of course, I was a total idiot for even contemplating parting company with the Ludwig kit,' comments Griffin ruefully.

Freddie Lee had made his first recorded appearances guesting on two

Screaming Lord Sutch singles, 'Good Golly Miss Molly' in 1961 and 'Jack The Ripper' in 1962, plus Danny Rivers and the River Men's 1962 single 'We're Gonna Dance'. Lee then cut two records of his own before he recorded with Ian Hunter. The first was a 1963 Decca EP entitled 'Everybody Surf' by The Surfin' Savages, followed by a 1964 single 'The Midnight Race' issued as Freddie Lee and the Upperhand on Columbia Records. Freddie produced three more British singles and Ian played on one, a novelty record, 'The Friendly Undertaker' and the B-side 'A Little Bit More', recorded at Regent Sound, and released on Fontana in 1965. Hunter did not appear on Fred's other singles, 'I'm Gonna Buy Me a Dog' and 'Bossy Boss', issued in 1966, but Lee confirms that Ian did play bass on several demos, some of which were cut onto acetate discs.

In the winter of 1966, Hunter finally made his move south for the glamour of the capital and Diane took the children back to Shrewsbury temporarily, while Ian looked for accommodation. He rented a flat for £5 a week and the family rejoined him. After a year, Diane thought the rent was excessive, so they moved to Cheverton Road, near the Archway in North London. 'I had the flat for £2 10s a week, so you can imagine what it was like, but at last I was in London, which is where I'd always wanted to be, all my life. I felt very proud walking round the streets. I always felt jealous of these guys who were born in London, because they didn't have to go through all that drama to get there.

'When I came back from Germany I was Jimi Hendrix crazy. I loved Hendrix and wrote down all his lyrics like 'The Wind Cries Mary', which I thought was amazing. I went back to Hamburg, trying to get something going for myself, doing Hendrix covers, but that wasn't happening at all, so I returned to London and starved, literally. They talk about starving now but they don't know what they're talking about. Starving is eating fucking toothpaste. There's no phone, there's no heat, and you go down to the dole and sit in offices for eight hours waiting for a lousy two quid.'

Ian got a factory job with an engineering company named Fryers in the Archway, but would sometimes telephone a recording engineer called Bill Farley, who was the only music person he really knew in London, the contact having been made originally through Freddie 'Fingers' Lee. Farley was boss and chief sound engineer at Regent Sound, a small, four-track recording studio in Denmark Street, affectionately known as Tin Pan Alley. Ian got to know Bill well and started to demo tracks at Regent Sound. Hunter recalls, 'The Stones did their first album there and Andrew Oldham went in to Bill and said, "How much?" Farley said, "Four pounds an hour." So Andrew replied, "Two quid an hour and I'll give you half the proceeds of the album," but Bill told him to fuck off. Jimi Hendrix played at Regent, but Bill kicked him out because he was too loud. Little Richard rehearsed there too. It was quite a famous studio.'

'Really, Bill Farley did all of us a lot of favours in those days,' says Freddie Lee. 'Regent Sound helped us too, because none of us had any money or anything, but the funny part about it is, we never got any money either for all the records we made, so therein hangs another tale!'

Hunter recalls Farley approaching him one day, laughing heartily and brandishing a cheque. 'Bill had never written a song in his life, but he said, "Look at this," and I asked, "How did you manage that? It's a royalty cheque." Bill said, "Well, I co-wrote 'Rosalyn'." He was in there with The Pretty Things and they had this real good riff but no words, so they said, "Here Bill, what shall we call this?" And Bill said, "Sounds like Rosalyn to me." So they said, "Well, write the lyric." Farley said, "Well the lyric is, 'Rosalyn where ya been? Where ya been Rosalyn?'" And for this, he's sitting with a cheque for £1,800!'

Bill Farley let Ian work on demos, while he still had his factory job and he started to develop some credible songs. Two of Hunter's early compositions were 'Broken Dreams and Promises' and 'Lucinda Brown', although these were not picked up by any other artists. The first of his songs to be covered was 'And I Have Learned to Dream', recorded by Dave Berry on the B-side of his Decca single 'Forever', released in April 1967. The song was produced by Mike Smith who Freddie Lee had met at Southern Music. Hunter also wrote 'Seasons', which was recorded by Louisa Jane White. 'Ian did his own writing. It didn't fit in with my activities at all,' says Freddie. 'I don't recall him working on "Seasons" but I remember the song; it was beautiful and I take my hat off to Ian for that.'

Freddie and the Dreamers are thought to have recorded Ian's 'Gilbert the Ghost' although Freddie Garrity, their lead singer, has no recollection of this number and the track was never issued commercially. 'I remember writing the song and I spent a bit of time on it too, but whether it was ever covered or not I don't know,' says Hunter.

It was inevitable that Ian would return to a group situation and this materialised when he met a guitarist named Miller Anderson, and auditioned for a group called The Scenary. 'Somehow I bumped into Miller who was living just two streets away from me and he was serious about music.'

Miller Anderson was born in Houston, Renfrewshire near Glasgow on 12 April 1945. He came to London in March 1965 with top Scottish R&B band The Royal Crest, who changed their name to Karl Stuart and the Profile at the suggestion of their agent. 'We made four singles for Philips' Mercury label, but after a year we were just about falling apart when we met up with a Scientology offshoot called The Process and became their "house band",' says Miller. 'The group was still Karl Stuart and the Profile initially, but they wanted us to change the name to something more in keeping with their message, so they came up with The Voice. They liked the lyrics that I was writing, which they said were close to their beliefs, but I don't know how they worked that out. I was the first to leave the group and they all went to Mexico and the Bahamas later on, and lived in a commune.'

When Miller handed in his notice, The Voice searched for a new guitarist and he agreed to stay on for one month, so that they could locate and blood a replacement. 'It was practically my band, so I auditioned all the candidates,' explains Anderson. 'A lot of people came for the job because we were getting paid £15 a week, which was a fortune in 1966. I chose a guy called Mick Ronson, who I thought was excellent.'

The original Scottish drummer from Miller's group had been replaced by Londoner Dave Dufort, whose sister, Denise, became the drummer in Girlschool. 'Dave and I stayed together as a duo after The Voice and decided that

we would look for a bass player. We were in his mother's house one day when Ian
Patterson turned up,' recalls Miller. 'Ian was six years older than me and probably eight years older than Dufort, so, immediately Dave, who was very image
concious, thought Ian was too old. But I liked Hunter and I could see something
you couldn't really describe. He wasn't a fantastic musician or a fantastic singer,
he just had a rounded talent, ironically, like Bob Dylan I suppose. You couldn't
put your finger on anything, Ian just had that undefined quality.

'We formed a group from that audition in June 1966 called The Scenary and
then recruited a keyboard player called Dante Smith to make a quartet, with Ian
and me as singers. After a short while we got another drummer called John
Vernon Smith and we were actually a really good group. Ian was a fine bass player
and had a couple of kids by then. He thought I was a good guitarist and I had
one baby, Miller Jnr, so we got on well and we're still friendly after all these years.
The Scenary made a few demos at Regent Sound for Bill Farley, one of them
being a song called "Queue Jumping", which Ian mostly wrote with help from
me. We composed another song, which I later stole for The Keef Hartley Band
and called "Waiting Around", although it was inspired by something we'd been
writing together. However Hunter did pinch one of my riffs for "Whizz Kidd"
later on in Mott, which he credited me for.'

Miller found out, much later, that "Queue Jumping" came out in Japan as an
EP. 'We never saw any money from it and I don't think we ever realised it was released in Japan until somebody showed me the cover a few years later. I think it
was on some two-bit, "Let's con these guys out of this song" label. There was a
company run by Jeff Kruger who had something to do with Radio Caroline at
the time and a record company possibly involving Bill Farley. Jeff wanted to sign
Ian and me to a nine-year contract, which we turned down. Can you imagine
signing that, what for? He wasn't offering us any money, he just wanted us under
contract for nine years.'

In addition to their efforts as a *bone fide* group, Bill Farley put The Scenary on
a 1967 tour backing new singer–songwriter sensation, David McWilliams, from
Belfast, most famous for his single, 'Days of Pearly Spencer'. Anderson, Hunter
and Vernon Smith were the only electric outfit on the concert package, which included folk groups The Dubliners and The Corries.

As The Scenary, Ian and Miller also provided accompaniment for former Joe
Meek star Mike Berry, and for The Young Idea, a UK duo who had a hit single
with Lennon and McCartney's 'With a Little Help from My Friends' in June
1967. 'The Young Idea was my first brush with teenage hysteria,' recalls Hunter.
'The curtains would open and young kids would just go nuts. I'd never experienced that before. Mike Berry was England's answer to Buddy Holly.'

'The Young Idea were a couple of nice guys but totally inexperienced,' says
Miller. 'I don't know what they'd done before that but they needed a backing
band and Ian and I were like veterans compared to them. We more or less told
them what to do when we went on stage. It was nothing much, just a few gigs.
The work with Mike Berry was "by the gig". He'd ring up and say he had a
couple of concerts at the weekend and we would go and back him.'

Whilst The Scenary continued to play as a band and a supporting unit to various acts, Hunter and Anderson still took time to attend an interesting audition that they thought might break their careers. 'Me and Miller went down to an audition in South London in this horrible little room covered in dirt with a tiny gas fire. We sat on a filthy sofa and this guy Paul Raven came out in a blazer and flannels and started jumping around in front of us with no music, no backing, nothing, just him singing. Me and Miller were sitting there trying to keep straight faces. I remember we came out and walked down the road, pissing ourselves laughing and that was Gary Glitter. We thought it was a joke, and it was a joke until he got with Mike Leander, who was a very clever, talented guy.'

Hunter first saw Mick Ronson around this time when Miller took Ian to see The Voice, at the Swan public house in Tottenham. A few months later Hunter met Ronson when The Scenary played a one-off gig with The Rats at the Flamingo Club in London. 'That venue was a big deal then, even if you didn't get paid, because people like Georgie Fame performed there and you thought if you played, maybe you could become famous overnight,' says Anderson. 'Mick was coming down the stairs having just finished his set and we were going up and I said, "Mick, this is my friend, Ian Patterson." That's where Hunter first met Ronson, on the stairs of the Flamingo in Soho. Mick had an undefined quality as well; he was a very talented guy.'

Ian and Miller played together in various guises throughout this period, but it was proving extremely difficult for them to penetrate the London music scene. 'It was like a big institution and if you were a little lad from the provinces, you just didn't know where to start,' says Hunter. 'Bill Farley was our only hope. We would ring him and he would say, "You never know, just keep going and I'll do a demo for you now and again." We did various gigs, and got conned by various agencies that wanted to sign you for ten years, purely to sell you when you caught the eye of some more reputable agency. We still worked together in Fryer Brothers factory in the Archway and hated every minute of it. It was dismal.'

'Ian got me the job there,' says Miller. 'I'd been an apprentice engineer in Scotland and we worked on capstan machines. I was useless. There was more scrap coming off my machine than product. We stood side by side making small screws. It was like being in hell. Ian was there before me, so it pissed me off when he eventually went to work at music publishers, Francis Day and Hunter, and left me stranded in Fryers.'

For a short while, Miller left The Scenary to join a psychedelic group, The Paper Blitz Tissue with drummer Dave Dufort, while Ian went back to play with Freddie Lee during a brief rock 'n' roll resurgence that had rapidly taken hold in Britain at that time. In the end, Fred left his wife and children in Northampton and moved down to London, to live with Ian in Cheverton Road. This renewed popularity of fifties rock 'n' roll appeared to be a window of opportunity for Hunter and Lee and they formed a group, At Last the 1958 Rock and Roll Show, as Freddie recalls.

'There was a massive upsurge in rock 'n' roll and there were not any real rock 'n' roll bands, except us, who were already playing. When it all started though, I was away and there was an advert for a group and Ian phoned me up to tell me about it. I got the job and a band was formed. We had a residency at a pub called the Angel at Edmonton and used to play there every Friday, Saturday and Sunday. I suppose that's what paid the rent. It spanned roughly a year and the other artists who came out at the same time were Tommy Bishop, who made a record called "Longback Train" and Jerry Tempest, who sang "Loving Up a Storm". It was short-lived, purely a fad. People wanted something different, then they moved on to something else. The idea for our band was dreamed up by NEMS record agency but then we were also approached by Chrysalis.'

'Suddenly there was interest,' says Ian. 'We were playing an awful lot of gigs, mainly colleges, and Fred was bringing the house down. Chrysalis came to a pub called the Ship one night and we talked, then we rang up NEMS and said we were going to sign with Chrysalis and within about twenty minutes, Colin Johnson, who went on to manage Status Quo, was there saying, "You've got to come with us, it's better with us."'

At first, the group was effectively The Scenary with Fred on piano, but they decided they needed a more powerful drummer and recruited Pete Phillips, who played with Del Shannon. Phillips got the job because the selected drummer, Johnny Banks from The Merseybeats, had his kit stolen the day he joined, and an alternative was needed quickly. The original guitar player with At Last the 1958 Rock and Roll Show, Chris Mayfield, was sacked but went on to form Mayfield's Mule, a relatively well known band, around 1969. 'Chris wasn't a bad guitar player but he wasn't a patch on Miller Anderson,' says Freddie. 'Also, Miller wanted regular money, because he had a wife and child, but we got him in because he was really good.'

'Ian and Fred were recording with this other guitar player who wasn't working out, so they got me to come along to CBS Studios to record on "I Can't Drive" and tricked the other guitarist into not being at the session,' says Miller. 'The record worked out well and the management wanted me to join the band. Even before they told the other guitarist he was no longer required, I was taken to Carnaby Street to be fitted out for clothes. When I was in the fitting room trying out these clothes that Ian had picked, a green and gold shirt and a pair of pink flares, the guitar player walked in, and I was told to hide in the changing room while they all fled and left me stranded.'

'Miller was phenomenal to work with,' confirms Lee. 'We ended up joining NEMS and that's when the band became At Last the 1958 Rock and Roll Show. The reason we went with NEMS was because, like everybody else, we didn't have a lot of money and they said they'd buy us a van, new gear and clothes. We had top of the range stuff, playing top of the range gigs.'

NEMS was run by Dick Lewis and former Beatles roadie Tony Barrow acted as publicist for the company and the group, who recorded a single for CBS Records, produced by Jimmy Duncan: 'I Can't Drive', backed with 'Working on the Railroad'. 'Fred wrote "Railroad" in about five minutes and Tom Jones covered it and Freddie made a lot of money out of that,' says Ian.

'I re-recorded "I Can't Drive" because I couldn't write anything else that was good enough at the time,' admits Lee. 'I'd got an original recording, but the session with the Rock and Roll Show is far superior, partly because we used a group called Grapefruit for the backing vocals. They were quite popular at the time.'

Grapefruit scored two top-30 British hits in 1968 with 'Dear Delilah' and 'C'mon Marianne' for RCA Records and one of the group, Peter Swettenham, became a tape op. on many of Mott The Hoople's AIR sessions. Aimed at cashing in on this short-lived British rock 'n' roll revival, At Last the 1958 Rock and Roll Show's single was issued around the same time that the band appeared in a documentary with Bill Haley. 'I had to present him with a 78 rpm record of "Rock Around The Clock" in a frame, from his English fans,' says Lee. 'At the party afterwards in The Revolution Club, I managed to get the record back and it's still hanging on the wall in my studio!'

Freddie was more popular in Europe than the UK, so they toured Germany again playing a week at the Star Club in Hamburg and performed 'I Can't Drive' on German TV's *Beat Club* in Bremen. 'We were on a programme with Chuck Berry and we were classed as one of the heroes of German rock and roll,' says Lee. 'For a while, we rode the crest of a wave in 1968. We did TV, radio, colleges and even made a documentary with Bill Haley. As a stunt, I climbed to the top of Nelson's Column without getting arrested, on April Fool's Day 1968, to promote the single that was being released. As a former steeplejack and scaffolder, I decided I'd climb the Column, with a broken toe, got to the top, tied my coat on Nelson's elbow and it gave us the publicity we needed. It was in every newspaper in Europe and got us right off the ground, ahead of the pack, before anybody got going.'

'Climbing Nelson's Column was supposed to be easy as a steel erector,' says Miller, 'but I've never seen anything like it. Fred was up the outside in sixty seconds. He was amazing. Fred had only one eye and that was firmly fixed on publicity. We did a gig at a south London college on a very bouncy stage and on each side there was a big PA column and on top of that another PA column. I kept looking at one of them moving from side to side and thinking it might fall and, it did, and landed on Pete Phillips. He was lying on the stage unconscious with this load on top of him and before anybody could do anything Fred's first reaction was, "Quick, somebody phone the press!" Publicity was always a laugh with Ian and me.' If you tripped up a kerb, Ian would say, "Call the press." It was a standing joke.'

On Rock and Roll Show gigs, Patterson, Anderson and Phillips would come on stage ahead of Lee and open the show, Miller singing 'Lucille' and Ian taking lead vocals on 'Keep A-Knockin' '. 'Ian was *mein host*, because I was shy then and he would get the audience going ahead of Fred's appearance,' says Miller. 'But it was Fred's show, with us as his backing band, singing harmonies. However, Ian and I were writing songs which weren't being used and we had other ideas. We wanted to go further than just being in a backing band and playing old rock 'n' roll covers.'

Ian and Miller were becoming increasingly worried about the longer term future of the group. 'Fred used to say, "It beats me why you fuckers bother to turn up." Fred thought he was the whole show, which he was basically, standing on his head whilst playing the piano,' admits Ian. 'But it was good money. Then Fred wanted us put on wages. Fortunately, Colin Johnson wouldn't have that because he could see we were getting into something else and thought the future might lie more with Miller and me. We were all paid equally, but Fred couldn't understand that, he thought it should be like Lord Sutch all over again, that we should get three quid a week and he should get the rest. So it made us think about changing things around a little bit. I said to Fred, "This is going to go out of style and die a death and we're not going to have a gig, we've got to progress a bit." So Miller came up with the idea of changing the group name.'

'I had this character that I'd read about in a book who was a half-breed Indian called Charlie Woolfe,' recalls Anderson, 'and I thought it was a good name for the group. Plus, you really had to have some kind of image then and I figured the pseudo-Indian clothes would be better than green-and-gold shirts with pink flares! I remember in the Rock and Roll Show days we kept our stage clothes in hanging bags in the back of the van and our roadie ran up one day ashen saying, "Miller, your clothes have been stolen," and my reaction was, "Thank fuck for that!" '

'We had some promotional pictures taken in Red Indian style clothes,' says Lee. 'We wanted to be different. I was losing my hair, so I tied a bandanna round my head to cover it all and hold it in place. But we didn't really do anything as Charlie Woolfe compared to the activity and laughs we'd had with The Rock and Roll Show. We'd had some piss-ups, especially in the American bases, and we'd had some women. Miller was the only guy who was nice and straight. I don't think I've ever seen him drunk. The women were largely down to Ian and myself, misbehaving, as boys do.'

Charlie Woolfe recorded a single, with Jimmy Duncan as producer once again, this time at Olympic Studios. They were still signed to NEMS who now wanted them on their own label, albeit CBS Records manufactured and distributed the single, released in August 1968. The A-side featured a cover of Carter/Lewis/Stephens's 'Dance, Dance, Dance' backed with 'Home', which was written by Fred, Miller and Ian, the first time Hunter had recorded one of his own songs. Lee recalls 'Home' as a joint composition, and that they never got a penny for doing it, but Anderson says it was predominantly written by Ian and him, not that it mattered, as the band was falling apart anyway and the single was a last ditch effort.

'Charlie Woolfe didn't last long,' says Hunter. 'Colin Johnson was looking at Miller pretty hard, thinking the blues was coming in and Miller looked the part. He looked great, played great and sang great. So we decided to leave and started doing colleges, playing blues. Miller liked my voice, too, so he let me sing.'

Freddie Lee parted company with Hunter in November 1968, joined The Wild Angels and started touring Germany again. 'They weren't a very good band at all, in fact I was the only one playing anything right and I had to learn to play everything wrong, the way they were playing it! When we came back in January 1969, I ditched the band.' Nowadays, Lee lives in County Durham and consistently tours Europe. He has issued several albums on the Charly, Big Beat and Rockhouse labels, but now releases material through his own record, publishing and production companies. 'Nobody will rip me off anymore, like they used to in the old days,' says Fred. 'I can't even rip myself off!'

Miller Anderson soon answered an advert in *Melody Maker* and joined drummer Keef Hartley who had once replaced Ringo Starr in Rory Storm and the Hurricanes. Keef played in Hamburg in the early sixties and joined The Artwoods and John Mayall's Bluesbreakers, where he provided a strong jazz-slanted style. The Keef Hartley Band merged jazz-rock and blues-rock traditions on many of their albums recorded for the Deram label, their third LP, *The Time Is Near*, being dominated by Miller's songwriting. However there was always a certain friction, and the band began to fall apart, Hartley's next two LPs being effectively solo albums with session support. In 1974 Miller joined a re-formed but short-lived version of Savoy Brown, then re-united with Hartley and formed Dog Soldier, releasing one album. Anderson has subsequently played with T. Rex, Donovan and The Spencer Davis Group and still tours and records in the UK and Europe. Miller and Ian have remained firm friends throughout their separate musical careers.

By the time of his split with Lee, Hunter was a reasonable bass player and he got a further opportunity to work as a backing musician with sixties' British pop idol, Billy Fury, playing clubs for a few weeks at £5 to £10 pounds a night. Originally a tugboat worker from Liverpool, Fury had leapt into the rock 'n' roll limelight in 1959 with the help of promoter/manager Larry Parnes and a hit single 'Maybe Tomorrow'. He tasted further chart success with 'Halfway to Paradise', 'Jealousy' and a highly regarded rockabilly album *The Sound of Fury*, which, although American sounding, featured Billy's own material and Joe Brown on guitar. Fury found his greatest success with a switch to big ballad cover versions but his UK chart run ended around 1965, at which point he earned a steady living on the cabaret scene.

'Billy was winding down,' says Hunter 'so half the gigs would be working men's clubs where they'd queue up for miles and he'd go down a storm, and the others would be "hip" clubs where Emerson Lake and Palmer were starting to play and Billy wouldn't do so well in these. He'd come in about a minute before we went on stage, looking amazing, sounding incredible and he would leave the minute we went off. He was a very nice man. I went to his Mum and Dad's house in Liverpool and I couldn't believe the number of gold discs and platinum records she had on the walls. In the end, Billy asked me to get a different guitar player and quickly parted company with us when we couldn't find a replacement. I always thought Fury was his own worst enemy because he was lazy, but Billy was a star. You'd walk in a room and it just reeked out of him. Trouble was he wasn't a motivator. He needed a manager and when you're only as good as your manager, that makes you vulnerable.'

Fury appeared with David Essex in the 1973 movie *That'll Be The Day* but, long affected by ill-health, he died of a heart attack in 1983 amid attempts at a career comeback. Freddie Lee accompanied Billy on his last live television show, and wrote a song for him called 'Chains'.

Ian and Diane were now drifting apart and Hunter was reaching desperation stakes in terms of his musical career. 'I'd always had problems with my parents but I looked at myself in the mirror one day and there wasn't much left and I thought, "Why don't you go and see your mother and your father?" So, I got a ride to Blackburn with Tony Dangerfield, who was doing a gig and then hitched

to Blackpool and sat down with my Mum and Dad. My wife wanted to go back
to Shrewsbury. She was perfectly normal and thought I was crazy and she was
probably right. We had two kids and I felt terrible about the fact that I wasn't
really supporting them like I should be. Diane had said, "It's the band or me,
make up your mind." There was no hope. So I told my Mum and Dad about it
and said, "Look, I just believe my future's in music. I feel I've got to do that."
They went in the other room and came back and my Dad, who had never given
me a dime in my life, said, "We'll give you £200." I nearly died. My Father was
a very individual man who wound up in MI5, and who believed you should do
what you felt strongly about. That two hundred quid gave me some leeway until
I got the call from Mott. I could give Diane maintenance money and stay in
music.'

Hunter moved into songwriting with Francis Day and Hunter, part of
Affiliated Music Publishers Limited, one of Britain's biggest publishing companies, located in Charing Cross Road. Their roster included Tom Jones, Engelbert
Humperdinck and Tony MacCauley, who became a well-known writer for middle-of-the-road artists of that style. Ian secured a job as a staff songwriter at
Francis Day and Hunter composing to order, still as Ian Patterson at this point.,
and also wrote for Leeds Music and Peer International, part of the same organisation, based in Denmark Street.

Mike Smith, head of A&R for CBS Records heard a demo of one of Ian's
songs and decided to record it. 'Mike had turned The Beatles down and signed
Brian Poole instead,' says Hunter. 'He had gone round to Bill Farley at Regent
Sound and heard a demo of one of my songs. He decided he liked it a lot and
recorded "Season's Song" with acclaimed British actor Nicol Williamson and a
24-piece orchestra. They spent about £400, but they hadn't got me to sign a contract beforehand. I was still working in this factory in the Archway and playing
at weekends. Mike Smith made a big mistake, and even as dumb and as stupid
as I was at the time, I realised it was my chance, so I turned round and said, "I
don't want to sign anything unless you give me some money." There was a bit of
a flap around Francis Day and Hunter and the upshot of it was that they signed
me on a contract. It was a bit of a fluke and really funny. I asked for three months
at fifteen quid a week and, if they liked me, an option of another three months.

'There were other writers there too, like Roger Glover of Deep Purple. We
took solace in each other. In fact, we both left at the same time. He was the
same as me, they liked the songs but they couldn't really get them recorded. I'd
had the odd cover here and there, like "And I Have Learned to Dream", which
was a good song, but by and large, they were giving us money to keep us going
because they felt we were good, but didn't know what to do with us. Initially I
asked for three months to get me off work, so I could play and write more
songs which was very valuable. I regarded it as a summer holiday, but they kept
me on for a year!'

Ian began feeling guilty when he picked up his wages every Friday. 'I was getting a bit embarrassed because they weren't using much of my material. The lyrics
were schmaltzy. I had to contrive, and in the end I found I couldn't do it. I used
to sneak in for my wages when they were all out to lunch. I didn't want to take

their money. They'd been very good to me. I wanted to find a band that would pay me the equivalent.'

As Ian recalls, he then got involved, briefly, with The New Yardbirds, a four - piece group with Hunter on bass, Mick Strode on guitar, drummer Dave Dufort (who would shortly play with East of Eden) and vocalist Johnny Gilpin. 'The New Yardbirds had the guitar player from Plant's group, Band of Joy, and the singer was a delicate, troubled kind of guy, who couldn't make his mind up if he really wanted to be in music or not. Mick used to play with picks on all his fingers. I think it was just a scam. Peter Grant had Jimmy Page over in America saying The New Yardbirds were still going, which they were, and in London there was about three sets of New Yardbirds desperately rehearsing, one of which was going to be chosen. I remember Mickie Most came to see us rehearse in an old church hall and there was a football which he was kicking around. When we started playing, he stopped kicking the ball because we sounded great. Our singer was really excellent. Mickie liked us and started giving us wages, until Grant came back from the States, and the payments suddenly stopped.'

Hunter's options were now almost exhausted. Bill Farley, at Regent Sound Studios, had already tried to help Ian in his pursuit of musical recognition. Farley was about to play a vital role in helping him achieve that goal.

3
Little flame, tormented soul

'Walk on Water' – Ian Hunter

During the latter part of 1968 and for the first four months of 1969, while Ian Patterson was employed at Leeds Music in London, Mick Ralphs, Pete Watts, Dale Griffin, Verden Allen and Stan Tippins played gigs together around Herefordshire and Wales without any greater success than before.

In the autumn, the group had made two crucial decisions: they decided to name the band Silence and, to up the ante, acquired a new Ford Transit van, amplifiers and PA system, with assistance from Mick Hince, who was later to become part of Mott The Hoople's road crew, along with Richie Anderson, Philip John and John Davies. Silence was now signed to an agency called Jay-Vee Entertainments Limited in Swansea, working a great deal in South Wales.

Although the Welsh audiences were quite progressive in their musical outlook, the gigs in South Wales were the beginning of the end for Silence according to Watts. 'We wanted to play our own songs and no covers but the agency complained. They demanded a pop approach and even suggested that we add a small brass section and play Blood Sweat and Tears type material! We used to swap instruments occasionally on stage. We did a Buffalo Springfield number, 'Child's Claim To Fame', in which Phally played bass, Mick went on to slide guitar and I used Ralpher's Gibson SG Standard which was very nice to play, with a sideways tremolo, and a frontways neck!'

Silence's performances embraced various cover versions including Moby Grape ('Hey Grandma / Fall On You'), Electric Flag ('Another Country'), Buffalo Springfield ('Mr Soul / Rock & Roll Woman'), The Byrds ('My Back Pages'), The West Coast Pop Art Experimental Band ('Miss Rose / Excuse Me') and Elmer Gantry's Velvet Opera ('Flames'). Ralphs had also started to write material like 'Yellow Van' and 'Wide Asleep', which was also played live. 'We would sneak one or two of our own songs into the set and pretend they were Stones B-sides, so we wouldn't get dragged off stage and beaten up,' says Mick.

Whilst Silence were able to get a reasonable number of gigs, their equipment was unreliable and devouring all their profits in repair costs. Vivian Phillips, friend and former road-crew man from their Italian days, re-emerged as a tour manager for Island Records' band Traffic who were rehearsing in the area.

Traffic guitarist and singer Dave Mason was the 'founder' of the original Doc Thomas Group and had played temporarily with The Buddies in 1966. They also knew Traffic drummer and vocalist Jim Capaldi, from his days in The Hellions with Mason. The Island connection was starting to connect.

Kingsley Ward of Future Sound Studios was now trying to support Silence behind the scenes as much as possible. Charles Ward had written 'If Your Heart Lay with the Rebel (Would You Cheer the Underdog?)', which Dave Edmunds' Love Sculpture performed on a BBC *Top Gear* radio broadcast in September 1968. 'The Rebel' was subsequently recorded by Joe Cocker and Black Sabbath but has still never been released commercially in any form. The Wards assisted Silence by making recordings at their Monmouth studio, including 'The Rebel', which the band believed was a strong enough track to secure them a recording contract. The song still means a great deal to Pete Watts. 'We began to do demo recordings at Rockfield, or Future Sound as it was then, when it was a hayloft. We recorded "The Rebel" and a couple of other tracks, including "Transparent Day", around December 1968 and January 1969. "The Rebel" has a major significance in the story of Mott The Hoople, being our audition song for Guy Stevens. I always wish we'd done it properly with Ian later on. It would've suited our early period well.'

Kingsley submitted Silence's version of 'The Rebel' to his contact at EMI, Malcolm Jones. 'Malcolm wanted to release it but was over-ruled at an A&R meeting by Tony Hall, a consultant and much respected figure in the UK music scene,' explains Dale Griffin. 'We were hugely pissed-off, but he was quite right of course. Our performance was pretty rough and ready, with the exception of "the Paul Newman of Pop" – Stan Tippins.'

In spite of the slick new transport, equipment and demo tapes, it now seemed the group was falling apart. During early 1969, Silence considered splitting and going their separate ways, however, hedging their bets, they came to London collectively but also to attend individual auditions. 'At that time we were still trying to do something as a band,' says Watts. 'We kept going back to Italy every summer and it was great, but we weren't getting anywhere over here. We were running our own gigs at village halls but of course it doesn't really help. So we decided to go to London and try and get record deals. We started going to different agencies up there and we'd get involved in all these ridiculous projects, like backing Tommy Steele's brother, Colin Hicks. He was a bit religious. At the rehearsal room, he was terrible. He couldn't tune his guitar and kept tuning it higher and higher and higher. It was awful, so that was knocked on the head.'

This was followed by opportunities for Silence to back two girl vocal groups, The Paper Dolls and The Pearlettes, who needed a band to accompany them on tour. 'We rehearsed "Yakety Yak" with The Paper Dolls, and "Something Here In My Heart", one of their hits,' remarks Pete. 'They got us to play some of our own numbers, which were cover versions mostly, and they thought we were great. Then their manager, George, came in, a little bloke with glasses who was fifty or sixty. He asked how they were getting on and they said they'd found the group they wanted. So he said, "Okay boys, here's your sheet music. Let's hear something." We all looked at each other and said, "We don't read music." He said, "You're joking! Well, that's the end of that isn't it!" The Pearlettes, from Sweden, were quite brilliant. We rehearsed with them, for Chris Wright and Terry Ellis (later of Chrysalis), in a building that was derelict, with lath and plaster falling down everywhere. Nothing ever developed because they didn't tour in the end.'

Silence then trudged off to see an A&R man at Apple Records. 'He was a gay bloke, and he liked us – well he would at that time, wouldn't he,' says Watts. 'He thought the accents we had were incredible, and he wanted to sign us and call us The Archers. We had no tapes, so he was going to fix up some time to record demos. We came out of the Apple Shop in Baker Street feeling that something might happen, but it never quite came off in the end. I recall seeing him a lot later, when we were in Mott, and goading him about it. I remember saying, "Ha, ha, you missed us, didn't ya? You didn't get us, did ya?" And he always used to say, "Yeah, I will in the end though luvvie!" And I thought, "You won't mate!"

One day, in Shaftesbury Avenue, the band chanced upon The Searchers' drummer, Chris Curtis. 'It was a shame,' says Watts. 'We didn't know at that time, but he'd flipped apparently. He gave us a shifty look as we walked past him in Charing Cross Road. Then, ten minutes later, we came back the same way to the group van, and he was there again and he spoke to us. "Are you a group? I've got it all worked out. You're going to be called Roundabout. Come with me, now." So he took us up to Polydor Records and asked the secretary for an appointment with somebody, and we sat there for four or five hours. And of course, we were there all bloody day. Next day we met him in the Giaconda Café, and he was planning out our careers. We went up to Polydor again and they wouldn't let him see anybody. They didn't have the heart to throw him out. The funny thing is that the same thing happened to Ritchie Blackmore and Jon Lord, who eventually became part of Roundabout, a nucleus of musicians who would be fronted by Curtis.'

Immediate Records was another label that seemed keen on Silence, but Pete is amazed, looking back, that the group went round record companies without demos, seeking a deal. They became desperate. Watts and Ralphs resorted to busking one rainy Sunday afternoon outside a cinema in Muswell Hill, whereupon two girls took pity on their version of Don Partridge's 'Rosie' and paid for them to see Sidney Poitier in *Guess Who's Coming to Dinner?* at the ABC Cinema.

'We even carried boxes of records around for this jerk once, who promised us an audition,' admits Watts. 'He was called Jeff, and I think Peter Grant threatened to break his legs years later. We eventually did an audition, in another hell hole, and he thought it was great and was going to sort out another audition and a deal, but, of course, nothing happened.'

Switching between London and Herefordshire, Silence continued to gig heavily in the Welsh borders and journalists started describing them visually as 'sex-laden smilers', and likening them musically to the loud heavy blues of Moby Grape. Watts said in one article at the time that the group wanted to build up a following and be 'interesting rather than successful'. Ralphs also expressed great respect for Welsh bands. 'They are not worried by being individual and way out. The Midlands scene, which we came into contact with a lot, is a drag. Here we meet up with good musicians like Man, Love Sculpture and The Dream.'

During one Silence gig at the Top Rank Suite in Swansea on 11 February 1969, supporting The Small Faces, Mick Ralphs and Steve Marriott enthused about guitar playing together before the show and took to the empty stage to experiment in front of the gathering audience. Joined by Dale Griffin and bass player Ronnie Lane, then Ian McLagan and Verden Allen on keyboards, this odd combination jammed for fully thirty minutes before Silence's set. Marriott was full of praise after their Welsh visit. 'We specifically came down here with the intention of having a rave up and some boogaloo. Silence were great to work with. This is how stage shows should be.'

'The Small Faces were a nice bunch of lads,' says Stan. 'We went out for an

Indian meal with them after the gig and they even paid the bill, which I thought was amazing, as I think they were getting ripped off left, right and centre. We took them to the railway station for the train back to London at 5.45 in the morning.'

Silence were also invited to Olympic Studios in Barnes one day to see Dave Mason, an event that Watts recalls had a devastating effect on Verden Allen. 'Dave was in Studio 2 and there were lots of hangers on. The air was thick with dope and there were joints going round but we never touched that kind of stuff really. Phally however, ended up with a joint between every finger of both hands, eight in all. Then we went in to Studio 1 where The Move were recording and we chatted with them and tried to impress, rather than appear like country hicks. By this time, Phally fell off a stool he was on and Ralpher and I were worried he would show us up. We took him out and left him safely in the group van parked outside and went back in to hob nob. When we departed about midnight, we discovered both van doors wide open and Phal was gone. It was a miracle the gear wasn't nicked. We drove around and tried to find him, terrified he'd drowned in a nearby lake, and eventually went back to our flat in Muswell Hill. Verden arrived the next morning having walked fifteen miles. A lesson in avoiding that kind of stuff.'

In May, fortunes improved for Silence when Overend saw an advertisement in *Melody Maker* – 'Tough, aggressive bass player required for Island Records group.' Watts phoned and was told the group was called Free, seeking to replace Paul Rodgers and bassist Andy Fraser who had 'left' the band. Watts ventured to London, accompanied by Ralphs, who would provide moral support. 'When I arrived, there were hundreds of tough, aggressive bass players in the street, all dressed in German metal helmets, chainmail waistcoats and tattoos. Horrible looking blokes, waiting to audition,' says Pete. 'Mick was with me, because he had nothing to do that day and he decided to come along. He said to me, "I met Guy Stevens, Free's manager, with Dave Mason, last year. I wonder if he's in there, because, if he is, I might be able to get you in ahead of this lot." So Ralphs, like he always did, pushed his way down the front, got in, and then emerged saying, "Come on in." He'd talked to Guy who had said, "Bring him in now." So I pushed ahead of all the others and there was Kossoff and Kirke. I'd learned some Free numbers in preparation, "Broad Daylight" and a couple of other songs from the first album and said, "Well, what do you want to play then?" and they said, "We'll just jam." They were really good and it was particularly good to play with Simon. As we played, Kossoff shook his head, and Guy shook his head and Guy kept putting his ear in my bass speaker to hear what I was doing. It went well and Guy got talking to me, and it turned out that he liked the way I looked, because I had a buckskin fringed jacket and lace up, knee-length boots and very long hair. Guy liked the image and he asked if I was in a band and I said I was in Silence with Mick and we were great, but couldn't get any work because we wanted to do our own material. I didn't get the job in Free, nobody did, because it was a temporary split and Rodgers and Fraser soon returned, but meeting Guy Stevens was invaluable. He said he'd like to hear Silence.'

Mick Ralphs didn't delay in making an appointment to see Guy Stevens and play him a demo tape. 'I was the one who would save money from the Silence gigs, to buy petrol, and take my car down to London, before the M4 was constructed, in prehistoric days. It used to take me forever. I'd leave at six in the morning and get to London at midday, try and park somewhere and go round the record companies, and just sort of sit there like a lemon and be told, "Sorry, Mr So-and-So has gone home for the day." I was in Island Records and they told me Mr. Stevens was a bit busy, so I said, "Well sod this, I'm not taking this any more." I went into his office and said, "I've been coming down to London for the last four or five weeks, I've got a tape here and we're good and you prats keep making excuses when you should be listening to this." And Guy said, "I like it, I like it, come in." He admired my attitude, so I learned there and then, it's not what you play, it's how you present it. He was so taken aback that he asked me to sit down and I played our demos to Guy, who wasn't particularly impressed, but I cajoled him to actually see us play and we ended up coming to London to audition.'

Ian Hunter later acknowledged the importance of Ralphs' determination in getting a record deal for Silence. 'He's a born hustler and he hustled for the original group. He kept on going to see Guy. Jim Capaldi of Traffic had also put a word in. Mick Ralphs knew a lot of people, I guess through Capaldi. He knew Luther Grosvenor of Spooky Tooth, too.' Ralphs met Grosvenor back in Evesham, where they used to practise guitar together on Luther's Les Paul Junior in the relative quiet of a telephone box after work because they had no amplifier.

'It was a bit hard convincing Island at first,' admits Ralphs. 'Guy wasn't too knocked out with our tapes, but we got him to hear us at a small rehearsal studio and he really dug us. The very next day he had us recording demos and not long after that we made the album. That's how a record company should work, putting the music first. The fact that Guy had an executive position with Island cut out any of the usual negotiations and traipsing round record companies. My initial impression of Guy was that he was a record company person, but I didn't realise how great he was then, he was just another guy who was probably saying, "Put your tape in the basket and I'll call you right back." But he wasn't, he liked me, and we found out we were both the same star sign, Aries, and got on really well.'

Island Records had been founded by Chris Blackwell, who was born in London on 23 June 1937, the son of Blanche Lindo and ex-Army officer Middleton Joseph Blackwell. When Chris was three months old, the family moved to the affluent Terra Nova area of Jamaica, returning to England some three years later. Blackwell attended prep school and Harrow Public School but didn't go to university. By the late fifties he 'commuted' between Kingston Jamaica and London. On one visit in 1958, he was stranded on a coral reef and suffered serious dehydration and sunburn but was rescued by a group of Rastafarians. This incident, and the people who aided him, made a great impression on Blackwell.

In the early sixties, Chris's mother was friendly with the James Bond author Ian Fleming, and Chris worked with Harry Saltzman on the *Doctor No* movie.

He was offered more film work, but opted for a career in music instead. Ironically, Blackwell was never a pop fan, being influenced by jazz music, particularly artists like Pine Top Smith and Jelly Roll Morton, and, later, R&B. Before Blackwell started making records, he imported discs into Jamaica, then began recording and producing records, which he sold to local shops. He became involved with the Sound Systems in Jamaica, travelling discos owned by various liquor distributors, and started going to New York, buying cheap 78s, scratching the labels off and selling them profitably back in Jamaica. Sound Systems also started up in England and New York and Blackwell began selling more and more records in the UK, which led to the opening of a British business.

He made deals with Jamaican producers, purchasing the masters of artists like Leslie Kong, Coxsone Dodd and King Edwards and started pressing up 500 records at a time in England, selling them personally to specialist retail outlets from the back of his Mini Cooper or his stall in Portobello Market, West London. Then Blackwell set up Island Records' London office in May 1962, operating from a rented flat at Rutland Gate Mews, to distribute Jamaican records and promote reggae music, or blue beat / ska as it was then known. The company formed subsidiary labels, Jump Up and Black Swan, becoming a considerable influence in the development of British rhythm and blues particularly after signing a distribution deal with American R&B label Sue Records in 1964. Guy Stevens, a London disc jockey at the time, was put in charge of the Sue label in the UK, which provided hits by James Brown, Bob & Earl and Inez & Charlie Foxx.

The release of Island's first record coincided with Jamaican independence from British rule and Blackwell had a number one hit in Jamaica with Lowell Aiken's 'Little Sheila'. Shortly afterwards, one of Island's early singles was to provide them with substantial UK and worldwide success. Chris brought fourteen year old girl singer, Millie Small, to England and recorded a cover version of 'My Boy Lollipop', licensing the track to Philips' Fontana label in 1964. The record sold six million copies worldwide, aided Island's financial position significantly, and helped popularise West Indian music, opening the market for artists such as Desmond Dekker, Toots and the Maytals and Jimmy Cliff. Blackwell became increasingly fascinated with reggae, Rastafarian religion and the musical message of artists like Bob Marley, who he eventually signed in 1973.

Blackwell bought a large property in Hope Road, Kingston as a base for his expanding reggae interests and named it Island House. It was also an attempt to re-establish his roots in Jamaica. His family had sold domestic property there in the Blue Mountains, the area from which Island's publishing company, Blue Mountain Music, got its name. Island Records was now establishing itself well in Britain, but it was to branch out even further, firstly with R&B and then progressive rock. Back in 1965, Chris Blackwell had accompanied Millie to a Birmingham television show, because he had been told of good local bands including The Spencer Davis Group, who played tough R&B. The Spencer Davis Group, featuring singer Steve Winwood and his older brother Muff, was signed instantly to Island and had several hits licensed on Fontana, including 'Keep On Running', 'Somebody Help Me' and

'Gimme Some Lovin' '. The band split when Steve left and formed Traffic in 1967, Island Records' first 'rock' signing.

Island was now starting to revolutionise British music by adopting a different approach, geared towards the album-orientated, progressive market and further independent record labels followed such as Planet and Immediate. Whilst these were valuable additions to the developing UK scene, most independents tried to compete directly with the major labels such as Decca, EMI, Pye and Philips by releasing standard pop. Island was different.

The name Island Records had been conceived by Blackwell in Jamaica, inspired by the movie *Island In The Sun*. As they moved away from Jamaican reggae, they tried Aladdin Records as an alternative label name for the British market, but without success. Chris reverted to Island, although changed the style of the company by introducing a vibrant pink label and a pop-image pink sleeve for Traffic's debut top-five single, 'Paper Sun'. Armed with their first progressive hit, and the follow-up, 'Hole In My Shoe', Island's image began to attract the best of the new groups including Spooky Tooth, King Crimson, Free and Jethro Tull, who gave Island their first number one album. Tull's managers, Chris Wright and Terry Ellis, subsequently set up Chrysalis Records from their deal with Island. Other rival labels were formed such as Track, Blue Horizon, Charisma and most notably Richard Branson's Virgin Records, part distributed by Island, all of them playing an important role in the development of British rock music. The majors struck back with their own progressive house labels such as Deram, Harvest, Dawn and Vertigo, but they could not compete with Island, who began to distribute other independents and set up their own record pressing plant.

Chris Blackwell surrounded himself with people like David Betteridge, Guy Stevens and Muff Winwood at Island, moving next to Oxford Street and then setting up their corporate establishment and two recording studios in a converted church at Basing Street near Notting Hill Gate in West London. In 1974, they also acquired a property in St Peter's Square, creating another basement studio christened 'The Fall Out Shelter'. Merging with Trojan Records to release and promote Jamaican music, Island concentrated on the progressive market although Blackwell returned to his roots in 1969 with Jimmy Cliff's hit single 'Wonderful World, Beautiful People'.

Island continued to sign a string of rock acts and developed a roster equivalent to the 'Who's Who' of popular music; Emerson, Lake and Palmer, Fairport Convention, Roxy Music, Sparks, Bad Company, Brian Eno, Robert Palmer, Steve Winwood, John Martyn and Cat Stevens, all recorded for the label throughout the seventies. They continued to explore other idioms, including Salsa and African pop, using their original reggae blueprint to generate further markets, but avoided certain musical areas. Punk rock was conspicuous by its absence at the label, apart from The Slits, and Eddie and the Hot Rods, Blackwell saying that he appreciated the attitude of the new wave, but not the non-musicality of it.

Chris Blackwell's musical contribution in terms of exposing reggae and progressive rock to a wider market is inestimable. Island had created a fundamental shift in popular music and will always be regarded as Britain's most successful and

important independent. In 1969, Mott The Hoople were about to join the ad-
mirable stable that will always be associated with Island, and the catalyst was to
be Guy Stevens, who to many was an unsung hero in terms of developing the
label.

'Island was the first real independent record company,' says Mick Ralphs.
'Guy Stevens found most of the bands and if it hadn't been for Guy I don't think
Island would have lasted five minutes. Chris Blackwell had the money but he
didn't possess Guy's vision.'

Stevens had become head of A&R at Island in the late sixties and the demo
tape that Mick Ralphs took to Guy, recorded by Kingsley Ward, contained 'Find
Your Way', 'The Rebel' and 'The Silence', an instrumental, all recorded at Future
Sound Studios. A Pete Watts track called 'The Wreck' and a cover version of The
West Coast Pop Art Experimental Band's 'Transparent Day' did not make it on
to the demo. Although he liked 'The Rebel', Mick remembers Guy wasn't particularly impressed with the Silence demos but he told Ralphs he would like to
see the group. 'I went back to Herefordshire and told everybody that this bloke
Guy Stevens wanted to see the band, and he's quite a wild man, so the main thing
is to go down there with a wild attitude because he seems to be impressed by that,
rather than the music.'

Guy arranged for Silence to audition for Island Records in a third floor room
at Spot Studio, South Molton Street in London's West End. 'We were nearly all
crushed to death again, carrying Phally's bloody Hammond organ up the stairs,'
recalls Dale. 'I say nearly; not Verden of course. He always seemed to escape unscathed.' Stevens recalled the audition once in an interview with Charles Shaar
Murray. 'I knew they had to be right. I saw these blokes lugging an organ up the
stairs. It was enormous, a Hammond the size of a piano, and I thought, 'I don't
care what they sound like. They've done it. They got the organ up the stairs.'

There was one problem however, as Tippins was not able to sing at the audition due to a newly-acquired broken jaw. 'Stan had tried to break up a fight in
Hereford and was punched from behind' explains Watts. 'Nobody could really
punch him from the front, he was a good fighter. The next night we played a gig
at the Liverpool Cavern with a group called The Bitter Suite and did two sets.
Stan struggled through the first and we went down a bomb, but he couldn't do
the second. We were furious with him. I pulled a piece of wood off the stage that
night and took it, because it was all rotting and was still the same stage that The
Beatles had played on. The atmosphere was incredible even then, in 1969.'

'The Island audition was in a small studio, a tiny room,' says Ralphs. 'We set
up for Guy and we'd all agreed earlier that we should just go full on and hope for
the best. So we did the songs with some madness.' Recalling his audition for Free,
when he had noticed Simon Kirke and Paul Kossoff raving and shaking their
heads a lot, Pete prompted Silence to do the same, which they did, with some
vigour. Performing self-composed material, which Watts likened to early Yes, the
group had practically made their minds up to split if they failed Guy's audition,
largely because of the dwindling work situation back in Herefordshire and Wales.
Pete is adamant that Guy Stevens was the group's last hope. Fortunately, he loved
them.

Several of the songs Silence played at the time were the autobiographical 'Mystic Balls', penned by Watts, plus 'The Rebel', but most of the numbers were Ralphs' originals like 'Lena', 'Yellow Van' (a Move rip-off), 'Find Your Way' (reminiscent of Hendrix and Spooky Tooth), 'Wide Asleep' and 'The Silence'. 'We would slip odd songs of our own amongst all the cover versions in our live set. Most of my early efforts were pretty awful, but when you start to write songs that's what happens really,' admits Mick. 'Songwriting, I've learned over the years, is a bit like building a bridge or knocking up a chair, you learn after a while there's a way of doing it that actually works. In the beginning, the construction of your songs is usually dreadful, but you've got to begin somewhere. It was a good start. They were early attempts at commercial songs, but with a wild side!'

Silence's repertoire was usually rounded out with covers of Electric Flag's 'Another Country', East Of Eden's 'Northern Hemisphere', Strawberry Alarm Clock's 'Tomorrow' and 'Transparent Day'. 'That was sort of our acid period man,' jokes Ralphs. 'We didn't take acid because the only acid we knew about was sulphuric, and we didn't think you should take that. So we pretended to be wild hippies, and wore kaftans, and did peace signs, and sang these songs, but it was a good experimental period. Pete was generally very good at finding these obscure tracks by Backward Love and people like that. He always had great ideas and was very innovative, opening up our minds to other ways of doing stuff.'

Having heard the group play, Guy Stevens agreed to hold a second Silence audition at Regent Sound Studios. 'We did another session about a week later,' recalls Watts. 'Guy noticed that Stan didn't feel comfortable with the material and he agreed with this. It came down to parting company with Tippins or keeping him and trying to find another deal. Stan didn't want to stand in anyone's way and said he'd leave the group. We didn't know what to say. We hadn't even asked him, we hadn't even talked about it. He just went next door to the shop in Denmark Street and sold his P.A. He gave up on the spot. It was just amazing. Stan didn't give up singing completely, as he went back to Italy that summer and did some solo work out there, while we were getting Mott together.

'It got to a stage in Silence where it was difficult for Stan, because we got in to this progressive stuff with long, long solos and Tippins was a vocalist and didn't play an instrument. Music went through a horrible phase at that time with lengthy songs and feedback for quarter of an hour and all manner of shit. Guy had got this thing in his mind about Dylan and The Stones and he didn't want the long drawn out progressive stuff like 'Mystic Balls' that I'd been writing. He wanted to go back to basic rock and a cross between *Blonde on Blonde* and 'Jumping Jack Flash'. Before Stan had even started to sing, Guy said to us that he wanted a fusion of the two things. When he heard Tippins, who had a big powerful voice, it wasn't what Guy had in mind. It left us in a very horrible position because we wouldn't throw Stan out, we couldn't do it, it was partly his group. The rest of us were upset because we didn't want him to go, but Stan said, "There's the chance of a deal, you can't turn it down," and he just left the band.'

Tippins recalls that he wasn't happy with the direction of the group by this stage in any case and so, he played his final gig with Silence on 26 May in Herefordshire. 'I hated "The Rebel" to be honest. Really it wasn't my kind of style at all and they would keep suggesting I sing it like Dylan, but I was more of a beat singer like Johnny Kidd and it was all getting a bit too psychedelic for me. Also the band's songs weren't really strong enough. I'd talked to Buffin for months beforehand anyway, and told him they really needed someone who could play guitar, write songs and give them their own style. I was very apprehensive about the Island audition in the first place. I wasn't enjoying the music and obviously that came through because Guy Stevens didn't really like me and felt it was better to have someone who could play an instrument rather than a solo singer. At the end of the audition he said, "Well, I can take the band but I can't really take the singer, because he doesn't add anything to what you've already got." It was a mixture of sadness but also relief when I finished, because really, I hadn't felt comfortable for about year.'

'It was bad in a way because Tippins had been with us for so long,' confesses Ralphs. 'Stan was an excellent singer with a really good voice, so how on earth do you tell someone that, that's been with you for years. Stan realised we had a real chance with Guy, so he graciously stepped aside. I said to him at the time, "If and when we do have any success, we want you to come back with us in some capacity." I'm glad he did too because, of course, he went on to become a very successful tour manager with us and several other large name bands.'

Dale comments that it took a man with the big heart of Tippins to walk away without anger or recrimination. 'Stan accepted his departure from Silence with good grace. He'd already had offers of gigs and film work in Italy, where he'd been dubbed 'The Sinatra of Beat'. He took up the offer to return to Italy and make solo records and undertake television work. Luckily for us we were not to lose contact with him for long and, after a year, the Italians had botched his career and he returned home, becoming Mott's tour manager for life.'

'When my singing role was over, they wanted me to continue with them,' recalls Stan, 'because I always used to do the organising in Silence anyway, trying to look after the bit of money we had, trying to get us to gigs on time and trying to keep some sort of professionalism about the whole outfit. I didn't start with Mott straight away, because they had a record to make, but when the touring started I went out with them from day one. There was me organising them and Mick Hince doing the equipment, so Mott The Hoople started with only two people on the road.'

On 13 May 1969, Watts's birthday, Guy took Silence into Morgan Studios for a recording test, to finally decide whether he would sign the group or not. 'We did two tracks,' recalls Pete, ' "The Rebel", with Mick on lead vocal, and "Find Your Way", which we just did as a backing track. We were enthusiastic at the end because Guy said he had to sign us up, but there was a problem in that we had no singer. He really seemed to like our unusual clothes and accents. We were obviously not Londoners and we had a fresh approach and a naivety which attracted him to us initially, rather than our playing ability. We were quite good though. I remember around the time we met Guy, we played a gig in Swansea Top Rank supporting Vanity Fayre. It had a revolving stage and there was nobody in the room apart from Vanity Fayre when we came on, and they just clapped us all the time. We were like a group's group. It was similar when we

played with The Small Faces at Swansea; they went down badly and we went
down a storm.'

Silence returned to Herefordshire after their second session with Stevens.
Ralphs had already decided that if no record deal with Island was forthcoming
by June, it was time for him to move on, so once again he began casting around
for other groups to join, amongst them Scottish band Cartoone, managed by
Peter Grant. Doc Thomas Group guitarist, Dave Tedstone, had originally pursued a place in Cartoone, who toured quite successfully in the USA. When the
band returned to London, the Hereford contingent had also moved back and
into their basement flat. 'I nearly joined Cartoone, but it was a good thing I
didn't. I auditioned for Tony Rivers and the Castaways instead,' admits Ralphs.
'God knows why. I had to drive all the way to some council house in Essex to
meet them and auditioned in their living room. They said I could have the job
and I panicked and ran away. I don't think I wanted it. I think I only went because I thought, "Am I actually good enough to join anybody else?" I didn't really
want to, I just wanted to find out.'

'Mick was thinking of joining Cartoone, in fact he was thinking of joining
everybody,' says Pete. 'Ralpher's biggest ambition was to get into any other group
besides us. They were usually putrid groups too, like Tony Rivers and the
Castaways – a middle of the road, polite, poor man's British Beach Boys. Who
would want to be in a group like that? It was funny because Ralphs always ended
up back with us no matter who he tried to join. Cartoone were great blokes
though, Scottish guys, who shared everything they'd got with us and they'd got
next to bugger all. They got home from a disastrous tour of America, about to be
dumped by their record company and manager, and found all of us living in *their*
flat. Mick said, years later, that he would never have left Mott The Hoople if he'd
known they would become so influential, and that is typical Ralpher. He always
opted for safety. Bad Company, his post-Mott group, were a very safe band, they
couldn't fail. They were run to a formula.'

Whilst Ralphs continued to be restless and impatient, Guy Stevens had
already placed an advertisement in Melody Maker, with a very clear idea of the
vocalist that he needed to complete his brainchild.

Very little is known about Guy Stevens' history. The members of Mott The
Hoople claim Guy was vague about it, and they never enquired about his background in any great detail. Maverick, unorthodox, whirlwind, firecracker, instigator and psychic puppeteer can all be used to describe the creative, crazed and
destructive side of his personality, but 'hidden' from view was Guy the football
fan, the routine family man – playing with his son or reading his daily newspaper over breakfast. His musical foresight and innovation received similarly modest recognition. It is absolutely impossible to describe or distil the essence of Guy
Stevens into the one dimensional, monochrome world of the printed word with
any hope of true success. A complex, complicated, dysfunctional character, the
tales from many of those who worked with him are such that he is often crudely
represented. The picture was invariably one of wildness and eccentricity, which
masked his attributes and rendered his talents almost invisible to those not on his
wavelength.

Guy Stevens was born on 6 April 1943 in South London. He lost his father when he was only six years of age, a tragic event that would have a marked effect on his life and personality in later years. His mother, Lillian, came from Oldham in Lancashire and his father George from Forest Hill in London. George Stevens was an entrepreneurial character and, apparently, made a significant amount of money from selling army surplus materials after the Second World War. Guy's elder brother, Roger, was a commodities broker, before devoting his life, more recently, to ecology and conservation. The two brothers shared a passion for Arsenal Football Club and became season ticket holders and regular attenders at Highbury Stadium in North London.

When Guy was eleven years old, he heard 'Whole Lotta Shakin' Goin' On' by Jerry Lee Lewis. He claimed that it marked the end of his school career, and that he was never the same person again. Stevens was instantly fanatical about music and started buying records, running a record club at his boarding school, and procuring many of his singles by mail order from Stan Lewis's Record Services in Shreveport, Louisiana.

Guy was expelled from school at fourteen and went to work for Lloyds insurance brokers. He was first introduced to his future wife, Diane Elizabeth Cox, in 1960, through a mutual friend on London Bridge. Guy was impressed, because Diane had seen Buddy Holly play live, although she was originally a jazz enthusiast. When they met, Guy had an interest in rock and roll and collected a lot of singles, records like 'Money' by Barrett Strong, and they went to Jerry Lee Lewis concerts together. Diane recalls Jerry Lee would often play in large cinemas that were only one third full but he created unbelievable rock and roll. Guy was mad on Jerry Lee, then it was Dylan. He became manic and obsessional over records, frequently visiting unusual shops in Holloway Road and Islington that he thought might stock what he wanted. Initially Guy kept the records in long boxes and then had a huge chest on legs built for albums, with a slot for his best singles.

Guy's other obsession was films, for which he became equally enthusiastic and intense. He would write down the details of every movie, religiously, in notebooks, James Dean films and *On the Waterfront* being particular favourites. Guy and Diane married and had one son, James.

Searching for records led Guy to a job as a disc jockey, and he became well known for the imported vinyl that he played at gigs. Jeff Dexter also worked as a DJ at the Lyceum Theatre in London and first met Guy in 1961. They became friends and, in 1969, Dexter recalls Guy raving about a sensational new 'Dylanesque' band he had discovered, Mott The Hoople. In 1963 Guy became a rival DJ at 'The Scene', a damp, dingy, spit-and-sawdust basement club in London's Ham Yard, near the Windmill Theatre, in Soho. The site had previously played host to various jazz clubs, and then a blues club called The Piccadilly, which closed in 1962, whereupon the property was leased by future Radio Caroline founder Ronan O'Rahilly. Although the rhythm and blues market was still limited, Ronan knew Guy had a large record collection, so he offered him work at The Scene, where, between 7 pm and 1 am, Stevens started to lay down his definition of R&B every Monday night, diligently announcing and playing artists like Louisiana Red, Lazy Lester, Little Al and Boogie Jake.

Initially known as the high altar of Mod, The Scene became an important meeting place for The Mod movement, including a young Steve Marriott who once admitted that his group took pills and stayed at The Scene Club until midnight before moving on to The Flamingo for 'the all nighter'. Although pills were frequently distributed at the club, Diane Stevens is adamant that Guy did not get involved at that time. The Mod audience widened and artists like The Stones, The Beatles and Eric Clapton would attend, many of them coming specifically to hear Guy. People would travel from across the UK for the Monday night sessions, and from France and Holland too, according to O'Rahilly.

Tony Brainsby, who became Mott's publicist midway through their Island period, recalls that Stevens was one of the first 'names' he ever met in the music industry. 'Guy soon became a friend and I first worked with him at the Scene Club. We used to give out cards at Piccadilly Circus with our initials on the back and anyone who turned up with our initials on their card earned us two pence commission! I actually took over Guy's flat in Leicester Square and shared with Brian Jones for a while. Clapton was on the top floor, there was a strip joint on the ground floor, a coffee bar in the basement and the rent was five pounds a week. Guy was always an instigator and he turned me on to Chuck Berry from the very early days.'

By 1963, Guy's record collecting mania was in full flight and, having no car, his vast armoury of discs required that he use taxis as his mode of transportation to and from the Scene. Georgie Fame and Eric Burdon were listeners at the club, and Guy became highly respected for his musical knowledge and taste, so much so that he supplied The Rolling Stones and The Animals with obscure records for their repertoires. For the sum of £5, he also furnished The Who with a compilation tape that gave them most of their early material and helped the Spencer Davis Group find songs, by passing copies of new American R&B records that he played at the Scene to Chris Blackwell. Such was the competition between the DJ's, that they often scratched the name of the artist or song title off the labels to keep their musical discoveries secret! There was a consensus in many circles that Guy created the 1964 British R&B boom single-handed.

Stevens would work in the City of London during the day and, in the evening, continue to seek out R&B records. The Who, Eric Clapton and Steve Marriott became regular visitors to his one-room Leicester Square flat, to listen to his vast array of singles. Guy once claimed he possessed every Motown and Stax single and then went to Stax in Memphis to try and explain to them that the company didn't really understand the importance of what they were doing. Whilst deejaying at the Scene, Guy was asked by Chris Blackwell to run Sue Records, a subsidiary R&B label at his young and progressive Island company, quite separate from the American original. Sue was originally started by Juggy Murray in New York with Charlie and Inez Foxx's 'Mockingbird', and Blackwell sent Guy over to the USA to find material for the British equivalent, which would have no business link with its American counterpart. Sue issued material from various labels up until 1968.

Blackwell saw Stevens' boundless energy and wanted to harness it, so Guy was paid £15 a week by Island and was able to fan the flames of the blues boom he'd helped to create, with the first UK releases for Ike & Tina Turner, Elmore James and Bobby Bland. Sue's *modus operandi* was that if Guy liked the song, and believed it had some musical relevance, then it was released. Issuing a few dozen singles from the American label, Sue UK developed into a fully-fledged label which had Ike & Tina Turner, Betty Everett and Rufus Thomas, amongst others. Guy operated as a blazing flame rather than a business person, and so Chris Blackwell and David Betteridge tried to instil some commercial focus. The label probably only made money on every fifth single according to Betteridge, the counter-balance being four successful compilation albums, collated by Guy, entitled *The Sue Story*.

In 1959, Chuck Berry had been jailed for an immorality offence, taking an underage girl across state lines. He completed his prison term in 1964, whereupon he planned new recording sessions and his first overseas tour. Guy had taken charge of the British Chuck Berry Fan Club and went to meet him in the USA when he was released from jail. Legend has it that two people met Berry, Guy Stevens and promoter Don Arden. Arden offered him ten thousand pounds for a British tour and immediately Stevens offered twenty thousand. An astonished Chris Blackwell questioned Guy later and wondered why he hadn't bid twelve or fifteen! David Betteridge was also amazed at Guy's approach and his ability to meet and stay with Chuck Berry, who he described as one of the top five most difficult people in the world to deal with!

Diane believes that some of these legendary Guy Stevens tales are untrue or at least distorted and heavily embroidered. In practice, Guy wrote for *New Musical Express* and *Record Mirror* and, through the journals, was instrumental in getting Chuck out of prison via his articles, and in setting up UK work for him. Guy's features could often be read in publications such as *Jazz Beat R&B Supplement*, where he would review American records, meticulously setting out the tracks, label and catalogue numbers, alongside his musical opinions.

Muff Winwood recalls that Guy then got the opportunity to dabble in record production. 'I got a job with Island as an A&R man and booking agent. At the top of the Basing Street building was a big office with a huge round table, and Blackwell and the rest of us would all sit around this table and work. Then, one day, Chris came in and said, "Great news, Guy is joining us tomorrow." And we're all going "fucking hell" and holding our heads. The next day, we're sitting there, and you can hear this kerfuffle getting nearer and nearer, and the door bursts open, and Guy leaps up on to the table, hair everywhere, dressed in these amazingly tight trousers and suede creepers and shouts, "We're going to make this the best fucking record company in the world!" And he just continued to jump around from then on.'

Guy was skinny, gangly and hyperactive with a large frizzy hair style and rolling, bulging eyes. He could be charming and urbane but was unpredictable and his enthusiasm, at times, could take him to incredible extremes resulting in chaotic sessions and occasional damage. Guy became one of the first house producers for Island, having previously produced a 1965 live album, *Larry Williams On Stage*, for Sue Records. Like Stevens' charted course, Williams had already followed a demonic trail, having been arrested and imprisoned on drugs charges in 1959. One of Stevens's other early projects was to put out a 1966 album of organ instrumentals, provocatively entitled *The Most Exciting Organ Ever*, by a young Billy Preston. Guy wanted everybody, including Dylan, to be on Island, so he started importing records for the label and nearly bankrupted them. Guy once described his introduction to record production as a result of complete musical enthusiasm. As he was so into sounds, it was natural to start creating them, but he knew clearly the sort of sounds that he wanted to make, and they were never to embrace any commercial consideration.

Stevens' Sue label operated from 1964 to 1967 and helped bridge Island's transition into progressive rock music, specialising in American R&B, blues and soul, whilst its parent was still almost exclusively an outlet for West Indian releases. Although they both featured the 'WI' prefix on their labels, Sue and Island would release material by UK bands such as The Circles, Smoke and The Belfast Gypsies. One group, called The VIPs, from Carlisle in the North East of England, formed their first link with Island when they provided the musical accompaniment for a Sue single by The Baron and his Pounding Piano, released in December 1965. The Baron, reportedly an East End dock worker, recorded brutal versions of 'Is a Bluebird Blue?' and 'In The Mood', produced by Stevens. Guy's session undoubtedly helped The VIPs to a contract with Island a year later, when they were signed by Stevens and subsequently became Spooky Tooth. Guy simply commented that they 'ambushed' Island Records at the same time he did.

The VIPs were the first band Guy ever produced. Formed in 1964 they released two unsuccessful singles and tried a temporary name change to The Vipps but, by October 1966, they reverted to The VIPs and were signed to Island Records. The key members of the band at this point were vocalist Mike Harrison and bass player Greg Ridley, but they recruited new blood in drummer Mike Kellie and lead guitarist Luther Grosvenor. Guy produced two VIPs singles for Island; a cover of Joe Tex's 'I Wanna Be Free', released in October 1966, and 'Straight Down to the Bottom', issued in February 1967. Island's most popular band at the time was The Spencer Davis Group who were released via Fontana Records and had The VIPs received similar treatment, they would undoubtedly have had a greater chance of chart success. Guy remarked that he liked The VIPs because they were 'incredibly heavy' and because they were all taking 500 'blues' a week!

In France, Fontana Records released four EPs featuring The VIPs, but within a few months keyboard player Keith Emerson, who had been added to the line up, left to form The Nice. The VIP's continued to work with Guy, but were soon re-named Art and became more progressive. Supervised by Chris Blackwell, they released a Stevens-produced album *Supernatural Fairy Tales* on Island in December 1967, preceded by a single from the LP, 'What's That Sound' (aka Buffalo Springfield's 'For What It's Worth'). All the tracks apart from the single were composed by Harrison, Ridley, Kellie and Grosvenor and the album was presented in a stunning psychedelic sleeve designed by Hapshash and the Coloured Coat.

Guy then decided to use Art as backing musicians for another of his projects involving two poster artists, Nigel Weymouth and Michael English, who had originally devised Art's sensational album cover and sleeves for Cream. Stevens produced the sessions for a free-form improvisational album entitled *Hapshash and the Coloured Coat Featuring the Human Host and the Heavy Metal Kids*. The recordings did not make for comfortable listening.

'One record that I really put a lot into for a long time was the first Hapshash And The Coloured Coat album, which was done in 1967, an intense year,' said Guy. 'That was when I left Island for a short time. It was recorded in about four and a half hours, with Art doing the backing, and they were the only musicians out of about thirty five people in the studio. I'd hired twenty different instruments and there were children there and people wandering in and out just banging things. Half the people were on acid, the rest were on something or other and everybody was just going berserk from beginning to end. It was amazing.'

The Hapshash album was released in 1968 on Liberty Records' subsidiary label, Minit, with initial copies pressed in red vinyl, which was innovative at the time. Re-issued on a 1994 CD, the sleeve notes remarked, 'Hypnotic and hilarious, the whole album is an idiosyncratic treat, and, alongside "Ptoof" by The Deviants, Britain's truest underground statement.' The five tracks on the album, described as an LSD opera, and featuring one song called 'A Mind Blown is a Mind Shown', were all composed by Stevens, Weymouth and English.

As Art evolved into Spooky Tooth, Guy suggested that they should add keyboards to create a Procul Harum / Bob Dylan sound, so American organist and pianist Gary Wright was recruited. Spooky Tooth did not really meet Guy's specification however, and he didn't stay around to produce their first album, *It's All About,* moving on to fill this Dylanesque void in his musical expectations a year later, with Mott The Hoople. Chris Blackwell felt that the original VIPs were stronger than Spooky Tooth and a group that 'slipped through the cracks'. At an early gig at the Star Club in Hamburg, he recalls the band being unbelievably raw and exciting. Blackwell felt, with hindsight, that the VIPs needed the right producer and manager, to spend twenty-four hours a day with the band, and drag out what they had in them. Ironically, the same could be said of Mott The Hoople's career with Island Records, and Guy's periodic disappearances and 'binges', after he had produced each Mott album. Twenty-four hour a day management would never have been in Guy Stevens' remit.

In 1967, Guy guided a lyricist that he knew to musician Gary Brooker, thus helping to form Procul Harum. Keith Reid worked in a solicitor's office but brought lyrics to Guy one day which he thought were vaguely Dylanish. Stevens told him the words were excellent and pointed him in the direction of a good songwriter. Guy found the name of the band, Procul Harum, on the pedigree of a friend's Burmese cat and, according to Diane, Reid also picked up the title of the song from Guy, when he was present at a small, late night party at the Stevens' Gloucester Avenue flat. Around 4.30 am, Guy offered Keith a lift home, in spite of their amphetamine intake, and turned, in the presence of Reid, to a nauseous Diane as he left saying, "My God, you've just turned a whiter shade of pale." Chris Blackwell was to turn down the song that resulted from the Brooker–Reid collaboration, but 'A Whiter Shade of Pale' went on to sell millions and became a worldwide number one hit. Guy was extremely unhappy about this lost opportunity and described it as the worst thing that happened between him and Chris, as he claimed Blackwell had the song on his desk for a week but did nothing with it. Stevens missed out on Procul Harum's success in any case, when he was jailed in 1968 on a minor drugs charge, his second prison term.

Around this time, Guy's massive record collection was stolen from his mother's house, and he suffered a nervous breakdown. He claimed to have owned every Miracles and Muddy Waters record and every Chess pressing, to have been present at a session with Phil Chess in 1964, when Chuck Berry recorded 'Promised Land' and 'Nadine' and to have pressurised Pye Records, who handled Chess in the UK, to release 'Memphis Tennessee' as a single. Guy had previously assembled several vinyl anthologies culled from the Chess label and released compilation albums of fifties material such as *Guy Stevens' Testament of Rock 'n' Roll* in 1968 and four volumes of *The Sue Story* in 1965 and 1966.

In Spring 1967, Steve Winwood asked Guy to work on the first Traffic album, *Mr Fantasy*, at Aston Tirrold, a Berkshire cottage to which the band had been despatched by Chris Blackwell. Stevens claimed that Winwood wanted him to produce Traffic and live with them, that he devised the cover, and that some very 'weird incidents' occured during the project. They did in the sense that Blackwell's neighbouring cottage kept getting broken into and, when the police eventually trapped the culprit, it was a Mr G. Stevens who had been entering, eating, drinking and lounging around. Blackwell had to go to the police to prevent them pressing charges and the *Mr Fantasy* album was produced by Jimmy Miller.

Stevens returned to work with Steve Winwood in 1970, when he produced a solo album, tentatively titled *Mad Shadows,* which he later used for Mott's second LP. The unreleased tapes apparently feature astounding takes of Bob Dylan's 'Visions of Johanna' and Jerry Lee's 'Great Balls of Fire'. Winwood decided to invite Chris Wood and Jim Capaldi to assist on the record and Traffic were re-born. The resultant *John Barleycorn Must Die* was their fourth LP, featuring only one Stevens-produced track, 'Staying Together', the remainder of the record masterminded by Jimmy Miller once again.

According to Diane Stevens, Guy didn't have any involvement with drugs in the early sixties, in spite of The Scene. Nevertheless, he was a compulsive and addictive figure; speed, when he discovered it one weekend in 1967, unlocked an uncontrollable side of his personality. In a short space of time, Guy started to take large quantities, and his general behaviour became extreme. Island Records would continually lose him 'on binges'. But for Blackwell, he would have been sacked. However, Guy was now the guardian of Island's taste and style and Chris liked him.

Island employee, Tim Clark, remembers, 'Guy was a one man army, a whirlwind who was always eager to get things done. He was a dervish, full of jibberish, ideas and enthusiasm for music and constantly alive with musical involvement. His opinion was always sought on how the music and, increasingly, on how an artist should look. He used to keep a little black book with names that he'd thought of. If he stumbled across a band and thought they were great but didn't like their name, he'd consult his list to come up with something better.'

Steve Hyams who befriended Mott The Hoople in their early days, experienced personal problems with drugs and remembers Stevens' involvement. 'Guy was a kind of enigma because musically, he was cloth-eared. Personally, I thought he was pretty useless as a producer and he would always be watching other people like Jimmy Miller very closely. Guy first got busted in 1967, the summer of love, with Brian Jones, for having some cocaine, which was unheard of in those days, and I think Guy took the rap for it. He was a speed freak and was always on uppers. You'd always get a messy sound with Guy and he'd switch moods depending on whether he'd had speed or coke or whatever. He'd generate this wildness and try to capture it on tape, but of course you can't sustain that, because drugs wear off and so does the enthusiasm. Blackwell really used to put good things his way like Spooky Tooth, Free and Traffic, then on things like the *John Barleycorn* LP, Chris eventually had to come in and take over.

'I'd often go round to Guy's flat in Swiss Cottage with my girlfriend. People like Chris Wood would be with him, and I remember Guy answered the door one day wearing nothing but a suspender belt and stockings. He had piles of bizarre magazines and he'd cut out pages and stuck them on the wall with butter. The only furniture was an enormous television and there were masses of records everywhere. He could be sad and mad, but Guy had a humourous side too and was always fantastic with potential names for bands. I once asked him, "Have you got a good name?" and he said, "Two grand," before he'd even tell me!'

Having already worked with Spooky Tooth and Traffic, Guy enhanced this track record with Free, who were to become one of the finest and most influential bands of the seventies. Formed in early 1968 from offshoots of two London R&B groups, Black Cat Bones and Brown Sugar, Island Records signed Free in April of that year after Alexis Korner had booked them to play at his club, and invited Chris Blackwell along to hear their set. Guy Stevens was lined up to produce their first album. He immediately suggested a change of name for the group to The Heavy Metal Kids, but this was resisted vigourously, particularly by Andy Fraser, only 15 years of age at the time, who refused to sign to Island unless they were called Free. They had originally developed as a live band, playing cover versions but, armed with enough of their own material for the debut album, they entered Morgan Studios with Stevens producing, to record *Tons of Sobs*. Guy's game plan for capturing Free on tape seemed simple.

Simon Kirke their drummer recollects, 'Guy was instrumental in getting Free off the ground. He wanted us to be called The Heavy Metal Kids, which was actually way before its time, and also *Tons of Sobs* was his title. He was pretty knocked out with us, that we could turn on such a wailing, bluesy wall of sound and it just triggered this phrase in him. We were really wet behind the ears when we went in to record. We were nervous and we didn't know what to do. They were partitioning us off and Guy came in and said, "Get rid of these screens and just play your set." Guy was careering around saying, "Great, great." It was a fabulous vibe. He was very talented and was forever buzzing around the studio. *Tons of Sobs* was recorded in a week. When I think about that today, it seems amazing. Now it takes a week to get the right snare sound!'

Tons of Sobs, released in November 1968, featured tracks that would become Free classics. The band were very young when they recorded the album, so their earthy and blues influenced 'I'm a Mover', 'Walk in My Shadow' and their passionate cover version of 'The Hunter' are quite remarkable. The way was paved for huge success with singles such as 'Alright Now', 'The Stealer' and 'My Brother Jake' plus the sensational albums *Fire and Water*, *Highway* and *Heartbreaker*.

In the summer of 1968, Stevens was arrested for possession of cannabis, found guilty and sentenced to a prison term of twelve months, of which he served nine. Guy paid his dues, but it wasn't a good experience for him and he was subdued when he was released from jail. He was soon back in the musical fold, however. During his term in Wormwood Scrubs, Guy had read a 1966 novel entitled *Mott The Hoople* by New-York-born author, Willard Manus. The book was a humorous fictional story of Norman Mott, described as a seventeen-stone, cigar-chomping, card-playing, wise-cracking hero, who rode in a balloon above Tulsa, Oklahoma and made a living by selling signed photographs of Christ! Hunter explains, 'It's about an eccentric guy who didn't fit in anywhere and ended up in a circus of freaks. Finally he got in a hot air balloon and dumped the sandbags. He was last seen two miles from heaven. In retrospect, that seems more or less right for us.'

Willard Manus recently explained the derivation of the word Hoople. 'Years ago in America there was a popular comic strip called "Our Boarding House". The leading character in the strip was a large, overweight guy named Major Hoople, who in England would, I guess, be called a layabout. He was forever hanging around the house, avoiding work, and spouting a lot of nonsense interspersed with lots of "ahems" and "cough-coughs" and "harhars". I was fond of the strip for as long as it lasted. I worked on the Mott book – on and off – for seven years. The original version was much bigger and more ambitious. The book was published in England, where it got rave reviews from all four main Sunday papers – and didn't sell a copy. Then it got put down in a New York review and that effectively killed off the book's chances of breaking through and making waves. Not long after that, I heard that a rock group had named itself after the book. I was never asked for my permission (which I would have given) nor have I ever made a penny from any of the band's activities (no problem there, either). The Mott novel was translated into Italian and was later re-published in 1980.

'Hoople is also an old American slang word, meaning variously, fool, rogue, buffoon and even *sucker*. That's why my character, Norman Mott, sometimes thinks of himself as a Hoople, because at different times in the book he is all of those things.'

Guy had borrowed a copy of Manus' novel from a young heroin addict in prison, and wrote to Diane, asking her to keep the title secret, which she thought was absolutely ridiculous. Nevertheless, Guy put it on his secret list of possible band names. When he subsequently learned, however, that the boy who possessed the book had died in jail, he wouldn't let Silence use Mott The Hoople, as he considered it a bad omen. The group hustled and eventually convinced him otherwise. Dale says, 'We each had a copy of the book very early on but I do not recall who gave them to us – possibly Guy. We met the author's secretary out in the States once, purely by chance. She was knocked out we knew the story and told us Manus was living as a recluse in the Greek islands.'

'Though it's true my wife and I lived for many years on a Greek island,' explains Manus, 'we did not consider ourselves to be recluses or people who had withdrawn from life. We simply found Lindos, on the island of Rhodes, to be a congenial place to live, especially on a writer's limited budget. It was a backwater in those days, but people from the rock world like Rick Wright and David Gilmour of Pink Floyd found their way there, among others of that ilk. All that's changed now, owing to the impact of mass tourism.'

Dale Griffin recalls Guy Stevens as a pencil slim man with receding, electric-shocked hair and a multiplicity of facial expressions. He could be an explosion of energy, enthusiasm, ideas and inspiration one minute, or a crumpled heap of despair the next. Tormented by his shortcomings, Guy could also destroy the things he loved and had nurtured, including himself, and yet the members of Mott invariably recall Guy's positive aspects rather than his negative side.

Verden Allen remembers Guy with affection but also the darker side of Stevens' personality. 'I respected Guy. I could never talk to him properly because I always thought he was superior in a funny sort of way. He was like a whizz kid and something special I thought. He pulled things out of people, not just us, because there were other great bands that he started off too. They just couldn't have happened without Guy. Nowadays, you go to London and play demo tapes to A&R people and they've got to ask somebody else's opinion. But Guy had the power to sign anyone he wanted and he liked our band. Guy was also destructive. He'd create then destroy. He would start something off, and if it developed into something and slipped from his grasp, he'd demolish what he'd created before it had developed into anything.'

'Guy was very, very strange to say the least,' comments Stan Tippins. 'He had outlandish ways, but his main thing with Mott The Hoople was that he had this confidence in them, and, in football terms, he was a really good coach. He believed in them and guided them in the right musical direction from early on. In football terms again, he believed in them winning games and climbing the league, which they did. On the other side of things like management and money, he wasn't good at all.'

Johnny Glover and Alec Leslie ran the Island Artists Agency, booking gigs and working with Traffic, Free and Mott The Hoople, and they acknowledge Stevens as an important character through the early development of the company. Guy would wander in to the office with 'projects' then disappear. He convinced Chris Blackwell that he should produce Mott but when he started, it wasn't a band, it was an idea. In spite of his 'genius', the Agency felt Guy was not really appreciated by the majority of Island Records' people because of his unreliability and 'lunacy'.

Muff Winwood, who became a senior figure at Island and producer of Sparks' acclaimed *Kimono My House* album in 1974, remembers Guy as a fun-loving but mad figure. Winwood recalls the discovery and naming of Mott, with Guy careering round the offices leaping on top of tables and chairs screaming, 'Mott The Hoople, Mott The Hoople.' Muff felt Stevens was a vibe for Mott, not a producer. He also expected Guy to settle down when he reached his middle twenties and married, but he never did, simply continuing his wild and manic journey through life with ever increasing ferocity. 'I loved Mott as a band and they were lovely, nice guys. Ian was older than the others and wasn't as mad. Guy was always way over the top, running around like a mad puppy dog. You couldn't settle down and discuss anything with him in a sensible way. He had outrageous ideas and was like a child with a new toy with them. Eventually, we would have to say, "For fuck's sake Guy, we've had enough now. Wonderful." '

In addition to his involvement with Spooky Tooth and Free, Guy also worked with several lower-profile bands. One project was with Heavy Jelly, who were actually Skip Bifferty, a sixties flower-power group. They used the name for a recording, to avoid contractual complications with their record label, and in an attempt to cash in on a favourable, but joke, album review for a band named Heavy Jelly, that never existed! With no long term aspirations to use the name for any subsequent work, they recorded 'I Keep Singing That Same Old Song' as an Island single in 1968 with Guy. A Stevens-produced album entitled *Take Me Down* was also prepared for release but never issued. Watts believes that Guy subsequently considered Heavy Jelly's lead singer, Graham Bell, as a candidate to replace Hunter in Mott The Hoople.

Another Stevens collaboration was with Britain's answer to The Grateful Dead, Mighty Baby, who played floating, melodic, progressive rock, inspired by West Coast psychedelia. In 1969, Guy assisted them with the production on their self-titled debut album, characterised musically by delicate melodies, accomplished musicianship and improvisation. The group issued a second LP in 1971 but disbanded shortly afterwards.

Guy auditioned bands and set up recording tests for Island in abundance, including Lindisfarne amongst others, who were then known as Downtown Faction. Drummer Ray Laidlaw recalls that Stevens was interested because he said the group had a similar sound to Creedence Clearwater Revival, a band they hadn't even heard of at the time! The test was unsuccessful as Guy felt they had potential, but were not ready to make records. Packing up their equipment to leave, it was the house engineer who asked if they would be interested in making an album, and the highly popular Lindisfarne was born and signed to Charisma Records.

Guy tried unsuccessfully to bring Creedence Clearwarer Revival to Island, but he was still charting another important course, assembling in his mind, the band that he had dreamed of with Spooky Tooth – a group that would fuse the crucial elements of Dylan, Procul Harum and the Stones.

4
Two miles from heaven

Mott The Hoople – Willard Manus

Guy Stevens had no real musical or technical knowledge but he did have an intuitive sense of musical quality. He could not play an instrument, could not sing and had only a slight grasp of the mechanics of record production, but he loved rock music and had an uncanny instinct for a musical 'vibe'. Having agreed to sign Silence to Island Records, he was very clear on how his new group should sound and their future direction. He still wanted to merge a Rolling Stones rhythm section, Procul Harum keyboards and a front man capable of combining the anti-establishment poetry of Bob Dylan with the aggressive vocals of Mick Jagger. Ian Hunter explains Guy's theory. 'He was always a Stones fan and a Dylan fan and he wanted a group that was a cross between the two. That was what he was after and we tried our best to live up to it.'

Stevens placed an advertisement for a new vocalist in *Melody Maker.* 'Island Records Ltd needs Pianist/Singer to join exciting hard rock band playing Bob Dylan influenced country rock music. Immediate album recording work. Ring Regent 6225.'

Freddie Lee, Ian Hunter's former colleague, confesses that he enquired about the position of vocalist but turned it down. 'I phoned up, but the wages on offer were a total insult. I was earning more a night in Germany than they were offering per week. Anyway, the vacancy was right for Ian and he did a better job than I ever could have done. My style of music was totally different, more rock 'n' roll and country orientated, which has made me a fantastic living, but Ian was tailor made for Mott The Hoople. I saw them play quite a few times and they were a really good band but just weren't my style. They were very important for British rock though. Ian's also proved his songwriting capabilities; he's very, very good, but he's his own man. Nobody can tell Ian anything and he'll only tell you what he wants you to know.' Dale Griffin states that Lee applied for the job in Mott The Hoople but was not considered for the post.

In spite of a limited response to the advertisement, Silence were asked to attend Regent Sound for auditions on 5 June 1969. The basement and ground floor studios at 4 Denmark Street were owned by Ed Kassner. The property became a comic shop some years later and has now regained credibility as a music book stockist.

'Only four people turned up for the audition,' recalls Dale Griffin. 'An old rocker like Cliff Richard, an over-the-top gay guy called Max from One Stop Records, a total fool who whined about spending two shillings on a bus fare, and a nondescript bloke who was so shy that he took five minutes to tell us that he was there for the audition. He'd been hanging around, moving screens and cables. We thought he worked at the studio. Depression set in and Guy was doleful.'

Watts agrees that all the candidates were terrible and the group was now regretting the departure of Stan Tippins. Silence and Guy had spent six horrendous hours auditioning without any success, so they decided to take a break and reflect on their predicament with Spooky Tooth's roadie in Denmark Street's Giaconda Cafe, Tin Pan Alley's temporary home to the rock world. With two hours of studio time left, the quintet finally trudged back to Regent Sound. Bill Farley, who ran the studio, said he knew someone who might be interested and called him. Guy cheered up and decided that if no one viable appeared, he would continue to place advertisements. Farley decided to telephone Hunter at his Archway flat.

Ian remembers, 'Bill rang me up one night and said there was this weird band in Regent Sound. I'd seen the ad in the paper for a pianist – singer but I wasn't feeling good when he called. At the time I was still making demos at Farley's in Denmark Street. He'd only charge four quid an hour. I sang in this odd Dylany voice, because I couldn't sing properly. Bill rang me up and said, "You've got to come down and see this band. They've been trying out people and don't like anyone but they're weird so they might like you." I wasn't in a very good mood, I had a headache and I was tired and, even though I was looking for a job, he'd got me to go to auditions before and they never turned out to be any good.'

In the interim, Hunter spoke to Miller Anderson. 'Ian said he was going for this audition with Guy Stevens for a piano playing singer and he wasn't sure about it because he couldn't play piano. I told him not to bother about it because I thought they'd probably see the same qualities in him as I did. Guy was a forward thinking person. He certainly gave Ian direction because everybody needs a little bit of help and other people can usually see you better than you can see yourself. I think Guy did that with Hunter.'

Richie Anderson, who met Ian when he joined The New Yardbirds, recalls Hunter's hesitation over the Island audition. 'Ian had turned up at some pub for a bass player audition in The New Yardbirds, which didn't last very long and didn't do anything much. Then, one day, Ian called me up and told me, "Someone at Island Records wants a Bob-Dylan-sounding singer and I think I might go for it, but I'm not very keen." I said it was worth him trying, if he wasn't really doing anything else.'

Farley rang Ian again. 'Bill was telling me they'd got down to the last two and they hadn't liked any of them so far. He was saying to me, "It's Island Records, It's Island Records." I'd never heard of Island. Traffic, Spooky Tooth and Free were all big at that time but I had no records. I still didn't bother but Bill rang again and said I'd better get down there as the job was still vacant, so I relented. And a funny thing happened on the way. I got out to the Archway and there were two buses you used to have to catch, and you always had to wait about half an hour for each one. That particular night the first bus was there, I got on it and got off, the second bus was right there, I got on the second bus and I was down there within half an hour, which anyone who lives in The Archway will tell you is impossible.

'I walked into Regent Sound and there were these long-haired people and I couldn't distinguish between them. But one person became apparent as the evening wore on and that was Guy Stevens. I didn't know if he was in the band but he started off serious and by the end was raving. I played Sonny Bono's "Laugh at Me" and then launched in to an aggressive rendering of "Like a Rolling

Stone". I didn't really play piano, C , F and G, that was about it and I'd never sung before, but I hammered away at the keys like a drum kit. It caught me at the right moment. I had nothing to lose. I remember Verden Allen, the organist, knew about half the chords. The guitarist looked just like the bass player, and Guy Stevens was this outrageous freak, hopping about. It was all very strange to me. I didn't know Guy was a Dylan freak as I was. I only had Dylan's singles, I didn't have any albums. All I had was a little plastic singles player, but I'd got "Like a Rolling Stone" and "Laugh At Me".'

Ian's electrifying and direct interpretation of Dylan immediately appealed to Stevens, but less so to the band. 'The rest of them were saying nothing but Guy was cheering up and so then I sat down in the flow of excitement and played this bass opus I'd just invented which killed the excitement immediately and it was left like that,' says Ian.

Of Hunter's arrival at Regent Sound Dale Griffin said, 'He wore open toed sandals with socks, a wretched faded black cord jacket that was too big for him and his hair, which was red and curly, tried, without success, to be long. Plus he sported big black shades. He was "basically a bass player" with The New Yardbirds.'

Pete Watts recalls, 'Ian hadn't seen the advert, but Guy explained, "We're look-ing for someone like Dylan and The Stones, can you play anything?" Hunter could hardly speak and mumbled, "Well, I can have a go at 'Like a Rolling Stone' I suppose." He looked horrific but he sat at the piano and started playing and singing, and it was pretty bad, but we sort of joined in and it went along. At least he had an idea. He wasn't a good piano player and he certainly wasn't a good singer, but there was something about him, the vocal meant something to him and he looked like he'd lived. Guy was standing behind Ian pulling horrific faces and making ridiculous gestures at me and giving the thumbs down, trying to get my reaction and I couldn't respond, because Ian was looking at me as he was singing. After that we all got talking and Ian said he was a bass player and had an idea for a symphony and could he borrow my bass guitar. I gave him the bass and he played this awful thing at the speed of sound, high on the bass. We all laughed about it afterwards.

'After Ian had gone, Guy asked, "What do you think?" and we said, "Well he's better than everybody else, but he's not exactly what we had in mind is he?" So Guy said, "Let's just get him in for a couple of weeks so we can say to Island we've got a complete group and a few weeks later we'll find somebody better and get him out." Guy's general plan was to get someone in even temporarily, so he could present a full band to Chris Blackwell. Our early photos in Kensington Gardens had the four of us and Guy in them.'

'When we did "Like A Rolling Stone" with Ian, Guy was in two or more minds,' recollects Dale. 'As I recall, Watts and I were the most pro-Hunter, Mick and Phally were wary. On that day the band was called Savage Rose and Fixable and we arranged to meet Ian at Island Records, in Oxford Street, the next day.'

'After the audition,' says Hunter, 'Guy rang up and said, "The way you look Ian, we're worried about the way you look." At that time I must have weighed about 170 pounds, I was fat and I had short hair and I'd worn shades to go down there because I looked horrible. I even think I had a corduroy suit on. So I said, "No problem. Whatever you want me to do, I'll do." '

Ian lost weight, grew a moustache and Stevens took him to a Berwick Street tailor and spent £100 on a black Dylan-style suit which was the signal that Hunter was in. 'I was back home for half an hour with my new suit and Miller came round saying I had to get a job as I was no longer with Francis Day and Hunter. He had the *Evening Standard* jobs pages with him and I said, "We're not going to need that Miller, I think I've got a gig." '

Asked if Miller Anderson might ever have figured in any Mott plans Hunter remarks, 'I always thought me and Miller were going to do something together, but that was the way it worked out. I think it was more timing than anything. We never seemed to coincide. Plus, Miller was my best mate, so it might not have gone down too well with the rest of the guys in the band.'

Ian had been continuing his songwriting, helping Leeds Music, run by Barry Mason and Les Reed, who would often say that he liked Ian's material although none got published. 'They wrote songs for people like Ken Dodd. I would write a song and Les would decide if it was good enough. I felt very paranoid about the whole thing,' said Hunter, 'so when Mott offered, I just seized the opportunity.

'I had my wife and two children and told Guy I'd been earning fifteen pounds a week with Francis Day and Hunter so he said he'd give me fifteen quid a week which he got from Blue Mountain Music. I joined and started this strange relationship. It was really funny because half the time I thought they were lousy and half the time I thought they were ten times better than I could ever be. I know Pete Watts was worried because he didn't think I looked right. The others said they liked me but they were very shy. Guy told me they were living in Lower Sloane Street and so I went down there and I saw the drummer and he walked straight past me as I went downstairs. I walked in the flat and nobody said a word to me for about twenty minutes and all of a sudden this guy came over who happened to be Stan Tippins. I was worried about him because I figured I'd taken his job but we got on great.'

Mott's accommodation was a basement flat at 20b Lower Sloane Street in Chelsea and this was to house the group members in the early days until they all moved to 17 Stonor Road in West Kensington. Hunter took the smallest room, at £4.10s, because he was paying maintenance by that time. Thereafter, Hunter moved to Wandsworth and then Wembley, Ralphs to Shepherds Bush, and Watts to Gayton Crescent in Hampstead where Paul Samwell Smith of The Yardbirds and Allan Clarke of The Hollies were his neighbours. Griffin and Allen continued to share Stonor Road until 1973.

'Mott were the weirdest people,' recalls Ian. 'The only person who would talk to me at first was Stan, who they'd effectively just fired and who ended up becoming our tour manager. I thought Stan was going to hit me, but he was the one that knocked all the barriers down. They never said a word and were a very insular mob who stuck to themselves. They were like a little local band from Hereford up in the big city and they seemed scared of everything and anybody. It was very odd; I spent half the time thinking I was dragging the whole show along and the other half of the time I spent running after them trying to catch them up. It was a strange sort of thing. They were country lads and there was this country-city thing. I'm city-inclined and there was a difference in view. I could-n't really see it happening at the time. I didn't think the band were very good and I was aware of my own inadequacies. I'd not been playing piano very long and I'd never sung before, so it scared me to death.'

'It was really funny,' says Watts. 'Hunter was in the group but we never saw him. He lived in Archway with his wife and kids and we all lived in the basement dwelling in Lower Sloane Street. We spent most of our time raging around the King's Road, very scared. Ian didn't think we were any good, but he needed the money at the time.'

'When I started writing songs they got really excited,' admits Hunter. 'I knew I was going to be the front man. I'd been waiting for that all my life. I guess I was real paranoid when I first joined Mott. I was scared stiff of people and wasn't singing very well. I didn't know how to do it. So the sun glasses were a defence mechanism and also a privacy mechanism and they just stayed there. In the end I became known for it so I just left them. I'm really quite handsome without them! If I took the shades off they would scream and shout like idiots. I did have bad eyes but I had ordinary prescription glasses. I can remember Mick Ralphs howling at Stan, "He's taken them off! He's taken them off! Get him to put them back on again!" '

Guy was delighted and relieved that he had found his Jagger/Dylan figure and Ian Hunter joined the group on 5 June, the five members actually signing a con-tract with Stevens, not Island Records. In the case of the youngest 'Mott', Fred Griffin signed the document.

The next stage was rehearsals and these were booked at the Pied Bull in Islington, North London commencing on 9 June. During these sessions Mott worked on 'The Rebel', 'Laugh at Me', 'At the Crossroads', 'Little Christine', 'Rabbit Foot and Toby Time' (originally entitled 'She's a Winner'), 'Half Moon Bay' and 'If the World Saluted You' (which became 'Backsliding Fearlessly'). Other rehearsed material which didn't survive for the first album sessions in-cluded Watts' 'The Wreck', Hunter/Ralphs' 'Back in the States Again' (a 'Back in the USSR' copy), Ian's 'Lavender Days' (a song in waltz time which would have been a great Dusty Springfield track according to Dale!), Dylan's 'Desolation Row', Chuck Berry's 'Little Queenie', the bizzare and reggae-flavoured 'Yma Sumac', 'The Parrot and the Cat' (an ode to Hunter's friendly club owner in Kiel), the Gothic and highly progressive 'Jekyll and Hyde' and 'When My Mind's Gone', which was to resurface for their second album.

Pete recollects, ' "Half Moon Bay" came out of the first rehearsal and things didn't seem so bad after all. But rehearsals at the Pied Bull were so boring. We booked in from 10 am to 6 pm and used to arrive at 2 or 3 in the afternoon. Ian would be there at 10 in the morning on the dot, writing stuff at the piano, all conscientious. The rest of us would arrive with hangovers from the night before and couldn't give a shit about anything. Poor old Ian, he was really putting a lot in to it and we didn't care. In the end Ian used to say, "Where the bloody hell have you been?" I felt sorry for him in the early stages because he was the only one trying. We didn't realise the significance of what was going on with the record deal, it just seemed easy for us.

'Ian, at that time was writing stuff that Guy told him to write. Guy was saying, "We want Bob-Dylan-type songs," so Ian would come back to rehearsals with songs like "Backsliding Fearlessly" and "Road to Birmingham". He could write to order after Francis Day and Hunter. Guy told him that we needed a combination of the Stones and Bob Dylan and as Guy had 'his' group mapped out, the whole direction came from him. He was lucky with Hunter in that he could tell him what he wanted and Ian would translate it in to actual songs. Ian eventually did start writing for himself when Guy got messed up with drink. He lost a lot of his direction. Hunter saw that the only way was to forge ahead on his own, without listening too much to Guy. Guy had given birth to Mott The Hoople but he couldn't handle it. In the beginning Ian's role was to write the Dylan-type songs, but Mick wrote "Rock and Roll Queen" and so Ian started to write songs like "Walkin' with a Mountain".'

When Mott met Stevens, he interested the group in American music. They were already familiar with Neil Young but he played them obscure records like Ford Theatre and the first Chicago Transit Authority album. In the group flat, they regularly listened to Delaney and Bonnie's debut LP, Buffalo Springfield and The Beatles' *Abbey Road*. Guy was still inspired by Dylan, however, and used to come to rehearsals and make Mott play 'Highway 61 Revisited', 'Can You Please Crawl Out Your Window', 'Desolation Row' and 'Just Like Tom Thumb's Blues'. They played 'Laugh at Me' because Ian liked the song and Guy suggested 'At the Crossroads' by Doug Sahm. 'We rehearsed "Crossroads" and then I reversed the chords and it became "Half Moon Bay",' says Ian. 'That's when they thought, "Maybe he can write". Pete said, "You're a better writer than me, so I'll leave it to you." Pete was really good about it. It's very hard to imagine that in Watts, because Pete is a very selfish guy, but in other ways, not in musical ways.'

After eleven days of rehearsal, and without doing any gigs at all, Mott went in to Morgan Recording Studios in Willesden High Road, North London on 20 June, with Guy Stevens as producer and Andy Johns, brother of Glyn Johns, as engineer. Glyn was to become one of British rock's major engineers and producers working with Steve Miller, Traffic, Led Zeppelin, The Rolling Stones, The Beatles, The Who, The Faces, The Eagles and Wings. Andy Johns had assisted Glyn as engineer on recordings for the Stones.

John Glover of Island recalls, 'Guy really put the entire Mott album together, recorded them at Morgan Studios and went way over budget. In those days Blackwell's budget for an album was about two thousand quid. Guy spent five, which was outrageous. It was all Guy's concept and Ian wasn't the dominating figure he later became. He was the new boy, didn't say too much and Guy's word was law.'

The album sessions started with the group still called Savage Rose and Fixable, further evidence of Guy's Zimmerman fixation, as the name was 'lifted' from the sleeve notes for the album *Highway 61 Revisited* in which Dylan had written the strangest of pieces, featuring the characters White Heap, Madan John, the

Cream Judge, Savage Rose and Fixable. On 27 June, three weeks after Hunter's recruitment, Stevens opted for Mott The Hoople.

Dale remembers the christening of Mott. 'Guy had several names ready for us. He was keen on Blue Egg, which we had to reject, then he was going to call us Savage Rose and Fixable. Griff Fender was another contender along with Brain Haulage; both were UK trucking firms. When he found out that a Danish group already used Savage Rose he eventually settled for Mott The Hoople, saying it would "look good written down".'

On completion of the recording sessions in July, Guy Stevens enthused wildly about Dylan and the new Mott The Hoople LP to Pete Frame, fan of the group and editor of *Zig Zag* music magazine. 'The record is amazingly like Bob Dylan in places, simply because Dylan is like, in the sky to them. They are completely and utterly on their backs about Dylan. I've got an unbelievable thing about Dylan myself. We're calling the album *Talking Bear Mountain Picnic Massacre Disaster Dylan Blues,* after the unrecorded Dylan song "Talking Bear Mountain". And we're having a picture of Dylan inside the sleeve, because it's all about Bob Dylan. But at the same time they have a thing of their own.' No wonder the group were soon having to fight shy of heavy *Blonde on Blonde* accusations, although musically the album was more reminiscent of *Highway 61 Revisited.*

Another potential title for the first Mott record had been *The Twilight of Pain Through Doubt!* which came from an Italian record that Mick Ralphs found in 1968. The song was an awful pseudo re-write of 'A Whiter Shade of Pale' and a literal translation of an Italian phrase. 'Guy Stevens loved it and it almost became the title of the first album and/or a song, but Guy didn't think of it himself, so it was quietly discarded. It is, though, an archetypal Hoopleism,' explains Dale.

The album title eventually ended up plain and simply, *Mott The Hoople* and like so many of their future LPs, it amply demonstrated Mott's schizophrenia. Hunter said at the time, 'We've always been schizoid. We like slow, quiet stuff, then there's that bit of madness that you've got to get out, like a kind of orgasm.'

The opening track was sheer lunacy, a wild and brutal high-octane version of Ray Davies' 'You Really Got Me', which had originally been a UK number one hit single for The Kinks in 1964. Initially, Mott recorded this as a ten minute instrumental with an increasingly frenzied coda, which Guy considered releasing in its entirety as a single! For once, sanity prevailed and a three minute version was prepared with added Ralphs lead vocal, before the instrumental made the final pressing. It was one of only two real 'rockers' on the album and a cover at that, as they were struggling to come up with anything other than slow songs. 'You Really Got Me' was attempted because Mott saw The Kinks going into Pye Studios as they drove to Morgan Studios for their session that day.

Ian says, 'It started just like The Kinks, a three minute song, and I think it was Mick who said, "Let's put this at the end and see what happens." A year later it was going for twenty-five or thirty minutes, pulling the places apart. And the funniest thing was we went to America supporting The Kinks, and we were in this really odd situation where half our show was that song, so we had to tell Ray Davies, "Look if you don't let us play this song, we can only do half an hour before you come on." And he said, "Well, do it." Then he used to do a medley at the end of their set and he would say, "We'll do a medley so Mott the Hoople can figure out which song to nick next time." '

The three remaining tracks on Side One illustrated the Guy Stevens' Mott concept so well; Doug Sahm's 'At the Crossroads', suggested by Stevens, Sonny Bono's 'Laugh at Me', proposed by Ian, and Hunter's 'Backsliding Fearlessly'.

Texan Doug Sahm, brought a mixture of blues and country to San Francisco music during the mid-sixties and first found success with The Sir Douglas Quintet and the single 'She's About a Mover'. It was later said that Mott's atmospheric version of 'At the Crossroads', taken from Sir Douglas Quintet's 1969 *Mendocino* album, was particularly enjoyed by Bob Dylan. Of Sahm's 'At the Crossroads' Ian says, 'That was the first song we were ever known for because it was on a compilation, the first number when people actually started clapping before we did the song'.

Mott's cover was included on the second in a series of Island sampler albums, *Nice Enough To Eat,* including contributions from stately stablemates King Crimson, Jethro Tull, Free and Traffic. To launch their contemporary and progressive acts, labels such as CBS, United Artists, Vertigo and Island conceived periodic budget LPs, often retailing from as little as a few shillings, aimed at tempting the impoverished student market with representative music from their catalogues.

The third track on Mott's debut, Sonny Bono's 1965 top-ten US single 'Laugh at Me', had been played by Hunter at his audition for the group. Sonny and Cher's 'I Got You Babe' remains one of Ian's all-time favourite tracks. Hunter explains, 'There was a gap of a few weeks and one day when we were in the studio, Guy came in and said, "Try 'Laugh at Me'," so we did it a second time. I thought at the time it was released it had a lot more to it than Sonny Bono put into it. But all his songs were very strong ones and they adapt well to changes of tempo. We did "Laugh at Me" much slower than the original for instance.' One journalist was to comment, ' "Laugh at Me" is done truly beautifully. From the tone of Ian Hunter's voice, you can tell that "I don't care if you laugh at me" is a line that he really means.'

Dylan and Bono had a style which convinced Hunter that he should sing in the first place. 'Sonny Bono couldn't sing that well and I sort of listened to people who couldn't sing very well because I couldn't sing very well,' admitted Ian. 'It was a good song and people used to laugh at me. I wore shades when it wasn't fashionable to wear them. People used to think you had a big head if you wore them and I did have a big head. I was extremely arrogant and I kind of liked it that way. And a lot of people would laugh at you, so I guess it was appropriate.'

Ian still acknowledges that Dylan's singing style encouraged him. 'I was lucky because Dylan came around and he couldn't sing either but he had this great delivery, like Leonard Cohen and Randy Newman. And it became easier for me and Mick Jagger if you like, phrase singers, people who haven't really got great chops. Rod Stewart and Paul Rodgers have got great natural voices, but we had to adopt different ways of getting across. Dylan really helped me a lot. At the time I couldn't sing a note. I was only using my vocals to get the words across like a lot of people do. It was just coming out that way. I didn't have *Blonde on Blonde*, I didn't have any albums, I couldn't afford them. I subsequently acquired the record, and I can see the parallels, but they are parallels in as much as the Byrds were a parallel. In America we were regarded as parallel. There seemed to be this thing that Dylan had gone off from *Blonde on Blonde* one way, but we had mainly come from *Blonde on Blonde* and gone another way. But in England it was passed off as a bunch of blokes trying to be like Dylan. I mean Dylan's a genius, he changed the world, he made music into a culture. He gave the whole rock and roll syndrome validity. I should imagine he's an influence on nearly everybody. Anyone who says that they aren't influenced by someone else is a liar!'

Having opened with three covers, Side One closed with 'Backsliding Fearlessly', written by Hunter but given a Guy Stevens' title just before the album was finally pressed. The song was originally called 'If the World Saluted You', and was very much in Dylan vein being a thinly disguised re-write of 'The Times They Are A-Changing'. The sound of the band and Hunter's lyrical imagery blended beautifully.

> Three cheers for the innocent though he is perverse
> Three screams for the hangman as he cries for the hearse
> I weep for the rebel conventional ways
> For he loses his mind while the devious say
>
> So come all ye faithful and slaughter your lambs
> For your minds have been witched by experienced hands
> I wish we were children I'd welcome the change
> For the mind of an old man you can't rearrange

The second side contained original group compositions and started with Mick Ralphs' 'Rock and Roll Queen', a mixture of The Stones and The Byrds. Roger McGuinn was later to enthuse about this LP and the song survived in Mott's live act almost indefinitely. Having completed the entire album by August and departed from Morgan Studios, Guy began to panic that it needed a tough, rock number. He telephoned, and instructed Mick and Ian to get something written '*quickly!*'. Much to the amazement of the other band members, Ralphs composed 'Rock and Roll Queen' on demand and under the severest of pressure. Recorded in early September, it was unlike anything he had written before and was strange, being a fantasy ode to a lady of the road from a self-proclaimed rock star, when Mott hadn't even played live, yet alone secured celebrity status. 'It was a fictitious story, written about being on the road in America using a load of cliches, but it was a good song,' says Mick. 'The right song at the right time.'

> Listen woman, you needn't look so stupid when I call your name out loud
> 'Cos everybody thinks you're a sweet little girl,
> with intelligence and you know how
> I wouldn't want anyone else to know, about the way you really are

You're just a rock 'n' roll Queen you know what I mean,
and I'm just a rock 'n' roll Star

Ralphs' instrumental, 'Rabbit Foot and Toby Time', originally conceived as a
vocal number and titled 'She's a Winner', prefaced the stunning, eleven minute,
'Half Moon Bay' which had originated during rehearsals at The Pied Bull and
showcased languid piano and dramatic organ. Written by Ian and Mick, and
originally called 'Half Moon Bay, Part One', the song was reminiscent of Procul
Harum but was intended to be another crossbreed of 'Like a Rolling Stone' and
'At the Crossroads'. The dynamics, time changes and various musical themes
were astonishing from such a young ensemble and hinted at the musical and lyrical maturity that was to develop in the future.

'Guy got me writing by getting us to do strange things,' recalls Hunter. 'I was
actually playing songs backwards and reversed chords. Guy was egging me on,
and Verden Allen waded in there, "Moonlight Sonata" and all that, and before
we knew where we were, we had our first epic; and it came out as "Half Moon
Bay". I still believe it's one of the best things we've ever done. I always think of
that as the essence of Mott because it had everything in it, all the jumbled ingre-
dients of those early days, thrown together in one bizarre track. I remember Mick
and I loved the riff. Later on, many years later, we were going down that road between Los Angeles and San Francisco, and there's "Half Moon Bay" on a sign. At
the time I'd just made it up. The whole song was just visual words.'

Well the colours crossed my mind, anyway
And the feelings that I find, so very hard to say
I've gone, with the rain, making out
But you never felt the same, you are in doubt
Too soon my eyes grow dim, and I try
To recognise the figures, drifting by
And too late the same man comes, with the key
And I fight the loneliness, that just ain't me

'That was one of the most important tracks we did,' says Ralphs. 'We didn't
know about the Californian village at the time, nor did we know that a Hell's
Angel chapter lived there, which we found out later.'

The album finished with a short blistering instrumental fragment entitled
'Wrath 'n' Wroll' which was credited to Guy Stevens, albeit he had simply salvaged and edited a section of tape from the riotous outpouring at the end of the
lengthy 'You Really Got Me' take. Ian said at the time of the LP's release, 'That
number developed into a jam which lasted about fifteen minutes, it was the best
thing I've ever played. We cut the last bit off and stuck it on as the final track on
the album.'

'The original take of "You Really Got Me" was frenzied nonsense, some ten
minutes long, getting faster and faster until chaos prevailed.' says Dale Griffin.
'We played "You Really Got Me" very fast, very high energy, very uncool for
those days. "Wrath 'n' Wroll", which completed the LP, caught the tail end of the

full take, as with "The Wheel of the Quivering Meat Conception" and "The Journey" on *Brain Capers*.'

Watts recalls that most of the album tracks were recorded in one take and that the sesssions seemed so easy with Guy and Andy Johns. Island were already prepared to put Mott back in the studios in October to capture each stage of their early development.

Verden Allen has particularly fond memories of the first Mott The Hoople album. 'That was the best one for me really. It was recorded on eight track and when we did it, there was no messing about. We had one track each and that was it. We went in and laid it down and the feel was there and maybe something went on afterwards, like the vocal. There is something nice about that album. Thinking of it, I wrote part of "Half Moon Bay" in Hereford but later Mick Ralphs said he did it, although I didn't mind, we just wanted to record. I also remember on that session, Chris Blackwell had a new girlfriend at the time. When we did that grating organ bit she said, "What's that sound? I like that. Fantastic. What's it about?" I said, "I haven't got a clue, I don't know." She said, "Well it sounds nice anyhow." So Blackwell says, "Carry on lads," and walked out.'

Dale recalls Blackwell arriving at that early recording session. 'Chris demanded to hear something we had done. A playback was made and Blackwell looked bemused. He turned to his blonde and beautiful companion and asked her opinion. "I like it," she said. We felt that a negative response would have seen us ejected from the studios, so thank you, Marilyn Rickard.'

Several additional tracks and jams were recorded at Morgan Studios including backtracks for Dylan's 'Desolation Row', Chuck Berry's 'Little Queenie', 'The Rebel', Ralphs' Hendrix-sounding 'Find Your Way' and 'Little Christine'. Griffin recollects Guy's original plan to produce a double album containing the full ten-minute version of 'You Really Got Me'. 'We were very crestfallen when Guy announced this idea had been shelved and it became a single LP.'

Mott The Hoople was preceeded by a single issued on 1 November, 'Rock and Roll Queen', backed with 'Road to Birmingham', which was supposed to be unavailable on the LP. An initial batch of the album was mispressed, however, with 'Rock and Roll Queen' omitted and 'Road to Birmingham' included in error. Furthermore some of the tracks on the rapidly withdrawn discs were early mixes including an extended introduction to 'Rabbit Foot and Toby Time' and a different mix of 'Wrath 'n' Wroll', which included the original coda of 'God Save the Queen'. In the USA Atlantic issued 'Rock and Roll Queen' as a single with 'Backsliding Fearlessly' as the B-side.

'Road to Birmingham', composed by Hunter, tackled the controversial topic of racial prejudice and almost delayed the release of the album. Ian explained, 'The song's about Birmingham USA as well as Birmingham in the UK. They've got the same racial problems. I know it's been said before, but it still hasn't been said enough – I think it's scandalous that we should set up offices in the Commonwealth countries to try and attract black people to come and live and work here, then treat them like shit. I just can't stand racial prejudice.'

Watts had been ill with a serious ear infection during the recording of this track, so Mick Ralphs made his bass-playing debut on record.

For in your youth, you think the truth, will always win the game
Some men are kings, some men are rooks, some men are pawns to blame
But if your skin, is coloured black, well the dice are hidden in
The minds of fools, who twist the rules, so you can never win
Birmingham, Birmingham, underneath your face
There's nothing but a space, you're hollow

Island Records promoted the group with full page music press advertisements proclaiming 'Mott The Hoople is Two Miles from Heaven', a slight re-write of the opening line from Manus's book. Their first photo session with Julian Allason, at a rainy and windswept Kensington Gardens, featured Ralphs, Watts, Allen, Buffin and Guy Stevens, as stand-in for Hunter, who had missed his bus and couldn't afford to take a taxi! They also shot an early publicity photograph at a site found by Guy in Notting Hill, used for the gloomy set of the Fellini film *Leo the Last,* the entire band pictured in front of dull and dilapidated brick buildings, all of them painted black.

Mott The Hoople was released by Island in November 1969 when The Beatles were topping the UK charts with *Abbey Road.* By the time the LP entered the British charts on 2 May 1970, The Beatles were at number one again with their next album, *Let It Be. Mott The Hoople* only stayed in the charts for one week, reaching number 66, but it received several excellent reviews. One journalist drew the inevitable comparisons with Bob Dylan, saying, 'This is a collection of good sounds. I always wanted more of the *Highway 61* stuff anyway.' Another held a different musical view, noting, 'Mott The Hoople play the type of heavy music that I was disturbed not to find on *Led Zeppelin II.* A rather bold statement you say? Well just give this disc a little listen and you'll see what I mean. Mott The Hoople – too good to be believed – much too good to be missed.'

For American distribution of their recordings Mott signed to Atlantic Records on a three-year contract worth 125,000 dollars. Like Island, Atlantic had been a label that, from its inception, championed black artists. Formed in 1947 in New York by Ahmet Ertegun and Herb Abramson, their first major signing was Ray Charles, and they kept in the forefront of soul music by cementing a distribution and recording deal with Stax, before merging with Warner Seven Arts Corp in 1967 and Kinney Communications in 1969, eventually becoming part of WEA Records. Like Island, Atlantic diversified successfully into the rock arena signing major acts throughout the late sixties and early seventies including Iron Butterfly, Buffalo Springfield, Yes, Led Zeppelin, Crosby Stills Nash & Young and Foreigner.

Atlantic Records did not release Mott's debut album in the US until Spring 1970. Ian recalls, 'We didn't get any action off the album at all. I think it got to about 175 in Billboard. In England it sold about 8,000 and everybody hated it. They didn't like it when we posed. In England no one seems to like what you're doing at the time. They always like it afterwards. It's a pain in the ass.' The group didn't know, but they were already starting to garner attention for Hunter's Zimmerman-like rasp, their odd choice of covers and their combined swagger of heavy Rolling Stones ('Rock and Roll Queen') with Dylan's poetic fervour ('Backsliding Fearlessly'), delivered with such anglicised vocals.

John Glover remembers completion of Mott's first LP. 'Once Guy brought the album in, he then went off on a drugs spree and we never saw him again for ages. He always went off on these benders. But Blackwell had put a deal together where Guy would manage the band. I don't think the management lasted long enough for the record to come out. He was off. So the agency took over. We all looked after Mott as agents. The album did okay and Ian began to get stronger within the band.'

Diane Stevens recalls Guy's infatuation with Mott. She feels it was the first time he could create rock and roll, and Ian soon tapped into that as he had the same psyche, although obviously not the same problems as Guy.

The *Mott The Hoople* LP was housed in a gatefold sleeve containing a repro-duction of Maurits Cornelis Escher's 1943 lithograph *Reptiles*. Originally from a lithographic stone, the drawing illustrated the 'bringing to life of an abstract structure', one of Escher's predilections. The drawing was also used as an illus-tration on an Italian chemistry text book! Legend has it that Mick Jagger had pre-viously written to Escher during his lifetime seeking permission to use one of his drawings for an LP cover and the artist turned him down. After his death, Guy simply blazed ahead, using one of his lithographs for the *Mott The Hoople* sleeve.

'We had nothing to do with the first album's cover,' admits Dale. 'Guy just presented that to us. We thought it was great and a very unusual sleeve. We had not seen anything like it before and, as far as I know, nobody had used Escher before, in the rock music world anyway. Where he got consent to colour in an Escher drawing I don't know. He probably didn't get permission and just did it.'

Verden recalls Guy arriving with the lizard print. 'We were in Morgan Studios when, all of a sudden, the door opened and Guy was struggling to get this bloody great cardboard sheet through and it wouldn't come in. So we gave him a hand and had to bend it round the door. He got it in and put it up against the wall. We said, "What's this Guy?" It was huge. He said, "Oh, this is your album cover." And somebody quipped, "Not that size, is it, Guy?" '

The inner gatefold photographs of each group member's head were all super-imposed on the same picture of Mick Ralphs' body, with a London Transport bus as the backdrop. 'The inside photo was taken outside Island's Basing Street stu-dio,' says Verden. 'They were the good old days in the beginning. I remember Guy bringing in the sleeve mock up and he said, "Right, we're doing the sleeve now. Your name, Terence Allen. The name. We can't use that. You've got five min-utes to think of one." So I said, "Well, I can always use my father's name. Verdun with a 'U', put an 'E' in instead. Verden Allen." Guy said, "Oh yeah, Verden. That's not bad." He just walked off. Next thing it's on the sleeve.'

Watts recalls, 'Guy's whole idea was that Mott would be a band surrounded in mystique and he went round all of us trying to find names. Buffin was Dale's nickname at school and Guy liked that, then he got Verden to use his father's name. Hunter was Ian's middle name but he didn't like Pete Watts at all. "It doesn't sound big enough," he said. I told him that my middle name was Overend and he started leaping about and shouting. "That's wonderful! Overend Watts! Not for him the turgid bass riff!" And he began a long Shakespearean-style monologue. He was so excited, you couldn't help getting caught up in it.'

Mott were satisfied with the finished album as Mick Ralphs explained. 'We're very pleased how it turned out, but the next one will be recorded at Olympic Studios, so that we can get better instrument separation. After you make a record, you always feel that it could have been improved on somewhere, that certain passages should have been re-arranged, but we're much wiser now, having done this first one. The next will be so much better.'

The first album and single had been released and Mott The Hoople had still not played a single live concert. 'We never did a gig before the album,' said Hunter. 'In fact, if we'd done gigs before we did the album, we'd never have done it! Rehearsing for two weeks before going in to the studio was remarkably fortunate, because subsequent live shows were pretty bad and I think Island would have given us the boot if it hadn't been for the fact we'd already got the album in the can.'

To kick start their live career away from the British press, the band arranged a 'get it together' residency at the Bat Caverna Club in Riccione, Italy, where The Doc Thomas Group had played during the previous two years. Mott left for Italy on 2 August and played their first ever public performance on 6 August with Thane Russell and The Trip and I Nomadi, who were subsequently to record an uncredited cover version of a Hunter song, 'Waterlow', from Mott's third LP. 'Why did they claim to write this?' questions Dale. 'I reported their plagiarism to Island Music, but did not hear anything further.'

The week of Italian Mott The Hoople gigs was poorly received, according to Griffin. 'The opening night was remarkable. They loved us far more than we could justify. The next night nothing – why? The first night audience believed Ian to be blind and with all the stumbling, fumbling and bad chords who could blame them? When they realised that our boy was sighted they lost all interest, and the Bat management was howling for the return of Stan, the Paul Newman of Pop.'

Ian recalls, 'It was certainly an inauspicious start. We went out to Italy for a few weeks to get things together and were told by the promoter after four days that we were on half pay or we could go home. Things were bad at the time so we took the cut and treated it like a rehearsal. I died a death there; they liked the band but they hated me because I was doing slow songs. I also had an electric piano which made more noise than it had notes and I couldn't play it very well anyway. I remember sitting on the toilet there one night thinking, "You've got to do it, you've got to get through it." I mean the gig really was hard.'

Guy Stevens accompanied Mott to Riccione to 'help', but felt absolutely alien and trapped in Italy according to Watts. 'Guy was like a fish out of water over there, because he meant nothing to anybody. They just thought he was a nutter. Nobody could understand him and I can remember him on the beach – he weighed about six stone and was almost translucent with whiteness. He had this big ball of black hair and was as thin as a rake, he looked ridiculous. The club owner threw him out and they wouldn't have him back in the Bat Cavern because they thought he was disruptive. It was frightening and we had no coherence as a band on stage, it just wasn't happening. We lasted about ten days and then they threw us out! I think all the rest of the groups thought, "My God, how did a pile of shit like that get signed up to Island Records?" '

Mott's early live repertoire contained several unrecorded songs including 'The Hunchback Fish', 'Rung From Your Ladder' (a 'jazz' jam added to 'Hunchback Fish'), 'Brand New Cadillac', 'Opus in D_m', 'Jekyll and Hyde' (a 5/4 time monster epic), 'Half Moon Bay' with a special introduction of drums and percussion and 'Darkness, Darkness'.

After their residency at Riccione, Mott played their first British live dates in early September supporting King Crimson and Free. Dale Griffin acknowledges that Mott were trounced. 'The Italian gigs hadn't been good. They were very rough and ready, not helped by the fact that three or four groups were playing on the same night. By the end of our trip the feeling wasn't good. Guy was depressed and Ian wanted me replaced with a drummer named Terry Slade, who was in one of the other groups and was a muso-type like Hunter. But in my diary I wrote, "This is a chaotic opening but it is going to work." Back in England our first gig was at Romford Polytechnic, as support to King Crimson, who were absolutely stunning and took the place apart.'

By this stage however, Watts recalls Stevens was already distributing advance pressings of *Mott The Hoople* in appropriate circles. 'Guy had got white-label copies of the album done and sent them exclusively to all the hip DJs like Jeff Dexter, John Peel and Andy Dunkley, who hung on everything Guy did. He had a lot of respect from people on the music side and because it was a Guy Stevens project, the name was weird and nobody knew anything about the band, they all took to it and thought, "Christ, this band's incredible." We weren't!

'We had this gig supporting King Crimson. Guy already had it worked out that Mick and I would do the talking and Ian would sit there as a mysterious character in shades, not saying a word, playing the piano, in a black suit, like Dylan. And that's how we were on the first gigs, Mick and me all cheerful introducing numbers and Ian sitting like an albino Ray Charles! Anyway, we did this set at Romford and it was fucking diabolical, and we knew it was terrible. But after every number, the audience just looked at us in disbelief, while tables of DJ's near the front, invited by Guy, all gave reverent applause. Because it was like the Emperor's new clothes; Guy had told them that this band were hot, so therefore they were going to clap. We knew we were awful, but they thought we were amazing.

'King Crimson were so great and halfway through watching their set, I had to go glumly to the toilet. When I was standing contemplating packing it all in, a guy four stalls along spoke to me. "Hey mate, were you in that first group?" So I said "Yeah" dejectedly, to which he replied, "You were better than this bloody lot!" I thought he was totally mental because Crimson's lights were spot on with the sound during all these complex numbers like '21st Century Schizoid Man'. I thought there was no way in a million years Mott would ever be good enough, but when the bloke at the urinal said that to me, I thought maybe there was some sort of hope for us. He thought we were better than them!

'In fact, after this, Crimson's guitarist Robert Fripp used to come and see us quite a bit in the early days of Mott. I was always quite surprised to see him there because I couldn't quite figure out what we had in common with them. They were such perfectionists and one of the most incredible live bands at that time. I got talking to Robert one night and asked him why he kept coming to see us. I said, "We're kind of not your cup of tea really are we, because we speed up and slow down all the time." And Fripp's reply to that was, "Yes, but you all do it at exactly the same time. It's fantastic!" I thought that was great.'

The opening concerts were soul destroying for Hunter too, particularly their second gig with Free in Sunderland, which he compared to Beatlemania for them at the time. Mott had been reasonably well received but then the crowd went wild for Free. Ian was down, but Watts was already becoming realistic enough to appreciate that Mott The Hoople still hadn't clicked yet as a unit, although he knew they had a long way to go. Verden Allen recalls that it only took a few gigs for things to happen. 'Hunter used to sit down at the piano and play all the time, but one night I ran across the stage with the maraccas at Ian, and he got off his keyboards and everything went crazy and took off.'

Chris Blackwell witnessed this developing madness when he turned up at the side of the stage during a King's Road gig one evening to watch Mott The Hoople live for the first time. Hunter, furious at the roadies with a faltering electric piano, hurled the instrument towards the wings, the flying keyboard missing Blackwell's face by inches. Ian admits he was shaken, but Island's figurehead re-marked to Guy Stevens that at least the band's committment appeared unquestionable.

Mott The Hoople was still ramshackle, awkward and self-conscious at these initial live tests, but over subsequent months the band developed and Hunter found enormous confidence and a stage presence that later distinguished him. Engaging in much concert work, Mott quickly built a rabid live following and soon they generated their first major audience reactions at Harwell in Oxfordshire and Letchworth in Hertfordshire. 'It took us a little while to find our feet,' says Dale. 'Then at a small show in Harwell, at the Atomic Energy Authority Research Station Social Club I think, it was the first gig where we used half the guitarist's amplification, a Marshall with one cabinet instead of two, and suddenly it just clicked. That night became the first typical Mott The Hoople night. It's difficult to know why and impossible to analyse. Something just snapped into gear.'

'After Harwell, we only ever used half our equipment,' recalls Pete. 'We were using Marshall stacks, then, when we went to America in May 1970, we got Acoustic amplification. In the early days of Mott I had a 200-watt bass amp, but I always used a black Laney cabinet, which had belonged to Spooky Tooth, and it sounded better than a Marshall. I still have the cabinet in my shed today, nearly thirty years on, and full of mice, so it's useful even now!

Letchworth Youth Club was the first time Mott The Hoople ever received an encore. 'They went spare at Letchworth and we couldn't believe it,' says Hunter. Then the following night we did the same again. It was all over one weekend, it just suddenly happened. It became more like a performance. We started to develop 'You Really Got Me' and it went on for twenty minutes and got a bit crazy. It began to be obvious that they didn't want to hear the slow stuff, they wanted to hear the fast stuff. I started moving around, kicking the piano over, things like that. Maybe it was in desperation, to try to get a reaction. I still stayed at the side but I started to dominate. I now wanted to play guitar and get in the middle.'

The group were soon to become a regular and major attraction at the Friars Club in Aylesbury, a town that was to remain big in Hunter's affections. 'I often thought about living in Aylesbury because I don't know what it is, it's like Toronto, it's like Cleveland, it's just that weird one off place,' said Hunter several years later. 'It's one of those strange places where everything seems to start. I know Mott happened in Aylesbury long before they happened anywhere else. So did David Bowie. They seem to sense what's going to happen. Similar to Newcastle, they have their own people who know each other and when they go to a gig they go to enjoy themselves. Newcastle, Aylesbury, maybe Glasgow, they just go determined. You get off on them and you always seem to deliver more. You get up and you think, 'Good God, look at them,' and then you've got to deliver.'

Watts also feels British crowds were best in the North. 'The further north you went, the wilder they got. They used to hang on to the bus while we screamed round corners. Glasgow and Newcastle were fantastic crowds.'

Mott were still fairly short of material at this early stage in their career so some songs were played twice in the same set. Mick Ralphs acknowledged that they were a different band after their initial London gigs at the Country Club, the Lyceum, the Speakeasy and the Roundhouse. But Watts recalls they were concerned initially with Alec Leslie and Johnny Glover and Island's bookings. 'When we came from South Wales, we were playing gigs as Silence for between £60 and £100 a night, which was good money. Then we were with Guy at the Island Agency one day and he asked them to get us some work. So they said they might be able to get the odd gig. And we remarked, "Well we had no record deal in Wales and we were getting at least three gigs a week." So Guy said, "What kind of money can you get?" Island replied, "Well, they'll have to play the Speakeasy for nothing and we can get £10 for doing a club in Tooting." And we were saying, "We got gigs for a £100 down in Wales." To which Alec Leslie replied, "But yeah, it's the law of nature isn't, you've got to start at the bottom, it's the law of nature." I wanted to stuff the law of nature up his arse.'

'I never liked the Roundhouse,' says Hunter. 'It was too hippyish, like Kensington Market, full of patchouli oil, joss sticks and filth – pretty disgusting, really. I remember doing the Speakeasy, and the whole Island record company was there. We died the most abysmal death. I'm sure everybody wanted to get rid of us. Guy held the whole thing together quite honestly. I never saw any hope for us.'

'The first "Speak" date was a disaster,' recalls Dale. 'The power blew and stayed off for over an hour. We fooled around on stage minus electricity and it was *not* appreciated. We regularly did the Speakeasy and were traded to the Pheasantry in King's Road for a string of gigs if Joe Cocker would play one. He blew them out and our contract was torn up!'

It was apparent that Mott had little knowledge of their financial situation and royalty entitlement from Island Records. 'Guy negotiated it for us,' said Ralphs at the time. 'We trust him and Island. Now we're on a retainer. The gig money goes straight into the office and they pay us £15 a week each. We're doing about two or three bookings a week now and it's good, because the promoters, who had no idea what we were like musically, have asked us back for return gigs each time.'

Hunter subsequently clarified Mott's financial arrangement with Island Records. 'I think the deal we had with them was 7 per cent; Guy got 3.5 per cent and we got 3.5 per cent amongst us. It sounds pretty stupid now, but at the time it wasn't that bad. I think Hendrix was on 3 per cent and he got less than one point because he was paying a manager and the other two guys in the band weren't. But I do think Island were a bit out of order with Mott The Hoople, because I don't believe it's right to manage, publish and record a band and handle the agency. They should be separate. They had individual sections within Island Records, but put simply, Island ran Mott totally. We were making some money on the records even though it didn't look like we were, but that money was going to pay for the tours. Conversely we were losing money on tours when everybody thought we were making a fortune, selling out everywhere.'

Reflecting some years later on their beginnings, Ian felt Mott really didn't fit in musically at the time. 'That's why we were doing it. It was hard but we loved it. We went against the grain because it was all blues and then the hippie thing happened and we didn't fit in to either of those categories. We wanted to be stars. We kept telling Chris Blackwell, "We want to be stars," and Chris didn't know what we were talking about, because he had Traffic and people like that, who were really good at what they did. But we wanted a different approach.'

Mott adopted a new approach when they went into Olympic's No. 1 Studio on 15 November 1969 to tape Mick Ralphs' heavyweight 'Thunderbuck Ram' and a group composition entitled 'Moonbus (Baby's Got a Down)', which was in the style of The Beatles' *Let It Be* Album and laced with electric tension. At a session on 29 November more new self-penned material followed – Ian's Dylanesque 'The Hunchback Fish', inspired musically by Guy Stevens' copy of Ford Theatre's *Theme For The Masses* LP. 'Hunchback' was played live and taped at Olympic, but with no finished lead vocal, partly because Guy got bored with it.

' "The Finchback Hush" was a nice old devil,' recalls Pete. 'Live, I could rest during this, before the onslaught on the unsuspecting audience. They had no idea of what was about to hit them.'

> The Hunchback Fish is weak, his money does not speak
> He has no argument, his money's all been spent
> He laughs at one who once, had dared to laugh at him
> He pleads for just one chance, but still he sighs askance
> And you're proud and you're handsome, but you're cruel
> You've got no time for the beauty of the fool
> If I had my way, I'd separate your thighs eight miles wide
> The Hunchback Fish is lost, and that's where he ought to be
> Deprived of fortune's cost, from true society
> And from the shattered wreck, self pity and decay
> Died from a broken neck, a slow deliberate way

This was Hunter's most obscure lyric to date, and Mott's second album, which was already just around the corner, was to be in similar vein, representing the first of several dramatic changes in musical direction.

5
When both of my minds have gone

'When My Mind's Gone' – Ian Hunter

At the beginning of 1970, Mott The Hoople undertook their first British radio and television session work. On 2 February they recorded 'Laugh At Me', 'At the Crossroads' and 'Thunderbuck Ram' at BBC Maida Vale Studio 4 and the session was broadcast on John Peel's *Top Gear* show on 21 February. 'In the old days, artists had to audition before they were accepted for a broadcast session,' says Dale Griffin. 'By the late sixties, the first broadcast session was the audition, played to a BBC panel for assessment. From the seventies, the producers and DJ's just made their own choices. No more "panel".' The notes for Mott's first session–audition gave 'this Dylan-influenced group' a unanimous pass.

The BBC accommodation in Maida Vale, West London was rather dull, uninspiring and not conducive to creativity, originally comprising various studios running off long corridors, decorated in unimaginative brown and cream colour schemes. Furthermore, many of the engineers were not keen on rock and the equipment was antiquated when Mott The Hoople first recorded. Tippins considered the sessions boring, and hated the whole process because Mott were asked to keep the volume down. The band would tape three or four numbers just as they did them on stage, and overdub lead vocals, lead guitar or backing vocals, the total session taking three or four hours.

'We always had to record at Maida Vale from 2.30 to 6 pm,' says Hunter. 'The engineers and BBC staff treated it like a gardening or bricklaying job. John Walters, who worked with John Peel, was the worst. He'd sit and read the *Daily Mirror* and we'd run through a few things and he'd tell us to do the shortest songs. Then, while we were recording them, he'd still be reading the newspaper. It was a fragile moment in our careers and I've never forgiven him for that attitude. I felt we were treated really badly at those early sessions.'

'Generally, the sessions at Maida Vale were painless and no great hardship,' confesses Watts, 'apart from the first one with John Walters. I felt very sorry for Ian then. We'd done the backing tracks and Ian was trying to do vocals and he couldn't hear himself when he eventually got headphones. He kept saying, "Can you turn it up, I can't hear myself?" Walters was saying, "Yes you can, there's plenty of level there, I've checked it." And Ian was going, "Look, I can't hear it." Then Walters would say, "Well try it now," and he wouldn't do anything, it would be the same. In the end, Hunter went mad, screaming, "I can't fucking hear it!" Walters was behaving like a prat, in my opinion. I got him back, though, on behalf of the band, and screwed one of his staff!

'I'd always loved John Peel's *Top Gear* radio show on a Sunday afternoon around 1967/8. It was fantastic and I never missed that show. He played Pink Floyd and Yes who were great in the early days. I've still got some recordings of those programmes, taped off the radio with a microphone, on horrible cheap cassettes.'

Only one of Mott's first BBC tracks has survived and most of their subsequent radio sessions and in concert work has been lost. Although the BBC appear to have been oblivious to the fact that they were actually developing an unprecedented library of rock recordings, it was routine procedure to wipe most tapes two months after they had been broadcast. Lamentably, their play and discard policy meant that a vast array of unique material was destroyed. In total, only five of Mott's session tracks and one concert recording have survived, largely because that material was pressed up on *Top of the Pops* transcription discs for distribution to worldwide radio stations. The lost Mott recordings would later include their stunning interpretation of Neil Young's 'Ohio' which they did not record in the studio, 'The Debt', a rare single B-side, and Dylan's 'Like a Rolling Stone', never fully committed to tape elsewhere.

In February, the same month as their radio session debut, Mott also made their first television appearance when they were featured on BBC's *Disco 2* programme playing 'At the Crossroads'. '*Disco 2* was fantastic really, because the guys who did that show apparently did it for nothing, just because they liked music,' says Watts. 'They weren't paid for that. It was a black and white television show, and although the film is lost, several stills still exist from the programme. After the T.V. session, we drove straight down to Swindon and played McIlroy's Ballroom, which Buff and I had done with The Soulents. We often used to do 'doubles' in the early days. We might play something like Maidstone College of Art, drive back to London and do the all-nighter at The Temple. If we were lucky, we had time to get back to the group flat, have a shower and get to the next gig.'

Mott The Hoople fulfilled around 200 gigs in 1970 and would go on to produce four studio albums in two years at Island. Asked if the band played too often and recorded too quickly, Watts is ambivalent, but he feels that the Island Agency didn't maximise financially on Mott's live drawing power. 'It was tough, but when you're that age, you can do it. Nowadays it's harder to get gigs. We got regular work. The way rock music's evolved, people are much more blase; a gig was quite an event in our day. Our live work tightened us up so much, unlike today's bands. I quite like groups like Oasis, but they can't ever really be any good live because they haven't got the experience to draw from. They can't really play. You could see Mott gigged constantly because we were spot on.

'If the Agency had done their job properly they could have booked us out seven nights a week for far more money in my opinion. We were going down incredibly well at all our gigs by this time, so at any venue where we were getting £50, we knew we could go back next time for at least double that. The first time we played The Lafayette in Wolverhampton, a 1500-seater, we had about twenty people there, but went down a storm. They said we were the best group they'd ever seen. We went back four months later and they were turning people away, just through word of mouth from that one gig. But Alec Leslie and Johnny Glover weren't used to that kind of thing. They built things up gradually with all their other acts, but we were suddenly realising all this potential and they never came to gigs and so didn't see that a lot more money was out there. They didn't realise. They were like the rest of Island, musos who loved serious musicians like Traffic, a nice safe group bordering on jazz, which gave them respectability. We were just kids up from the country who banged around a bit – at least that was the label's view. Defries optimised later on for us by creating demand. He would say, "Oh no, you're not getting my band for that money." Leslie and Glover would say, "Oh well, maybe we can get fifty quid!"

Having made their British TV debut, Mott also recorded a session for the *Beat Club* television show in Bremen, West Germany, performing live versions of 'You Really Got Me' and 'At the Crossroads'. 'We had to use Beat Club's Orange gear, and kicked it all over and smashed it,' recalls Pete. 'The Germans didn't know what to make of us. There was a small audience, probably producer's sons, mistresses and those kind of people. After we stopped at the end, there was a pregnant pause, then they went absolutely mad. We found it quite challenging in Europe, because they weren't used to groups like us. We went to The Zoom Club in Frankfurt; it was supposed to be a hard venue to play. At the end of our set they did nothing, there was dead silence, and they must have thought, "Where did they get this lot from?" But we didn't care because we knew we had something. We played a few days there and won them over in the end. It was very seldom that we failed to get a crowd going. I remember the crowd, cheering and clapping, watching films of Nazi soldiers. Creepy!'

In early 1970, Mott The Hoople toured heavily, having built up a strong UK following with an amazing stage act that included most of their first album, some rock 'n' roll covers and Hunter's classic, 'The Hunchback Fish'. 'We were at last breaking through live,' recalls Ian. 'I began to see there was a strain in Mott that could happen. I was getting inspiration from within the band too, from Mick Ralphs especially, who I firmly believe is one of the greatest guitarists there is.'

Having had the steadfast and ineffably eccentric Mick Hince as their lone roadie since the beginning, Mott recruited Richie Anderson as a technical crew member in March 1970. He would stay with the group right through their career and was aided a year later by John Davies, Phil John and as the band grew, supplementary hired crew. Anderson recalls that the work was tough.

'I joined Mott's road crew when I was aged just 22. We did about six nights a week, or even seven, and it seemed to be all Universities up and down the country. It was manic stuff and a lot of hard work, but it was good and there was lots of enthusiasm. We travelled all over the place, basically just being booked almost at random by Island, without thought for the mileage in between. Alec Leslie and John Glover were bookers who'd been roadies for Spencer Davis, and they thought because they'd done the miles and the distances with Spencer Davis, then we could do it. They never took no for an answer. Once they had us going from Vienna to Madrid with one day in between, and it just wasn't feasible. The difference was they'd done it before the days of border documentation in their little Transit van.

'The purse strings were always tight in those days with Island but as Mott developed, the band acquired a Ford Zodiac to travel in the UK or used planes when they were abroad. The crew used two trucks and we frequently made 400 mile journeys through the night. I remember once, in one seven day week, I got ten hours sleep. The European gigs were the worst. They were two years behind on the continent and they hated Mott The Hoople. I don't know why we went touring there at all. It was hell on earth. Customs and the officials at the border controls treated us like shit.'

To say that Mott The Hoople had dressed distinctively from an early stage in their career would be an understatement and Dale maintains they also started a trend in seventies footwear. 'It's not something to boast about, but I think Mott The Hoople really did start the craze for platform boots. We used to get boots made at Ken Todds in Kensington Market and he started making boots with a double layer of leather on the sole. So we thought, why not make double as much leather and have an even bigger sole with stacked heels? It developed from there with Ralphs and Watts getting taller and taller boots. Of course, Watts always got the tallest, and then people like Slade, the Sweet, Elton John and T. Rex picked up on this. They had them made even more tasteless with all the money they had, but it was Mott The Hoople's fault. We also started the whole thing of dressing up on stage again, although we wouldn't want to be aligned with the glam rock groups – we just thought of ourselves as 'flash'. Things were very boring when we started, with bands all wearing blue denim, staring at the floor and being very serious about music. We tried, with our rather small budgets, to put some life and colour and movement into our act, but, whilst we didn't have much money, we had a tad more taste!'

Hunter had been wounded by the Dylan accusations placed on him after the first album, so he started listening less to other artists and concentrated more on writing his own material. Soon, Mott settled down to start their second LP, tentatively titled *Sticky Fingers,* which was recorded discontinuously throughout February, March and April, at Olympic Sound Studios in Barnes, West London. Two new recording studios were still under construction during early 1970, in a converted church at Basing Street, which would become Island's new headquarters. When the Island studios opened later that year, they had a new 16-track 2-inch recording machine and Chris Blackwell employed some of the best recording engineers.

While Mott The Hoople were in Studio 1 at Olympic recording an entire album, The Rolling Stones were working in Studio 2 completing one track. When their album was released, the Stones had 'acquired' Mott's title, and *Sticky Fingers* became one of their most highly regarded records, and a successful exercise in post-sixties reinvention. Guy Stevens was credited on the inner sleeve of the LP. 'The *Sticky Fingers* title could have been nicked because Guy hung out with the Stones as well as us. Guy always had a lot of titles,' says Ian. Mott's second LP was changed to *Mad Shadows,* which Guy had originally thought of using for Steve Winwood's solo album. To complete the circle, a Rolling Stones bootleg CD of Olympic session recordings from this period was released in 1993 as *Mad Shadows.*

Once again, Guy was Mott's 'producer' for the *Mad Shadows* project but in practice he was more of a psychic puppeteer, creating vibes and atmosphere to draw contributions from the band. Intimidation, mood creation, frustration, elation and arrogance were all key techniques in the Guy Stevens 'production' handbook. He would motivate Mott by telling them they were The Stones or they were Bob Dylan, as the mood required. Stevens was Mott's mentor and almost a sixth member of the group by this stage, crediting himself with providing 'spiritual percussion and psychic piano' on the *Mad Shadows* sleeve. Assisted by engineers Andy Johns and Chris Kimsey, Guy had decided that he would capture Mott The Hoople 'live' in the studio.

Verden says, 'Some of it was recorded on 16 track and there was a lot of space and room to record different things, but I think we were genuinely a bit short of material. We were put in the studio to do something and it took a few months, but it was largely written in the studio.'

Ian Hunter does not have fond recollections of *Mad Shadows* or this period in the group's career. At the time of its release Ian said of the LP, 'It's very introspective, not contrived, but that's how we felt at the time. We were in this peculiar mood and we went into the studio with the numbers but no lyrics written – they just came as we recorded. It rather frightens us now. It was done at a time when we had a lot of personal hang-ups in the group. We are trying to express what we have been through in terms of music. It was recorded over a period of about six months, although we only had eight or nine sessions in the studio. We had a very heavy work schedule and just had to fit it in when we could. The album is a mixture of various moods we went through.'

Ian admits the album was much more difficult to record than their debut because Guy was trying to give the band speed to keep them awake. 'Instead of recording, we'd have twelve hours sitting in the studio control room talking. We were a bit unhappy with some of the record because Guy went purely by feel. It was a crazy album. Guy wasn't well when we did it and I was in the midst of dramas.'

Shortly afterwards Hunter felt that at least it was an honest record, saying it was a 'creative nightmare and a scream for help but everybody was too embarrassed to say so'. Guy Stevens had claimed that Side Two conveyed the kind of despair that drugs can lead to, particularly 'I Can Feel' and 'Threads of Iron'.

Mott The Hoople taped two *In Concerts* at the Paris Theatre in London for Radio One during 1970. The first for John Peel's 'Sunday Concert' was recorded on 23 April and broadcast on 3 May, shortly before Mott embarked on their first American tour. The tapes have not survived but the set included 'No Wheels To Ride', 'Rock and Roll Queen' and 'Walkin' with a Mountain'. Peel also introduced 'Wrong Side of the River' from *Sticky Fingers* which he intimated would be released on 5 May, although the LP was subsequently delayed until September.

Because of volume restrictions and the small seated audience, BBC concerts were never going to get out of hand like a normal Mott The Hoople gig. 'I remember the Paris Theatre and the Maida Vale Studios,' says Ralphs. 'The BBC was like going to school again, a bit like an institution. I really didn't like working there because they made you feel that you shouldn't be loud and you shouldn't be wild because it wasn't acceptable, so we always felt a bit inhibited in those places.'

'The Paris was a lovely little venue, but it was slightly restrictive,' says Watts. 'You really had to work on the audience, so we used to go in amongst them and goad them and poke at them a little bit. Worse was a live television show we did in Paris, France around that time. We played on a parquet floor and the crowd sat cross-legged in front of us. They gave Ian some stick and somebody threw something at him, so I kicked one guy in the head. The audience grabbed at my legs and I was kicking them off and punching them. That got nasty and was in all the papers the next day – 'This group are not human, they are animals, they are pigs.' We didn't mind, it was great, but the French were just a bunch of bastards, they really were.'

Mott would often 'attack' an audience if they were subdued or restrained, even to the extent of walking into the crowd with long guitar leads and pursuing the physically retreating mass. 'We would never accept a passive audience,' says Pete. 'When we first went to The Lafayette Club at Wolverhampton, there were only twenty people, and we had the most incredible gig. In the end everybody was going mental, just twenty people and us. It was wonderful. We often went into the hall and prodded them and stared at them from point blank range just to get reactions. They were fine, they didn't mind. I knocked a bloke's teeth out one night in Cleethorpes Winter Gardens. He jumped up as I swung round and I hit him with the head of the bass. He came to me afterwards with half his teeth gone, and I thought, "My God, here we go!" but he praised me, blood everywhere, saying, "Thanks Overend, it was wonderful, I'll never forget this." He was pleased!'

Mott played a nine-week American tour throughout May, June and July supporting Ten Years After, Traffic and The Kinks. The *Mott The Hoople* album was promoted heavily, as its release had been delayed until Spring 1970 by Atlantic Records in the US, but the live set already included tracks that would appear on *Mad Shadows*. The concerts typically featured 'Darkness, Darkness', 'No Wheels to Ride', 'Rock and Roll Queen', 'At the Crossroads', 'Keep A-Knockin' ', 'Thunderbuck Ram', 'Laugh at Me', 'You Really Got Me', 'Half Moon Bay 'and 'Keep A-Knockin' ', played for a second time in each show. Watts felt proud appearing at legendary venues like the Fillmore East and Fillmore West, where the great West Coast bands that he loved had played before. Mott The Hoople also performed at the Atlanta Pop Festival in Macon, Georgia to 400,000 people, Spirit's singer Jay Ferguson frantically taking photographs of Mott from all over the stage, much to the group's amazement.

Richie Anderson's experience following the Georgia festival was unpleasant to say the least. 'I had to get our equipment back to Atlanta Airport, and the arrangement to take it there was some guy simply turning up with a truck and we stuffed it in the back. So we were driving along in the middle of the night, just me and this bloke and the equipment and he said, "Can you open the glove box?" which I did. Then he leant over and pulled out a revolver and pointed it at me and said, "Right, here we are, you're in the middle of Georgia, miles from anywhere, I've got a gun, if I say get out, I've got all your equipment, what are you going to do about it?" I'd worked out by this time that he was a bit of an idiot, and a typical American male groupie-type, who seemed to want a job as a roadie. So I said, "Well, if you do that, then I won't give you a job on the next tour," so he put the gun away and we drove on to Atlanta! We were always ready for violence of one sort or another, especially at concerts, and you sometimes had to resort to it yourself. We hit and kicked people if they deserved it, by behaving like an idiot, or if they were stealing something. Someone got on the stage once and we just picked him up and threw him six feet down some stairs on to his head. He shouldn't have been there. Cowboy boots were also great weapons.'

Guy Stevens had decided he would accompany Mott on their first U.S. tour, to a mixed response from the band and Hunter. As manager, he decided to join the group on a radio talk show with The Kinks. The results were devastating!

'It was a strange kind of affair because it was a joint interview,' explains Watts. 'The four members of the Kinks were sat with the five of us, and Guy, at this radio station in New York. The Kinks by this time were a bit of a cult band over there, but they weren't doing very much in England anymore and we were nervous and didn't say much. The Kinks seemed very close knit and insular and Guy started getting on his high horse and began to goad them. It transpired he didn't have much respect for them which surprised us. When one of them said they liked football more than playing in a group, Guy went berserk and said, "Well why don't you fucking leave the group and play fucking football then. You don't deserve to be in a group." And The Kinks just sat there and took it all. To their credit they didn't get up and thump him. We felt very embarrassed with the whole thing. Guy went mental at them.'

Hunter believes it was Stevens' total commitment to what he was doing that ignited these passions, and the fact that Guy insisted others should feel the same way.

Mick Ralphs had favourable memories of Mott's first US sortie. 'America judged the band on its own merits. They cared about us and went out of their way to find out about who we were. The album was constantly played on the FM stations and while people in England always said we were trying to sound like Bob Dylan, in America they took the comparison for what it was. They tried to understand what we were playing.'

'The only thing that really struck me around that time when we went to America, was I couldn't believe that we actually would be heard,' says Hunter. 'I saw a guy leaning up against a lamp post on his bike, with a little radio strapped to his crossbar, and I could hear "Half Moon Bay" coming from it which just blew me away. It was amazing. I also remember some guy wrote to Rolling Stone's letters page and said that, on his new album, Bob Dylan was trying to sound like Mott The Hoople, which was total bullshit, but we thought, "What! Us little chaps from England!"'

In the UK some commentators had swiftly likened Hunter's vocal inflections and visual image of corkscrew hair and sunglasses to 1966 vintage Dylan, but in the US the reaction was different, much to Ian's relief. 'I wasn't criticised for Dylan. In England I was passed off as a copy, but in the States people accepted me. On the first tour we played pretty safe, doing things from the first album and being very cautious in approach. Apart from the fact that we were playing to such large audiences when we appeared with bands like Ten Years After and Traffic, the thing was that the audiences were so receptive. They were really open minded musically and we did well there.'

On their first tour of the States, Mott also supported Mountain, a heavy rock band featuring the colossal Leslie West on guitar, Corky Laing on drums and bass player Felix Pappalardi, who had previously produced Cream. West played with passion, precision, power and delicacy and Mountain was to become revered by both fans and rival bands. On many of their concerts, musicians would crowd the wings of the stage to watch the group in admiration, as they careered through classic tracks such as 'Nantucket Sleighride', 'Mississippi Queen' and 'Long Red'.

'I always remember Guy Stevens right at the beginning of Mott coming back and enthusing madly about this huge person who was playing guitar around the New York clubs and concert venues,' says Ian. 'He said this bloke was about 25 stone. Guy was always prone to exaggeration. We eventually saw Mountain and Leslie West when we went over on our first tour. Ralphs was in tears because Mick was going somewhere with his guitar playing and he saw Leslie West was already at that journey's end, he saw the actual result.'

'It did poor Mick in when he saw Leslie West play with that sound that he got from his Les Paul Junior,' remarks Verden. 'It looked like a toy he was such a big bloke. I remember Mick saying, "That's it. It's too late. I've had it. He's got the sound I want." I said, "You'll just have to get that sort of sound, only better."'

The Mott The Hoople – Mountain connection was to continue over subsequent years; in 1971 Mott covered 'Long Red', Watts and Ralphs recorded with West and Laing, and Leslie approached them as a possible guitarist to augment their line up. Hunter would also work in the studio with Felix and Corky in 1978 and appear on a Mountain LP in 1985 with Miller Anderson. Tragically, Pappalardi, who was reputed to be medically deaf from playing on stage with Mountain, was gunned down by his wife in 1983.

For the American tour there was no means of transporting Verden's weighty Hammond across the Atlantic or around the States, so equipment was hired in, usually a Hammond B3. At this time, Mott also started using much heavier amplification and Allen plugged the organ direct into an Acoustic amp as well as using a Leslie tone cabinet. Watts recalls onstage antics whereby the equipment was used to 'terrorise' audiences. 'The Acoustic amp had a horn on it which you could lift off the top and Phally and I used to have a laugh on stage. During one of the quieter passages, and at an agreed point, I would rip this horn off the amp and push it straight into someone's face in the front row, at which point Phally would blast on the keys. We used to single people out and get them. They must have been horrified in the crowd.

'I'd switched to a 1956 Fender Precision bass by this time and one night on the first American tour I was playing it on stage and suddenly it just stopped. I never had that before or since. The only other bass I had at the time was a black Silvertone which had no poke to it at all. Back in London, I found a Gibson Thunderbird which were very hard to get in those days. I'd played Eric Haydock's when The Hollies came to Hereford years before and I loved the way they looked. So I had to have this orange Thunderbird, £250, a lot of money in those days. I didn't get on with it at first and it was top heavy, so I went back to the Precision but it didn't seem any good after the Gibson. I had about six Thunderbirds altogether, mainly from pawn shops. The single pick ups had more power than the twin pick ups.

'I broke the neck on every single Thunderbird I owned, because I used to throw the bass up into the air on stage. If it was a low ceiling, the guitar smashed through it, there was plaster and dust everywhere and I used to leave the bass swinging from the hole in the ceiling. If it was a high ceiling, I'd throw it as high as I could and catch it with one hand, while I looked at somebody in the audience. One night though, at Newcastle, I had a mind block and it crashed to the floor and smashed to bits. I broke two others at the same gig that night and ended up humming the bass parts into the mike for the encore. Terrible, really. Stan used to take them to a guy called Sam Lee in the West End and they were £24 each to repair. The group always used to moan because they had to pay. I've smashed a few ceilings in my time. I designed an elasticated guitar strap, so that I could throw basses down to the floor and when they bounced back up I could catch them and it would look great. The only trouble was, it didn't quite work out in practice, because they used to bounce back up and hit me in the face. I only tried that twice.'

One lesser known reaction to Mott on their US tour was the American's assumption that they were heavily drug-orientated. 'Mott The Hoople was not a drugs group, we never got into that,' says Dale. 'Although, when we started working in America people were saying, "Jesus Christ man, what were you on to do that gig or make that record?" And we said, "Cider? Brown Ale? Mateus Rose?" "But what drugs?" they would question. And people would get nasty when we said, "None".'

'We never used to get stoned in the early days,' says Hunter. 'When we first went to America none of us would even have a joint. I remember at the Fillmore West people were saying "What do you want?" The name of the band was kind of strange and they thought we were strange. I remember this black girl sitting there and she went through all these abbreviations for illicit substances, trying to find out what we were on. I kept saying, "No. No. No," and her eyes were getting wider and wider. She thought we had this great stuff that nobody had heard of and we were just sitting there terrified.'

Hunter confesses that he would take the occasional prescribed mandrax tablet and a glass or two of wine to settle his nerves, or ease insomniac tendencies, but is scathing of current young bands who are now cavalier about drugs in general. 'You need a little bit of help now and again, whether it's a bottle of wine or a joint, but you can't recommend it in any way because some people have addictive personalities and some haven't. Some people can handle it and some can't. That's why most artists, even if they do, say they don't. The problem is that idiots take ten mandrax and two bottles of wine and of course there's adverse publicity. There are some great things in the world but always some bastard who comes along and ruins it for everyone. Like Oasis's "cocaine-on-our-cornflakes for breakfast" claim. That's bullshit. They treat drugs as though they're oranges or something. It makes for good newspaper copy, but I wouldn't feel good making those kind of headlines.'

Island Records didn't release *Mad Shadows* until 25 September 1970, when Mott had returned from their American tour and were able to promote the album in the UK. It entered the British charts on 17 October and stayed for two weeks reaching number 46 while the upper regions of the top thirty were led by

Black Sabbath's *Paranoid* and Pink Floyd's *Atom Heart Mother*. *Mad Shadows* was considered an excellent package by the press and received favourable reviews. 'They're not easy listening but on stage they're devastating. Ask Free: they found it hard to follow this band when they were on tour,' remarked one journalist. Another commented on the tremendous power behind their songs and even said, 'Musically, *Mad Shadows* is such a phenomenally tight, beautiful work that you can go mad happily and safely. Don't take it all *that* seriously, it's only music – but don't *dare* underestimate it.'

The album opened with Mick Ralphs' stunning 'Thunderbuck Ram', which Watts recalls was originally a song with no title. 'We found the name scrawled on a toilet wall in the Pied Bull. I think it was the name of a group. We first played the number at the Country Club in Hampstead, North London. Guy had never heard it before and he went pots over "Thunderbuck Ram". He thought it was great.'

The second track, 'No Wheels to Ride', (Mott's first 16-track recording, made at Island's studio where Led Zeppelin taped 'Black Dog'), was written by Ian and had started life entitled 'Pale Ale' and then 'The Coalminer's Lament'. Hunter can only remember having to sing all the songs in a row, one after the other, so unsurprisingly he is scathing of his vocals on the record.

> No wheels to ride, no wheels to travel
> No tracks to take on down
> The road I walk, is getting heavy
> But I must still go on
> And in the night, I hear the calling
> As the train goes by
> But all I hear is my footsteps falling
> Upon the tears I cry

Tracks three and four were written by Hunter, the jaunty and peculiar 'You Are One of Us', followed by 'Walkin' with a Mountain', penned in response to Ralphs' 'Rock and Roll Queen'. Although Ian acknowledged he had trouble writing faster rock material, he composed 'Walkin' with a Mountain' quickly, while the band took a 'tea break' during one session. Buffin wondered if an early 1960s Parlophone LP by Spike Milligan, *Milligan Preserved*, featuring a track called 'I'm Walking Out With a Mountain', had inspired Hunter! Like 'Rock and Roll Queen', 'Walking with a Mountain' became a live Mott staple and has remained a concert favourite for Hunter throughout his solo career. Ian recalls the coda, containing 'Jumping Jack Flash', was spontaneous, because Mick Jagger came in to see the band during the session.

'That was written in the studio in about ten minutes. It was done out of panic when we needed a rock song. That particular night, none of the Stones were in, so Jagger came in with us. That's why it goes in to the Stones thing at the end, because he was dancing in the control room. At one point Buffin breaks a stick and misses a beat. We said, "We'll have to re-do that Guy, he's missed a beat." But Guy said, "No, no, it's fucking amazing as it is!" And of course every time you listen to it that mistake just gets bigger and in the end you can't bear to hear it anymore.'

Watts also recorded this track with only two bass strings. 'I'd broken them the previous night and there was nowhere to get new bass strings so I just carried on with two. I was used to that because once in Italy, I broke a string and there was nowhere nearby to get a replacement, so I played for ages with three. If it was a string like the bottom E you could get away without it. The best string to break would be the top G. Often in Mott I'd play runs on the A string rather than change and go up because I liked the sound of staying on one string, it sounded more full. I think "Walking with a Mountain" was played on an A string, the whole lot!'

Side Two of the LP contained potent and powerful material. The gospel tinged 'I Can Feel', written by Ian, was dramatic and majestic, with fine bass and tasteful Ralphs' lead guitar. Buffin's squeaking bass pedal is accidently audible but creates a chilling effect. 'There's a squeak on the foot pedal of the drums through the whole damn album and we didn't even know at the time,' admits Hunter. 'We found out later. If you notice it, you can never listen to that album again without hearing it.

' "I Can Feel" could be a great song,' opines Ian. 'It's a basic thing, like a declaration, but I was upset with the way I sang it. I wasn't good enough to do it justice vocally, but if somebody had got hold of it that had the right voice, it could easily have done it for someone. I was a powerful lyricist then. I don't know what I was doing, but there were some good lyrics.'

> The truth is here in me
> It does not matter what you see
> For my face is living on borrowed time
> But still I feel
>
> So bury me alone
> You can take your flowers home
> For there ain't no peace in this world that I know
> But I can feel

Ralphs' manic riffing on 'Threads of Iron', originally titled 'Sticky Fingers', with lead vocals shared by Mick and Ian, is possibly the closest Mott ever came to 'heavy metal', Ian's screams at the end leading into the album's closing track, 'When My Mind's Gone'. This was supposed to be a spontaneous composition and stream of consciousness song, credited to Hunter, and as legend has it, recorded under the influence of Guy Stevens while Ian was 'hypnotised'.

> So I'll take my secrets – I'll take them with me to my grave
> And if I'm taking yours – then I will try to make them safe
> There ain't nothing going right
> There ain't even nothing going wrong – that's right

And day is day – and night ain't night
And night is day – and day is night
And spring is summer – and autumn's winter
When my mind's gone – when my mind's gone
When my mind's gone – everything has gone

'It was really weird because there was no real lyric. I just looked at Guy and sang,' said Hunter. 'He was very, very forceful. I had two chords in my head and just made it up as we went along. That's the whole atmosphere of Mott The Hoople. All the songs relate to enormous changes we were going through at the time. A lot of it was scary because I was always used to scoring songs before we ever recorded them, but this time it was different. When I'd finished there was silence for a couple of minutes and then Guy pushed the switch down and started screaming at the top of his voice. You wanted to work for him, to be great for him, because he was so excited when you were, and if you weren't he'd look at you with such a hurt expression.'

'I think Guy probably got the studio lights down and he did have a mesmerising effect on all of us, but it wasn't hypnosis,' says Watts. 'Ian just did the track straight off. It was quite amazing really.'

On the sessions at Olympic Studios, Mott also recorded backtracks for 'The Wreck of the *Liberty Belle*', 'In the Presence of Your Mind', 'Enough is Enough', Ralphs' country-flavoured 'It Would Be a Pleasure' and 'The Ballad of Billy Joe'. A proposed cover version of The Small Faces' 'Tin Soldier' was never committed to tape or rehearsed and 'Wrong Side of the River' was recorded but shelved, as Guy felt it did not fit in with the overall mood of *Mad Shadows*. Two other studio out-takes from the sessions, 'Going Home' and 'Keep A-Knockin' ', were later issued on a 1980 compilation *Two Miles from Heaven*. 'Can You Sing a Song Like I Sing?', was a ten-minute Stevens-inspired epic, and an attempt at doing 'When My Mind's Gone' with the whole band. 'It was incredibly boring but Guy wanted to release it as a single!' admits Dale. 'At Olympic, Ian used to shake with panic at the thought of the studio costs – £14 per hour.'

Ian was soon to declare that he was embarrassed with *Mad Shadows*. 'It was badly produced and badly mixed and I couldn't listen to it. I haven't even got it at home. It was a diary of bad periods we were going through at the time and was recorded live in the studio.'

Many years later he is still disparaging towards it. 'I hate that album. We were mental when we did it. I think I single handedly ruined the *Mad Shadows* record. I mean you can hear the poor guys trying to play and I'm all over it. The singing is real bad. *Mad Shadows* was really me egoing out. It's just stupid to me. I was out of control at the time. My personal life was chaotic and so was Guy's. I can't talk about it really but a lot was going on, incestuous relationships, things like that. Guy was in love with me by this album and the band was resenting it. There's some good stuff on there though, if somebody got a hold of "I Can Feel" and made it a three-minute song, or "No Wheels to Ride", but they're all silly lengths. They could have been a lot shorter.'

Ralphs believes Hunter was finding it hard to deal with Mott's live success. 'I was just along for the ride, but Ian got pretty serious about the whole thing. We were very much into being us I think on *Mad Shadows*. We'd done the first album and Guy had got the Escher cover and it was all a bit avant garde, avant garde a clue! So on the next album, Guy was very much into mood and delving into the mind. I think he was going through a mental state at the time and was a little unhappy, and he encouraged Ian to get a bit dark.'

Guy expressed his view of *Mad Shadows* in a Mott concert programme one year later. 'Everybody involved in the making of it, including the engineer and the producer, and most probably even the studio walls, went to the brink of madness, but somehow none fell into the pit they all saw none too clearly beneath them. The songs on this record tell a story which will be clear to any who have been tempted by the forces of perversity and self destruction, knowing or unknowing. Six months after the release of *Mad Shadows*, John Lennon came out with 'his' comparatively mild album which covered much of the same territory Mott had already explored, and the phrase 'identity-crisis rock' was coined. Mott The Hoople was there first.'

Dale Griffin recalls that most of the problems around the time of *Mad Shadows* related to Stevens. 'There was never a big drug thing in the band, ever. It has to relate to Guy, who became erratic. Guy even wanted Ian out of the band again at this time. He just said, "That's it. Ian's out." We said, "Oh no he isn't." He said, "He is, he is. He's finished." The rest of us had to say, "If he goes, we go." Guy backed down. He was like a kid with building blocks. He would build this structure and say, "Look at that, isn't it great," – then smash! The next thing he wanted to do was knock it over. I think there was a bit of a power struggle because Ian wouldn't submit to Guy. I would. Guy could scare the shit out of me!'

Stevens attempted to dismiss various members of Mott at different times according to Watts, but it happened with Hunter on more than one occasion. 'Guy wanted Ian out of the group around the time of *Mad Shadows* and I believe Graham Bell, Heavy Jelly's vocalist, was a contender as his replacement. I think at that time he was considering other people to join us because Guy suddenly took a dislike to Ian. He thought Hunter had got too dangerous and was maybe rivalling him in terms of being the main creative force. When Ian started writing more and more good songs, Guy felt his own hold might be slipping a bit. Hunter may also have said a few things to Guy that insulted him. So Guy got hold of me and Ralpher one day and said, "I think we should get rid of Ian. He's got to go, he's trying to take over the group." Which he wasn't because he was only doing what he'd been asked to do by Guy, which was write Dylan and Stones type songs. So we said, "No", which surprised Guy because we'd never shown that much affection towards Ian really.

'I feel very sorry for Hunter, in retrospect, because it must have been difficult for him in the group. He probably believed the four of us were a lot closer than we actually were, and maybe thought he was the outsider, but it wasn't like that really. He did take a lot of responsibility though. I didn't give a shit, I just wanted to be out buying clothes and eyeing up girls, while poor old Ian was always trying to write songs. It must have been quite hard for him, and then there was this business of Guy wanting him out. Guy had tried to oust Ian after only a month or two as well, after we'd done "Half Moon Bay", when he probably realised there really was something there!'

'Guy wanted to fire me but Pete and Mick wouldn't have it,' admits Hunter. 'At first we didn't go down well at all live. Apparently Guy would rave saying, "Ian sits at the piano, he's over there, we need a focal point, we need a front man, we need a Jagger, we've made a mistake with Ian." But Pete and Mick had decided by this time that something was going on and they didn't want to change the band.'

Pete recalls that drugs were a problem in Guy's life by this time. 'One day during *Mad Shadows,* when he was going through a bad drug period, he came in and he had a great big bump and cut on his forehead, and just looked like he was on another planet. Now Guy always used to have hundreds of clothes the same. If he saw a pair of trousers he liked, he'd buy twenty identical pairs, and he always used to wear tight red trousers and striped jackets, like boating jackets. This particular night when he arrived, he had this shirt on that he'd got from Stirling Cooper, and again, apparently, he'd ordered twenty of them. It was an ordinary red shirt with tight sleeves and a tight body, but the collar, instead of being straight, had one point at the front and one at the back, and the neck was on the side of the shirt! It just looked absolutely bloody ridiculous and he was completely gone. So I asked, "Are you sure you're alright Guy? Are you okay?" And he just said, "Who are you?" and turned round and walked off. Quite extraordinary. I don't know exactly what had happened to him, whether he'd fallen over and got concussion, or it was drugs, or a mixture of both. Needless to say we didn't get much recording done that night!

'Some of the sessions during *Mad Shadows* were totally unproductive. We didn't record a thing and just had big meals, and we started to wonder who was paying for all this. Of course it was us, but we didn't know at the time. It got to the point where we were going in and not recording anything. That's partly why we got rid of Guy for a while because we thought we couldn't afford all that. Too many unproductive sessions and no recordings and it was costing us all this money.'

Contrary to Hunter's reservations, Verden Allen likes the 'croaky' sound of Ian's voice on the album. 'I like the vocals on "When My Mind's Gone" and 'I Can Feel". I remember Guy looking up and he wasn't very sure at the time. And I said, "I like that, that's great, that is it!" ' However, Verden was considerably less happy with 'Thunderbuck Ram', as Guy had mixed down the organ track when it appeared on the finished disc, although the original version was included shortly afterwards on Island's *Bumpers* sampler LP. The band all knew that the organ had been forgotten on the *Mad Shadows* mix, and that Guy didn't give a damn, but it was too late to argue. Nevertheless, Verden exploded during a listening session at Guy's Swiss Cottage flat in North London, and destroyed a copy of the record in front of Stevens and the group.

'I was annoyed. It had a rasping organ sound originally and the guitar was a backing to the organ in a way, but it wasn't on the final LP. When Guy mixed *Mad Shadows* he was on some sort of speed. I was very upset. I actually failed to

smash the album but I bent it back and forth. Guy was sitting with his mouth
wide open in disbelief. I couldn't tell him in words. I tried to explain, but nobody
would listen. So I said, "To tell you the truth this is what I think of the mix on
that track," and I bent it over on itself.'

The original artwork for *Sticky Fingers* and *Mad Shadows* comprised various
Guy Stevens 'possibilities' all of which were aborted, including a drawing of
Frankenstein on one cover, eventually used by Verden Allen for a solo album release in 1994, a tartan design shortbread tin and two alternatives featuring photographs of Mott. Guy had to abort an amazing failed photo shoot with Pete
Sanders for one of the *Mad Shadows* covers, the group dressed in druid's cloaks
with silver foil obscuring their heads. Verden recalls the photo session vividly.

'That was bloody hell. A total disaster. Can you imagine being bunged in all
that stuff, with silver foil over your face. The idea was for the foil to explode into
light, so that it gave off a certain effect, but it didn't. I remember there was another sleeve where Guy had these massive scissors made out of cardboard. The
idea was that the scissors chased us, and caught us, and were wrapped around the
complete band chopping us in half. Anyway, it didn't work out and Guy was driving around London for a month with huge scissors sticking out of his car.
Somebody made money though, because we used to do endless photo sessions in
Mott The Hoople and yet they kept using the same early ones, taken on top of
Basing Street.'

Dale adds, 'For the scissors sleeve, we were in a room that had been purpose
built as a visual deceit and we were trapped in it. It didn't work for Guy and so
it wasn't used. I remember being in the little house that was built, and the scissors coming towards us, and it being explained to us how this was all going to
work. I don't know what the idea was. I don't think it was any idea other than
being put in this strange situation where the house was closing in on us, or appeared to be closing in on us, and these big scissors were coming at us. What that
had got to do with anything I don't know. I don't think there was any kind of
method in that madness, it was a just a crazy idea that Guy ultimately discarded.
We didn't see everything nor were we privy to everything that happened.'

During their Island years, Mott worked with various photographic friends of
Guy including Peter Sanders, Richard Stirling, Richard Polak and the imaginative Mike Sida, who had created the *Nice Enough to Eat* sampler sleeve. Sanders
worked a great deal with Mott The Hoople taking a number of studio and live
photographs. 'Mott were wonderful in concert. They were one of the more interesting bands at a time when there was so much music, we couldn't really absorb it all.'

The final *Mad Shadows* sleeve appeared like a monochrome demon's head
when it was in fact, a sideways double image of a smoking fire grate! Taken by
German photographer Gabi Nasemann, the overall cover design by Peter Sanders
and Ginny Smith received an award at the Art Director's Club of New York 50th
Annual Exhibition. *Mad Shadows* was Mott The Hoople's black album, a bleak
and chilling document enhanced by the cover and an extract from Charles
Baudelaire's *Fleurs du Mal* ('Flowers of Evil') on the back of the sleeve:

Descend the way that leads to hell infernal
Plunge in a deep gulf where crime's inevitable
Flagellated by a wind driven from skies eternal
Where all your torments, and for all the ages
Mad Shadows never at the end of your desires
Shall never satisfy your furious rages
And your chastisement be born of loveless fires

Mott continued to tour extensively in 1970 and although Ian had private reservations, at the time, he was quoted as saying that the new album was quite different from the first, comprising original songs which were more representative of what Mott played on gigs. By this stage, the volume of their playing and Hunter's control of a live audience was receiving feverish press comment. Ian had now developed a confident on-stage persona and vocal style which ripped and tore at lyrics with ragged exaggerations and pronunciations. Writing of a triumphant sold out concert at London's Lyceum one journalist said, 'What was amazing was that Ian Hunter was able to control the mass hysteria which prevailed with just a mere gesture of the hand, or a well chosen command – it would even have done Mick Jagger proud!'

'Mott was always wild and magic in concert,' says Ralphs. 'We were a pre-punk punk band I think, who just went on and went berserk. We had the ability to bring out the wildness in people that was probably within all of us. We used to go and see bands play and people would sit and listen, but we always thought something was missing. We always went for contact with the audience from the minute we went on. Once you've won people over you've got them for life, but we did it in a natural way. Mott was rough round the edges and we weren't the same every night. We were not particularly musical, but pleasantly acceptable and quite vulnerable. Crucially, Mott The Hoople was exciting, and that's more important I think.'

Internationally renowned promoter Mel Bush first saw Mott the Hoople at McIroy's in Swindon and then at venues in Devizes and Yeovil. 'Mott was like an army on stage. They generated a wall of sound and were incredibly impressive. I started to book them on individual shows and then eventually on a headlining tour in 1973.'

Around this time, independent publicist Tony Brainsby, was also introduced to Mott, having already worked with Cat Stevens and Free from the Island label. Brainsby went on to represent Thin Lizzy, The Strawbs, Steve Harley and Paul McCartney. 'I received a call from Guy asking me to go over and see Mott The Hoople, who I seem to remember were a raggedy rock band that could deliver live but were never able to capture it on record. That was their big problem. Whether it was the producer or the material or what I don't know, but they never caught their live show on record. So I went along for a meeting with Guy, and Mott, and heard this sob story. But I could see something in Ian Hunter. He was a journalist's delight because you could wind him up and away he'd go. He was good copy, like Steve Harley and Phil Lynott, although he was ahead of them. The media always had time for Ian. So I wanted to become publicist for the band

and I soon learned that they really worked exceptionally hard. They were always on tour, virtually non-stop.'

Hunter seemed keen to release a new single following *Mad Shadows,* to broaden their appeal and transport them to a wider audience, like stablemates Free had recently done with their hit, 'All Right Now', but no Mott single was forthcoming. Instead, they toured Europe with Grand Funk Railroad, a combination that contributed to the misguided prejudice that Mott The Hoople were a heavy rock group, and the inter-band rivalry that the press tried to generate, much to Mott's ambivalence. 'Grand Funk never bothered us much,' says Watts. 'I never really looked at them and didn't know much about them. They didn't do anything for me at all because I didn't know what they were supposed to be, whether they were a metal band or what the hell they were.'

The concerts seemed endless and Mott maintained a live work rate which today's bands would regard as unthinkable. 'We toured too much,' says Ian. 'Island Records tried to keep us from going into debt but we were getting overexposed. After *Mad Shadows* the band was exhausted.'

Mott was becoming a huge draw, selling out most venues that they played and were a dynamic and energetic band on stage. They decided that they would record and release a live LP next, in an attempt to capture their unique sound, so Mott played two shows in one evening with Free at Croydon's Fairfield Halls on 13 September 1970, both of which were taped with Guy as producer and Andy Johns as engineer. However, the audience beseiged the stage and according to Guy and the band, cables were wrecked and very little of the material could actually be salvaged. They recorded using a portable eight track machine borrowed from The Who, which meant if one or two lines were inadvertently pulled or damaged by advancing and 'participating' fans, instruments went down and the track was effectively rendered unusable.

Verden does recall the invading audience at Croydon. 'I remember Jim Capaldi getting smashed over the head with a maracca. He came on with a tambourine and suddenly someone jumped on the stage, picked up the maracca and bang! There were peas rolling all over the floor.'

Mott started to break new ground, experimenting with dynamic clothing that could be seen on stage, a tactic soon employed by Marc Bolan, Elton John and Slade who attended their Midlands gigs. Ralphs recalls that Mott's antics and head shaking were copied too. 'Croydon was always a good gig for us, although you can't imagine Croydon being wild. Status Quo came to see us there and that's where they learned to shake their heads up and down and change their image from a pop group to an incredibly successful rock band. I think they're a great group but they nicked the head-shaking business from us and Elton John copied the outrageous boots and togs pioneered by Wattsy.'

Slade were regular attendees at Mott's concerts according to Pete. 'Jimmy Lea, Slade's bass player, told me they used to have great arguments about where our huge sound was coming from. He said they came to see us at Wolverhampton Civic and they had a fight afterwards about it. One would say that when the guitar player stopped playing the sound was still there, and another thought when the organist stopped playing the sound was still there. Apparently they nearly came to blows over it but I could have told them – it was bass and drums – but then I would say that wouldn't I!'

Guy ditched the proposed *Mott The Hoople Live* LP but 'Keep A-Knockin' ' was taken from the tapes and included on their third studio album, which was originally scheduled to contain a live take of 'Thunderbuck Ram'. Over twenty years later, reappraisal of the Croydon tapes reveals the scrapping of the recordings to be a considerable misjudgement on Guy Stevens part, as the tracks survive unscathed, intact and almost wholly useable in Island's archives. The set for both shows comprised 'Ohio', 'No Wheels to Ride' including a coda of 'Hey Jude', 'Rock and Roll Queen', 'When My Mind's Gone', 'Thunderbuck Ram', 'Keep A-Knockin' ' and 'You Really Got Me'.

The live piano sound on some of Mott's early material *was* restricted by the technology of the time and Watts had sympathy for Ian when he played live. 'There wasn't such a thing as amplified grand pianos when Hunter joined us. The nearest thing we could get was a terrible RMI electric piano which wasn't touch sensitive, so if you made a mistake in a quiet passage you couldn't obscure it, it just blurted out a horribly discordant note. It was a difficult instrument for him to play and it sounded average. Later on, grand pianos were specified on a rider in our contracts and things improved.'

Mott now performed an excellent live version of Crosby Stills Nash & Young's 'Ohio'. Once descibed by Neil Young as CSNY's greatest cut and probably the biggest lesson learned at an American seat of learning, it was the first political song that Young had ever written. In the summer of 1970, American National Guardsmen opened fire on demonstrators at Kent State University in Ohio and killed four students. Composed in an afternoon, alledgedly recorded in fifteen minutes and released as a single within eight days of the shootings, this highly topical and controversial song pointed an accusing finger directly at President Nixon and was banned from nationwide US radio.

'I liked Neil Young and so I introduced "Ohio" to the band,' recalls Ralphs. 'I remember at the time of the Kent State University incident, he was so moved that he went into the studio the next day and did this song spontaneously and so poignantly. I thought it was great that he just reeled off this song about a news story. I ended up singing it for Mott because I had a high voice then!'

As *Mad Shadows* had hit the UK charts, Mott postponed their planned October US tour until the new year to consolidate on their success. Hunter explained, 'We seem to have got five times bigger in England just in the last few weeks and we're especially grateful to Free for that, because they brought in so many people on the tour that we did with them that it gave us the chance to get across to so many people.'

Their plans to help the record cruise further up the chart were thwarted however when Buffin was taken seriously ill with glandular fever and several live dates were cancelled. Dale was still dragged off for one provincial concert. 'The bastards took me to Bristol for a gig despite the pain I was suffering, then took me all the way back to London rather than on to Hereford which was closer!

Guy Stevens meanwhile, decided to line up a Mott The Hoople concert for the inmates at Pentonville Prison in North London. 'No sooner was the gig announced than it was cancelled. Who knows why,' remarks Griffin.

In October, Mott made their second appearance on BBC's *Disco 2* television programme playing 'Walking with a Mountain' and 'Rock and Roll Queen', and taped their second BBC *In Concert* at the Paris Theatre. 'Ohio' and 'The Debt' were included in the set but once again the tapes of this recording were 'wiped'. Well organised with writing material for their third LP, Mott had already gone into the studio to tape some new tracks and a possible single. However there was to be a significant change in their future recording plans and their relationship with Guy Stevens before they even started the next album.

Following the episode with Verden concerning the 'Thunderbuck Ram' mixes, Guy's next move was to try and oust Allen from the group. 'After I'd buckled that album, Guy wanted to get me out of the band and there were apparently discussions about this. Guy disappeared for about three days and then I had to go and see him and apologize. I went to Island Records because I had to meet the boys there and they said, "Guy wants to see you upstairs." So I went and sat in this room and explained to him why I'd done it, and my conscience was clear because to me he'd done wrong. Guy's mouth was wide open. I said, "Well, really I think you were wrong actually, but I couldn't get a word in to explain, nobody would listen to me. That was the only way I could express the way I felt about things and you should sympathize with my feelings as a musician. I was frustrated."

'Anyway the boys were outside listening to all this, but I didn't know that, and they came in and said, "We've been having a good talk about this Guy, and we've decided Phally's got to stay in the band and we're going to have to find another producer!" '

6
Maybe I'm just a loser

'Home Is Where I Want to Be' – Mick Ralphs

Mad Shadows had been dominated to a large extent by Hunter, so Ralphs was eager to see a change in Mott's direction. Ian recalls, 'After the debacle of *Mad Shadows*, it was Ralphs, the voice of reason, who suggested we do some nice songs. Mick said, "Look, the hell with this, we're going in too deep, so let's do a nice quiet album. Let's produce the next one ourselves." Mick liked country music a lot, so as much as *Mad Shadows* was towards me, *Wildlife*, the next album, was Mick's. Neither of us was right. We were just searching around, I suppose. We didn't have much idea how you did it.'

Guy had faded from view because of personal problems although Dale recalls he was 'around' initially for the odd session. 'We were all bitterly disappointed with *Mad Shadows*. It was followed by an unbelievably heavy tour schedule which left me exhausted and ill. I was sent home with glandular fever, so bad that I couldn't touch things or sit upright. Island was still insisting that I go out on gigs. It took a couple of months for me to recover and the *Wildlife* album was written then. After *Mad Shadows* we wanted to be rid of Guy. There was no conscious veto of Ian's songs, he'd just not written much, and no rock stuff. Also, especially with Mick, there was a muso-snob thing that made him want us to be proper, serious musicians.'

Due to lack of material from the band, a *Mad Shadows* reject ('Wrong Side of the River'), a rough live track ('Keep A-Knockin' ') and a Melanie cover ('Lay Down') taped in September 1970 were all dragged in, all of them produced by Stevens. 'Guy had no connection with the actual recording of *Wildlife*,' says Dale. ' "Lay Down" was not even originated during the sessions.'

Wildlife was recorded on 16-track over a period of two months from November to December 1970 at Island Studios 1 and 2 in Basing Street, produced by Mott and engineered by Brian Humphries who was assisted by Richard Digby Smith and Howard Kilgour. The album is clearly lightweight compared to its predecessor and untypically the only Mott LP where Ralphs' songs are predominant. Mick replaced Ian in the spotlight, writing and singing lead on half the tracks, but Hunter still contributed an exceptional trilogy of songs. One of these tracks, 'Waterlow', he continues to rate amongst his best work.

In January 1971, Mott played their first headlining tour, a short series of dates at major halls, supported by the very fine Wishbone Ash, who were soon to be voted Britain's most promising new act with their highly acclaimed *Argus* LP. Watts recalls that Mott enjoyed their time with the band. 'We got on very well with Wishbone Ash, nice blokes and a really good group. I always liked their guitar styles and Martin Turner was a good bass player too. He bought one of my two pick up Thunderbirds and I saw him using that in many photographs. He was a bit of a Gibson Thunderbird fan like me, can't blame him!'

Immediately prior to the release of *Wildlife*, the band were at great pains to explain that the new record was much lighter than the previous two and, in their own words, 'a lot less weird'. They had tried to produce an album that wasn't too emotional or heavy, and felt the recording was different from other efforts, because it was the first where they'd had full control. Hunter said *Wildlife* was designed to make people finally understand that Mott The Hoople had musical ability and to lay to rest their perceived hard edge, and the misguided belief that they couldn't record as well as they played live. The group had never had so much say in the making of an album and they made it more musical because previous write ups and reviews had put an accent on the visual and live aspects of the band. For most artists the tactic in recording an album was making their stage act live up to it; to date it had been the other way round for Mott.

All of Ralphs' musical inspirations are laid bare and demonstrated to the full on *Wildlife,* most notably his interest in American country rock with 'It Must Be Love', and his Buffalo Springfield influences on 'Whiskey Women' (Stephen Stills style), and 'Wrong Side of the River' (Neil Young variety). The Nashville Room in West Kensington, near the group's flat, became a regular haunt for Mott, and they saw several country and western bands there including pedal steel player Jerry Hogan who they desperately wanted to feature on some tracks of their own, which they did with 'It Must Be Love' and 'The Original Mixed-Up Kid'.

'Whiskey Women', originally titled 'Brain Haulage', opened the album, and was a good example of Mott's new approach, a lighter touch but still a powerful punch, although in retrospect the band, and Dale in particular, was very unhappy with the sound. The song was inspired by the Whiskey-A-Go-Go club in Los Angeles and its collection of jaded and faded first generation groupies. 'The Whiskey was an horrendous place where people could go and pick up the odd lady, and then go to the doctor about three days later,' says Ralphs.

> What do you want from me – clutching to my blue jeans
> You don't know where those old jeans have been
> Why do you look so hurt – when I'm telling you where to go
> You've been there before from what I've seen

'Angel of Eighth Avenue', one of three stunning ballads that Hunter wrote for *Wildlife,* is the story of a relationship that Ian had with a girl from The Bronx, written after a drunken evening at Nobodies club in Greenwich Village. 'That was the first time I discovered New York,' said Hunter. 'This girl worked in a band and her whole family was a bunch of idiots – prostitutes, God knows what else. She was trying desperately to keep it together.'

> Somewhere a siren sounds and she is turning
> She moves my arm around for she is burning
> She has so much to give but so little time to live
> My angel of eighth avenue – Manhattan morning
>
> And as I look down the streets are slowly forming
> And the ladies of the night have stopped performing

> And the trash collector's horn salutes the dawning
> And soon the workward bound will awaken yawning
>
> And the soft warm hands behind that give no warning
> Tell me for just one hour have I been learning
> I have so much to say but so little time to stay
> With my angel of eighth avenue – Manhattan morning

'Wrong Side of the River' was penned by Mick Ralphs and was lyrically significant. As one reviewer remarked, 'The song starts softly and builds to something very meaningful. There is a good message in this song, be sure not to miss it.' 'It's about me really,' admits Mick. 'A lonesome, reflective song.'

The fourth track on *Wildlife* was another Hunter composition and featured Mott's first-ever string arrangement, using members of the London Symphony Orchestra conducted by Michael Gray. 'Waterlow' concerned Ian's painful divorce and separation from his wife and two young children whom he used to take to Waterlow Park. The song, originally titled 'Blue Broken Tears', summed up the total tenderness and absolute pain of Hunter's personal situation.

> I followed the night 'til the morning sunlight
> And I thought of the changing times
> And I followed the child with the evergreen smile
> And the blue broken tears start to cry
>
> Blue broken tears – hide away the years
> The misty highway – seems colder today
>
> And I saw Waterlow where the evergreen grows
> And the wise man who knows why he cries
> And I heard a child call 'you're away from us all'
> And the blue broken tears start to rise
>
> Blue broken tears – ain't nobody here
> Lost in the sun – my pretty young one
>
> Blue broken tears – our love disappears
> The evergreen dies – drowned in my eyes

'I was married at eighteen and had two kids at twenty,' says Ian. 'When I changed, and the hair got long, and I started going out to weird places and doing weird things, apparently they were weird, she was dead against it. She considered it a threat, so it naturally disintegrated and Diane went back to Shrewsbury. One of the things with me and Diane was she hated London as well, and it came down to the fact that if I stayed in bands, she left. I wrote 'Waterlow' in Stonor Road for Tracey. It's about a park in North London up by Suicide Bridge where we used to go and feed the birds. To me, it's the best thing I ever did. I was going through the divorce about that time.'

Side One closes with 'Lay Down', the aforementioned cover of Melanie Safka's 'Lay Down (Candles in the Rain)', a gospel rock piece featuring Stan Tippins and Jess Roden of Bronco on backing vocals. The track had originated with Guy Stevens, but he soon abandoned it and Mott completed production. 'It was the first decent piano part I ever put down so I thought "I'll just shove that right out front," explains Ian. 'I loved the song. By this time we had our eye on a single too.'

The second side kicks off with Ralphs' 'It Must Be Love', straight country music complete with pedal steel guitar, and then moves into Hunter's third ballad, 'The Original Mixed-Up Kid', (christened 'The Original Poxed-Up Sod' by Watts), which was also included on another of Island's compilation albums, *El Pea*. Ian subsequently admits that this was an example of where he was truly living his lyrics. 'This was probably one of the best songs I ever wrote,' says Hunter in retrospect. 'I like *Wildlife* better than *Mad Shadows*, well parts of it. It is a very uneven record but I like some songs on it. There are some very truthful songs on *Wildlife*. Every time we tried to do something decent like on the first record and on *Wildlife*, people would say it was crap. And every time we would do something completely nuts they would say it was great. But it wouldn't sell. It sells more now than it did then. I know because I get the royalties. I get more money from it now, than I did when it came out.'

> The original mixed-up kid – sleeps with the ladies all night
> Home in the morning light – to nothing
> Climbs into an empty bed – pillows around his head
> Hides the tears he sheds – for no one
>
> And he can't make up his mind where he wants to go
> Ain't there a heaven, ain't there a hell – well he just don't know
> For in a crowded street he can see the sleet – while the other men just see
> the snow

Ralphs fourth composition is the penultimate track, 'Home Is Where I Want to Be', much admired by Ian at the time of release. ' "Home" is my favourite track on *Wildlife*. We all had our little parts on it. Phally's organ playing was beautiful. Mick writes some great songs.'

> Maybe I'm just a loser
> Maybe it's because my boots ain't as clean as they could be
> I came to town with an even chance
> Now I'm feeling down the people I meet ain't fair with me
>
> Maybe I'm just unfortunate
> Maybe I'm alone in thinking that I've got a lot to say
> Too far in to be anywhere
> Lost in this place where nobody seems to know the way

Home – is where I want to be
Home – is where you'll always see
A friendly face that'll never turn you down – say goodbye

'I always felt very drawn towards home, especially when I was on the road,' says Mick. 'So it's about missing your security and whatever it is you miss when you're away, a bit soppy really!'

The musical peace is then shattered as the album finishes with eleven minutes of mayhem, the live version of Little Richard's 'Keep A-Knockin'' salvaged from the Croydon gigs in September 1970. During this musical madness, Mott acknowledge their other rock 'n' roll influences such as Jerry Lee Lewis by including segments of 'Mean Woman Blues', 'Whole Lotta Shakin'' and 'What'd I Say'. The track is also notable for Ian's policy statement that, 'rock and roll is the best possible form of music there ever was.'

'*Wildlife* kind of illustrated where we were,' says Hunter. 'I mean a couple of people in the band were Buffalo Springfield fans and Bob Dylan fans, and we were stuck with this rock and roll thing by this time, so then we were doing *Wildlife*, which was to be all the material we wanted, and we'd stick on 'Keep A-Knockin'' from the live show. Twenty minutes of total stupidity that I had in me too. I mean, I loved doing that live, but somehow when we went in to the studio, we always wanted to do these quiet little songs. It doesn't make any sense. We recorded the whole gig at Croydon for a live album and that was the only thing that was salvageable. Whenever we'd play live, it seemed like half the audience would get on stage with us. It was hopeless trying to record. The kids would be pulling leads out and knocking over mikes. I have more of a fondness for *Wildlife* than practically all the other albums, because I really like the songs on there, but it was a total departure and the worst selling album we ever did.'

Wildlife was released by Island on 19 March 1971 in a sleeve featuring a live colour photograph from Croydon on the inner gatefold and a woodland shot of Mott taken in County Durham on the front cover. It entered the UK album chart on 17 April where it stayed for two weeks peaking at number 44. If only *Wildlife* could have displaced Andy Williams' *Home Loving Man* at the top of the charts that month! Mott had threatened to disband if *Wildlife* didn't outsell *Mad Shadows* and 'officially' it just managed to edge past it, so the group survived and staggered on for several more months. Hunter couldn't understand it, claiming that the new record had sold 15,000 more copies than its predecessor. The LP also received very favourable reviews – '*Wildlife* must be the clincher' – 'A true labour of love, *Wildlife* contains a wealth of fine material' – 'Mott is just about the best rock and roll band around. An excellent album' – were just some of the compliments offered by the British rock press.

Rolling Stone magazine in the USA made the following observation. 'The outcome of the battle has yet to be conclusively determined, but my scorecard gives the race for "The Most Beloved Rock and Roll Band in All the English Isles" to Mott The Hoople by two full lengths over Free. Mott The Hoople has clearly gone beyond any Dylan comparisons you might have heard. Ah, had only Dylan this much fresh energy!'

At the time, Ralphs believed Mott had possibly issued *Wildlife* too soon, and that they weren't really big enough to have made such a drastic change. Years later however, he considered the record essential light relief after the intensity of *Mad Shadows*. 'We needed that to survive. Nice is a horrible word, but it's a nice album. And it was the first time that the band got a say in what went on. On the previous two we were just told what to do.'

Privately, the group were to dub the record *Mildlife,* having discarded *Original Mixed-Up Mott* as a genuine title. 'We produced *Wildlife* ourselves, assisted by Brian Humphries, and it was grim,' says Watts. 'All Brian ever talked about was West Bromwich Albion Football Club. "Can you give us a bit more treble on the bass Brian?" "West Brom 2, Arsenal 3. Oh shit!" You knew it would be a bad recording session that day. "Can you get us some repeat echo on the voice Brian?" "Oh no, you can't do that at this studio, it can't be done. West Brom 3." Repeat echoes can be done anywhere, as we found out later with Bowie, but Brian would just get out of things at every turn.'

Dale too is at a loss to understand Humphries' negative input. 'Brian went on to work with The Who at their Ramport Studios and did some great things with Nirvana earlier, but he seemed to put no effort into Mott The Hoople at all. Everything was a problem to Brian. He limited the bass guitar on "Until I'm Gone" and made it sound pedestrian rather than make it rich, and get full value from each note.'

As with the two previous LPs, some *Wildlife* out-takes remained unissued until 1980 when 'Black Hills' (originally titled 'Green Valley Monday'), 'Surfin' UK' and 'Growing Man Blues' appeared on the *Two Miles from Heaven* compilation of new and rare tracks. Richard Digby-Smith also recalls a rare one man recording during the *Wildlife* sessions.

'Mick Ralphs turned up one Saturday and the studio was all set up, but on that day none of the band arrived because there had been confusion over the booking. So there was only Mick, and rather than go home and waste the day, and as all the instruments were miked up and we had a reel of tape on, he said, "I've got an idea I want to demo." So he went out there and put a bit of acoustic guitar down first, then he put some drums on the top, then bass, electric guitar, vocals, percussion and backing vocals. Then we did a little mix, it probably only went on a cassette, it probably never even went on quarter inch, and off went Mick with his little tape which was a demo of "Can't Get Enough of Your Love". I never heard that song again for years until it came on the radio in Los Angeles by Bad Company and I nearly crashed the car!'

Another recording around this period presents a fascinating document of Mott's live capability from their early career, the tape from a 16 February concert played at The Konserthuset in Stockholm, as part of a short Scandinavian tour. The show was taped by a local FM radio station and circulated for years on bootleg cassettes until a CD, entitled *Long Red,* was issued in 1990. The set included 'The Original Mixed-Up Kid', 'Walkin' with a Mountain', 'Laugh at Me', 'Thunderbuck Ram', 'Keep A-Knockin'' and a cover version of Mountain's 'Long Red'. If confirmation were ever needed that Guy's planned live album was a tragic loss, then this is it.

In early 1971, Mott played several dates supported by Bronco who had Jess Roden and guitarist Robbie Blunt, later of Robert Plant's band, in their ranks. Mott agreed to help them with two tracks on their Island album *Ace of Sunlight*. Hunter and Ralphs played organ and piano on 'Amber Moon' and Allen played organ on a track called 'Discernible'. Verden had previously recorded a spoof of Joe Cocker's 'With a Little Help from my Friends' for John Peel's Dandelion label in 1970 with Jim Capaldi, Henry McCulloch, Alan Spenner, Sue and Sunny and Bill Oddie of *The Goodies* singing 'On Ilkla Moor Baht' At'.

Zig Zag magazine, edited by Pete Frame, had continued to give Mott The Hoople regular support and features, and in 1971 they published a readers rock poll: Ian Hunter and Verden Allen were placed eleventh and seventeenth respectively in the British keyboard players listing, with Overend Watts in thirteenth place in the bass players poll. However, Watts is not afraid to show the honest and humanistic side of Mott and recalls that whilst they seldom played a bad concert, there were one or two notable exceptions. 'One of the worst gigs we ever played as Mott The Hoople was at Southampton University with Brinsley Schwartz as support, who had a lot of hype at that time but were a very good band. I don't know what happened that night but it was dreadful. The sound that we got on stage was awful and we played abominably. What Brinsley Schwartz must have thought of us I just don't know. We were diabolical and I was in the Gents afterwards and a student said, "You were in that group weren't you?" And I said, "Yeah, I'm afraid so." He said, "It was some kind of joke wasn't it; the group is like a spoof is it?" And I replied, "Yes, that's right, we just take the mickey out of groups a bit, you know." We didn't have many gigs where we were diabolical, maybe three or four in the whole of Mott, but that was the worst. I make a formal apology to the members of Brinsley Schwartz, Nick Lowe included, because that was bad.'

Mott were now eager to release a second single and tried to do this with a re-recording of 'Lay Down', however they couldn't recreate the sound they wanted and all plans were abandoned. Ian made it clear that whilst Mott could have released a 12-bar single which might get into the charts, they wouldn't be proud of it, so there was little point. They spent time in Island's Basing Street Studios between 11 and 21 April recording various tracks – 'One of the Boys', 'Until I'm Gone', 'Long Red', 'It'll Be Me', 'Where Do You All Come From?', 'Ill Wind Blowing', 'Downtown' and 'The Debt' – before embarking on an American tour. Hunter had mixed feelings about their second US assault. 'For the kids it was great, but our American record company, Atlantic, did nothing to promote it. We came in through the back door and went out through the back door. We lost six thousand dollars on the tour, went in as second billing, lost four gigs through Free splitting up and two gigs were stopped by the police before we played. We won't be going back until we get some kind of chart success over there because there's no point in going to lose money.'

'Atlantic Records had no interest in us after Ahmet Ertegun came to a gig at Stonybrook University, New York,' says Dale. 'Phally's organ was on the blink and out of tune with Ian's piano. It was a complete mess and a fiasco. Blackwell was there too.' Watts used the meeting with Atlantic's head to create another of his spoonerisms, re-christening Ahmet Ertegun, ''Urt his arm again!'

During their American tour, it was arranged that Mott would take time out to record their elusive hit single. Immediately following a concert with Emerson, Lake and Palmer in Milwaukee they flew to Long Island to work for one day with legendary New York producer George 'Shadow' Morton, selected at the suggestion of Atlantic Records. A former member of The Marquis and The Gems vocal groups, Shadow had been a partner in the influential Red Bird record label founded in 1964 and was famous for his production and writing for artists such as The Goodies, Vanilla Fudge, Ellie Greenwich and most notably The Shangri La's, who had a huge hit with 'Leader of the Pack'. Morton was later to go on to produce The New York Dolls and Isis but many felt that his subsequent work paled into insignificance against his classic tracks of the sixties. Similar to Guy Stevens in some respects, Shadow Morton had a tremendous amount of raw talent but couldn't play an instrument, He once proclaimed of his work, 'We're not talking about talent, we're talking about sound.'

Hunter and Ralphs had been working on a song called 'The Hooker' as a possible single, which was subsequently to be issued as 'The Road to Rome' but became 'Midnight Lady' upon release. The single was recorded on 12 May with Shadow at Ultra Sonic Recording Studios in Hempstead, Long Island. Steve Marriott happened to be around the adjoining studio during Mott's visit, so he was included on backing vocals, but had to be isolated at the opposite end of the room because he was so loud.

Hunter feels Mott did not fully exploit the potential of the session. ' "Midnight Lady" could have been great but we worked with Shadow for only one day and we were in a bad state, having flown in to New York from Milwaukee on an early morning flight. We'd been five or six days on the road with ELP and were shattered after a party the night before. The band played badly, but the second verse makes it. Shadow never got a chance, but we enjoyed his company immensely. He was an amazing guy. He had this crocodile shirt on and I remember saying, "I love that shirt, Shadow," and he just ripped it straight off his back and it was mine. He was larger than life.'

'We'd played this gig in Milwaukee and Fred Fishpool had moved there,' says Watts. 'We hadn't seen him for over five years, so you can imagine what state we were all in at 6 o'clock the next morning when we flew to New York. It was something of a comeback session for Shadow as he had been recovering from serious alchohol problems.'

The evening with Fishpool was a nightmare, as he insisted on taking Mott round various Hell's Angels bars. Griffin could hardly play next day at the session. 'Horribly hungover, I was lying across the drum kit, feeling like death and the colour of Kermit The Frog. Meanwhile, Shadow was trying to engage me in meaningful discussions about the drum parts. *Never* go drinking with Fred Fishpool.'

'We only did the one track with Shadow Morton,' says Verden. 'If we could have had a hit without calling somebody else in it could have been better. We were just looking for someone to give us a commercial type mix, that's all it was, because it was nearly three years of ground work with Island and they were starting to worry.'

Ian invited his new girlfriend, American, Trudi Ligouri to the recording session on Long Island. Trudi came from New York, although her Mother was Austrian, and Ian had met her originally in England, where she dated friend of Mott and fellow Herefordian Richard Weaver during her stay. 'I'd met Trudi a few times,' says Ian. 'When I was in New York, Tru rang me up to find out where this guy was and I told her when he was coming to New York, but said I had to see her about something. She was going to St.John's University and working in Greenwich Village to pay for it at night. I was going out with about seven women and one of them was her mate, and Trudi was horrified by this and thought I was a complete asshole. Then I went with one girl. It took a little while to win Trudi, but eventually I did. I proposed to her during the "Midnight Lady" session, outside the Gent's!'

The single was released in the UK on 11 June in a picture sleeve, and one reviewer remarked, 'More an album group really, but they can also create a commercial touch without losing that powerful and authoritative style. A hit I'd say. Possibly a sizeable one.' The single also received a European release, with Mick Ralphs' "It Must Be Love" as the B-side, but was not issued in America.

The British single was backed with "The Debt", written by Ian and recorded at Island's Basing Street No. 2 Studio on 21 April. Described by Watts as 'puny and miserable', 'The Debt' was one of the most Dylanesque-sounding songs that Mott ever recorded. Dale recalls the group always laughed about it because it was never a loud, dynamic number and on vinyl, the surface noise on the record almost drowned out the track. 'I remember doing "The Debt",' says Verden. 'Chris Blackwell came in and said, "That's a good title, yes, there is a bit of a debt building up now." And we said, "We're having strings put on the next album." And he replied, ' "Yeah, there'll be an even bigger debt then. Don't go over the top lads!" '

Ian commented at the time that if their single hit the charts, then Mott would make another album. If it failed they planned to record another single, their aim being 'quality single success' like The Rolling Stones and The Who. The band received adverse radio comment about 'Midnight Lady' from Radio One DJ Tony Blackburn, although Hunter responded during several live concerts at the time. 'Tony Blackburn says he'll hang himself if our new single is a hit,' he would tell audiences, 'and I want to be a fuckin' witness!' Ironically, Blackburn was to select a Mott single as his 'Record of the Week' one year later. Initial sales of 'Midnight Lady' were so promising that the BBC offered Mott their first ever appearance on *Top of the Pops* during July. Dale points out that the day after the show aired, the single stopped selling, a feat that deserves a place in the *Guinness Book of Records*.

In 1971, Mick and Overend embarked on some extra curricular group activity with several high profile names from Island Records. 'Me and Ralpher did a session with Leslie West, Corky Laing and Paul Rodgers and recorded a twelve-minute song, "Sail On", which Free did later on *Free At Last*,' says Watts. 'It was all done live, with Paul playing piano and singing, Mick playing rhythm, Leslie lead and Corky on drums with me on bass. I think Mott were recording at the time at Island Studios and Leslie and Corky came along and asked if we wanted to play something when Paul happened to be around.'

Mott recorded three further BBC sessions in 1971. In April they appeared on BBC Television's *Disco 2* playing 'Whiskey Women' and 'The Original Mixed-Up Kid' and on 8 March they also taped these two songs plus 'Angel of Eighth Avenue' and 'Keep A-Knockin'' at Maida Vale studios for Mike Harding's *Sounds of the Seventies* programme. On 6 July they recorded 'Midnight Lady', 'Like a Rolling Stone' and 'Angel of Eighth Avenue' (again) for John Peel's *Top Gear*. This latter session is highly noteable because, whilst Hunter originally auditioned for Mott with Dylan's 'Like a Rolling Stone', they never committed the entire track to tape anywhere else. Dale was particularly surprised to learn several years later that Mott had recorded this at the BBC, although they had rehearsed the song especially for an appearance at the Royal Albert Hall.

On 8 July, Mott played the Royal Albert Hall, in London, for the first and last time. Their performance caused scenes which one reviewer compared to Beatlemania and several seats and boxes were damaged. The group were sent a substantial bill for repairs and rock concerts were cancelled indefinitely at this venue as a result, one front page headline proclaiming 'Mott banned – RAH cracks up'. Mott were denied a December re-booking by the management because of 'the riotous actions of the audience' after several floors 'cracked' and two boxes 'collapsed'. The band was presented with an account for 'damages to property' amounting to £1,467. 'Originally it was just for damage to two boxes, but somehow it changed to thirty,' remarked Hunter. 'Perhaps it's Mott's contribution to the Royal Albert Hall Restoration Fund. I can tell you it's expensive publicity being banned. We don't need it. To be truthful we can't afford it.'

Verden says of The Royal Albert Hall gig, 'Apparently a crack appeared in one of the balconies above the press which was just right and we had a nice bill and every venue wanted us then. I remember a coach pulling up outside with all our parents on it and people from Hereford and Guy Stevens saying, "Bloody hell, most bands would want a coach full of women turning up, but Mott The Hoople want their parents to come down and see them." That was the first gig that I used my C3 on, and in one write up some girl journalist said we had a good organ sound. It was a nice feeling. Guy came up to me and said, "That's the best thing you've ever done buying that organ, great." I used the C3 with two Leslie 145 speaker cabinets combined with two 150-Watt Acoustic stacks plus an additional horn for my direct sound. When using this combination in the UK, I had to wear ear protectors. So did Buffin!'

Ian's friend Miller Anderson joined Mott for their Albert Hall finale. 'Hunter ran off the stage and grabbed me and brought me on to sing 'Keep A-Knockin'' with him. Ian's parents were there that night and I remember he had a funny relationship with his Dad who was a military man and was very strict. He never had much good to say about Ian because he wasn't an obvious singer and I suppose you could say I was. Coming off stage, his Dad should have been so proud of him being at the Albert Hall, but all he could say was, "Just as well they had you up there Miller, they needed a good singer." I thought that was a terrible thing to say. I think that was part of the reason Ian's able to write such good songs, because he's got all that experience and angst behind him.'

Following the Royal Albert Hall fiasco, Mott The Hoople were also banned from gigs at Cheltenham Town Hall and Brighton Dome, but they capitalised on this 'opportunity' and hatched a plan with Tony Brainsby to publicise the various threatened bans from UK concert halls. The group announced that rather than cancel various live dates they had acquired a 2,000 capacity mobile fibreglass theatre called the Caraivari, which would be erected on village greens around the country, enabling Mott to play. Inexplicably, this ludicrous tale is still believed to this day.

Around this time, Mott The Hoople was approached by brilliant American lead guitarist Leslie West. His group Mountain had just split and he offered to produce, co-write and play gigs with Mott. Hunter used this as a platform to put people straight on the Mott versus Grand Funk comparisons which frequented the press at the time. 'If we were some potty little band trying to get banned and some cheap publicity as the next Grand Funk Railroad, why would a musician of Leslie West's calibre and status want to work with us. I can tell you that he is really keen on it.' After much deliberation however, it was decided a Mott-West collaboration wasn't feasible. Even though the group believed Leslie West to be the best guitarist in America at the time, they agreed that they'd started as Mott, and they'd finish as Mott.

Watts jokes that West wasn't compatible for other reasons. 'I don't know whose idea it would have been for Leslie to join Mott. It's a bloody good job he didn't. The bloody plane would never have stayed in the air! What would Ralpher have done anyway. Mick and Ian on rhythm and West on lead? You always got the feeling with Leslie that he might have been another Dave Mason, somebody who was pushy. When you're in bands you often get people coming along who seem that way inclined. They want to get in on things and you feel they're going to take over. When we recorded "Sail On" with Free and Mountain, Leslie played lead all over it. He never gave Mick a lead break, so Ralpher was just hanging around on rhythm. I don't think we'd have had Leslie West in Mott. We loved his playing but Ralpher was our guitarist.'

Mott The Hoople played a BBC concert session at the Paris Theatre on 17 July for *The Rosko Show*. It was broadcast in a week when they had no live gigs, a rare occurence. Dale recalls, 'This was live – real live, as it happened, with rioting skinheads in the audience and just a handful of dear old geriatric BBC commissionaires to keep order. They had no chance, and Rosko was encouraging the brawling through his PA system.'

Mott The Hoople had become one of Britain's finest and most-in-demand live acts, so much so that a number of more established groups refused to work with them as they feared their ability to match or even top the audience excitement that Mott generated. 'They say on its night, Mott The Hoople was the best live band going,' says Hunter. 'And Jagger said that he felt that we would be the next ones up, which amazed me, because he was always bitching about everybody.'

However, whilst they were a live sensation, record sales remained weak for Mott The Hoople and the group were becoming increasingly concerned. 'I was worried because Miller Anderson was playing with Keef Hartley and they had a similar situation,' said Hunter. 'It was totally different music, but he had sold out everywhere in England, not had a hit and now that band was sliding and I knew if we didn't get a hit, we weren't going to be able to sustain this business of sell-ing out everywhere. Somewhere down the line, people always want a record to hang on to, they want it on vinyl. So I was beginning to panic and really panic after *Wildlife*. I thought we'd had it.

'Island Records was pretty bland,' says Ian. 'I kept telling them we were Led Zeppelin, that we needed lots of hustle and push. They said, "Alright, we'll do it," but they never did. In retrospect I don't blame them that much. Then they said, "You've got to do another album." I had stuff and I didn't even want to record it, which was amazing to me, having wanted to record all my life. We knew we were wrong. There just didn't seem to be any niche for us. Yet by this time we were the biggest live act in England. We were very honest live; it used to be a very chaotic experience. We filled the Albert Hall with no success whatso-ever on record.'

Their staggeringly successful live concerts had sometimes been a source of amazement to certain commentators but Mott continued to attract a die-hard support. 'The kids who follow us, follow us everywhere.' said Hunter. 'They know us back to front. We call them the lieutenants. They're the ones that are nearest to us and come with us nearly everywhere we go. Then we've got divisions who'll travel anywhere. It's great, because when you go to a gig there are always these people there. You know you're going to make somebody happy.'

The group had begun working on their fourth Island album during April 1971 and resurrected the sessions in August, but in the interim they decided to release another single. Once again Ralphs' Buffalo Springfield – Neil Young influence floated to the surface as they opted for a cover of Crazy Horse's ode to West Coast drug culture, 'Downtown', taken from their stunning 1971 debut LP which also featured 'Gone Dead Train', 'Beggars' Day' and 'I Don't Want to Talk about It'. 'Downtown' was written by Neil Young and Danny Whitten, who subsequently died from a drug overdose in late 1972. Neil had previously written 'The Needle and the Damage Done', an account of Whitten's slide into heroin addiction.

Mott The Hoople's 'Downtown' single had been recorded with 'The Debt', at Island, on 21 April and was issued as a UK single in September. One reviewer said, 'Mott have waited relatively patiently and now they've got their hit. It's a blatant aim at the commercial market which works.' As with the previous 'Midnight Lady' single, Downtown was not released in the USA. The B-side was Ralphs' 'Home', printed on the label with an abbreviated title, from the recent *Wildlife* LP. ' "Downtown" was great by Crazy Horse – God knows what went wrong when we got hold of it.' says Pete. 'Definitely one of our worst efforts. I blame Muff Winwood, or anybody else!'

Mott also made a promotional film for 'Downtown' but the single failed to chart. Verden Allen recalls, 'Guy came in one day with the Crazy Horse album and said, "Look, I think you ought to do this track as a single." There's a good video of that filmed in the Basing Street Studios, but that single was mushy and Ian wouldn't sing it for a start. It wasn't his cup of tea. It didn't really suit him. So Mick sang it.'

'I never really liked "Downtown" either,' admits Ralphs, 'and I can understand why Ian didn't want to sing it. It was pretty naff. We were desperately trying to get a hit but it was an ordinary cover of an ordinary song.'

Mott The Hoople had become recognised as a rock band but wanted to promote their lighter side. 'We'd love to do *Wildlife* live,' said Ian. 'We even considered doing it at the Albert Hall and using the London Symphony Orchestra We
could have got good reviews for it, but how can you kick 3,000 kids in the teeth
for the sake of four or five reviewers? We've always worked our act so that there
is 50 per cent quiet stuff and the rest faster things – with a couple of rock numbers at the end. But the rock has mushroomed. People have latched on to it.'

Around this period Mott were unwittingly thinking in ground breaking terms
when they gave serious consideration to recording an interpretive album of cover
versions, long before Bryan Ferry and David Bowie embarked on similar projects
with *These Foolish Things* and *Pin Ups*. Inspired by complimentary remarks about
their earlier treatment of Ray Davies, Doug Sahm, Sonny Bono and Melanie material, some of the songs that were debated by the group included James Taylor's
'Fire and Rain', Tom Rush's 'Driving Wheel' and Dylan's 'Watching the River
Flow', the spirit and tempo of which they had revamped as 'Where Do You All
Come From?' However, feeling trapped in a musical hinterland after *Mad
Shadows* and *Wildlife,* and with fans always craving their harder live edge, Mott
decided to adopt their stage persona in the studio instead, and recorded an
aggressive, energy-laden album which was ahead of its time. Sadly the record did-
n't sell in quantity, but was perhaps one of the finest LPs of the decade and probably the most underrated but important single influence on the 'New Wave'
movement six years later.

7
We ain't bleeding you, we're feeding you

'The Moon Upstairs' – Ian Hunter / Mick Ralphs

Mott returned to Island's Basing Street Studios in August to commence work on their fourth album. Again it was an attempt to come to terms with their live – studio quandary but the dilemma was no nearer resolution. The LP was originally to be titled *AC/DC* because the group was still schizoid and the songs were half fast and half slow. They were even considering having a rock side and a slow side on the record and wanted Guy Stevens to organise the sleeve. 'I'd forgotten about *AC/DC*,' says Dale Griffin. 'It was ditched because we were worried about the sexual connotations. Odd, considering the imminent involvement with Bowie and his camp.'

Mott had worked on various tracks at Basing Street in April immediately following *Wildlife*, including Mountain's 'Long Red', Jerry Lee Lewis' 'It'll Be Me', 'Ill Wind Blowing', 'One of the Boys', a rough and rocky instrumental version of 'Where Do You All Come From?' (later re-recorded and released in 1973), and 'Til I'm Gone' (about Ralphs' first wife, Nina). ' "Til I'm Gone" was one of Ralphs' best songs,' remarks Watts. 'It made me come over all unnecessary and run away and hide. I think the others were quite affected by it too. I really felt for Mick and his split from Nina. I'll never forget the night he did the vocal. It got right through to me. I loved doing "It'll Be Me" live – it just pounded relentlessly on – until it stopped!'

The new album was to be self-produced by Mott but they decided to invite Guy Stevens back to help them after only one week of recording when it was thought the sessions were going awry. Only recently, during a 1996 review of the Island tape archive, was it revealed that Mott had actually recorded astonishing self-produced versions of 'The Journey', 'The Moon Upstairs' (originally titled 'Mental Train') and 'Death May Be Your Santa Claus' (working title 'How Long') prior to Stevens' involvement. 'I Don't Know', 'A Year Ago Today' and 'Show Me the Bottle' were also taped over a seven-day period commencing 4 August 1971 at Island's Basing Street Studio 1, before Guy was brought in during September to complete proceedings.

'The early Mott-produced versions are relaxed and atmospheric whilst the subsequent recordings with Guy Stevens have a raw and aggressive manner,' remarks Griffin. 'The original take of "The Journey" for instance, recorded before Guy ever got involved in the *Brain Capers* sessions, is staggeringly beautiful. Over nine minutes long with an elegiac pace and overpowering majesty, the dynamics and build up executed by the ensemble is, to my mind, the best of Mott The Hoople ever captured on tape.'

Mott The Hoople was frequently volatile and the group were often on the verge of splitting, and yet there were numerous times where there was genuine harmony, 'The Journey' being a prime example. Mott's version displays incredible melancholy whilst Guy Stevens' 'Journey' is almost neurotic. On cover versions, the group could sensitively shape other writers' material sufficiently to place their own stamp upon it. When Guy influenced Mott he could almost twist the music out of recognition, as with 'The Wheel of the Quivering Meat Conception', which illustrates how crazed 'The Journey' had become.

Pete Watts recalls how Mott's attempt at a new album faltered before Stevens returned to produce the group. 'We'd tried to do an album on our own and it wasn't quite happening. We'd recorded those three tracks but we were probably having trouble getting anything else together. *Wildlife* had been gentle and tepid so we wanted to get some of the Guy feel back, but technically better. The initial tracks were good, but we were a bit stumped and we were frightened it might go the way of *Wildlife*, so we made the decision to call him back. Guy came in and said, "Right, we start from scratch and scrap everything you've done." He wouldn't have kept anything that wasn't initiated by him. Like "Growing Man Blues", which Buff found later. That was a good track that we never completed. We probably did it without Guy and he would have come in and said, "That's no good, forget that and we'll start again. He liked to have his mark on things from inception to completion."

Mott was still touring the country on an ongoing basis and on 30 August, they decided to play an open-air date at Hereford United Football Club's Edgar Street Stadium. Because the concert was scheduled for the British Bank Holiday weekend, there was concern at one stage that the event might be poorly attended, but Tippins came to the rescue and spread the rumour that Mick Jagger would arrive by helicopter to join Mott. Suffice to say, Stanley succeeded in attracting more people to Hereford with this announcement, and ticket sales were significantly enhanced. While he didn't subsequently appear in court, Hunter was charged for using abusive language on stage during this concert. 'That was a nice little gig,' recalls Overend. 'It was great because Hereford United was on a high at the time and had come from nowhere up to the English Second Division. It was really happening for them and it was happening for us with a huge fan following.'

From 19–23 September Guy Stevens was scheduled to produce Mott's new album, which turned out to be their Island swansong, demanding a thousand pounds up front before he would work on the project. 'He was a smart bastard with money,' remarks Hunter. 'This one we were forced into doing. We went in to the studio with very few songs, because we toured endlessly and I never wrote on the road. Guy was pissed off because we hadn't asked him to do it originally. We'd been looking for him, but hadn't been able to find him because he was off on another one of his binges.'

Engineer Richard Digby-Smith was present when Stevens made his return to Island. 'I saw Guy and Andy enter the building on the first night of recording sessions when Mott decided that what they needed was to get Guy and the old team back. The door to the Basing Street reception flew open and in ran Andy Johns and Guy Stevens, wearing capes and Zorro masks. They ran round with enormous water pistols and created absolute mayhem.'

For the sessions, Guy procured a case of wine and insisted the tracks were mainly first takes, the result being a complete contrast to *Wildlife*. *Brain Capers (featuring the Brain Caper Kids)*, as the album became known, had an amazing atmosphere and last gasp energy, capturing Mott in wild and manic mood. However, Guy's enthusiasm and creativity was to emerge in an extreme way during completion of the LP, for which the band had been given five days of session time. On the first day, Guy didn't even turn up and for the next three days things went very slowly. Hunter recalls Stevens' response to this.

'Guy came in dressed like a highwayman and Andy Johns was behind him feeling no pain because he'd been with the Stones for a while. I remember about half way through the sessions, we had no material. It was kind of like Pooh, Piglet, Kanga and Tigger, and Guy was Tigger. He said, "I know what we have to do, we've got to set fire to the studio. This will inspire us to greater heights." So we set fire to the studio and while the fire was in progress, I felt responsible and I felt bad about it. I thought it was bullshit too. I said, "Look somebody's got to talk to Chris Blackwell about this." Chris was upstairs in the flat and the studio's on fire. Now, I'd never talk to Chris because he upset me once, but I had to talk to him about this and I said, "Chris your studio's on fire." And he said, "Are you talking about the console or the actual studio itself?" I said, "The studio itself." And he said, "Was it really necessary?" So I said, "Yeah," and he replied, "Fine," and that was it. When I left it was still going. It was all a pile of chairs in the middle of the room and clocks and stuff that's in studios, all piled up in the studio upstairs. I just felt disgusted. I mean Guy was nuts and the band was nuts but I never felt the madness that Guy felt.'

John Glover of Island recalls, 'Guy had a plan for a manic album. Blackwell had a soft spot for him and let him in to Basing Street Studios. I vividly remember walking in one morning and they'd finished the album and gone totally berserk. Guy always incited them in to being outrageous and the whole place was wrecked. Blackwell blew his top and Guy was banned. The band had played the album back and gone wild. The whole thing was total lunacy.'

During the sessions one of Island's senior engineers came in to warn Guy that they were running over time and that he needed the studio for other purposes. Stevens freaked, and smashed a clock, screaming that he didn't care about time when he was creating. The rest of the band cheered and joined in. Pressured by Island to get the record out, Mott recorded the bulk of the album in only five days, but came up with probably their most consistent LP to date.

'Brain Capers was all done fairly quickly,' confirms Watts. 'On the last day we just went straight into the studio, Guy got us drunk out of our heads, we put the tracks down, then smashed up the studio. Like an absolute disaster, it was chaos. Guy and Andy were running around the control room with Zorro masks and capes on, squirting us with water pistols while we were playing. They didn't do any proper recording. They just got us to play a bit each and set the sound levels, said, "Okay. Go!", pressed "Record", left the desk immediately and chased each other round while we recorded the numbers. They didn't touch the desk, that was it, just left running. We'd finish a song and they would say, "Right, that's it, next one," and we'd do that and the tapes just kept rolling. Nothing was adjusted during the recording. Andy Johns didn't stop to ask if we wanted a bit more guitar or anything like that. I think I bust a string in the middle of one song and just carried on without it. In the end we stopped because Buffin collapsed and fell into his bass drum case unconscious.

'We were all out of our heads completely. Guy ordered meals in the end and chefs with big tall hats were bringing these trolleys in. It must have cost us a fortune because we didn't know at the time we were paying for it all. There were great big steaks but no plates so I threw something at this large studio wall clock to loosen it and I remember laughing at it as it swung there, then I ripped it down from its lead and ate my dinner out of the back of it, steak and salad! I was going out with a school teacher, Jenny Morgan, at the time and I recall going to her Hampstead flat at five in the morning, drunk and yelling to be let in, still clutching the clock and being told to go home.'

Pete also remembers Stevens damaging the Island reception. 'Guy went out into the lobby and tore down all the framed album covers. He'd pick up something like King Crimson and smash it on the floor. "Fucking King Crimson," he'd be going. "They're shit. Mott The Hoople's the biggest band in the world." Chris Blackwell came in the next day and asked Guy what was going on. Guy said, "We were recording and it got a bit out of hand." Blackwell said, "Did you get any tracks done?" And Guy said, "Yeah, five." And Blackwell said, "Well that's not too bad then." Funnily enough, the American reviews said it was the best album to date, they really liked it over there. I can see in a way why hardcore fans like it, because it is the most aggressive, the most panic stricken.'

Verden Allen also confirms the studio mayhem associated with the session. 'I remember a big pile of chairs got slung all over the place and some of them were sticking in the walls in Studio One downstairs. Guy wanted to start something off but it went further than he thought. When you walked in to Island Records there were pictures of bands and album sleeves on the wall – Mott The Hoople, Blodwyn Pig, Quintessence – and they got destroyed, except Traffic, because that was Chris Blackwell's band. We never touched drugs but we got drunk at that session, and when Buffin got drunk he really did.'

In retrospect, Dale is somewhat critical of the recording methods employed. 'Guy and Andy Johns were brought in at a very late stage for the *Brain Capers* project, and it drove me crazy when Andy positioned a microphone on my drums that made it all-but impossible to get from one side of the kit to the other or to lift the sticks up. There's a lot of clicked sticks, missed beats and even a breakdown on "Sweet Angeline". It was horrible. They did get some good guitar noises though. Mick had acquired a Sunn amp which had an amazing sound.'

Looking back, Mott's own production of 'The Journey', with acoustic guitars, sensitive backing vocals and swirling Hammond, was astounding and technically superior to Stevens' approach. Conversely Guy had successfully captured the aggression and frustration contained in 'The Moon Upstairs' and nobody could deny that the record's attack was unprecedented and truly ahead of its time. *Brain Capers* opened with 'Death May Be Your Santa Claus', the first ever Hunter/Allen composition, and a pounding track with fearsome guitars and wailing organ, carrying a trademark message of defiance.

How long will it take to turn you around
How long will it take to bend you down
Eventually you will exchange
How long will it take for me to rearrange
How long – how long – 'til you realise that I'm strange

Well I don't care what the people may say
I don't give a – anyway
I don't care what the people may say

The song was originally titled 'A Duck Can Swim With Me' and then 'How Long?' before Guy plundered 'Death May Be Your Santa Claus', the title of a little known 1971 film and accompanying soundtrack album by a group called Secondhand. This art house movie, supposedly masterminded by a black power leader and filmed in and around 10 Rillington Place (home of murderer John Christie) and Notting Hill, featured disturbing scenes including an Earth Mother breast-feeding black and white children and a gang of hooligans who castrated passers-by in Hyde Park. 'I thought Guy took the title from something written by Kerouac,' says Dale Griffin. 'We never knew it might have been taken from a film.'

Tracks two and three were imaginative and tasteful cover versions of Dion DiMucci's autobiographical 'Your Own Backyard' and The Youngbloods' neglected classic, 'Darkness, Darkness' written by Jesse Colin Young for their 1969 album *Elephant Mountain*. New Yorker Dion had fought heroin addiction in the mid-sixties and 'Your Own Backyard' was an anti-drug song. Selected by Guy for *Brain Capers,* this could have referred directly to Stevens' worsening personal problems and the direction he should have taken. 'Darkness, Darkness' featured Mick Ralphs on vocals and contained some excellent guitar, although Verden refused to play organ on the studio version. Mott had performed this song live in 1969 and 1970 so it was already a long standing group favourite. Two separate reviews of the album commended the group's approach to cover versions, one reviewer crediting Mott with the panache to re-interpret other writer's material with feeling and understanding.

Side One closed with Ian Hunter's 'The Journey', a sad introspective masterful ballad, some eight minutes long. The band often made apologies for playing it live and in a short space of time dropped the song from their set. Ian said, 'It's always been schizoid ever since the word go. Sometimes I go through moods when I just like to play quietly. My dearest wish is to play a proper piano on stage rather than an electric, which I don't play nearly so well. There are times when I'd like to play quietly all the way through and get a respectful reaction, but we have this degree of madness and it's still there. It's a really weird band. I've been an advocate of the slow music, mainly because I write it, from the very beginning. I think that Mick and myself have written some really reasonable numbers, but somehow when we get on stage, it's like a minor explosion, every time, we just can't help it.'

'The Journey' started life as a poem and Hunter had explained previously that he'd worked on the piece for a considerable time. 'Its theme is a bridge at the Archway in London, which is now known as Suicide Bridge because so many people have jumped off it. Peter Sellers once saved someone there.'

> So for forty days – and for forty nights
> Well they tied my hands – made me see the light
> And the angels screamed – in my nightmare ride
> And the changes, Lord – well they will take their time
> Well, I guess he lost – just a little bit on the journey
> For his mind was split – by little things that didn't fit on the way
> Oh I know he lost – just a little bit on the journey

One reviewer remarked, ' "The Journey" yet again demonstrates that Hunter is a writer who in time may well become a major contributor to rock music.' The song was also a personal favourite of Verden Allen, whose keyboard playing excelled throughout *Brain Capers*, most notably on this opus.

The second side opened with 'Sweet Angeline', written by Ian, and originally titled 'Indian City Queen'. This remains a favourite in Hunter's solo sets, but in retrospect Ian was not happy with the studio recording. '*Brain Capers* almost has me in tears. It was done as a rush job. We did all the backing tracks live and then I added all the vocals. You can hear my voice getting progressively croakier. It really upset me, because I obviously wasn't doing the songs justice. "Angeline" was one of the best numbers I'd ever written, but the way it turned out makes it sound like nothing more than just another rocker.' Dale actually wanted to re-record the track and protested to Stevens but without the support of the remaining group members at the time. 'I pleaded unsuccessfully to Guy to let us do it again properly. Just Griffin being difficult again I suppose!'

'Second Love' was the first song that Verden Allen ever wrote and it was an intensely personal debut. Asked about the intimate nature of the lyric and the original take of his own lead vocal intended for the LP, Verden is emotional. 'Oh that's bloody awful. I've heard that, it's terrible. I couldn't do it, I couldn't get away with the emotion of that song. It was about religion, nothing to do with physical love. I was going out with this girl called Elaine Pampel, I thought the world of her. She was a Jewish girl and the "second love" was religion. It was her that got me in to writing. Her father was an orthodox Jew and he said, "It's either the family or him." Emotional blackmail. She was torn between her love for her family and religion, and her love for me. The relationship ended in 1974. Elaine came to see me at the Marquee in my new band The Cheeks. She'd gone from eight-and-a-half down to four stones in weight.'

> I know you have a second love
> Another one you're thinking of
> What is there now that I can do
> I'll always feel the same for you

I'm crossed between your second love
It ain't just me you're thinking of
What is there now that I can do
I'll always feel the same about you

Hunter recalls the session for 'Second Love'. 'This was Verden's first stab at songwriting and what a day we had with that! Phally was singing it at the time but I ended up doing it. I couldn't say, "Phally you're not up to this song. I've got to sing it." He was so intense about it. Finally Guy told him. Verden was always trying to get his songs in the band and legitimately so, since we hadn't had any success with our stuff, but they were the first things he was composing.'

'We didn't want Verden to refrain from writing,' says Dale. 'But we didn't want him to expect a song would go on an album just because he'd written it. Ian and Mick had songs turned down by Mott but when we said the same thing to Phal he took it very hard.'

The penultimate track, Hunter/Ralphs' 'The Moon Upstairs', (originally titled 'Who's Cheating Who?' – an old Buddies stage number – and then 'Mental Train'), was one of the most powerful tracks that Mott ever recorded. The song was unquestionably six years ahead of its time, being a frightening 'New Wave' fuzz-tone premonition that, musically and lyrically, rendered late seventies 'Punk Rock' tame, clumsy and lacking in any real substance.

Dale recalls, ' "The Moon Upstairs" began life as a godawful country song, very Band / "The Weight" orientated. It was a Ralphs composition with a chorus lyric, "Red, red wine and the moon upstairs, are gonna make a big fool out of me." The song died, but the title lived on. Sadly, Andy Johns missed Ralphs' opening guitar chord on the master take.'

'Originally it mentioned the lunar factor and red wine which both have the same effect, they make you go loopy,' says Ralphs. 'But rather than analysing it, it was just a way of making words hang together well. The "moon upstairs" sounds better than the moon in the sky. It meant nothing really.' The final lyric carried a very different message as Mott, truly at the end of their rope, discharged desperation, frustration and anger in astounding style.

Well I wandered freely as a bird, that had broken both its wings
And I hated them, and they hated me, and I hated everything
I realised that to survive, well my body is not mine
And I feel neglected, feel rejected, living in a wrong time
And to those of you who always laugh – let this be our epitaph

And my head is down and I'm called a clown, by comedians that grace
The living stage and every page, of worthless, meaningless space
But I swear to you before we're through, you're gonna feel our every blow
We ain't bleeding you, we're feeding you, but you're too fucking slow

' "The Moon Upstairs" made sense to me,' says Ian. 'I liked the line, "We ain't bleeding you, we're feeding you, but you're too fucking slow." That still applies to this day. You know *Brain Capers* to me was five days of chaos. I didn't think anything came out of it, but when I listened to it recently, you can actually hear The Sex Pistols loud and clear. I was quite chuffed. I like *Brain Capers* better than I did. I was very surprised, because I never listened to it for many many years and then the punks started talking about it. I remember it as three days of total madness. I did the vocals all in one go because Island weren't too flush with the money there. It's not like we were doing well. We were still failing miserably. I hated Island Records. I hated every fucker. Me and Guy really didn't know where the fuck we were. There was real heavy shit going down but it all seemed to contribute to that so I guess it's all right.'

Brain Capers' coda was a two-minute instrumental 'piece' named 'The Wheel of the Quivering Meat Conception'. Once again, Guy played the part of a jackdaw, lifting the title from Jack Kerouac's 1958 *Poetry for the Beat Generation.* Similar to 'Wrath 'n' Wroll' on the first album, which had been edited from the finale of 'You Really Got Me', 'The Wheel of the Quivering Meat Conception' was nothing more than the climax of 'The Journey', from an end-of-session jam and another of Stevens' tape reclamation initiatives. Once described as 'music publishing and royalties seams', Dale remarks, 'These frenzied edits were orchestrated lunacies and are, quite justly, credited to Guy Stevens.'

' "Death May Be Your Santa Claus", "The Moon Upstairs" and "The Wheel of the Quivering Meat Conception" were Guy Stevens' ideas,' admits Ian. 'You never knew where they came from. He was full of it. We were living quite crazily at the time, I was especially and so was Guy, and these were just stream of conciousness things.'

'Guy came up with these titles simply to sound outrageous,' says Ralphs. 'He really just wanted to shock, as we did. *Brain Capers* is my favourite of all Mott The Hoople albums and the cover was brilliant.'

Stevens devised the sleeve after several of his original ideas were once again aborted. 'We did a photograph session at Guy's flat near Marble Arch,' says Dale. 'We'd done a session at the old British Coal Headquarters just off the Westway down towards Maida Vale and we got thrown out of there when they found out we were photographing. Then we went to a little park down by the canal just off Warwick Road tube station and those photos were a disaster. So we ended up in Guy's flat which was reasonably near by and that's where the back cover photographs were taken for *Brain Capers.'*

Unable to decide between *Bizarre Capers* and *Brain Damage* for an album title, Stevens eventually opted for Dale's suggested compromise, *Brain Capers,* and then credited his sleeve concept to Bizarre Damage. Released on 19 November, the album was packaged in a plain scarlet cover with heavy white text, Guy and Richard Polak's simplistic approach being heavily inspired by supermarket packaging of the time according to Diane Stevens. Initial copies of the record were slightly more elaborate internally, with a liner containing a photo collage of bomber planes and a free highwayman's mask! Guy dedicated the LP to one of his heroes, James Dean.

The overall feel of *Brain Capers* was barely controlled chaos but it remains a brilliant and crucial album. Once described as the great lost hard rock LP of all time, the record drew a line in the sand between sixties and seventies music, revealing almost everything called rock, and the subsequent punk movement six years later, to be nothing short of fraudulent. The album charts were being led by John Lennon's *Imagine,* Led Zeppelin's *Four Symbols* and T. Rex's *Electric Warrior* at the end of 1971. *Brain Capers* didn't register with the record buying public at all and although the album failed to chart, again Ian claimed that it actually sold more copies than its predecessor *Wildlife.* The reviews of Mott's latest offering were excellent however, with one headline – 'Mott Near Perfection'. *Brain Capers* was the primer for punk rock and remains a highly influential and neglected classic to this day.

Just before Mott embarked on their UK tour to promote *Brain Capers,* they recorded three tracks from the album at Maida Vale Studio 5 on 25 October. This was their fourth BBC studio session and 'The Journey', 'Darkness, Darkness' and 'The Moon Upstairs' were broadcast on Radio One's *Sounds of the Seventies* on 4 November to showcase the new LP. The live studio version of 'The Moon Upstairs' was particularly stunning with an interesting treatment of Hunter's vocal and the offending expletive in the final verse replaced by a humorous cough.

By the time *Brain Capers* had been released, Mott The Hoople had already started an eleven date promotional concert tour of Britain with Paul Rodgers' new band Peace as support. The tour opened in Oxford on 27 October and finished in Wolverhampton on 29 November taking in the London Rainbow, Birmingham, Glasgow and Newcastle *en route.* Island produced an attractive fold-out programme for the shows featuring notes from Guy Stevens.

During these concerts Hunter considered inviting Rodgers into Mott as a fully-fledged group member, Ian concentrating on songwriting and leaving Paul to take over as lead vocalist for his material. He also thought of expanding the group with a brass section and female singers for live work, much to Watts' chagrin and disbelief. 'I just could not believe it. Ian wanted Paul to be the singer and Hunter would just play piano and do some backing vocals. I remember looking at Ian and thinking, "What's the matter with you? Are you totally fucking mad or something?" I shouted at him, "But *you* are the singer in Mott The Hoople. *You* are the singer!" And Ian replied, "But he's the best singer in the world." And we had to assure him it didn't matter. These were the sort of ridiculous arguments we had in Mott. I never went for the "best in the world mentality". That's why Ian liked Leon Russell, because he was supposed to be the best rock keyboard player in the world. Like Hunter's later solo album, *All American Alien Boy,* where he got Jaco Pastorius in on bass because he was the greatest bass player in the world. Well the record didn't sell millions and it wasn't that great to me. All these people who are "great musicians". In the end, it doesn't really matter. The Beatles weren't the greatest individual musicians in the world, but together they were. It was the sum of the five people in Mott The Hoople that counted.'

None of this proposition to expand Mott materialised, but Rodgers and Ralphs did get to know each other musically, and the seeds were sown for their future collaboration.

In December, Mott played a series of Continental gigs with Grand Funk Railroad and once again, road-life in Europe was dreadful for Richie Anderson and the crew. 'We were doing this tour, and were down in Munich before we had to drive north to Berlin,' says Richie. 'We crossed over into East Germany at a place called Hoff, and that was pretty horrific. They took away our passports and did nothing, leaving us freezing in the cold, but eventually we sorted the documentation and moved along. The images were horrible. It was dark and there was lots of searchlights, snow, minefields, machine guns, razor wire, concrete walls, dogs and soldiers in grey coats. Then, when we had to cross out of East Germany into West Berlin, they opened up the truck and equipment boxes, anything they could, looking for defectors. The real killer was, we got stopped behind a lorry loaded with Christmas trees and the soldiers were on top of the truck, thrusting spikes into the trees and continually checking for blood as they pulled them out. It was frightening. So much for the Democratic People's Republic. It made me think of Red Robbo and the Communists in England at the time, and how they might have squared with what we were seeing.'

Mott's fourth and final BBC *In Concert* was recorded on 30 December at London's Paris Theatre, released several years later as two bootlegs – *Sticky Fingers* and *Hoopling Furiously (Guy Stevens' Testament of Rock and Roll Part 1)* – and officially by Windsong as *Original Mixed-Up Kids* in 1996. The live set comprised 'The Moon Upstairs', 'Angel of Eighth Avenue', 'Your Own Backyard', 'Walking with a Mountain', 'Whiskey Women', 'The Journey', 'Thunderbuck Ram', 'Death May Be Your Santa Claus', 'Rock and Roll Queen', 'Midnight Lady' and 'Keep A-Knockin''.

In the opening weeks of 1972, Mott continued to tour heavily but they squeezed in a session at Basing Street Studios on 24 January, with Muff Winwood as Executive Producer, taping three new tracks scheduled for March release to coincide with yet more British live dates. The single, 'Moving On', was shelved, and the recordings, including 'Black Scorpio' and 'Ride on the Sun' remained unissued until Island released a rarities compilation and promotional album in 1980.

Ralphs' 'Moving On', which catalogued the strains of touring and his fear of flying, was offered as a single for new Island stablemates Hackensack. 'I'd had "Moving On" for ages,' says Ralphs. 'It was about being on the road and was written in open tuning which is a good way to write rock songs, because it restricts you to basics and you can't go wandering off onto posh chords. The hardest song to write is a rock song that sounds simple, but different.'

Following several February concerts Mott announced a major UK tour with a difference – 'Mott The Hoople's Rock and Roll Circus' – planned for April and comprising 16 dates in 18 days. The package featured Hackensack, knife thrower Barry Winship billed as La Vivas, and as special guest star, stand-up music hall comedian, Max Wall. Juggler Frank Paulo departed during rehearsals and a performing dog troupe left after two gigs, the conditions on the tour bus becoming unbearable for the travellers and the animals.

However, before the UK tour took place, Mott had to play two tortuous live dates in Switzerland. At one concert Watts recalls that Dale got drunk, could hardly play and stepped forward on stage wanting to do all the lead vocals! 'We were in a posh restaurant after the gig and Buff was still out of his brains. He tried to leave but the taxi driver refused to take him and some fans outside went mad at the driver, which resulted in a big punch up, while Buff was shuffled into the restaurant, where he passed out, semi-naked, in the toilets.'

Group spirits were low and, on 25 March, crisis ensued on a cramped stage in Berne, where Mott were astounded to find themselves playing in a disused gas holder that had been craftily converted into a youth club. Time was they would never ever have played such a concert; they would certainly not have taken a boat and trains through Dover, Calais and Ostend to perform two meagre Swiss gigs and return via Basle, Calais and Folkestone to get home to London. A minor fight ensued on stage between Hunter and Griffin and Mott The Hoople decided to break up. The band had become increasingly frustrated with Island Records as they applied relentless pressure to perform more and more live dates, with less and less technical support.

'The Island Agency kept asking us to play more gigs with less lights, less PA, less crew and cheaper hotels,' says Dale. 'We told them to fuck off. How apt that we were in a gas holder when some ill-timed drum beat, wrong chord or missed cue would become the catalyst for an explosion of furious insult trading and punch throwing. There was this terrible, general frustration, because we were rudderless under Island, rather than any personal abuse between the band members.'

The Swiss dates were absolutely pointless according to Richie Anderson. 'I don't know why we even bothered to go to Europe to be honest. Nobody liked us there. It just seemed like a waste of time and they always seemed to be two years behind the times. In Britain, it was brilliant most nights. Mott were a cult band and the students and kids just couldn't get enough of them. Because so many of the British gigs were so good, you tended to notice how bad Europe was when you went there. The only good thing about Europe was the nights out, but the shows were crap! It was also a pain to travel around because of all the customs and check points, long before border controls were taken away. You would have daft situations, like going from Germany to Belgium in the middle of the night, and you'd exit Germany at midnight but they wouldn't start letting you into Belgium until six next morning. So you'd sit in the truck for five hours in the middle of winter, and it did give you time to think how much you don't like Belgians!'

The two concerts at Zurich Volkshaus and Berne Youth Centre, were full of idiocy and disenchantment for the group and Hunter recalls how their self worth was at an extremely low ebb. 'We thought, "If this is fame, forget it!" We genuinely felt that nobody wanted us.'

'We were just fed up with being unsuccessful,' admits Ralphs. 'And as bands always do, they point fingers at each other, but it wasn't really anything to do with us, we just couldn't get a hit for love nor money. We were always working at a loss and of course the record company thought we were a dead loss and whilst we made a bit of money on gigs it was a low point when we seemed to be getting nowhere. So somebody had the bright idea to split up, which was a relief at the time, but only for about five minutes.'

The absence of any significant record sales was a bugbear for the band, and Watts questions whether their efforts ever covered any of the recording costs. 'A number of things contributed to the split,' confesses Pete. 'We'd being going a long time and nothing had happened. Record sales hadn't gone up. We were doing great on gigs but nothing else was really happening for us. In Switzerland a punch up broke out on stage. I just thought I can't go on like this, it turned ugly, everything we'd had turned horrible. So we came off and I said, "I've had it, I'm going." We went back to the hotel and at breakfast next morning Ian said he was jacking it in as well. We all went to see John Wayne in *The Cowboys* at the local cinema in Berne, then decided to come back together and all got pissed on the train. It was an amazing journey because all the tension had gone. We had a laugh and were joking as to what we were going to do next. Ian was always on about digging holes in the road, that was always his dreaded terror. If anything went wrong he used to say, "I'll be digging holes in the road next week." None of us knew what we were going to do but we didn't care.'

Dale however, recalls being relatively laid back about any potential split at the time. 'The band members had been butting heads, but without really butting. I thought it was a storm in a teacup and we'd be potty to kill off the group at this stage, having made such great efforts to make a name for ourselves.'

Verden Allen also puts a slightly different slant on the Swiss incident and re-calls what actually happened when they went to see Island Records to say they didn't want to continue with the Rock and Roll Circus tour planned for the following month.

'I remember being extremely sad coming back and they were saying it was the end of the band. I think it was because we weren't selling records, unless Ian and Mick were quibbling about something. I personally wasn't at all. We hadn't made it as far as I was concerned. We had gone out to be successful and have a hit and we hadn't had one. We got back and had to have a meeting with Chris Blackwell and went upstairs to his flat in the Island Records building. So we sat down and Chris said, "How is it going boys?" We said, "All right." And he said, "Somebody said you're thinking of packing up." "Yes," we said, "We've had enough." "Well I've got this tour arranged for you. The Rock and Roll Circus." And I think Mick said, "Oh we don't want to do it, we've decided to pack it in." "Oh I see," said Chris. "I've spent two to three thousand pounds on organising this for you. You don't have to do it but I shall tell you now. I'll only tell you once," he said. "If you don't do this tour, I shall personally see to it, that not one of you will ever do anything again, ever, ever, in the music business. That's it." So we said, "Oh well, perhaps we'll do it!"'

'The Rock and Roll Circus tour was not of Chris Blackwell's making,' re-marks Griffin. 'It was Hunter's idea I think, borrowed from The Rolling Stones 1969 film. In fact, Ian was upset in front of Blackwell when forced to do it. I think he had thought he was free at last to pursue his solo career after Zurich and now he was being dragged back into Mott The Hoople again. I couldn't under-stand what all the fuss was about. I could not imagine anything better than being in Mott, ninety per cent of the time anyway. We had great fun together, on stage and off, for most of the time and there is no group, past or present, with which I would rather have been involved.

'We were heavily heavied to honour the Rock and Roll Circus tour dates,' says Dale. 'There was considerable resistance, but behind the scenes exciting developments developed.'

'The Ballad of Mott The Hoople (26th March 1972, Zurich)'

I changed my name in search of fame, to find the midas touch
Oh I wish I'd never wanted then, what I want now twice as much
We crossed the mighty oceans, and we had a few divides
But we never crossed emotion, for we felt too much inside

You know all the tales we tell, you know the band so well
And still I feel, somehow, we let you down
We went off somewhere on the way
And now I see we have to pay
The rock 'n' roll Circus is in town

Buffin lost his child-like dreams, and Mick lost his guitar
And Verden grew a line or two, and Overend's just a rock 'n' roll star
Behind these shades, the visions fade, as I learned a thing or two
But if I had my time again, you all know just what I'd do

Rock 'n' roll's a losers' game, it mesmerises and I can't explain
The reasons, for the sights, and for the sounds
The grease paint still sticks to my face
So what the hell? I can't erase
The rock 'n' roll feeling, from my mind

8
I'm a dude, Dad

'All the Young Dudes' – David Bowie

In 1972, Britain officially joined the European Economic Community, the Watergate scandal broke, and terrorists murdered nine Israeli hostages at the Munich Olympic Games. It was an unprecedented and eventful year in musical terms too, for having witnessed a recent rise in bland, middle of the road pop acts such as The Osmonds, The New Seekers and David Cassidy, the UK singles charts were about to receive a welcome injection of exciting rock artists including Alice Cooper, Roxy Music, David Bowie and, at long last, Mott The Hoople. However, before securing their eagerly awaited chart success, Mott would have to encounter considerable but beneficial upheaval.

Early 1972 found the group exhausted by its live success and frustrated by its failure to make a commercially successful recording. Due to their lack of record sales and the high cost of touring, Mott was falling heavily into debt. They perceived that they were misunderstood and unwanted by Island Records and divisions were forming between the group, the label and, inevitably, Guy Stevens. A tripartite divorce was looming. 'We were in debt with Island and we desperately wanted a good producer, but how could you go and say, 'Get us Bill Szymzyck,' when they were losing money on us,' says Ian. 'Island didn't know what to do with us. It wasn't a case of bad management, just non-management.'

Hunter reflects that perhaps Mott were not appropriate for Island Records, suggesting that they didn't even fit in with the other artists signed to the label. 'We looked absurd to the rest of the Island bands. I did especially. I was up against Jess Roden, Mike Harrison, Steve Winwood and Paul Rodgers, the cream of the cream of British singers and me, I was like a cut-price Bob Dylan. I'm sure Traffic's song, "The Low Spark of High-Heeled Boys", was about Mott. I asked Winwood once, at Media Sound Studios in New York, and he smiled and was totally non-committal about it.'

> The percentage you're paying is too high price
> while you're living beyond all your means
> and the man in the suit has just bought a new car
> from the profit he's made on your dreams
> but today news has spread that the man was shot dead
> by a gun that didn't make any noise
> no it wasn't the bullet that laid him to rest
> was the low spark of high-heeled boys

'We always felt like the runts of the litter, the outcast band,' Ralphs concurs. 'Guy liked us, so that was all right, but the other bands were perceived to be more musical and we were a bit of an embarrassment to Island, I think. We were always very nice to people, got on with everybody, never made any money or had any hits and became a bit of a joke. But we were always fun, while all the other groups were very serious.'

'Although we had fun, Island was the wrong label,' says Ian. 'Ralphs was sold on them from the start, so we went with them, but we never even approached anyone else. I remember the day Island died for me was when Chris Blackwell came back from a trip to Nashville, and he said he'd been working with Steve Winwood in the studio, the way it should be done, "9 'til 5". I nearly wept when he suggested we adopt that sort of approach.'

Mott gradually became despondent about their lack of achievement with Island Records and although Ian Hunter may have had mild praise for Alec Leslie and John Glover who ran the Island Agency and arranged tours, he believed the all-encompassing deal Mott The Hoople had signed for agency, management, recording and publishing was unfair, and agreed at a time when they were total-ly inexperienced. Mott were tied to Island Records, Island Music and Island Agency – an arrangement that was possibly unprecedented – but Hunter's aware-ness was changing.

'I'd never been in a cab, I'd never been in a Chinese restaurant and I'd never had a lawyer. The cabs and the Chinese restaurants we could have done without, but the lawyer situation was quickly remedied, although it was too late. I got them back good later on though. Originally on the publishing, Lionel Conway of Island Music had got me in and of course, I had this deal where they gave me 50 per cent of the writer's share and they kept 150 per cent. I always remember a couple of years after that, Lionel said, "It's not right." And me still saying, "What do you mean, it's not right?" "Well, we should be giving you more," he said. And I'm thinking Lionel's a wonderful guy. He's giving me 75 per cent of my money and keeping the other 125 per cent. At that meeting I said, "You know Lionel, I'm paying maintenance now on my first wife and my two kids, Tracey and Steven. I need some kind of guaranteed income. Can you give me twenty quid a week for three years and then I'll sign another three year contract?" And Lionel said, "Oh I'll get back to you on that," which he never did.'

Mott's Island period had been tough – endless concerts, four commercially unsuccessful LPs recorded in two years, three failed singles – but they were one of the country's best live bands. However, Island Records had allowed Mott The Hoople to develop and grow, something that Hunter acknowledges would never happen nowadays, where groups are often ditched after the second album. Watts agrees. 'Even though things tailed off horribly with Island at the end, you have to bear in mind that they kept letting us carry on. Their idea was to develop artists, not just to sign someone for a quick buck, but after four Mott albums they were starting to think, "How much more are we going to plough into this group?" Our career was always very volatile and they could see that, and the fact that Mott really could have broken up at any second, literally. There were always rows and threats of people leaving. We weren't a nice diplomatic band like Traffic!'

Ralphs expresses the view that touring was a financial loss-maker for Mott, but their records made money, a view with which Griffin concurs. 'According to Island Records' figures, all four Mott The Hoople albums were in profit by the time we left the label in 1972,' says Dale.

Watts nonetheless, remains exasperated by the financial side of Mott The Hoople. 'The first album sold 20,000 in America which sounded good, but then I thought, hang on, there's quite a lot of people in America. We didn't make any money from the albums and I wouldn't even think they covered the recording costs, because Guy went to town when it came to recording. There was a lot of time booked in, but half of the time we were eating meals out of the backs of studio clocks rather than recording! Studio time wasn't cheap even in 1969 – it was probably £20 or £30 pounds an hour, and sessions were twelve hours a time, so it mounted up. We ended up in terrible debt to Island, £50,000, and we still owe them thousands of pounds today and probably always will.

'The money side was another reason we left the label. They called us in one day to a meeting and said, "You're going to have to cut back on your lighting and PA systems now, because you owe us too much money." That was the first time they did a turn around. We said we wouldn't do it. We'd always agreed as a group that if we didn't keep going up, we'd split up. There was no way we were going backwards with less PA and lights because all we'd really got was our live following, that was our strength. We couldn't get back on our feet with Island from there on.'

Mott The Hoople were at the end of the line. They would have to honour their remaining tour commitments but decided they would then split from Island and disolve the group. Mott hadn't counted, however, on the intervention of an emerging singer/songwriter by the name of David Bowie, who was soon to take the music world by storm and become a rock phenomenon. He had been secretly watching and admiring the band and had previously offered one of his songs by sending them a demo tape. When Bowie learned of their intention to break up, it would trigger an astounding chain of events.

David Bowie was born David Jones, in Brixton, South London in 1947. Initially a commercial artist and a saxophonist in semi-pro groups around 1963, David was eventually contracted to Pye Records in 1966 and then Decca. He cut several pop and novelty singles but changed his musical approach after the UK arrival of 'flower power' in 1967/68, releasing his album *Space Oddity* in 1969. Encouraged to return to the studio by his new record label Phillips, he had formed a band in 1970 which included guitarist Mick Ronson, who would later play a similarly important part in Ian Hunter's career. Ronson enhanced Bowie's work with crunching guitar and stunning musical arrangements and David enjoyed one of his most fruitful artistic periods. Switching to RCA Records, they went on to record a profusion of chart-topping singles and classic rock albums including *Hunky Dory*, his blueprint for stardom – *The Rise and Fall of Ziggy Stardust and the Spiders from Mars* and *Aladdin Sane*. Eventually splitting from Ronson in 1973, Bowie became a musical chameleon, moving into soul, disco and electronic music, eventually working in other arenas including film, theatre and art. Fascinated by technological frontiers, his creativity currently finds expression through computers and the internet and he has recently led a remunerative move in the financial markets towards issuing junk bonds, whose payments are based on artists' back catalogue recordings.

Bowie remains as unpredictable as ever today and is unquestionably one of rock music's greatest and most influential talents. Of important and crucial note however, is the fact that, back in early 1972, he had just released *Hunky Dory* and was still a relatively unknown and emergent force. He was about to provide Mott with new lifeblood, but he would also gain inspiration and knowledge from them. Never a fan of The Rolling Stones like Hunter, Bowie was to record Jagger/Richard's 'Let's Spend the Night Together' within a few months of his Mott The Hoople liaison.

Before he ever reached 'Starman' status, David had been an admirer of the group. It is said he liked the *Wildlife* album and Verden Allen recalls he particularly enjoyed *Brain Capers,* which had an edge and an air of madness that Bowie loved. 'I never asked David why he took such an interest in us, but I was told by numerous sources that his image of us, was that of Mott The Hoople being the only true punk band ever in England, and that *Brain Capers* had turned him on to this,' remarks Hunter. 'And I'd agree with those sentiments exactly, even though the word is over used. I mean, when I used to read Marc Bolan, saying he was a street punk – don't make me laugh.'

Bowie had previously sent Mott a demo tape of a song called 'Suffragette City', which he later included on his *Ziggy Stardust* album, hoping the group would be prepared to record it. 'We received the tape at Island Studios one day, just after the *Brain Capers* sessions,' says Watts. 'It was a seven and a half inch spool in a box and it said something like, "This may be of use to you. Give me a ring. Love David." I was actually knocked out, because I'd bought *Hunky Dory* and seen him on stage and thought, "Bloody hell, he's brilliant."'

Mott would not attempt 'Suffragette City' as they felt it was not a hit or a Hoople-type song. They didn't even respond to David, but after the nightmare of Switzerland and the Zurich split, Pete returned to his Hampstead home and inadvertently set new wheels in motion. 'David had left his telephone number on the tape, which I kept, and when I got back from our European disaster I thought, well it's all over now, what do I do? I've got to play with somebody. Who would I like to play with? Bowie. There's his number on the tape, phone him up. So I rang and said, "Thanks for the tape of *Suffragette City,* but the group's going to split up, what are you doing these days?" I was hoping he would say he was looking for a bass player. We got talking for an hour and I was telling him about the group and Island, and all the problems we'd had. I don't think Bowie had ever seen us, but he'd got our albums and seemed quite into the band. David said, "You *can't* split up. Look, leave it with me for a while. I've got a great manager, he's the business."'

Bowie was about to play a truly vital role for Mott The Hoople behind the scenes, healing their Zurich split by offering them a classic song, which facilitated one final attempt at recorded success and a change of record label.

'He phoned me back about a couple of hours later and said, "I've got this song, it might be ideal for you," says Pete. 'He had the title, "All the Young Dudes", and said, "I'd like you to hear it and meet my manager." He asked me to listen to the song, saying that if it was any good, just to record that one track.'

Renowned photographer, Mick Rock, was with David Bowie during the genesis of the song that would save Mott. 'I remember cabbing through Hyde Park with David one afternoon in the spring of 1972, on our way to Bowie's management office near Oxford Circus. He was full of that crusading zeal which would be a hallmark of his rush to stardom in the summer of '72. The subject was Mott The Hoople (soon he would expend the same creative and emotional energy on Lou Reed and Iggy Pop).

'Mott were on the brink of extinction, he told me. They were about to be dropped by their record label, and were totally broke. After talking at length with Pete Watts the night before, David had vowed to rescue them. They were fabulous and unique and he would get Tony Defries to take them over, get them a new deal and David would write them a hit song! He was very excited.

' "I started it this morning, the first few bars. You'll be the first to hear it," said David. We were just passing Marble Arch – "All the young dudes, carry the news … , " he sang. It's not often one gets to be present at the birth of an anthem.'

Watts had explained to Bowie that he didn't really know how the rest of the group would feel about staying together and recording a new song, but said he'd come over and see David anyway. 'In fact, he and Angie came over and picked me up in a beaten up old Jag one Sunday afternoon,' says Pete. 'He was nervous to meet me, and I was nervous to meet him. I'd first seen David at a gig at Imperial College and thought he was great. I'd bought *The Man who Sold the World* and I loved that album; I used to play it a lot with Steve Hyams. But I think when I mentioned him to the others, they didn't even know who he was. Bowie was obviously a fan of the group when I met him and knew everything we'd ever done. He had clearly analysed all the albums and was so keen on Mott. He seemed frightened and Angie said he'd spent three hours getting ready to meet me. He was more frightened when he eventually came to meet the rest of the band. It was strange really. He had his ear to the ground musically, and he'd heard we were sensational live and liked the wildness of it all. He raved about *Brain Capers*.

'When David and Angie picked me up, we went to Park Lane and looked round an art exhibition, then Tony Defries turned up and we went to The Inn On The Park and had tea. Defries seemed quite uninterested to start with. He was asking me a few questions and seemed very off-ish, but David was goading him on a bit and it got more and more positive. Then we went back to Tony's place in Chelsea in the evening and David got a 12-string acoustic and played me "All the Young Dudes". You could tell it was a great song; he'd got the chorus words but he hadn't got some of the verse words, but I thought, "Christ, what a song," straightaway.

'Then Defries started to change, saying things like, "Yeah, what we're going to do is get you off Island and get you away from them, they're no good. I know a good contact at Columbia, we'll get you on there." He was talking like it was all going to happen, so during the course of the afternoon it had all turned around. They dropped me off back at the flat in the evening and I was all excited by then, and yet it was me who had been the first to leave the group in Switzerland. I phoned the rest of the lads next day and told them what had happened and said, "Look, if you're willing to give it a go, I will too," and they all said they would.

When the rest of Mott heard the song, they thought it was amazing. Then it transpired we had to fulfil the tour obligation with Island, so we hadn't actually broken up and David came to one of the gigs. Everybody met him and Defries, and the group was fired up, it was all back on again.'

For a second time, perhaps by chance more than anything, Watts had proved to be a vital connection in the history of the group, the first being the 1969 Guy Stevens audition with Free, and now the liaison with David Bowie, both of which were possibly the two most important events in the development of Mott The Hoople.

'David's arrival on the scene really gave us a new lease of life,' admits Pete. 'The Rock and Roll Circus tour went amazingly well, which was a bonus. It was great with Max Wall, the nicest tour we did.'

Mott The Hoople's Rock and Roll Circus, an idea of Hunter's 'lifted' from The Rolling Stones' aborted film project, saw the group playing 15 UK concert dates, supported by Island stablemates Hackensack, circus knife throwers and comedian, Max Wall. Max was one of Britain's greatest funnymen in true music hall tradition. He made his stage debut in 1925 and switched from his trademark eccentric dancing to comedy, becoming a star of stage, radio and television. Ian and the group invited Max to guest on tour and it was a new experience in entertainment for him. Playing in arenas was very different from the usual music hall atmosphere, and it was a challenge. In the smaller towns and universities he was accepted, but in Liverpool, Glasgow and Edinburgh the greeting was more hostile, and Ian often had to introduce Max and intervene to keep the crowds in order. Max once said he 'died like a louse in a tramp's beard' at the bigger venues, but he won most of them round in the end and the touring party became one big happy family. Mott loved him and Max marvelled at the way the group worked, and the behind-the-scenes efforts of people like the road crew, which was completely foreign to him. However, financial remuneration remained low for Mott; Max Wall was paid £75 a night, and each band member £50 per week!

The tour was not without incident and Ray Major, guitarist with support group Hackensack, recalls some of the circus mayhem. 'We all got included in the knife act at some point. I was thrown on stage in Glasgow and Hunter was caught one night, standing against the board with his guitar. This guy did the knife act with his wife, and he nicked her toe at one gig and it was bleeding. But they had to come back later and do this Apache dance as a prostitute and a sailor, so she had to hobble round trying to do the act. When it came to the part where she was supposed to hit him with this metal tray, she really whacked him on the head and dented the tray, and we had a sailor literally staggering around cursing like hell.'

Mott's live set contained three new songs, 'One of the Boys', 'The Ballad of Mott' and 'Till I'm Gone', plus 'Darkness, Darkness', 'Angeline', 'Thunderbuck Ram', 'Mr Bugle Player' (a variation on Dylan's 'Mr Tambourine Man'), 'Honky Tonk Women', 'The Moon Upstairs', 'Rock and Roll Queen' and 'Midnight Lady.'

Bowie now started courting Mott, bombarding them with flowers during their Rock and Roll Circus tour and offering to manage the band and negotiate a new record deal with CBS Records. He also went to see the group perform at Guildford Civic Hall, where they fixed a secret recording date. Hunter remembers Bowie was extremely nervous at the Guildford gathering. 'David was trembling. He had this big thing and he thought we were very heavy. We were really just ordinary people who would get legitimately upset about things.

'When David came to us with "All the Young Dudes" we were still with Island, and suddenly we're sitting on this song and know it's a big hit,' explains Ian. 'Then Lionel Conway took me and Trudi out to a French restaurant in Ladbroke Grove and offered me quarter of a million dollars to re-sign with Island Records. He could have had it weeks before for three thousand pounds. I said, "Lionel it's not enough," and it wasn't.'

Stan Tippins was not a great lover of Blackwell's label in any case. 'I don't have fond memories of Island and didn't feel welcome there. They were much more into groups like Free and King Crimson and they definitely had resentment for Guy Stevens. Traffic and Free were their babies, and I think they really lacked ambition for Mott The Hoople, who came in a little later. Island seemed a bit small time to me, and it felt great when the band went to CBS.'

Mott were now able to link up with a new record label and Bowie's manager would be the catalyst. Anthony Defries was born in Rickmansworth, Hertfordshire of Dutch ancestry. His parents ran an antique and restoration business in Shepherd's Bush and Tony was their fourth child. He joined Martin Boston Solicitors in London, at a time when few companies specialised in music business law. Defries assisted Mickie Most in a dispute concerning the Animals and dealt with New York accountant and future Beatles manager Allen Klein, then left Martin Boston and became a freelance 'legal adviser' working part-time for Godfrey Davis and Batt. Defries also went into artist management with Laurie Myers at Gem Toby Management, whose sphere of activities included accountancy, legal services, music publishing and, subsequently, GTO Records. Gem Toby represented Mike Leander, Gary Glitter and The New Seekers. Myers eventually assigned Gem's contracts to Mainman Ltd, a new organisation formed by Defries after he acquired a trading company, Minnie Bell Limited, in 1971. The term 'Mainman' was street slang for a drug dealer.

Hugh Attwooll, former drummer with Bill Wyman's sixties proteges The End, was drafted in as a complete novice to be the agent for Bowie, Mott The Hoople and sundry others at Mainman in 1972. 'I was a musician and knew nothing about being an agent, but that was how Defries liked it. He didn't trust experts and never hired them. Tony was a highly intelligent, charming man. People took him to be a trained lawyer but he wasn't, so Tony in turn liked people to be untrained individuals who would do something from a different and original perspective or, more cynically, people he could mould to his way of thinking. So he was thrilled to hire a complete idiot like me to be the agent. Why pay 10 per cent to an outside agency you don't trust anyway?

'Defries thought that he could do things better than other people and he was right, he could. It was almost a game. He wanted to see if he could manipulate this strange world of pop music, where he saw there were a lot of incompetents doing a bad job. He had an insight well ahead of his time and he thought, "Most of these people aren't very bright. I am bright. I'm not frightened of them. I can do this much better than anybody else," and simultaneously he found the artist with whom he could it, which was old D.B.'

Attwooll believes Defries' genius was that he had unbelievable insight and faith in David Bowie and felt he could make him a star where others had failed, using unconventional means to achieve this. 'He took Bowie away from previous labels and managers and stirred up a lot of trouble in the process, because he operated in a way that hadn't been seen from an artist's manager in the UK before. It was no secret that Tony, semi-humorously, modelled himself on Colonel Tom Parker, whom he admired for the way he had single mindedly made Elvis's career. By hiring me and lots of others who really knew nothing, Defries could also totally control the way things were done.

'The reason people perceived Defries to be the villain of the piece is because Bowie arrived at a point in the mid-seventies where he was fantastically famous, but didn't have very much money, because Tony had ploughed all previous earnings from Bowie into running the organisation that was Mainman. The whole of Bowie's rise to fame was achieved, initially, on a shoestring, but Defries told David he would make him a star and he did. I don't think David would have made it as far as he did without Tony. Defries accomplished things because he did them in a way that people weren't used to. He didn't respect the hierarchy. As a manager, he would never phone up the Product Manager or the Head of Promotions at the record company and complain about something. He only ever spoke to the Chairman, the Managing Director or the President of the US company, so that when things were referred, you already had power over the next man down, because the next man down knows you've already spoken to the boss. He started the whole "no photos, no interviews" syndrome and made people scream out for anything to do with Bowie. David only ever went into RCA Records in London once in the eighteen months I was with Defries. Tony created this mystique, was way ahead of his time and the manner in which he operated made it possible for all other managers who came after.'

Defries was persuaded by Bowie that he should take on Mott The Hoople, which Attwooll feels probably wasn't a good idea from either party's point of view. 'Tony wouldn't have understood remotely what Mott were about musically. He would understand there was something there, although he wouldn't know what it was, but it was probably convenient to add to the roster at the time, which included Dana Gillespie and dabblings with Iggy And The Stooges and Lou Reed. In the light of Defries wanting to create this huge empire fine, but as right as Defries was for Bowie, he was completely wrong for Mott The Hoople. He was the wrong manager for Mott and Mott were the wrong band for him, because they didn't conform to something which could be moulded into something else. Mott were Mott and the very individual thing they were.

'Unfortunately for Mott The Hoople, being managed by Defries didn't get them very far, because he didn't have any grand plan or grand design for the band or, if he did, it didn't suit Mott. There was a hit record and there was me or Stan Tippins in the office, booking gigs, and really the hit record didn't do very much for the concerts. I'd tell Stan there was a gig at The Dreamland in Margate and

Stan would tell me they'd played it before and didn't want to play it ever again, but, it was money. Mott was an amusing thing to have along with Bowie, but what wasn't so amusing was when they had to be paid. When Defries went to New York to set up an office, I was left in Fulham, part tea boy, part booker, part Chief European Executive, running the London office, when there was essentially no money to pay this huge entourage. I'd be calling Defries a great deal and he would magic up money to fund the cause. The cause was make Bowie a star and world domination. When he first took David to America, he took an unprecedented entourage and put them in The Plaza Hotel in New York, to make the record company and the press and the public think Bowie was twenty-eight times bigger than he really was in Britain. He convinced people. The con worked and it was brilliant.'

Defries oozed confidence and aimed to surround his artists with the apparatus and expense of major stars, regardless of financial capability. Bowie confessed that Defries believed if he simply told the world David was a superstar, and treated him accordingly, stardom would happen. Tony had successfully convinced RCA Records in America that he could replace their king of rock 'n' roll, Elvis Presley, with a new queen of rock, Bowie. Encouraged by David, he adopted a similar managerial approach with Mott The Hoople and CBS Records.

Verden Allen recalls considerable reluctance to handle Mott. 'Defries actually didn't want to take us on. David liked the band and didn't want to see Mott finish. He obviously had "All the Young Dudes" in his mind and could imagine us doing it and he convinced Defries that we were a good proposition. So Tony went to CBS, who had turned Bowie down before he went to RCA, and he said, "Look, we've got Mott The Hoople now and they're going to be big. We're going to make Mott The Hoople. You made a mistake with Bowie, do you want to make the same mistake again with Mott The Hoople?" Defries used his business sense with CBS and I'm glad he did, because I don't know what would have happened otherwise.'

Columbia Broadcasting Systems had begun business in 1965 and were a major international operation, but their subsidiary, CBS Records, was generally regarded as a label who put more of an emphasis on MOR and AOR artists, having signed Simon and Garfunkel, Barbra Streisand and Bob Dylan.

'By this time, Guy Stevens was crazy,' says Hunter. 'We were still paying him to keep out of the way. So Bowie persuaded Defries to manage the band. David falls in love with ideas and he just had to have us. I think David was interested in Mott because he wanted to be a little more human. At a Bowie gig you tended to gravitate towards Mick Ronson. Bowie wasn't the kind of guy you rocked with. I think he was also looking for balls, because his rock songs weren't very good.'

Dale also believes that Tony was only really sold on Bowie, and that Mott and Iggy Pop became Defries caprices. Hunter says he was also slightly wary of the new situation with the result that Mott The Hoople never signed any management agreement with Mainman, even though Defries circulated contracts amongst the group members. 'I immediately collected them and took them home and put them under the piano stool,' admitted Hunter. 'Now and again he'd say, "Where's the contracts?" and I'd say that somebody forgot.'

'Defries was the first full-on "travelling with the artists" type of manager,' says Ralphs. 'He was a bit of a blur with Mott because he was very, very much into Bowie and I really didn't get to know him to be truthful. He was a bit too show-biz for me!'

Defries started to negotiate severance with Island Records and secured an advance of $50,000 from CBS, whilst Mott The Hoople secretly commenced work on their new single with Bowie at Olympic Studios on 14 May. Hunter explains; 'We got off Island for virtually nothing. By this time Island figured, "They're never going to do anything." But we already had "Dudes" in the can. We'd been down to Olympic on the quiet with David and Blackwell didn't even know. We did "All the Young Dudes" in a day and a half and on the second night we did "One of the Boys". Bowie loved that and said, "Maybe this is the single". I said, "You've got to be fucking joking." Towards the end of the second day we knew "Dudes" would be the A-side.'

Having taped both tracks secretly, with Bowie and engineer Ted Sharp, but still legally contracted to Island Records, Mott started to record for CBS through GEM, who licensed the recordings to Columbia USA as Mainman Productions. With the single completed, Bowie took the band into Trident Studios at St Annes Court off Wardour Street in Soho and supervised about twenty album sessions, Mott re-vamping 'Black Scorpio' (now called 'Momma's Little Jewel') and 'Ride on the Sun' (re-titled 'Sea Diver'), and recording more recent self-composed material plus, Lou Reed's 'Sweet Jane'. 'David was supposed to have written some more songs on the album but he came down to rehearsals and he liked all the tracks we'd written, so that's how the record turned out like it did,' says Ian 'He heard "Sucker" and said, "Look, I don't see why I should have to write anything, you sound like you're writing great." That was because when David came in there was a resurrgence of energy. I still think "Sucker" could have been a lot heavier, but David heard it that way.'

During Mott's sessions, Lou Reed was in London and was invited to Trident by Bowie to record a guide vocal for 'Sweet Jane', in order that Ian could pick up the phrasing and spirit of the lyric. Bowie described Mott backing Reed as fabulous and praised their material and outlook. He originally thought he would have to contribute a lot of material but believed Mott's new songs were their best ever, saying the band were now riding on a wave of optimism after the general apathy of their previous management and record label. 'Everybody was so excited about them when they first came out, but, because they didn't click immediately, it fell away,' said David. 'When I first saw them, I couldn't believe a band so full of integrity and a really naive exuberance could command such enormous followings and not be talked about.'

People around Mott The Hoople at the time believed that David looked up to Ian and saw himself having the same control over an audience as Hunter al-ways had. Ian stressed that by working with Mott, he felt Bowie also hoped to acquire the live prowess that they possessed, but he remains complimentary of Bowie's studio work. 'David is one of the few people who can walk in and there is magic in the room. He has a very inquisitive mind, he's fast, and you feel that the guy knows more than you do, so you put yourself in his hands. That has never happened before or since with me. But the type of thing that Mott had, that he never had, was humanity. I think he was upset because he never had riots at his concerts!'

When the *All the Young Dudes* album was finished and released, the concensus view of the press and most fans was that the LP would perhaps not have reached such a high standard without Bowie. He had given Mott renewed confidence in themselves and injected fresh enthusiasm into their music, and Ian accepts the sessions, and David's production, were significant learning processes. 'You can't compare it to our other albums, this one is how Mott should have sounded all along,' said Hunter upon release. 'David likes a very perfect record and this one is so much cleaner and clearer, after the muggy sound on previous albums. In the past we just didn't know how to record. I think we could have done this album a year ago if we'd had the right producer.'

Hunter realised Mott had started the climb to commercial success. They knew the standard now, and accepted that they just didn't reach that benchmark. To survive, they would have to reach it with their next album. Although they may have been learning and striving in terms of studio capability, Ian would not be secondary in terms of concert work. Just before the release of their sensational new single, Mott The Hoople were lined up behind Bowie for the 'Friends of the Earth – Save the Whale' concert at London's Royal Festival Hall on 8 July, but Hunter declined to play second fiddle. David was supported by Lou Reed.

CBS released the 'All the Young Dudes' single on 28 July 1972. It entered the UK charts on 12 August, where it stayed for eleven weeks, reaching number three, was an international top ten single and reached the top thirty in America. The group received tremendous reviews – 'Mott have a smash 45' – 'The most brilliant single I've heard in ages' – 'If you want to buy yourself a number one record, get this'. Mott also made a promotional appearance on *Top of the Pops* and produced a video, part-filmed during one of their concerts at Bristol Top Rank, and directed by old friend, Richard Weaver.

On the original session recording of 'Dudes', Hunter had sung the line – 'Wendy's stealing clothes from Marks and Sparks' – and this was included on the album pressings. When the single started to break however, BBC radio decided to ban the song because of the Marks and Spencer reference. Ian was rushed back to Trident studios to overdub an amended lyric – 'Wendy's stealing clothes from unmarked cars' – which was edited into the original mix by Ken Scott, then specially cut and pressed as a radio edition of the single. It wasn't long before BBC Radio One began playing the original version again. The B-side was an edited version of 'One of the Boys', minus special effects that Bowie later included on the re-mixed album cut.

The LP, released on 8 September, opened with Mott's version of Lou Reed's 'Sweet Jane'. Reed had been leader of New York's sixties pioneering band, The Velvet Underground, who were connected to pop artist Andy Warhol, and his writing blatantly explored subject matter which had previously been taboo in music – 'Heroin', 'I'm Waiting For the Man' and 'White Light, White Heat'. Sweet Jane was regarded as one of The Velvet's classic tracks from their 1970 album, *Loaded*, a record which had influenced Bowie's *Hunky Dory* LP. Ian confesses that around the same time as 'Dudes', Bowie played a riff and the band reacted instantly, wanting to know what it was. 'It turned out to be "Sweet Jane". I couldn't understand what the song was about, not being a New York gay. So David stood next to me and I sang line after line exactly how he was telling me. Lou Reed came in to do the demo and I had less idea of what to do than before. Plus, I told him a joke that went wrong, so Lou glared at me. This slob comes in and goes 'eeaugh' all over the microphone. We didn't know if he was kidding or what. Lou and me just did not get on. When I heard the Velvet Underground I thought they stunk as well. "Sweet Jane" wasn't really us.'

Mott The Hoople had no idea that the original Velvet's version was so slow. 'Lou turned white when he heard how fast we had played it,' says Dale. 'We just recorded it the way David strummed it to us on his acoustic guitar.' Watts even thought the song was called 'C. J.', until he saw the title on Mott's own LP cover, three months later!

'Momma's Little Jewel' was a re-recorded version of Hunter/Watts' 'Black Scorpio', Pete writing the guitar riffs to complement Ian's basic song and lyrics. The musical construction was interesting, the song snapping into shape after a languid introduction, and Bowie replacing Mott's guitars with his own sax work. The unusual lyric was inspired by Ian's wife. 'Watts wrote this with me while we were still at Island,' says Hunter. 'We recorded it then but it was too fast. It was one of David's best tracks. He really had got the knack of knowing what to do, just a little thing makes all the difference. Lyrically, it sounds like Trudi. "Momma's little jewel, just left school." Nuns. Catholics. Scorpio. There's probably a bit of her in there.'

'All the Young Dudes' commenced after an abrupt jerk on the master tape and ended with a novel talk section devised by Ian, probably the first time that 'rap' had ever been done on record. The original Bowie guide vocal, backed by Mott, was finally released on 1998's Mott The Hoople *Anthology* and Watts feels strongly that this shows the importance of Hunter's input to the finished version. 'I thought Hunter was brilliant on "All the Young Dudes". If you listen to Bowie's vocal, it shows what a fantastic job Ian did on the final recording. Dave's vocal is fantastically "cosy", like a friendly Uncle, whereas Ian's is "cool". Hunter made that song. His vocal was a killer, especially the rap section at the end. Part of Ian's ad lib was taken from the *Billy Cotton Band Show*, a lunch-time family variety programme on the radio in the fifties and sixties, featuring the old band leader Billy Cotton, with horrible singers. One part of the show had an American voice, meant to be an alien in a spaceship, who flew down and said, "Hey you down there, with the glasses," to Billy Cotton, or Thrilly Bottom as I called him.'

On the fade out, 'I've wanted to do this for years' [have a hit record], and 'How do you feel, sick?', was slanted at Island Records, Blackwell and co. After the lack of success with their former label, Mott were excited to be sitting on a guaranteed hit record. Hunter and the band loved the song but, as Ian explains, he didn't get obsessed with analysing the lyric.

'I never saw anything all that sexual about "Dudes" as a lyric. I know it sounds daft, but to me it was just a great song. I don't ever tire of "Dudes", because great songs are great songs, but Bowie's done it as well, and you can make up your own mind how much he had to do with it. It was one of those sessions where it was entirely mutual. The talk was thought up by me. Just when we were thinking the song was sounding a bit bland, I said, "Let me try this." I'd done this talk section onstage at the Rainbow to a kid who had heckled me, and I just did the rap to try to brighten the song up a bit. Mick Ralphs also contributed the guitar intro to the song.

'After "Dudes", we were considered instant fags. It was comical. A lot of gays followed us around, especially in America. We were scared at first because we all happened to be straight but then we started talking to people and there wasn't anybody pushing you. I met some incredible people. It's like another nation. It's just scary at first because we were small town boys, but once we knew nobody was going to grab us every minute of the day, everything was fine.'

Bowie claims that 'Dudes' shared a similar theme to 'Five Years', from his *Ziggy Stardust* album, where it had been announced the world would end because of a lack of natural resources. Ziggy was in a rock band, but his audience no longer wanted rock and roll because there was no electricity to play it. He told them to collect news and sing it, but in the absence of any news, Ziggy died to create headlines for them.

'When I first heard "All the Young Dudes",' says Dale, 'sung by David Bowie, strumming an acoustic guitar, I heard it as an anthem – and I think that goes for all of Mott The Hoople – but I'm not sure David thought of it that way. This is probably why our approach to it worked so well. It sounded like a great rallying call to all the disaffected and dispossessed youth – worldwide – and with the addition of Ian rapping and ranting, the whole thing coalesced into an instant classic. I do remember when Blue Weaver joined the ranks later on, he played us an ancient, early 1900s, French recording of a melody identical to the melody of "All the Young Dudes".'

'Bowie producing "Dudes" was the best thing that ever happened to us,' opines Ralphs. 'He saved our bacon really. When we met Bowie, I realised he was an artist who used music as a vehicle for his painting. He was very unconventional which I liked, and he looked unconventional which he did for effect, but he was a very intelligent man. I remember when we were trying to get the sound of an anvil on "Sucker" and he said, "Why don't we just get an anvil?" and of course we never thought of that. So I said, "How the hell do we get an anvil in the middle of Soho?" but he said he'd just find one, and sure enough, an hour later, a bloke arrives and says, "Sign here for this anvil, Squire," and there it was!'

The sadistic 'Sucker' was principally a Hunter composition with contributions from Pete and Mick. Watts wrote a heavy guitar riff to the song originally, but Bowie changed it to a 'Volga boatman' style vocal, much to Pete's horror. 'At first I didn't like it, but it was interesting, and it grew on me. Bowie was a strange bloke, very talented, but he could be difficult and a bit moody.'

Ian always stressed this track illustrated the essence of Ralphs' guitar playing. 'If people can't relate to the guitar solo on "Sucker", then there's something wrong. It's funny with guitarists, the emphasis often seems to be on speed, but character is important and I think Mick's guitar playing is very individual.'

Hunter's 'Jerkin' Crocus', a song about a dominant female, closed Side One of the album. Originally titled 'Rock House', it had been written just before Mott went into Trident and for once, Bowie tried to emphasise Ralphs' biting lead guitar and Hunter's rhythm. The final title was adapted by Pete from the name of a wild old tramp in Ross, called Creeping Jesus; on this occasion, Watts was able to corrupt the tramp's nickname to 'Jumping Craparse' and then, 'Jerkin' Crocus!'

'Momma's Little Jewel', 'Sucker' and 'Jerkin' Crocus' saw Mott lurching into new lyrical territory and rather bizarre sexual imagery, as Dale acknowledges. 'It does seem as though Ian was going through a torrid time in the lead up to the album. I think a lot of the lyrics were about fantasies rather than anything else. Perhaps Ian was finding his sexual feet again after his marriage break up – if you can have sexual feet – I don't know, and I don't want to see them, or sniff them. Those songs were a fresh turn for the band to get into that sort of thing, on record anyway, not that they weren't doing it off the record!'

Side Two kicked off with Hunter/Ralphs' 'One of the Boys', completely re-vamped from the original demo taped at Island in April 1971, although many of the band felt the new version was too long. Bowie added a telephone dialling effect to the intro at Trident, plus a central portion where the phone rings, is answered, the track dies away and the music comes out of the telephone receiver.

> Well I borrowed Gypsie's Gibson just to show them
> And now I'm a rock 'n' roll star I don't wanna know them
> If they want Slade they better go out and grow one!
>
> One of the boys, one of the boys
> I don't say much but I make a big noise
> And it's growing

Hunter acknowledged the song was derived from a riff that Ralphs had been working on and the press were later to latch on to the suggestion that it had been 'Can't Get Enough'. Neither Ian or Mick possessed the range to sing it in its original form.

'Ian wrote most of "One of the Boys" and I'm not so sure that it did come from "Can't Get Enough", although it probably has got similar construction,' says Ralphs. 'Ian did have some difficulty with singing some of my songs because his voice was more suited to the material he wrote. That's not detrimental to him, but I was writing songs, and as I was writing them, I was singing them to myself and not thinking about Ian having to sing them. I don't think "Can't Get Enough" really suited Mott anyway, it was a different style and it was more the direction I was going in, and didn't fit the way Mott The Hoople was at the time.'

'"Can't Get Enough" is "One of the Boys",' remarks Dale. 'It's the same bloody riff, same bloody song!'

'Soft Ground' was Verden Allen's second composition for the group and, in this case, Watts rates his contribution highly. 'I thought "Soft Ground" was brilliant and even now, it's the best song on the album for me. It wasn't very Mott-ish, but it was more futuristic than anything else we'd ever done.'

Ian recollects that Verden had wrestled with this piece for months and become totally absorbed by it, until the completed song materialised at rehearsals just before the album sessions. When questioned about the inspiration for this track, Verden admits it was band politics. 'It was funny. It was like a build up. Something was going on then within the band. There was a lot of back talk and the boys weren't open. Things were happening that I knew nothing about.'

> Too many people about
> Telling me what to do with myself
> It's hard to get around
> Walking on soft, ground

Mick Ralphs contributed a superb composition with 'Ready For Love / After Lights', which was essentially one song with two hook lines. Bad Company decided to omit the second hook when they re-recorded this for their debut album in 1974, because the section was actually written by Hunter. 'I couldn't sing like Paul Rodgers,' says Ian. 'It was more difficult for us because of my voice, so I put that second bit in because I thought I could handle it. Ralpher went along with it, but I don't think he liked it.'

This stunning song still pleases Mick immensely. '"Ready For Love" is one of the best songs I've ever written. "After Lights" was the coda, a kind of drifting off into dreamland type thing. I used the echoplex for the effect on the guitar. I like that sort of drifty stuff, it's like an after-sex cigarette really; you've said what you want to say and you're just musing and reflecting I suppose.'

The album closed with the emotional 'Sea Diver', originally written and recorded at Island six months previously as 'Ride on the Sun'. For this version, Bowie brought in his co-producer and lead guitarist Mick Ronson, who arranged and conducted dramatic strings and brass. Ian confirms that the lyrical subject matter was the trauma of songwriting. 'Writing songs is almost a perversion. Most writers can go six months and not get a song. They panic, and then suddenly they start again. That's what this song is about. It's a story of one verse trying to get into the studio, and the other verse in the studio. I remember "Sea Diver" being very intense and it was hard not to cry during that one, for some reason. I think I could see myself, twenty or thirty years ahead, and knowing this would be all I did, and hoping not to be pathetic, not to be one of these guys falling about the stage and fucked up!'

'It was nice to have a hit record,' says Verden, 'but I think Ian felt a bit rejected in a way and disappointed he hadn't come up with what we were looking for. I think he was a bit like a sea diver, heavy and down, and "lost in space", is a reference to Bowie the Starman.'

The album entered the UK charts on 23 September and stayed for four weeks, reaching number 21. The critics acknowledged that it was a much cleaner sounding Mott The Hoople and, predictably, noted a Rolling Stones 'atmosphere' on many tracks. The British album release contained black and white group photos taken by Mick Rock, the back of the US jacket featuring colour live shots of the band members. The original album sleeve concept had comprised a photo of a

young boy brandishing a cardboard cut-out guitar, but the selected front cover
was a rather bland illustration of three finely attired but slightly threatening
'young dudes', much to the group's dismay. 'We didn't like the sleeve for *All the
Young Dudes*,' remarks Dale. 'We put up with it because we were just doing what
we were told. It was very dull and boring, a typical seventies browny sort of
colour. But what do you do? We'd had works of art before and they hadn't sold,
so what did it matter?'

Whilst Mott The Hoople spoke highly of the LP and David Bowie's contribution at the time of release, retrospectively, the group has a different opinion of
his input. Dale feels that Bowie's only real involvement was the backing vocals on
'Dudes', Ralphs writing the guitar intro and Hunter devising the vocal, ad-lib
sections and rap without credit. 'David did nothing in terms of arrangements
and little to Mott's material because of budget constraints. The main Bowie contributions were the addition of effects like the telephone on "One of the Boys",
saxes, acoustic guitar and the anvil on "Sucker".'

Mott were 'banned' from David's mixing of the basic studio tracks and Griffin
believes the finished product suffered, rendering many of the songs 'puny' instead
of powerful. ' "Sucker" sounded phenomenal when we first played it back at
Trident, the heaviest, hardest hitting track Mott had ever done, and just how we
wanted it. When mixed it was weak, led by Bowie's acoustic guitar. Why was
Mick Ralphs' soaring guitar solo at the end of "Sea Diver" all but lost? Why was
everything made to sound so thin and small? At the end of "Jerkin' Crocus" Ian
says, "That's much better". He was referring to the powerful, controlled feel of
the track. That is not apparent in the mixed version. All the power and size have
been removed. It recently emerged, during the mastering of the *Mott The Hoople
Anthology*, that Bowie's penchant at that time required that bass guitar and bass
drum should feature very little in his mixes.'

During initial tape research for Sony's *Anthology* box set, it was originally intended that some of the *All the Young Dudes* album tracks might be 'reinstated'
by Dale Griffin, who had hoped to re-mix 'Sucker' and 'Jerkin' Crocus' to their
original, pre-Bowie, overdub status, removing acoustic guitars and added effects.
Tragically, it was discovered that the multi-track tapes had been 'destroyed in
error', in February 1992, and this exciting plan was thwarted.

At the Trident sesssion in 1972, Mott had also taped Hunter's 'politically
incorrect' 'The First Third' (aka 'It's Alright'), and a demo of Hunter's 'Henry
and the H Bombs', which although never completed, was eventually given commercial release in 1993. Neither of these tracks featured Verden Allen. Ian and
Mick had also wanted to develop a song which was a descendant of the piano instrumental on the outro to Derek and the Dominos' 'Layla', but this was not pursued. Other rehearsed tracks included Ian's Beatles-inspired 'I Don't Dig It',
Verden Allen's 'The Black Staff', 'Beside The B-side' and 'Electric Robot', Mott's
attempt at 'machine music'!

The Everly Brothers' 'So Sad', plus Johnny Kidd and the Pirates' 'Please Don't
Touch' and 'Shakin' All Over', featuring Stan Tippins on lead vocals, were also
taped on 5 July during the 'Dudes' sessions and, at long last, included on Mott's
Anthology CD set. The recordings were made one evening when Bowie didn't

attend Trident Studios after a *Top of the Pops* appearance, much to Hunter's frustration. 'We did these on the night Ian stormed out of the studio when Bowie failed to turn up,' says Dale. 'We wouldn't waste valuable studio time. Bowie had gone home in a huff because he'd been upset at a BBC recording. Ian had gone home in a huff because Bowie had gone home in a huff.'

'Stan liked to sing, so we asked him to sing with us again,' recalls Mick. 'We asked him what he'd like to do and we did some of the numbers that he loved. He sang very well too, but they were done for fun, and for Stan.'

'When Ian left, the boys said, "Why don't you do a couple of songs?"' says Tippins. 'They came up with "So Sad", which I'd never heard of, but they just talked me through it, and I sang it, and that was that. But "Please Don't Touch" and "Shakin' All Over" annoy me. Half the chords are wrong because they didn't really know it. I still do "Please Don't Touch" and "All the Young Dudes" on stage, at sound checks with Simple Minds to test the PA. It seems to amuse a lot of people every day.'

Watts claims that Bowie actually asked Mott if they wanted to make an album with Stan, after hearing him sing. 'Bowie would get ideas and go into something like that for a short while and then that's the last you'd hear of it,' says Tippins. 'He'd be very keen on something for a few seconds and then the enthusiasm would evaporate.'

The record marked a fresh beginning for Mott The Hoople and Griffin suggested to Mott's new manager that he should adopt a new stage name. 'I never liked being called Buffin. It wasn't my idea. It was all down to Watts. Watts, the bane of my life. By 1972, I desperately wanted to dump the name and I thought the new era with CBS and Defries was the time to relaunch myself as somebody who was not Buffin. I wanted something that was dynamic and tough sounding, like a comic book character, so the name I came up with was Johnny Smack, which was quite punky in hindsight. I had no idea that smack was heroin. So I put the idea to Tony Defries thinking he'd go for it, but he didn't, the swine. I had to stay Buffin for many more years after that. No wonder I'm such a bitter and twisted old bastard!

'Having refused my request to be Johnny Smack, Tony decided to place us with a new PR person – Caroline Pfeiffer. As a ploy to get the national press interested in us, she decided to let it be known that I had romanced and swiftly got engaged to another of her clients, an American, who was coming to Britain to promote her new film. The film was *Cabaret* and my fiancée-to-be was Liza Minnelli. Regrettably for me – because this 'job' would have involved me in a lot of high living, being chauffeur driven hither and thither with my intended and attending all the best parties, shows, receptions and high society do's – Liza arrived in London, met up with Peter Sellers, a big romance ensued and my high-life bubble popped as I descended back into the hell that was 17 Stonor Road – the group's flat in West Kensington. I have corresponded with Liza from time to time since then, but, despite my pleading, she won't 'have me back', at any price!'

The album completed, a revitalised Mott The Hoople undertook an extensive UK tour from September to October to promote the record. They were supported by Home, who featured Laurie Wisefield, later of Wishbone Ash, on lead guitar. Mott were well received during their tour although it was not the whirlwind they had anticipated and their dates at The London Rainbow, the climax of the schedule, were disappointing. Mott The Hoople never played this venue again. Dale recalls that the group still tried to break new ground and attempted to introduce some theatrics to their Rainbow concerts.

'It was one of those stupid ideas. What we wanted was a bit of theatre and the idea of the show was "Past, Present and Future". Hunter used to back Billy Fury and had been around him in the sixties. We were going to try and get Fury, Adam Faith and John Leyton – all major sixties British pop stars – to do a couple of numbers each, then Mott were going to play, and then we would have a final number by a young group. Richard Weaver had devised a way whereby Mott could 'disappear' and be replaced by a different set of people who would be playing the same number, but they'd be young kids. So you would have the past, which would be the pop stars from the sixties, then you'd have Mott The Hoople who were the contemporary, then you'd have the future of rock. The future of rock was going to be, amongst others, Mick Jones of The Clash, and they would have been playing punk music. That's how we had it set up, except Billy Fury was ill and wasn't available and Adam Faith wouldn't hear of it, so we didn't bother John Leyton. Since we couldn't get the past, we didn't bother to do the future either. The whole idea really was that the future would have been like punk was going to be.

'That plan having fallen through we thought, "What the bloody hell are we going to do? It's just going to be another stage show". So Richard Weaver or Pete Watts said, "Why don't we have a bit of theatre where somebody runs amok on stage and then he's chased off stage?" Internally, the Rainbow was almost like a Spanish Castle, with a very special interior and there's a window you can get to above the stage, with an open space out into the top of the hall. So we decided to have a fight up in that window, and the person who was chased up there would be thrown out of the window, and this would cause a sensation in the audience. We had one of the road crew dressed like a scruffy old tramp, and then a dummy was dressed exactly the same and the roadie was chased upstairs. Of course it all went wrong, it wasn't lit properly and at some point the dummy was thrown and landed in the audience and nobody took much notice really, a total farce.'

In retrospect, the band considered that the 'All the Young Dudes' tour had been relatively unsuccessful, as it was evident that a lot of their traditional fan base, who felt Mott were an album group, had been lost, whilst the gains were low because others mistakenly considered the new single to be a first record. It was to be a temporary aberration, as their follow up records were to generate substantial new support, but the group did find it worrying at the time. ' "All the Young Dudes" didn't do us any good in the way of live gigs and, of course, there was that nagging thing that we hadn't written it ourselves,' says Ian. 'Having said that, I was really brought down when David decided not to release his version of "All the Young Dudes" on *Aladdin Sane* – *Aladdin's Vein* it was called at the time – because then people would have seen just how much of a

Mott The Hoople song it really was. He wrote it and produced it, but that was our song, for our audience!'

Watts feels Defries was very effective for Mott at this time and recalls how he managed to significantly increase the live earning potential of the group. After performing at The Oval cricket ground in South London, the band had previously agreed they would never play any festivals again. 'Tony Defries knew that, but phoned one day to say we'd been offered £3,000 to play another festival. We said, "no thanks", but he came back again and it was suddenly £5,000! We still turned it down though.'

In October 1972, Island Records attempted to cash in on Mott's new found success with CBS, by releasing an album of early tracks compiled by Muff Winwood. Originally titled *Mott's Greatest Misses,* but issued as *Rock and Roll Queen,* it contained examples of the band's more aggressive, up-tempo songs and avoided their softer side. Amazingly 'No Wheels to Ride', 'Waterlow', 'Angel of Eighth Avenue' and 'I Can Feel' were omitted, but the disc marked the first issue of 'Midnight Lady' on album. The cover design by Philip Castle was interesting, but with no rare or previously unreleased material or sleeve notes, the *Rock and Roll Queen* compilation was a somewhat rushed and thoughtless affair.

Ian was also unduly scathing of Mott's earlier work at the time it was released. 'I'm not keen on the idea of these tracks coming out. They were done a long time ago. I don't think we were good enough at the time. Even if Island/Atlantic had been behind us then, it probably wouldn't have made any difference because we just weren't ready as a band. It embarrasses me, the songs don't. It's the way they were done – the mixing. "Thunderbuck Ram" is characterised by its terrible, awful, disgusting mix – it's the worst of them all. I know it isn't good, but some of it could have been so good. It infuriates me when I hear *Brain Capers* for example. I can hear it a million times better. It was a mess but it was how we were feeling. We thought the whole damn world was against us and it was our way of spitting and saying, "the hell with you". We thought we were going out, so we figured we'd go down blasting.'

'Island never treated us with much respect,' says Watts. 'You always got the feeling that all the staff at Island were into "proper groups" like Traffic, people who had jazz inclinations, whereas bands like Mott The Hoople were just sort of, "We can't see what anyone sees in them, but they're on Island, so we've got to talk to them." I remember one of the greatest feelings I ever had was when "All the Young Dudes" was a hit, and I went to the Greyhound in Fulham Palace Road one night to see a group. Johnny Glover and Alec Leslie were there and I went to the bar dressed in a leather suit. I had money and we had a hit. Now they'd always said, "Oh, you'll never get anywhere," but now Alec was saying to me, "Well done mate, you've done well, I knew you'd do it." And I thought, "No you fuckin' didn't." They never had any faith in us at all but I said, "Yeah, we enjoyed it at Island, but it's all over now."'

Mott spent a day in the studio on 18 October before their next US concert tour to record demos of three new songs for CBS; an early, medium-paced version of Ian's 'Honaloochie Boogie', which had a significanty different lyric from the eventual single, a Hunter/Allen composition, 'Hymn for the Dudes', which they had been performing on stage for some six months, and the auto-biographical 'Nightmare', written by Verden, which illustrated his increasing paranoia about the band with the lines, 'take good care what you say; if you don't they'll call you insane.'

Watts remembers being miserable during the latter recording, and the demo sessions, at CBS's new studios in Whitfield Street, were an episode that Dale Griffin would also rather forget. 'A nightmare indeed. I've never heard a sound like it at a professional studio. We sounded like we were imbedded in thick mud at the end of a long, damp concrete sewer pipe! It was a hellish day. We tried "Nightmare" early on in the session and the backtrack was much better – we lost the will to live by the time we did the second take later on. Poor old Phall – just his luck.' Allen had also written 'For Each Other' around this time, but it was not attempted by the group.

Next on the new Mainman agenda, was a five week American tour to promote *All the Young Dudes,* originally scheduled to commence on 22 October in Atlanta, but put back to 24 November starting in Hollywood and running through to 22 December in Memphis. During these US concerts, Ian kept a daily tour diary which he eventually published in 1974, but that aside, the sojourn was often frustrating for the group as Griffin recalls. 'We'd been to America twice before, by the time we went under the aegis of Columbia Records in New York and the Mainman organisation, or as far as that tour went the Mainman disorganisation. We were a bit distressed because a lot of the gigs were not what they should have been, several concerts got pulled hours before we were due to play them and we found ourselves flying from city to city, sometimes without playing in a particular venue, which was very frustrating. Generally, it was rather low key and disappointing. It was something of a bad news tour and the trip where a promoter pulled a gun on Ian because he rightly made certain demands backstage.'

At the Tower Theatre, Philadelphia on 29 November, Mott was introduced and accompanied on two encores by David Bowie, in a show which was broadcast by local radio and subsequently bootlegged as *Mott The Hoople Live with David Bowie.* The concert repertoire was now focused almost entirely on Mott's new album, and included 'Jerkin' Crocus', 'Sucker', 'Hymn for the Dudes', 'Ready for Love', 'Sweet Jane', 'Sea Diver', 'Angeline', 'One of the Boys', 'Midnight Lady', 'All the Young Dudes' and 'Honky Tonk Women'. Mott soundchecked on the tour with a new Hunter/Ralphs blues composition, 'I Can't Get No Breakfast in Texas!'

Watts was intrigued at the manner in which Mott The Hoople's association with Bowie was swiftly and grossly misconstrued in the US, 'gay hangers-on' suddenly appearing in abundance. 'As soon as certain Americans knew we'd had something to do with David, they thought we were gay. We had people following us round, like The Petit Bon Bons, a group of guys from L.A., who realised very quickly that they were on to a loser. At one gig in West Palm Beach, Florida the hall had signs which said, 'Those costumed cuties – Mott The Hoople', and we just thought, "Oh Christ!" The link with Bowie also got us banned on some radio stations who wouldn't have anything to do with "gay music". I had blokes crying outside my bedroom door. "I'm in love with you Overend, let me in. I've loved you for two years." I had to leave the girl I was with and open the door, and pat some guy on the shoulder and say, "Sorry mate, there's no chance, ever!" Pathetic, really.

'We had girls too of course, like The Hot Motts, although I had little to do with them. I also had a bloke in Boston who took a shine to me and insisted on taking me to see a cheap Les Paul in a pawn shop, but of course there was no such guitar. The bloke became a nuisance. The night of the gig, Stan came for me and took me down to the lobby and the guy was sitting there. He leapt up saying, "Oh, Overend," and Tippins pushed him back into the chair by his throat and said, "Not you. You fucking stay there!" which had the desired effect. Hunter had it too with a guy called Wayne, a photographer in New York. We weren't nice to him and he got pissed off in the end and went after Badfinger. There were people who could be a pain in the neck.'

The band were glad to reach the end of the tour, not least because it was becoming more and more apparent that Mick Ralphs was having great difficulty with getting on an aeroplane and making flights. To get to their final gig in Memphis, Mott had to fly down the east coast of America on a commuter plane, landing every fifteen minutes to deposit and collect passengers, much to Ralphs' increasing distress. At one location he refused to continue and decided to disembark and travel the rest of the way by road, taking Verden Allen for company.

'Watts, Hunter and I continued with the flight to Memphis and it was chaos when we arrived,' recalls Dale. 'Verden had charged us with looking after his guitar, but the airline lost it, and because the promoter insisted on a police escort, we were hustled into town very quickly, minus Ralphs, Allen and Allen's guitar. In Memphis, we discovered the road crew, Mick and Verden had all disappeared, and even with Joe Walsh as support act, ticket sales were very grim. The missing entourage arrived at the last minute but then Ralphs' hotel room was robbed. Suddenly, we got a telephone call from Stan at the hall, to say ticket sales were rising rapidly. When we got to the auditorium, the place was full and there was a great electric atmosphere so we decided to do a first, and entered the arena from the rear, walking through the crowd to the stage. The place went mad and the gig was a riot. After all the craziness of trying to get there, and all the gloom that had settled upon us, it was an incredible triumph wrenched from the jaws of disaster. Put together properly it would have made a great film, but Hunter immortalised it in song instead.'

Mott delivered a stunning show at Ellis Auditorium and one of their guitar heroes, Joe Walsh, returned to jam with the band on stage. After the concert Walsh even joined Hunter and Allen in an attempted 'assault' on Elvis Presley's Gracelands mansion. 'Me and Joe got very drunk and we just felt we wanted to do something funny,' explained Ian. 'It was no different from anybody on a Saturday night, trying to get in somewhere just for the hell of it. I was in Elvis' house and, all of a sudden, I sobered up and thought, "Christ, this is trespassing." They knew we weren't breaking and entering, or villains, because Dobermans were barking but they didn't let the dogs go. I was inside and I saw Alberta, and she just told me to get back out in a nice way. It was just because

we were in Memphis and it was something to do. My heroes were always Little
Richard, Jerry Lee Lewis, and Dylan. But it was there, it was Elvis.'

Verden also recalls the Gracelands incident. 'I remember the front gates being
opened and I saw Ian going one way, and I went the other way. I got to the front
door and a Land Rover picked me up because they'd seen me on the cameras.
They took me down to the gate and I thought, "God, they could have shot me."
Then Ian came and got in the car and said, "Here you are," and put a load of
leaves in my hand and said, "We've got a memory, me and you were there." They
gave us a card, "Merry Christmas from The Colonel" so I wrote on it and posted it, because we were coming home the next day. When I got home, I'm in a
pub the next night in Hereford, and I said to this friend, "Incredible last night,
I nearly got shot at Elvis Presley's house," and they thought I was round the
bend.'

The entire episode, pre- and post-concert, was to inspire one of Hunter's
finest songs, which he dedicated to two of Mainman's entourage who helped the
band on the road; 'Leee Childers, Tony Zanetta and Memphis Tennessee,
December 22nd 1972'.

> Forgot my six string razor – and hit the sky
> Half way to Memphis 'fore I realized
> I rang the information – my axe was cold
> They said, 'She rides the train to Oreole'
>
> Now it's a mighty long way down the dusty trail
> And the sun burns hot on the cold steel rail
> And I look like a bum and I crawl like a snail
> All the way from Memphis

The after-gig celebrations at the group's hotel, with Joe Walsh, were bizarre to
say the least according to Watts. 'I remember in the middle of this wild party
there were policemen rolling joints, half-naked girls on the floor and wild music
going on, and me and Joe playing chess on the bed!'

Mott returned to London on Christmas Eve and Ian went to spend the holiday with his friend, Colen York, in Northampton, where he was telephoned by
David Bowie who asked to see Hunter urgently to discuss Mott's future. When
Ian and Trudi, tired and jet-lagged, drove all the way to Beckenham, Bowie
played peek-a-boo with a cushion on his sofa and had nothing to say. Ian felt he
could either ignore David or hit him, but he avoided the latter in Angie Bowie's
presence. Driving to his Wembley flat, Hunter realised that Bowie had probably
acquired all he could from the group. The Mott – Mainman association was
reaching the end of the road, but Verden Allen wasn't surprised. 'I don't think Ian
knew just what to do. I remember him coming up and he said about Bowie doing
the next single. And I said, "You can forget about that, he's taken off, he's too
busy. David won't write a single, we've got to do that ourselves." It had to come
from the group. It was obvious, because don't forget, he hadn't made it when he
gave us "Dudes", so helping Mott helped him as well.'

Dale believes the novelty of Mott had worn off as far as Bowie was concerned. 'He'd lost interest. I think one of the things that bored Bowie was, there wasn't anything to suck from Mott. We were desperately boring for him, when the image was, "these crazy guys, are they gay or out of their brains on drugs?" We weren't any of those things. Once David had sussed that, it all became rather tedious for him. But Bowie taught us to be more organised and I don't think we have too much to complain about as far as he is concerned. The best thing David did was offer us "Drive In Saturday" as a follow up to "Dudes", and then not give it to us. That made Ian very keen to write a hit single, which he did four or five times. In a way, dangling that carrot and taking it away made us all more determined, particularly Ian. Let's face it, "Drive In Saturday" isn't the greatest song in the world. Bowie's instinct to withdraw it was good for all concerned.'

With David departed, Mott The Hoople were then to go through further significant change, not only in terms of attitude and management, but also group personnel.

9

Verden grew a line or two

'The Ballad of Mott The Hoople' – Ian Hunter

David Bowie had recommended at an early stage in their relationship that Hunter should take control of Mott The Hoople and lead more forcefully from the front, a move that would lead to two significant group changes during 1973.

'What actually happened was that David took me out to The Stage Deli in New York and advised me to take over the band, because Defries was getting really pissed off,' explains Ian. 'Mott was a diplomatic group, but not only was it diplomatic, it wasn't 3–2, it had to be 5–nil. So obviously one guy was going to say no just for fun. That's the way Mott The Hoople always was and still is actually. Now I wasn't big on responsibility, but I understood what they were saying because they could never get a "yes" or a "no" out of us. So I went back and told the band that David thought things were slow because we didn't make a decision about anything. When I said Bowie recommended I take over in that regard, Mick Ralphs said, "Fuck you," and that was the end of that. I never ran Mott. I think certain people will have you believe it, but if I was running Mott, it sure didn't feel like I was running it to me.'

'I can't recall Ralphs' exact response or him reacting against Ian's suggestion,' says Dale, 'but it was discussed and, to be honest, it made total sense and was inevitable. We'd started as an equal five-man billing and had set up in a straight line across the front of the stage for live performance, even the organ and drums. That changed with the Mainman liaison when Ian went out stage centre and switched to rhythm guitar, but in any case, everybody associated his face and image with Mott The Hoople. Who would you remember most – me, Ralphs or a shaded Hunter? Ian's leadership was discussed and met with the explicit approval of the band. It was the right and sensible thing to do.'

The threat of change was increasingly in the air however and the first departure from the original line-up was organist Verden Allen, who quit after two gigs in mid January 1973, following increased tension between himself and the rest of the band, particularly Hunter. Emotions had reached boiling point on stage during two consecutive concerts, firstly at the Glen Ballroom in Llanelli, when Mott played an indifferent show to a half-empty hall and vented their anger on the crowd.

'It wasn't a good gig musically,' recalls Stan Tippins. 'The band got frustrated and Ian knocked a mike stand off the stage in a fury and it went into the audience. Then in the dressing room afterwards, bottles were smashed and windows were broken. One journalist wrote a review with the headline "Mott lean on Llanelli", which I liked, and he said, the singing was off key, even though they had a hidden vocalist in the wings – me!'

During the next gig, at Sheffield University on 19 January, with Nazareth as support, Verden refused to play on stage and heckled Ian. A parting of the ways was now inevitable. 'I told them, "I think you've got to carry on on your own now, because I can't do any more with the group, I'm off." I'd said it a few times

before and didn't really mean it. I didn't really mean it then. I left because I honestly don't think anybody knew what to do at that particular time, because Bowie
wasn't coming back. There were a lot of things going on and I had some ideas,
things I wanted to do. I couldn't see any way under the sun we were going to get
them done.'

'The Sheffield gig was horrible,' confesses Watts. 'I remember Verden being
abusive to Ian between songs as he announced the numbers. And I thought,
"God, what's going to happen next?" I think a bottle was thrown or something.
Then, when we came off, Phally said for the umpteenth time that he was going
to leave the group.'

Hunter confirms that Allen often threatened to depart, but he also felt that
Verden had engaged in increasing outbursts and moods aimed at him, culminating in the flashpoint at Sheffield. 'He'd always leave and nobody would ever take
him up on it. Mick would say, "Don't be so stupid. Everything will be all right."
Then, at the Sheffield gig he pulled the usual. I was on stage saying, "I'm going
to do this slow number. The band doesn't really want me to do it, but I forced it
on them." And from behind I heard Phally saying, "You're fuckin' right you
forced it on us!" Afterwards, in the dressing room, he said, "I'm leaving." So
Mick turned round and said, "When do you want to go?" That was it. Mick had
finally decided enough was enough.'

Verden was out and the music press carried front page headlines – 'Mott
Shock: Allen Quits'. The official line was a difference in musical policy, Verden
wanting to develop more as a songwriter, a vocalist and to work in a band that
was more organ-based. The announcement confirmed that Mott would continue
as a four piece, all the players remaining 'friends'.

'Sheffield was the bursting of the boil that had been festering for some time,'
says Dale. 'Phally had become increasingly intense and I remember he actually
had Ian by the throat after a gig at Portsmouth once. Even worse, he jumped the
queue to get him. He couldn't understand why we repeatedly wouldn't let him
have a more prominent role and position within the group. This went on for
months, but even after he freaked at the Sheffield gig and left the group, the
wound took some time to heal. Verden and I still shared adjoining flats at Stonor
Road, which became difficult, as I was exposed to Phally's wanting to be allowed
back into the band. The others could, and did, avoid contact with him, but I
didn't have that luxury. I had to say no, it wasn't possible and he couldn't return
to Mott, which caused him – and me – great upset.'

'Verden always had this thing about composing songs and when he saw Ian
was writing, he wanted to write,' says Stan. 'But in a band, you've got to know
your strengths, and Phally wasn't up to scratch in terms of songwriting.'

'He started getting very heavy and pushing for his songs to be used, to the
extent that he wanted the whole sound changing completely,' said Hunter. 'What
he was into was a combination of Black Sabbath and Lou Reed, which sounds
weird, but there's no other way to describe it really. Anyway, it just wasn't Mott.'

'We were very sad to lose Phally because he was the joker of the group,' says
Watts. 'Verden played the fool a lot, but he was great and we all loved him. Then,
suddenly, it all changed, and he started writing and wanted to be taken deadly

seriously. It was very hard for us all to change our attitudes towards him. I think he was worse when he'd gone home and seen his folks. He'd come back to London demanding his songs were recorded by the band.'

Several record labels, including CBS, were interested in Verden's signature immediately after his departure from Mott but he refused to sign, which still causes Hunter dismay. 'Phal's written some good songs, but he's been in re-mixing them twenty times. There's people that were interested, but he's ruined that by his intenseness. We told him he was fat one day; at the time he weighed 179 pounds. Within a month he was 155 and then he went down to 130. We'd get in the car with Phal and I'd say to him, "What's the matter with you? You don't look too good." He'd sit and think for 300 miles and you'd be talking about something completely different, almost to the gig, and he'd turn round and say, "Well, you don't look so good either." '

'I think the group changed after Bowie,' admits Ralphs. 'We became commercially acceptable and Ian found the knack of writing hits and I would help him with little melodic bits on "Honaloochie Boogie" for example. Verden didn't really feel the same after that. The band was different.'

Although Allen has subsequently released several solo singles and an album, his career, post-Mott, has been erratic and perhaps hasn't received the coverage or profile he deserved. His first single was recorded in July 1973 with Mooni, and released by Polydor later that year, featuring two of his own compositions, 'Wine Ridden Talks' (from the *All the Young Dudes* era) backed with a re-recording of 'Nightmare'. Verden sang the B-side but let Mooni take the lead vocal on the A-side, something in retrospect that he feels he should not have done. 'After the split from Mott The Hoople, I was introduced to Polydor Records by Nicky Graham. Nicky worked with David Bowie prior to being with the label, but it was Hedley Leyton, John Leyton's brother, who signed me. Looking back now, it was all very rushed and the deal with Polydor didn't mean that much.'

Verden's next project was a band called The Cheeks, formed early in 1974 with drummer Martin Chambers and guitarist James Honeyman-Scott, both from Hereford. 'It took a year after Mott before I finally moved out of London to go back to Hereford. I first met bass player Kelvin Wilson there and then went to see Martin playing with The Dave Stuart Sound at the Hillside Ballroom. After a brief chat, the three of us got together at a local studio in Bridge Street, Hereford. The night of that rehearsal, Martin had a gig with his band, but at the end of our session, we had to carry him to my car, an old Ford Zodiac, and drive him to the gig minus his drums. He stumbled into the ballroom and laid flat out on the floor. Dave Stuart went crazy. Martin groaned and got up and said to Stuart, "I won't be playing for you any more Dave, you can stuff your band, I've just teamed up with Verden and Kelvin." That night was the birth of The Cheeks and after that unforgettable first session, we started the hunt for a guitarist. I placed an advertisement in *Melody Maker* and over a period of a month we had various people who came up from London, but we just couldn't find anyone to suit. Then, one night, in a local pub, Jimmy Scott turned up. Back at the studio we ran through a song called "Eight O'Clock at the Corner" and James Honeyman Scott became a Cheek.'

The Cheeks survived until 1976 and played numerous live dates under MAM Agency, including support slots with The Arrows, Hot Chocolate and Trapeze, and three appearances at the London Marquee, cheered on, on one occassion, by Hunter and Watts. The Cheeks, under encouragement from Jack Nelson of Queen fame, recorded three Allen compositions at Trident Studios in October 1975 – 'On the Rebound', 'Sweet Sweet Girl' and 'Hypnotised'. Sadly, they never released any material as Verden did not sign a new deal after Polydor and 'Hypnotised' is the only surviving group recording.

By 1978, Chambers and Honeyman-Scott joined ex-*NME* writer Chrissie Hynde, originally from Akron, Ohio, and Hereford bass player Pete Farndon in The Pretenders. Stan Tippins subsequently became tour manager for the band and, whilst they enjoyed enormous chart success, they were to be plagued with tragedy – the sacking of Farndon because of his drug abuse, the death two days later of Honeyman-Scott from a heroin and cocaine overdose and the demise of Farndon in the following year, also from a drug overdose. Chambers has continued to work with Hynde in various reformations of The Pretenders, and Martin subsequently recorded some singles with Verden.

In August 1975, Allen was re-united briefly with Guy Stevens at AIR Studios in London, when he was asked to play with a group called Little Queenie, featuring Kelvin Blacklock on vocals and future Clash guitarist Mick Jones. Mick was considered superfluous when the band did a showcase for Warner Brothers and Guy, who wanted to recreate a keyboard dominated group in Mott The Hoople vein. They re-recorded 'No Wheels to Ride', plus a Blacklock composition and a Flaming Groovies cover, and Guy re-named the band Violent Luck, but the project was aborted at an early stage.

Verden Allen's Seven Inches was the next group formed and, like The Cheeks, they were prominent on the college concert circuit. Then Verden decided to record a single with guitarist Luther Grosvenor. Signed to Don Arden's Jet label by Brian McMenemy, brother of football manager Lawrie McMenemy, the single featured two new Allen songs, 'On the Rebound' backed with 'A New Way', produced by ELO's stage mixer, Jake Commander. Issued in July 1978, as Verden & Luther, the disc was reviewed by a couple of music journals but sank without any active promotion or live support, Grosvenor refusing to play any gigs. 'Luther was a loveable bloke,' says Allen. 'The trouble was I had a band called Seven Inches before that, and we were going great on college gigs. As soon as Luther turned up, he didn't want to do any playing and said, "Don't worry we'll have a number one" and started drinking. I felt ten years older from being with him.'

By 1982, Verden decided to launch his own record label, Spinit, and invited Grosvenor into the studio again, to record with Martin Chambers and bass player Norman Jarrett. Allen's first release on Spinit was 'Colleen', backed with 'Through and Through', although this was soon re-issued with 'Sweet Sweet Girl' as the A-side and 'Colleen' moved to the flip. Verden then worked with Watts and Griffin and recorded 'This Way Now' and 'Tomorrow', the label proclaiming, 'Arrangement and Production by Mott the Hoople Minus Two.' The singles were difficult to find because of limited distribution, so Verden remixed 'Sweet Sweet

Girl' and put a new song, 'Come On Back', on the A-side, then re-issued 'About Tomorrow'. ' "Come On Back" sold well. I should have held on and pushed it. Then, the Independent Record Labels Association I was working with went bust, and it all stopped. "About Tomorrow"with Pete and Buff was issued too soon after "Come On Back".'

At this point, Verden's recorded output ceased and he played in various bands around South Wales and Hereford. By 1990 he had joined a group called The Business, who played frequent gigs and asked Allen to contribute new material. When Verden took more control, the bass player and singer departed, and they recruited Rob Hankins as replacement. The group continued gigging for a further year and a half, but in 1992 changed their name, at Hankins' suggestion, to Thunderbuck Ram and Verden put together an album of material for commercial release.

Eventually, a 14-track Spinit CD, entitled appropriately, *Long Time No See,* was released in 1994 as Verden Allen and Thunderbuck Ram, for distribution at gigs and through a mail-order company. The CD featured older singles, several new tracks and re-recordings of Mott's 'Soft Ground' and 'Death May Be Your Santa Claus'. On the live circuit, Thunderbuck Ram also played 'At The Crossroads', 'You Really Got Me', 'All the Young Dudes' and 'Two Miles from Heaven', the last composed by Verden some years previously in Mott The Hoople and aired live with The Cheeks. The *Long Time No See* album also contained another Allen composition written for the *Mott* LP, 'Son of the Wise Ones'. Originally entitled 'Black Staff', Mott The Hoople had put the song down on rehearsal tape at Hunter's request, but never finished the recording.

In early 1995, Verden returned to Chapel Lane Studio in Hereford with Thunderbuck Ram to record four new tracks, including 'Two Miles from Heaven', but the band subsequently split.

When asked about his career with Mott The Hoople and their contribution to music, Verden is philosophical. 'It's nice knowing a mark was put down, but we'd made it and I left the band, instead of holding on a bit longer and keeping myself quiet. When I started writing things as well, if we'd got them on the next album the original Mott might have developed more. To be truthful, I shouldn't have left when I did because as soon as you break the circle it starts going wrong.'

Pete Watts opines that Verden was probably the best musician in Mott The Hoople, but he was sometimes uncomfortable in the studio. 'He wasn't so natural in the studio and often had a great deal of trouble recording. Sometimes we used to go out because his hands wouldn't actually touch the keys. It happens with other keyboard players, they go to play but it's almost like there's a forcefield in the way. Phally could be like that and get in quite a state over his keyboard parts. We used to leave him quite often and he'd do it on his own or at some later date, but his playing was always great. If you listen to early Mott The Hoople, his keyboard work was inspired.'

Dale Griffin looks back on Verden's contribution to Mott with affection. 'At the time Verden Allen left Mott The Hoople, he was one of the best and most original Hammond organ players in the world. He had also developed a unique sound using a blend of "Leslie" tone cabinet and "Acoustic" guitar amplifier, fed direct from his Hammond. He was a first-rate musician who could play the sensitive and subtle, the brutal and bellicose and all musical steps in between. In a song like "The Journey", his playing and sound ranged from celestial to industrial, from a whisper to a scream, always complementing the mood and intent of the song. When Verden Allen left, it was the end of the Mott The Hoople that played so hard and fast, that having heard recordings from those early days, I cannot imagine how we did it. It was the end of the Mott The Hoople "wall of sound" that bands like Slade used to hear, and then argue about just what made that sound. Well, much of it was Verden Allen Esq.

'So why did he leave? In essence, because he had ceased to pull with the team and had, for some time, seemed to be an opposition force within the group. In no way did we ever think "as one", but there had never been such a wide gulf of attitude in our ranks and something or someone had to give. Verden wanted to share more of the limelight afforded to Hunter and Ralphs, but lacked the songs or vocal style to come across strongly on stage. On this basis his wishes were opposed by "the band". We felt that his song writing was improving but doubted his vocalising would ever truly stand the scrutiny of recorded or even live performance. So the discussions on this subject grew more heated and Verden became more frustrated and felt more alienated.

'Finally, early in 1973, at a university gig in the north of England, Verden's on stage outbursts at Hunter throughout the performance led to a back stage row during which he ended his association with the group. It was a time of sadness and relief. Sadness, because Verden had been a pillar of our group for so long and was a good humoured, kind hearted man. The huge stock of 'Phally stories' are testament to the affection in which he is held. Relief, because the tensions caused by the endless arguments had become unbearable and a huge strain on all concerned. This too was the end of the Guy Stevens' Mott and there was never again that close camaraderie that existed between the founder members.'

'In a way when Verden Allen left, Ralpher kind of left mentally too,' suggests Hunter. 'He likes to look after somebody, because he has this maternal instinct. When Phal had gone, Mick was left a bit stuck.'

10

'73 was a jamboree

After Verden Allen left Mott The Hoople in January 1973, the band was forced to cancel some immediate concert dates, however they were soon back on the road as a four-piece, in February, playing a five-date 'mini-tour' of Scotland and the north of England, with The Sensational Alex Harvey Band as support.

Dale and Overend recall seeing Harvey live, several years before, playing bass in an early sixties group in Ross, and Hunter knew him slightly through his work in Germany around that time. Like Mott, Alex had worked hard for many years to achieve musical success and, at last, it was imminent. SAHB promoted their debut album *Framed* on the Mott The Hoople tour but went on to secure several hits with *Next, The Impossible Dream, Tomorrow Belongs to Me* and a hilarious cover version of 'Delilah'. Harvey came from the tough Gorbals area of Glasgow and was once frank in his views and political opinions to journalist Charles Shaar Murray. 'Politicians don't know a light. When I see these poor men, Wilson and Heath, walking about and blustering and saying, "We'll do this and we'll do that," with their silly suits on, they're a hundred years out of date. They've got nothing to do with what's going on. I'd rather see Ian Hunter in charge of the lifeboat, 'cause at least I can trust his motives.'

The songs played in Mott's set during their tour with Harvey included 'Drivin' Sister', 'Sucker', 'Hymn for the Dudes', 'Sweet Jane', 'Ready for Love', 'Ballad of Mott', 'Angeline', 'Jerkin' Crocus', 'One of the Boys', 'Rock and Roll Queen' and 'Honky Tonk Women', but, in truth, the band badly missed Allen's keyboard sound in their live performance. Mott also tried to sever the Bowie connection by dropping 'All the Young Dudes' from their repertoire.

Hunter was lyrically and musically active at this point with the band rehearsing songs like 'Silver Needles' and 'Did You See Them Run'. Watts had even written a number entitled 'Symphony in O Minor' which featured Ralphs on organ and Hunter on lead guitar!

In addition to Verden's New-Year exit, Mott also parted company officially with David Bowie, Mainman and Tony Defries. 'I got on fine with Defries but I think he was a svengali,' says Hunter in retrospect. 'His whole trip was that Mott The Hoople and Bowie shall inherit the earth, but when was the pay off? We could never pin him down on an exact date. And Tony was irritated with us too, because we were very much a democratic band. With David he only had to ask David what he wanted to do. With Mott, he had to ask everybody.'

If Defries was becoming frustrated, then so was Hunter, for he believed there was a critical need for Tony's undivided attention in terms of management, if Mott were to make the big break. 'When David got enormous in America and then Japan, Defries was gone and we had no effective management at all. I knew we'd got to get back to America, I knew the time was right and we did get back to America under different management, and the time was right. But Tony was trying to bring David in, bring David out, bring us in, bring us out, but we were impatient, we wanted to get back there and he couldn't handle the two things at once. We felt were getting neglected.

'Defries did a good job up to a point, because he knew that David would be enormous, the one thing that David didn't himself know. I kept on to Tony from the beginning to get another guy in, because there was no way he could be in two places at once, but he wouldn't take on anybody else to be on the same level as him, which was what we wanted. This is why the split came about. Defries will only have his one baby, and we weren't the first. I got very upset about it because the *Dudes* album was in the American charts for over twenty weeks and we had a number three single in Britain.'

Another sticking point with Ian was that Bowie had promised to give Mott 'Drive In Saturday' as a follow up single to 'All the Young Dudes', then changed his mind. 'David had offered us "Suffragette City" and we turned it down because it wasn't strong enough. It was a good song but Mott had three missed singles already so the radio was shut, and when the radio's that shut to you, you need something not far short of a classic to open the door again. Then he offered us "Dudes" and then I wanted "Drive In Saturday", although now I don't know why. I can't imagine what I was going to do with it, although Verden and I had discussed how we'd handle the chord run down. David had "John I'm Only Dancing" and "Drive In Saturday" and played me them, and it was obvious he was going to do "John I'm Only Dancing" and we weren't. I tried to get "Drive In Saturday" but he wouldn't budge and by this time he was slightly miffed he'd given us "Dudes". So we then had to go and write our own, but one of the things we had learned from Mick Ronson and Bowie was the work effort was a lot higher than we thought it was. So by the time we split with David we had a good idea of what to do.

'David's kind of like Peter Sellers in a way,' explains Hunter. 'That's about as near as I can explain him. He's almost like a transparency. He constantly absorbs and when he wants to absorb something about something, he goes to that area. And he has great charm and he has great talent and then he gets what he wants and moves to the next area. David was great to work with, but he'll pull stunts on a personal level. He's very Jekyll and Hyde. A lot of David's genius, if you want to call it that, is an almost Dracula-like quality of draining what he wants before moving on to the next victim. And then he has this great quality of converting it into what he believes the public wants, which is very often exactly right.'

There was now another financial crisis for Mott The Hoople, so much so that roadie, Richie Anderson, was encouraged to take time out and work with Black Sabbath, while Mott tried to re-group, cancelling a proposed five week American tour. Griffin recalls that the Mott–Bowie–Defries split led to some panic within Columbia Records and the band. 'Bowie's and Mott's careers were very paralleled in America. In fact we were ahead in national terms and I think David felt that Defries couldn't serve his and our interests. So the Mainman involvement began to grow remote. Wages became erratic and contact problematical. Suddenly, it cut off and we were left to the mercy of CBS who quickly got cold feet. So did Ian. He panicked and decided he'd gone solo but told

Ralphs, Watts and me that he'd like us to play on his first single, if we wanted to. The three of us discussed it and decided to do it, having nothing better to do, I was furious with Hunter though. So we went into AIR Studios and did "Honaloochie Boogie" and "Ballad of Mott" as Ian's backing band. The tracks came out beyond our wildest dreams, or those of CBS, and the solo career was forgotten, for the time being. They did originate as solo recordings though, and I recall Ian remarking as we finished them, that they sounded very Mott-ish and should perhaps come out as such.'

Ian counters the claims that the recordings were originally intended as a solo project. 'Halfway through the *Mott* album, Buff and Pete came to me and said, "Is this your solo album?" And if I'd have had any fucking brains I would have answered "Yes", but it never dawned on me. I said, "No, of course it's not. It's our album." I never thought in those terms. I was in Mott The Hoople and very glad to be so. In retrospect, it wouldn't have been a bad move though. I guess I was in a position of power and I didn't even know it. I was doing all the writing for them and was too busy to think about it.'

Mott were now without management, although by this time a lawyer named Bob Hirschman was already representing the band in the UK. An American, Hirschman had previously been a trombone player, and made a fleeting contribution to a Spencer Tracy movie. Dale recalls he also keen to make contributions to Mott The Hoople's work. 'Bob always wanted to play trombone on a Mott track and we kept saying, "But we don't want trombone." Eventually we told him to get lost, which had the desired effect, especially as he was petrified of Hunter!'

Whilst, according to Ian, Hirschman was extremely keen on Mott The Hoople, Hunter wanted separate management in the UK and USA because he strongly believed the band's future was in America. Watts recalls the search for new managerial blood. 'Clive Davis, the head of Columbia in America, came over after we'd split from Defries and just done the *Mott* album, and he was instrumental in the Hirschman/Heller set up. Hirschman got involved with us initially as a consultant lawyer. Then Clive Davis had a meeting with us and suggested a couple of people like Bud Prager and possibly even Peter Grant. We were aiming big with managers, we wanted somebody strong. So we had Prager over, but didn't think he was right and rejected him and he didn't like that. He was very upset and never forgave us. Then Hirschman was retained to oversee all the band's business affairs while we looked for another manager in the meantime.'

Mott were soon to engage Fred Heller, a New Yorker who had studied International Finance at the University Graduate School of Business Affairs before becoming tour manager for Blood Sweat & Tears in 1970. 'Columbia Records recommended a few people because we were worried about the American situation,' admits Hunter. 'Hirschman was already our lawyer and had more or less entrenched himself as Mott's manager in England. We met a couple of people and finally wound up with Fred Heller. Fred and Bob were on 10 per cent each but Heller had kittens when we told him he was on 10 per cent and said not to tell anyone. Fred was managing Blood Sweat & Tears and he also managed Lou Reed a bit. We liked him. He was young, he was fresh, he was a nice guy, but it all fell apart in the end with Fred, because his father owned a

chequer cab firm in New York and it was the whole Julian Coulter thing in
Northampton, all over again. "You've got to stop doing that and come and help
me out because I'm getting older." The Heller family were Jewish and Fred felt
very obligated to his father as they do. But Fred was all right initially.'

'Bob Hirschman was very boring,' says Ralphs, 'but Fred Heller was a young
kid, from New York, tough, with a lot of drive and very positive thinking.'

'Hirschman harboured no real imagination,' says Stan Tippins. 'Fred Heller
came over and was very keen and could have been the best. Ian liked him because
he was young and very enthusiastic but I wasn't so sure. I could suss these people out a lot quicker and easier than the band and I didn't like him after a while.'

Watts observed that Hirschman made a strong play for a joint management
role with the group. 'I remember Bob at a meeting saying, "Look, why don't I become your manager over here too, I know the ins-and-outs of the group, I've
been running it for two or three months." And Ralphs said, "I think it's better
you doing what you're doing Bob, it's good, we should keep it like that." We
didn't in the end and he became the other half, because it seemed sensible to have
one manager here and one over there. But even Hirschman and Heller didn't
seem to trust each other.'

Mott signed a management contract with H&H Enterprises, Fred Heller
looking after their US affairs based in New York, and Bob Hirschman as associate, located in London, handling Europe for the band and acting as legal adviser.
Heller helped structure plans for Mott's assault on the American market and
secured the deal for the publication of Hunter's 1972 tour diary.

The band started recording their new album, *Mott,* in early February through
to April, at AIR No. 2 Studio in Oxford Street, with some final overdubbing
done at EMI Abbey Road in St John's Wood. They were two London studios they
hadn't used before, which had strong connections with The Beatles' producer
George Martin. AIR was originally formed in 1965 and Abbey Road was, of
course, home to the majority of The Beatles' recorded work. Because of George
Martin, there were old BBC Radio connections with people like The Goons, so
two of Mott's tape operators were Goon prodigies, Peter Sellers' son, Mike and
Spike Milligan's son, Sean. Bill Price, now one of the world's leading engineers,
was a mainstay at AIR, often working sixteen hours a day with Mott The Hoople,
always unflustered and sustained by his chain smoking – 200 plus St Moritz
Menthols every day!

The first tracks that Mott taped for their new album were 'Honaloochie
Boogie', 'Hymn for the Dudes', 'Ballad of Mott', 'Drivin' Sister' and 'Rose', the
latter two introduced live for the first time on their February tour. Ian had wanted Roy Wood, of Move, ELO and Wizzard fame, to produce the sessions. Roy's
recollection is that he was too busy at the time but he particularly remembers that
Hunter liked the horn section in his band, which Wood had used to stunning
effect on the hit singles 'Ball Bark Incident' and 'See My Baby Jive'. On the
spritely 'Honaloochie Boogie', Mott featured Paul Buckmaster on electric cello,
and Roxy Music's Andy Mackay on sax, in a manner reminiscent of Roy's style.
Mackay was invited to guest on two Mott tracks, as Roxy were in the adjoining
studio during February recording *For Your Pleasure,* their second album.

'Ian idolised Roy after "See My Baby Jive", and we had a few arguments about Mott adopting that style,' says Watts. 'Ian often went on about Roy Wood and The Stones, asking Buff and me to play like Charlie Watts and Bill Wyman. I never liked Wizzard's records much, simply because everything was Automatic Double Tracked. I thought they sounded messy. Roy was managed by Carl Wayne at the time and so Stan, encouraged by Hunter, phoned him and he got quite nasty saying, "What do you want? What's your game mate?" All we wanted was to see if Roy would produce one album!'

Casting around for producers, Mott seriously considered asking John Lennon to assist them. Although it was only discussed amongst the band, Watts says it proves that Mott The Hoople were now thinking big league. 'He was the only guy that all of us respected. Everybody in the group wanted that because we just loved him. He would have been good for us and I'd have loved to have met him.

'We weren't going to produce *Mott* initially,' says Pete, 'but we went in and did "Honaloochie Boogie". Roxy Music came down to listen to it and they said it was a hit. We were worried about getting a producer and I think it was Andy Mackay, the sax player, who said, "No way. You don't need a producer." We looked up to them from a sound point of view, because they were very much into sound. Eno was another one that said we should do it, so we thought, "If they think we can, we'll do it." Andy Mackay used to come and sit with us at AIR a lot, because he didn't like being in the studio with the rest of his group. Andy was really nice and tried to join us on several occasions. I got quite friendly with him and we were going to go to greyhound racing at White City but it never quite happened. He did say he didn't want to be in Roxy Music anymore and could he join Mott. Sadly there was no way, because we really only needed sax on about two songs.'

Hunter reveals that he also asked Mike Leander to produce *Mott*. 'I liked Gary Glitter's sound and I thought Leander was great. I figured it would be different for Mott The Hoople but it would be good, because he was an intelligent producer. Sadly, he was too busy. I liked Roy Wood's singles, his voice and his songs. Then it was funny how Roxy all came in from AIR 1 and said we didn't need outside help. Really *Mott* was produced by us purely because Roxy Music wanted us to!'

Encouraged into self-production, with Hunter credited as arranger, Mott knew that they had to utilise the lessons learned from David Bowie and surpass, rather than maintain, his standards. George Martin observed some session overdubs and then, with the bulk of the recording completed, the band moved to Abbey Road where Pink Floyd were completing *Dark Side of the Moon* in an adjoining studio. Dale confirms that little recording work was done at Abbey Road but the band thought the name would look good on the record sleeve!

Bob Hirschman was able to confirm to Mainman on 2 May 1973 that Mott The Hoople had delivered finished master tapes of their second album directly to CBS, constituting fulfilment of Mainman's obligations under the Columbia contract of 1st June 1972. All recordings subsequent to the *All the Young Dudes* album would be between Mott and CBS directly.

The new LP, titled plain and simply *Mott,* was crucial for the group and, as it turned out, a seventies milestone that has received much acclaim over subsequent years, being voted number 2 in one recent retrospective chart. The production techniques were excellent and the playing, most noticeably Mick Ralphs' guitar work, was exceptional. *Mott* was a loose concept record in many ways, which addressed the travails of rock stardom, the highs and lows of touring and the battle for, and pitfalls of, success.

'We opted for *Mott* because, first and foremost, we wanted to consolidate and further establish the group's name,' explains Watts. 'We'd had all these wild Guy Stevens titles during our early period. *Mott* was simple and direct for a change!'

It was now nearly ten months since the release of 'All the Young Dudes', so, on 25 May, CBS rush-released 'Honaloochie Boogie' as the first single from the LP, without the picture sleeve originally planned. It entered the UK singles charts on 16 June, staying for nine weeks and reaching number 12. Mott appeared on *Top of the Pops* with Andy Mackay and, directed by Richard Weaver, produced a promotional video in a basement room near Hyde Park, for the princely sum of £150! Ian recognises that it was a critical single for the band. 'If "Honaloochie Boogie" stiffed, we knew we had a big problem. At the time, everybody looked incorrectly on "All the Young Dudes" as David's single and said we couldn't do it on our own, so that was a very important track.'

The single B-side, 'Rose', featured Watts on fretless bass and Ralphs playing volume guitar. Written by Hunter, this was to be the first of three excellent B-sides co-credited to Mott. 'They were just handed out to the group in their entirety,' admits Watts, 'partly because the general feeling in the band, which Ian agreed with, was that people were contributing towards the numbers he'd written without getting any credit for it. A lot of it was arrangement, like Buff would suggest a particular verse went in later on, or I'd have ideas to change a chord.'

The *Mott* album was issued on 20 July, entering the British album charts on 11 August, where it remained for fifteen weeks. The upper reaches of the chart were monopolised by The Rolling Stones' *Goat Head Soup*, Status Quo's *Hello*, David Bowie's *Pin Ups* and Roxy Music's *Stranded* albums, but *Mott* had a strong run too, peaking at number seven, the band's first top-ten LP. The record would also be voted 'Album of the Year' in US magazines *Rolling Stone* and *Creem*.

In the UK the LP was released in a limited-edition gatefold sleeve with colour photo collage, before the package was changed to a simple single cover. For the first time ever a Mott album sleeve was different in America with a colour photo of the group on the front. CBS had asked Hipgnosis to submit proposals for the sleeve. 'Their best idea was a girl's face with no mouth and a tear trickling down one cheek,' recalls Dale. 'In the USA Columbia refused point blank to use the original UK artwork. Instead, they utilised a "do not use" photo from a bad colour set made in Bayswater.'

Mott opened with the remarkable US touring saga, 'All the Way from Memphis', one of Hunter's finest compositions and a future single. The song was a rock and roll chronicle dedicated to the audience at their recent tumultuous headlining gig in Ellis Auditorium. 'That was a magical night in Memphis,' says Ian. 'Nobody was in the hall at seven o'clock and we thought it was a total disaster. But the turnstiles were broken and they were all outside, so at the last minute, from nothing, it was full, and we came running down through the audience from the back of the auditorium. Some of the lyric is true and some fictionalised.'

The original working title for the track had been 'Rocker in Sea Sharp (and Bristol Fashion)' and it featured blazing saxophone played by Andy Mackay, but not without prior traumas as Dale recalls. 'The sax part was done originally by Ronnie Ross and it was all wrong. Then we tried Bobby Keyes, a total failure, before Andy Mackay. I remember we thought the stop–start accents of "Memphis" bore more than a passing resemblance to Procul Harum's "Conquistador".'

'Bobby Keyes was out of his depth,' says Watts. 'His playing was so far off what we wanted that we didn't know what to say. We just said it was great and that we'd sort out bits later and, after he left, we wiped the tape. C sharp is not a saxophone-friendly key. "Memphis" was a true and remarkable story. Shame it sounds so insipid on record!'

'Whizz Kidd' (spelt 'Whizz Kid' on the cover – a CBS track listing error) was one of two songs concerning failed relationships. Buffin recalls that Ralphs hated the song because he thought it mirrored Free's 'Catch a Train'. Mick's working title for 'Whizz Kidd' had been 'Catch a Cold'! Musically, the song was complex and, for the one and only time, Ian had to encourage the rest of the group to accept it. 'It was a very troublesome song when it was written, because it went down and we just didn't know what to play on top of it. The backtrack was very involved and sounded weird on its own. They were a bit worried about it then, but I could see the finished article. That was the only time I ever pushed. We thought at one point that it had to be orchestrated because the chords and progressions were so strange but then, Mick Ralphs just came in with a guitar part and filled it up beautifully.'

'Hymn for the Dudes', written by Ian and Verden, had been played live for some months and was taped with Allen in October 1972 but re-recorded for *Mott*. Ian directed the lyrics at his young and enthusiatic audience. 'I just feel passionately about young kids. They're amazing. They've got all the energy in the world. The song is just to say 'somebody cares about you' without sounding too corny. It's very hard to live at that age today.' But Hunter seemed also to be predicting musical change and, like 'The Moon Upstairs' and 'Crash Street Kidds' to follow, it could be construed as a premonition of the New Wave which would arrive some four years later.

> Correct your heads, for there's a new song rising
> High above the waves
> Go write your time, go sing it on the street
> Go tell the world, but you go brave

Ian's lyrics also appeared to demolish the pedestal Mott had placed Bowie on.

> You ain't the nazz …
> You're just a buzz …
> Some kinda temporary …

Dale Griffin recalls, 'It was written before Bowie and amended. Ian had to be dissuaded from ending the final verse with the phrase "temporary twat!", which was on the original demo. Not very classy!'

'Honaloochie Boogie' was a song which recalled Hunter's early days in Northampton where he discovered bands and rock music. The references to 'steel toed shoes' and 'this friend' who 'has converted me to rock and roll' were acknowledgements of his sixties mentor, Freddie Lee. Ian admitted seeing the film *That'll Be the Day* which reminded him of his days as a youngster at the local dance hall, waiting for a punch up, but he is no longer convinced it inspired the song whose lyrics he now considers virtually meaningless. 'I don't know what "Honaloochie Boogie" is about. I can't figure it out at all. I used to say to people, "It doesn't mean anything." But it didn't matter, it sounded good.'

Side One closed with the frantic and relentless 'Violence', which culminated with insane violin and a 'fight scene'. The track was a follow-on, in many respects, from 'One of the Boys' and featured manic violin played by Graham Preskett each time 'violence' was mentioned on the choruses, before ending with the 'punch up' in a blazing fade out.

> Gotta fight, nothing right, living nowhere
> Watch out for the gun, snake on the run, hide in my hair
> You keep your mouth shut, or you'll get cut, 'cos I like to scare
> I'm a battery louse, a superstar mouse, I don't care
> Get off my back, or I'll attack, 'cos I don't owe you nothing
> Head for your hole, you're sick and you're old, and I'm here to tell you
>   something …
> Violence, violence – it's the only thing
> That'll make you see sense

Watts recalls how violinist Graham Preskett was always around the studio. 'He looked like Keith Moon, invariably unshaven, and we didn't know who the hell he was but we sort of liked him. We'd come in and he'd be sitting on a couch and we'd say hello to one another. Normally, I'd have asked Stan to sling him out, but, somehow we didn't mind. When we got talking, it turned out he was doing a session in another studio and he had a fag packet and was writing. We said, "What are you doing?" He said, "Writing a string arrangement – I haven't done it yet." We enquired, "What do you mean?" He said, "Well I'm writing the orchestra arrangement." So we asked, "How many pieces in the orchestra?" He said, "Fifty two." "And you're doing it on a fag packet?" He said, "Yeah, I forgot to do it at home." And we thought, "Great!" We liked him straightaway then, writing an arrangement for a fifty-two piece orchestra on a cigarette packet. We wondered what he was really like, so he worked with us and wasn't wooden like most classical musicians. Graham was on to things immediately and whatever you suggested to him he would do it better. I could do the same thing later with Ray Major.'

'Violence' was meant to be a parody of the group's anger and frustrations, but real angst eventually exploded in the studio. Alan Harris, Mott's engineer, stepped in between Hunter and Ralphs to break up a fight, but the damage was done and it led to a deterioration in their relationship. ' "Violence" was the crunch between Mick and me,' admits Ian. 'It would be the crunch between a lot of people. Try listening to that for three days. It's murder. It was supposed to be a maddening song and was the last track recorded for the album, and I think a combination of being out to lunch, being extremely drunk and it being the end of the record, I got a little loose. I'd sat with the whole album like a mother sits with her baby and Mick Ralphs called me a name and I flew at him. I just went ape shit. I went for him and he went for me. It was never the same after that.

'I had this feeling that Mick was going to leave. I knew he was hanging about with Paul Rodgers, but I couldn't believe he could do this at a time when we were doing such good work. I rang him the next day and apologized but I could tell things were different between us. He really steered clear of me. I think that severed any cord that me and Ralphs had. We were never close, you couldn't get close to Mick, but it severed things musically.'

Watts feels that the original menace of 'Violence' was never recreated in the studio. 'I've got a rehearsal tape where the idea for the song took shape. Hunter remarks that it sounds "really violent". It's threatening, heavy and unrelenting – not like the record. I still like it, but it could have been much, much greater!'

The second side of the album started with 'Drivin' Sister', (originally called 'Rolling Fingers'), another title lifted by Guy Stevens, this time from The Stones 'Drivin' Sister Fanny'. Dale was unhappy with this take because he felt the track was lacklustre and small when it was intended to be hard, raunchy and 'big'. Ian explained that the song was based on a wild car journey Mott had taken with their former manager. 'Guy raced his Volkswagen through Hampstead Heath but he was driving it to the beat of a track from our first LP, "Half Moon Bay". The song had at least ten time changes and Guy raced the car to seventy, then abruptly dropped down to two miles per hour and back again, in time with the music.'

'The Ballad of Mott The Hoople (26th March 1972 Zurich)', obviously referred to the time and place where the band temporarily split in disillusion, before linking up with David Bowie, and was dedicated to 'The Sea Divers', Mott's fan club. If anyone needed to know what it took to succeed in a rock band, then this was the primer. Totally autobiographical throughout, this piece catalogued the ups and downs of rock and roll and Hunter's fight for, and mistrust of, success. 'In the lyrics on the *Mott* album, I tried to get it across that rock isn't superstars and God in the sky,' said Ian. 'There's losers and winners and varying degrees of losers and winners. It's honesty really. Mott's a very honest band. Bowie was very dishonest but I still think he's incredible. I'm just saying, "Wait a minute, this is how it really is." '

The track remains one of the group's favourites from the LP as it ended up almost exactly as intended. 'Ian managed to put into words what we all felt on "Ballad of Mott",' says Watts. 'A lovely piece of writing – sad and pessimistic.'

Mick Ralphs got the penultimate spot for the second LP in a row with 'I'm a Cadillac'. 'Ready for Love' on the *Dudes* LP was a hard act to follow, but 'I'm a Cadillac' was a fine pop song, bridged by an understated acoustic passage, 'El Camino Doloroso'. 'Mick and I were very much into US motors from 1972 onwards,' says Watts. 'We had Cadillacs and Mustangs but Ian preferred a sensible Ford Anglia with gold stripes, although he bought a Jaguar later on.'

The working title for 'I'm a Cadillac' was 'Nice One Stan' and there were several titles for 'El Camino Doloroso' including 'Elephant's Gerald' and 'No Jive'. 'The instrumental was a jam that just happened and then Mick overdubbed slide guitar,' says Dale. 'It was really a Ralphs, Watts, Griffin "composition". Doloroso is one word. We got it wrong on the album sleeve!'

' "El Camino Doloroso" meant "The Road of Sadness", and was simply a coda like "After Lights",' says Ralphs. 'I just came up with these little titles so it was almost like a different piece, but it was really just the tail end of a song.'

'I Wish I Was Your Mother', written by Hunter, was the final track on *Mott* and was recorded late in the sessions to replace the original closing number, 'Rose', as Dale Griffin recalls. ' "Rose" was dumped because we wanted a more upbeat song for Side Two. "I Wish I Was Your Mother" was the fastest we got. There was a mandolin hanging around the studio – not ours, plus bells – not ours, both of which appeared on "I Wish I Was Your Mother" together with the timpani which we used on "Hymn for the Dudes". They were all in the studio and if it was hanging around, we used it!'

Featuring Mick Ralphs on mandolin, this heavily Dylan-flavoured piece addressed the personal matter of heavy jealousy with Ian highlighting extreme possessiveness towards his wife, and yearning for the close-knit family upbringing that he seemed to have missed in his own life. Hunter once joked that Trudi's mother got the real message behind this song and suggested they shouldn't marry!

> I scream at you for sharing
> And I curse you just for caring
> I hate the clothes you're wearing they're so pretty
> I tell you not to see me
> I tell you not to feel me
> And I make your life a drag it's such a pity
>
> I wish I was your mother – I wish I was your father
> And then I would have seen you – would have been you as a child
> Played houses with your sisters – and wrestled all your brothers
> And then who knows I might have felt a family for a while

Ian dismisses any suggestion that Mott and CBS considered releasing 'I Wish I Was Your Mother' as a follow-up to 'Honaloochie Boogie'. 'I don't think it could have been a single because it's a bit psychological. I don't think it's quite simple enough.'

Hunter was highly optimistic about *Mott* at the time of release saying that the group had received an incredibly positive reaction from everybody in Britain and America and that the album seemed to be a hit before it even came out. The press also praised *Mott* universally: 'This album marks a giant step forward for Mott'; 'Truly great albums aren't released every week – in fact I can only name six this year that fall into that category. Now here's the seventh and I assure you it is the finest Mott The Hoople have done'; 'Unreservedly, I'd say this was a superb album, from the heart of the songs, through the excellence of the band's playing to the bright imaginative production'; 'John Peel thinks it might easily be one of his albums of the year'; ' Each track is a gem'; '*Mott* is an exceedingly impressive album.'

Mott The Hoople's music was angry but intelligent, verging on anarchy but just for the fun of it. 'A Sane Revolution', a poem by D.H. Lawrence on the back of the album sleeve, captured the character of the group, claiming that the revolution should not be done in ghastly seriousness or in deadly earnest, for equality, money or hate, but strictly for fun. *Mott* reached number 7 in the UK charts and the top 40 in the USA. The group wanted to give much more attention to the American market at this stage. Hunter questioned why they shouldn't and said the band wanted to leave Britain for a period, because it seemed to be swamped with what he considered 'below standard rock and roll.'

Mott The Hoople had a two-part US tour planned for the summer and autumn of 1973, 15 dates on the east coast in July and August, followed by 36 concerts from September to early November. T. Rex pulled out as support act and instead, Mott would play with Joe Walsh and The New York Dolls. Mott The Hoople were one of very few British bands to achieve major success on American soil. They were about to receive considerable attention and would leave T. Rex, Slade, Status Quo and even Roxy Music in their wake.

Immediately after the release of *Mott,* the group flew out for their American concerts, starting on 27 July in Chicago and finishing 19 August in Washington. Morgan Fisher and Mick Bolton augmented the live line up on keyboards but were not taken on as full band members, although Fisher had an interesting musical background and was subsequently to become official replacement for Verden Allen.

Morgan was born Stephen Morgan Fisher on 1 January 1950 at The Middlesex Hospital in North London. He was educated at Hendon County Primary School where he enjoyed mathematics, science and gymnastics, and received classical piano tuition between the ages of ten and fifteen. His musical influences were Georgie Fame, Alan Price, Dave Brubeck, Keith Emerson of The Nice, Leon Russell and, like Verden, Booker T and Jimmy Smith.

Morgan formed his first school band, The Private Eyes, in 1965 and this soon evolved into The Beat Circuit. He joined his first semi-professional outfit, The Soul Survivors, featuring vocalist Steve Ellis, in February 1966. They had a residency at London's Marquee Club for a while and cut a two track demo disc, Morgan's first recording. When they discovered an American group with the same name, they became The Love Affair, named after a TV series, and signed to Decca Records in early 1967 releasing Jagger/Richards' 'She Smiled Sweetly' as a single in February of that year. Morgan left the band temporarily to concentrate on his studies and by the time he returned, The Love Affair had signed to CBS Records and recorded two singles, a fine cover version of Robert Knight's 'Everlasting Love' and 'Rainbow Valley' which reached number 1 and number 5 respectively in the UK charts. Morgan re-joined Love Affair in August 1968 and went straight into the studio to work on an album, *The Everlasting Love Affair*, on which he co-wrote three songs.

Steve Ellis left The Love Affair in December 1969, formed his own group Ellis and eventually went on to work with Luther Grosvenor in Widowmaker. At Olympic Studios, around August 1973, Hunter and Griffin were lined up to produce Ellis on a cover version of 'I Wish I Was Your Mother'. 'The whole thing was poorly organised,' said Dale. 'The drummer was hours late and he was the first person we needed. Even when he arrived, the band had no real will to do anything. It was decided to abort the session without any recording. What a waste. We had the impression that the group were being coerced into recording Ian's song and working with us.'

The Love Affair recruited a new singer, Auguste Eadon, ex Shakedown Sound, and released several more hits, notably 'A Day Without Love', 'One Road' and 'Bringing On Back the Good Times'. Their second album, *New Day*, was issued under the name LA and featured three tracks co-written by Morgan. The band was then dropped by CBS but Love Affair cut two more singles for Parlophone Records before splitting in early 1971, although the group name is still used at various times for revivalist concerts.

Morgan decided to form a new group and, in the summer of 1971, acquired one of the first synthesizers in the UK, recruiting vocalist/guitarist Tim Staffel for classical rock band, Morgan. They were to form an early link with future superstar group Queen, Staffel becoming the original lead singer in Smile before they changed their name and replaced him with Freddie Mercury. 'Morgan played complex progressive material but I was sort of winging it, flying by the seat of my pants,' admits Fisher. 'It was just an experimental era I went through. Joining Mott later was a breath of fresh air for me, because I could forget all that intellectual stuff and let myself get out of control and see what would happen then.'

Morgan's first gig was at the Marquee in September 1971 and they subsequently held a weekly residency there, playing for several months but failing to secure a UK recording contract, and signing instead with RCA Records in Italy. Their first album, *Nova Solis*, was recorded in Rome in the summer of 1972 but sold very poorly and Morgan returned to RCA's Rome studio in February 1973 to record a second LP. This project was aborted and the group were dropped. Morgan split the band that summer although the recordings were eventually issued in 1976 as *Brown Out* and *The Sleeper Wakes* on Cherry Red Records in 1978. During the February 1973 sessions, Fisher had also worked on tracks for a solo album to be called *Morgan Fisher's Hand Job*, released in 1984, re-titled *Ivories*.

Morgan joined The Third Ear Band for two months via a music paper advertisement but only played two gigs and one radio session. He kept a continuing watch on the music press and, in June 1973, pursued a further opportunity. 'I spotted another likely looking ad, called this number and they rang me back, but they didn't tell me who the band was; they never do when they put ads in *Melody Maker*. So I went down to this audition and it turned out to be Mott The Hoople. Their rehearsal room was in Chelsea, in a basement under an off licence and I'd arrived early. It was a lovely sunny day and I was thirsty, so I thought a little drop of wine would be nice to relax me for the audition. I popped into the ground floor off licence and they were selling sachets of wine and I asked for a glass. Suddenly Pete came in and said, "Morgan, would you like to come down and play with us?" So I strolled into the rehearsal room carrying half a glass of wine. I think that probably impressed them a bit because they'd been used, I'm sure, to dozens of nervous guys coming in shaking. They just ran through a couple of songs and I played them right off. I've always had a good ear although I'm not good at reading scores.

'That night Stan called and said, "Morgan if you want to join the band, we'd like to have you." He mentioned they were impressed about my history with the Love Affair, who'd had some hard times after they admitted they hadn't played on their records. Mott felt I'd been through the mill a bit and knew what it was all about. They seemed a very nice bunch of chaps so I joined and within a few weeks found myself on a plane to the US, my first glimpse of America, and it was a real eye opener. I'd seen Mott once at Cooks Ferry Inn and thought they were a good rock band with a really great image. I wasn't a Mott fan, so I think I was doing it for the travel and a chance to play new music, which is always good in my book.'

Fisher joined as pianist and before departing for the States, went into AIR Studios with Mott in June to record a new track, 'Roll Away the Stone', and made two television appearances for *Top of the Pops* and *Hits a Go Go* in Germany. Mott had already auditioned Mick Bolton as piano player, but he became organist after Fisher's session. Bolton was virtually unknown before joining the group, having played with White Myth and Blind Eye, but he confesses Fisher was a much better pianist and that he was lucky to be given the job of organist simply because Mott perceived some potential. Morgan recalls Mick Bolton as a quiet, unassuming and charming man. 'He used to read his bible while I got up to high jinx in hotel rooms. We shared rooms often in those days. I think Mick was brought in as he was the total opposite to Verden, who was brilliant, but extremely intense. A bit of peace and quiet for us all. Nice guy.' Mick Bolton left Mott at the end of 1973 to become a Jehovah's Witness and subsequently recorded a series of demo tracks including 'The Last Love Song' and 'London Never Sleeps', which were never released commercially.

Having sorted out their keyboard dilemma, Mott The Hoople were delighted with their American live dates in July and August which were highly successful, none more so than a headlining concert at the Felt Forum in New York. Morgan remembers his first Mott show at the Aragon Ballroom in Chicago with Joe Walsh and Barnstorm as support.

'Joe was a real nice guy, we did several gigs with him, and before he went on he came to the dressing room and said, "Hi, I'm Joe. I'm staying in the same hotel as you guys. That might be kinda dangerous!" Ian happened to remark, "Joe, you can't go on stage like that, you look like a scruff." Hunter had just bought this really flash new leather jacket, it was all different coloured patches, a really nice piece of work. He just took it out of his bag, handed it to him and said, "Joe it's yours, wear it for Christ's sake," and Joe did. They were one of the nicest bands I toured with. The combination of Walsh and Mott was really great because he warmed the audiences up for us with his organic, non-aggressive gutsy rock, and then we came on with our attitude and smashed them to the back of the wall. In contrast, I remember on "Ready For Love", Ralphs' playing his solo in this vast antique ballroom under a huge mirror ball, with the spots of light whirling round gracefully and Mick's notes echoing out over the crowd. It was one of the most moving moments in my whole career and the perfect example of how delicate a rock guitarist can be.'

Mott The Hoople were supported on several dates by the up-and-coming New York Dolls, fronted by lead singer David Johansen, who regularly made off-handed remarks about Mott and became a 'public' rival of Hunter, even though the Dolls were really admirers of the band. Watts recalls, 'We had quite a lot to do with The New York Dolls and they were good guys. Johansen was so quick witted, like Noel Coward or something, and such a lovely bloke. He was super-intelligent, and used to give Ian a lot of verbal, but Hunter never said anything back, because he'd probably think of great things to say ten minutes later. I think David loved Mott The Hoople, but he pretended he didn't, and created this feud with Ian. He was always real friendly to us afterwards and used to show us round New York a lot in 1975 and 1976. When we first played with The Dolls in '73, they treated us like establishment and claimed they were now the rebels.'

Although Morgan Fisher describes The Dolls as 'punk before punk', Mott had been there already with their music and clothes, Arthur Kane copying Overend's outrageous boots, but extending it into cross-dressing. 'Arthur, the bass player, couldn't even stand up and had to have three or four of his fans holding him up most of the time at airports,' says Watts. 'Arthur used to like the platform boots I had made so, when I'd finished with a pair, and had new ones on order, I'd sell a pair to him but, in between them getting to Arthur, their roadie would wear them to carry the equipment. I can still see the roadie, with little round glasses and curly hair, Max, carrying a Marshall cabinet, wearing my leopardskin boots that were trailing along the floor, four feet behind him, because he hadn't got them done up properly. He really could have broken his neck because the plat-forms were a foot high and dangerous!'

Another admirer of Mott's was Ozzy Osbourne, who often tried to get back-stage according to Pete. 'I didn't know much about him and had never met him, because he was never allowed into the dressing room unfortunately. He turned up at a few gigs and the first I knew of it was when somebody said, "Oh, Ozzy Osbourne's been to the gig," and I asked where he was and they said, "Stan would-n't let him in, he's too noisy." That happened three or four times with Ozzy.'

Whilst attracting secret admiration from several US bands, Mott also received critcism from America's MOR darlings, The Carpenters, who claimed Mott The Hoople was the most outrageous and unprofessional looking group they had seen. Hunter was initially blase when questioned about this verbal attack saying The Carpenters were part of a different department, but he was subsequently scathing of Karen Carpenter. 'She dresses like a twelve-year-old and she looks about ninety-five. When she said she didn't like the guy with the shades and the boots I was upset, because Pete had the boots and I had the shades. That was two guys. So she's obviously not only stupid, but she's fucking blind as well.'

Watts says the band were actually extremely grateful for publicity that really worked! 'When they did that interview, obviously about The Carpenters, most of the article was about us, saying how dreadful we were and that we weren't human and we didn't play music. It seemed to double our following and, coupled with a rush of TV shows that we did at that time, I could feel the interest in us rising. The first time I noticed it was when we went to Disneyworld in Florida, horrible place, and people were looking at us and stopping us everywhere and asking for our autographs. It was an overnight thing and The Carpenters really helped us. Mott The Hoople couldn't have wished for better publicity!'

The group had wanted to aim high for this US tour including stage performance, equipment and PA. Richie Anderson recalls that the two best American sound organisations at that time were Clair Bros Audio of Pennsylvania and Show Co. of Texas, and the band urged Fred Heller to engage the former. In practice, Anderson soon discovered that a smaller sound company was retained by Mott's management, run by a former Clair Bros employee, and the tour was not without problems. Griffin remembers the nadir when one side of the PA died at the prestigious Radio City Music Hall in New York. The sound 'expert' was regularly chastised by the group and eventually suffered a nervous breakdown.

The differences in British and American touring were notable, as Richie describes. 'On the road in England we usually travelled short distances, but it was hard work with lots of stairs to navigate at the venues. We were filthy all the time, using dirty trucks, living on fish and chips and staying in crappy places or driving back through the night. The motorway services were absolutely appalling in those days. In the States however, travelling and driving was a lot more fun; the trucks were shiny; you could get a shower and a decent meal; the shows were usually a lot easier to get into and they weren't as tough physically. England was just hard graft.'

Just as the big breakthrough was starting to happen for Mott, stories started to filter back to Britain from the USA that a second member of the group was about to depart. Hunter was soon to confirm this to the press, adding that no replacement would be made, leaving Mott as a trio. 'I know for a fact that another member will be leaving. David Bowie told me that I should lead Mott. This decision has already cost the band one member – and now it may cost another. It's been four years now and people are growing up. If someone wants to leave home for a couple of years, we can't blame them.'

In August, CBS decided to release a second single from *Mott*. Back in June the band had recorded 'Roll Away the Stone' as the follow up to 'Honaloochie Boogie', but this was held in reserve to make way for an edited version of 'All the Way from Memphis', CBS's preference, which was forced on to the group. 'Memphis' was issued on 31 August, backed with 'The Ballad of Mott', and was highly praised in the rock press again – 'This is magnifico' – 'Genuine rock 'n' roll' – 'This number illustrates there's more vitality in the band, plus wonderful writing capabilities'.

Several publications selected 'All the Way from Memphis' as their Record of the Week and it rapidly entered the UK singles chart on 8 September and stayed for eight weeks, reaching number 10, battling against The Rolling Stones, David

Essex, Wizzard and Roy Wood. Once again, *Top of the Pops* was on Mott's promotional agenda. Filmed on Wednesdays and transmitted every Thursday
evening on BBC Television, it was becoming a regular slot for the group, much
to Watts' despair.

'*Top of the Pops* was hell, absolute hell! It was always a day of grind and misery. You *had* to get there for ten in the morning but they didn't need you. You'd
arrive and hang around in your dressing room for two to three hours. Then, at
about one o'clock, you'd go up for a camera angle rehearsal. They'd play the
record and you stood there while the producer sorted out the cameramen and
told you where and where not to move. That took half an hour, then you'd go
back to your room and you couldn't go out of the building, so you'd stay and
have something to eat. At four o'clock in the afternoon you came down for a
dress rehearsal and ran through the song, miming, before you came back down
again and did the filming at seven or eight o'clock. Then without fail, after
every show, you would want to go to the BBC bar for a drink on the top floor
at Shepherd's Bush Studios, and the old blokes with the caps wouldn't let you
in because you weren't a BBC Club Member. Stan would wrangle, argue and
eventually fight with them, and after an hour you got in. You'd end up talking
to other artists and be legless by the end of the night. It was horrible at *Top of
the Pops*. I hated it!'

There was however, one humorous incident during the filming of 'All the Way
from Memphis' for *Top of the Pops*, which looms large in the band's legend,
involving BBC disc jockey Tony Blackburn. 'Blackburn just didn't like Mott The
Hoople,' says Watts. 'He used to say mildly offensive stuff about us and our material on his breakfast show, and our supporters didn't like it. We had one fan who
used to come to all our London gigs and, during this telecast, he jumped on
Blackburn, pulled him to the ground and punched him a couple of times.
Blackburn came up to me afterwards and asked what it was all about, so I said,
"You want to be careful what you say on the radio, some people won't like it."
He replied, "I can say what I like," and I said, "Yeah, you can, and you can ex-
pect to get what you get as well." He just looked at me and walked off.'

'Tony Blackburn had an abiding dislike of Mott The Hoople,' says Griffin.
'We're not quite sure why, but perhaps because he was always trying to pull Pete's
girlfriend, Pam. She wouldn't have any of it and would be talking about her
boyfriend in Mott, while Tony was desperately trying to engage himself with her.
We figured this was the reason he loathed the group. He had played "Midnight
Lady" on the radio and was very critical of it and he was always taking swipes at
us. He was a popular DJ on Radio One, the only national pop music station in
the UK at that time, so he became a bit of a *bête noire* for the group. Ian particularly disliked him and this went round the group's fans, who were predominantly teenage boys, sadly. We would have preferred girls! During the show, one
of our fans got involved in a fracas with Blackburn and physically assaulted him.
We thought we couldn't have fans hitting him on our behalf – we'd rather do it
ourselves. So I decided to find Blackburn and apologise for the unfortunate occurence even though we weren't responsible for the lad's action. My girlfriend,
Paula, and I found him in one of the rooms off the main studio and made the

appropriate apologies, offering a handshake, but he wouldn't look at us. The apology wasn't accepted. Nice!'

Years before MTV and the critical promotional medium of video, Mott The Hoople's history is spartan in terms of film to say the least – a tragedy for such a visual band. 'It's a problem and very sad that there is nothing remaining of the group, in terms of concert footage or live recording that's any good, to reflect what we were really like,' says Pete. 'Richard Weaver did a fantastic job on some promotional films for us, but he did those for next to nothing. The budget for each one was £150!'

When the time arrived to perform their 'dreaded' promotional slot on *Top of the Pops* for 'All the Way from Memphis', Mott had a new guitarist. Immediately upon their return from America in August, the headlines in the music press confirmed the earlier speculation – 'Ralphs quits Hoople!'

11
I've got to move on

'Moving On' – Mick Ralphs

Mott The Hoople's management gave the following official statement concerning Mick Ralphs' departure – 'Mick has now left to join singer Paul Rodgers and drummer Simon Kirke. He left Mott when they returned from the States because he felt that after a long time he wanted to do something else. There are other reasons like lack of recognition and his fear of flying, but really Mick just wanted a change. It has taken from February for him to make the decision but Mott had to know sooner or later.'

With that announcement, founder member Mick Ralphs left to join Bad Company. Watts feels that Ralphs had run with the safe option because a group with half of Free couldn't fail, but he also recalls how bad flying had become for Mick, which was another contributory factor. 'It was sad to see him. He was just terrified. On the ground, Mick was a nice controlled guy, but up there he just freaked. It was most peculiar really. He used to take sleeping tablets before he boarded the plane, but he'd be terrified on the flight and then slump down and fall asleep afterwards, or hardly be able to do the gig. Nothing could stop it. I admire him for going on and doing the whole Bad Company thing afterwards, although they had their own plane and he would sit in the cockpit with the pilot apparently, to try and overcome his fear. People like Bowie and Mick Abrahams wouldn't fly and just point blank refused. It was brave of Ralpher to keep on playing despite his phobia.'

In early September, Dale Griffin explained about Ralphs' exit. 'We're sorry that Mick left, obviously. We were very much a unit. I think, though, that it will be good for the group in a way. Verden leaving was a kind of relief for us, and for him, because he was growing away from us, and it's difficult to be in a group where one member is not feeling part of what you're doing. It was the same with Mick, he was wanting to do other things. He wasn't happy because he wasn't able to write songs, I guess because the environment wasn't right, I don't know. We're sad to lose him, he's a great guitarist.'

Morgan Fisher had shared a Chiswick flat with Ralphs when he joined Mott and feels that Mick's departure was inevitable. 'It was, I think, already on the cards when I joined, and had been building up for some time. I had no idea though that Mick was leaving, and he never really spoke about it. Then he mentioned he was jamming with a couple of the guys from Free and I went to a rehearsal in the country and jammed with them, although I made the mistake of taking my synthesizer along! I think they were a bit put off by that. In the end, I believe Bad Company suited Mick very well. I hardly felt involved with Mick leaving, as a newcomer, whereas I'm sure Pete and Buff were very affected by it.'

At the time of Ralphs' departure, Hunter referred to the recording of 'Violence' again and the mock punch up sequence at the end. 'If they'd waited quarter of an hour they could have had the real thing. I was calling Mick Ralphs everything under the sun and saying I'd never work with the bastard again. Mick

hated the *Mott* album. His hands were there but his head wasn't there at all. In
the course of the album Ralphs was talking with Paul Rodgers. I said, "Tell me
what's going on. Put it like this, do you want to join his band?" He said, "Well,
he ain't got a band." "If he asked you to join a group would you go?" Mick
replied, "I'd have to think about it." Then I knew. He wanted to leave because he
had songs I couldn't sing. We'd done "Ready for Love" and he wasn't too happy
with that. He had "Can't Get Enough"; we'd used the riff already for "One of the
Boys". He felt they were really good songs. It was also the old thing of Ralpher
needing somebody to take care of. Paul Rodgers didn't know what he wanted to
do; he was vegetating. Maybe it was a relief for Mick to be able to do that again.
His playing improved tremendously. For that alone, it was well worth him leaving.'

However, Ian also explained that he had done everything possible to convince
Ralphs to remain in Mott The Hoople. 'I didn't want Mick to leave. I spent three
hours with him in Fred Heller's house trying to talk him out of it, but it was
getting ridiculous. I wanted Mick to stay. I even offered him half my royalties
on a total co-writer basis and he was writing maybe an eighth of what I was
writing. I believe in Mick Ralphs. I can't deny it. There's something about
Ralph's guitar playing that turned me on. His taste is impeccable, that's why I
say he's one of the best guitar players there is. Ralpher used to be perfect for my
stuff, but he wasn't too keen on doing it. He played great considering his heart
wasn't really in it.

'Mick avoids hassle like the plague. He's very nervous and he doesn't want to
hear it. He just wants to float along the surface. He was very forceful with Mott
when I joined; it was him that was doing all the hustling. I must have been too
strong. There are guys who, if somebody's in the room talking, they'll just leave
it to them. If nobody's there talking, they'll take over. With Ralpher, I'd walk out
of the studio if I thought he had something I wasn't hearing, and he'd come into
his own. But when I was there, he'd never say too much.'

Verden Allen confirms that he can imagine relationships between Hunter and
Ralphs became strained after he had departed. 'I was piggy in the middle with
Ian and Mick when we were rehearsing. I would often say, "Oh I'm not keen on
this, I can't get off on this at all." So when I left the group, Ian and Mick couldn't
get on because they were fighting about what to do next. So Mick left. When I
was there, and Ralphs was trying to push a number, I might say, "To tell you the
truth Mick, I just can't get off on this. It's not right." So we didn't do it. Maybe
I was a stabilising influence. Perhaps they didn't know that.

'I went to see Mick after I left. He was sitting down and he said, "I don't know
what to do. I don't know whether to leave the group or what." I said, "Well I'll
tell you something, you can't smoke two bloody cigarettes at the same time for a
start." He had one in each hand. I said, "I think you've left the group now. Go
with Paul Rodgers if you're that screwed up." His head had gone totally. I knew
him. I got him the job with Jimmy Cliff in the first place.'

Ralphs admits he left because he felt the band had changed. 'We'd struggled
all these years to have a hit and Ian was on a roll writing hit singles, but I'd started
writing songs and didn't think they would fit in the vehicle known as Mott

The Hoople. Also, as much as we were having success, the success was because we were writing songs like "Honaloochie Boogie" and we'd lost a bit of the wildness.

'Mott survived on struggle, adversity and disappointment and that gave us the spirit to carry on. We'd always said, sod convention, sod the system, but there comes a point where you can't be famous and be like that. We were always the underdog and that was part of the reason we were so spirited and so exciting. And then we got into this thing with Bowie, which was a great success and helped everyone, but in a way we'd become part of the system we were always dead against. We'd had success, but there was a different feeling in the band and it was time for me to move on. I didn't have the same commitment and interest because of the change. Mott was like my adolescence and I decided it was time to go off and do my own thing. I just wanted to play some different music. It was like leaving your parents; it's not that you don't love them, you just want to go and do something else.

'When we did the tour with Peace in 1971, I couldn't believe that someone of Paul Rodgers calibre was supporting us, although his band weren't that great. We all loved Paul and got him up to sing with us one night, and I said to him backstage that I'd got some songs we weren't doing in Mott and would he like to do them. So I played him "Ready for Love" and he liked that, and then I played "Movin' On" and he liked that too. Initially, I was just going to do some recording with Paul, but when I started working with him, it was obvious I was more interested in that.

'We were doing the *Mott* album and Paul wanted to record and put a band together but I told him Mott The Hoople had a US tour coming up and I had to do that, I couldn't just tell them I'm leaving, it wouldn't be fair. So I said to Mott I was going to leave, but not straightaway. I'd do the American tour and that would give them time to get somebody else in to take my place. Because I did the tour they probably thought I wasn't going to leave. I remember Ian saying to me, "You're playing great, why are you leaving, you seem so happy?" So I explained I was leaving but wasn't going to look miserable.'

Ralphs looks back on his fellow Mott members with affection. 'Ian Hunter is a very strong character. I respect him enormously, he's an excellent songwriter and he has a great handle on the business. He's also very good at dealing with the press, much better than I am, because Ian has the art of always saying something interesting. He's a very good wordsmith and a great chap to have in a band as he's so assured, although, like all of us, a bit insecure underneath. My old mate Pete Watts is an easy going guy but can be stubborn. He always had lots of great ideas and was always doing something interesting, like he'd have a guitar made in the shape of a bird, or a three dimensional chess set or would wear platform boots long before anybody else did. Buffin often underestimated his strength in the band, because he was always pushing the thing along and was a real driving force. He was also underestimated as a drummer I think, because a lot of people took something from his style. He believed so much in Mott The Hoople and still does. He has had more commitment to the band than anybody and has shown it over the years. Verden was a good, passionate man, often a touch impulsive and, if he had an idea, he was always very single minded and determined. But he was extremely musical and had great ability. He wasn't afraid to try something different for effect and would often play a wild style rather than adopt a conventional approach, which all contributed heavily to the Mott sound.'

Mick Ralphs formed Bad Company (named after the Robert Benton western) in late 1973, with vocalist Paul Rodgers and drummer Simon Kirke of Free. Boz Burrell completed the line up and was the least known of the four, although he had previously been with King Crimson, where he learned bass under the tuition of lead guitarist Robert Fripp. Bad Company joined Island Records in Britain and in America were the first addition to Led Zeppelin's new record label, Swan Song, managed by the late Peter Grant. 'He was a lovely man,' says Ralphs, 'and another big influence, as Guy Stevens was, but in a different way. If it hadn't been for Peter, Bad Company wouldn't have been as big as they were, just like Guy with Mott.'

Bad Company played their debut gig at Newcastle City Hall on 9 March 1974 and from the start were enormously successful. Their first album was a huge hit that year reaching number 3 in the UK and number 1 platinum status in the US charts. The album *Bad Company* had been recorded at Headley Grange Hampshire during November 1973 using Ronnie Lane's Mobile Studio and was produced by the band. It included two recent Mott tracks, 'Ready for Love', which now featured Mick Ralphs on keyboards and 'Movin' On', released as Bad Company's second American single. Ralphs also co-wrote two fine ballads with Paul Rodgers, 'Don't Let Me Down' and the acoustic 'Seagull'. The debut single from the album was 'Can't Get Enough' which reached number 5 in the States and number 15 in Britain.

The group became the most successful new British band in the USA achieving almost instant recognition. They departed on their first American tour for six weeks as a support act, but were so popular that they were instantly promoted to headlining status and eventually returned to the UK three months later. The band were a completely self contained musical unit, working both studio and live with the minimum of frills. Whilst many felt the group were lyrically pedestrian on some songs, the sparse tight rhythm section of Ralphs, Kirke and Burrell turned in some memorable melodies and riffs, and were the ideal foil for Rodgers' powerful and explosive vocals.

Bad Company's popularity increased on both sides of the Atlantic with the release of their second album, *Straight Shooter*, which they recorded and produced in September 1974 at Clearwell Castle in Gloucestershire, a location to be used later by Mott. The LP, issued in 1975, reached the top three in the UK charts and spawned two hit singles, Ralphs' 'Good Lovin' Gone Bad' and 'Feel Like Makin' Love' composed by Ralphs and Rodgers, which both reached the top twenty. Mick co-wrote two other songs with Rodgers – 'Deal with the Preacher' and 'Wild Fire Woman'. 'Once I got working with Paul I got into a roll,' says Ralphs. 'I unleashed a lot of songs because I had the perfect vehicle; I had the greatest singer in the world and the greatest drummer, and everybody was into the blues, so I was able to exploit my songwriting to the degree that I did.'

By 1975 Bad Company decided to live in the USA and Ralphs temporarily abandoned his Oxfordshire home. 'We lived in Malibu when the tax in England was ridiculously high and everybody was leaving the UK. We decided to cushion the financial burden and ended up living in California for six months in a rented house. We picked Malibu because it was about forty five minutes from LA, to try and get away from the madness, but of course we didn't, it just followed us out there.'

For their third album, the excellent *Run with the Pack,* released in 1976, Bad Company worked in Grasse, France recording and producing the LP using the Rolling Stones Mobile Studio. Once again they had a top-three hit album in Britain and, whilst the title track failed to chart as a British single, their US single, 'Young Blood', reached number 20. Mick Ralphs composed three songs for the LP, 'Live for the Music', 'Simple Man' and 'Sweet Lil' Sister', and co-wrote 'Honey Child', a second US single.

Manager Peter Grant's policy of a world tour every two years kept audiences hungry and perhaps explained the band's lifespan of ten years, but their subsequent LPs were not as strong as their opening trio and to some, not truly worthy of the adulation they received. The material seemed weaker in parts and bereft of new ideas on the albums *Burnin' Sky, Desolation Angels* and *Rough Diamonds,* although their 1979 single 'Rock 'n' Roll Fantasy' reached number 13 in the American charts. For a time, the band folded and Paul Rodgers departed, leaving them to reform in 1986 with Mick Ralphs and Dave Colwell on guitars, Simon Kirke and former Ted Nugent vocalist Brian Howe. They enjoyed considerable renewed success with several hit albums for Atco Records in America, including *Fame and Fortune, Dangerous Age, Holy Water* and *Here Comes Trouble,* the latter two being the strongest and achieving platinum awards. The band were produced by Terry Thomas who also co-wrote material with Howe. Rick Wills, formerly of Roxy Music and Foreigner, eventually joined on bass guitar.

Although they were always a major concert attraction, Bad Company didn't issue a live album until 1994, the excellent *What You Hear Is What You Get,* produced by Simon Kirke, and thereafter, vocalist Brian Howe departed. For a time, it was rumoured that Paul Rodgers might return to Bad Company but this did not materialise. As a solo artist Rodgers produced an excellent tribute album in 1993 entitled *Muddy Water Blues.* Initial copies of this CD housed a second disc containing re-recordings of Free and Bad Company hits including the Ralphs' tracks 'Feel Like Makin' Love' and 'Can't Get Enough'.

Bad Company's strongest albums are undoubtedly *Bad Company, Run With The Pack* and *Straight Shooter* and their 'Best Of' collection, *10 From 6,* issued in 1985, relies heavily on material from this era. It is however, short in content and the definitive CD compilation of their repertoire has yet to be produced.

In 1984, during Bad Company's temporary demise, Mick Ralphs released a solo LP entitled *Take This,* but with no singles and no promotion, the album died. Ralphs composed all of the songs including 'All It Takes', 'Give You My Love' and 'Another Lonely Day' and included one cover version, Chanel/Cobb's 'Hey Baby'. Assisted by Simon Kirke and bass player Micky Feat, all other instruments and vocals were handled by Mick. Ralphs arranged and produced the album at The Townhouse Studio in London and mixed the tapes with Max Norman, who had by this time, worked with Ian Hunter as a solo artist.

'I enjoyed doing my solo album. I had all these songs I'd written for Bad Company and Bad Co. wasn't functioning, so I got the songs, arranged them, booked the studio, hired the players, mixed it, put it all together, did the cover but basically lost a fortune! The record company said, "Oh, great Mick. Yeah, nice one!" but when I came to get a deal, I couldn't, because people just wanted Bad Company, they didn't want a Mick Ralphs album. I should have known that. It cost me quite a lot of my own money even though the record wasn't that expensive to make. The singing let's it down because I'm not a very good vocalist, but I had a great band. We rehearsed endlessly and that also cost me a fortune as I was paying their wages. It was a shame, it went nowhere and I had to split the group.'

Mick played only four live dates to promote his solo record with Dave Colwell, AC/DC drummer Chris Slade, Micky Feat and Lindsay Bridgewater on keyboards. The concerts were all pub gigs in the London area and the songs played in Mick's set included Little Feat and Ry Cooder covers. Ralphs also worked briefly with a lesser known group which he christened Cold Turkey. 'I was off the road and was in the pub one night and met these local musicians and said, "Why don't we just do a gig for the hell of it? We'll do R&B, blues and rock and just wing it." And they said, "Aren't we going to rehearse?" and I said, "No". So we booked a place to play and I wrote down the titles of some songs and unknown to me, they went off and learnt them all. We only did one gig.'

Over the years Ralphs has played on an array of sessions, appearing on album tracks by Jon Lord, Ken Hensley, Amazing Blondel, Ian Thomas, Lonnie Donegan, Jim Capaldi, and The Who's re-recording of *Tommy*. Mick also produced other artists, including Maggie Bell, Wildlife, and Scottish band Gun. 'When the original Bad Co. stopped working and Paul went off to do his own thing, I did my solo record and Simon became the drummer of Wildlife, who were later FM. It was quite a good band but obviously that was never going to go anywhere either, because the business really wanted Bad Co. to get back together again. Anything we did wasn't going to happen.'

Ralphs continues to live in Oxfordshire and has done so on and off since 1974. 'It's a lovely area. Most of the people are not natives because it's not far from London, so it's good if you are connected with business. Dave Gilmour of Pink Floyd moved into the area years ago. He's a wonderful man and probably one of my best friends bar none. I went on the road with him in 1984 for a year and had a super time. He saw me doing my solo thing and said, "Mick, you're wasting your time, just come on the road with me and save yourself some money." I also worked with another neighbour, George Harrison. I used to go over to his house and play with him and other musicians in the area like Jon Lord, Jim Capaldi and Dave Gilmour. George and I wrote a song called "The Flying Hour" together and then he used it on one of his Dark Horse albums, and gave me a credit, which was very gracious.'

Summer 1995 saw the release of a self-produced Bad Company album entitled *Company of Strangers*. A new singer, Robert Hart, had been added to the group, and his vocal similarity to Paul Rodgers was astounding. Five tracks were self-penned or co-written by Ralphs and the band undertook a lengthy promotional tour of the USA including a supporting role with Bon Jovi. Griffin Music of the USA also re-issued Mick's solo album *Take This* on compact disc but Ralphs has stated he won't do another solo album. 'Not after the last LP. It was a mistake. I'm a band person really.'

Bad Company's *Stories Told & Untold,* issued in 1996, contained seven new compositions and acoustic versions of 'Can't Get Enough', 'Silver Blue and Gold', 'Weep No More', 'Shooting Star' featuring Richie Sambora of Bon Jovi, and a superbly revitalised 'Ready for Love'.

Ralphs has remained committed to Bad Company for over twenty years and, more than any other, has been the one original Mott member reluctant to see any Hoople reformation. 'I personally think that Mott The Hoople was great as it was and should be left as that. I always think you can't really recreate something that was unique. I love everybody involved in it, and love to get together and see them, but we talked about a reformation a few years ago and I said I'd find time to do an album then. But, of course, you have to do an album and a tour and this and that, and it's too much. In all reality, I now hope to be away from home a lot less in the future, lead a more non-music biz life, be around my kids and try and find some peace of mind. I doubt therefore if Mott The Hoople will ever do anything commercially together again because it would be too involved. In fact we've had more success since we finished than we had when Mott was alive.'

Recently, Pete Watts has reflected on Ralphs' guitar playing, admitting that perhaps he didn't receive the recognition he truly deserved, particularly for his live work. 'When I heard Mick recently on the 1970 Croydon live tapes, some of his guitar playing that night was just so blistering. I've never heard Ralphs play like that. He was a natural in the studio and very adaptable, but Mick always liked to have his guitar playing quite refined. On reflection, hearing his live work, it was so much better than anything I ever heard him do on record. It was nastier and had more of a rough edge.'

12

Ladies and gentlemen,
the golden age of rock 'n' roll

'The Golden Age of Rock 'n' Roll' – Ian Hunter

As a result of Mick Ralphs' departure to form Bad Company, there was now substantial pressure on Mott the Hoople, with the second part of a major American tour to complete and no lead guitarist.

'We had to go on an American tour, as it turned out, before the *Mott* album was released in the USA, and it was decided along the way that there would be a two week break, the record would be released and then we'd go back and tour again,' explains Hunter. 'So all through that first tour it was on everybody's mind, "Is Mick leaving?" and Ralphs would not say he was. Fred Heller was trying to get Mick to commit to the next tour, and he was hedging his bets, but we were working, so what could we do.

'Mick decided that he would leave. This gave us two weeks to find another guitar player, so everybody sat down and said, "Well, who are we going to get?" And it really wasn't a question of who are we going to get. It was a question of who can learn the songs, in the next fourteen days, because we're playing the Hollywood Palladium a week on Saturday!'

'We knew before the tour that Mick wanted to leave, and we discussed ideas for replacements,' says Dale. 'We *did* all hope that he'd change his mind though.'

Mott considered various guitarists to replace Ralphs. Initially they thought of Mick Ronson from Bowie's Spiders From Mars and whilst he was interested, 'contractual difficulties' between Mainman and RCA at the time prevented any swift move. Hackensack guitarist Ray Major was also considered ideal by some members of Mott, although Hunter was less enthuastic about the prospect. Zal Cleminson of The Sensational Alex Harvey Band was another British candidate, alongwith American guitarists Joe Walsh, Tommy Bolin, Leslie West and Ronnie Montrose. Mott eventually decided to approach Luther Grosvenor, formerly of Spooky Tooth, an old friend from their Island days. He was delighted to accept their invitation.

'People were flying names around but the fact of the matter was who was available and who was reasonably good at that point in time that could do the gig, and it turned out to be Luther Grosvenor,' says Hunter. 'Once he was in, all these other guitar players that we were thinking about subsided. Somehow we felt loyal to Luther, so we just didn't broach the subject any further, but yes, Leslie West had been discussed, as had Joe Walsh, Ronnie Montrose and Tommy Bolin.'

'Bolin was named, definitely,' says Watts, 'but I was against him from the start. I didn't want any Americans in the group, that was my big thing. I didn't mean to be prejudiced but I wanted Mott to be a British band. I used to say to Ian, "This group is English mate, and it stays English!" He had this thing about America and wanted an American guitar player. Hunter wanted sax players and backing girl singers joining the group and we used to have arguments about that.

We nearly had a punch up in Sweden over it. We might not have argued so much over Joe Walsh because we loved him, but I don't think he would have joined anyway. He was a laid-back American guitarist and Mott wasn't that kind of band.'

Miller Anderson affirms that Ian thought about bringing him into Mott The Hoople at this juncture. 'At the time Ariel Bender joined, Ian thought about inviting me to join Mott but there was already a little bit of friction in the band. The rest of them weren't too keen on having me in, because I was Ian's mate and he was already becoming the front runner in the group. It was starting to look more and more like Hunter's band after Ralphs left and I think they felt, and probably rightly so, that if Ian got his friend in on guitar, it would strengthen that position. I could certainly play well enough, better than bloody Ariel Bender anyway. I never joined, but I probably would have been wrong for them because, although I looked okay, I was never really into dressing up and they were pretty image conscious. I would have joined though, because I like working with Ian and I liked Mott. I saw them several times.'

So Luther Grosvenor was selected and he too was pleased that Mott remained British. 'Mott The Hoople felt they had to have somebody in who was English, and perhaps a little bit flash and flamboyant. If you'd brought in an American player, you'd take something away. Don't get me wrong, all these guitarists were fabulous, they were probably better guitarists than myself. But it's like The Stones having an American guitarist, it doesn't really work, they're English, they're ours. Mott kept it British, which was important.'

Grosvenor was soon asked by Hunter to adopt the pseudonym Ariel Bender, a name which had been thought up for Mick Ralphs by Lynsey de Paul during a trip to Germany in June. 'We were doing a TV show in Seeheim, and Ralphs had been a little bit out of it and walked down the street bending these car aerials,' says Ian. 'I thought maybe we'll use Ariel Bender with Luther and make it sound like a guitar player out of nowhere and give him a new start. I felt so embarrassed about it that I carted him out to a Hampstead pub to break it gently to him over a quiet drink. I said, "Luther Grosvenor's a great name." He said, "I know, I love that name I wouldn't change it for the world." So I had to say, "Well that's the problem. We don't want to call you Luther Grosvenor, we want to call you Ariel Bender." He said, "Ariel Bender. I love that name. I wouldn't want to change it for the world. Call me Ariel, not Luther, call me Ariel." So we did, and he learned all the songs and we went back and played the Hollywood Palladium and went down great.'

'When I joined Mott, Ian took me to this pub and said, "The job's yours, it's secure, but what would you think of a change of name?" explains Luther. "And I thought it didn't matter – they could have fucking called me Joe Bloggs." Hunter went on to say, "Look, I'm a little bit embarrassed about this but would you mind being called Ariel Bender?" It was a great name for a guitarist who happened to be Luther Grosvenor, but Ariel really was created that night, in a pub, in North London.'

Luther Grosvenor was born in Evesham near Worcester on 23 December 1946. His parents came from Birmingham and Luther, named after his oldest sister's husband who was a GI, was the youngest of seven children – four girls and three boys. He was educated at Swan Lane School from the age of five to eleven and Four Pauls in Evesham, where he made his first public musical appearance, before he was fifteen. 'When I was at school, I played a couple of times in the hall, on my own, with an acoustic guitar doing Shadows songs, which probably sounded absolutely awful at the time. It didn't matter, it was what it was and it started me on my way to being a professional guitarist, which is all I ever wanted to be in my life. I began playing when I was eleven, on a guitar which my Dad bought me for about five quid. I was totally self taught and learned to read music but found out that, realistically, all you had to know was the fretboard.'

Luther's musical influences were predominantly Hank Marvin, the Shadows, Jeff Beck, The Rolling Stones and latterly, Led Zeppelin and Joe Walsh. 'I used to get pocket money from my Mum and Dad in the early sixties and go and buy "FBI" and "Apache", and rush home and play them on the Dansette which we had. I'd spend hours and hours getting these solos worked out and then run downstairs days later and let my brothers and sisters hear what I'd learnt, and my parents if they were interested. Money was very tight, but I remember my Dad bought me a Futurama Three, red and white like Hank Marvin's, and I used to look in the mirror and dream of myself playing on the big stages one day, which came true. I was very lucky.

'Jeff Beck, to me, is the ultimate guitarist. He does everything that I wish I could do. Even today, certain things that he's done, like the solo on "Shapes of Things", are magnificent. That was thirty years ago and for somebody to have done that then is incredible. To try and emulate it is virtually impossible. Joe Walsh is a great American guitarist and Jimmy Page is a favourite of mine. He was around before he was known, on Tom Jones and Peter and Gordon singles, and he played on The Kinks' "You Really Got Me". Some of his guitarwork with Led Zeppelin was brilliant.'

Grosvenor started his professional career in a band called Deep Feeling, formed in Birmingham around 1966 as an offshoot of The Hellions, who featured Dave Mason and Jim Capaldi. Deep Feeling recorded two unreleased singles, 'Pretty Colours' and 'Poltergeist of Alice', produced by Giorgio Gomelsky, who had worked with The Yardbirds, but they subsequently split when former Spencer Davis Group member Steve Winwood and Dave Mason collaborated and recruited half the band to rehearse an early version of Traffic. 'I got loosely associated with Spencer Davis and Island Records. Jim Capaldi, my good friend, joined Traffic. Through Steve Winwood and his girlfriend, they got me the job with a band called The VIPs and I joined Greg Ridley, Mike Harrison and Mike Kellie.'

The VIPs recorded two singles for Island Records, produced by Guy Stevens, and three EP's released by Fontana Records in France. The band maintained their connection with Guy, changing their name to Art and recording *Supernatural Fairy Tales*. In the following year, Stevens used Art as the backing band on an improvisational album. 'I didn't play on the VIP single "I Wanna Be Free", only the follow up, but I remember Guy particularly on the Art album. He was absolutely amazing, very inspirational and extremely good at drawing you out of yourself.

Guy was highly energetic and very speedy. Two artists, Weymouth and English, effectively financed the *Hapshash* album and with Guy, it was sort of organised, but disorganised. Whoever turned up at the studio could come in and play a bongo or a tambourine or do a bit of shouting, while Art were the nucleus or the musical roots of the project. I can't look back on it with particular pride, but it was of its time and, of course, was effectively a jamming record.

'Guy, in 1967 and 1968, was pretty much like everybody else at that time. Everyone in the Island stable enjoyed a smoke and uppers and downers, but unfortunately with Guy he did tend to be off his head more than he was sober. He grew up normal and drug free but, regrettably, as a young man, was always high on something. He was a great inspiration although often out of control and he suffered greatly from come downs and depressions. He was a mini-genius really but sadly drugs were a burden for him. The sixties were amazing. We were in control and we were out of control with one thing and another – speed, coke, mandrax – which were all around the scene. I didn't meet a lot of people that were totally straight, it was unheard of.'

After two commercially unsuccessful albums, Art changed their name to Spooky Tooth who became an integral part of the progressive rock boom, but without attaining major status. With Luther in their line up, between 1968 and 1970, they released four albums – *It's All About, Spooky Two, Ceremony* and *The Last Puff* which was co-produced by Chris Blackwell and multi-instrumentalist Chris Stainton, later to work with Ian Hunter. The *Spooky Two* album was marked by one of rock music's earliest marketing gimmicks – five different coloured sleeves. It was also linked with a controversial US court case years later, when Judas Priest's cover version of 'Better By You, Better By Me', alledgedly inspired the death of two fans.

An unknown part of Luther's career at this time was his consideration as replacement guitarist in The Rolling Stones after Brian Jones' death. 'I was in the running for the job with Mick Taylor and various other guitarists. It was done discreetly through Island Records and, although it didn't happen for me, it was a great honour to be linked with them.'

Spooky Tooth enjoyed considerable European concert success, undertook two tours of the USA and appeared in a documentary film, *Groupies,* with Joe Cocker and Ten Years After. 'It was a "why not?" situation,' says Luther. 'We were offered the opportunity to take part in a corny film about life on the road and being with the girls. I was a young English guitarist in America, women were there for the picking and I slept with lots of girls and enjoyed every part of it.

'Around 1969, I married Githa, my first wife, who was a Swedish model. We met at the Lyceum ballroom and we were together for about five years but it was a stormy partnership. She was modelling, I was here, there and everywhere – a real rock and roll marriage – but we still remain great friends. My children Emony and Jem are from my second marriage to Brenda, and now I'm married to Cathy, who I lived with when I split up with Githa.'

Having folded in September 1970, Spooky Tooth reformed in 1973 without Grosvenor, bringing in future Foreigner guitarist Mick Jones to record two albums before finally disbanding in November 1974. Looking back, Luther still regards Spooky Tooth as one of the highlights of his career. '*Spooky Two* was a great album and it was really where I belonged musically.'

After leaving Spooky Tooth, Luther started work on a solo album, *Under Open Skies,* writing material for the project in Spain over a three month period. 'Chris Blackwell thought it would be nice for Luther Grosvenor, ex-Spooky Tooth, to do something of his own and I went and spent two months in Chris's villa in Spain to have a holiday, get some material together, come back and possibly record a solo album. I had a wonderful time and didn't do all the writing I should have done, but I got six or seven songs, all as a very rough structure and played these to Chris who said go ahead.'

Recording sessions were completed at Island Studios in London, during the summer of 1971, and a single issued in August, 'Here Comes the Queen', later to be included in Mott's live set when Luther joined the band. *Under Open Skies* was released in October in the UK and Germany, featuring seven new songs written by Luther, who handled all guitars and lead vocals. He had co-produced the album with Tony Platt and sought help from Mike Kellie, Jim Capaldi, Mike Giles, Trevor Burton and Mick Ralphs. The record incorporated a number of different musical styles and was not a brash guitar dominated album as had been expected.

'There are a couple of soft songs on the album, but it's not really what I'd call heavy as far as crashing chords go. "Here Comes the Queen" and "Love the Way" were written with Gita in mind, but the inspiration for several of the tracks was me being free of Spooky Tooth. The single didn't really represent what the album was all about, but it just happened to be the most commercial track on the record and it actually did quite well. I was very happy with the way the LP turned out and I will always love the title track until the day I die. I could re-record it and make it into something quite special. The album was a very special part of my career because I wrote all the songs, co-produced it and arranged it. I still love the record.'

Grosvenor intended to form a live band to promote his solo record but when this didn't materialise, he planned a second LP using several of the musicians from *Under Open Skies.* In the interim, Luther played on Mike Harrison's *Smokestack Lightning* album then, in November 1972, accepted an invitation to join Stealers Wheel, originally formed by Gerry Rafferty and Joe Egan. They had recorded a self-titled album produced by Leiber and Stoller but before the record made any commercial impact, Rafferty quit and the group recruited Grosvenor on guitar as his replacement. 'It was a pleasure to work with two guys like Egan and Rafferty. Gerry wasn't there when I joined originally, I actually took his place, but he was a great songwriter and a great guy. Musically, however, it wasn't right, a blues rock guitarist joining a melodic outfit. It didn't really work and was one of the more uninteresting years of my life. There were some good periods but there was nothing really solid overall.'

Luther played on two tours with Stealers Wheel, singing vocals on 'Stuck in the Middle with You' and 'Here Comes the Queen'. He also recorded two singles, 'Everyone's Agreed' and 'No More', but then, 'Stuck in the Middle with You', a superlative folk-rock song, became a hit. Rafferty was encouraged to re-join the fold in July 1973, at which point all band members except Egan were dismissed. Grosvenor was asked to re-join Spooky Tooth but declined, at which point another door was opened by Ian Hunter and Mott the Hoople in August.

'I'd left Stealers Wheel in a little bit of limbo wondering what to do next and I was living in Hampstead with Githa. I was actually lying in bed one morning, and shall never forget until the day I die, the phone ringing, and it was Ian Hunter. He said, "Look, we know you, we're from the same stable, Island Records. You know Mick, he's leaving the band, we're in the middle of a tour, we've all spoken and narrowed everything down, do you want to join Mott?" and I said, "Of course!" '

Ian explained publicly at the time, 'I rang Luther – as he then was – from Memphis. I've always been in awe of him because Spooky Tooth were so incredible. I thought he was totally honest. That was another reason why I liked him. We gave him the job and within eight days this maniac had the whole act off and we did two TV shows.'

Luther immediately spent a week rehearsing with Mott at Manticore, Emerson, Lake and Palmer's unconverted former cinema near North End Road in Fulham. In hindsight, Dale recalls that whilst Grosvenor quickly perfected Ralphs' solos note for note, the sound and the feel wasn't quite right, even bearing in mind the short acquaintance of the band and Luther.

'We rehearsed the two hour set very quickly, which really wasn't fair,' says Luther. 'We all knew the time wasn't enough, but that's the way it had to be because they had to get back to start the second half of their US tour. We did what we could – it could have been worse, it could have been better – but it was all the time we had and any guitar player could have done with a week or two more. Then we had a few days in a US auditorium with the lights to do the final run through of what we'd "under-rehearsed" in London.'

'We anticipated a bumpy ride in the USA – into the great unknown without a safety net,' says Dale. 'It got the adrenalin pumping, though.'

Mott appeared on *Top of the Pops* with Bender to promote 'All the Way from Memphis' before flying back to America on 9 September to commence the second leg of their tour, starting at the Palladium in Los Angeles on 14 September. On the previous evening they played the *Midnight Special* rock show on US television with The Rolling Stones. 'I shall never forget the first night at the Hollywood Palladium, it was chock-a-block,' says Luther. 'Everybody was sympathetic, but I was absolutely petrified. You had the first number in your head and then you've got to remember all the others in this new set. It wasn't quite polished but we had a blinding first night and it was wonderful. I looked the part and we played the part. After that, I could settle down to being a member of Mott The Hoople, but it wasn't easy.'

Mott's headlining US tour included two nights at San Francisco's Winterland supported by Joe Walsh and Bachman Turner Overdrive (re-christened Bachman Turner Overweight by Fisher). 'Luther got rather too "relaxed" at the first Winterland gig,' says Griffin. 'He was all over the place. It was a nightmare.'

The end of the schedule also included a major appearance at Radio City

Music Hall in New York City. 'The stage manager there had an ego the size of
New York,' recalls Morgan. 'During rehearsals we decided to use the elevating
front section of the stage to give the opening a little more drama. Pete, Bender
and Ian were going to stand on that section while it was lowered way down in
the orchestra pit 27 feet below the stage. During the intro tape, it was going to
rise gradually to reach the stage just as we went into the first song. We were all a
little concerned that it would go right, but the stage manager looked at us as if
we were amateurs when we suggested rehearsing the stage entrance and said, "Are
you kidding – I'm a pro – trust me, it'll be perfect." He blew it that night and
was a full minute late, an eternity. The intro tape had ended and Buff and I sat
there in full view of the audience feeling like complete idiots, waiting for the
front half of the stage to rise out of the pit. So much for "pros".'

'I had to climb, in total darkness, ten feet up onto the drum rostrum –
arriving, in full view of the audience, covered in cobwebs and black dust,' says
Dale. 'Very professional!'

Grosvenor's arrival in Mott The Hoople was certainly greeted favourably by
press and fans and Bender soon adopted 'Walking with a Mountain' as his showcase at the end of their live act. Playing blistering, manic solos, Luther tried to
steal more of the centre stage at various points during the show, goading Hunter.
Ian would remain relatively impassive during these taunts until finally his patience snapped and, in a wild act of showmanship, he would grab and wrestle
Grosvenor round the stage before hurling him, still playing, on the floor. Hunter
liked Luther's taunting. 'It is a game that we play, but it's great. After laid-back
Ralpher, I love to see this punk come and challenge me for my turf. When he
comes on at me, all the underdogs and the rebels in the audience that feel like
they aren't making it, get off on him.'

In hindsight Luther agrees the visual chemistry was strong from the start and
that it got stronger with every show. 'The part that I`played with Ian on stage
was very powerful. Ariel started to steal a bit of the limelight, which Ralphs
couldn't do because he didn't have Bender's explosive, livewire persona on stage.
Grosvenor obviously wasn't like that with Spooky Tooth, but Mott was a different
musical approach. Ariel felt he could come on to Ian and take away some of
Hunter's glory. All of Mott's songs were structured but I was able to adapt
"Walking with a Mountain" as my freelance guitar showpiece. It became
dynamic, with me out front playing up to Hunter and he'd shout to the audience, "Who is the star of Mott The Hoople, Ariel Bender or Ian Hunter?" Then
Ian would throw me on the floor and drag me across the stage by my hair, literally. Bender brought Mott back to life and they'll admit the spirit returned.
Before I joined, I think it had started to become a bit angry and, in some ways,
jealous with Ian's writing. When Ariel joined the band they woke up again.'

'On that tour, Luther and I also devised that whole thing where we started
having these bullshit arguments for the press and that also developed well, got
attention and was a lot of fun,' recalls Hunter.

'The comments we each made to the press were meant to be taken lightly, but
it fired them up and was made to sound malicious,' says Luther. 'It was all a load
of nonsense. I knew Ian too well. We were great friends. We went to Bermuda on

holiday together for three weeks, we shared hotel rooms together and we genuinely liked each other as people and as artists. The jibes were purely a publicity stunt, and it worked.'

Bender's fun loving personality and spirit were also enjoyed by the rest of the band, as Watts recalls. 'I remember Stan getting Bender to a plane one day. Luther had his glitter cap on, leftover make up from the night before running all down his face, and Stan had him by the scruff of the neck with one hand and the arse of his trousers by the other, dragging him across the tarmac to the plane. It was all in fun. Luther was saying to me as we got onboard, "Oh, Pete, never again mate, I'm not drinking again today, that's it, I'm tee-total from now on. Eh, excuse me Miss, can I have a whisky and coke please?" Luther was always such a scream and when he was out of it he was a puppy and easy to handle.'

During the second leg of their US tour there was almost a third change in original Mott personnel when Watts started receiving messages from Bad Company's management. 'After Mick had left, they tried to lure me into Bad Company! Ralphs didn't ask me straight away, because they probably thought they'd get somebody easily, but on our tour we were arriving at hotels, would walk in together and the receptionists would announce, "There's a message for Mr Peter Watts." And there were telegrams saying, "Can you phone me urgently, Peter Grant." So I telephoned him and he said, "It's like this, Bad Company want you, the boys want you in the group." I thought God, how can you say no to Peter Grant, he'll have your bloody knee caps off. So I had to be really tactful and said, "Well I'm really happy doing what I'm doing at the moment to be honest Peter, but I'll think about it." "But they really want you, but they want you in the group," was his response, as if you'd got to drop everything. But I think he could tell eventually from my tone of voice that I was going to stick it out in Mott The Hoople. I know Mick wanted me around because we always got on well. Ralphs was like a big brother to me, he wanted to look after me in a way. I turned the job down but I think Boz Burrell was probably better for them than I would have been, because I'd have kept trying to change them all the time. I was like that in The Buddies and I never wanted Mott to stand still for long.'

Hotel high jinks were the order of the day as Mott played across the USA, in particular a night in Bethlehem, Pensnylvania when Watts' room was trashed. 'We'd done this gig, with Aerosmith as support, got back to the hotel, and there was no party, no birds and nothing to do,' recalls Pete. 'It was totally boring, so everyone came to my room and we thought we'd have a bit of a party. We had a few drinks and somebody came on telly we didn't like the look of, so somebody threw a cigarette at the television, then somebody threw a drink at the telly, then a glass, then a bottle and it just got totally out of hand. People were turning the bed upside down, smashing it, setting fire to the curtains and getting pictures off the wall and breaking them. Behind the pictures it said, "Picture Taken". There were feathers everywhere and then the telly went bang. It was terrible. There had been other incidents when damage was done, but this was the worst. There were fifteen people going berserk around me and I was sitting thinking, "this is my room". So I moved my cases to another room along the corridor. Next thing I knew, there was a knock on my door and it was Stan saying, "Get up, get dressed and get out. See that limo? Get in it, don't say a word to anybody, get to the plane, get on it and leave. I'm staying behind to sort this out." '

'The maids had gone in early before we left,' explains Stan, 'saw the state of the room, freaked, called the manager, who called the police, and obviously they grabbed me because I was the tour manager. I said, "Look, it got out of hand last night, it was a party and it got wild." I eventually talked my way out of it and paid up. The hotel people were happy because they'd got a new room, so I asked if I could take the television, having paid for the room repair, and they agreed. Hours later, driving to the airport, I stopped to fill up with petrol and started talking about the TV in the back and sold it to the garage. Next thing we know, Aerosmith use the entire story in *Circus* magazine, and say *they* did it!

'If Bethlehem wasn't bad enough, I arrived in Indianapolis hours later and joined a meal that the band and a local promoter were having in America's oldest Holiday Inn. Once again things soon got out of hand. The lighting guy and Bender were creating a fracas so the management called the police and they arrested the crew member. As I was ushering Bender out of the way, Ian decided to 'handle' the situation and addressed the cop: "Right, I'm telling you, you can't do that, we've got rights, my Dad's a policeman in England," and, as he pointed, the cop grabbed his arm, threw him through the front doors of the hotel and he was gone, into a police car and off to a cell for the night. Just another night!

'Every evening was wild with Mott on the road, because every night we had a party. We could often manage to hide it, but one week we had a damage bill of $2,000. Statements would say, "Six plants in the foyer ruined, Paintings removed, Curtains torn down …". The main culprits were myself, Bender and Morgan Fisher. I remember a fan's room where there was food and bed covers trampled into it all over the floor, and the police arrested the fan!'

Watts isn't proud of these tales but says they are a blueprint for the majority of rock groups. 'It happens with all bands. It's regular group behaviour really. It's part of what you do and all rock bands would say the same thing. Now we're older it seems totally stupid really, but when you're young and exuberant and things are going your way, it's like letting off steam. Especially after doing a brilliant gig or if you have a lousy gig. Ian wasn't prone to doing damage much but he did it more in anger if something went wrong. Same with Buff, kicking in a dressing room door once, that wouldn't open after a bad show.'

Morgan explains that the band would take turns every night to have a party in their room with Stan or the roadies, Phil and John, going out into the audience to organise the invitees. 'We'd make a few requests like, "That one in the fifth row!" It went on with American girls, one, two, three in one night sometimes. Pete used to keep a score and was always asking the next day, "Right. How many did you have last night?" I pissed him off one month, when I finally beat him. I think I got 27 in one month. Of course we were taking a risk, but nothing like the risks there are now with Aids. We'd have to go and visit the doctor sometimes in Harley Street and you'd see *all* sorts of music people there.'

'Most of the room wrecking generally took place in the States,' admits Richie Anderson. 'In England and Europe, they would get nasty about any damage, but in America, as long as you paid, they didn't care too much. I remember a Holiday

Inn room that was systematically destroyed and almost reduced to four walls. Often, Phil and I were already on the road each night, travelling to the next gig, so we missed a lot of the parties and didn't always experience the crazy times. The road crew generally had to try and stay alive and get some sleep, at any opportunity.'

The treadmill was now spinning faster and faster for Mott The Hoople and having successfully completed the second leg of their American tour, they returned to Britain on 5 November, four days before their new single 'Roll Away the Stone' was released. Once again they received encouraging reviews – 'Just a motter of time' – 'A hit if ever I heard one' – 'This single is another sharp and laconic gem.' The track, reminiscent of the Ronnettes and Phil Spector, entered the UK charts on 24 November and stayed for twelve weeks, reaching number 8, although it actually sold more copies than their previous number 3 success, 'All the Young Dudes', and gained a silver disc for the group. The B-side, 'Where Do You All Come From?' was a Hunter composition, originally written in 1971, but now credited to the group and recorded live in the studio. Both sides of the record featured Ralphs' original lead guitar parts and Mick joined Mott on one of their *Top of the Pops* promotional appearances.

Hunter and the band had now mastered the singles and album charts, a far cry from the desperation and lack of sales they experienced at Island, as Tony Brainsby their publicist recalls. 'I remember Ian coming into the office one day saying, "I've cracked it! I've cracked it! I've got the knack of writing hit records. I know how to do it." It had just dawned on him. He'd discovered the thrill of writing hit songs and it was great to witness his exhilaration.'

' "Roll Away the Stone" just happened quickly,' says Ian. 'I was playing in the key of C and it was the first time I realised you could bung an E major in. I thought great. It made it melodic.'

On 11 November, thirty US radio stations broadcast *The Pioneer Concert*, featuring Mott recorded at San Francisco's Winterland earlier in the year, but the music was not live. The 'concert' consisted of studio versions of Mott's songs sandwiched between a live recording of band introductions, and the audience reaction to those songs, with added crowd noise on top. In spite of vigorous complaints about the tactics employed, the group could do nothing to prevent it.

Mott The Hoople continued their heavy concert commitment with a 22-date UK Winter tour opening on 12 November 1973 at Leeds Town Hall and culminating with two performances at London's Hammersmith Odeon on 14th December. Queen joined Mott as their support act on all dates. Relatively unknown at this juncture, they promoted their *Queen II* album at the time and swiftly went on to become one of rock music's most successful bands.

Jack Nelson of Trident, Queen's management company, approached fellow American Bob Hirschman, Mott's UK manager, in September 1973, to ask if Queen could participate. Hirschman had reservations but, after consultation, Queen joined the billing for all the British dates. Trident made a down payment of £3,000 to contribute to 'on the road costs', in practical terms a fee, which was normal procedure at that time. With Mott's star rapidly rising, Queen thought the tour would generate considerable publicity but, in practice, the British press

did not universally praise the band, who subsequently complained to their management that they did not get sufficient exposure. The two groups became great
friends nonetheless and Queen subsequently joined Mott again on a US tour in
Spring 1974, the only two occasions in their history that they supported *any*
group.

Tony Brainsby was already promoting Queen at the same time as Mott The
Hoople. 'They were both in the office a lot. Freddie and the group had great respect for Ian and Mott, and similarly Hunter could recognise that Queen were
going to be a big band. The joint publicity situation helped that little initial tie
up and friendship between the two groups, but it was still quite normal at that
time for a support band to pay to go on the bill with a headlining act.'

'Queen were wonderful guys and very down-to-earth, although Freddie was,
of course, flamboyant and eccentric,' says Luther. 'You just knew they were going
to become stars.'

Watts also speaks highly of Queen's members. 'We got on fantastically well
right from the start. The day we met them, we were rehearsing at Emerson, Lake
and Palmer's studio, and we were looking at a little cine film Morgan had taken
on the road, projected on to the wall. They came in and introduced themselves
and every one of them was a really nice guy. Travelling on the bus also helped to
cement friendships and the two teams of roadies worked well together.'

Mott's British tour was a huge success, with eighteen of the venues sold out
and the rest over 90 per cent full. Their performances were highly praised by the
press – 'These are the REAL Dudes,' said *Sounds*, while *Melody Maker* described
their show as 'Very Flash – Very Rude – Very much '74 rock 'n' roll.' During their
Oxford concert they were presented with a silver disc for British sales of the *Mott*
album whilst at Southend, Freddie Mercury, Brian May and Roger Taylor of
Queen joined the group to help out on backing vocals during 'All the Young
Dudes'. The set for Mott's live dates included 'Drivin' Sister', 'Sucker', 'Sweet
Jane', 'Hymn for the Dudes', 'All the Way from Memphis', 'Angeline', 'Rose',
'Roll Away the Stone', 'All the Young Dudes', a stunning closing medley of
'Jerkin' Crocus', 'One of the Boys', 'Rock and Roll Queen' and 'Violence' and an
encore of 'Walking with a Mountain'.

Mott The Hoople's final show at Hammersmith ended in a riotous debacle,
the band's road crew and fans grappling and fighting with stewards, successfully
preventing the Odeon management lowering the safety curtain on a swashbuck-
ling Mott, before they had finished their encore. Their efforts enabled Hunter
and Bender to advance down the catwalk amongst the chaos, still playing a brutal
version of 'Walking with a Mountain'. 'Ian and I just kept on playing,' says
Luther. 'It was absolute chaos. I believe somebody broke their leg and the management were screaming at us to get off, but the adrenalin was flowing and it was
indicative of the power of Mott The Hoople at that time.'

A review of the show in *Sounds* said, 'This was a touch of the old Mott, the
shambolic rebel rousers. It's good that they're not falling into a cozy middle age
of success. It keeps you on the edge of your seat when you know such things can
still blow up at a moment's notice'. *Melody Maker* gave the show front page headlines – 'Mott Riot – rock 'n' roll is here to stay!' The two shows at Hammersmith

were recorded and it was announced before Christmas that Mott would be releasing their first live album early in the new year. Mick Bolton left the group at
the end of the UK tour to become a Jehovah's Witness but Morgan Fisher was
taken on as a full band member.

Another event at Hammersmith, had been the surprise announcement of
Buffin's marriage to Paula Greaves, a well known Page-Three model. No one ex-
cept Ian, who was best man, knew of the previous day's registry office wedding
until it was announced on stage. The celebrations after the gig involved all of
Queen, Andy Mackay and Eddie Jobson of Roxy Music, Guy Stevens, Paul
Rodgers and Mick Ralphs of Bad Company, Andy Williams, Mick Jagger and
David Bowie.

'Bowie and Jagger strung us along the whole day,' recalls Morgan Fisher, 'saying they will come, they won't come, they will come. In the end they showed up
about half an hour before show time. During most of the concert they danced in
the wings about two yards behind me, arms around each others' shoulders. It was
a great night.'

Fisher already had huge admiration for the road team that supported Mott.
'Phil John, Richie Anderson and Mick Hince were an utterly dedicated road
crew. God knows what hours they put in, but they always delivered the goods
and I'd not had that before I joined Mott. Roadies were always temporary
members, whereas it seemed that Mott had this solid team around them. It was
so important on the road, not only in terms of gear and making things work,
but having a bunch of guys going through the hassles with you. Mott's team
was A1.'

Watts also admired the road crew, and explains that each of them were characters in their own right. 'Richie was so slow we used to call him "Snail Shit". He
was like a vile Clint Eastwood and used to wear a shirt I called "The Riverbed
Shirt" – brown and grey – it looked like something that had been buried underground for a thousand years. He'd wear it all the time. Richie had a sick sense of
humour and would laugh if something horrible happened to somebody. He
always had a cigarette hanging out of his mouth but he was a very clever bloke.
He knew about electronics and we never had problems or any shocks. You always
felt safe with Richie and knew if you picked up a guitar you were going to be
okay.

'Phil John was Phil Carruthers Pilkington Neasby Smythe, the Earl of
Leicester, and he dealt mainly with the drums. Mick Hince was nicknamed
Booster and he was rough and ready and loud. He was fired in the end, because
he kept shouting at Ian and insulting him in front of fans while he was signing
autographs or chatting. Mick came around with us in the early days. He got his
thumb cut off at work and with the compensation he got, we made him buy a
van which we pinched off him, on the condition he became our roadie. He nearly
became The Silence's bass player for a while when I stayed in Italy. He played a
couple of gigs and was horrified when I came back!'

Dale acknowledges their roadies worked beyond the call of duty. 'When we
went to the States, all the bands there had about four times the amount of road
crew we'd got. How our guys kept it up I don't know. We do owe them a great

debt of thanks, because they never got any credit. Nobody could have worked harder than them and they were not paid very much, in fact they were paid very poorly.'

In November, Ian was already talking about Mott The Hoople's plans for their next studio LP, to be recorded in January. Hunter had ideas for six songs and wanted the new record to be more aggressive than the last. His original idea was a concept album, titled *Weekend*, about a group of British kids and their experiences and lifestyle over a typical weekend. Ian explained the idea to the band driving on the M1 one day and already had several songs written in outline, including 'I've Got My Mum', later re-titled 'Trudi's Song'.

By the end of December, the group were rehearsing at Advision Studios in London. The new album was now to be called *The Bash Street Kids* after Leo Baxendale's cartoon strip of the same name, which had been instrumental in significantly boosting sales of the *Beano* comic. The Bash Street Kids were a gormless gang who would cheerfully plot to blow up their school or drive their teachers to the brink of dementia. Academics once debated which stratus of the British educational system the gang belonged to; Baxendale explained they were the reluctant products of a bizarre alternative to secondary and grammar school.

Ian had written the title track and the story was still to be loosely based around the gang of youngsters, following the earlier *Weekend* theme. The concept idea was a good one, but Thomson Publishing, who produced the *Beano* comic and held the copyright to the Bash Street Kids, refused permission and prevented the group using their planned title. As a result, the song was changed to 'Crash Street Kidds', the concept was shelved and *The Hoople* album was born. 'Ian had several possible titles, but he was very strong on *The Bash Street Kids* which was actually a great title for a Mott the Hoople album,' says Luther.

'*Mott* had been effective as an album title, so *The Hoople* was a natural progression,' says Watts. 'We should have done a trilogy though – *Mott, The* and *Hoople.*'

The original schedule was for Mott to record the album for release by February at which point they would undertake an extensive European tour. However these plans were delayed as a result of significant studio problems. Mott had wanted to use AIR Studios and engineer Bill Price for the recording in January, but neither was available. 'We made a demo of "The Golden Age of Rock 'n' Roll" in December 1973 with "Dudes" engineer Keith Harwood in Olympic No. 2 studio,' recalls Dale. 'AIR was booked up and we were searching for a suitable venue to record *The Hoople*. Keith was fine, but the studio was looking ragged and in need of upgrading, so we passed. Sadly, Keith died in a car crash a short while after.'

Mike Dunne was then brought in as engineer for the album at Advision Studios with Alan Harris as executive engineer, although Harris took over when Dunne stopped turning up for the sessions and had a nervous breakdown. Morgan Fisher describes Alan as 'ex-Harrow and gung-ho'. The LP was produced by Hunter, Watts and Griffin with Dan Loggins, brother of Kenny Loggins, who had signed Mott to CBS, as production supervisor.

There were significant political developments in the USA and the UK at the beginning of 1974. The Watergate affair gathered considerable momentum as American President Richard Nixon was further implicated in the 1972 break-in and bugging scandal, resulting in his eventual resignation. Of more direct consequence to Britain, December 1973 had seen the country move into a three-day working week because of a miner's strike, which had escalated to the rest of the power industry causing public havoc. By the following February, Ted Heath's Conservative Government were ousted from power when Harold Wilson's Labour Party won the General Election. This undercurrent was to surface musically and lyrically in several tracks on the eventual album, and Ian actually spoke about the country's economic plight to the press. 'I'm amazed by it all. We've gone back to the Middle Ages in a week. One minute it's 1973 – now it's 1073. If I ran my group the way Ted Heath runs his Government, we'd be out of work in a week.'

Dale Griffin directed production of *The Hoople* album more than any other member of Mott around this chaotic period and describes the sessions as horrendous. 'It was a ghastly experience. Wrong studio, wrong engineer, country in crisis, strikes, electricity cut offs, petrol shortage, Bender oddly disconnected, not enough songs …'

Watts' memories of the Advision sessions were not good either, from day one! 'I arrived the first evening for a recording session in my '58 Cadillac Eldorado and asked the uniformed doorman where I could park. He proceeded to go mental at me for owning a huge flash car, which used an obscene amount of petrol, and "ruined things for the poor people". Were they paying for my petrol without me knowing?. I told him to "fuck off" and there was almost a punch up. A nice start for *The Hoople* album, and things went downhill from there.'

In February, the newly recorded tapes were re-mixed by Bill Price at AIR Studios with some guitars and vocals overdubbed on to the tracks recorded at Advision. Harris and Price helped rescue the recordings because, on playing the basic tracks back at AIR Studios, Mott discovered the sounds on tape were not good. There were frantic calls between Advision and AIR and tests run on tapes and machines, but in spite of these technical checks, it still sounded dismal. 'We felt that it had been okay at Advision,' says Dale. 'At this point any other group would have scrapped the Advision tapes and re-recorded the lot at AIR with Bill Price. Mott The Hoople however, were forced by management and record company to mix the album as it was.'

On *The Hoople* sessions, Mott used backing vocalists Barry St.John, Sue Glover and Sunny Leslie replacing Thunderthighs who had worked on *Mott*. Howie Casey and Andy Mackay played saxophones, but Andy was credited as Rockin' Jock McPherson. Howie wanted to be left off the credits, because he thought Mackay was a dreadful saxophonist and people might think it was him playing badly. Mick Ralphs was also around for several of the sessions and appeared on two tracks.

'I remember Ralpher came in one day with a picture of Bad Company from the States,' says Watts. 'It said Nick Phelps under Mick's photo and Paul Rodgers was labelled Jock McPherson, nothing to do with his name at all. We laughed and thought it was a great name, so we used it with Andy Mackay. Andy was

unconventional, almost avant garde in his playing and Howie Casey was a pro
session player, one of the old brigade, and didn't like it much. To be honest I
wasn't too keen on Andy's sax on "All the Way from Memphis".'

The Hoople album was the first to feature Morgan Fisher, who was a fully
fledged band member by this point, and Ariel Bender, who opted for stiff power
chords and riffs, quite different from the more tasteful Ralphs. Bender said of the
recording sessions, 'Of course there were suggestions made, which I followed and
which were good ideas. They came out really well. But generally I played what I
felt was right for the song. I played a lot of slide guitar, a lot of tremolo, and on the
whole I think the album is much stronger than what Mott have put out before.'

In January 1974, Hunter was saying of Luther, 'He's a great guitarist. He's
worked on *Spooky Two* which is one of the all-time great English rock albums as
far as I'm concerned.' But it was noticeable that *The Hoople* was largely keyboard
dominated and, looking back, Ian speaks differently of Bender's input. 'He was
fine at first because he just copied Mick Ralphs' parts, but when we got to do the
album we found out he had a lot of trouble with creativity. That's why it's geared
so much towards keyboards; he didn't know what to do. He put a solo on "Trudi's
Song" that was like Jimi Hendrix. It didn't make it at all; it's only a simple little
song.'

Morgan Fisher endorsed Hunter's concerns. 'Bender couldn't relax in the studio. Onstage he was speedy too, four bars ahead of everybody else. Doing *The
Hoople* album was quite tricky, we had to talk to him and encourage him a lot.
Bender was trying to adapt himself too much to the feel of the band, to replacing Ralphs. It didn't happen in the studio for Luther as it should have done.
Consequently, there's a lot of keyboards on *The Hoople*. I just steamed in and did
anything I felt like doing. I had plenty of ideas and it was a very enjoyable way
of recording. Overdubs were done in one or two takes and I think keyboards
added colour to Mott, as Verden's special style had done.'

The group spoke privately about Bender's lack of creativity at this time, but
he was a popular guitarist with fans and critics in America and as projected sales
of the new single and album were high, and with a major US tour planned, Mott
accepted the situation, at least for the time being. Publicly, everything seemed
fine, as Bender was pushed forward and did more interviews than any other band
member.

The new single release from *The Hoople* was Hunter's 'The Golden Age of
Rock 'n' Roll', issued on 15 March 1974. The lyrics concerned Leeds City Council
who tried to impose a 96-decibel noise limit on local rock concerts in 1973, an
issue which became big news at the time. Buffin remarked, 'Rock 'n' roll is for
the young and to be enjoyed, and now these old bastards are trying to tone it
down. The song is telling them to leave us alone.'

> Everybody move, everybody groove
> There ain't no trouble in the streets now
> So if the going gets tough
> Don't you blame us
> You ninety-six-decibel freaks

Ian explained that it wasn't really a nostalgia song as the title suggested. 'If anything, the golden age of rock 'n' roll has been in recent years, where the industry has picked up phenomenally even without people like The Beatles. The secretary of the students' union at Liverpool Polytechnic wrote to me and asked if I could do something about the 96-decibel limit. It's very difficult to do, because when you write to a Town Hall you only get the same reply as them. I did write to the Town Hall, asking them specifically not to send me a reply, as she'd sent me the reply she'd got, and I didn't really want that. This was about the time I was writing "Golden Age", so "The Golden Age of Rock 'n' Roll" is meant to be, "what would it be like if these 96-decibel idiots got their own way?" I don't think they know quite what they're letting themselves in for. To me, it's ridiculous, the whole thing.'

'The Golden Age of Rock 'n' Roll' entered the UK charts on 30 March and stayed for seven weeks. The single attracted favourable press headlines such as 'Mott's rock and sleaze' but one reviewer expressed concern about the scale of the single's hit potential. The song peaked at number 16, a slightly less favourable chart placing than Mott's recent run of hit singles. Hunter now describes 'Golden Age' as an average song which should not have been put out as a single, and Watts says bluntly that he 'can't bear it!' The song had lyrical reason, but the band consider that the recording and musical feel were below par. Once again, Mott used Richard Weaver to direct a promotional video for the single.

The B-side, 'Rest in Peace', was credited to Hunter, Watts and Griffin, but was not included on the new LP, having been recorded live, without any overdubbing, by Bill Price at AIR No. 2 studio, during the mixing of *The Hoople*. ' "Rest in Peace" was too churchy,' remarks Pete. 'Good for a breather on stage though, and a few swigs of booze!'

The early part of the album sessions had also yielded a recording known as 'The Advision Jam', described by Dale Griffin as 'crap' and regarded as something of a skeleton in Mott's closet. The session was no more than an impromptu take of Jerry Lee Lewis, Hank Williams and Ray Charles standards, namely 'Whole Lotta Shakin' Goin' On', 'Your Cheating Heart' and 'What'd I Say', featuring Dan Loggins on lead vocal and Hunter on drums! The group having had a fairly unproductive day and rather too much to drink, decided to forget serious recording and have fun instead. 'There were certain bits of magic there,' says Luther. 'I wouldn't say it was crap or wonderful, I'd say the time was great and it was only a jam.'

The Hoople album was issued on 22 March in Britain and was certified gold in both the USA and Britain before release. All the songs were composed by Ian apart from one track, 'Born Late '58', where Overend Watts made his writing debut. 'The Golden Age of Rock 'n' Roll' single, with its pseudo Alan Freed DJ introduction, opened the LP in rousing style, but on the second track, Mott went straight for the jugular and delivered the cornerstone of the album.

'Marionette' was a frantic operetta, and a production masterpiece, about the business side of rock and the manner in which it could affect musicians manipulated by management and large corporate organisations. Around this time,

Hunter remarked on the strains of Mott's new found success: 'It's heavy these days, it's not like it used to be. You've got to be pretty insane to keep your sanity. The pressures are intangible, but it's a 24-hour rush of arguments and people expecting so much of you, not understanding when you can't quite deliver, right from the kids up to the top brass of Columbia Records. You've got to be healthy to keep up with it all.'

> And when the coffin comes – make sure there's room for two
> You lied – I led
> I died – you're dead

Once again, Hunter was unconsciously leading the field with his interpretation of the industry's pressures and its dramatic effect on rock stars, a script that was to be mirrored on film, with the subsequent release of the David Essex movie, *Stardust,* in 1975.

'I thought Essex was great in *That'll Be the Day* and *Stardust.* He was a really good artist. I think he just got lumbered with the wrong audience. *Stardust* was pretty much how it is though, when you get near the top, and I was saying that in "Marionette". In fact, in the film, his girlfriend says he has become a marionette, which might be a total fluke, but I got a little chill when I was watching the movie, because that was right where I was at. Once you've got something successful going, you have to keep it going, because a lot of people are getting paid, so it all has to be planned ahead and that's when I started to get a bit funny about it. If somebody asked me at the end of a tour whether I wanted to do another one, I'd be perfectly happy, but there's something about it all lined up in front of you. It looked like too much to me.'

Ian described 'Marionette' as the best track that Mott had ever done and heaped praise on Dale Griffin's production involvement. The song featured Andy Mackay and Howie Casey on saxophones, Mike Hurwitz on cello, in the absence of Paul Buckmaster who was unavailable, and Graham Preskett on violin. Watts observed that Hurwitz was not as rock orientated as Buckmaster had been on *Mott* and he ended up guiding Mike on the cello parts for 'Marionette'. Ian, Ariel and Overend contributed 'Voix grotesques à la Quasimodo' backing vocals and Bender was responsible for the manic laughter in the central portion of the song. Watts was also instructed to hit Grosvenor over the head repeatedly with a tin tray to create the crashing noises on the choruses. 'There was a huge row at Advision about the damage caused to this bloody tin tray, too,' says Dale. 'That place was a total nightmare.'

'Marionette' was a nightmarish mini-opera of five minute duration, a concept that would shortly be used by Queen for their multi-million-selling single 'Bohemian Rhapsody'. At the time of release Ian explained, 'It's something I've wanted to do personally as a songwriter for a long time and that is to do a five-minute opera, as opposed to an opera that goes on for forty minutes, which I feel might be a bit trying. I mean *Tommy* wasn't trying at all, neither was *Arthur,* but when I listen to music I like to hear a hook all the time, and I think we got it with "Marionette". I think perhaps this is the first track where we've really got it all the way through. One thing hits you, another thing hits you and you don't get room to sit back.'

Hunter is adamant that Jeff Lynne and the Electric Light Orchestra, whilst influenced by The Beatles, were watching Mott The Hoople. 'I was messing with European against American influences on "Marionette". "Memphis" was another one, a European staccatto verse and an American groove on the chorus. Sometimes I don't think we influenced people when they say we did, but then on some occasions we did, and they don't admit it. Queen said they were influenced by us but Lynne didn't, and yet he went for the same quasi-European zig zag feel, saxes against cellos, very dramatic.'

The third track on the album was 'Alice', a New York song about a 42nd Street prostitute, featuring Lynsey de Paul and the whistling 'moog mouse', Overend playing bass through a Leslie cabinet and a cultured, relaxed Morgan Fisher on organ. The bass line was 'lifted' from Nils Lofgren's group Grin. It was a very 'busy' and ambitious track with an excessive lyrical out-pouring from Ian which demanded careful listening. Mott attempted one concert version of the song, but the panoply of words caused the group to abandon it.

Watts was a huge admirer of Nils Lofgren and forced Tippins to go out and find him when Mott played in Washington. Stan returned on the night of the gig, holding Lofgren by the shoulder, much to Watts' amazement. Pictures were taken and Pete gave him various stage rings, Nils being somewhat mesmerised by it all. Years later they both met at The Venue in London and Lofgren helped Watts on a market stall that he had started in Portobello Road.

Side One of the album closed with 'Crash Street Kidds' which was an extension of 'One of the Boys' and, more directly, 'Violence', being about boredom and maltreatment. Ian explained that he had an absolute preoccupation with New Towns which didn't seem to have any heart or centre. The song was the tale of a street gang in such a town, who were so disaffected and disenchanted with the way things were run by local and national government, and the police force, that they decided to form their own 'army' and take over Britain.

Heed my faults – and heed my curse
Heed my frustration – you just don't know
New Town nothing – send for the hearse

Hear me swear – hear every word
I ain't just a number- I wanna be heard
The TV announcer – he talks to the scum

The Crash Street Kidds are comin' to get you
Better run, better run, better run
The Crash Street Kidds are comin' to get you
One's your son, one's your son, one's your son

'Crash Street Kidds' was a sinister and brutal rocker featuring hard guitars and an amazing finale where Ian was 'gunned down'. Dale Griffin confesses that one slight problem was the ending, which had the puniest sounding machine guns imaginable. ' "Crash Street Kidds" was meant to end in a cacophony of machine guns and explosions to denote the coming insurrection, *coup d'état* or Armaggedon. Sadly the effects available to use were woefully inadequate and it all ended up a tad Mickey Mouse.'

Hunter had already given us 'The Moon Upstairs' and 'Violence' and this completed his aggressive triptych, as he hammered home premonitionary, threatening lines of discontent and frustration, further fuelling the punk movement that would rise three years later. Ian is unphased by any visionary claim and feels that the New Wave and British street riots were predictable, but Dale praises his writing and the uncanny vision contained in his lyrics. 'Ian was capable of astonishing flashes of percipience and, with "Violence" and "Crash Street Kidds", he brilliantly foretold the coming and the mood of the punk era in the UK, not to mention the civil unrest of the early eighties. In many ways Hunter was a punk, in that he had within him great feelings of anger and frustration.'

One reviewer remarked, ' "Crash Street Kidds" is a number which has the Hells Angels and The Monattoes (people who removed corpses during the time of the Great Plague) alongside the James Dean legend and the romantic myth of *A Clockwork Orange*.'

Side Two opened with 'Born Late '58', Overend Watts' songwriting and lead-vocal debut. It was the only number, other than 'I'm a Cadillac', that Mott ever recorded without Hunter, in a week where he had gone to the USA for interviews, telling the group to 'get Bender fucking sorted out!' Following the overlying theme adopted on 'Drivin' Sister' and 'I'm a Cadillac', Watts used car terminology to mask the underlying subject matter, not a 1958 automobile, but a girl who would actually have been below the age of consent had she been born on the stated date. Hunter declared in 1974 that not only was it a highly creditable debut from Watts, but the song was also single material.

The track had Overend on 12-string, rhythm and 'Manfred Mann's bass guitar' and featured excellent slide Strat from Ariel. Watts recalls: 'I used a single pick up Gibson SG Special for the riff on "Born Late '58", and sold it for £80 to pay a gas bill three months later, we were so hard up. I was gutted. This was 1974 – at our peak! I also used a baby Rickenbacker 12-string on it – solid body. I had to sell that too – £120 – Bastards!'

Watts writing style was of simple construction, compared to most of the material on Side One, and there was more emphasis on beat, which offered a nice break in the proceedings, but Pete is less than convinced. 'The band, particularly Ian, had always tried to get me to compose, but I felt the chemistry of Hunter and Ralphs' writing shouldn't be interfered with. When Phally started to write, and then pushed to get his songs on albums, it really worried me that it might upset the balance too. Even after Mick left, Ian said to me again, "Look you've got to try and write something." And I didn't really want to, because I didn't feel like a natural writer and found it very difficult, particularly the lyrics. What inspired "Born Late '58" was, I was told, "There aren't enough tracks for album, you've got to write something. Ian's going to America to do interviews, we need another track, it's got to be a rock number and you've got to write it." That's it, plain and simple. There was nobody else to do it. For my first recorded song, it's almost half okay, but lacks a decent hook. It had a good riff, but with an average lyric stuck on it. Wookie (Pam Chuck), my girlfriend, and Mick Ralphs actually helped me with the words. She even came up with the title!

'I remember trying to finish off the lyrics upstairs at Advision Studios in the middle of a party! There were about ten people there, including Wookie and Ralpher in gleeful mood. Everyone was drunk. Ralphs was already with Bad Company, but he always hung out with us when he could, and we liked that too. When I got to the line, "Listen feller, never gonna sell her", I changed it to, "Listen Heller" – a reference to our manager. Then, somehow, Ralpher and I got on this stupid roll with lyrics like, "Hirschman – log's in a dan" (Manager Hirschman and Dan Loggins – CBS A&R man). We didn't like any of these "officials" much. I can see Mick crying with laughter and repeating the lines over and over again. We went almost hysterical about it. On the lyric sheet, the words were perceived as "Hush man, doves in a tan," which I liked a lot. The poor devil at the publishers must have played it again and again to try and decipher the undecipherable. He did well in the end!

'Later that night, damage was done and a posh glass table top was broken. Advision went potty the next day. The culprit never owned up. They went even more potty when the old tea lady reported angrily, that her metal tray had been rendered useless (like tin foil). I'd smashed it over Bender's head at least five hundred times during the recording of "Marionette" to get the crashing noises on each chorus. He begged me to hit him, "'arder, 'arder", so I did. They never liked us at Advision!'

'Trudi's Song', a quiet, gentle love song, was self explanatory in content, Hunter emphasising that it was a simple piece inspired by the vocal sound on Dylan's *Nashville Skyline*. Ian enthused about Fisher's excellent playing and, in spite of his recent introduction, the fact that it seemed as though he had been with Mott since the beginning. Morgan's piano, played through a Leslie organ cabinet, added beauty and life to the track. Every Mott The Hoople album featured one ballad and this was a charming gift from Ian to his wife. ' "Trudi's Song" was really solo album material and had no place on a Mott The Hoople record,' says Dale.

Hunter made a further stinging comment on the state of the country and the British political system in 'Pearl 'n' Roy (England)', originally titled 'J.C's Alright'. But Ian's success meant he could now look at life from a slightly different perspective. 'I'm not a working class hero anymore, but I have been,' admitted Hunter. 'I really feel that social class, because that's where I come from. There's no difference between people in the street and myself. "Pearl 'n' Roy" was a great backtrack, really buoyant, and was finished, but I hadn't written the lyric. I took it home and these words came pouring out. I couldn't alter them because the lyric was good, but it was a down lyric.'

> Now I'll tell you something
> It seems to me that the rich dudes live in the sun
> And if Eton be a democracy – well I'm gonna get me some

> They got no chins and they always win
> Piece of glass hides the class from the mass
> Uni-own Jack is starting to crack
> The greed breed's killing off the grass

'It's about all politicians really, but in particular it related to the state of British politics just before the 1974 election,' remarks Dale. 'It was saying that they'd blown it.… What were they going to do about the mess they'd presided over.'

Sadly, 'Pearl 'n' Roy's' lyrics were overtaken by events as they referred to the Conservative Prime Minister of the day, Ted Heath, whose government was ousted shortly afterwards by a Labour Party election victory. The song featured Blue Weaver on the choruses and 'opening saloon bar scene'. Blue was to replace Mick Bolton on organ for Mott's 1974 tours and this was his only studio appearance with the group. Mick Ralphs also appeared on the choruses.

'Ralphs used to hang around the studio to see how things were going and he came on *Top of the Pops* with us,' says Luther. 'Mott was still his baby and I think he genuinely came along just to see how things were developing for me, and for the love of his old band. You know, you don't play for fucking Liverpool for twenty years and move on, and have no love any more. You'll always go back and sit and watch. It's the same with music. Mick loved Mott The Hoople and liked me, and it was nice.'

'Through the Looking Glass', previously titled 'Why My Love Slipped Away', was effective and extremely dramatic but, in truth, possibly not a Mott The Hoople album track, as it didn't really showcase the band in any case. The song was constructed in 'Hymn for the Dudes' mode, building and falling against a stunning orchestral arrangement, written and conducted by Graham Preskett. Like Watts, Morgan Fisher admired Preskett greatly. 'Graham had a really good sense of what the band needed. He was a first-class arranger but he sensed what fitted over a rock group like us. I complimented him one day and remarked that his input must have entailed a lot of work, but he told me he just jotted arrangements down on his way to the session!'

> And you're my voyeur, see every line
> Chase them to destinations, on through time
> And you're my diary, the bitter truth
> Unexpurgated, my mis-spent youth

Mott also prepared an alternative 'private' version of 'Through the Looking Glass' featuring a coda of abusive language which horrified and fooled CBS when it was explained that the obscenities were necessary to demonstrate the inner conflict and alter ego of the writer. The stream of invective filth was a mimic of Mick Hince, Mott's former roadie, and this 'profanity' version was included on Columbia's 1993 *Ballad of Mott* compilation, much to Hunter's chagrin. 'Dan Loggins, Kenny Loggins brother, had signed Mott to Columbia and was our benefactor. You could do things like that in the studio with Dan, and play it back and watch for the record company reaction. So I did it and we played it for him, as if that was the version that was going on the record, just to get him going. And he didn't do anything bless him, until a few days later when he phoned in a panic about the ending, and I explained we were pulling his leg. I was a bit pissed off though when somebody had the brilliant idea that it should come out in 1993. It was strictly for the studio.'

Dale Griffin recalls a lot of grey-faced sweating CBS people after the playback, some of whom said they could even understand the need for the outpouring of profanity. 'We earlier played the same kind of trick on the same A&R man at EMI during the "Memphis" vocal/sax dubbing sessions. Another episode was after Verden Allen's 'resignation', at a time when CBS were nervously bank-rolling the band. There was a wonderful scene with Dan Loggins at Abbey Road Studio 2 over money. We were all feeling the pinch, but Watts was the group profligate and a situation was set up so that when Loggins arrived, Pete would ask for more money. His "Cadillac needed repairs and the butcher was threatening to repossess the meat in the freezer." John Leckie, the engineer, got all of the non-sense on tape and Watts did a great acting job. Dan was totally taken in and began to whine about "all the money we've spent on you guys", before adopting a slightly more aggressive stance. Just what we'd anticipated.'

'Roll Away the Stone', the last track on the album, meant *The Hoople* was framed with two hit singles, effectively an overture and finale. The album version had some minor changes though as Mott used the original backing track, added Bender's harmony line and got Lynsey de Paul to re-voice the spoken section in the middle of the song. Sue and Sunny were also engaged as backing singers for *The Hoople* sessions. 'They were very professional and easy to work with,' observes Watts. 'They were married to Alec Leslie and Johnny Glover and we were always jealous. We'd be driving back from Manchester at five in the morning in the freezing cold and would say, "Look at Johnny Glover and Alec Leslie, look at 'em, lying in bed now with Sue and Sunny and colour TV's, and look at us". We only had black and white televisions!'

Roslav Szaybo had designed the *Mott* album sleeve and was commissioned for *The Hoople* cover too. He came up with a simple idea and replaced the male face on *Mott* with a female's face, Kari Ann Moller, a popular and much-in-demand Norwegian model, former lover of Bryan Ferry and wife of Chris Jagger. *Mott* had pink running into white on the cover and *The Hoople* repeated the theme in blue. A simple Dylan quote was included on the rear of the sleeve this time – 'It's life and life only.' Ian appeared on BBC radio and talked about the LP enthusi-astically. 'This album's about ten times better than the last one. I can't believe it, it's great. I'm knocked out with it. This time we concentrated even more than we did on the *Mott* album, and that got five awards, so we'll be able to get half a dozen with this!'

The Hoople received excellent press reviews and dramatic headlines: 'Mott – Fragments of Madness' – 'Hoople's Blood and Thunder'. 'It's jagged, fragment-ed, punctuated with bursts of maniac laughter, arrogant and eerie. The whole band sound as if they find the studio acutely claustrophobic and are fighting des-perately to get out. Ariel's playing is as uncomfortable as a high speed dental drill while Hunter's voice seems all out to provoke a row with the listener,' said one critic, clearly animated by the record. 'The album adds up to Mott at their biggest and best, their most ambitious production yet. It has denser colour than before, each number sprung in Hunter's new punk-poet imagery. With this album, Mott absolutely establish themselves as Britain's major new band.'

Luther feels that *The Hoople* was probably the best record Mott made. He had written some material but didn't contribute any compositions for his first studio outing with the group. 'Mott was geared around Ian Hunter and, to some extent, Buff and Pete, and should have been. If I'd been there another year I would have been writing material for Mott. In the meantime, we knocked around with "Here Comes the Queen" and they felt I should come forward in the stageshow and do that live.'

But Mott had become privately frustrated with the lack of imagination that they felt Grosvenor displayed on *The Hoople,* and the group was further alarmed upon hearing a live recording of Bender. In hindsight, Dale Griffin feels that Luther wasn't entirely at fault, as Mott really weren't ready to record *The Hoople.* 'Ariel had to be told what to play. To be fair to Luther, he was a very, very big name in Spooky Tooth. He was classed in the top ten guitarists in Britain. Whether he lost it, or what happened, I don't know. Certainly he didn't have it once he joined us. Something about the set up seemed to stifle his creativity. It's a great shame. You could not wish to encounter a more easy-going, generous, likeable character than Luther but the record was just forced on us. "You've got to do a new album. You've got to go on tour." All the usual record company management stuff. Then, in 1974, with the union troubles, petrol rationing and the three-day week, we would be in the studio halfway through a take and the power would go out. It was a dreadful, dismal, awful period. It just didn't happen.'

'This album was the beginning of the end,' admits Ian. 'A lot of stupid things were going on. I was really upset with Bender and the trouble was that I liked him a lot. We were working hard, we were successful, but I didn't like it. I knew I had to find a guitar player but we were touring constantly so there was no room to stop, get Bender out and put another guy in. I think we knew we were cheating ourselves, that we could only get away with it for so long.'

Nevertheless, *The Hoople* entered the UK album charts on 13 April where it stayed for five weeks reaching number 11. Immediately after its release, Mott played six live dates in England to break in the new set for their forthcoming US tour and Judi Pulver accompanied the band as support.

'Me and Mick, who were just guitar mad, immediately homed in on Judi's guitarist because he had an original Les Paul,' says Watts. 'We got talking to him quite a bit throughout the tour, and he was a really nice American bloke, but he wouldn't sell the guitar. Years later, when I started to listen to Warren Zevon, I liked the guitar playing a lot and it was Waddy Wachtel. Then someone told me he was the guy who played with Judi Pulver in 1974, which was amazing.'

'During our English mini-tour, we introduced "American Pie" as a preface to "The Golden Age of Rock 'n' Roll," says Morgan. 'We decided to change the key from E to F, I think, as it would suit Ian's voice better, but the first night we tried it, I completely forgot. I was the only one accompanying Ian before the band came in, so there was no way that he could know we were in the old key. Half way through it, I realised my mistake and had no choice but to simply switch into the new key, before the band came in. The expression on Ian's face when I abruptly changed key was one I will never forget!'

The group attracted press headlines such as 'Solid Gold Mott' in reviews of these successful British concerts, but their next exhaustive American tour was about to feature a unique event which was truly gold; Mott The Hoople were to become the first ever rock and roll band to play a week of Broadway concerts in New York's theatreland!

13
It's got to be the greatest show
on Broadway

'Broadway' – Ian Hunter

As Mott the Hoople embarked on their US Spring tour, Ian finally saw his book *Diary of a Rock 'n' Roll Star* printed by Panther. Hunter's original title had been more modest. 'It was called *Rock 'n' Roll Sweepstakes* but then they explained to me that to put it in airports they would have to call it something more Elton John-ish,' said Ian. ' "Star" is a funny old term. To me somebody like Barbra Streisand's a star but obviously if they put star on the front they reckon they'll flog a few more, so I think that's the rough idea of it.'

Diary of a Rock 'n' Roll Star was an amazing day-by-day account of Mott's five-week Stateside tour in November and December 1972, cataloguing the stresses and strains of life on the road and exposing to view the ordinary, down-to-earth man that Hunter was. It was never meant to be a work of literary merit or an 'unreserved' exposé of the rock business, but Ian did take care to explain recording processes, touring and his impressions of the stars he met and admired such as Keith Moon, Frank Zappa and David Bowie. Furthermore, he was never frightened to air his criticisms, always acknowledging that his views were merely a personal opinion. Guitarist John McLaughlin certainly incurred Hunter's wrath.

Ian also took the opportunity to discuss the characters that made up Mott The Hoople describing Buffin as being 'unsure, quick tempered, polite, messy, loveable and paranoid about his nose.' Ralphs comes across in Hunter's writing as 'the ultimate loner', perplexed and uncertain but loyal, as he stuck out for Ian and Verden when Guy sought to axe them from the band. Humorously described as 'a hypochondriac, fanatic and self-dramatist', Ian felt Verden had great difficulty in living because he always sought perfection. Unpredictable but generous, Phal maintained stability 'with the help of God, his girlfriend Elaine, and his C3.' Overend whilst considered by Hunter 'unreliable, eccentric and selfish', is portrayed as the backbone of the group, always good humoured in the face of any crisis and 'forever trying to bolster band morale'.

Thankfully, Ian commented on the man he regarded as the central core of Mott, their former singer and road manager Stan Tippins, whose actions and falsely credited names became legendary in group circles. Chiffon, Tilkins, Timkins, Rippoff, Ticktock, Pippins, Chickens, Repunzel, Jippinger and Abdul Ganges were some of the aliases given by numerous hotels that Mott visited, much to Stanley's annoyance. Group spirits could also vary depending on Hereford United Football Club's results, which Tippins still follows with a passion. Described as the ultimate eccentric Englishman, Hunter commented on Stan's love of 'arguments, panic, rows, chaos and bull-shitting' and his propensity to start inventive rumours and swell concert attendances for the group.

Hunter's character descriptions were laced with humour and there were further hilarious and dramatic episodes in *Diary of a Rock 'n' Roll Star*, such as Ian's drunken attempt to get into Elvis Presley's Gracelands mansion, meeting Frank Zappa after a madcap drive with Keith Moon and leaping off stage mid-song to physically quell a Rhode Island heckler who had thrown a bottle at Mick Ralphs. The minutiae of road life was a charming contrast as Ian recounted the endless trail of airport lounges, planes, sound checks, hotels, highs, lows and mood swings. Equally fascinating were the trials and tribulations of Mott's absolute preoccupation with guitars, chasing round every available pawn shop in each American city that they played, frantically trying to enhance their collections.

'The roadies always used to be upset because we'd go to America with six guitars and come back with about forty-five,' recalled Hunter. 'They're beautiful things to look at. I've always been in love with guitars. Mick and Overend turned me on to it. It was just a thrill and a craze. You could pick up Gibsons in the US for fifty or sixty dollars, while in England you're paying £150 for them. The Maltese Cross guitar that I had, which used to get photographed more than I did, cost $75.'

Perhaps the most significant acquisition was Overend's American purchase of what is believed to be the second production Fender Stratocaster ever built. Serial number 0052 and sunburst finish, this is only surpassed by model 0051, now owned by Dave Gilmour of Pink Floyd. However, Watts recalls that the purchase of guitars from pawn shops was often a risky hobby. 'Shawn pops were good fun but very dangerous, because we always had to go to the nastiest areas in each town to get the best stuff. I was buying a Mosrite 12-string guitar in St Louis one day. We'd got this old black cab driver to take us down to the pawn shop quarter and it was a rough area, all run down, with wrecked fifties Cadillacs with no wheels and people living in them. I was standing in this shop with glitter in my hair and make up on, and a black guy three yards along the counter was staring at me, buying a gun. And the shopkeeper asked him, "This is the gun you want?" And he says, "Yeah." So the owner says, "Well, I'll just wrap it up for you," and the black bloke, still looking at me says, "No, don't wrap it up, I'm gonna use it." I left the money on the counter, took the guitar and ran. We barely made it back to the cab with the rest of the gang waiting outside.'

Mott became legendary for their guitars. Notable amongst these was Hunter's white Thomas Maltese Cross, acquired in a Milwaukee pawn shop, and later given to an Aylesbury group, a brass-finished 'H' shaped guitar, known affectionately as 'The Weapon', and Overend's silver swallow-shaped bass, christened 'The Beast'. Both of these instruments were specially constructed by Bruce Evans of Nimbo, a Badfinger-sounding London-based group who had Mari Wilson's brother, John, in their line up and with whom Overend anonymously played some gigs. Watts describes the guitars as technically ghastly instruments and Hunter eventually wrecked the 'H' on stage because of frequent tuning problems.

'We were playing at Richmond, Virginia and, being the end of the tour, it was a wild night,' says Pete. 'Ian always had problems with the "H" because it would never stay in tune as the strings splayed out on the head. It looked great, but he'd had enough of it. So he took it off and swung it round and round on stage and broke it. Bender, not to be outdone, took an original Gibson Les Paul Junior, and

smashed it to bits. It was crazy. The Who broke Rickenbackers in 1965 but they
were being produced then. Bender's Les Paul was a 1957 and irreplacable!'

Ralphs had always utilised Les Pauls in Mott; an early fifties gold top in 1969
with white P90 pick ups and, after playing with Leslie West and Mountain in
America, a 1957 Les Paul Junior sunburst with single P90. Mick also owned a
valuable Les Paul with F holes and an original natural wood Gibson Flying V, one
of only 100 made. Mott never used Stratocasters throughout their career until
Grosvenor's arrival in the band.

Overend's design for the Swallow bass was based on face masks that he sometimes wore on stage in the early days of the group. 'They were theatrical masks.
I had hundreds of them and the design of the bass came from the shapes of those
masks. The electrics comprised a rewound Precision pick up and an independent
Guild Bluesbird pick up. The swallow body was just two sheets of chipboard
glued together with £17 worth of chrome sheet on the front. It played well, although the neck was a bit like a tree trunk, but it was too heavy, which we had-
n't thought of. It used to double me up if I played it too long, so it became an
encore guitar in the end and I would pick up the spotlights on the silver body
and blind people in the audience. Lemmy of Motorhead always wanted to buy
the Swallow, but I never sold it.'

Diary of a Rock 'n' Roll Star was a vitriolic and compulsive work, which managed to capture the real flavour of rock on the road. It received excellent press reviews, had advance UK orders of over 50,000 when it was published in May 1974
and subsequently ran into several reprints. But the book would also stimulate
Mott The Hoople's forthcoming LP, Hunter's songwriting adopting a similar
documentary tone. 'I think I was working myself up to writing the *Mott* album
and used the diary as a form of self control. Also, at the time, a lot of people
thought we were a bit of a joke, especially journalists. There's some journalists I
enjoy reading, but the majority are con merchants who appeared to be in a position of responsibility directing my career and I wanted to clarify a few points
about the group. I remember I had my picture in the *New Statesman* because of
the diary. My father, who was never too mad about my rock 'n' roll career saw
that, and a review in *The Sunday Times*, and it was his crowning glory. He
thought it was incredible.'

In 1976, the diary was re-issued in America as *Reflections of a Rock Star* and
having achieved cult status over many years, was eventually re-published in the
UK in 1996 by Independent Music Press. Promoted with a cover quote from *Q*
magazine – 'This is the greatest music book ever written' – a new introduction
described the diary as 'quite simply, the finest and funniest insight into this life
we call 'rock' ever committed to the back of a boarding pass.' Again the first print
run of 3,000 copies sold out in weeks, which for a 25-year-old tour account emphasised its importance in music circles. The press for the re-issue was widespread
and highly complimentary, *Vox* magazine reviewing it as their 'Book of the
Month'.

With the passage of time, Hunter confesses that parts of the story were sani-
tised, as there were sometimes outsiders around who shouldn't have been there.
The book didn't declare for example that Keith Moon was accompanied by a

'rather famous girl' when he and Ian went out in Los Angeles, much to Moon's relief when he met Hunter again a few weeks later in London's Speakeasy. 'You're in the book Keith, but I've left her out,' said Ian, to which Keith replied, 'Stout fellow Ian, stout fellow.'

Watts believes Hunter's proclamation that certain band members remained entirely faithful to their ladies back home was stretching the truth somewhat, although, on this topic, Ian subsequently professed no interest, having recently got married at the time of writing the book. 'To be honest, that side of it never really impressed me that much. You could get into big trouble with some of those women. There were some who were going out with the sole intention of fucking you up, especially if you had money. There were some very clever and professional women out there. But the fans were amazing, the ones who genuinely got off on your music. I've still got friends now who started off as fans.'

'We had the Hott Motts, a die-hard group of fans from New York,' remarks Pete. 'I never had much to do with them because when I refused one of them access to my room once, I was accused of playing the "big rock star". There was very little about girls in the diary for marriages' and relationships' sakes. It was always hinted at that Buff, and by implication nobody else, was involved, with lines like, "Buffin was dutifully chatting up the ladies." When he subsequently got married, Paula went berserk when she heard about the book. We had to ban our girlfriends from tours in the end because they really could cause a lot of trouble, especially when they got talking when we were on stage. I would come off and my girlfriend wouldn't be speaking to me. I suppose Nina, Elaine and Pam used to talk about our alleged exploits. It was rumoured at one time that they were going to employ a private detective to follow us to see what we did on the road. But I actually never made any secret of it to Pam. I used to tell her I was going to do what I wanted to do and that I couldn't be celibate, so she should do what she wanted to do. It's a horrible, cruel thing to say but I knew it was going to be true. At the end of the day – girls, damaged hotels – every band on the road does that, it's nothing new!'

Following the publication of Hunter's diary in 1974, there was the possibility of Mott The Hoople making a movie for Paramount Pictures. Ian saw an excellent idea for an unusual film followed by a thirty-page screenplay draft, the impetus for the project coming from CBS, but the plans were never developed.

Mott's 1974 US and Canadian tour lasted for two months, from 11 April to 1 June, comprised 45 concerts and, like their UK schedule the previous winter, Queen joined them as support, a cameraderie having developed between the two groups. The highlight of the trip would be a week of sell out concerts at the Uris Theatre on Broadway. Blue Weaver was added as a sixth member of the live Mott The Hoople line up for the American tour, playing organ. Morgan knew Blue from his 'teeny pop' days and as he was otherwise unengaged and Mott knew he had the ability to do what was necessary, Weaver was in.

Derek 'Blue' Weaver was born in Cardiff, Wales on 11 March 1947. He describes his musical influences as 'all organists and pianists' but was a particular fan of Booker T. Jones. At one time he lived in a flat above Zoot Money, and Georgie Fame and Alan Price were frequent visitors who jammed there regularly. With vocalist Andy Fairweather-Low, Blue helped form the seven-piece mod/teenybopper group, Amen Corner, in 1966. Originating from the Cardiff area, they were highly successful and had several hit singles including 'Bend Me, Shape Me', 'High in the Sky', 'Hello Susie' and '(If Paradise Is) Half As Nice', which went to number one. They disbanded in 1970 during the progressive boom and became Fairweather, releasing a top-five hit single, 'Natural Sinner'. Blue then replaced Rick Wakeman in The Strawbs and cut two LPs, *Grave New World* and *Bursting at the Seams,* a top three album which also featured their two biggest hit singles, 'Lay Down' and 'Part of the Union'. This latter track stormed up the UK charts as it was released during the aforementioned miners' strike and received much publicity with the *Sun, The Times,* the House of Commons and the Conservative Party all claiming that it should be banned. Blue left The Strawbs and worked briefly as a taxi driver, but did occasional session work before playing on Lou Reed's *Berlin* album and teaming up with Mott The Hoople.

After leaving Mott, Weaver played with Roger Chapman in Streetwalkers and worked with the Bee Gees in America from 1974 through to 1982, appearing on various hit albums and singles. Blue stayed in America for several years doing production and session work before returning to London. He has since worked with Ian Hunter, The Pet Shop Boys and a re-united Strawbs, but spends most of his time on music for television commercials and shows, films and corporate work including advertising.

'Blue was a wonderful guy to have on tour and a great keyboard player,' says Luther. 'I knew him very early on when he was with Amen Corner and I was in The VIPs, and we used to share the same hotel in Paddington. Lo and behold, years later we're in the same band, Mott The Hoople, which was incredible.'

During the start of their American tour Mott were dogged with ill health; Ian had laryngitis, Luther tonsilitis and Overend and Morgan viral flu, but 85 per cent of their concerts were sold out with average attendances of around 9,000 per show. Mott played two concerts at Santa Monica Civic Auditorium in California on 13 April, one of which was recorded for FM broadcast and has subsequently appeared on various bootlegs including *Behind Enemy Lines, Rest In Peace* and *Flash and Crash.* Their concert of 28 April at the Exposition Hall in Portland also featured on a bootleg album, *The Golden Age of Mott The Hoople.* The live set for the tour typically comprised 'American Pie' / 'The Golden Age of Rock 'n' Roll', 'Sucker', 'Roll Away the Stone' / 'Sweet Jane', 'Rest In Peace', 'Here Comes the Queen', 'One of the Boys', 'Born Late '58', 'Hymn for the Dudes', 'Marionette', 'Drivin' Sister' / 'Crash Street Kidds' / 'Violence', 'All the Way from Memphis' and 'All the Young Dudes'.

Mott attempted other live material in the lead up to their Broadway extravanganza. At their Palace Theatre gig in Waterbury, Connecticut on 4 May they played 'Alice', the only time they performed this in concert. 'My guess, through the mists of time,' says Morgan, ' is it was a one-off attempt, as "Alice" may have been a song we were considering for the Uris shows. That was really a studio song and would have needed to be re-arranged and toughened up for live performance. I really enjoyed playing that song in the studio. As you can hear on the album, there is plenty of piano and organ on it. Hats off to Al Kooper and Garth Hudson!'

The Hoople album version had seen a lyrical out-pouring from Ian. ' "Alice" in particular was difficult to re-create live because there were so many lyrics,' says Watts. 'Also, Hunter is the first to admit that his memory isn't the greatest. He came across stage to me on more than one instance to seek prompts on the next line after the middle eight. We also used to finish near the end of our set with a small section from "Blowing in the Wind", and Ian would sometimes get the venue wrong – "The answer, my friend, is blowing in the wind, the answer is blowing in the ... Goodnight St Louis, you've been great"... and we were playing in Atlanta!'

Mott played two nights at San Francisco Winterland, supported one evening by Aerosmith, and although five years or more their junior, one journalist wrote that Mott's set had much more of a seventies aura. During 'Hymn for the Dudes', and the lines, 'I got an idea, go tell the superstar, all his hairs are turning grey,' Ian pointed at a Grateful Dead logo, thus blatantly mocking San Francisco legend, but the audience loved it. The use of Don McLean's 'American Pie' as a prelude to 'The Golden Age of Rock 'n' Roll' also sent the US crowds into raptures.

A Mott The Hoople concert now featured Watts parading the stage in his '21st-century centurion's costume', including hooved cherry red, black or white boots and silver hair, Fisher in white suit with piano key lapels and trilby, and Buffin surrounded by exploding dummies. Meanwhile, Hunter and Bender taunted each other throughout the proceedings, until Ian sent Ariel sprawling across the floor at the climax of each set, beneath raking blood-red spotlights used to devastating effect on 'Violence'. Ian also embroidered his vocal delivery with sneers and accents, further enhancing the lyrical impact of his songs with mocking gesticulations.

Watts' silver hair treatment caused a few problems. 'I started off using Ford silver car paint and went on to Rolls Royce Silver. Then I used Nestlé's Streaks and Tips, which is actually designed for it, but, in the end, I'd buggered my hair up completely. The paint wouldn't come out when you washed it, so you'd just re-spray it. I had pinks and blues mixed in with it sometimes. My scalp went horrible and my hair was coming out in clumps. It was so bloody stupid really. I should have had it dyed blonde and tinted all the colours I wanted. Crazy, but image is everything!'

Visiting several new cities on this tour that they hadn't played previously, Mott The Hoople then became the first rock band to sell out a week of Broadway concerts, spending five days at the 2,000 seater Uris Theatre in New York's theatreland. After their Waterbury concert Mott had returned to New York for two days of rehearsal before their Broadway premiere. 'That rehearsal location might have been the Capitol Theatre, Passaic, New Jersey,' said Morgan. 'I seem to remember such a place, where on the first day of rehearsal I downed a whole bottle of Tequila, with salt and lemon ... "my misspent youth".'

Mott's Broadway debut at the Uris Theatre lasted from 7 to 11 May and the concert on 8 May was recorded to supplement their proposed live album.

Channel 2 in the US did a television report on Mott's opening night but, regrettably, Columbia did not see fit to film this unique event, which is unfortunate, as the group introduced some fine theatrical elements during the show.

'I really never want to say much about Mott's management,' says Morgan. 'I guess they pulled off some great strokes, like the Broadway show, which was quite a scoop, but the failure to film it was bad management, as was the failure to bring us to Japan. Heller was only interested in Ian. His attitude, generally, was that Hunter was the man, and we were just supporting him. He considered the rest of the band to be completely dispensable. I recall Heller once said to Buffin during some argument in the dressing room, "Well, what are you going to do if you don't do this job – pump gas?" I later tried to remonstrate with Fred about something at a very auspicious gig at Avery Fisher Hall in New York with Sparks. I started complaining about something and he simply turned and walked away, leaving me screaming at his back. Thank you very much.'

'To the best of my recollection, the Uris show was only recorded on two nights,' says Dale. 'I think that CBS did a deal with *King Biscuit Flower Hour* to pay for the recording, whilst Columbia retained the rights to the master. You can see the stupid way that our management and record company "planned" things. Nobody records just two nights of a seven day run. We did! And did they film or video the event or even a dress rehearsal? No, nothing!

'At the Uris, we utilised a marionette theatre. Ian felt he was being manipulated by everybody, which was Ian's paranoia, because Ian was as much a manipulator as anybody on the business side of things. He wrote "Marionette" as a result of those feelings of being twisted and turned by record company executives and the music business in general. So, on Broadway, we had marionettes as well as the figures from the Teddy Shephard Puppet Theatre, some of which were larger than life size and some of which were worked by the puppeteers on stage and moved around the stage and interacted with the group. Others just hung down from the top of the proscenium.

'We also had Roger Ruskin-Spear, who was in the Bonzo Dog Band, make two creations, one of which looked like a French policeman and the other a clown. At a certain point in the act, these two figures would spring into life and explode feathers all over the stage and the eyes would flash and the bow ties would spin around. It was good fun. We also had the "Cookie Monster" who played piano with Morgan at one point, which was probably a bit a cheeky, because I don't think they had permission from Frank Oz or Jim Henson to use that character. Also, a pink, feathered ostrich ballerina puppet danced on stage during the introduction to "Rest in Peace". All rather gooey for nasty rockers Mott The Hoople!'

At the climax of 'Marionette', five life-sized puppets were lowered down on to the stage while two puppeteers whirled other figures around the band. As Ian sang, 'Oh God, these wires are so tight,' he was dominated by the real marionettes, who pushed him into a crouch, whilst a smaller puppet thumbed its nose at him.

'Broadway was great,' says Hunter looking back. 'Big deal. All the major companies were there: NBC, CBS ; we didn't know who they were at the time, so it was good because we were really relaxed about it. I made them all wait actually, for about an hour and a half, because the sound check was really bad and we had to get it better. Fred Heller was having kittens because he knew the weight of these people, but I said they'd got to wait until we got things right. The first night I looked out and freaked because there was not a person in the audience under forty five that I could see. It was all heavy duty business people. I thought, "They've come for a show, a Broadway show. They don't even understand what we're doing here." The first night was okay, but the rest of the week was great.'

Mott had problems backstage before their Broadway debut however, when Robert Plant, Jimmy Page and John Bonham of Led Zeppelin arrived from a celebratory lunch, and Bonham insisted on playing on 'All the Young Dudes'. Hunter declined, explaining it was Mott's night, and a scuffle broke out, the episode turning rather unpleasant when Buffin was kicked and Zeppelin's crew antagonised Mott's roadies. Page later apologized but as one journalist remarked, 'Who needs that aggravation. There's a time and a place for games and Zep should have known better.'

Stan Tippins remembers it was an unpleasant experience. 'Zeppelin came in and stood by the side of the stage and interfered with some of the marionettes that were coming down. I wasn't there, just at that time, but the bloke who was working the puppets got upset and explained that somebody called Jimmy Page had tried to halt the marionettes. Then Page appeared and tried to force his way into our dressing room, so I went crazy, stopped him coming in, and threw a bottle which smashed above his head.'

'At the end of the set Bonham came across to me and asked what we were going to play as the encore,' says Watts. 'When I mentioned "All the Young Dudes", he flipped. "Let me do it, I've got it on our jukebox, my son plays it, I know it inside out." So I tried to say we did a different arrangement from the record, but he kept pleading, "Let me do it, let me do it." I said "I'm sorry." Then he turned to Buffin and asked to play.'

'Bonham was prodding me saying, "Yeah, I'll play on the encore, I'll play on the encore," recalls Dale. 'I said, "I don't really know. You'd better talk to Stan Tippins." I was in awe of him and he was out of his head. In the end, I had to hide in the toilet because he kept following me around. Eventually, there was a scuffle. One of their road crew booted me in the knee just before we went on. My knee went up like a balloon. It was our first night and we wanted it for ourselves. We didn't want to say, "And here's some of Led Zeppelin." It was horrible playing with Bonham standing in the wings. I was painfully aware of his prowess as a drummer and quite froze, feeling more and more inadequate.'

'Zep arrived from a lunch well sauced and it was all hell let loose,' recalls Hunter. 'That's all we needed. Our first night on Broadway and there were pitched battles going on. Plant and me were the only ones that kept out of it. Buff got kicked. Page was being real crafty going in and out. Stan went in to help and Al Smith was bouncing for us and got stopped by two of Page's minders. It was pretty ugly. After it had all settled, Peter Grant came up to me and said,

"Sorry about that," and I think it's the only time Grant apologised for anything in his life.'

'It was difficult at the Uris,' explains Watts. 'Zep probably didn't mean any harm, but it was very important to us. It's not that we objected to anybody playing with us, but it was the first rock night on Broadway, in an all seated theatre, the press were there in abundance, and we didn't want it to turn into an out of control jam. We had a precise set, with the marionettes, and it was a showcase. You couldn't have somebody coming on botching it all up! I'm glad we had Stan that night. He was a human dynamo. You needed someone like that around. He could handle just about anybody, in a nice way at first and if they refused to leave or problems persisted, he got them by the scruff of the arse and they were out. Even in his younger days, if it came to it, he could really fight.'

The Beach Boys' Mike Love attended the Uris to see Mott The Hoople but they didn't know who he was. 'He must have been quite miffed that nobody said hello to him. You wouldn't expect to find one of the Beach Boys at a Mott gig,' confesses Dale.

Like the Zeppelin incident, one initial high point turned out to be another Broadway 'downer' for Mott. When a telegram arrived 'from Willard Manus', saying 'thanks for taking the name Mott The Hoople to Broadway', the group were stunned and ecstatic. They were subsequently distraught to learn that it was in fact a hoax, ill-advisedly sent by a Columbia Records A&R man.

American journalist Ben Edmonds summed up Mott's Broadway appearance admirably. 'May 7, 1974. All the way from nowhere to the Uris Theatre in New York, where the ghost of Broadway tradition exchanged its top hat and tails for a pair of shades and a week long electric seizure. To my thinking there could've been no better rock and roll band to open up Broadway's belly than Mott The Hoople. They earned the right to that much frosting on the cake with five years of diligently rendered service.'

Queen's guitarist Brian May had been feeling increasingly unwell since the sixth date of the tour with Mott in Louisiana. Immediately after the last Uris Theatre show, he was diagnosed as having hepatitis and, within a couple of days, flown home secretly to the UK. Queen were forced to pull out of the remaining tour itinerary as Mott's support, and were replaced by Kansas. Back home in England, May started to write new songs from his sickbed and 'Now I'm Here', a hit single from their soon to be released *Sheer Heart Attack* album, was inspired by their touring with Mott, containing the lyric 'down in the city just Hoople 'n' me.'

Of Mott's 1974 US Tour, Morgan Fisher says, 'Bender had just injected a large amount of new energy and fun into the band, and I personally felt I had become a fully-fledged Mott by that time. I guess that was a peak time in terms of showmanship, record sales, tension, fun, girls, all of it, but no drugs – just lots of drink. I never ever saw any drugs going down with Mott The Hoople. Now I may have been naive, but I didn't want any, and I don't think the rest of the band did either. Of course the Americans believed we couldn't do anything or create the energy we did without chemical assistance. Perhaps that's why these shows still stand out in people's memories?'

Luther Grosvenor describes Mott The Hoople as being on the crest of a wave at this time. 'There were loads of women, loads of parties, loads of wonderful times, you're playing on Broadway and it's full every night, what can you say, it speaks for itself. On stage though Mott were absolutely sober and professional. Before we went on we might have had a couple of beers but nobody got out of order, although after the show we *did* party. At rehearsals and recording everybody was very together. It was a business-like band.'

Because of Mott's earlier association with David Bowie, Morgan recalls the considerable interest that the group still generated amongst the gay community, particularly in the USA. 'We attracted a lot of gay people and some of them would try and chat us up. We never got involved, but we sometimes went to gay bars, partly due to the fact that we had a gay guy as our wardrobe man, Leee Black Childers, a brilliant photographer and part of the Mainman set. He would be out at four in the morning getting our clothes dry cleaned. He was very energetic and positive. With most gays there is a courage to show the world they're gay and they don't give a shit. I think the attraction of the kitsch gay bars was that there wasn't the normal boy – girl pressure and it always seemed much more light-hearted.

'I recall a bar in New York run by lesbians with short cropped hair, which had acquired a mystique because you had to drink champagne in this establishment with your trousers down. I went there one day with Mick Ralphs and Mick Jagger and Led Zep walked in. At Peter Grant's suggestion we went to the Plaza Hotel and they picked up two ounces of white powder en route. At the reception I remember Grant saying to Jagger, "Oi, son, wipe yer nose." I think Peter was the only person in the world who could call Jagger "son". I only drank that afternoon, but the last thing I recall, was all of us sitting in the bathroom, for some obscure reason, being "lectured" by Jagger. Very strange!'

Mott The Hoople returned to the UK on 3 June, four days before CBS released their next single, and their New York to London flight remains notorious for the invitation extended by Hunter to a rather famous guitarist. Dale confirms. 'By now we had realised the horrible truth about Bender, and the fact that we would have to part company with him. On a flight from the States to England, Ian saw Eric Clapton and had eyeballed him a few times. As he was leaving the plane, Hunter was feeling no pain after a few drinks and sleeping tablets, and he decided to check out whether Eric would like to join the group or not. He didn't join, nor did he come to any rehearsals, so the answer must have been in the negative, but he was quite jolly about it and at least Eric Clapton was afforded the opportunity to join Mott The Hoople.'

Hunter recalls Clapton complimenting him on his recent *Diary*. 'Eric said, "'Ere, I half like your book." I said, "What do you mean, half?" "Well, I've only half read it!"'

Mott's next single, 'Foxy Foxy', recorded during *The Hoople* sessions, was released on 7 June, backed with 'Trudi's Song' from the LP. The press proclaimed, 'Foxy Mott: best ever' but the single received very little radio airplay and the group was acutely disappointed with the eventual sales and chart placing. Entering the British charts on 22 June, it only stayed for five weeks reaching number 33, their worst CBS position. In retrospect, most of the band didn't share Hunter's enthusiasm for the track, particularly the vocal and Phil Spector production sound, which was a notable aspect of the song. ' "Foxy Foxy" was a good song but it wasn't really for us,' admits Watts. 'We half did it as a demo for Ronnie Spector. It was nice to do a different project, but it wasn't really Mott The Hoople.'

'I just wanted to do a song like Phil Spector but I never offered the song to Ronnie. I've never offered anybody a song in my life,' stresses Hunter.

'I never shared Ian's enthusiasm for "Foxy Foxy" because to me it wasn't really Mott, it didn't make it,' says Luther. 'It was a good song, but too much of a Spector kind of number. Phil could have written the same thing himself anyway.' At the time of release, Luther had commented on the imminent recording of two new Hunter songs which were much more in "All the Way from Memphis" singles mould.

Management was actively planning future activities for the group during June and the pace was quickening at an horrendous rate of knots. The latter half of August was set aside for recording a new single at AIR and the studio was also booked for the months of January and February 1975 to record a new album. September was pencilled-in for European concerts and October for a four-week US tour, failing which, Australia, New Zealand and Japan would be lined up, 'providing the terms were right'. A concert during September at Wembley Stadium with Judy Collins, The Band and CSNY was also explored. Further US concerts would commence in March or April through to June, which meant the new studio LP would have to be rehearsed over Christmas, sessions commenced in January and the recordings completed by early February. July and August 1975 were being investigated to tour Australia and Japan. The machine was moving faster and faster.

Meanwhile, on 5 July, Mott The Hoople played at the Buxton Festival, Derbyshire, in what turned out to be their last UK mainland concert, and, the following day, stormed the Douglas Palace Lido, Isle of Man where Morgan ended up pushing his white grand piano off a six-foot-high stage! Mott were scheduled to play the London Music Festival at Alexandra Palace on 31 July, but the event was cancelled.

Having mixed the Broadway and Hammersmith concert tapes at AIR Studios during June and July, Dale Griffin flew off to Los Angeles to cut Mott's long awaited live album in early August. The LP was originally going to be a US-only release, but this was changed when it was decided to have one side each featuring highlights from both shows. The idea was to use almost thirty minutes of material on each side using a special disc-cutting lab in Los Angeles to achieve appropriate preservation of sound quality. Dale remembers piecing the album together and having to cut Bender's brutal solo on the live version of 'Walking with a Mountain'. 'When it was mixed the engineer said, "We're gonna have to edit this. We can't have the whole thing." I said, "Well how the hell do we edit it?" The guy said, "I know what we'll do." He rolled the tape, closed his eyes and made chalk marks. "All right we'll cut it here." He pulled 200 feet of tape out. It worked. It was one of those things you couldn't do musically or scientifically. In the event, I found out that the LA studio's claims for cutting lengthy sides on to vinyl were bullshit; returning to London, Howard Thompson cut the disc, and the bullshit, at Trident's mastering suite in Soho.'

During early August, the music journals turned their attentions to a 'feud' between Ian and Luther, which had actually been devised by the band to generate press coverage, and it worked. Ian had appeared on BBC television's *Old Grey Whistle Test* and, in an interview, made disparaging remarks about Ariel. Bender subsequently referred in the press to Hunter's age and the fact that he should have retired from music years before. Luther explained later, 'When we were in the States, Ian and I spent a lot of time together and for a bit of fun simply decided to cook up some trouble between us. Ah, publicity!'

August saw Mott play Avro's Top Pop Show on Dutch television to promote 'Foxy Foxy', but the record was not matching the group's recent single success in terms of chart placings, and this was to be Bender's last appearance with the group. Early in September there was news of Mott's next single and future touring plans. *Record Mirror* ran a front page headline 'Mott Bounce Back' and featured Morgan Fisher who explained that the group had spent its five-week summer rest from live performance working on musical ideas for a follow up to 'Foxy Foxy'. 'We want something back in the old vein, something that is not such a departure from what we usually play.' It was also confirmed that Mott would play an extensive European tour in October, UK concert dates in November and December and another US tour in Spring 1975.

The group had been in the studio working on a number of new tracks including 'Three Blind Mice', 'One Fine Day' and 'Colwater High', which was a strong contender for a single in Ian's view. Dale also recalls 'a relatively boring 12-bar,' proposed as a single by Hunter. 'The Saturday Kids' was eventually selected.

Suddenly, in the 21 September weekly editions of the music press, there was speculation about Grosvenor's possible departure from Mott The Hoople and his likely replacement – 'Bender to quit Mott?' – 'Is Ronson joining Mott?' The papers spoke about the rumoured replacement of Luther after it was learned in London and New York that Hunter was shortly to make an important announcement concerning the band. In the same features, Mott's Winter tour arrangements were also announced, encompassing October dates in France, Holland, Germany, Spain and Denmark followed by 25 British concerts, commencing in Glasgow on 10 November and finishing in Wolverhampton on 12 December with a further two shows at London's Hammersmith Odeon.

Within seven days it was confirmed by the press that Bender had in fact been writing solo material for three months and had left Mott to begin recording a new solo album immediately, and to plan an American tour. 'Luther was one of the best friends I've ever had in my life and was a great morale booster for the band, but he never was a Mott The Hoople guitarist,' confesses Ian. 'You had to play a certain way, as Luther found out, and it wasn't as easy a gig as you would think. It was a very eclectic band; it went across the board from ballads to rockers and all kinds of stuff in between. You had to be a good guitar player to play with Mott The Hoople.'

Mick Ralphs reflects on Grosvenor's role in Mott as his replacement. 'Luther's a great personality and he has his own way of playing but I don't know if it was actually quite right for Mott. With a band like Mott The Hoople it's the combination of the all people within it that makes it, and once you change one of the elements things are bound to be different. It would have been hard to replace anyone in Mott, I suppose.'

Hunter felt that the band was a compromising and difficult post for a guitarist, but Watts believes it was wider than that. 'All the positions were difficult to fill in Mott The Hoople actually, because there were so many instruments in the group and you had to fit in amongst everything else. If you're in Cream and you're Jack Bruce or Ginger Baker, you can play what you want virtually as much as you want. In Mott, you've got lead guitar, rhythm guitar, organ, piano, bass and drums, minimum. I couldn't be like Jack Bruce, I had to keep it heavy and low. I had to play for the group I was in and it would have been different, I'm sure, if I was in some other band.'

Mott more or less broke up in August after the 'failure' of the 'Foxy Foxy' single, as Dale recalls: 'We were all frustrated with Bender's lack of input, none more so than Ian. I was very unhappy to have "Foxy Foxy" as Mott's final single and tried to persuade Ian that we should put out a proper single. He was unenthusiastic. I convinced CBS that we had a great song, so that we could book studio time – we had nothing. I plotted with Morgan and Overend to get the band into the studio to do a ghastly number that I had written, "Sunset Summer Nights", on the pretext that it would be great as Mott The Hoople's final single. We recorded the backtrack, we even got Howie Casey to do a sax part and solo on it. All the while Ian looked more troubled as the rest of us enthused over this "wonderful" song. After I had put my guide vocal on to the backtrack, and desperation had begun to grip me, Ian said, "I've got an idea for a song," motioned us over to the piano and began to play the first draft of "The Saturday Gigs" – it was "The Saturday Kids" at that stage. Bender played a solo on the first version. The guitar solo on "Saturday Gigs" was his last chance. He blew it, sadly.'

Morgan Fisher had much admiration for Luther's playing in Spooky Tooth but was increasingly puzzled. 'I knew he was a brilliant musician from his work with Spooky Tooth. He was a character and great to have in the band, so different from Mick who was a very quiet, down-to-earth chap. Bender was a nutcase – boozing, raving, running after women. Every night the dressing room was like a flea market. A fan would come in and say, "That's a nice hat," and Luther would say, " 'Ave it, 'ave it. It's yours." He was such a nice guy. But I think Bender compensated for not fitting in musically by being a character and a lunatic and letting Ian drag him around the stage by his hair. Sadly, Luther didn't deliver the goods in a way I knew he could have done.'

'Bender truly was one of the boys,' says Stan Tippins, 'a local Worcestershire lad, very much the same as the rest of the band. But by now, Ian already knew that Bender couldn't contribute any more in the studio and as much as he really loved him, he had to go. It was tragic, because Luther was one of the greatest people to have on the road that I have ever been out with.'

Ian accepts that Grosvenor had been a whirlwind of energy and that he helped the morale of Mott, but as a guitarist he wasn't compatible. 'Bender was an incredible bloke, but the two styles, his and ours, would not go together, no matter which way we tried it. It was upsetting him and I got depressed about it. We just couldn't work it out but I would have done anything for Bender to have suited us. Luther had been great at covering. When Ralphs left, Luther was there and he was available. He was a wonderful guy, but he wasn't a natural player for Mott and so it skidded a bit through *The Hoople* situation, which is why it's so keyboard orientated. I finally decided we had to make a change.'

Much was made of the Ralphs/Bender comparisons and Luther's suitability which he feels was unjust. 'In hindsight, the only answer I have for people who say that Luther Grosvenor or Ariel Bender's guitar playing didn't suit Mott is that you have to listen back to the material that was recorded on *The Hoople* LP, which contained some very fine songs and guitar playing. The performance I gave was very good I think. I was never knocked out with the live album and my own personal performance on that although, if you were there at a concert, you could relate more to Mott and it was great.

'As for the Ralphs comparisons, I love Mick and we go back a long way. We played in telephone boxes with electric guitars as youngsters and we were buddies and had the same dream of being in Mott The Hooples and Spooky Tooths and we achieved that. It's not fair to compare a guitarist to another guitarist, because we both had a little bit of magic here and there and we were each better at some things than others. You also have to appreciate that when I joined Mott, I got one week's rehearsal and had to play Mick's parts which isn't easy. *The Hoople* album let me play my own parts, but on stage Ralphs was still alive in Mott. I think the comparisons aren't fair to me or Mick.

'Looking back on my departure, I don't think that I *was* cut out to be a Mott The Hoople guitarist in reality, although I think they have to be very thankful for what I brought back into the group. Apart from musical ability, I reintroduced some spirit and everybody woke up a bit really. When Ralphs left, the morale of the band was very low. They didn't need another guitar player, they needed a kick, a spark. I think I gave them a wonderful fourteen months.

'I don't know the complete story of the end but Stan Tippins came to see me, at Bedford Gardens where I was living, almost in tears and he said, "Look, the boys don't know how to say this, because they love you dearly, but they feel it's time for a change of guitarist." In other words I was getting the sack. I can't say I was very happy at the time. I was actually most sad that Stan had to tell me and the guys couldn't, because they didn't have the heart. I was a little bit upset that Ian or Pete or Buff didn't say, "This is the story. We don't think things are suitable for both parties, for you or for us." I guess it was just another chapter in life but, at the end of the day, I can honestly say I gave them as much as they gave me.'

'For *The Hoople*, Morgan and I worked out a lot of the guitar parts,' says Watts. 'That was okay to a degree, but the old saying, a chain is only as strong as

its weakest link, started to come more and more to the foreground. His departure was very upsetting for us. I was very immature for my age really and probably just didn't want to be around when it happened. Luther had good technique
and most of the time he was alright and straight, I think, but some of the live
things Luther played were so diabolical, I don't think he could play that way
unless he was out of his head.'

The press swiftly intimated that Mick Ronson, formerly of Bowie's Spiders
From Mars, was first choice guitarist to replace Grosvenor but then 'negotiations'
appeared to have fallen through. Derek Griffiths, who had previously played with
Colin Blunstone and guested on Argent's *In Deep* album, was then suggested as
successor. By the end of September, however, the music press confirmed the continuing rumour that Mick Ronson was joining after all: 'Mott moves for Ronson
as new Hoople.'

Luther started to record demo tracks with Pete Gage, formerly of Vinegar Joe,
however, planned UK and US tours as The Ariel Bender Band never materialised.
He began to put another group together, Widowmaker, with Gage and Steve
York, Vinegar Joe's bass player, but was then asked to join Sparks, through Island
Records, turning the opportunity down to concentrate on his own project. 'I was
actually singing all the material through the rehearsals for Widowmaker and just
wanted to play the guitar really. Then Roger Chapman from Family, a good
friend of mine, suggested Steve Ellis and initially he wasn't interested. I was quite
persistent, as he's a great singer, so he did a few rehearsals with us which were
amazing and he joined. It was very flattering to be offered the job in Sparks but
I was never their sort of guitar player anyway. At that particular time it didn't
really move me like joining Mott The Hoople. I was in the process of doing
my own thing. I had the songs for an album and Widowmaker was already on
the boil.'

Eventually Grosvenor, retaining the name Ariel Bender, signed up with
manager Don Arden and concluded the formation of Widowmaker in June 1975
with Steve Ellis, Hugh Lloyd Langton, Paul Nicholls and Bob Daisley. Their first
album was recorded and produced by the band in London during August and
September and issued on Jet Records in April 1976. *Widowmaker* contained ten
tracks, including a re-make of 'When I Met You' from Luther's solo LP. He also
composed 'Shine a Light on Me' and co-wrote four other titles. Jet released three
singles to promote the album and the group supported Ted Nugent and The
Electric Light Orchestra on a US tour before they dispensed with the services of
Steve Ellis.

Sessions for a second LP were held at Olympic Studios in December 1976,
with Chris Kimsey as producer and a new vocalist, John Butler. United Artists
released the album *Too Late to Cry* in April, containing nine songs including a re-
working of 'Here Comes the Queen'. Once again, Widowmaker toured to promote the album, but by the end of 1977 the band split. 'John Butler joined us for
about a year and we did the second album which was great,' says Luther. 'We had
a good tour of the States but because of management problems, we decided to
call it a day and that was the end of my career. The biggest problem with
Widowmaker was that we signed with the wrong manager and it was difficult.

We did two successful albums and were promised this and that, but after two years, I decided to pack it all in and I never went back.'

Luther teamed up with Verden Allen in 1978, recorded one single for Jet, 'On the Rebound', and re-appeared on another Verden single, 'Come On Back'. 'We did various projects and it was a good time, but nothing came out of it because there was never anything there in the first place. It filled a space, but I never wanted to play live with Verden. After Mott The Hoople and Widowmaker I really wasn't interested. I was fed up with the whole fucking music business and packed up and left it completely.'

During his abscence from music throughout the 1980's Luther set up a painting and decorating business, and worked in removals and a shop selling electrical goods. Then, in 1992, he formed a new band, Blues 92, with amateur musician John Ledsom, playing the 1993 Wirral Guitar Festival and drawing the second biggest house at the event.

Luther played occasional live dates with Hugh Lloyd Langton in 1994, including a concert at the Marquee, then, early in 1995, ex-music journalist, Bob Laul from New York asked Grosvenor if he would like to play on a Peter Green tribute album. Luther worked on 'Crying' and 'Merry Go Round' for the *Rattlesnake Guitar* sessions, the first recordings he had made for fifteen years. The album also featured Mick Abrahams, Rory Gallagher, Snowy White and Zooy Money.

'I told Bob I'd try and get my fingers back and I recorded two tracks in May 1995 and got very positive feedback,' says Grosvenor. 'Through that album, Bob asked me if I wanted to do my own record and he offered to pay for it. I got six or seven songs together and brought in Mike Kellie and some other guys and rehearsed the songs. Then, just before Christmas, I told Bob I was ready and booked a studio near Evesham, and *Floodgates* was born.'

Luther selected all the tracks for *Floodgates,* wrote most of the material himself or with John Ledsom and chose two cover versions, Joe Tex's 'I Wanna Be Free', which he had done in the sixties with The VIPs, and 'Fire Down Below', a Bob Seger song he had always liked. With Jess Roden and Jim Capaldi helping out on the sessions, the album was recorded in a scant ten days and offered a varied and diverse range of songs which were melodic, musical and understated, both in terms of their structure and production. Mike Kellie's 'Fullness of Time' was particularly spritely, 'Evesham Boy' recalled Luther's early years and 'Cathy' was a beautiful instrumental dedicated to Grosvenor's wife. In 1996, the CD was released in America and Europe and received a very favourable reaction in the USA, where Luther was offered live showcases to promote the album in New York and Los Angeles.

A further solo album, *If You Dare*, and recorded work with Spooky Tooth are in the pipeline for Grosvenor, but he still retains affection for Mott The Hoople. 'When I look back over twenty years and my time with Mott, I think of Ian Hunter as a great musician and songwriter but also a great friend. Pete Watts was a loveable rogue, Buffin was the moody one but a lovely guy and a good drummer, and Verden was perhaps muddled in a way, but a truly great keyboard player.

'Before I left Mott though, there was a bit of unease in the band, and I do believe strongly when Mick Ronson joined, they were split in half anyway. But
Ariel Bender brought a new persona and energy to Mott The Hoople and gave
them injection and he's proud of that. He wasn't proud of the way things happened when he left, but he was honoured to have been part of Mott The Hoople.
It was a privilege.'

14
Ziggy played guitar

'Ziggy Stardust' – David Bowie

Mott The Hoople had picked a high-calibre guitarist as replacement for Luther Grosvenor and, on paper, the combined musical potential of Mott and Mick Ronson was earth-shattering.

Michael Ronson was born on 26 May 1946 in Hull, the eldest of three children to George and Minnie Ronson. He had a great love of music and showed considerable aptitude when he started playing piano at the age of five. He took music lessons and one of his teachers was the grandmother of Trevor Bolder, who would later become his bass playing partner with David Bowie. Michael went to Park Grove Primary and Wyvern Road schools and by eleven years of age could play the violin, recorder and accordion. He also played music in the family's local Mormon church. His first love was the cello, but his parents could not afford to buy him one.

'I was brought up on classical music, so I was very conscious of melodies,' said Mick. 'Learning classical music was a great help to me but it also hindered me a bit too, as everything has to be relative. For example, the relative minor to a C chord is A minor and so you end up playing by the rules, because they are so strict and forced into you. In some ways classical training was good, but in other ways I wish I had never known anything about it at all. I was still into classical music when I was sixteen. I played the violin but I always had one eye on The Everly Brothers and The Shadows. I thought it looked better than playing the violin. Then, when the Stones came along, it was all over. I wanted to be one of them.'

Mick left Maybury High School at fifteen without any O-levels and worked in the warehouse of the local Co-op and as a delivery man. He wanted to be a music teacher at first and dreamed of being a concert pianist, but then bought his first guitar, inspired by Duane Eddy and The Yardbirds. His desire to be a musician was to cause some friction with his father, who didn't approve.

As Mike Ronson, he joined his first group, The Mariners, in November 1963 and made his stage debut with the band, at Elloughton Village Hall on the outskirts of Hull. Like most developing musicians, Mick moved from group to group and played in The King Bees – no relation to David Jones (Bowie) and the King Bees – John Tomlinson and the Buccaneers and a seven-piece band, The Crestas, who supported The Rolling Stones at Bridlington Spa, an experience which thrilled Ronson and fired his musical dream.

Mick once recalled his early rock influences and groups. 'I started off in groups where we played Everly Brothers' and Beatles' songs and later on, progressed into a soul/blues band. I liked listening to Eddie Cochran, George Harrison and Hank Marvin and, having played classical music, I was fond of good melody. The Shadows were great at that I thought, a good instrumental band. George Harrison was a big influence, but I was more of a Rolling Stones fan early on, and then I got into The Beatles' guitar playing and Jeff Beck.'

In 1966, Mick moved to London and found work as a garage mechanic. He replaced Miller Anderson as lead guitarist in The Voice, sponsored by Scientologists and a semi-mystical religious organisation called Process who took a substantial part of the band's income. The Voice went to the West Indies a short time later, so Ronson joined semi-professional outfit, Wanted, who played Tamla Motown and Soul. Mick tried to supplement his musical income with day jobs but was soon in debt. Without any money and literally starving, he returned dejectedly to Hull and ended up taking employment in a paint factory but was soon asked to join The Rats, a group who had been highly regarded locally, but were now in decline.

The Rats' vocalist, Benny Marshall, first became aware of Mick when he played in The Crestas in 1964. 'I used to go and watch The Crestas when I started in bands, because their lead singer was one my heroes. Mick had a nice Gibson 335 at the time and they would play Hollies material and old rock standards. I was already in a group who'd done some recording and TV work, and this interested Mick who seemed really keen to get on. We used to joke with him that we'd put him on the transfer list and get him in our band and he went along with that. The Crestas were a good group and I used to see them regularly. One gig Mick played at had a DC electric mains and he put his hand on his guitar strings and got hold of the microphone stand. It gave him a nasty shock and threw him clean off the stage. Ronson somersaulted and landed across a table before Eric Lee, the singer, kicked the guitar away from his body. It had stuck to Mick though, and burned him quite badly, so he was out of action for a while.'

The Rats virtually split in 1966 when their lead guitarist, bassist and keyboard player left the band, but Benny Marshall and drummer Jim Simpson picked up the pieces and recruited Ronson and bass player Geoff Appleby. Simpson left shortly afterwards and was replaced initially by Clive Taylor and later, John Cambridge, who was soon to provide the Bowie/Ronson link.

'The last I'd heard of Mick had been The Crestas and then he returned to Hull by which time The Rats were on the way out, so I suggested to the drummer that we try and get Ronson in the group,' recalls Marshall. Mick came back from London playing soul music and we started doing Four Tops material which was weird for us. He'd talk about Jeff Beck and Eric Clapton and was experimenting with sounds on a Telecaster he'd bought. Then we went back to playing R&B. Mick was still quite strictly into the Mormon faith and was a great one for shaking hands with everybody, as they do, which rubbed off on all of us. Contrary to popular opinion, he never drank much, certainly in the early days. We used to drink, but Mick didn't like to, although he eventually settled on Guinness and cider mixed. He only needed one, and that set him off and made him very entertaining.'

The Rats played regularly around Yorkshire and Mick, now regarded as one of Hull's most outstanding rock musicians, soon became the focal point of the group. Various Rats singles exist from this period but Ronson does not play on any of the recordings as he did not join the group until 1966. The origins of the band go back to 1962 and a group called Rocky Stone and the Stereotones who became Peter King and the Majestics with Benny Marshall on vocals (Peter was

Benny's middle name). In 1964, their agent, Martin Yale, suggested they change their name to The River Rats or The Rats, and during September in London, they recorded 'Young Blood', 'I Gotta See My Baby' and 'Spoonful', which was issued by Columbia Records in February 1965. The Rats gained TV exposure when Yale set up a 'Battle of the Rats' contest against their even more obscure namesakes from Lancashire. It was this rival outfit rather than the 'pre-Ronson Rats' who recorded two singles, 'Sack of Woe' and 'Parchman Farm'. The Hull-based Rats released their second Columbia single in June 1965, Chris Andrews' 'I Gotta See My Baby', and the band appeared on a Bristol TV show, *Discs-A-Go-Go*, performing live versions of 'New Orleans' and 'Chicago Calling'.

In early 1967, The Rats secured a one month residency at a club in Paris and played further dates in Dieppe and Rouens. Benny Marshall recalls how Mick became intrigued with one of his lesser-known influences. 'Ronson used to listen to an album of Jango Rheinhardt and Stephane Grappelli and it was the only record he took to France. Mick played that until it was worn out and scratched. He used to listen to the violin and tried to mimic it in his guitar playing.'

In 1967, Fairview Studios were opened in Hull by a local musician, Keith Herd, who had been in headlining group, The Keith Herd Band, at The Rats first gig with Ronson in Elloughton the previous year. By the winter, The Rats recorded a psychedelic group composition, 'The Rise and Fall of Bernie Gripplestone', at Fairview, making use of basic studio effects and gimmickry in Beatles style. Marshall admits that they 'lifted' chords from 'Eleanor Rigby'.

Ronson had become a great admirer of guitarist Jeff Beck who was part of the developing heavier R&B sound of the period. The Rats started to adopt this style and in March 1968 supported The Jeff Beck Group at a venue in Grantham. 'Jeff was always Mick's guitar idol,' says Benny. 'He used to copy Beck and listened to everything he did. I never ever went to Mick's house once, where he wasn't in the kitchen with a guitar in his hand. He really persevered, practising Beck's style and was always hungry to learn. I remember Mike Chapman came down once and he was going to let us use some of his original songs. Mick started preaching the Beck gospel to Mike and played him 'Jeff's Boogie'. Beck actually taught Ronson how to play that when we supported him. That was the best thing that ever happened to Mick Ronson.'

In 1968, The Rats changed their name to Treacle at the insistence of local musician and entrepreneur Don Lill, who claimed to know Robert Stigwood, later of RSO Records. They soon reverted to The Rats when they realised Lill could not advance their quest for recognition. As Treacle, they taped three tracks at Fairview Studios early in 1969, Gladys Knight's 'Stop and Get a Hold of Myself', and two songs from Beck's repertoire, 'Morning Dew' and 'Jeff's Boogie', renamed 'Mick's Boogie'. This latter track showcased Ronson's guitar abilities but his playing volume had to be supressed by Keith Herd placing blankets over the speakers in an attempt to maintain sound clarity during the recording.

Drummer John Cambridge left The Rats to join London-based band Junior's Eyes, who had secured a record deal with Regal Zonophone. His place was taken by Mick 'Woody' Woodmansey, and the group continued to play local concerts, performing cover versions including Hendrix's 'Red House', Led Zeppelin's

'Dazed and Confused' and The Beatles' 'Paperback Writer'. Cream, Jeff Beck and virtually all of the first Free album, *Tons of Sobs*, also provided much of their live material at this time. The Rats, now comprising Marshall, Ronson, Appleby and Woodmansey, used Fairview again for their third and final recording session, John Mayall's 'Telephone Blues' and the self-composed 'Early in Spring'. Most of the foregoing material remained unreleased until a 1995 album, *The Rise and Fall of Bernie Gripplestone and the Rats from Hull*, brought together their two Columbia singles, six unreleased session tracks and live material.

Mick continued to play in The Rats, but the group were virtually broke by 1970, so Ronson, who left the family home at this stage, secured work as a municipal gardener with Hull City Council, which he enjoyed greatly. His former colleague from The Mariners, Rick Kemp, noticed Mick tending a flower bed on a roundabout in Hull one day, and explained that he needed a guitarist for some studio work in London. Mick, still musically determined, headed south and recorded what was to become Michael Chapman's *Fully Qualified Survivor* album, released the following year. Ronson met Gus Dudgeon and Paul Buckmaster on the sessions and in May 1970 recorded an early version of 'Madman across the Water' with Dudgeon and Elton John, during sessions for his 1971 LP, *Tumbleweed Connection*.

Although they never married, Mick was now living with his girlfriend Denise and they had a son, Nicky. Suddenly, Ronson was diverted by John Cambridge to a second musical opportunity in London. Junior's Eyes had become involved with a singer, David Jones (Bowie), who was produced by Tony Visconti. In February 1970, Cambridge took Mick to meet David but had to persuade Ronson to go, on the basis he could return to Hull if he was unhappy. Two days later Mick recorded his first BBC radio session with Bowie for John Peel, and, within a few weeks, Ronson joined David's band, The Hype, and moved in to his Victorian home, Haddon Hall in Beckenham.

Mick recalled his first impressions of Bowie. 'I loved David's music from the start. I just thought he was the most creative person ever. He knew what he wanted to do and he got on and did it. He was quite a giving sort of person too, a kind person, and that's what really struck me about him. You knew he was going to be a star.'

On 22 February, Bowie and The Hype, (who sometimes appeared under the pseudonym Harry The Butcher), played at London's Roundhouse wearing specially designed stage costumes inspired by photographer Ray Stevenson and his passion for comic book heroes. The audience that night included Marc Bolan. The Hype died a death, but it was a landmark performance in terms of style and a significant precursor to 'glam rock'.

Mick's first studio session with Bowie soon followed, a single re-recording of 'Memory of a Free Festival' from David's LP *Space Oddity*, but the first major Bowie/Ronson collaboration was on the doom-laden *The Man who Sold the World* album, recorded in late 1970. Featuring Mick's high volume, aggressive playing style, it was a bleak LP, filled with themes that Bowie would develop in his future work. David seemed to be unsure of his musical direction at this time and The Hype, comprising Ronson, Woodmansey and Tony Visconti, signed independently to Phillips and recorded demos before looking to Bowie for more work.

As David seemed to have lost interest in live peformance for the time being, and had not yet got material fully prepared for his next record, Ronson held auditions in Hull for a new band – Ronno. They recorded several instrumental backing tracks for a proposed album and released a single on Vertigo Records in January 1971, 'Fourth Hour of My Sleep' written by Tucker Zimmerman (an American friend of Visconti's), backed with Marshall and Ronson's 'Powers of Darkness'. The band also recorded two Visconti songs, 'Invisible Long Hair' and 'Clarissa', and shot a private promotional film for the single at London's Marquee Club. 'The *Ronno* album was never fully completed,' said Mick. 'Tony Visconti was acting as producer. I think we only recorded four tracks and after a time we started playing gigs with David.' The group comprised Ronson with Woodmansey, Visconti and Benny Marshall on vocals but when they played live, Visconti dropped out and Mick recruited former Chicago Style Blues Band bass player, Trevor Bolder.

Benny Marshall recalls, 'I was heartbroken when Mick first went to London. Then he came back and for a while, with Ronno, we were back on course but it didn't last. We had to write to order and weren't good enough at that which disheartened Mick. I remember saying once, "If this band doesn't get anywhere now, it'll never get anywhere," and I think that's what convinced him to go back to Bowie. It wasn't a happy experience playing the Ronno material because when you're playing songs, and you know they're second rate, it's really not satisfying. Even Woody told me recently, the best years of his entire musical career were still in The Rats.'

The trio of Ronson, Woodmansey and Bolder were about to become Bowie's greatest-ever band during the finest and most creative part of his career. Visconti, who had acted as arranger for David, wanted to work more in production with Marc Bolan and T. Rex, but Ronson had been watching Tony mixing and working out arrangements.

'I used to think it was amazing what he did. Tony Visconti was my teacher,' said Ronson. 'I'd never written a string arrangement before, but I could read and write music and I thought, "If he can do it, so can I." We went out for dinner with Dana Gillespie who wanted strings on some tracks she was recording. David said, "Oh, that's all right, Mick does string arrangements, he's going to do it." Bowie was really good at pushing you forward to do something. That was one of the greatest things about him. It was great, ploughing in head first. I did my first string arrangement with Dana and Bowie heard this and liked it a lot, so he started to give me his arrangements.' Mick worked on four tracks for Dana's 1972 RCA album, *Weren't Born a Man* – a re-recording of Bowie's 'Andy Warhol', 'Mother Don't Be Frightened', 'Lavender Hill' and 'Never Knew'.

Hugh Attwooll of Mainman admired David's ability to draw the best out of people, talented or not. With Mick's considerable abilities, he viewed the Bowie – Ronson liaison as a marriage made in heaven. 'Bowie got out of Mick Ronson ten times more than Mick Ronson himself would have thought to give. Ronson had the talent, but Bowie was the catalyst that knew how to extract that talent from Mick. The albums they recorded together are still marvellous records and Ronson was a very, very important part. He was a wonderful and unique player, in the sense that less was more with Mick.'

The Man who Sold the World was released in April 1971 and, although not commercially successful in the UK at first, it helped David on a promotional trip to the USA where he met Detroit vocalist Iggy Pop and renowned pop artist Andy Warhol. Already intrigued by American music, the Warhol look and New York sound were highly inspirational in terms of Bowie's next two LPs.

Hunky Dory was recorded in the summer of 1971 and released in December. A somewhat 'quirky' album, it was critically acclaimed and subsequently regarded as a highly influential work by many musicians. The LP featured the first of several string arrangements from Ronson on 'Life on Mars?', but he retained his biting guitar style on 'Queen Bitch', which was written in direct response to The Velvet Underground's *Loaded* album and pointed towards the direction Bowie would take next.

Within three weeks of *Hunky Dory's* release, Bowie, Ronson and the band were back in the studio to begin work on *The Rise and Fall of Ziggy Stardust and the Spiders from Mars*. More confident and optimistic than ever before, David had dreamed up a concept that would put him on radio, television and front pages all over the world. Bowie became the incarnation of the Ziggy character and moved towards stage theatrics, outlandish costumes and disturbing imagery, his sources of inspiration including Iggy Pop, Lindsay Kemp's mime troupe and the nightmarish movie *A Clockwork Orange*. Bowie put a softer and different spin on the malicious, malevolent, vicious quality of Kubrick's gang, by dressing his group in florid, bright, quilted jump suits, but still retaining a terroristic, ready-for-action look. Even the photographs on the inside sleeve of *Ziggy* owed a lot to the sinister Malcolm McDowell look from the film's poster. Anthony Burgess's mock 'Russianspeak' used in the film, and the idea of 'droogs', also fitted in with the futuristic, fake society that Bowie created to replace the dreary world of suburbia from which he came. David later acknowledged that crazed, fifties, US rocker Vince Taylor, also influenced the Ziggy character.

The horrendous visions of *A Clockwork Orange* provided a backdrop to the story of a doomed rock star of the future, whose rise and fall coincided with the end of the world. *Ziggy Stardust* became enormous, but a key element of Bowie's rapidly increasing success was the muscular sound of Ronson's firebrand guitar and his reflective style of playing, which added untold depth and range to recorded and live performance.

Mick felt that Bowie and the Spiders injected a new impetus into early seventies music. 'Just before the Ziggy Stardust period happened, there was a bit of a lull. I remember groups like Bread and The Carpenters, a very middle of the road period in music. The rest of the rock scene was basically all jeans and shirts, just like anybody else walking about the street. It seemed like it needed something to give it a kick up the rear end. Early seventies music freed up a lot of people and that was a great relief from their everyday boring life. There were groups like Mott The Hoople, David Bowie and Roxy Music. The music was great.'

Around this time, Bowie became the first rock star to proclaim publicly that he was bisexual, which caused Ronson some shock. 'When David said in a *Melody Maker* interview that he was gay, it kind of embarrassed me a little, but only because of what people would say about me. My family got a lot of flak for it. I remember I gave my mother and father a car and somebody threw paint all over it. It was not really a normal thing then, it was pretty outrageous. It was a pretty shocking thing to say at that time, and a very brave thing to do.'

Ronson's obvious production and musical capabilities meant that he started to attract extra-curricular work. Bob Ringe of RCA Records asked Mick if he would like to produce stablemates Pure Prairie League in Toronto. Ronson wrote orchestration for the album and played bass and sang on 'Amie' which became a US hit single. The album, *Bustin' Out,* featured 'Angel No. 9' and 'Woman', which would be subsequently covered by Mick as a solo artist.

During 1972, David and the group, now officially headed by Mick, toured to promote *Hunky Dory* and *Ziggy Stardust* which was released in June. The album was a rock landmark and glam opus containing several eternal classics including the title track, 'Suffragette City' and the stunning 'Moonage Daydream', which showcased Ronson's innovation, arranging and guitar playing to the extreme.

'*Ziggy Stardust* was a very quick album to do,' said Ronson. 'In those days, you had a song, you would go into the studio, you'd record it and leave. It was as simple as that. A couple of overdubs and it was done. We didn't do that many takes on each track. Plus they were great songs which had good melodic content. Even just playing the chords had some sort of melody to it which I liked. The guitar sound on the records was played with a Les Paul. I used a Cry Baby pedal and used to press the wah-wah on, set it, and leave it to get this middle, honking tone. You can't help get a decent sound when you turn an amp full on, although I think a lot of it is in the way one actually plays too. It's in the fingers and your own personality. If you're going to play rock music, hit the chord, don't tickle about with it!'

Bowie and Ronson produced Lou Reed's 1972 LP, *Transformer,* Mick playing guitar and piano, scoring the string and brass arrangements for the album and writing the bass parts for the controversial hit single 'Walk on the Wild Side'. Reed has credited co-producer Ronson with making the greatest contribution to the completion of *Transformer.* Mick's nasal guitar, often played through his half closed wah-wah pedal, gave the record a very identifiable sound and he played wonderful piano too, from the languid arpeggios of 'Satellite of Love' and 'Perfect Day', to the comical 'New York Telephone Conversation'.

Looking back, Mick clearly favoured the swift and simple method of recording that was adopted. 'I think we recorded *Transformer* in two weeks. We'd go in at eleven o'clock in the morning and finish by six in the evening. It was a very good experience to work with Lou, because he was so laid back. He didn't care if his guitar was in tune or out of tune, he just wanted to sing the song. We'd bring the musicians in, whatever song was going to be done that day, tape it and leave. It was done very quickly, which is always great, because you can still feel the energy from it by the time you've finished. These days people spend that long on albums, you're sick to death of the songs before you've demoed them, let alone recorded them. There were great things captured back then I think. You can lose a lot in today's technology, so I found it very fortunate to be growing up in that period of music.'

In May and June 1972, Bowie produced Mott The Hoople's *All the Young Dudes,* and the LP featured another fine string arrangement from Ronson on 'Sea Diver', marking Mick's first involvement with its writer and his future life-long partner, Ian Hunter. Ian recalls meeting Mick in a King's Road restaurant. 'We all sat on the floor, which you were supposed to do then apparently, and ate. I got slightly more involved with Ronson on "Sea Diver". I said to him, "I want a string arrangement on this," because I'd heard he was an arranger. "How much do you charge?" and he said, "Twenty quid." So I didn't even argue!'

Bowie took Ziggy Stardust to the USA in September 1972, while he continued to storm the UK charts with two hit singles, John 'I'm Only Dancing' and 'The Jean Genie', both of them most memorable for Ronson's prominent guitar work, inspired in the latter case by The Yardbirds' 'I'm a Man'. 'We recorded "The Jean Genie" in Nashville Tennesee,' said Mick. 'All we had with us were little practice amps. We just went in, plugged in, turned it up and I think we recorded "Jean Genie" in two takes. We did it once and messed up, and we did it again. We'd never played the song before. The riff comes from Muddy Waters and John Lee Hooker – "I'm A Man" – very simply done.'

'Jean Genie' screamed straight into the UK chart at number 2 and had been written, like most of the next album, touring in the United States during late 1972. 'Jean Genie' focused on New York City and Detroit while the next single, 'Drive In Saturday', was inspired by a journey between Seattle and Phoenix. Originally promised to Mott The Hoople as their follow up to 'All the Young Dudes', Bowie decided to hold on to the track in the end, securing another top three British chart hit.

On their US tour, David and Mick recruited avant-garde jazz pianist, Mike Garson, for The Spiders and he was soon astounded at the manner in which the band lived. 'I'll never forget it. They put us up at the Beverley Hills Hotel in bungalows. I remember to the right of me was Elton John, and to the left, Perry Como. The room service bill alone, not the hotel bill, for just the band and the entourage, in 1972, must have been ten grand for the ten days we were staying there, and we were playing one concert!'

Woody Woodmansey spoke highly of Tony Defries and the way the tour was organised. 'It was marvellous fun, because we toured as though we were millionaires. It was on that level. The way Defries actually arranged it, he was very good in those areas. He kept any problems, trouble, and hassles off the musicians.'

Ronson's fourth album with Bowie, *Aladdin Sane,* was released in April 1973 and stormed straight to number 1 in the British charts with advance orders of over 100,000, the first such figures since The Beatles. The album, jointly arranged and mixed by Ronson, centred on global destruction as its main theme, and maintained Ronson's unique stamp, particularly in the raw guitar power of 'Watch That Man', 'Cracked Actor' and 'Panic in Detroit'. Bowie described the record as 'Ziggy goes to America' and a treading-water album, but accepted that, in retrospect, *Aladdin Sane* was probably the more successful work, being more informed about rock 'n' roll than Ziggy was. Absorbing an array of images as he travelled across the USA, Bowie had found the alternative world he had been talking about – the violence, the strangeness, the bizarreness was really happening. Detroit caught the imagination and made *A Clockwork Orange* seem tame.

After the release of *Aladdin Sane*, Bowie and the Spiders' 1973 UK summer tour took the country by storm, culminating in two shows at London's Hammersmith Odeon. The final concert was filmed and marked David's 'retirement' from live performance, when he announced on stage that not only was it the last show of the tour, but also the last show the band would ever do. This was the final time that Ronson, Bolder and Woodmansey played together on stage. When questioned about the Spiders' demise, his live work with Bowie and their stage presence, Ronson remained modest. 'That last tour was pretty wild. Places were mobbed with screaming fans. At the Hammersmith concert, the rest of the band really never knew anything about the split until David announced it. I don't know what people saw it as, but I have been told that it was great, the way David was on stage and I was on stage. I think a lot of people saw it as a good counterfoil between us, because he would be more delicate and womanlike and I was stomping along on the side, a bit more like a — bricklayer.'

Ronson's final album collaboration with Bowie was a reworking of favourite sixties pop hits on *Pin Ups,* recorded at Chateau d'Herouville in Northern France and released in October 1973. Trevor Bolder was brought back in to play bass as replacement for Jack Bruce who became unavailable. The final track was a cover of The Kinks' 'Where Have All the Good Times Gone?' – apt, given the imminent end of the Bowie–Ronson partnership. The album gave David his second chart-topping LP in six months.

Having already collaborated with Lou Reed and Mott The Hoople, David and Mick joined forces with Lulu and arranged, produced and recorded four tracks. 'The Man who Sold the World' backed with 'Watch That Man', was released early in 1974 on Polydor and became a top-3 UK single. In November 1973, David and Mick made what would be their last recordings for twenty years, *1984* and *Dodo*, which both featured in The 1980 Floor Show, filmed at the Marquee for US television. 'David started to work on some ideas for a Broadway musical which never saw the light of day and we started the recording of *Diamond Dogs*,' recalled Mick.

Bowie subsequently parted company with Ronson and, in the years ahead, strayed into new areas such as soul, R&B and electronic music. An attempt to get back to his roots with a new group venture, Tin Machine, failed to live up to expectations and it was the re-issue of Bowie's back catalogue by EMI on compact disc in the early nineties which generated greater interest.

Ronson had contributed a vast amount to the quality of Bowie's early albums and set the pattern for his music. Mick's association with David had lasted for three years during which time they produced five classic hit albums, eight chart singles and played over 200 concerts. In 1973, Bowie's albums had been in the UK top 50 for a record 182 weeks. Much of the credit for the overall strength of these recordings and stageshows is due to Ronson, although he seldom received proper acknowledgement. 'Queen Bitch', 'The Supermen', 'Moonage Daydream', 'Ziggy Stardust', 'Suffragette City', 'Watch that Man', 'Cracked

Actor', 'Panic in Detroit' and many of Bowie's other compositions would never have crystalised in their recorded form without Mick's considerable influence.

Bowie's career has been a barometer of change ever since and his output has embraced numerous musical styles, but many still believe that his material and arrangements were never again to reach the creative peaks and excitement that he achieved with Ronson.

Of the split Mick said, 'There were a lot of changes going on around that time and David had all these projects – The Astronettes was one – they just weren't my cup of tea. I never really left. David stopped working on the road and wanted a rest, so if I had stayed with him I would have sat down and done nothing. I didn't know how long he was going to stop for, so I went into the studio for fun. The newspapers wrote about disagreements but, in truth, David is very obliged to me. His albums are very much based on my character too and I often realised musically, things he just had in his mind.'

When Bowie and The Spiders split, Ronson formed a new band, The Fallen Angels, with Trevor Bolder, Aynsley Dunbar and American Scott Richardson who played with hard rock blues band, SRC. The group was almost a prototype to The Pretenders, who would soon surface with three British musicians and a mid-West American singer in their line up. The Fallen Angels attempted recordings which have never been released, but the group folded with Richardson returning to the USA to pursue a solo career. The liaison nevertheless produced material that Mick would utilise in his solo work, Richardson and Ronson co-writing 'Only After Dark' and 'Pleasure Man'.

Similarly, a 1973 production session with the New Seekers, for a single, 'Milkwood', allowed Mick to meet Laurie Heath who played a demo of a song called 'This is for You'. Recording with Al Stewart was less productive. 'It didn't work out too well,' admitted Ronson. 'He asked me to play like Tim Renwick and I said, "He lives round the corner, so phone him, here's his telephone number," and I left.'

Tony Defries soon turned to Ronson and tried to establish him as a star in his own right, securing a substantial solo contract for Mick with RCA Records and stirring up significant publicity, including a six storey advertising board in Times Square, New York, to promote his first album release. 'Tony had this idea that I was to become the next David Cassidy or something like that, a total money making venture,' said Ronson. 'Bowie wasn't quite sure what he was going to do, so Tony said to me, "Okay, we can make you a big star and get you a deal with RCA." So I said, "Wonderful" and went off to make my own record.'

Suzi Fussey, who eventually married Ronson and had devised the Ziggy hairstyle for Bowie, felt Mick wasn't ready for solo stardom. 'He was pushed into it by Defries and the Mainman machine. It was a very hard thing to do after coming off something like David, and Mick wasn't ready.'

Ronson's first solo album, *Slaughter on 10th Avenue,* had been loosely conceived during an Italian Mainman vacation before the *Pin Ups* sessions. The LP was taped at Chateau d'Herouville in France during September 1973, two weeks after *Pin Ups,* with additional recording at Trident Studios in London during October and final mixing at RCA Studios in New York. Mick produced the album and, for the sessions, worked with Aynsley Dunbar, Trevor Bolder and Mike Garson. The result was a fine mixture of ballads and hard rock, although surprisingly, not a guitar-dominated record. Ian Hunter recalls the sessions were not without controversy. 'Mick told me he was doing his album, and David came in with the gang and sort of took over, but that was all right with Mick, because he was always fine that way. But then there was less and less time to do Ronson's album, and Mick was left to complete the record in two days – but he did it.'

RCA released *Slaughter on 10th Avenue* in March 1974, preceded by a single, a cover of Elvis Presley's 1956 hit, 'Love Me Tender', which also opened the LP. Although Ronson's version was nicely sung and arranged, it was probably stronger as an album track. Bowie's 'Growing Up and I'm Fine' and 'Only After Dark', (subsequently covered by The Human League, Def Leppard and Siouxsie and the Banshees), would have been better single releases. Side One closed with 'Music is Lethal', a song originally recorded in 1972 as 'Io Vorrei ... Non Vorrei ... Ma Se Vuoi' by Italian artist Lucio Battisti. Mick had recently become interested in Italian music and his version featured new English lyrics.

Annette Peacock's 'I'm the One' opened Side Two, followed by Ronson/Richardson's 'Pleasure Man' which segued into David and Mick's only joint composition, 'Hey Ma, Get Papa', a tale of a street killing which interestingly prefaced the lyrical theme that Queen would follow on their 1975 hit, 'Bohemian Rhapsody'. The climax of the LP was Ronson's stunning guitar interpretation of Richard Roger's 'Slaughter On 10th Avenue'. Originally a ballet score for *On Your Toes* and covered by The Shadows in 1969, the track was issued as a second single to promote the album. At the time Mick said, 'Although I had the idea for the album in Italy, it has a lot of New York in it. The concept is basically the same as the original version, except it's brought up to date a little.'

Mick had launched his live solo career prior to the LP's release with two February concerts at London's Rainbow Theatre, and a further 13-date UK promotional tour was played during April, Ronson's band supplemented by female backing vocalists and a brass section. The London shows were recorded for a live album, *Bowing Out,* but this was never released. Cover versions of 'Something to Say', 'Music Maker' and 'Green Power' remain commercially unavailable but a live version of Pure Prairie League's 'Leave My Heart Alone' was released as a single B-side.

Ronson said of the album and tour, 'When *Slaughter* came out it went straight into the charts at number nine. I hadn't expected that at all and, though it was very nice for me, it came as quite a shock. I suddenly had to set about lining up dates much quicker than I'd anticipated. I think *Slaughter* did pretty well for somebody's first solo album, although there are one or two things I'd change if I could. Being on your own all of a sudden is a bit strenuous. You've only got yourself to talk to, so you end up asking yourself questions and you answer your own questions and it's really a bit strange. When you're working in a group, each member has other ideas of his own, which makes it a little easier. When it's down to one person as a solo artist, people are saying, "Mick, what do you want?" – it's a bit difficult. I find that I like the company of other musicians and I also like to hear what other musicians have to say, because that's valid to me. I trust the judgement of other musicians too.'

Whilst *Slaughter on 10th Avenue* stayed on the British album chart for seven weeks, it soon became obvious that Mick was not wholly comfortable as a solo artist. Leee Childers, one of Mainman's entourage, recalled, 'Mick always had a lot of girls screaming and reaching for him and Tony Defries saw this and thought there was money to be made. The trouble was, Ronson wasn't Bowie and Tony just didn't know how to sell him.'

Up until this point, Mick had always been seen, largely, as a sideman to David, and it could be argued that he was written off too soon and given no real chance as a solo artist. Nonetheless, Ronson subsequently believed he had been fooling himself, and more importantly his audience. 'I was sort of bamboozled out of the last David Bowie concert and approached with the offer that I could be the next star, and, being really impressionable, I went with it. It's something that I think everybody would like to do, but while I was on the road I started to think, "Is this right for me? Why am I doing this?" I found I was starting to feel very uncomfortable within myself.'

Ronson spent time during the Summer of 1974 helping RCA artist Bob Sargeant record, arrange and produce his album *First Starring Role*, but Mick tried to form a permanent band for a 'better' tour in support of a second solo record. By July, Ronson had commenced work on *Play Don't Worry*, which he arranged, produced and conducted at Trident and Scorpio Studios in London and Strawberry Studios, Juan-les-Pins in Southern France. His first choice musicians, Aynsley Dunbar and Mike Garson, were unavailable so various session players were used although Mick also played several drum, bass and keyboard parts himself. Ironically, *Slaughter* had been a concept approach but *Play Don't Worry* appeared to 'gel' more in terms of songs and musical flow.

The album was preceded by a single, 'Billy Porter', issued in October 1974 with a non-album B-side, 'Seven Days'. *Play Don't Worry* was originally scheduled for November release, but this changed when Ronson was approached to join Mott The Hoople in September and RCA delayed the album until February of the following year. It entered the UK charts on 8 March 1975 where it stayed for three weeks rising to number 29.

The LP began with Ronson's 'Billy Porter' and although it was commercially stronger single material than previously, it failed to chart. In many ways, a lyrical and musical descendant of 'Hey Ma, Get Papa', Mick handled all the vocals, guitars, piano, drums, bass and harmonica. 'It was the first time I had written lyrics for one of my own songs,' said Ronson. 'We'd had this friend named Billy Porter and he told a lot of jokes, so the song was originally a joke song. Then, I was talking to Lou Reed, and the lyrics became things Lou had told me, about getting mugged in New York, plus the joke parts I'd already written.'

Craig Fuller's 'Angel No. 9' was another Pure Prairie League track from *Bustin' Out*, and the beautiful ballad, 'This is for You', whilst written by Laurie Heath, could have been a Ronson composition it suited him so well. 'I worked with the New Seekers and Laurie had this song, but they didn't record it so I did!' explained Mick. 'He might just have taped it on demo, that was all.' Side One closed with a supercharged cover version of Lou Reed's amphetamine-fuelled 'White Light, White Heat', originally featured on the *Velvet Underground* LP and shortlisted for Bowie's *Pin Ups* album. An incomplete backing track had been taped with David, but shelved. Mick salvaged and completed the recording for *Slaughter on 10th Avenue* but replaced it with 'Love Me Tender' late in the sessions.

'Play Don't Worry' opened Side Two and was co-written by Ronson and Bob Sargeant during their collaboration on *First Starring Role*. 'Hazy Days', which featured as the B-side of the 'Billy Porter' single in America, was a simple acoustic track, written by Mick following guidance from Lou Reed on lyrical composition. A cover of Little Richard's 'The Girl Can't Help It' with 'Ian Hunter & The Microns' on backing vocals, was recorded live in the studio and would soon be introduced by Ronson to Mott's live set, together with 'Angel No. 9'. 'The Empty Bed' reprised 'Music is Lethal', being another Italian song ('Io Me Ne Andrei'), written and performed by Claudio Baglioni. Mick re-vamped the piece, and Baglioni, flattered by his cover, wanted to record a 1977 version using Ronson's English lyrics. The album closed with Adam Taylor's 'Woman', Ronson's third Pure Prairie League cover. 'That was a last-minute track that was just thrown in,' said Mick. 'It came out a bit messy. I just never got it to sound the way I wanted.'

Play Don't Worry marked quite a progression for Ronson, because he had begun to write lyrics for several of the songs and, whilst it featured a wide variety of material, it was still a tremendously coherent and even record. However, Mick was less happy. He hadn't really wanted to make the LP but was committed to it, so with his second solo album completed, but not actually released, he was unsure of his future. 'I decided that solo vocal projects weren't quite right for me. I felt uncomfortable as I didn't quite believe in what I was singing, so I decided to knock my solo recording career on the head.'

In the autumn of 1974, it was rumoured that Ronson was a contender to replace Mick Taylor in The Rolling Stones, but, in September, Ian Hunter swooped and invited Ronson to join Mott The Hoople instead. It was a combination that press, fans and the group considered to have enormous potential.

15
I'm just a marionette

'Marionette' – Ian Hunter

By the end of September 1974, the British music press confirmed that Mick Ronson had joined Mott The Hoople as their new lead guitarist. Although Ronson's second album was ready for release, Mick had apparently agreed to forsake his solo career in exchange for a major role with Mott, the deal being that he would feature three of his own numbers on stage with the band and would share vocals with Ian Hunter. Ronson was to remain under contract to Mainman and would continue a parallel career as a solo recording artist.

Ian and Mick announced the news to the press at receptions in London and the following day in New York. Beginning with a congratulatory note for Mick Ralphs, whose *Bad Company* album had just reached number one in the USA, Ian said he had asked Ronson to join the group as early as a year ago, but Mott recruited Luther Grosvenor when these arrangements went awry. Hunter explained that Mick's presence would give Mott The Hoople 'a more electric sound' and that they had already recorded two sides of a single together. Angie Bowie sent a telegram to the band saying that Mick joining Mott was 'the wedding of the year'.

'I'd been panicking slightly, because we were on the slide and we needed someone quick,' confesses Hunter. 'Mick Rock, the photographer, kept saying to me, "Why don't you talk to Mick Ronson?" I didn't know Mick, apart from saying hello and a quick arrangement on "Sea Diver". So I rang him up and Ronson asked me round and he was great. We sat there for about six hours and, in the end, he rang up Defries in the States. Mick had a record coming out and Defries was figuring, "Get him out on the road with Mott and I can plug the album." They'd tried him as a solo artist and it hadn't worked, so it just seemed like a great move from Tony's point of view too. It was the start of endless complications, but I didn't care, and neither did Mick, because we were getting on great and Ronson was really on form at that time. In the studio, he was brilliant as an arranger and a producer. He was right at the top of his game so I thought, naturally, this is going to be wonderful, because all the creativity will come back.'

Mott The Hoople's recruitment of Mick Ronson generated immense publicity but they had already been in AIR No. 2 studio working on new material. In September, Ronson overdubbed guitar parts for 'The Saturday Gigs' single that Hunter, Watts, Griffin and Fisher had already recorded in August, and the entire group taped Hunter's 'Lounge Lizard', a medium-paced, heavy rock number and the only Mott The Hoople track ever originated with Ronson on guitar.

Mick was pleased about the new arrangement and the single. 'It worked out very well. "Saturday Gigs", as a backing track, was already laid down. During the final stages I came in and played guitar and then I did some mixing on the single. The B-side was like a jam and it felt very good. Everybody is really happy about it and seems to think that it has been a good move. It wasn't planned, it really just happened. It was what I was looking for and I guess what they were looking for.'

Dale explains that no one was actually auditioned to replace Luther Grosvenor and the band had temporarily decided to halt Mott The Hoople activities, when the name of Ronson came up. 'Ian was very enthusiastic. Watts and I were concerned, because it meant "getting in to bed" with Mainman and all the attendant nonsense again. We'd had nine months of that in 1972 – it was quite sufficient – but Mott did perceive that Ronson's solo career might be flagging, and the band were certainly very keen to engage his services as a guitarist. At that time, Mick Ronson was one of the elite. A fêted and widely respected musician. We were looking for a toweringly talented guitarist after the difficulties with Luther, and were all thrilled with the prospect of having Mick join Mott The Hoople. It was said Griffin, Watts and Fisher were envious of Ronson. Why would we be envious? It was desirable for the media to be clamouring for interviews. Would we want a guitarist who was of no interest, who gave no boost to the group? A nonentity? The truth is there was no envy of Ronson from within the ranks, just an air of breathless anticipation at the thought of great things ahead, with the group firing on all cylinders again, as of old.'

Mott The Hoople's final single, the elegiac 'Saturday Gigs', was released on 18 October (it should have read '*The* Saturday Gigs'). The lyrics were a précis of Mott's history, mentioning Croydon and Broadway, seat-smashing at the Royal Albert Hall and the March 1972 split. The press gave it a mixed reaction – 'With Saturday Gigs, Mott The Hoople are back on course and showing the kind of form that brought us the *Mott* LP, one of my top 10 LPs of last year,' said the *Sounds* review – but one journal carried the headline 'Mott blow gig' and was less complimentary in its appraisal. The single entered the UK chart on 2 November, two weeks after release, and Mott recorded an unscreened promotional film for *Top of the Pops*. However, 'The Saturday Gigs' stayed in the charts for only three weeks, peaking at number 41, Mott's lowest single placing since their Island era.

'I loved "The Saturday Gigs", but it didn't sell,' says Hunter. 'When it stopped at 41, I think the writing must have been on the wall, because that was a good single. The production's brilliant. We were all involved in it, but it was mainly Ronson.'

Although not a major chart success, Dale described it as a moral hit and a thank you to the people who'd come to Mott The Hoople shows over the years. 'It said goodbye to them and the group. Sadly, in hindsight, the song was just too downbeat. The introduction was muted and didn't make its presence felt.'

'I played my old 1954 Stratocaster all over "The Saturday Gigs",' says Watts. 'Nobody else seems to realise this, even though it's quite clear in the quiet bits, the heavy riffs and chords. The guitar solo by Ronson was the same solo I wrote for Grosvenor. We wanted Mick on the record, so we swapped Luther's solo for Ronson's, doing the same, but with his own expression.'

Believing they had recorded a major hit, the lowly chart placing started to demotivate the group in Watts' view. 'I do like "The Gitterday Sags". It's a lovely, nostalgic number and a shame that it wasn't a top ten hit. I thought that was a good record, one of the best we ever made, and that it would do well. It went straight to number two on the Capital Radio chart and we thought it was going to be big, but then it failed to climb on the main chart and that was a crippler.

Things like that do affect you psychologically as a band. Perhaps if it had been a bigger hit, the atmosphere in Mott might have lifted. Then the *Top of the Pops* session with Ronson was all wrong and horrible, and Buff threw an absolute wobbler on it.'

'I am supposed to have complained about Mick getting too much attention,' says Dale. 'I complained that the front line – Hunter, Watts and Ronson – was getting all the close ups, while Morgan and I got nowt. The same discussion happened every time at *Top of the Pops*. It had nothing to do with Ronson; he wasn't directing the cameras.'

'Lounge Lizard' was intended as the B-side to 'The Saturday Gigs', but was dropped at the last minute, much to Griffin's annoyance. 'Watts and I were desperate to release "Lounge Lizard" on the single, the only Mott recording originated with Mick in the band. The two tracks were a really great package and we always liked to have a good B-side, one that wasn't previously available to the record buying public. All well and good, until Ian turned to me in the control room of AIR No. 2 and said, "We're not going to use 'Lounge Lizard' for the B-side; you'll have to knock something together out of the live material." I was enraged Hunter was "witholding" the track and, with Bill Price, compiled a hideously edited-together three song live medley ("Jerkin' Crocus", "Violence" and "One of the Boys"). That's why the B-side of "The Saturday Gigs" is so crap! It was by way of a two-finger job at Ian!'

'Lounge Lizard' (another CBS error – it was intended to be 'Lounge Lizzard'), remained in the archives until 1993, when it was issued on *The Ballad of Mott* retrospective CD. 'The powerful, almost modern, sound, particularly on the drums, was the result of a long heart-to-heart between Bill Price and me,' says Dale. 'He did a brilliant job creating the drum sound. It took years and digital reverberation before the rest of the world caught up.'

'We taped "Lounge Lizard" in a day or two, and it was the first and only full recording with Mick Ronson,' says Watts. 'It was an uncomfortable session I thought, because Mick fancied himself in production and was sitting in the control room saying, "Oh, could you play an E there instead of a B Pete?" Ian seemed happy to let him try and take over, whereas I felt that before you let someone go to town on you, they've got to justify themselves, and Mick hadn't really done that since he'd been in the group. Plus, Ronson did no guitars "live" like Ralpher would have done. Instead, he would come back later and put down a fully worked out solo, and it seemed rather clinical to work that way.'

Mott The Hoople's European tour started in October and was to be followed by 25 concerts in Britain, recording sessions for an album (working title *Showtime*) in January and a US tour in April, May and June of 1975, including Mott's first appearance at Madison Square Gardens in New York. Ronson said of the proposed European and US dates, 'We'll start off by playing the basic songs that they have been playing. Then, by the time we do the English tour, we'll have a few new numbers, and by the American tour we will have recorded a new LP and will be doing, probably, a completely fresh set.'

The European tour opened in Lund, Sweden on 10 October and included 19 dates in Denmark, Germany, Switzerland, Lichtenstein, France and Holland, several with Titanic as support. The live set remained largely unchanged, containing all the familiar Hoople standards but with the two new songs, 'The Saturday Gigs' and 'Lounge Lizard', and two of Mick's tracks from his forthcoming solo album, 'Angel No. 9' and 'The Girl Can't Help It.' Ronson also added an interesting section of Hendrix's 'Voodoo Chile' to 'Born Late '58' and Mott amended their taped introduction to the show, prefacing the customary 'Jupiter', from Holst's suite *The Planets*, with Bryan Johnson's 1960 hit, 'Looking High, High, High'. The complete live set comprised 'American Pie' / 'The Golden Age of Rock 'n' Roll', 'Sucker', 'Roll Away the Stone' / 'Sweet Jane', 'Rest In Peace', 'One of the Boys', 'Angel No. 9', 'Lounge Lizard', 'Born Late '58' / 'Voodoo Chile', 'Rose', 'The Saturday Gigs', 'Sweet Angeline', 'All the Way from Memphis', 'Drivin' Sister' / 'Crash Steet Kidds' / 'Violence', 'All the Young Dudes' and 'The Girl Can't Help It'.

The concerts received excellent press coverage and crowd riots in Sweden were a measure of the excitement and expectation surrounding the combined potential of Mott The Hoople and Ronson. British headlines for the European dates included 'Cancel the Wake', with one journalist saying Mott The Hoople now had added 'Mick Ronson fuel injection'.

'We couldn't believe it when we went to Sweden,' says Watts. 'We got out of the bloody plane and we were greeted like The Beatles. The last time we went there, we played to two people in a village hall in the middle of nowhere, with Fairport Convulsion.'

'On our arrival in Sweden, for the first date of the tour, we all had an evening meal together at the hotel,' recalls Dale. 'The road crew was also included. We sat around a huge table and it was a very pleasant event. Sadly, this was to be the *only* occasion on that tour. The Stockholm gig was astonishing, with very Beatlesque scenes inside and outside the gig, as Swedish fans – where had they suddenly appeared from, had they just been too shy before? – swamped the stage and then the streets surrounding the venue. Absolute mayhem, not seen since the last time we'd played in Boston. The next day, the Swedish press was full of pictures and reports of the wild events – they'd had riot police with rubber truncheons inside and outside the hall. Again, things seemed to augur well for a great tour of Europe, for just once.'

Conversely, Stan Tippins was worried from the start that the Mott–Ronson live combination didn't seem right. 'The sound was very weak, that's what surprised me out front in the audience. Mick didn't seem to come through forcefully. Added to the developing personality problems, another disappointment was that the tickets for the British tour certainly weren't selling well, and that was also feeding back to the band and Ian.'

'It didn't sound great on stage and Mick didn't feel comfortable with us,' agrees Watts. 'Maybe it would have done, given more time. The future looked ominous to me from here on! It seemed so great on paper, the idea of Ronson joining us. I read articles later, where we're supposed to have said we didn't want him in the group, which was shit! It just seemed like Mick Ronson and Mott the Hoople was going to be the perfect match, but it wasn't. It was very sad.

'We had to have this image change and we felt awful. I think it was probably

Tony that suggested we get rid of the thigh-length boots and get our hair cut short. I ended up without *any* image. I just felt naff. I was in a blue boiler suit, Ian was in dark denim and the clothes were all dowdy, except Mick, who was in a sparkling white jumpsuit which stood out brilliantly under the stage lights. It seemed like Ronson was being made to look really good, and the rest of us to look really bad. We didn't see much of Hirschman and Heller by this point. Stan managed us more than anybody.'

Group morale was still shielded from public view when Ronson appeared in an interview on BBC Television's *Old Grey Whistle Test* and talked excitedly of his plans with Mott. 'When we first started rehearsing, it was a fixed set of numbers which only required me to play guitar on top, but I'm enjoying it. It's really good, because I can just pick up a guitar and walk around stage and play. It'll be nice when we record a new album in January, because then I'll feel I've added more to Mott the Hoople. I'm looking forward to it very much, because it'll be new material and I'll feel as though I'm really contributing something, which will be much more fun for me.'

Before the forthcoming British tour, CBS released *Mott The Hoople Live* on 1 November. The album came in a single sleeve but initial copies contained a fold out souvenir handbill with pictures and features of the infamous Broadway and Hammersmith concerts. Mott's sleeve notes dedicated the record to the departed stable of 'Guy, Phally and Ralpher, without whom …'

The first side of the record had been taken entirely from Mott's Broadway shows taped in the USA in May 1974, and the second from the London Hammersmith Odeon concerts in December 1973. Columbia Records would not countenance a double album or have a bonus 10-inch disc, so material had to be sacrificed with the result that live versions of 'Marionette', 'The Golden Age of Rock 'n' Roll' with 'American Pie' intro, 'Hymn for the Dudes' with 'Blowing in the Wind' coda, 'Born Late '58' and the 'Roll Away The Stone' / 'Sweet Jane' medley were dropped.

Dale Griffin produced the LP and had to edit some of the selected tracks and adjust running orders, but explains the aural differences in each side of the album. 'The sound from the Uris Theatre on Broadway is a lot more compact, because the hall was smaller. The London audience was younger and perhaps a bit more excited. In our early days, there used to be quite a lot of wrecking going on at our British gigs, and it was like that at the end of the Hammersmith concert. Worst of all, we had only two shows recorded from the UK tour – both at Hammersmith – and on one of those, the organ was miles out of tune – plus, only two nights from the Uris run – and we played like prats on both of them. Most bands' live albums are made up from a great number of different performances. Not The Hoople!'

The energy and sound on the Hammersmith side was better, as exemplified in 'Angeline' and the power of Mott's closing medley featuring 'Jerkin' Crocus', 'Rock and Roll Queen' and the sado-masochistic finale, 'Violence'. One American reviewer acknowledged, 'The medley closing Side Two is as close to the spirit of Little Richard as anyone could hope to be in 1974'. The LP also contained superb versions of 'Rest In Peace' and 'Rose', the former with classical piano introduction from Morgan Fisher, showing once again that Mott were always capable of sensitivity and dynamics, as well as gut-tearing rock and roll. Press reviews for the live disc were mixed however, one headline saying 'Uninspired Mott' and another 'Whole Lotta Nothin' Goin' On'. Nevertheless, the album entered the UK charts on 23 November for two weeks, reaching number 32.

Mott played a stunning show at the Paris Olympia on 2 November and completed their European concert trek at the Concertgebouw, in Amsterdam, the following day. They were scheduled to commence their British concerts one week later at the Glasgow Apollo on 10 November. Externally, all seemed well, and the band were embarking on potentially the most successful and exciting part of their career. Hidden from public view however, the personality problems which had developed during the European tour had taken their toll, with the band effectively broken into two factions; Hunter and Ronson on one side and Griffin, Watts and Fisher on the other. They had often travelled apart, and they even dined apart.

Between the European and UK concert dates, Hunter made a business visit to America. According to press reports, Ian collapsed during dinner whilst staying at Fred Heller's house in New Jersey, was taken to Riverside Hospital, Morristown, where he was diagnosed as suffering from physical exhaustion, kept under sedation over the weekend and detained for five days complete rest. The first four dates of Mott's British tour, in Scotland, which had completely sold out, were re-scheduled for late December. The opening concert became Leeds on 15 November, but the dates were never to be played.

One week later, Mott's UK manager, Bob Hirschman, confirmed to the press that the entire British tour was cancelled. The reason given was that Hunter had been ordered to take two months complete rest, with doctors saying that he could suffer 'permanent health problems' if he attempted to fulfil tour commitments. Accordingly, he was to stay in America at Fred Heller's home and was not expected to return to the UK until after Christmas. An official statement said, 'It is hoped that the dates will be re-scheduled for next year, subject to their itinerary and Ian Hunter's health. Mott's plans for recording a new studio album in January are not affected.'

Mott The Hoople had sold over 50,000 tickets for the tour and were expected to lose a five-figure sum as a result of the postponement. It seemed, on the face of it, that Hunter, as the focal point of the group, had finally succumbed to various pressures – writing all of Mott The Hoople's material, interviews, management liaison, personality problems – and had reached overload status. Speculation had already started to grow on both sides of the Atlantic that Mott The Hoople were breaking up, and rumours were particularly rife in New York, where it was suggested that the band's next album would be recorded with a changed line up and possibly under a different name. One press feature confirmed, 'Fred Heller has been talking 'cooperatively' with Mick Ronson's manager, Tony Defries, about what's next.'

On 23 November, there was further major speculation about a Mott The Hoople break up – 'MOTT SPLIT? – Run its course with Hunter' – was the bold headline in *Sounds*. The article stated that sources in London were suggesting, 'Mott The Hoople may split up early in the New Year despite the new burst of life given the band by the arrival of Mick Ronson as new lead guitarist. It is likely there will be a farewell British tour and a last studio album, after Mott's American tour in January and February.' The feature also referred to one off the record comment that, 'Mott The Hoople would seem to have run its course with Ian and the appearance of Mick Ronson has not changed the basic plans.' Ronson, like Hunter, was said to be in America.

The next reported development was that Ian had arrived back in Britain earlier than expected and that he was in a London studio recording a solo LP, assisted by Ronson, who was co-producing and playing on the sessions. They hoped to complete all the tracks before Mott started work on their album in the New Year. This increased the mounting speculation and rumour surrounding a possible Mott break up, but official sources still maintained that no such split was on the cards.

Then, in the music journals of 28 December, Mott's fans got the Christmas news they feared and dreaded – Mott The Hoople had definitely broken up: 'Mott split? – Now it's official', 'Hunter, Ronson split Hoople' and 'Ian and Ronno leave but Mott soldiers on', were the headlines. The features confirmed that Ian and Mick had broken away from the rest of the group in order that Hunter could pursue a solo career, both for recording and live work, with Ronson as his second in command, although they also planned to form a new band. There were rumours in the press that Ian had been offered a large sum of money, a reported $750,000, by CBS for a solo deal, speculation that Hunter strongly refuted.

Ian explained, 'Mott was just getting *negative* and I didn't want to go on unless it was positive. After five years I'd just had enough. Mott had gone as far as it could.' It was confirmed that Hunter would finish a solo album in January and February using studio time originally booked at AIR for Mott the Hoople, before teaming up with Mick Ronson and going to America for a year.

Stan Tippins had been swiftly despatched to New York to try and persuade Hunter to re-think his decision to leave Mott The Hoople, but it was pointless and almost a charade. 'Hunter went over to see Fred and we had the call back, from Heller to Hirschman, that Ian was in a collapsed state in New York, that he was very depressed and had suffered a breakdown,' says Tippins. 'Everyone was surprised and Bob Hirschman sent me over to see if I could retrieve the situation, but when I got there I couldn't do much about it. Ian was adamant that he had left the band. I tried to coax him back, but it was no good. In fact, I don't think there was much to be said. When I was going over, I thought I was going to say a lot more, but when I got there, and saw the situation, it all seemed cut and dried. It was a complete waste of time saying anything to be honest. I think the management had it in their minds that they would have Ian as a solo artist, or as a duo with Mick Ronson!

Tippins feels that the group, and the atmosphere within it, gradually became an increasing source of worry and upset to Ian. 'When we'd got Bender in, everybody loved him and the spirit within the band was very high. Then, Hunter heard the material for the live album and although the guitar playing had sounded great during live performance, it wasn't good on tape, plus ideas and creativity had already been a difficulty for Luther in the studio. So we got Ronson in, but Buffin and Pete seemed uneasy almost from day one; they felt Mick didn't want to be a group member and he seemed to be all over Ian. Buff always sensed happenings and became a bit upset about what might be happening, but the band was already drifting apart. Ian got worried, then nervous, depressed and finally stressed, although there's a difference between a breakdown in a hospital, completely gone, out of your mind, and really being at the end of your tether.

The other members of Mott The Hoople split at first – Morgan decamped and left the country, Blue composed with Overend and Dale wrote at home. Watts and Griffin then made some demos, while Fisher wrote film music to be shown at the Institute of Contemporary Arts in London and Blue Weaver left for Miami to record an album with The Bee Gees. Finally, Watts, Griffin and Fisher decided to stay together in a re-shaped line up and look for a new vocalist and lead guitarist to replace Hunter and Ronson. Their press officer Tony Brainsby said, 'They had every intention of changing their identity and coming up with a brand new name, but they've had requests to stick with the Mott tag. One supporter was even organising a petition to persuade them. So they have now opted to stay as Mott The Hoople.' Brainsby confirmed that the trio had already recorded five tracks together and were very pleased with the results.

Journalist Bill Henderson wrote a Mott The Hoople valediction in the 18 January edition of *Sounds*, expressing the view that even before Mick Ralphs had left, Hunter was Mott The Hoople, in effect. 'Mott without Hunter, is The Stones without Jagger, The Who without Townshend. For Hunter, it was obviously the end of the line within the group.'

Reported rows between Ian and Dale about the production of the live album were *not* true, but increasing tension between the original members and Hunter and Ronson were undoubtedly significant factors to Ian, although not the only reason for the demise of Mott The Hoople. Even the private pleadings of their original mentor, Guy Stevens, couldn't change Hunter's mind. He had carried the weight of Mott, its direction and creativity for too long and, after two singles, which had failed to storm the charts, he had possibly exhausted any musical possibilities that remained. It was time to change course, even if it meant removing the group's composer and focal point. In the months that followed, there was some enmity over the split, but emotions were obviously running high, given the tremendous musical and commercial opportunity that had been lost.

Griffin still stresses that the whole point of getting Ronson in Mott, and the reason they were so excited by the prospect of Mott The Hoople with Mick as lead guitarist, was because of his musicianship, both on stage and in the studio, and because it would mean renewed and strengthening press/media interest in the band and in Ronson himself. The group's intent was also to make Mott The Hoople an equal-shares five-man group again, as it had been initially, even though Mick was still part of the Mainman regime.

'A short while after Mick joined Mott, we realised that he had not been receiving his Hoople wage of £75 per week, and decided to discuss this with him at an upcoming meeting at his flat – a huge, Mainman-funded apartment, in a select mews where Sir Winston Churchill had lived.,' says Dale. 'Once there, it was left to Watts, Fisher and me. Ronno looked taken-aback, startled, even, at our suggestion that he should be paid Mott money, and he was casting panic-stricken glances at Ian. We left it with Ronno agreeing to sort things out with Stan, since he was already owed "back-pay". We did think it weird that Mick seemed so ill-at-ease with the concept of being paid by Mott, just the same as the rest of us. To the best of my knowledge, Mick never did accept his Hoople wages.

'After the difficulties with Bender, we desperately wanted a guitarist who could be part of the group and contribute musically. Mick seemed perfect, but the whole Mott The Hoople – Ronson business is a puzzle. We were thrilled at the prospect of his joining the band as a full member. We had enormous respect for him and we had every artistic and financial reason to want this version of Mott The Hoople to succeed and have longevity. We felt that Mick was the man to put the musicality firmly back in place in Mott The Hoople and to contribute a strong stage presence too. It was the dream that all too soon became a nightmare.

'At each airport we arrived at, two limousines would be waiting,' explains Dale. 'A CBS limo for Mott the Hoople and an RCA limo for Ronson. One day, the Mott limo was over-full and the RCA representative was a very attractive girl, so Watts decided that he'd ride in the RCA limo with Mick and Susie Ronson and the rep! However, the RCA girl would have none of it and required him to depart the RCA transport immediately. Wattsy protested that he and Ronno were in the same band but was slung out, and we all laughed at his exasperation. However, if a CBS person had tried to pull that stunt on Ronson, he or she would have found themselves thumbing a lift home from the airport, with the full backing of Mott the Hoople.'

Watts agrees that 'on paper' Ronson joining Mott was a fantastic idea. 'We thought it was going to be amazing, and contrary to what some people have said, Buff and I *did* want him in the group. He seemed ideal to us. I'd loved what he'd done with Bowie and raved endlessly to the band about his work on *The Man Who Sold the World*. Mick looked great, he could do string arrangements and was obviously world class. We thought the band was going to soar.

'But from early on it didn't seem right. When I went to his flat, the atmosphere was horrible. It was real decadence and we weren't used to that. We were a very down-to-earth band. I was used to eating beans on toast and fish fingers; when we went round there, it was all caviar in the fridge and champagne everywhere. It was full of obvious Bowie hangers-on too, people with dyed purple and green hair, just helping themselves to everything in his flat. I felt very uncomfortable and didn't like it at all. I remember Mick wandering into the kitchen and he was very friendly saying, "Help yourself Pete, there's champagne there, vodka, whatever you want. I'll make you a special milk shake if you like."

'Then we rehearsed together a bit, but we'd still never spoken much, so on the plane to the first date of our European tour, I remember thinking I'd never actually had a conversation with him and he'd been in the band about two or three weeks by then. So I sat next to him, flying to Sweden, and I couldn't get a word out of him. I couldn't get him to open up at all to me. Then, Mick, funded by his management and record company, was being driven round in limousines and on the tour, he and Hunter ate together and led a champagne lifestyle. The rest of us couldn't afford to do this, but that didn't annoy us because we didn't want it. We did feel however, that the band should have been spending "eating time" together for bonding purposes – not being split into two camps. Ian had never flaunted money before, in fact he had a less flash car than me, even though he had money from his songwriting. So it became more and more apparent there was a financially contrived 'them and us' divide when the group was in Europe.

'I knew things were grim, but I thought when we got back for the British dates everything would be alright. Europe was always a strain and you had to en- dure things on the road over there that you didn't have to endure anywhere else. For the first dates in Sweden, we had to have police protection from the hordes of fans. The funny thing is the last time we were there in 1971, we were playing in village halls to two people, then we'd drive 500 miles across Sweden and play to three people, and then drive back across the country for the next gig. It was terrible, so when they said we were going on another Swedish tour we feared the worst.

'I describe the end of Mott The Hoople as a combination of everything going wrong at once; poor sounding European gigs with Ronson, the breakdown of normal relations within the group and the relative failure of "The Saturday Gigs". It all happened together at the wrong time. Ronson had been the "leader" of The Spiders group behind Bowie, who was the creative force. I don't know, maybe Mick thought he would lead Mott the Hoople as a band, supporting our creator?'

Pete also believes Hunter had simply had enough. 'Ian sounded coherent when he spoke to me from America. I think he was just at the end of his tether really. He must have felt a lot of weight on him as well. He was getting on with Mick Ronson, but it must have been pretty obvious to everyone that it wasn't happening as a group.'

Griffin stresses that he and Watts wanted Mott The Hoople to survive. 'We'd talked as a band about an Ian Hunter solo LP, which made absolute sense, and Pete and I wanted to be able to take time off to produce and pursue new avenues, because we appreciated Mott wouldn't last forever. That's why, on the original mix of "The Saturday Gigs", Ian was saying on the fade out that the band was just going to sleep for a little while and we'd be back. We wanted Mott to survive as long as possible. In retrospect, the strange thing is that our management and record label showed no real wish to do the same. All of them, including Stan, seemed to enter a period of slumber.'

The split meant that Watts' first royalty advances for writing would be used to 'float' the new group that would be formed from the remnants of Mott the Hoople, but Pete still regards the money-side of the business as a joke in any case. 'We never had any real money with any of the groups all the way through. In Mott The Hoople we had tour bonuses occasionally; I think once, I got a £750 bonus after an American tour. But the trouble is, you'd come back from a tour and it was gone straightaway on bills that had accumulated while you were away. When I got my Bentley, I nearly had to strangle Bob Hirschman to get the money to buy it. I had to threaten to leave the group. And Fred Heller didn't want me to get a house. He wanted everyone not to have any base. He wanted us to be 'mobile' he said, but the truth of the matter is he wanted to keep us on tenterhooks and if we had roots somewhere, if we'd got something that was solid, and an investment, they wouldn't have so much of a hold over us, that's the way I always looked at it.

'We were an image band, but all the money for clothes, apart from the last tour, came out of our wages. I was buying leather suits at £75 each and yet our top wage was £75 a week at the height of our fame in 1974! The guitars I bought in the States, I used to bring back and sell, to supplement my income so I could pay the bills at home. This was a group who'd had five or six hit records, was nationally known, had adverts on the sides of buses driving round London, *Top of the Pops*, the lot. £75 a week! I started to think it was a mug's game, but I foolishly held on for a few more years, thinking it might change.

'I saw a documentary on The Sweet, and they had Rolls Royces with Steve Priest saying they had so much money they didn't know what to do. Well, we were never like that. We had so *little* money we didn't know what to do. That was always a factor that irritated all of us. I had flashy cars, like Mustangs and Cadillacs, but they cost £700, cheap cars. Why didn't we have any more money? No one could ever answer us. Cash flow and expenses were reasons given and then we were told, 'You worry about the music and let us worry about the business'. The problem is, the advisors you have are smarter guys than you are, and you haven't got time to learn how to be an accountant or a lawyer.

'In the early days, I thought we could make some money out of a retail business separate from the group. I wanted to open a shop like "Mr Freedom" or "Granny Takes a Trip" and get designers working for us. I can remember mentioning it in the group car, and they were all luke-warm about it. Even if one other guy had been interested, it might have happened. We were also keen to invest in property, like Free did.'

The idea of a temporary halt to Mott The Hoople and a Hunter solo album, which the band should have done, would not have been feasible back in 1974 in Watts' opinion. 'In hindsight, Hunter made the mistake of officially breaking up Mott the Hoople, but, in those days you were either a band or you weren't a band. You did an album, toured and by the end of the tour, by God, you had to be back in the studio. The record company hounded you. They'd say, "There's three months booked for an album and six months for a tour," and if you hadn't finished the album in twelve weeks, tough! It wasn't so flexible back then, not like today when it seems you can just not bother to do anything for three years if you want to.'

Another problem for Watts was the possibility of the band moving to the USA. 'I hated America, hated it. That was another thing that caused the split really. There was no way I'd have ever moved over there. I just love it here. Ian wanted to go and Dale would probably have gone, but I never liked the idea of it. In 1974, it wasn't done to have a group split between two countries. Nowadays, people like Def Leppard do it, two in Los Angeles and two in Ireland, but it didn't appeal to me.'

Fisher confesses that he wasn't entirely shocked when Hunter departed. 'I think when Bender left, a lot of the spirit went out of the band, because for all his faults he was an incredible catalyst. We were thinking that Mick Ronson would be the ideal combination of Bender and Ralphs, the best of both worlds. Ronno was really good on stage, but he was too professional in a way. It wasn't totally unexpected, but the timing couldn't have been worse because we were about to become enormous in America. We were going to do Madison Square Garden and the Spectrum in Philadelphia. If it had happened six months later we would all have been in a much better position, including Ian. That's how strongly he felt about it.'

Morgan finds it difficult to shed light on the split even now. 'It happened so suddenly. There was no discussion before or after. It was just a *fait accompli*. We had so little experience of working together with Mick Ronson, because we'd only recorded a couple of songs with him, but we were quite willing to go Ronson's way. We changed our wardrobe and our hairstyles as soon as he joined. I actually had my hair cut in Mick's flat. But the problem was, we didn't have enough time to play together, and I'm sure Mick and Ian huddled together and Ronson said to Hunter, "You've got to get away from these guys." There was also this idea about moving to the USA, which was a big part of it too, because I think Mick and Ian saw America as a place where the streets were paved with gold. It's a great pity, because I think we were all good players in our own way. Buffin, as far as I'm concerned, was one of the best British drummers. He was unique and powerful, and had a way of delaying the snare just behind the beat which made the whole thing bigger and gave it more tension. I also liked the way Pete played the third or the fifth of a chord, instead of the root note; he was a very melodic, thoughful bass player. I don't think Mick Ronson took the time to really under-stand where we were as musicians, and then it was all over so quick.

'I'm quite a mellow person. I tend to find myself in the middle of things and I was watching this going on with Ian and Mick on one side, and Pete and Buff on the other, and I was just thinking, "I don't see any problem, let's just play and get on with this." Of course Mick and Ian went to the States and I didn't. I was-n't bothered about the crock of gold, although I could have gone either way. My response to being deserted, which is what it was in a way, was to shut down the emotion and not get angry, and not fight back. I decided it was time to start bringing out my ideas which I'd not felt any space for in Mott although, on 'The Saturday Gigs", I contributed a lot – I worked out and played the intro and the middle eight. I was surprised Ian let me at the time, but I guess he already had his eyes on America and "interesting stuff" like Todd Rundgren, with whom he collaborated later.'

'Being honest,' confesses Watts, 'one of the most annoying things about the split was the cancellation of the next American tour, because we'd been told we were going to be on big money, for the first time really. The gigs were large and we were looking forward to that. Frankly, it was time we thought about the money, because when Mott The Hoople split up, I was in a £20-a-week flat in Ealing, and when the roadies came round with my gear, I didn't know where I was going to put it. Phil and Richie turned up with a big van and said, "Well, there's your stage clothes and there's your amps." They had a wardrobe trunk full of silver hair spray and crab cream and I thought, "My God". That's when it really came home to me it was the end. I had to take all my stuff up a flight of stairs to this little flat and it was a horrible feeling. One of the worst days of my life.'

Ronson said of his period in Mott The Hoople, 'I enjoyed the idea of joining. I thought it was all going to happen. When I left David, I had some problems in finding musicians for my own band, so I soon accepted their offer to join when they asked me. But I was surprised after being with Mott The Hoople for a month. I soon realised that things weren't good. As soon as we started playing gigs, I knew what was going on. Mott The Hoople was really just something else to do, but I liked Ian, really more than I liked the band. It was Ian that I did it for, but I got disillusioned really fast, which was partly my fault I suppose. It just didn't gel.'

Richie Anderson believes that Hunter and Ronson possibly didn't stop to take a long term view, because on paper, the new line up was awesome. However he does feel that the split was probably inevitable in any case. 'Perhaps Mick was a little too eager too soon, and didn't wait to take stock. Then Ian latched on to him very quickly. But, these things happen in groups and they're never going to come to an end with everybody being all nice and smiley, especially when you've got a going concern. I can't think of many cases where it really worked when big names got together in the music industry. The odds are usually against it. Sadly, Mott The Hoople with Ronson was like Winwood, Clapton and Baker in Blind Faith – "supergroups" just don't work!'

Even today, Ian remains disappointed that the Mott – Ronson collaboration failed. 'Mick was 110 per cent but for some reason it didn't work out. I remember Buff coming round to my house in Wembley and saying, "What happened?" I said, "Ronson's in the band." And Buffin was floored. He was over the moon about it. But then, when the dust settled, and RCA had Mick, and Columbia had us, and two limos started turning up, and Ronson got in another one, it wasn't bothering me, but it started to have a real effect on Pete, Buff and Morgan. And that kind of pissed me off, because I thought this guy is probably the only guy in England that can really save Mott's bacon. They can't work with an ordinary guitar player, it had to be a really creative individual. Mick was the only person I knew. You couldn't have average guitar players in Mott The Hoople and Ronson, like Ralphs, was special.

'So here was Mick Ronson and our troubles were over. It was like a whole new band and I started writing again. Then, we did this tour of Europe and the atmosphere got real strange and hateful. For some reason, we'd come down in the morning and we'd be sitting at one end of the room and the guys would be sitting at the other end of the room. It really fucked me up. I knew we were having to make concessions but I understood it, particularly with Mick on RCA. However, the band had been so close knit even from before I joined, they just didn't like it. I think they thought I was on Mick's side, but I felt I was the diplomat and the bridge. Mick had all these ideas and some of the other members of the band just looked at him with suspicion. Ronson was the outsider. Then Mick came to me and said, "What do I need this for?" He'd only been in the group a few weeks.

'Also, at that time, I was doing all the press, I was the front figure and I was writing most of the material and it was too much to handle. By the end of the European tour I was gone. I remember sitting with Charles Shaar Murray one night, and I looked down and my hands were really shaking. My nerves were shot and Charlie said I should take a break, but it wasn't that, it was this horrible thing that was going on. I never really blamed anybody, it was more circumstances than anything. But it was a pain in the ass, because the band was already tired after years of failure and then, when the success came, they had to work extremely hard and now this. So I thought, maybe we should split this thing up and knock it on the head.'

In Mick Ronson, Mott The Hoople had recruited a guitarist of immense capability and a player who could combine the taste and feel of Mick Ralphs, with the presence and power of Luther Grosvenor. Tragically they were not able to work together in the studio for any length of time and the true potential of this combination never materialized on record. Interestingly, the first Hunter Ronson collaboration, the *Ian Hunter* LP released the following spring, was one of Ian's finest records. It featured several songs originally written and rehearsed, in whole or in part, for Mott, ('Lounge Lizard', 'Boy' – originally called 'Did You See Them Run', '3,000 Miles from Here' and 'Shades Off'), and was a stunning album, illustrating the Mott The Hoople that might have been, and the considerable opportunity that had slipped from British rock music's grasp.

Ian Hunter had highlighted earlier in the year that 'Marionette' was the most important song on *The Hoople* and, ironically, it contained premonitionary lines.

OK the show's been fun
but my wood's begun to warp
They won – I'm done
New one – begun

I did my best
It just couldn't last
Get me out of this mess
It all happened so fast
Now I need a rest
Where's my sanity gone – Mother?
I did my best
I'm just like all the others

They gambled with my life
And now I've lost my will to fight
Oh God, these wires are so tight...
I'm just a marionette

'Mott The Hoople was a lot of aggravation, a lot of trouble and total madness,' says Ian. 'When we split up in Switzerland in 1972, I remember we got pissed on the train coming back and we were great mates, when all that trouble wasn't in the way, all the pressure of trying to get there. I think my happiest days were actually in Hamburg, beforehand, because there was no pressure. With Mott, I was doing an awful lot and wound up a wreck.

'Mick Ralphs would probably mention intensity, and there was a lot of that and maybe that was my fault. Mott The Hoople were a very intense band, driven on by desperation. There were so many groups about at the time and I guess that's why we started dressing up stupidly, just to separate us from the rest. It wasn't so much music as desperation although I think Verden Allen and Mick Ralphs were trying to play music. You see music came to me late, I started learning with Mott. I wasn't even the original writer in Mott The Hoople. Pete and Mick were going to write. Pete turned round after a while and said, "Look you should start writing because you're a good writer." So then it was me and Mick that started doing all the songs. I was all for Mott happening, because I knew what the alternative was. I'd worked in a factory.'

Hunter still looks back on all of the Mott members with affection. 'I think Pete Watts was probably the backbone of Mott The Hoople. He was a lazy sod, and a selfish sod too, but I think he was the backbone. He was a tourist, always sunny and a lot of laughs, a lovely bloke. Dale was the facts and figures man. He had a tremendous memory and when it came to mixing the live album and all the incidental stuff, we got Buff because he seemed to have a clearer mind than the rest of us. Verden Allen was a really, really good organ player, excellent. When I listen to that old stuff now, he was a great organist. He could be his own worst enemy but he was funny, loyal and a great musician. I'm still a personal fan of Mick Ralphs. We've had our ups and downs, but I really rate Ralphs highly. He has good song sensibility and he's written some great material.

'Morgan Fisher was a very intelligent, warm character and a great player, and Luther was one of the best friends you could ever have in your life. I don't think he suited Mott musically, as most guitar players wouldn't, but what a great guy. Ronson, I thought, could and would have suited Mott The Hoople had he been given the chance, but I think Mick brought a lot of baggage with him when he came into Mott. We still had RCA to contend with, we still had the whole Bowie mentality when it came to dealing with his management and all-in-all it just became too much, but Mick could have revived Mott The Hoople. If he'd come in off the street with no management, walked in and taken the guitar job, I think, probably, it would have worked.

'Guy Stevens was a fantastic manager half the time, and the other half was your worst nightmare. He was always 100 per cent; there was never any middle line with Guy. But I think he brought something out of us that no other person would ever have brought out of us, and therefore, I don't think Mott The Hoople, had it been formed, would ever have done what it did without Guy Stevens.'

Pete Watts reflects that Mott The Hoople was extremely open-minded about music and their approach to it. 'It was a bottomless pit, we could have gone in any direction and I've never been in a band that's been like that, before or since. Even at rehearsals, we'd jam with a jazz or a reggae piece, like "Yma Sumac", which was weird but brilliant. We were never afraid to try things and go in different directions. I always felt that we only scraped the surface really. We weren't great musicians, we were okay and got better, but we were dynamite live and I don't know how we got to be in that position. I think the sound of Mott came from the rhythm section and Phally. I really wonder if when Bender and Ronson joined us, they were subconsciously in awe of our live reputation and that's why musically they didn't fit?

'I'm still glad I was in Mott The Hoople and did it, but I'm bloody glad I got out of it too. I didn't enjoy it any more in the end. It was very difficult after *The Hoople*, especially the tour with Ronson. Not pleasureable at all. There was a lot of decadence and I hated all that. But some of our work I thought was great, like 'The Saturday Gigs" and "Waterlow", and it's amazing when people say *Brain Capers* was so influential. After we'd recorded it, we just thought it was a mess, then Lester Bangs, the American journalist, said *Brain Capers* was the one everyone was waiting for. He had his finger on the pulse and picked up on the energy.'

Extensive touring didn't bother Watts too much, but the group finances lead him to question whether his efforts were worthwhile. 'We were young enough to take life on the road. I loved it for a time, but we only did short-ish tours of three months and we couldn't have kept it up longer than that because we partied *hard*. We weren't one of those groups who ate brown rice and lentils and went to bed after the gig. We really went for it and I'd rarely be in bed before five o'clock every morning, and even then it was with about four birds! We'd get half an hour's sleep and then you'd hear Stan coming along the corridor, knocking on all the doors. I'd lie there motionless, hoping he'd miss my door; he only did that once, the swine!

'I always felt I was a mug in Mott The Hoople because I never made any money. These days when a group forms, as soon as they get a manager, they go straight to lawyer and get the contract sorted out properly. In those days, you signed anything that was put in front of you. Record deals were terrible then too, you got a tiny percentage. In fact, we only found out a couple of years ago that Mott were actually signed to Guy Stevens.

'Whether the group made any money in the early days is doubtful, because with Island Records we were always on a wage – £15 a week to start with – which wasn't a lot at that time. Then, we had to buy our stage clothes out of our wages and we were a very flashy group. It's not like we were Status Quo who could go on wearing old denims. We had good clothes. Mott The Hoople always seemed to be a non-profit making concern. We all made nothing from it and I felt I'd been a fool long enough. We had such a complex set up that we don't know where it went. We were selling out gigs everywhere, but we had lots of on-the-road expenses. We got our first £150 gig at Glasgow Maryland Club and I think it went up to £300 for concerts like the Fairfield Hall, but expenses would include hotels, equipment hire, lighting rigs, lighting crew, roadies, sound systems, transport, support groups and so on. So much came out of what we actually earned.'

Watts feels the split was inevitable. 'Mott The Hoople wasn't right in the end. I suppose you can say that groups have peaks and troughs in their careers, and that we were going through a trough, but rather than go through it, we just broke up.'

Dale Griffin however, remains angry about the group's downfall and feels that a verbal agreement to observe certain protocols concerning departures had not been fully observed, although other group members have different memories. Dale also remains annoyed by inaccurate reports about the reasons for the break up of the group. 'There were many falsehoods surrounding the split. Several "rock encyclopedias" quote these inaccuracies as fact to this day and *The Ballad of Mott* CD booklet also repeated at least one of these bogus assertions.'

Trudi Hunter describes the final dissolution of the band as a Pandora's box, but stresses it is important to understand that the unravelling of Mott The Hoople was a process of evolution, not revolution.

Perhaps the demise really began with the suggestion that Hunter should take control of the group in 1972, or Mick Ralphs subsequent departure? Perhaps, in the end, Ian was not prepared to embark on further fundamental structural change? Perhaps the final group members simply missed the obvious and failed to observe the tremendous opportunity that they had to work together as musicians. Certainly, various events, hands and personalities were involved in, and became contributory factors to, the split; the complex web may never be unravelled and part of the 'Ballad of Mott The Hoople' will probably always remain unsung.

Hunter says, 'It was a long time ago and frankly, it reached the stage where I just couldn't take any more in Mott the Hoople, so I left to work with Mick Ronson.'

Mick Ralphs reflects that the group were extraordinary. 'It was a very memorable period in my life, the step from a local group to professionalism. Mott The Hoople were a special band. We always stuck to our principles and we always went against convention although, without the help of Guy, I don't think we'd have got any further than the village hall. I always felt Mott was ahead of its time and it was never accepted for what it was, which was part of the frustration.'

Mott The Hoople had finally split. The politics, neurosis, egos and volatility of the group, and some of the events and individuals around it, had gradually driven the members apart. Thankfully, they left behind a legacy of astounding, groundbreaking music, which was innovative, varied and dynamic. Most of that legacy was written by music's greatest observer, who would immediately continue in that vein as a solo artist.

16
Trapped halfway up

'Shades Off' – Ian Hunter

Ian Hunter had decided in November 1974 that he could no longer work within the confines of Mott The Hoople, and quit. Even though Mott's sell out UK tour had been partly re-scheduled in the hope Ian would play, he could not face anymore. Personality problems had finally taken their toll although the death of the band had been a slow and gradual decline.

'The difficulties really began when Ralphs left Mott,' admits Hunter. 'We got Ariel Bender, an excellent chap, but the magic left. Commercially things went a lot better, but artistically the bottom had gone out of it and we were living on our former glory. Then Mick Ronson came in and said, "Listen guys, this is not working and we have to take it in hand." We'd always had an excellent atmosphere in the group but, when Bender left and we got Mick with all his statements, the rest of the group went haywire. They didn't want it, not one single bit. So I got up and left.'

Ian says that the split was not entirely amicable, but he was not in good health. Examined by a doctor, it was discovered he was suffering from mental and physical exhaustion. 'There was another tour about to start and I simply couldn't pull myself together to do it. This doctor said that if I didn't get away from it and rethink my life, I'd be on the way to an early grave. Rock 'n' roll's not much good to you when you're lying on your back in a hospital. Really you get things in proportion. Your own well-being is far more important.'

Hunter was also quick to counter the journalistic claim that he left Mott The Hoople for money. 'Columbia Records didn't even know I'd left and it happened weeks before the press knew about it anyway. It really upset me that they would print I left Mott for money. I'd never think of that. There was something also that I argued with Buff over the live album, and that was pure conjecture. I didn't want anybody to feel upset because it just happened that way. I never really saw them after the split. I don't think they particularly liked me at the time. Morgan was okay, but I think the others were a bit upset with me.'

In addition to handling all the songwriting and press interviews, Hunter alludes to a further area of pressure that had been placed on him in the group. 'We had lawyers, we didn't have managers, so I would spend time managing and that's a drag, because it means checking everything that goes through.'

Ronson confessed that he had rapidly become disillusioned in Mott The Hoople and that Hunter was in a similar frame of mind. 'Ian was getting tired of the situation, so it was a good excuse to work together. He asked me if I would do an album with him if he left Mott and I said, "Sure", and that was it. He really wanted to be a solo artist and there were a lot of things he could do as a solo artist that he couldn't do with a group.'

After the demise of Mott, Mick flew over to the USA to visit Hunter who had moved into Bobby Colomby's house in Nassau County. Bobby was the drummer with Blood Sweat and Tears and a friend of Ian's, and as he was touring, he let the Hunters stay at his home. 'Looking back it was like a new beginning,' says Ian. 'Mick and I sat together in Colomby's house and wondered what to do. Ronson was a clever bloke, he knew I was emotionally charged and he said, "We have to make a record, right now! This is when you make 'em, this is when you make 'em." I got in such a state that I just had to do something.'

Urged on by Ronson, Hunter decided to record a solo LP and together they worked on material for about ten days, doing most of the pre-production demos at Colomby's home. Mick offered to go back to England and put a band together for the album sessions and touring. He recruited Geoff Appleby first, his former bass-playing colleague from The Rats, then lined up an unknown sixteen-year-old drummer. Hunter confirmed later that it was Simon Phillips, who went on to become a well-respected session musician with Jeff Beck and The Who. 'He didn't last long because his father wouldn't let him leave the country. He was just a baby at the time, but a great drummer. He made my songs come to life,' said Ian.

According to Dale Griffin, Hunter Ronson wanted Morgan Fisher in the new band but he turned down their offer to play keyboards. 'Morgan was incandescent with rage at Ian and Mick about the split, but time is a great rose-tinter, apparently!'

Hunter had returned to London by late December and explained that the proposed solo record wouldn't be a major change from his past work, and that he had written most of the songs for Mott in any case. The album was routined at a demo studio after which some material was discarded and, on 13 January, Ian and Mick moved into AIR No. 2 Studio in London's Oxford Street to begin recording, using two months of studio time previously booked for Mott The Hoople. Ronson arranged and produced the record with assistance from Hunter and engineer Bill Price. 'Looking back actually, how we started the album, it wouldn't have happened at all,' said Ian. 'It was really interesting. It just changed in mid-flight and something different came out. Some of the songs we went in with were "One Fine Day" and "Colwater High", but I found I was writing as we recorded. We were lucky. It's a good album, something special.'

For the sessions, they retained Geoff Appleby on bass and brought in Peter Arnesen on keyboards, who had played in Daddy Longlegs and Taggett before he helped form The Rubettes. Ian and Mick also decided to replace Simon Phillips with Dennis Elliott, former drummer with The Roy Young Band and If, a jazz-rock septet who had recorded for Island Records in the early seventies and were frequently compared to their American peers, Blood Sweat and Tears and Chicago. 'When I got back to London I moved in upstairs from Dennis,' recalls Ian. 'He was a swing drummer and I've always liked swing drummers, so Dennis came down and we decided he would play. I remember saying to Mick that the only problem with Dennis was he had bad teeth, but he turned up with a brand new pair of choppers. He'd had his teeth capped, so he was in the band!'

The first three songs on Side One of the *Ian Hunter* LP were a rock 'n' roll masterpiece and openly illustrated several of Ian's prime musical influences, including Chuck Berry and The Rolling Stones. The opening track, 'Once Bitten Twice Shy', started with 'Little Queenie' style chording and a spoken 'hello' from

Ian, a direct counterpart to the 'goodbyes' at the end of 'The Saturday Gigs'. 'Once Bitten Twice Shy' destroyed the rule book for singles chart success. Gradually growing in intensity, verse by verse, eventually hitting overdrive after a full two minute lead-in, Ronson's superb guitar solo culminated in an astounding, fifteen-second, single note vibrato held over the bridge to the final choruses of the song. Mick's playing was often concise and notable for its sustain and musical tone, but this simplistic technique was brilliant in its economy and effect.

'The first time I went round to Mick's place after Mott, I wrote "Once Bitten Twice Shy" because he had a little drum machine there that had real bossanova beats,' says Hunter. 'We found this weird beat and ten hours later I'd written "Once Bitten" and we took it to the studio. I think we used the drum machine on the track and put Dennis Elliott's drums on last. Dennis was great. I was saying something on "Once Bitten", but covered it up by using a girl. That was the best track on the album for me, I love it. I found that Americans heard it straightaway but the English thought it was just an average rocker. To me it's like soul, it really happens. The great song is the one that comes altogether at once, en block, words and music. "Once Bitten" took ten hours.'

Sixties-style harmonica and boogie piano featured heavily on 'Who Do You Love?', an 'on-the-road-song' to a Detroit female. Ian explained on release, 'I've just got the first reaction from America which was "Once Bitten Twice Shy", 100 per cent all the way through. Yet in England, everybody we play it to, "Who Do You Love?" hits them more.'

Mott The Hoople's 'Lounge Lizard' was ressurected for the Hunter sessions, but, featuring laid back 'Honky Tonk Women' rhythm and cowbell, and Johnny Gustafson, famous for his work with Quatermass and Roxy Music, on bass, Ian's version was stronger. 'It was a year before I met Trudi after I finished with my first wife, and I was pulling 'slags' out of the Speakeasy in the middle of the night,' said Ian. 'That was the subject matter for the song.'

'Boy' was a brooding, dramatic ballad, part-written with Mott, under the original working title, 'Did You See Them Run?', and concluded by Hunter with assistance from Ronson. 'That was probably the first song I wrote with Mick. We did deals on these things. I was probably being generous at the time. It was a bunch of bits and pieces that all sounded good, so we just threw a lot of different things together.'

There was much speculation on the lyrical content of 'Boy' – did the song refer to David Bowie, Bob Dylan or Tony Defries perhaps? It actually carried a multi-faceted message. ' "Boy" wasn't about one particular person, it was two or three people, and a bit of myself is in there,' admits Hunter. 'Everyone thought it was about Bowie, but I wouldn't give away eight minutes to David. Predominantly it was about Joe Cocker. I loved Leon Russell, who was getting all this bad rap about taking over Cocker's "Mad Dogs" tour and engineering it all. I just thought, "It's not Leon, it's Joe not applying himself." Somebody's got to take the reins and I always rated Leon Russell very highly. "Boy" was a bit of, "Come on, Joe!", because we'd known him a little at Island.'

Spanning almost nine minutes, the verses were tangled with both despair and encouragement, implicating the characters that Hunter had declared, and even reflecting on the demise of Mott The Hoople.

> Boy, you're getting out of hand
> You've got to make a stand
> So put the coke away
> Boy, you've got to do the show
> Got to let the people know
> You've got the strength to stay
>
> I can see you run, I can see you hide, oh your heart is aching
> Lost in a dream, of what might have been
> You're the guy, you're the number one, and your knees are shaking
> Stand and deliver, in an endless dream
>
> Cheer up mate put the drummers in the past
> See you did not have to grass
> Euphemism lasts and lasts …

Hunter then adopted an optimistic and futuristic tone.

> Boy, take a turnpike heading west
> Turn the people on to Beau Geste
> 'Cos that's what you did the best
> Boy, play the pipes 'til they're old and worn
> Sing the words 'til they fall forlorn
> Like the pieces of a jigsaw set

Side Two of the album opened with '3,000 Miles from Here', a gentle, sparse track which almost sounded like an unfinished demo. At a mere 2 min. 46 sec., the song had a beautifully atmospheric, natural quality and was another ode to a transient woman, featuring just Ian's vocal and acoustic guitar. Originally written with Mott, this was a stunningly simple, but highly effective piece.

> If you hear a young dove crying
> You'll know it's me to blame
> For I never got her number
> I never knew her name
> Now she's gone – disappeared
> But I hear a young dove crying
> Three thousand miles from here

'The Truth, The Whole Truth and Nuthin' But The Truth' was a new Hunter composition, structurally reminiscent of Free, and a showcase for a highly charged and emotional Ronson solo. 'It was an ambiguous lyric,' confesses Ian, 'but I wrote it musically with Mick in mind, especially the whole middle section,

where the scream occurs. The minute Mick heard it he was taken. That was
Ronson's speed. The slower the better. It was very simple and I knew Mick would
play the shit out of it, which he did, so I did that for Ronson. I remember he got
a review for *Play Don't Worry*, which was vicious, and it was personal. He went
bright red and we were doing "The Truth, The Whole Truth and Nuthin' But
The Truth" and went out to do the solo. We got it in five minutes flat. If he hadn't
read that review it would have taken us about three days!'

'It Ain't Easy When You Fall' dealt with the fragility of success and fame and
segued in to 'Shades Off', a poem which Ian had written two years before for
Mott. Effectively, they became one six-minute track of genius, and were really the
cornerstone of Side Two, featuring fine piano interludes from Peter Arnesen and
a powerful, melodic chorus. It seemed that the lyric was Hunter's song to himself, in the second person, written at the peak of his 'breakdown', but Ian later revealed the true source of inspiration. 'It wasn't anything to do with me. It was
written about Mick Ralphs actually. Maybe I was telling Mick how I felt, my side
of the story and how I was. He really did talk about boats and planes; he'd talk
about anything other than getting down to business.'

> You used to float, just like a boat, upon the tide
> You used to run, when things were done, you used to hide
> You talk of ships, you talk of boats, you talk of games
> And now you're down, you ain't around, it's such a shame
>
> 'Cos you've got, something to give
> Something to hold on to, why don't you live
> If you, just forget about, fixing on fate
> Maybe you'd stop, pick yourself up, now it's too late
>
> You didn't know, this world ain't slow, you gotta move
> You made no sound, I watched you drown, I watched you lose
> Your loneliness, you knew it best, but it's a drag
> 'Cos in the end, I lost a friend, I feel so sad

Ian explained why 'Shades Off' had reached tape. 'I always had a habit of
putting poems on sleeves. We'd had D.H. Lawrence (on *Mott*) and Baudelaire
(on *Mad Shadows*) and I'd written this poem and we thought it was good enough
to put on the sleeve. Then we were short of material. We had a long ending on
"It Ain't Easy When You Fall"; you know you do these long endings just in case.
Then we thought, why don't we put the poem in there and that'll make the side
a bit longer. I felt very embarrassed about doing it. It was easier to listen to me
singing, than it was talking.'

> Where do you go, when you've somewhere to run
> But the time isn't right, and there's things to be done
> And you're trapped halfway up, you don't want to go back
> So you keep going on, compromising the lack

And you see the green fields, as you travel on by
And you look at the things, you've forgotten to try
And you wish you were young, and you wish you were old
For the songs always sung, and the story's been told

And you thought you were different, but what did that mean
For you tricked yourself trying, life's still unseen
As it is, as it was, as it's always will be
Will you find out at all what it is to be free

See it never was easy to live with a head
So I've kept to the backroom, and I live there instead
What comes from the front room's only for friends
I have a bay window, but that's where it ends

And it's here I see pictures and my madness is clear
And there's no longer logic, so therefore no fear
And I'm almost dead with uncontrollable light
Sometimes when I've written a song, it's all right

'I Get So Excited' closed the album and was a pounding rocker with an abrupt mechanical scissor-cut at the end of the master tape. 'We had a hell of a job with this,' said Ian. 'We'd run out of songs, so we put that one together. I wasn't singing it that well so we added every echo in the book. That was left over from Mott. I kicked three songs off the *Ian Hunter* album. We had a number called "One Fine Day", but it just sounded terrible, so that went with another song called "Colwater High". They were epic, drama-type things and, all of a sudden, these funky tracks were coming through like "Who Do You Love?", "The Truth" and we were axing more. "Colwater High" I thought would have been an English single, but it was so blatant it made the rest of the album sound like shit. I don't think I'm really into singles. "Honaloochie Boogie" stands out like a sore thumb on the *Mott* album. I can't do that any more.'

The LP was not scheduled for release until late March so the British public had an opportunity to hear the new material live, in advance, when Hunter Ronson commenced a 13-date UK tour on 19 March. They played a warm-up gig at Exeter University and started the tour in earnest at Aylesbury Friars storming most major cities en route including Glasgow, Manchester, Birmingham and London's Hammersmith Odeon. The end of the tour was eventually re-scheduled as Ian, now a US citizen, had to leave Britain by 3 April. The live set alternated between Mott, Hunter and Ronson songs and included 'Once Bitten, Twice Shy', 'Lounge Lizard', 'Growing Up and I'm Fine', 'Angel No. 9', 'Who Do You Love?', 'White Light, White Heat', 'Boy', 'Play, Don't Worry', 'The Truth, the Whole Truth and Nothin' but the Truth', 'Roll Away the Stone', 'Slaughter on 10th Avenue', 'The Golden Age of Rock 'n' Roll', 'All the Way from Memphis', 'All the Young Dudes' and 'The Girl Can't Help It'.

The touring band featured Geoff Appleby and Dennis Elliott but keyboard duties were handled by former Mott The Hoople organist Blue Weaver, as Peter Arnesen was hospitalised following an operation. Blue had been recording with The Bee Gees in America, when he received an urgent request to assist Ian and Mick on tour, flying in to rehearse with them briefly before they played their first concert. 'It was great to join Ian again,' says Blue. 'I only had two days rehearsal and hadn't played piano on the Mott The Hoople material before, so I spent the time with chord sheets in front of me. It was an excellent tour though and there was really no noticeable difference between the earlier concerts with Mott. There were still Mott The Hoople fans and Mick's fans and the Bowie overflow. It was good for me to play piano and organ – I had played just organ before with Mott – piano is more physical and good fun. Hunter Ronson was a really good band. "Slaughter on 10th Avenue" made me a bit nervous though; I'd originally heard Mike Garson playing that and he was incredible.'

The audience and press response to the UK shows was excellent and most venues were sold out. Hunter Ronson were supported by new CBS band, Jet, whose members included Martin Gordon and Davey O'List, formerly of Sparks and Roxy Music.

Ian Hunter was released by CBS Records on 28 March 1975, the sleeve featuring a Martin Springett illustration, which used part of M.C. Escher's drawing *Bond of Union*, a counterpart to *Reptiles* used on the first Mott The Hoople LP cover. It entered the UK charts on 12 April and stayed for fifteen weeks, reaching number 21; in America the record hit number 50, also spending fifteen weeks on *Billboard*. The LP received excellent press reviews, one headline proclaiming 'Hunter Turns Killer!'.

'Once Bitten Twice Shy' was issued as a single on 4 April, entering the UK charts on 3 May, where it stayed for ten weeks. It was an edited version of the album track, backed with '3,000 Miles from Here'. A promotional video featured on *Top of the Pops* and the single reached number 14. In subsequent years 'Once Bitten Twice Shy' was recorded by Shaun Cassidy, Jigsaw, Steve Thompson, The Angels and Great White, who reached the top 5 in the USA with their 1989 cover version. It paid royalties, but Hunter was ambivalent, especially when Great White's singer was nominated for a Grammy, which Ian thought added insult to injury.

Before Hunter went back to America he appeared on BBC Radio One's *My Top Twelve* programme with Brian Matthews. His selection of favourite tracks and influences was varied – Jerry Lee Lewis ('Whole Lotta Shakin' '), Little Richard ('Good Golly Miss Molly'), the Righteous Brothers ('You've Lost That Loving Feeling'), Lorraine Ellison ('Stay With Me'), Sonny & Cher ('I Got You Babe'), Mountain ('Mississippi Queen'), The Rolling Stones ('Brown Sugar'), Randy Newman ('Sail Away'), Free ('Catch a Train'), Leon Russell ('Delta Lady'), David Bowie ('Life on Mars?') and Bob Dylan ('Like a Rolling Stone').

During the programme, Ian was asked how strong his desire for musical success really was. 'I can't compromise with what I write. It's just a question of timing, it's just a question of you zero in on that point where everybody thinks the same way you do, and then you become huge. If they don't, then you never become huge. If you're asking me if I'd like to be huge, I'd say yes, obviously, but on my writing, *not* on a compromise trip. Then it'll be me!'

Ian and Mick returned to the USA in early April, Hunter moving into his new home in a secluded estate at Chappaqua near Westchester, an hours drive north of New York City, as he had finally decided to make America his base, at least for the next year. When questioned why he was leaving the UK, Ian remarked, 'I like Britain. I've lived there all my life. I didn't like what was going on and it affected me deeply and emotionally. I thought I was better off living somewhere else. I don't think you can argue with politicians – they're concrete, a different breed of people all together.

'I guess it was natural I would gravitate towards New York, because it's the biggest fairground there is, and when it's bad, it's very, very bad, and when it's good, it's very, very good, and there's just nothing medium about it. It's always extreme. Even if you've got no money there, there's always plenty of colour, plenty of things to fill up your mind. I find New York a very fast place to live, I find London medium and I find Los Angeles slow and I find that I hate LA and I find London okay, so I guess it's a question of metabolism.

'I live at the New York speed. It's not really the States, it's the town of New York City that I want to go at. I think that every person, if they're fortunate enough to have amassed a few quid, should live somewhere other than England. I mean, if you're 75 and you look back on your life, and you didn't spend a year somewhere else, then I think you might be a bit narrow in your mind. I really want to go over there for a year. I'm drawn to it, possibly for the same reason Lennon was drawn to it. I live on nervous energy, so therefore I find it a little bit slow in England. I've given myself a year just to see what it's like, and if it does me in totally, then I'll be coming back, or I'll go somewhere else again.'

Ian also revealed that the move was necessary for artistic reasons. 'To be honest, I'm running out of lyrics. I really worked hard on the lyrics for this last album, but I'm having to get a little bit more into fiction and I don't want to do that, I want to live the lyric. New York has always got me. I can go there for a week and get two lyrics. Similarly, I can't write about London, but if I lived in New York and came here, I could. I'm always better as an observer in a different situation. Don't forget, if you try to write songs over any length of time which I've done, you run out of topics. You don't want to keep on approaching the same things. You've got to move to places that will keep you going, otherwise it can dry up. I like New York for lots of reasons. I think it's an incredible place.'

Hunter Ronson played a series of US concert dates in May, which Fred Heller had originally booked when Ian decided to go solo. They used the same UK touring band but Peter Arnesen was able to join them this time on keyboards. In several regions where Mott had never played, such as Grand Rapids, Hunter Ronson received an ecstatic reception. 'The Lid Blows Off' was one press headline for their raucous show at New York's Felt Forum. Some of the concerts were in smaller, more intimate halls than previous Mott tours, and in some cases these venues were less favourably attended.

'We toured before the album came out, billed as Ian Hunter and Mick Ronson,' said Ian. 'We played in places that were not full and people called it a disaster, but it wasn't a disaster. We never played to a bum crowd. I wanted to carry on because the record wasn't even out. One show in Toledo, Ohio was pulled by the promoter, but the rest we pulled because of the PA system. What we did after the Philadelphia Spectrum date, where we had sound problems, was to find out how many gigs we had to do without legally being sued, and do them with a different sound company every night. We felt it was a back door tour. It came before the album which was a stupid mistake, the classic Hunter Ronson fuck up!'

One British music paper wrote that attendances for the American tour were considerably lower than expectations and the claims of Hunter's management, much to Ian's annoyance. 'It simply wasn't true. The Hunter Ronson tour was portrayed as a disaster, but I remember it totally different to that. Our gigs were all over three quarters full and the audiences went away happy. I wrote to *Melody Maker* telling them to get off my back. I even sent Ticketron slips to prove the attendance figures and they eventually stopped. All the shows weren't sell outs, but neither were Jefferson Starship's, The Grateful Dead, Deep Purple or any of the big names. Spring '75 was a really depressed time in the industry, and yet Mick and I did the Spectrum in Philadelphia, with Aerosmith opening, and sold the place out. I thought it was a great tour and I really enjoyed it. I do remember Ronson's camp saying on the way to one gig that nobody was turning up. I also remember getting there and it was mobbed. All that stuff didn't help my career any.'

After the US dates, the band, who were contracted only for the tour, returned to England. 'We came off the road, split up and then we were offered gigs in Japan and Australia but it was too late,' admits Hunter. 'I couldn't keep the group together. Mick's management was supposed to be paying half the band and I was supposed to pay the other half. Then, Dennis Elliott came to me one day because he hadn't been paid for ten weeks. Mick couldn't do much about it. It's a pity, because that was the nearest we got to touring Japan.'

The members of Hunter Ronson's backing group subsequently pursued a variety of projects. Dennis Elliott acheived most commercial success joining Lou Gramm and Mick Jones in the highly acclaimed Foreigner. Geoff Appleby went on to join The Killers and The Jackals and formed Buzz, who later became The Screen Idols, releasing an album on EMI entitled *Premiere*. Peter Arnesen did session work and issued two solo singles, including a cover of 'Somewhere Over the Rainbow'!

1975 saw the release of a superb Mott The Hoople retrospective when Island Records in Germany issued the double compilation album, *Pop Chronik*. Carefully packaged and compiled with a gatefold sleeve and booklet, the collection contained no new or rare songs but an excellent track selection, including some of their more under-rated compositions including 'I Can Feel' and 'Second Love'.

On 25 July, CBS released a second UK single from the *Ian Hunter* album, 'Who Do You Love?', backed with an edited version of *Boy*. This received no airplay and failed to chart. The A-side was subsequently covered by The Pointer Sisters on their 1979 album *Priority*.

During the summer of 1975, Ian and Mick stayed at Hunter's US home writing and recording in a small basement studio. Their split label and management situation prevented them working jointly and, under their contracts, the next record was to be a Ronson album. Their intention was to use Elliott, Appleby and Arnesen again on the sessions. 'We've got two or three things done,' said Ian at the time, 'and we're starting to get down to serious writing. He panics but I don't. It's his album next. At the moment, we're fighting for a Hunter Ronson record, but it's difficult. I don't care about Ian Hunter solo albums. I want to get the name Hunter Ronson known.'

Ian estimated that he and Mick would be off the road for about six months and on the subject of future live work said, 'I don't want to go out and play a little bit of *Slaughter, The Hoople, Mott* and a little bit of the *Ian Hunter* album. I want to go out and play a total catalogue starting with the album we've just done, which I consider to be a Hunter Ronson album anyway, and also the record we're going to do next.'

The proposed Ronson album never materialised and Mick was soon to part company with Ian, who explained why some time later. 'The original plan was for us to start work on a new Ronson solo album. Then, we had to shelve that idea because RCA didn't want another album as the last two had lost money, at least that's how I understood the situation. By this time, I'd already got four songs that I was really pleased with, written specifically for Mick, and we were going to go in and cut them, but I think Mick was very relieved not to have to make another album. Even though RCA wanted him to cut some singles, he drifted off and had a whale of a time playing with Bob Dylan and Roger McGuinn.

'The business side of it got a bit twisted, as it inevitably does. Both CBS and my manager wanted me to be a solo artist, not linked with Ronson. So I offered him half my bread. I said, "Okay, the album will have to go out as Ian Hunter, but you'll make the same money as me." But he wasn't keen on the idea, he wanted us to form a group called Joe Soap or whatever, which would obviously have been a commercial disaster. The outcome of it all was, that to do a second album, Ronson's management wanted more for him than I was going to get. I said, "Mick, there's no way I'm going to put up with that." Mick would agree with me but then he'd see Tony, who's a very hypnotic character, and he'd come back different. Me and Defries were not getting along at all.

'Anyway, Mick and I drifted apart. He left my house, wasn't "able" to get a home near us and so moved into Dana Gillespie's vacant apartment in Manhattan. I think we both knew that it wasn't going to happen because we had a lot of business problems. In the end, I said to Mick, "I can't work with you any more as long as you're with Mainman." I'll never forgive Fred or Tony. I lost three years when me and Mick could have been working. We couldn't get agreement on anything and it ended up destroying our band.'

Mick met Bob Dylan shortly after he and Ian had decided to split, and joined Dylan's Rolling Thunder Review playing with an ensemble of world-renowned musicians including Roger McGuinn and Joan Baez. They remained close friends, but the business side of their affairs meant that Hunter Ronson would not work together again for three years.

17
Just a whitey from Blighty

'All American Alien Boy' – Ian Hunter

By the end of 1975, Hunter switched to writing material for his second solo LP and auditioned several highly respected musicians, whilst recording demos of his songs in New York. The players that Ian selected for the eventual album sessions were of the highest calibre.

Dennis Elliott came back initially on drums for rehearsals but was about to join Foreigner and was therefore replaced by Aynsley Dunbar for the album. Aynsley had played in Merseybeat bands, John Mayall's Bluesbreakers and The Jeff Beck Group before joining Frank Zappa's Mothers of Invention and Flo and Eddie. Dunbar had also appeared on Bowie's *Pin Ups*, Lou Reed's *Berlin* and Ronson's *Play Don't Worry*, but was a member of Journey when he recorded with Ian.

American David Sanborn, leading rock and jazz saxophonist, and former member of The Butterfield Blues Band, was also recruited. Sanborn had played alto on Bowie's *Young Americans* LP and worked with James Taylor and Stevie Wonder, before recording his first solo album in 1975.

The bass-playing slot was filled with help from Bobby Colomby. He had suggested Ian listen to Jaco Pastorius, who had backed The Temptations and The Supremes. Colomby produced the 1975 *Jaco Pastorius* album before Jaco featured on Weather Report's *Heavy Weather* LP. Pastorius' flamboyant technique, using fretless bass in a melodic fashion, was astounding. Jaco joined Hunter for his album and became good friends with Ian, staying with him and Chris Stainton at the Hunter's Chappaqua home. The trio would be driven up and down to New York City daily, for the sessions, by Trudi's brother, Kevin Ligouri. By 1980, Pastorius was to form his own group, Word of Mouth, and recorded with leading jazz musicians. Sadly, he suffered from depression and alcoholism and died in 1987 after receiving fatal injuries in a fight outside a Florida nightclub.

Hunter initially wanted guitarist Les Nicholls as replacement for Mick Ronson. Nicholls had played with Leo Sayer but the combination with Ian didn't work out, so Gerry Weems, a member of Bonaroo, who had supported Hunter Ronson on their 1975 US tour, was engaged for the sessions.

The nucleus of Hunter's 'band' for the LP was British bass player Chris Stainton, who had worked with Joe Cocker, Spooky Tooth, The Grease Band and his own group Tundra. Stainton acted as musical director and arranger during Ian's sessions and played keyboards.

'A lot of the musicians on the album I had seen playing, and just went up and asked them to join me on the record,' said Ian. 'We worked together really well. I dug Jaco's playing and he liked my lyrics. It was just so easy. When I did the album, I was petrified, because you're producing, writing and arranging all this stuff. There's all these people in the studio that are the best in their profession, so you've got to get organized. You don't have the technical ability of any of the other people, even though you might have something they haven't got in another direction.'

Bobby Colomby was credited on the record although he did not play. 'He helped considerably,' admitted Hunter. 'Bobby kept telling me how much he liked what I did. I needed that little nudge to do something completely on my own. He was very good for my confidence.'

Work started on Hunter's album at the beginning of January 1976 and was completed in only 26 days. There were three weeks of recording at Electric Lady Studios in New York City and a final week for Hunter and Stainton to mix the tapes at A&M Studios in Los Angeles. A total of twelve songs were recorded but four were left off the LP including 'Common Disease'. 'It just didn't work,' confesses Ian. 'Sometimes you don't have time to get it right and you just have to go on to the next track. There were a couple of rockers for the record, but they were wrong. They didn't fit the mood of the rest of the tracks.'

The completed album, entitled *All American Alien Boy*, was built thematically around Hunter's permanent move from Britain to the USA. Several of the songs were first or second takes and all the material was written, produced and arranged by Ian. Unusually, many of the lyrics were written in the third person and it appeared as if he had looked towards Bob Dylan, Randy Newman and John Lennon for some of his inspiration. Hunter had also become infatuated, it seemed, with the mythology of America and the excitement he had discovered there, and the album showed a new maturity and creativity. He certainly didn't play safe with this discerning and somewhat disturbing record, as he tackled Britain, the USA, young love, the Mafia, rapists, drugs, political corruption, rock and roll and God, head on! Lyrically, it is the most mature and potent record in the Hunter canon, each and every track deserving careful listening.

The opening number, 'Letter to Britannia from the Union Jack', originally titled 'To Rule Britannia from the Union Jack', was a song that Ian addressed to his homeland. Sounding a slightly discordant note of national pride and a plea for England to 'get it together', he was critical of the country but also sorrowful for the state of Britain.

> You – you been up, and you – you been down
> You been through many things, I know you been around
> I have fought armies for you in the conflicts of the past
> Britannia I implore you, do not lower me by half

Hunter reflects: 'The flag is talking to the nation but I'm singing to the audience. My feelings about England are very complicated and that's the only way I could get them down, somewhere between Britannia and the Union Jack. It's perfect and exactly the way I felt about England. I was really proud of that.'

'All American Alien Boy' started with piercing Weems guitar which cut in abruptly on the fade out of 'Britannia', taking the listener on an instant trans-Atlantic crossing.

I packed my bags – in the land of rags
'Cos I don't believe – in them dimmo drags
Don't wanna vote for the left wing – don't wanna vote for the right
I gotta have both – to make me fly

Hunter was jaded with British politics and government and was now able to write about the United States of America as a resident, rather than a visitor. He was humorously confused with grotesque Americana, TV commercials and guns. 'In America it's very sophisticated. It's like, "Here's all the dirt, isn't it great." All that is covered up in Britain. America is tacky in comparison to Britain. I'd toured there, but living there is different. "Alien Boy" is like a chronology of first impressions.'

'Irene Wilde' was a song to a girl from Hunter's youth and a poignant, fragile ballad which has remained in his live set throughout his career. His teenage dream rejects him in this true story of 'a Barker Street bus station non-affair' and pushes him towards ambition instead, away from his hometown of Shrewsbury. 'It's the truth,' says Ian. 'Irene really snubbed me at the bus station and inspired me to be a star. She's still there, married and enormous, of course, but I meant what I wrote in the song.'

When I was just sixteen, I stood waiting for a dream
At Barker Street Bus Station every night
When I tried to get it on, she just looked at me with scorn
My courage turned to dust and I took flight
For those looks they seemed to say, you ain't nothing go away
You're just some face in the crowd, so I went home and I vowed
I'm gonna be somebody, someday

Side One ended with 'Restless Youth', by far the hardest rock song on the album, but even then it was medium-paced. Stainton plays bass on this one track, in a style reminiscent of Joe Cocker's 'With a Little Help from My Friends'. Hunter tackled American criminals, underdogs and the Mafia in this pounding number, with direct references to Little Italy, hanging, gangs, Al Capone and government corruption.

He soon found out he could not work – the money was no good
This child of the city hit the welfare kitty – did some running for the
     hoods
And the logic of the street was such – that everything was bent
There's a lot of white collars stealing government dollars –
Wouldn't notice such a little per cent

'Rape' was originally recorded with 12 opening bars from 'Singing in the Rain', a throwback to the brutal scene in *A Clockwork Orange*, but this was edit-ed out for legal reasons. America's casual violence seemed to have both captured Hunter and disgusted him. Musically, 'Rape' had a haunting gospel flavour and stunning female chorus, while the lyrics expressed an horrendous sexual violation.

> A knife full of life penetrated the bait
> While he thinks of the sister and the mother that he hates
> And he thinks he'll get off 'cos he's sick, rich and stoned
> And justice was made to be honed

Ian then crucifies the injustice of the justice system.

> And his lawyer is smiling one hell of a smile
> 'N' he's lying all the lies of the lies in exile
> While she's dying of grief, he's defending his brief
> And justice would seem to be cheap

Throughout the song, Hunter has described justice as cheap and something to be abused. In an intense crescendo at the end of the track, he shouts in disgust: 'Justice just is … Justice just is … Justice just is … Not!'

'You Nearly Did Me In', was originally titled 'Weary Anger' on initial test pressings of the record and featured instantly recognisable backing vocals from Freddie Mercury, Roger Taylor and Brian May. 'Queen happened to be in New York and came down to the session', said Ian. 'They were at the studio for an hour before I knew they were there. Then someone told me they were outside. They'd sat there for an hour and Freddie said, "Isn't there *anything* we can do?" So I had one particular track that I was going to put girls on and I said, "Well, you can do this." Hunter's lead vocal demonstrated a new-found confidence and was stronger than ever. Some speculated that the title referred to Ronson or Defries, but the lyrics actually conveyed another stark and terrifying American landscape, as Hunter sadly observed drug addiction.

> See lonely shadows, silver needles
> Abandoned in the evening war
> Lost children of the night, come catch the candles bright
> I hear a hollow sound, falling to the ground
> Oh, she's lost before she's found

Many reviewers predictably drew parallels with Dylan on several of the album's tracks, but this song had no resemblance whatsoever to Zimmerman. 'Apathy '83' did. Featuring buoyant accordion and conga playing, it saw Hunter capture the vigour and anger which once characterised Dylan's work. It is perhaps one of the most perceptive songs ever written about the decaying rock scene, as Hunter sings in successive choruses – 'There ain't no rock 'n' roll no more, just the music of the young'; '… the sickly sound of greed and the music of the rich.'

'I used the word rock 'n' roll as a substitute for innocence,' explained Hunter. 'There isn't any rock 'n' roll now, just the music of the young. Rock 'n' roll was Little Richard and Fats Domino. It wasn't Soft Machine. You've got the apathetic seventies and a lot of apathetic bands. Bowie is the only one who did anything.'

Ian also included a refrain of 'Apathy for the Devil' in the song, which delightfully mimicked The Rolling Stones' 'Sympathy for the Devil'. Lyrically, Hunter had been 'inspired' by aspects of Dylan's Rolling Thunder Revue and a comment made by Dylan after a very 'uninspired' concert in New York. 'I'd just been to see The Stones at Madison Square Garden, and who should I meet on the Saturday night down the Village in New York but Bob Dylan. It was the first time I ever met him,' said Ian. 'When asked by Dylan what I thought of the Stones' concert, I replied "insipid". Dylan said, "Yeah – apathy for the devil." And that's how "Apathy '83" got written. He gave me the idea for the song.'

Hunter had been in the Bitter End club and was asked if he wanted to go to the next door restaurant to hear Dylan playing songs from his forthcoming album *Desire*. 'I wasn't pushing to meet him, but he was talking to everybody after his set, a little bit pissed on wine, and he looked me straight in the eye and said, "I know you from somewhere, don't I?" So Bobby Neuwirth told him who I was, and he charged around the pavement whooping "Mott The Hoople, Mott The Hoople!" I thought he was taking the piss, but he was being genuine. He knew all the songs from the first album. He was singing great chunks of "Half Moon Bay" and "At the Crossroads" right there in the street. I'd been told that The Byrds and The Band had listened to the early Mott albums, but I never dreamed Dylan would be familiar with them, especially not after six years.'

Hunter has always credited Dylan as his inspiration to take up singing in the first place. 'I never understood a word of what Dylan was saying, I just had this chill. His voice just felt right. I also like Keith Richard's singing; to me it's pure jazz. I got this amazing vibe from Dylan and I knew I couldn't sing properly be-cause people like Paul Rodgers had already informed me of that, so I was aiming at phrasing my vocals.'

However, at the time of *All American Alien Boy*, Hunter was becoming ex-tremely tired of repetitive Dylan comparisons. 'I'm sick of it now. I'm not in awe of the guy. I don't think he's been delivering for a while. I prefer my first solo album to *Blood on the Tracks*. Dylan is a genius and my mentor, but I think I'm lucky enough to be making better records right now. I'm a writer and he's a writer, and, at the moment, I think I'm better than he is.'

American malaise found further expression in 'Apathy '83' as Ian mixed Watergate, President Nixon and General Sheridan with his pop heroes.

> For the law is now the lawless
> And the flaw is now the flawless
> And the crime is now accepted
> And the criminal respected
> And now evil gets elected
> And now sinful gets selected
> See a president proven rotten, now officially forgotten

'God (Take 1)', originally titled '(God) Advice to a Friend', was unquestion-ably the most 'Dylan-ish' song on the LP, but was in actual fact a parody. 'I

wanted to let people hear how it would sound if I really imitated Bob Dylan,'
admitted Ian. The lyric was a witty and thought provoking dialogue between
writer and creator, with God being highly casual about good, evil, faith, super-
stition and the meaning of life.

> I said to God 'I found you out,
> 'cos I know what this world is all about'
> And God said, 'Stop – don't scramble your brain –
> my opponent's been messing you around again
> See him and me are enemies
> and we play little games for galaxies
> And he's inside you – and I am too –
> so here were are – just the three of you'

The entire record possessed a lyrical mastery and Hunter was aware of it too.
'I know this one's good,' said Ian at the time. 'I would love *All American Alien
Boy* to be a big album because I wrote it for me, really. I'm genuinely upset about
the political thing. It's a really delicate subject, as is rape, as is God. I'm proud of
those lyrics because I went where a lot of people won't go.' Ironically, Mick
Ronson was to acknowledge that this was his favourite Hunter LP, and Ian now
admits that his writing for the record, particularly tracks like 'Letter to Britannia'
and 'God', was fuelled by his manager's supplies of Colombian Red.

All American Alien Boy was released by CBS in April 1976 and entered the UK
album chart on 29 May where it stayed for four weeks hitting number 29.
Surprisingly, the record faired worse in America, where it only reached number
177, spending seven weeks on *Billboard*. The press reacted very favourably to the
LP: 'Hunter turns up trumps'; 'The eight songs are his most powerful and
thoughtful yet'; 'Altogether a peak album!'; '… by far the most adventurous and
expansive album Hunter has recorded'; 'This is a rock 'n' roll album and Ian
Hunter is one of rock's finest.'

CBS also issued 'All American Alien Boy', backed with 'Rape', as a single in
Britain but it failed to chart. For the Hunter collector, the A-side was, however,
a shorter alternate take from the sessions, with some lyrical and musical
differences. Ian had specifically recorded a more up-tempo funk version as a
thank you and compliment to his musicians. 'They played it my way on the
album, so I did the single their way.' CBS released a second UK single in July,
'You Nearly Did Me In' with 'Letter to Britannia from the Union Jack', but with
minimal promotion this also sank virtually unnoticed.

Ian subsequently reflected on the album and admitted that *Alien Boy* was
commercial suicide. 'I knew that when I did it. It was all slow and pretty boring
but it was something I just wanted to do. People like to think of me in terms of
rock 'n' roll and so I had a chip on my shoulder about slower stuff. I knew I had
to get the ballads out of my system, but I thought the record would happen anyway with all these great people playing on it. It comes as quite a shock when it
doesn't.

'Everyone was thinking the album was a piece of art, telling me how I was a genius. They had me fooled. I really thought I'd done something special, then we went up to Columbia. They told me how wonderful it was but you develop a nose. There's a difference between genuine wonderful and telling you wonderful. I don't know if I was trying to get away from rock 'n' roll permanently, but I knew I'd had enough at the time. I thought I wrote good lyrics and nobody took a lot of notice of them. There's no real songs on there; the melodies are vehicles for the lyrics. I came out of that album a lot bigger musically, and the fact that it died commercially was a total bummer. Ronson's typical; he hated the album, then he liked it a lot.

'I can see why it didn't sell. It's pretty boring on one level, if you want to look at it that way, but I don't. I can hardly see one of Aerosmith doing one like that. I'm quite special in certain ways. Maybe if it had been put out differently, instead of just another rock 'n' roll album, it might have stood a bit of a chance. It's a lyrical album. 'God (Take 1)' is great. It's one of the best things I've ever written.'

Ian says he also liked the record because it contained material and ideas which he had harboured for years. 'I had so much on my conscience after that turbulent Mott The Hoople period, that *All American Alien Boy* was a kind of relief to me. It is a reflection of what went through me at the time.'

Hunter decided that he would not tour to promote the album. He chose instead to play with a band he had seen live during Mott The Hoople's U.S. tour in 1972 and praised in *Diary of a rock 'n' roll Star*. 'All Columbia wanted to know was, "Do you want to become this kind of artist full time?" I didn't have an answer. So I went upstate and started rehearsing with The Fabulous Rhinestones. They were great and I was going to go out with them, because I really liked Harvey Brookes, the bass player. But after about a week of rehearsals, it suddenly hit me. I thought, "I can't go onstage and do this. I can't play a bunch of slow songs on their own. I have to play rock." It just didn't feel right without that bit of swagger attached to the front and the back. I have to do both. That was when I realised I didn't want to do that full time, so I dropped it and was stuck. I didn't do anything.'

Having exorcised his slower and serious lyrical material with *All American Alien Boy*, Hunter admits that his record company put him under pressure to revert to a more commercial musical approach. He found that he started to write harder rock songs again and the inevitable group situation was already on the horizon.

18
Don't let them tell you
that you'll never find fame

'Collision Course' – Overend Watts

Ian Hunter had got his solo career off to a flying start with Mick Ronson after Mott The Hoople disbanded in November 1974, but the other members of the group took a little longer to rise from the ashes. Initially shattered by Mott's split and the cancellation of their UK and US tours, Overend Watts and Blue Weaver gradually worked on material together while Dale Griffin wrote at home, and Morgan Fisher left the country.

Watts recalls that it was not an easy period after the demise of Mott The Hoople. 'When we split up, Ian left suddenly and there was a tour coming up and we weren't able to fulfill it. We didn't know what to do as it was so sudden, it didn't happen over a period of time. Everything I'd worked for was gone in a flash. It was almost like a bereavement. I just felt complete emptiness. We didn't know whether we were going to carry on as Mott or not, so we sat at home for a while and then Buff and I started to read all sorts of crap in press articles about Hunter Ronson, that we weren't really into music and we only wanted to tour to get money for Christmas presents, which was just awful. About three or four weeks after the split, I parked my car one day to go into a butchers in Ealing and, amazingly, bumped into Ian and Trudi outside the shop. Hunter made pleasant conversation but I wasn't in a very good frame of mind. He said, "I'm sorry about the split Pete, are you okay?" I said, "Well to be honest Ian, no I'm not." '

Gradually, Pete started to compose with Blue, although there was no intention of forming a group. 'We wrote some songs that weren't bad,' says Watts. 'One of the first was "Love Now", which was quite funky in its original form. Morgan was off doing his own thing, but then Buffin seemed interested, so me, Buffin and Blue decided to work together. We booked some studio time to see how it went and during this period we were still being managed by Heller and Hirschman. We played them our demo tape which contained "The Bright Days," "Love Me Always", The Everly Brothers' "Leave My Woman Alone", "Collision Course" and "Love Now". They thought the songs were great, and told us to keep going and try to make something of it by putting another group together, which we did.'

'There were however, debts to be paid after the split,' explains Watts. 'Fred Heller said he needed money to float the new band and asked if I wanted it to operate on a similar level to the old one, which I did. I had two $30,000 publishing advances for my writing and we used that finance for the new group. I ended up broke by the late seventies. $60,000 was probably worth over £30,000 – my house cost me £12,000 back then – so it was a lot of money.'

Unexpectedly, Blue was suddenly offered a £250-a-week post, playing keyboards with The Bee Gees, which Pete urged him to accept. Weaver soon notified Watts that The Bee Gees were looking for a bass player too but Pete swiftly declined at which point Morgan offered to take Blue's place. 'We used to go round to Pete's rambling house in Acton, which was a great place to visit because it was full of pin ball machines and juke boxes,' says Fisher. 'It became our pre-rehearsal rehearsal room, before we went into a real rehearsal studio. He had this horrendously out of tune piano there and Buffin would use cardboard boxes as drums, which sounded really good. I think Eddie Cochran did the same thing on some of his recordings.'

The trio discovered that they had several new songs between them and concluded they had to form a new band. They booked time at Gooseberry Studios in London's Gerrard Street and continued to record demos, Pete handling vocals, six string guitar and bass on the backing tracks. New material continued to flow in the studio, most of it eventually forming their first album, and by the end of the sessions they had over 20 songs on tape, the majority being self-composed tracks that would form the new record.

At first the band were petitioned by several fans to retain the Mott The Hoople name but they opted for The Hooples, before eventually settling on Mott, which they felt was simple, recognised and reflected the group which contained three-fifths of the old Mott. At one point they almost adopted Watts' suggestion, Shane Cleaven and the Clean Shaven! The biggest problem was the selection of a lead guitarist and vocalist, and they knew the task would be difficult. Pete felt the old band had a good reputation and wanted the new one to be even better.

Mott The Hoople had originally considered Hackensack's lead guitarist, Ray Smith, as a possible replacement for Mick Ralphs. The official story was that, contractually, he could not join in 1973, although Ray has a different tale to tell. This time he was not restricted.

Ray changed his surname from Smith to Major when he joined Mott because of confusion with his namesake, a member of Island group Heads, Hands and Feet. 'We were getting cross-referenced in PRS and were getting each others' publishing royalties. So I mentioned to Pete that I should change my name and reinvent myself and Major seemed good at the time.' Watts' suggestions for a new identity – Jesus Smythe Briggs, The Pink Punk or Damage Massacre – were not accepted!

Ray Major was born in Brixton, South London on 16 July 1949. He had one sister and his father, a motor engineer, played piano. Several other members of the family were musical too, so Ray was exposed to music from a young age. 'I had a pretty good childhood, but my Mum died when I was fifteen and that put me on a collision course with rock 'n' roll. My Dad will hate me for saying it, but he did me no real favours. My Mum had three jobs supporting us and he would play in pub bands and pull women, and my Mum was out of her mind with worry. I was good at art and got a place at Brixton Art College, but my Father hounded me to get a job.

'I was playing music then, but not that well. However, most of my cousins were players and there were guitars around so it was like a fever that was hitting me. There were always family parties and it was a very old-fashioned way of doing things; you'd turn the T.V. off and sing and play. I couldn't play until I was about fourteen when I learned on my cousin's guitar. After my Mum died, when

I was seventeen, I was straining at the leash to leave home and be a musician.'

Ray's musical influences were eclectic. 'I liked Jimi Hendrix, Johnny Winter and Big Jim Sullivan. I've always had this affection for blues because it's therapy in a way. I remember as an eight year-old kid, hearing Link Wray's "The Rumble". I didn't know what it was, but it affected me deeply. Then I liked the Ventures, the Shadows naturally, the Small Faces, The Beatles and the Stones.'

From the age of 15, Ray played in local semi-pro Brixton bands including White Stains and The Split. 'I lived in Brixton squats and rented accommodation most of my life, up until I was 25, when I joined Mott. I was just generally hanging out with musicians. But my family didn't like rock 'n' roll, so I had to get away and at 19 I joined my first pro band, called Opal Butterfly, which was a "hippie group", signed to CBS.'

Opal Butterfly recorded a single for Polydor, 'Groupie Girl' / 'The Gig Song', which Ray describes as 'trash', and featured in the film *Groupie Girl*. 'I was in that with my then-to-be first wife. She was half Jamaican-half English, a very stunning looking girl, a bit like Marsha Hunt. I think we were just caught on camera for about ten or twenty seconds, canoodling in the studio.'

The Brixton connection was proving troublesome for Ray, and he wanted to lose it. 'It was very heavy for me, with the police and drugs. I wasn't dealing, but a lot of my friends were, because there was no money. You got branded with them. I was a hippie, they were black, and the police didn't like either. They just kicked you, broke the toilets, broke the baths, slapped you in the face and blackened your eyes. People should know what was happening in Brixton in the seventies. Between 1971 and 1973 it was a hellish place to be, lovely people but everybody was hassled.'

In 1971, Ray Major joined Hackensack, but he does not have fond memories of the group, certainly in its latter stages. 'There was vocalist Nicky Moore, Stu Mills on bass and drummer John Turner who was great. At first the band was fresh, then it became sloppy, so we got Simon Fox in on drums, later of Be Bop Deluxe. Muff Winwood came to see us one day and said, "Yeah, this is a good little set up, I like this, I think we'll do a single." We did, and it was a great record.'

Hackensack signed to Island Records and released Mick Ralphs' 'Moving On', produced by Winwood in 1972. They had supported Mott The Hoople on their Rock and Roll Circus tour and Ralphs offered them the song. 'We did the Circus tour as the support band with fire eaters, knife throwers and Max Wall. We had one of our roadies, Jed, dressed up as a bear running round on stage and it was a lot of fun. We became friendly with Mott and used to phone each other up, and then Ralphs said he had this great song called "Moving On" and he played lap steel on it for us. Commercially it died, so we left Island Records, which was a mistake, because it was such a great company. Every band under Island's banner had something, but we got a deal from Polydor. It was a bad move. The money side of the business came into play!'

Island Records shelved an album of studio material (eventually issued in 1997 entitled *Give It Some!*) but, in 1972, Polydor finally released a Hackensack LP, *Up The Hardway*. The sessions were produced by Derek Lawrence, who had worked with Wishbone Ash, at De Lane Lea Studios in London. Ray co-wrote three of the tracks – "Up the Hardway", "Goodbye Bad Boy" and "Blindman" – on which he also sang lead vocal for the first section of the song. However, Ray dislikes the record and believes it resulted in the group's demise.

'Hackensack started to decline after the album. Simon was getting bored, I wasn't really interested, but I fell into the money trap with everyone else. It felt good for a while but then one of the group ripped us off. It was so painful. The only decent thing on the album was that Big Jim Sullivan played on two tracks. I told Jim at the time I couldn't stand the material and the record was not us, but he said, "Ray, it's part of the game. You do it and forget it." I actually threw my copies of the LP out of my flat window. They made great UFOs. Now vinyl copies are changing hands for £80! After that the band actually came to blows and Hackensack broke up. Our equipment was sold, we got no money and were all broke.'

Ray started to form a group with Andy Fraser and Frankie Miller, composing and recording tracks over a two month period at Fraser's Woking home, where Paul Kossoff was a regular visitor. Suddenly Andy decided to go and stay in America but, just when all seemed lost for Ray, Mott reared its head for a second time.

'I almost connected with Mott The Hoople when I was with Hackensack and Ralphs left, but we were on tour and I subsequently learned that Mott's telegrams didn't get to me. They needed to get a new guitarist rehearsed quickly to go back and tour America and we were out of the country. When I got back, I saw my old road manager and he said, "You should get in touch with Mott The Hoople, they've been trying to get hold of you." I didn't know this, although I'd had a feeling that Ralpher might hand in his notice. Mick had actually opened the door for me with Mott The Hoople, but I never received the telegrams, even though Hackensack will all deny it, or say they got lost.'

Tippins has a different summary of events. 'Ray wouldn't actually leave Hackensack to join Mott The Hoople. Hunter couldn't believe it. I remember talking to Ian and he was laughing saying, "He won't leave Hackensack to join us. He won't leave that piddling little group to join Mott." Hunter was flabbergasted.'

This time, Ray saw a *Melody Maker* advertisement for the post and approached Mott. 'After the sessions with Fraser and Miller in 1974, I did a few gigs and sessions in London and in the paper one day I read an ad: "Guitarist wanted – Vocalist wanted – Name band" – so I phoned up and asked for the name of the band. They said, "Well, we can't tell you that, but come down to Gooseberry Studios on Thursday morning at eleven o'clock, and we'll audition you." So I got down there, checked in, got a cup of coffee and the control room door opened and there was Overend Watts. He turned to Stan Tippins and said, "That's it, we've found the guitar player we want. This is Ray out of Hackensack, I like him, I want him in the band." Pete was a strong ally for me. I did the audition and Morgan said play something to this, and it was "I'll Tell You Something," with a beautiful run down in A, which I did, and Pete said, "You've got it." '

Mott had auditioned a number of other guitar players including John Cann of Atomic Rooster and Dave Ball ex-Big Bertha and Procul Harum. They also wanted John Miles at one point, and thought about Zal Cleminson from The Sensational Alex Harvey Band again, as they had done after Ralphs' departure in 1973.

In the meantime, CBS Records had been pushing for Russ Ballard of Argent, composer of classic songs such as 'It's Only Money', 'I Don't Believe in Miracles' and 'God Gave Rock and Roll to You'. There had already been a vague Mott–Argent connection when Derek Griffiths was suggested as a possible replacement for Luther Grosvenor. Russ Ballard's punchy rock songs had increasingly become at odds with Rod Argent's elongated keyboard work-outs, and he quit in 1974. Unfortunately, although Russ was a prolific songwriter, excellent guitar player and good lead vocalist, Mott rejected him, mainly in view of his age and omnipresent Hunteresque sunglasses! Ballard went on to pen further hits including 'I Surrender' and 'Since You've Been Gone' for Ritchie Blackmore's Rainbow. Mott had missed a great opportunity.

'CBS suggested Russ Ballard as a replacement for Ian,' admits Griffin. 'The trouble is, we were looking for a singer and songwriter who didn't wear dark glasses, who wasn't older than us, had a wide vocal range and who was unknown. Unfortunately we got a singer who was an unknown and who still is, which wasn't quite the plan. We didn't think Russ Ballard was a good idea because we thought there were too many similarities with Ian, when we were eager to distance ourselves from any Hunter comparisons.'

'I also wanted Nils Lofgren,' says Pete. 'An American, but small, and thus easy to hit around! I still think Nils is the greatest guitar player in the world. When you think of people in bands, how many can you think of who can write brilliant songs, is a brilliant singer and is a brilliant guitarist? I can't think of anyone except him, who can do all three. Even my favourite artist of all time, Warren Zevon, is a brilliant singer and songwriter but doesn't play great guitar.'

Ray Major's thoughtful playing style seemed to suit the new Mott perfectly and so he joined in December 1974, although this was not announced until much later. Having bagged Major, the position of lead vocalist proved more difficult to fill and Watts, Griffin and Fisher eventually received and heard over 200 tapes and auditioned around 60 singers. They tried John Otway during the auditions, but the group thought that they might inhibit him. Robert Palmer was suggested but they turned down that prospect immediately. The other contenders included Peter French, John Butler, Terry Wilson-Slesser, Graham Bonnett, Steve Wright, Brian Engel and Brian Parrish, who auditioned fully and recorded a demo of 'I'll Tell You Something'.

'The guy we really wanted was Stevie Wright from The Easybeats,' admits Watts. 'Stan had to find him and phoned all over the world trying to track him down. Eventually, he got hold of his mother in the backwoods of Australia and she said, "Steve? Oh yes, he's in a hotel in Birmingham, England." So Stan called the hotel, got hold of his manager and the manager wouldn't put him on the telephone. We couldn't get hold of Steve because they obviously didn't want to lose him.'

Major recalls, 'My original choice for a vocalist was Pete French who had been with Cactus, Atomic Rooster and Bogart & Appice. He had a Paul Rodgers-type range. Then we almost had Terry Wilson-Slesser in the band. Terry was a nice guy, but he got an offer from Paul Kossoff to join Back Street Crawler and if I was a singer of that stature, I would have gone with Kossoff to be frank. Koss was a brilliant player.'

'We first decided on Terry Wilson-Slesser as vocalist, having already recruited Ray Major,' explains Dale. 'Terry was from the north-east of England, like my wife, and had an excellent voice and great personality. We organised a "welcome to the group" do at my house in Wembley with the managers, road crew and friends. It was a jolly evening and we thought everything was great. The next day, we got a call from him, saying he'd decided to join Paul Kossoff's "Nightcrawler" group. It was a bit of a surprise really, since he'd joined us the day before. We didn't organise a leaving party for him!'

Around this time, Mick Ralphs spotted vocalist Nigel Benjamin playing at the London Marquee with a band called Royce. Ralphs recommended him to Mott and, after auditioning only three songs, he was asked to join. Nigel was born near Southend in Essex on 12 September 1954. His first group, Grott, featured Lee Brilleaux, who would later join Dr Feelgood. Grott was an early Deviants/Stooges-style band, who committed many outrages during their short career, such as pouring green paint all over the floor at a gig in the Brentwood High School for Girls. Benjamin's other local groups, prior to Royce, were Virginia Waters, Billion Dollar Band and Fancy. Nigel was influenced musically by The Beatles, The Rolling Stones and Captain Beefheart and whilst he had developed as a lead vocalist, he could also play guitar and piano.

Ray Major recalls that it took a few months of searching for a vocalist before Nigel came along. 'I was in a tube station one day, waiting to go over to Pete's place, and I saw this guy on the other platform with long red hair and snakeskin boots, singing away to himself, and I thought he had a great image. I got to Pete's and we went down to the studio, and this guy that I'd seen at the station came in. I thought he had a real attitude, a sort of, "I'm the best" approach and he certainly wasn't backwards in coming forward, which was good for a front man. As soon as he sang, that was it.'

'We got Ray four months before Benjamin came along,' says Watts. 'Nigel's voice was incredible. He was quite young and inexperienced but he seemed a nice sort of bloke. When he joined the group, he had to move from Southend and he stayed with me and we got on great. He had a lovely sense of humour. "Collision Course", which appeared on our second album, was the audition number we used when we started Mott. The verse had a very high A and we wanted a singer who had a good vocal range. Most of them couldn't reach it. Stan could!'

Benjamin admitted he wasn't really thinking of joining another group at the time, but during the audition he sang 'She Does It', 'Shout It All Out' and 'I'll Tell You Something', and was immediately excited by the prospect of joining Mott. Within only ten days, they had commenced recording of a new album. The sessions were held between 28 April and 20 May 1975 at Clearwell Castle in Gloucestershire, previously used by Bad Company and Badfinger, utilising Ronnie Lane's mobile recording studio. Master mixing and final overdubs were completed with Geoff Emerick at AIR London Studio No. 3, in Oxford Street between 23 May and 9 June. All the backing tracks were taped in two weeks and the entire album arranged, produced and directed by the band. Dale felt it was the best sound Mott had ever achieved on record, largely because they went back to 16 tracks. *The Hoople* had been taped on 24 tracks, which he thought got too complicated and meant the extra space was filled and embroidered with unnecessary decoration.

'To record the album we used Ronnie Lane's mobile studio, parked it outside the castle, multi-coiled the dungeon and just went for it,' recalls Ray. 'Then we found out about the Ghost of Clearwell Castle! I never saw anything, but it was extremely spooky. You had to come out of the basement studio and climb some stairs, and if you were on your own, believe me, you'd run out very quickly into the Airstream caravan that housed the recording equipment.'

The resulting album, *Drive On*, was released by CBS Records on 12 September 1975, Nigel Benjamin's 21st birthday. It entered the UK charts on 4 October for one week at number 45. The record was presented in an unusual silver foil sleeve and contained an insert featuring Mott's 'What a Bloke List', a tribute to their friends and influences. 'The What a Bloke List started life when we all said, "Who can we thank on the sleeve? Oh fuck it, let's thank everybody. Who do you want to thank? – Big Jim Sullivan?" So it developed from there,' says Ray.

The final running order for the album was selected from a total of fourteen completed tracks, most of the songs being written by Overend Watts. Eleven numbers were included on the LP with 'Shout It All Out', 'Phantom of the Opera' and one other being shelved. Mott had also considered recording a cover version of 'Milk Train', for release as a single. Bob Hirschman had received a publisher's tape of the song, composed by Bugatti and Musker, subsequently demoed by Gary Holton and recorded by Roger Daltrey. Mott liked the track, but didn't record it as once again, they felt it was too reminiscent of a Hunter-style number!

'By Tonight' opened *Drive On* in rousing style with a strong riff and verse, showing the new Mott to be both musically tight and mature, even before they had played any live dates. Benjamin's voice added a new dimension to the sound of the original trio, being more youthful, in Robert Plant / Steve Marriott mould.

The first single to be released from the LP was 'Monte Carlo', one of the lighter tracks on the record. The idea came from some Morgan Fisher keyboard antics during which he sang 'the man who broke the Bank at Monte Carlo', and the group latched on to this as a possible title. On August 31 Mott promoted the single on the first edition of a new BBC TV music quiz, *Disco*, hosted, inexplicably, by Terry Wogan. 'Monte Carlo' was backed with a non-album Watts' composition entitled 'Shout It All Out', lyrically 'pointed' at Hunter. 'Ian would often telephone Pete to tell him how well things were going for him, and that inspired the lyric,' claims Dale.

The lyrically banal 'She Does It', opened with stately and dramatic piano but exploded into a pacey and very hard rock track showcasing powerful drumming from Dale Griffin. The middle eight of the song featured Overend on vocals. 'I'll Tell You Something', on the other hand, was one of very few ballads on the album and was extremely melodic, featuring exceptional vocals and grand piano from Nigel and Morgan. This was an important song, being the audition piece that convinced both Major and Benjamin to join the band. 'Morgan had got these chords, and Pete had written some lyrics, and it was a ballad which I thought was very nice, and different from things I'd done with Hackensack,' remarks Ray.

Side One ended with *Stiff Upper Lip,* regarded by many as the cornerstone of the LP, being a comment about the political state of the country similar to 'Pearl 'n' Roy' from *The Hoople* album. Overend sang the slow pounding verses and Nigel the up-beat choruses. The track was the most complicated on the record with various fade outs and theme changes, a spoken middle section, a finale reminiscent of The Beach Boys plus a 'wry snatch' of the 'Memphis' intro.

Side Two opened in crashing style with Watts singing lead vocal on 'Love Now', another powerful rocker which followed a similarly blatant lyrical theme to 'She Does It'. 'Apologies' was a short piece, less than a minute in duration, written by Benjamin. Featuring only Nigel's vocal, this simple acoustic passage, was a welcome prelude to the two longest tracks on the record.

Mott attempted a thundering portion of heavy metal with Watts' 'The Great White Wail', originally inspired by the Ghost of Clearwell Castle and featuring Overend on rhythm and Morgan on bass guitar. In contrast, 'Here We Are' was a beautiful song with expressive vocals, sad synthesizer and a fine acoustic bridge between the choruses and verses, showing the true diversity of Mott's musical horizons.

'I wrote "The Great White Wail" in Clearwell Castle one evening, and it was very peculiar, because after I'd done it, I found a big set of jaws from a whale hung up above a door, and I hadn't seen them before,' says Watts. 'I'd written the song and titled it, without even seeing those bones. There were some very weird occurrences down there.'

Dale Griffin made his songwriting debut with 'It Takes One to Know One', possibly the most instant pop-rock track on the album. The chorus was particularly strong and although obvious single material, it failed to chart when CBS issued it in Spring 1976. 'A&R man Nicky Graham felt this was a sure fire hit, but, of course, it wasn't,' admits Dale, who included a quote from Willard Manus' *Mott The Hoople* book beneath the song title on the lyric sheet: 'The best time to hit a man is when he's down, the best place to hit him is below the belt' – a reference to the propaganda and press which followed Hunter's departure from the original group. This linked appropriately with 'I Can Show You How It Is', which was a stunning ballad to close the LP. Written by Overend and Dale, the lyrics were again directed towards Ian.

When questioned about the inspiration for the songs on *Drive On,* the major contributor, Pete Watts is frank. 'Desperation! Somebody had to write them and there was only me who could do it, there was no other reason. I was landed with it after Ian left because, although we got Nigel in, he wasn't a writer. It was soon pretty obvious that he wasn't going to write anything that was right for the group and suddenly, it was all on me, and it was horrible. I was writing songs that were half good, because I didn't know about choruses and wasn't composing complete songs. I was getting a riff that was okay and trying to finish it off without making any real song. Also, I seldom wrote about incidents directly, they were more general and imaginary.'

In spite of these self-confessed shortfalls, Watts does admit it was one of the more enjoyable albums that Mott produced. 'It was good fun recording *Drive On* and it was probably the lightest album we ever had to do. It was great shaking off the burden of Mott The Hoople and all the saxes and girl singers and orchestras. We could get down to basics again, but it's a shame the order that things happened in. I hadn't really got round to songwriting in a proper way at that time, and I didn't really understand about fitting choruses to things very well. A lot of the songs on *Drive On* are promising but they haven't got choruses. "By Tonight" has no chorus – it's basically a riff and a verse – if it had, it could have been a great track. Quite a few of the other songs I wrote are two-thirds of the way there, because I didn't quite have the grasp of it. By 1980, I did a demo of a track called "Caribbean Hate Song", the best song I ever wrote. I can certainly write much better now.'

Morgan, however, felt that the new line up presented opportunities for wider musical contributions, given time. 'I think the whole creative thing of the band without Ian became more rewarding for us, because we all had a chance to pitch in and write songs. That's not to say there had been any resentment about Ian being the main songwriter, because he was a strong passionate writer. He really had something to say and was a man with a message, although I don't think we paid too much attention to his lyrics at the time. We were all too busy getting on making the music.

'Ian would come up with a song and we'd say it was a good one and we'd go with the rhythm and the melody. We liked the way he wrote musically but he would never discuss or explain his lyrics and we never really asked him. It happens with a lot of bands. Ian used to invite us round to his apartment to play us a new song on his little upright piano, even with scat singing if he hadn't finished the lyrics. It was inspiring to see him do that, but when we wrote in Mott, and the Lions later, it was more like a musician's approach, looking for riffs and chords before melody and lyrics. Mott was more music-based and less vocal-orientated but, let's face it, Hunter was a better songwriter all round.'

Shortly after recording *Drive On*, Mott played a few continental gigs followed by an eight-date British tour commencing at Bristol Colston Hall on 18 September. Supported by Upp, they did further shows in Manchester, Birmingham, Newcastle, Aylesbury and finally London New Victoria Theatre. The tour was successful in terms of crowds and reviews with one feature headed 'Mott the Magnificent' saying 'the new band with their welcome influx of youth, look set not just to match but top their illustrious past'. The live set included most of the new album and a cover version of The Easybeats' 'Good Times' as well as 'Rock and Roll Queen', 'Sweet Jane', 'Violence' and encores of 'All the Way from Memphis' and 'All the Young Dudes'. A four-track video was also filmed to promote the group, containing 'By Tonight', 'Stiff Upper Lip', 'Apologies' and 'Monte Carlo', plus a comedy section showing the group arriving at Kensington's Royal Garden Hotel in a Rolls Royce.

CBS insisted on issuing two more singles from *Drive On,* 'By Tonight', backed with 'I Can Show You How It Is' and 'It Takes One to Know One', coupled with 'I'll Tell You Something'. Mott were opposed to the release of three singles from the album but CBS got their own way, although, with no real promotion, both records failed to make any impression whatsoever on the charts.

After the initial live dates with Nigel Benjamin, Morgan Fisher recalls that real reservations started to creep in quite quickly amongst the other band members about his suitability for the job. 'Once we'd got past the first impact of his voice and toured with him, I think we all realized he wasn't really the kind of guy we needed. There was just too much mucking about. We called Nigel "The Dome", as he had a rather large shiny forehead. I nearly came to blows with him in the end, and I'm not at all a violent person.'

By October 1975, Mott embarked on a 40-date tour of the United States, supporting Kiss and Aerosmith and playing with Sparks, Slade, Peter Frampton and Montrose. Mott received good receptions and reviews, one journalist's commentary of a show in New York with Sparks referring to 'one of the finest sets I have ever heard from any of the Mott incarnations'. The band toured until the end of December making appearances at Largo Auditorium and The Los Angeles Forum. They split the concerts between headlining and supporting, playing 25,000-capacity stadiums and smaller 1,000-seater halls, performing in Texas, where they hadn't appeared for five years, and reaching new markets they had never struck before. The tour was the longest in Mott's history and sales of *Drive On* exceeded 120,000 copies in America.

'A lot of Mott The Hoople fans came out to see us and they loved it,' recalls Major. 'But we would hit a lot of hip towns and people would be saying, "Hey where the fuck's Ian and Mick?" and we'd tell them, "This is it, they've left, it's Mott now." And Americans would pronounce it "Moch" on its own. They could say Mott The Hoople, but Mott seemed to be a problem, they couldn't understand it.

'Working with Aerosmith was a great experience, and we had some fun too. We had this large American guy in H&H Management who looked after us. He used to get on and off the stage and sometimes got in the way a little. On the US tour, we didn't have a road crew with us as such, and one day, one of the guys working for Aerosmith suddenly said, "Is this guy with you?" and I looked and said, "Oh, he's part of the management." So he says, "Is he a musician?" "No". "Hey fat boy, get off the fuckin' stage!" He flipped of course, because nobody had spoken to him like this before. But Aerosmith's guy persisted, "I'm talkin' to you. Get off the fuckin' stage, you're standin' all over the wires man."

'So I said, "Look, this guy is part of our management." But he still persisted, "He ain't a musician, and, listen, your gear's shit anyway. Let me fix it, all right." So I explained I couldn't pay him. "It's okay, just get me a bottle of 'Jack' at the end of the week and drink down to the label with me." So I agreed; my gear was sparkling and the shows were brilliant. In the end, we played a prank on the H&H guy when we got him absolutely pissed one night, ordered room service, put him in the hotel corridor and left him nude on the floor, with his belly completely garnished with salad and mayonnaise. We flew off the following morning and next time we saw him, his style had changed a little – "Hi guys, how ya doin!" – as if nothing had happened.'

Ray got to know his new Mott colleagues fairly quickly and liked them as personalities. 'Pete wasn't that serious about the business. He told me once he'd only ever been in music and played guitar for birds and money. I recall the first time we went to America. I'd never been there and we landed in New York and I was out of sorts with a terrible head cold and the time change. All Pete could think about was hitting the town. He would say, "You've got to come raging, because if you sleep now, you'll be messed up tomorrow." So we'd go to The Bottom Line Club and would end up drunk, with Pete always searching out his "children of the night".

'Dale on the other hand was serious, he wanted to get it right, and sometimes it wasn't right and we fell out a few times, but not to blows. Morgan was wild and would drink cognac and champagne. He was a typical English gentleman and a very talented man, but always seemed to be on the brink between sanity and madness to me.

'I saw Ian Hunter again and met Mick Ronson for the first time in New York on the *Drive On* tour. They were gentlemen. I went to pick up this message at the hotel desk and Ronson was there and said, "Hello, how are you doing?" I'd never met him before. "Are you playing with Mott and is this your first time in the States?" "Yeah". Ronson said, "You'll love it. It's great. They're all right, they're good guys." And yet there was all that crap about Mick, and Pete and Buff, calling his album, *Worry, Don't Play*. I told them I wasn't into that and they should have got it all out in the open and sorted things out with Ronson. I really think though, that when Ian and Mick left Mott The Hoople, the others felt cheated.'

Mott's 'on-the-road' antics continued across America, and most days were full of incident according to Major. 'One night down South, we'd played our set and Aerosmith were on stage, so we took cars back to the hotel. In the bar they told Morgan to "check" his hat, so he took it off and remarked it was fine, but the barman started to get abusive because he wouldn't remove it. Morgan looked great in this white suit and people were coming up asking him to sign things. After a few drinks he was singing John Lennon songs. Because he'd mixed medication with alcohol. The barman told him to shut up and pulled out a gun. So Fisher says, "Look, I'm English, how dare you point that thing at me." Chris Whitehouse, Stan's personal assistant, hurriedly got Morgan upstairs and I helped put him to bed and got him to cool down. As we left his room and closed the door behind us, I heard a click and felt a gun barrel in my face. The police had been called and we were then accused of creating a fracas, breaking crockery in the bar and abusing the manager's wife, which was not true. So we explained about Fisher and one cop hammered on the bedroom door. Morgan eventually opened it, with a tooth brush in his mouth and a towel wrapped around him. He was staggering about shouting, "Put that weapon away, I'm English, do you want to frisk me, are you looking for this?" and ripped the towel off before collapsing. We managed to calm things down, and retired to our bedrooms under threat that we would all see jail when the local judge was woken to charge us, ensuring that we missed at least the next gig. The following morning a police escort led us to the airport.'

Chris Whitehouse had been brought in to assist Stan Tippins on the road and is described by Watts as the most loyal person associated with the group. 'Chris, or Puss as we called him, was with Bad Company. Ralpher recommended him to us. I liked Puss, he was great. He would die for you. When we used to arrive in the limo at a gig, Chris would go in first to make sure everything was safe. In Atlanta once, he went in ahead, and I was thinking he seemed to be a long time. When he came back out, he told us it was okay to go in, but we didn't notice his hat was missing. A few days later, Stan explained that when he'd gone in, three blokes were waiting to attack us and Puss had laid them all out on the floor. That's why he was so long, but he hadn't mentioned it to us, because he didn't want to worry us. He was very loyal. It was sad, because when things got tighter financially, after the second album, we had to dispense with him.'

Richie Anderson had worked with Hunter Ronson on their British and American tours before linking up with Mott, but he felt things weren't the same as the original Mott The Hoople. 'It was very different. The spark wasn't there. Whatever Mott The Hoople had was gone. Whether that was because Ian wasn't there, I don't know, it probably was if the truth be known. It also changed after Allen and Ralphs left Mott to a lesser degree, but there again it was probably an impossible situation with Mick and Ian in the same band, pulling in different directions.'

A second American tour was quickly planned for May and June 1976 and by February, Mott, having previously worked on demos at Tony Pike's studio in West London, were in Manor Studios, Oxfordshire to commence work on their second LP, tentatively called *Shouting and Pointing*. The working title came from an interview with Oliver Reed in which he said he disciplined his sons with 'a lot of shouting and pointing'. The other possible album title, courtesy of Watts, was *The Side of a Wedding in Germany!*

'Tony was a lewd character,' says Dale. 'We'd work on songs and once they were down on tape and before we could think of a working title, he would devise something apalling to put on the reel.'

The first album had been carefully planned and worked out in advance of the recording sessions, but having played extensive live dates, Mott decided to make the new record tougher and more experimental, entering the studio with a less-defined idea of what they would commit to tape. There were to be fewer tracks on the LP, one ballad and two cover versions, including 'Good Times'. While Mott worked on their second album, CBS issued *Mott The Hoople's Greatest Hits* on 27 March, featuring their seven hit singles plus three album tracks.

Mott's proposed spring tour of America was postponed when *Shouting and Pointing* took slightly longer than planned to complete. The LP was eventually released by CBS on 4 June followed by a few British promotional concerts. Recording had begun at the Manor Studio, Shipton-on-Cherwell, Oxfordshire on 16 February 1976 with Eddie Kramer, veteran Jimi Hendrix, Led Zeppelin, Kiss and Bad Company producer, and tape operator Mick Glossop.

'Kramer was a bit of a coup for us,' admits Morgan. 'He was a bit of a star, but I suppose he delivered the goods. I guess he felt we weren't really up to his level which, when you've worked with Hendrix, I can kind of understand. Mick Glossop was really great to have in the studio, always laughing and always on the ball.'

'Eddie was out of this world to work with,' enthuses Ray Major. 'Being a guitar player, he had me in the studio for hours on end, sometimes until five in the morning. He would open up tracks and just let me play, which meant he had loads of stuff to process. He would also flash all these incredible sounds across us, left to right, spinning your head around, a bit like Hendrix's *Electric Ladyland*. I had a great time with Eddie Kramer.'

Dale recalls the troubled start to the album sessions and the problems encountered mixing the multi-track tapes in America. 'Things went swimmingly well at the Manor, until Morgan fell and dislocated his shoulder during some horse play with Nigel, which slowed matters down a little, but in just over three weeks, the basic tracks were ready. Pete and I then flew to New York to mix the album with Eddie Kramer at Electric Lady Studios. Eddie was desperate to mix in New York, so Wattsy and I went over but were unhappy with the quality of the sound. Fred Heller arranged a showdown with Kramer, Pete and me at the studio, telling us, "When I slap my knee, we walk out on him and close down the mixing." And we did! We were forced to return to England and search for a studio and an engineer to complete the album. Luckily, former Mott the Hoople engineer, Bill Price, came to the rescue. He had left AIR (London) and was then studio manager and engineer at Wessex Studios in Highbury. Work began on 23 March and the final touches were completed some three weeks later. The whole thing was re-recorded, except for the drums on many of the tracks.'

The record featured a 'Shouting' and 'Pointing' side instead of the traditional sides One and Two. 'Shouting and Pointing', co-written by Watts and Fisher, opened the album, a hard rock track with an immensely powerful introduction. The song had originated as 'Phantom of the Opera', but failed to make *Drive On* in its original form, only the intro surviving. The 'Shouting' involved all of Mott, all of their road crew, all of the staff at the Manor and several itinerant cats and dogs.

'Collision Course', written by Watts, started life in Gooseberry Studios in February 1975, lay dormant during *Drive On,* but returned at the Manor, due to a lack of material, complete with new chorus and up-dated lyrics. Watt's parrot, Toby, was allowed to make his recording debut on this one track! 'Storm', originally titled 'Ill Wind', was possibly the heaviest track Mott had ever recorded. 'Ray instigated this monster, Overend aided and abetted him and Morgan compounded the deed!' said Dale. 'This also featured Morgan as the Union Pacific Railroad!'

The only ballad on the album was 'Career (No Such Thing as Rock and Roll)', written by Nigel and Morgan, whose piano playing excelled on this track. 'Career' also featured some tremendous echo effects, courtesy of Bill Price, who cascaded the guitar parts across a second 24-track machine during mixing.

The 'Pointing' side of the LP opened with 'Hold On You're Crazy'. 'This was the first song Watts wrote in 1976,' explained Dale. 'Ray provided an amazing guitar solo, Overend took lead vocal and Morgan played lead crashing wave and a bowel-moving synth bassline on the outro!' 'To See You Again' was another new Watts song, written entirely at the Manor and originally titled 'Early Light'. Pete played guitar on this track, best described as an acoustic stomper, and it would have been a good single to promote the album. Mick Ralphs guested on bass, credited as Bert Fringe, of Bert Fringe and the Benefits!

'Too Short Arms (I Don't Care)', an infectious boogie, featuring Morgan playing stupendous piano and a schoolbell, was written by Major and Fisher, with the aid of a bottle of Rémy Martin! 'A lot of these songs came off the road,' says Ray. 'Morgan came up with some great inversions for certain things, and that's where he was great. He was classically trained so he could do that.'

The penultimate song, 'Broadside Outcasts', by Overend and Morgan, featured Ray Major's 'Russian' influenced guitar in the haunting intro, leading to a mildly manic Benjamin vocal, a 'strapping' chorus by Stan and Overend and a brief vocal appearance by Labour Prime Minister of the day, Jim Callaghan. The old Easybeats song, Vanda/Young's 'Good Times', a track that had become Mott's closing stage number and a live favourite, concluded the album by popular request.

Three songs from the sessions were shelved, a crazed Vodkabilly cover of 'Barking up the Wrong Tree', performed live in the studio, with a gloriously silly cod-American-intro and lead vocal by Morgan Fisher, a ballad entitled 'Brighter Days' and 'It Don't Come Easy', written by and featuring Mick Ralphs under the working title 'Ralpho's Folly'. 'Mick turned up one night and asked if we'd bash out a demo of a song he'd written.' says Dale. 'He did a pleasant little solo too.' Mott had considered taping a re-working of The Doors' 'Love Me Two Times', which they sometimes played live, including a mid-section incorporating the drum and bass parts from The Sorrows' 'Take a Heart'.

It was decided and intended that the *Shouting and Pointing* album cover should represent a rock and roll battlefield, a project which involved two weeks of organisation, two weeks of studio construction and eight hours of photography. The setting was strewn with over 1,500 albums and singles as well as musical instruments, amps and bric-a-brac. 'We were allowed to work with photographer Gered Mankowitz for the sleeve,' says Ray. 'Usually it was Roslov Szaybo from CBS. We got instruments and cans of film and tape and Fisher was like a regimental sergeant major, growling and shouting. It was a good image.'

Sadly, this very fine album failed to chart in the UK, which was unsurprising as, in spite of the group's wishes, CBS would not countenance any single release to raise the LP's profile. 'By the time of the second Mott LP, CBS had effectively lost interest and wouldn't release any more singles to promote us, and who could blame them after three stiffs,' says Dale.

A six-date tour of England was soon organised but three concerts were cancelled when Ray Major developed a cyst on his hand which prevented him from playing. The group rehearsed in time to play gigs at Cromer, Aylesbury (where 700 people were turned away from a packed show) and London Victoria Palace. Mott also played *Shouting and Pointing* live on Manchester's Granada TV show *So It Goes*, and, on 15 June, flew out for a three month tour of the USA, where the LP was scheduled for July release.

In September, Mott recorded Watts' 'Get Rich Quick' at Pye Studios in Cumberland Place, London but it was to be their last session with Benjamin and their final recording for CBS Records. 'On 8 September 1976 we recorded "Get Rich Quick" and Nicky Graham, A&R Executive of Columbia, enthusiatically said, "It's Top Ten!"' says Dale. 'On 9 September we were dropped!'

During October and November Mott played a 26-date UK tour with Lone Star as support and, on 16 October, taped a BBC Radio One *In Concert* session. They included two new songs in their live set, 'Get Rich Quick' and a cover of Little Richard's 'Don't Wanna Discuss It', but the tour was to be their last, in spite of an excellent reception from public and press.

Long-time fan of Mott The Hoople, Kelvin Blacklock, then played demo material to Watts and Griffin including Garland Jeffery's 'Wild in the Streets'. They were impressed with the song and Kelvin's performance, and hatched a plan to replace Benjamin with Blacklock in Mott. After the first rehearsal with Kelvin, however, they perceived him as unreliable and the 'plot' was shelved. Blacklock later joined The Tuff Darts as vocalist Tony Frenzy and appeared on their 1978 LP *Tuff Darts*, which also featured Ian Hunter on some tracks.

By December 1976, Nigel Benjamin had left Mott. Whilst he had the voice to handle their material, his musical ideas were different from the rest of the group and, consequently, they did not want to record any of his songs. Watts believes Nigel saw himself more in the mould of Peter Gabriel and Griffin recalls Benjamin as being stylised and unable to improvise. 'Pete and I realised only recently that we never jammed with Benjamin. He didn't know any of the regular old standards – too young – it was a generation gap problem!'

'There was a lot of friction and sarcasm, and Nigel ostracised himself,' says Ray. 'As far as I know, he went off to Los Angeles with a German girl that he'd met and had a kid with her. When he left, we were in dire straits and hit all sorts of problems with Mott Music and the taxman. Everybody came in grabbing. I had to sell a Travis Bean guitar that I'd purchased in New York to Ralphs, to get myself out of trouble.'

Nigel Benjamin went on to form English Assassins with former members of Merlin and Royce and keyboard player Ian Gibbons, later of the Kinks. They recorded an unreleased album for Arista, entitled *Hex,* which contained a Mott The Hoople 'tribute', 'The Last of the Dudes'. Nigel then formed London and was rumoured to have produced Little Roosters. He moved to Los Angeles around 1980 and joined glam rock group Satyr but pursued a solo career leaving Kevin Dubrow of Quiet Riot to take over as lead vocalist. A reported 1983 solo LP, recorded in California, never materialised and Nigel is believed to have left the music industry in 1984 to work in property construction and renovation in LA.

With hindsight, Morgan Fisher viewed the demise of Mott as an inevitability. 'I'm afraid I never felt that a Mott without Hunter had much chance. It didn't really work out. None of us were great songwriters and the main problem was we were getting singers in and trying to force them into an Ian-Hunter-shaped hole, which was not a wise thing to do. So, obviously, Nigel Benjamin never felt very comfortable in the role and we never really gave him a chance to do what he wanted anyway. Well, we gave him some chances, and then flattened him when he came up with something, because we really couldn't get into what he was doing. So there was a division in the band which never really closed. It was doomed.'

'Part of the problem with Mott not taking off was that the name was more charismatic than the band,' says Ray Major, 'apart from when Ian was in the group.'

19
Can you hear us?

'Overnight Angels' – Ian Hunter

In late 1976, there were two sensational press announcements concerning Ian Hunter; he would be joining Uriah Heep or a reformed Mott the Hoople!

Uriah Heep, having sacked front man David Byron, offered Hunter $5,000 a week to join them as lead singer on a ten week American tour. 'I was totally skint, sitting in the US after *All American Alien Boy*, one of the best albums I ever made, had died a horrible death and effectively killed me off. Then I got this call from keyboard player Ken Hensley, but I really didn't like what Uriah Heep did, nor did I see the point in it, and I don't think he did after a while. I think they were just looking for a face or somebody people had heard of. The interesting thing about the offer was that the money came first. The money was great, but I can't do what I don't believe in. Ronson was the same. If you can't do it, you should-n't do it.'

News also began to circulate in the music world that Ian would be re-joining Mott, after Nigel Benjamin's departure. Hunter immediately halted these rumours by forming his own band to record a third solo album.

Ian had already been watching groups in New York clubs and, during his search for new musicians, noticed Tuff Darts, who had an interesting guitarist in their ranks named Jeffrey Salen. Mick Ronson had worked with Sparks on some 1976 demos for their album *Big Beat,* but eventually, they used Salen on the sessions for the final record. The majority of the *Big Beat* album was demoed with Mick in Los Angeles, but only three of the original songs were re-recorded for the LP – 'I Want to be Like Everybody Else', 'Big Boy' and 'Everybody's Stupid'. The drummer for the Sparks album, Hilly Boy Michaels, had introduced Ronson to Ron and Russell Mael. Mick's offer to produce the Sparks record was declined and they worked with Rupert Holmes instead, although Ron Mael later admitted that the Ronson demos were better than the finished recordings.

Ian went to see Tuff Darts at Max's in New York City, met Jeffrey Salen, played with him and liked him. Around the same time, Mick Jones, former guitarist with Spooky Tooth, was keen to team up with Hunter on a project, but he was auditioning members for his new band Foreigner. Ian attended a number of the Foreigner auditions to see if any of the candidates might suit his own group. 'Mick Jones had been on at me over the years to get together, but you know how people are busy. Foreigner saw hundreds of people and none of them was any good. All of a sudden, I realised English players needed gigs, so I went to England. I tried to put the whole band together using English musicians but it didn't work out that way. I couldn't get the drummer I wanted and the guitar playing situation was weird. English guitarists are very few and far between.'

Back in America, Hunter finally decided on two members for his group, choosing Peter Oxendale, former keyboard player with The Glitter Band and Jet, and bassist Rob Rawlinson, who was recommended by Miller Anderson following sessions for Stan Webb's 1975 LP, *Broken Glass.*

The lead guitar role was more difficult to satisfy. Still searching for players, Hunter came across New Yorker Billy Schwarz, and then, courtesy of Mick Ronson, met American guitarist, Earl Slick, who was originally in a group named Tracks with Roy Bittan, later of Bruce Springsteen Band fame. Slick subsequently played with David Bowie before forming The Earl Slick Band, who cut two poor selling albums and amassed substantial debts in Los Angeles prior to breaking up. 'Slick rang me up right out of the middle of nowhere, just as I was really worried because I didn't think that Billy Schwarz was right,' explained Ian. 'Schwarz liked to play different every time he played and I like a more patterned approach. I was half-interested in Slick, so I tried him out on "Golden Opportunity" and "Shallow Crystals". Earl is good and he played beautifully, but he couldn't take something and develop it. I'd heard him on *Station to Station*. He wasn't Bender by any means, but he was another one who'd say, "What do you want?" '

By late 1976, Dennis Elliott was able to complete the line up for Hunter's album when he had a gap in his commitments with Foreigner. In January, Ian and the band moved up to Morin Heights in Quebec, fifty miles west of Montreal, to commence recording at Le Studio. Ian selected Roy Thomas Baker, former Decca Studios engineer who had worked with The Rolling Stones as producer and who was famous for his work with Lone Star, Queen and The Cars. This choice was to have a significant effect on the overall sound of the final LP.

'Roy's been a good friend for a long time,' said Ian. 'After "Alien Boy" I was really knackered. I was in LA and we got drunk together and he said, "Why don't you let me do your next one?" The last one was so slow that the other half of me, the half that does the fast stuff, must have been stockpiling material, because I started writing rock songs as soon as I finished that record. Plus, it hadn't done as well as the first solo album, so I wanted to be in a group again.'

The Canadian sessions began well but almost came to a dramatic and fatal halt on the night of 3 February 1977, when the rented house that Ian and the band were staying in caught fire and exploded. It was a very narrow escape for the occupants, as the entire building and its contents were completely destroyed. 'About seven in the morning, Earl Slick woke up to find his room on fire,' recalled Hunter. 'Roy Thomas Baker jumped from his third storey window and we all just managed to get out before the house was literally wiped off the face of the earth. We were left outside, four of us naked, because there had been no time to dress, with the temperature four degrees below zero.'

Hunter's entourage faced a pile of rubble, and were left with no instruments or personal effects. Engineer Gary Lyons, his girlfriend, bass player Rob Rawlinson and his wife were admitted to hospital, and Lyons was detained under observation. Ian's producer and engineer were still suffering from the effects of the incident some weeks later during mixing of the finished tapes, Lyons working with an oxygen mask at his side and Baker with a damaged hand.

By March, Hunter was back in London at Utopia and Olympic Studios recording vocals and mixing the new album, to be called *Overnight Angels*, a reference to the near-fatal incident surrounding its birth. It was also announced that the band would play a ten-date UK tour in June, as part of a wider European concert schedule including Sweden. These were Ian's first British appearances since the Hunter Ronson concerts two years before.

The new LP, *Ian Hunter's Overnight Angels,* was issued by CBS on 20 May 1977 in the UK and Europe, and was preceded by a single, 'Justice of the Peace', backed with 'The Ballad of Little Star'. All the album tracks, apart from one, were written by Ian. The gatefold cover featured a painting of Hunter by rock artist David Oxtoby, who famously captured Elton John, Rod Stewart and Joe Cocker in similar style. The record failed to chart and was not released in the USA. It received a mixed response from the British press, although *Sounds* praised the LP highly with the headline 'Overnight Sensation' and a four-star review.

'Golden Opportunity' opened the album in barnstorming fashion, commencing with a lengthy instrumental section which took several interesting twists and turns, before settling into the main tempo and pattern of the song. The lyrics seemed potent too, but like much of the *Overnight Angels* mix, they lacked clarity, a factor which seemed to annoy several critics, who commented accordingly. One thing was clear however, the new band that Ian had formed was musically capable and powerful.

'Shallow Crystals', originally titled 'I Think You Made a Mess of His Life', was a leisured and acidic piece featuring beautiful lead guitar work from Slick. Whilst Ian acknowledges Earl's playing contributions, he admits that he helped Slick construct the solo. 'Earl didn't understand my music that much,' says Hunter in hindsight. 'Slick is capable, but you have to sit with him. He was a bit like Luther, he sometimes had difficulty in the creativity department. On "Shallow Crystals", we worked out a lot of the solo together, at my house in Chappaqua. We were in my basement for hours sorting out his guitar. That happened with Ronson on occasion too. I can hear a solo but I can't play one.' The character receiving Hunter's criticism in the song was not clear. He suggests several years later that the subject matter may have been Guy Stevens, but perhaps David Bowie or Verden Allen was in here too, in a multi-character lyric like 'Boy'. 'I wasn't really focused for this album and I think "Shallow Crystals" may simply have been a selection of words that were attracted to each other,' says Ian. 'However, I have a better feeling about this track than just about any other on the record.'

> My friend don't speak, he's such a mixed up boy
> I wonder if she sold him his toys
> A kiss on the cheek, a conversation be coy
> In his cute little corderoys
> Oh she taught him how to win the game
> She taught him everything is your name
> Oh mother did you have to destroy

'Overnight Angels' was another powerful instrumental track, but the lyrics were almost inaudible in the mix; the song subsequently featured in the movie soundtrack, *Asphaltnacht*. Side One closed with a moody ballad, 'Broadway', a dramatic tale of show business traumas, showcasing fine piano, solo voice and an orchestral and vocal coda featuring Miller Anderson. 'I happen to think a lot of "Broadway",' says Hunter. 'I think it told me I was still capable of writing a good song. It's probably the best slow thing I'd ever done musically. The music was great, the verse was great but the hook was awful.'

'Justice of the Peace' opened Side Two in rousing style and was classic single material, described by Ian as 'nifty'. The song told the humorous story of a youngblood cowering in fear at the prospect of an imminent shotgun marriage. Starting with a section of 'The Wedding March' before Hunter's musical army charged in, the powerful pace and irresistible hook of the song were enhanced with impressive multi-faceted production.

> It's such a terrible shame, it was only a game
> Then her brothers found out, seven Johnny B Goode's
> We was only pretending at Mummies and Daddies
> They totally misunderstood
>
> Oh what a terrible waste, such a shocking disgrace
> To give me away, I'm too young to die
> A shotgun wedding heading straight for the sky
> And I'm shy, Mary Ellen, I'm shy

Sounds selected this as their 'Single of the Week' saying, ' "Justice of the Peace" is a natural-born radio hit, layered like expensive pastry to give more bits of half buried weirdness every time you hear it, so full of hooks that your hands bleed when you pick it up, pounding along with deranged zest in such a way that it's always potentially out of control. Such is Hunter's cunning that it never actually does though. Pure pop for now people – hear it!' Sadly, the writer had forgotten the arrival of punk rock, which rendered Hunter passe in some quarters, and criminally, the single failed to chart.

The Hunter/Slick composition '(Miss) Silver Dime', about Alice, 'a drunken Mona Lisa', was the only co-written song on the album, and at one time would have been potential single material, having an attractive theme and grand chorus. 'Wild 'n' Free', meanwhile, had the pace of a locomotive train and marked a 1977-style return to the atmosphere of *Brain Capers*. It demonstrated to the emerging New Wave of the time that their debt to Hunter and Mott was un-questionable, that they certainly had no monopoly on speed and that they had much to learn if they ever hoped to match Ian's lyrical prowess.

The pace and energy of 'Wild 'n' Free' snapped abruptly into absolute tran-quility – 'The Ballad of Little Star' – a peaceful song with sparse but effective key-boards. The lyric concerned a city hooker of Red Indian origin and was a reminder of the pain inflicted on her race. The subject matter had been covered by other artists before, but Hunter's quality shone through, lyrically and musically.

Lost, on a merry-go-round, on the game, you can never be found
'Cos you don't know who you are
The reservation killed your nation
And in some tourist's car, you feel the pain, little star

You know, you know – we grow and grow
We never slow – we always win
And you feel lost – and you feel crossed
And you feel tossed – just like the wind
Your father, will have told you, of the wind

Bowed, those proud heads that once prowled, round the plains
They sought nothing to gain
'Til our fathers civilised, and broken hearted arrows roamed the skies
Then you were born, to feel the pain, little star

'To Love a Woman' closed the album in an uncharacteristic style for Hunter, the song being a simple, pop/soul-flavoured love song. 'I always thought, and still think to this day, that Rod Stewart would do a really nice job of this song,' says Ian. 'We never got around to sending it to him, but I think it would suit him.'

One very interesting aspect of the record was the way that Hunter and Roy Thomas Baker had merged and segued most of the tracks to create an effective musical flow. However, on reflection, Ian is not happy with the production. 'This wasn't Roy's fault. He will tell you he wants commercial success for you, and he's absolutely correct. I just think too heavy, that's been my problem all the way down the line. My idea of sound is a heavy sort of sound. Roy likes it much lighter than that, which works for The Cars but doesn't work for me. I think Charles Shaar Murray had it at the time; he said it sounded like Mantovani trying to produce Johnny Rotten. I did the songs in the wrong key. I sang them too high, so it doesn't sound like me. I think this is the worst album I've ever done, and it's the only LP in my whole career which I really regret.

'Up until the final mixes, I'd never heard anything like it. The rough mixes were incredible. It really sounded amazing, but Roy had a way at that time of really squeezing the mixes for radio, which is what most good producers do. I was in total disagreement with this, because the thing sounded so panoramic, so huge, I didn't want it squeezing. I had glandular fever at that time and didn't fight. Right up until the final mixes it sounded incredible, and Roy gets upset with me when I talk about this, because Roy and I have been very good friends over the years, but I can't help the way I feel. It was just a matter of musical differences. I really felt if he had left the rough mixes on the record, and the album had come out, it would have done great. I'd never heard anything like it at that time.'

Aside from the production 'debate', the record was noteable for the fact that, for once, Hunter didn't seem to be living his lyrics and had swung more to fictional writing. 'I don't think I wrote that way,' Ian says, 'it just sort of occurred. It's like movies. You go in with the best of intentions and you come out with something else. But I was not happy with the songs I wrote on *Overnight Angels*. I'd done *All American Alien Boy*, which was very good lyrically, but it hadn't done well because it wasn't a rock album and it didn't have singles. So I thought I'd just walk in and happily do a rock album for them, but it didn't turn out like that. Rock and roll's harder to do for me than that. I'm not a mad fan of *Overnight Angels* but Roy was hilarious to work with as was Gary Lyons.'

To promote the new album, Hunter toured Britain in June playing eight dates, including Newcastle, Manchester, Birmingham and London. The Hammersmith Odeon show had replaced an original booking at the New Victoria Theatre with American singer-songwriter Elliott Murphy as opening act. However 'New Wave' was on the rise and The Vibrators were subsequently chosen as Hunter's support, without realising that punk rock had already been banned by the New Victoria's management.

In practice, many of the young pretenders, including The Clash and Generation X were largely influenced by Ian's earlier writing with Mott The Hoople, even down to appropriations of Mick Ralph's guitar playing. The New Wave was nothing new. Mott had voiced a stronger message of disillusionment and failure with *Brain Capers* in 1971, in direct contrast to the limp fantasy and self aggrandisement of many other rock bands that surrounded them at that time. 'Violence' and 'Crash Street Kidds' had already forecast, with uncanny accuracy, the emergence of the new generation of disaffected angry kids who were now trying to fight a similar climate of vanity and unreality. The difference was that Ian was literate and a genuine straight shooter, his popularity with some of the punk movement stemming largely from his Mott output, stage presence and attitude.

Ironically Hunter's new position as an early patron saint of punk was a noteable feat, as the new movement was based on public rejection of his generation of 'old wave' musicians. There was no question that punk was predominantly a clever PR move, designed at eliminating established artists and creating a record buying frenzy, just as the industry has done in the nineties with Britpop, which is already waning. Hunter reflects astutely on the new musical movement of the seventies.

'I think the term "New Wave" was a very clever invention. Whoever thought of that was a genius. It was designed to wipe us out of the way. By calling the new bands "New Wave", that meant that people like me were "Old Wave", and that doesn't sound too nice or too fashionable. I'm glad I wasn't living in England anymore, because it cut off a lot of people by virtue of this huge ageist stigma. Ageism is just as bad as racism. It was a very clever term but it never quite worked because, what they were trying to do was conveniently cut off half and sway public opinion towards the new, which would have worked perfectly had the new been good enough, but it wasn't quite good enough.'

Ian felt that the trend failed to remove established acts like The Rolling Stones and the Who in a decade that belonged to rock 'n' roll, and that punk wasn't particularly original or exciting anyway. 'I can remember Elvis Presley happening and Jerry Lee Lewis and Chuck Berry and I know what a changeover is. That's a changeover. That took over the world. I mean, don't come along and tell me that

these bands are going to take me away, because it's just not the same. They should
have found something else. I think they're very unimaginative.'

Hunter is still saddened today by the hypocrisy of the New Wave, and recalls
Jeff Dexter taking him to London's punk club, The Roxy, around that time. 'It
was pretty hypocritical,' says Ian. 'They were all supposed to be wasted little kids
from the streets but a lot of them weren't. I know one guy whose dad owned half
of Brighton and he was in a very famous punk band. He said to me, "Don't say
nuffin' like." So a lot of it was just bullshit. It was kids who knew C, F and G
and had that enthusiasm I'd had with The Apex, jumping around like maniacs.
I remember looking at The Damned with Jeff at The Roxy and I asked him, "Was
that what we were like?" meaning Mott, and he said, "Yeah, but you were great." '

Hunter used the *Overnight Angels* album line-up in concert apart from Dennis
Elliott who had to return to drumming duties with Foreigner. His place was
taken by Texan Curly Smith who had played previously with John Sebastian and
Jo Jo Gunne. The live set for the concerts featured several tracks from the new
LP plus old Hoople and Hunter favourites including 'Golden Opportunity',
'One of the Boys', 'Overnight Angels', 'All the Way from Memphis', '(Miss)
Silver Dime', 'Justice of the Peace', 'Once Bitten Twice Shy', 'Wild 'n' Free',
'Violence', 'Roll Away the Stone', and 'All the Young Dudes'. During the encores
Ian previewed a new song, 'England Rocks', and played Jerry Lee Lewis's 'Whole
Lotta Shakin'' plus 'Letter to Britannia from the Union Jack'. Hunter didn't re-
gard the dates as a great success. 'We did that tour of England and I hated the
whole mess I was in. I knew I was writing shit, singing shit and playing shit.'

'England Rocks,' featuring Jimmy Bain, ex-Rainbow bassman, on backing
vocals, was issued in Europe as a second Overnight Angels single with 'Wild 'n'
Free' as the B-side. The single got good reviews but failed to chart. Originally
written as 'Cleveland Rocks', it was to be re-recorded in its original form for his
next LP. Jimmy Bain had been offered the role of bass player in the Overnight
Angels, but his replacement in Rainbow lasted only a few weeks, and he rejoined,
leaving Rob Rawlinson to link up with Hunter. Ian says of the single, 'I hadn't
written like that since 'Roll Away the Stone' and 'All the Way from Memphis'. It
was basic, but it had that quasi-classical European chord sequence with the hal-
lelujah chorus at the back end. I was quite happy to have got that one.' 'England
Rocks' was subsequently recorded in 1988 by Little Angels.

In addition to the UK tour, Ian played live dates in Norway and Sweden but
wanted to terminate his management deal. Having parted company with Fred
Heller, he was then left in Europe with a group and no finance. To add to his
problems, Columbia had decided that they would not issue *Overnight Angels* in
America, although some US test pressings of the LP were made. Ian left
Columbia Records, when they didn't release his album. 'I split with Heller after
a gig in Leicester, and was stuck with a band and no money,' said Hunter. 'I had
no means of shifting $40,000 worth of gear back to the States, plus I had no way
of paying the band's wages.'

At this point, Don Arden almost came to Hunter's rescue. Arden had set up
the Jet Record label in the UK and his major signing was The Electric Light
Orchestra. Ian had created a storm over the prospect of his band supporting ELO

at Earl's Court in London and in Europe. 'We'll be supporting ELO at Earl's Court,' he said. 'I don't mind doing it. I could headline in London, but we'll support them, because they're completely boring and we'll kill them.'

Hunter and his band headlined at the Hammersmith Odeon instead, but at that particular show he met Arden. 'I was concerned,' says Ian. 'I explained to Don why I'd done the ELO thing and he said, "Ian, it's business," and we spoke about me joining his label. I nearly went with Jet Records. They were trying to buy the album off Columbia, but they couldn't get it so in the end they didn't want me. Columbia weren't interested, so it was easy to get out of that, and it was easy to get out of the management situation. It was Mott The Hoople's label and it was Mott The Hoople's management. Technically, I could have done another album, but I knew how it was going to turn out. So I was without a manager and without a record company, which was interesting and frightening. I knew I was in the shit, but now at least I was clear. I also knew I wasn't 21 anymore and would anybody want to pick me up?'

After the demise of The Overnight Angels, Hunter returned to New York and, at first, teamed up with Jeffrey Salen again, accepting his invitation to play keyboards on their LP, *Tuff Darts*.

Thereafter, Ian joined Corky Laing of Mountain and producer Bob Ezrin to help Corky with demos for his second solo LP. Ian also wanted to record a new album and the demos were so good that Laing's label, Elektra Asylum, asked the duo to work together as Hunter-Laing. They wrote several new songs, including a track called 'Pompeii', and agreed to record, bringing in former Lou Reed and Alice Cooper guitarist Steve Hunter. Rehearsals started well but the plans went awry when they couldn't retain the musicians they wanted to complete their chosen line up. Ex-Free bassist Andy Fraser soon tired of 'commuting' between Los Angeles and New York and keyboard player Lee Michaels left when he and Hunter couldn't agree. 'The guy didn't like me,' says Ian. 'I don't know what it was, but I couldn't get along with him. So, at a given time, it became clear we had to split up. It was a pity, because Andy Fraser was brilliant and a nice guy, although the music was different for me.'

Hunter agreed to try and continue his project with Corky Laing and suggested they speak to Mick Ronson which quickly led to a link with John Cale. 'John Cale was producing Bobby Neuwirth, with a Welsh guy who had a studio in Manhattan, but Neuwirth never turned up. So Cale rang us up and Ronson and me went down with Corky Laing and played and recorded for two nights. It was really good, but all the lyrics are stream of consciousness. Apparently, I'm one of the few people who can do that if I get excited enough. I can reel off words without writing them down. They just come. We had it going for two nights and it was great.'

In 1989, Ronson confirmed that John Cale's lawyer was seeking agreement for a release of the Hunter, Ronson, Cale and Laing LP but, to date, this has not happened. Mick was certainly happy to see it issued, describing it as a 'true rock 'n' roll album'. One of the unreleased tracks was a Cale composition, 'What's Your Name, Jane?'

In January 1978 former Mott The Hoople manager, Robert Hirschman, re-emerged and asked Hunter if he would return to England to work with Mr Big, a group who had enjoyed reasonable success with two albums and a hit single 'Romeo'. Stan Tippins had shown great interest in the band around January 1975. Mr Big's lead vocalist and writer, Dicken, wanted Ian to produce their third LP, *Suppuku,* at Chipping Norton Studios in Oxfordshire. The end result was a hard rock album, which delighted the band and their management, but horrified EMI, who thought they had a pop group on their roster. A single entitled 'Senora', co-written by Hunter, was issued but soon withdrawn and the LP was never released.

Hunter was now writing what he termed 'down' songs – 'Standing in My Light', 'The Outsider' and 'Bastard' – that would eventually appear on his next album. Mick Ronson heard Ian's new material and wanted to contribute, so Hunter Ronson worked with Corky Laing at Bearsville Studios and invited Mountain's bassist Felix Pappalardi to join the sessions. Mick confirmed they were forming a band, but not Mott The Mountain! Eventually recordings were finished at Levon Helms studio with Todd Rundgren producing and David Sanborn, John Sebastian and Paul Butterfield joining the proceedings at different stages. Nine tracks were taped including Hunter/Laing's 'I Ain't No Angel' and 'Easy Money', subsequently covered by Ian Lloyd on his LP *Goosebumps.* Although Leslie West added overdubs for Corky during mixing at Miami's Criteria Studios, the session recordings were shelved and also remain unreleased.

Importantly, Hunter was re-united with Ronson, and he was now focused on his next solo record. 'I really prefer to work with Mick,' admitted Ian.

20
Give me one more chance to run

'One More Chance to Run' – John Fiddler

After Nigel Benjamin's departure from Mott, Steve Hyams was asked if he would like to work with the band. Hyams had shared accommodation with Mott The Hoople at their Chelsea flat in the early seventies and had recorded one track with Watts, Griffin and Fisher at AIR London studios in 1974. Steve had developed as a lead vocalist and songwriter, securing a recording contract with Phonogram. On the face of it his material, visual presence and gutsy voice seemed an ideal replacement for Benjamin in Mott.

Steve Hyams was born on 4 November 1950 in London, the eldest of three children in a middle class family. By the late fifties, his father, who owned a shop in Tottenham Court Road and imported optical equipment from Russia, had made a considerable amount of money. This resulted in a great deal of moving around for the Hyams, before they settled in Brighton. During his teenage years, Steve's parents decided to get divorced and he was sent to boarding school. 'It was a very hard public school and the aim was to knock some sense into me. My father was the old generation, very strict, but of course it had the reverse effect on me.'

Steve found he had a real interest in music when he was about thirteen, and, at seventeen, travelled to India with three friends, having been tempted by psychedelic music. Upon his return to England, Hyams took a job working on the record counter at Chelsea Drug Store. 'It was like a little mall with a boutique, bars, a restaurant and the record shop in the basement, and that's where I met Pete Watts, just after Mott had recorded their first album. He came in one day and I was looking for somewhere to stay close by, so Pete offered me a room in their flat in Lower Sloane Street. Neil Hubbard, the guitarist with Arrival, had lived there and moved out, and I took a room which was only £4 a week. I think their rent was £18, but there were so many people living there, I paid £4. The basement was sectioned off and I had a bed above a structure which housed the heating boiler. There was also a room out the back, which had water sweating continuously out of the walls, and it was the only single room. Everybody else shared accommodation, except Pete, who was always quite canny and had made a den in a tiny front room.'

Hyams became friends with Watts and got to know Mott well. 'They would all get up as late as possible and were real night people. They were naive in many ways. At that time, I was already smoking hash and occasionally took acid. They knew nothing about this at all, and didn't take anything. I put some hash on the table one day in the flat, and they just looked at it. Booster, their roadie, even asked how to inject it!'

Musically, Mott The Hoople were not one of Hyams' favourite bands but he admired their attitude and liked them a lot as individuals. He perceives that ultimately, a 'pressure cooker' rivalry developed between Hunter and Ralphs. 'They were great people. When they played live, there was always this mayhem with "You Really Got Me" at end of their set, which became a total rave up. They found success with "All the Young Dudes", then Ian came up with "Honaloochie Boogie", "Memphis" and "Roll Away the Stone", and I think in some ways, the rivalry broke the camel's back. By this time they were flying high, and for Mick to leave a group that was in the charts and becoming so big was a brave gamble to say the least. Pete told me that he was asked to join Mick in Bad Company, but turned it down because he felt so much loyalty towards Mott The Hoople and Buffin. Then, when Bad Company became successful and Ralphs went straight to number one in the US with "Can't Get Enough", which had been a Mott track in any case, I'm sure Ian developed an even greater ambition.'

Watts encouraged Hyams to play music and, armed with Pete's Fender Precision bass, Steve joined a band called Dolls House in 1971, living and playing in Ireland, then a Sussex-based blues group, The Sam Brodie Blues Band, with Canadian guitarist Bruce Irvine. Hyams wanted to sing and write and couldn't handle lead vocals and bass at the same time, so he sold the Precision and acquired a Telecaster.

Music however, was to have a painful side for Steve Hyams, as he endured the nightmare of cocaine and heroin addiction over a long period of time. He was an addict from 1973 to 1989 whereupon he managed to quit. During several of the periods when he took substitutes to cure his addiction, alcohol also played a major and destructive role in his life. 'It all started with cocaine, which I took at weekends just for fun. Then I needed valium to get to sleep and I was soon introduced to heroin by one of the musicians at Island Records, and took cocaine at the same time. I was hooked and it was a very frightening situation to be in. If I'd put as much effort into music as I put into my addiction, I'd have been very successful. I would have a gig to play, but would have to wait for someone to deliver dope, just to become normal and do the show.'

In 1974, Hyams had received a call from Phonogram saying they liked his material and Tony Hall, who had signed The Rolling Stones, Joe Cocker and Black Sabbath, secured a solo deal for Steve. 'I did an album in the States with several name session players, such as Denny Seiwell, Wings' drummer, and producer Elliott Mazer. After two days, Mazer decided he was going off to work with Crosby, Stills, Nash and Young. In the end, the feel was better on the original demos I'd done in London with my own band. Record companies always say, "You do the singing and writing and we'll get you the band," but it's really a way of signing a group cheaply. If I'd taken Bruce Irvine with me, maybe it would have been better but, when I got out there, I was totally out of my depth with these people and they knew it.'

Hyams' solo album, *Mistaken Identities*, was completed in San Francisco and scheduled for release on Phonogram's Fresh Air label, containing self-composed material including 'Do It Again', 'Walking on a Tombstone', '1, 2, 3 ,4, Kickalong Blues' and 'Pick It Up'. Copies of the LP were pressed but destroyed before release and *Mistaken Identities* was finally issued on CD in 1997.

Around November 1974, at a session in London, Overend Watts agreed to help Steve record a track called 'World Cruise' with Dale Griffin, Morgan Fisher and Bruce Irvine. 'I had a record company behind me and Pete wanted to record at AIR London. We went in and came out with this massive wall of sound, then Tony Hall being the purist that he is said, "I'm really disappointed. I really don't like it." I was disappointed too, because songwriting is a craft and to write good songs isn't easy. Nothing happened with the track at that stage.'

In 1975, Steve returned to the USA, played live dates with a new band and then linked up with Watts again. 'Pete had my solo album, which had some rock things on it, but some funky tracks too. Then, in 1976, after Nigel Benjamin left Mott, Pete said, "Look Steve, we're getting all these tapes from different people and none is better than yours. Do you want to come and have a go with us?" So I went to Pete's house in Ealing and Mott were demoralised by this time. Mick Ralphs had gone, Ian had gone, the deal with CBS was up and the punk thing was happening. Nobody had any money so I asked a contact, Pete Warden, if he could get me some studio time, which he did through Arista Records.'

Following some 'front room' rehearsals at Watts' home, Hyams and Mott recorded five demos at The Argonaut, Richard Branson's floating barge studio on Regents Park Canal near Maida Vale in North London, between January and March 1977. Hyams had recorded versions of 'Dear Louise' and 'Brother Soul' at Argonaut during the previous year. They commenced the sessions with an relatively unknown engineer but then summoned Tom Newman, who had worked on Mike Oldfield's *Tubular Bells*. 'We went in and did these tracks, but I was going yellower and yellower by the day because I had hepatitis,' says Hyams. 'By this time I was on heroin daily.'

Steve attempted to persuade the band to revert to the name Mott The Hoople once again. 'I tried to explain to Pete that really the strongest thing they had got was the group name,' says Hyams. 'I said they really had to use Mott The Hoople, but they ummed and aahed. I think he agreed with me, but in the back of his mind he hoped Ian might come back some day, and he wanted to keep Mott The Hoople for that possibility. They were apprehensive.'

Nonetheless, a concert showcase and photo session were arranged at he Rainbow Theatre for *Sounds* music journalistics. Dale Griffin regards the whole episode as something of an embarrassment however; the quality of the recordings, their production and the live showcase did not meet with his, or the band's, approval. The resurrection of 'Mott The Hoople' lasted for one day.

Steve admits the recordings could have been better and, in hindsight, wishes Watts or Griffin had been given a chance to select another studio. 'In my opinion, Pete and Buff know how to get the best out of a good studio. However, at the time, we felt pretty good about the recordings. I still think they're good songs and the vocals were perhaps geared towards the New Wave. Hirschman and Heller heard the tapes, but nobody was sure what to do at the time, largely because of punk.'

'We went to Arista Records with the finished tapes,' explains Hyams, 'but they said they didn't see a future for the band and they were not really interested in signing us. So we went out into Mount Street and, although we were pissed off, we agreed to take the tapes to some other labels. However, I got home that night about seven, and got a phone call from Arista who said, "We like the songs Steve, and your singing, and you play guitar and write your own stuff, but Mott's had its day, why don't you sign with us?" Basically they offered me a good solo deal and, having a healthy drug habit, I didn't know what to do. I really liked all of Mott. I went to Ralphs' house that weekend with Pete, and then we went over to Alvin Lee's, and Mick and Alvin both said sign with Arista. I had to say to Pete, "I'm sorry, I'm going to sign," and I felt so bad because he was my closest friend. He'd been let down before I think, when Ian left, and he'd turned down Bad Company and stayed loyal to Mott, so I felt awful. It was tough.'

'I liked that band,' says Ray Major. 'It was very, very fresh, because we didn't work it and never went on the road. Steve wrote some good songs and I felt sorry for him over the Arista situation, because he felt terrible about it. But it's the usual story, when you dangle a carrot in front of a musician. "Oh I like your stuff, you're with Mott, great, but I wanna record you without them!" '

Steve recorded solo material for Arista. However, shortly afterwards, the record label recruited new management and dropped twelve acts; Hyams was one of the casualties.

The 1977 Mott tracks with Steve Hyams lay dormant until 1993 when See For Miles Records released a CD entitled *Mott The Hoople featuring Steve Hyams*. The songs were all written by Hyams except Garland Jeffrey's 'Wild in the Streets'. Steve had composed 'Dear Louise', an ode to his sister, 'Brother Soul', a reference to heroin and the drug problems that he was enduring, 'Hotfootin'', written on a mammoth car journey between Mexico and Texas, '1,2,3,4 Kickalong Blues', and the wonderfully punchy 'World Cruise', which was an optimistic reference to Steve's first American venture. Watts contributed the bridge section to 'Hotfootin' ' and was also credited with producing the recordings although he tried feverishly to prevent the release going out under the Mott The Hoople name in 1993.

'The See For Miles CD is not Mott The Hoople,' emphasises Dale. 'It is a rag-bag collection of hurried demos with the group "Mott" providing the musical accompaniment for Hyams vocals. It was never intended for commercial release and should not have been inflicted upon the public.'

'When Mott fell apart, nothing happened for quite some time,' says Morgan Fisher. 'We did try out a few singers and went through a dreadful process of auditioning once again. We even got to the stage of getting in Steve Hyams, who was a friend of Overend's, made some demos together, and approached Frank Zappa to produce us. We went to The Dorchester Hotel to have tea with him, but really, as we were sitting there talking to him, we knew we were wasting our time playing him the tapes. He tactfully pointed that out to us, and I think we also wasted our time talking to Zappa, because it's a bit like talking to a headmaster, it didn't really feel right.'

'I didn't meet Zappa, because I was in hospital with hepatitis,' recalls Hyams. 'Pete went with Morgan and Buff. We'd heard this Grand Funk Railroad album that he'd produced, called *Good Singin' Good Playin'*, and they really liked this. Our tracks from The Argonaut were crying out for good production, but Zappa was apparently too busy and was fed up; he hated England and couldn't wait to get home.'

Zappa listened impassively to the Mott tapes and when they complimented him on his work with Grand Funk, he took no credit and claimed the band just sounded good and he simply recorded them. Dale says, 'Zappa was very matter-of-fact, talked like a human being and didn't give us any typical record producer bullshit jive. I really admired him for that. He laid out what had to be done by the band.'

'Mott Mark II didn't really take off,' admits Watts. 'Steve had a very unusual voice and he had great capabilities, but it was always dragged down by drug problems. He was also quite an indecisive person. He was a nice guy though, the first friend I made when I came to London.'

After his dealings with Mott and his attempted solo career with Arista, Hyams moved to Brighton and tried to change his life becoming a registered drug addict, eventually kicking his habit in 1989 after sixteen torrid years. His personal tragedies included the death of his younger brother and his first wife, who was found overdosed in Africa, nine months after they married. 'She was an heiress and was crazy. I remember Pete told former Doc Thomas Group guitarist Dave Tedstone, "One of them is going to end up dead." And he was right, one of us did end up dead!'

More recently, Hyams has worked with Ray Major again, playing in The Dig Band and writing 'I Fall Over, I Fall Down', for Marianne Faithfull, originally intended for her album *Broken English*.

With Steve Hyams' departure, Mott were undecided over their future. 'We knew we couldn't carry on as Mott as we'd played it out,' says Watts. 'Morgan and I were absolutely penniless, so we thought about forming another group. John Otway nearly joined us and Hunter was there at the time. We didn't think Otway would be right in the end. Ian and I used to keep in touch quite a bit then, and he often used to come over and see me each time he came back to England. I had a grand piano and he would play two or three new songs on it and ask me what I thought.'

Morgan Fisher had known John Fiddler for a couple of years in his former group Medicine Head, a progressive duo who released several acclaimed albums and singles in the early seventies. Comprising John on guitar and percussion, and Peter Hope Evans on harmonica and jew's harp, Medicine Head's music was sparse and understated with a quaint mixture of exotic love songs and skeletal rhythm and blues in Fiddler's writing.

John Fiddler was born in Darlston, Staffordshire on 25 September 1947, and he went through school and Stafford Art College with Peter where they first played music together. Parting after college, they met up again and started performing R&B plus a few of their own numbers, in small clubs around the Midlands, playing variously as The Mission, Doctor Feelgood and the Blue Telephone and Medicine Head, which were effectively the same group. They played a gig at Wolverhampton Lafayette in front of John Peel and reached a wider audience when he asked them to send a demo tape for his Radio One *Top Gear* show. Peel formed The Dandelion Record Co. with Clive Selwood of Elektra, and, in 1969, Medicine Head were one of the first acts to sign for Dandelion.

They released two albums, *New Bottles Old Medicine* and *Heavy on the Drum* plus five singles, including the 1971 hit 'Pictures in the Sky', which reached number 19 in the UK charts. Hope Evans left the band at this point and Fiddler formed a trio with ex-Yardbird Keith Relf and drummer John Davies, switching to Polydor Records to record the LP *Dark Side of the Moon*. Hope Evans rejoined and three more hit singles followed – 'One and One is One', 'Rising Sun' and 'Slip and Slide', plus three albums. Medicine Head finally disbanded in 1976, Peter Hope Evans securing a philosophy degree and becoming a teacher.

Morgan Fisher had guested on Medicine Head's sixth and final LP, *Two Man Band*. 'Fiddler asked me to do Medicine Head's farewell tour. He just fancied having me there on keyboards and we got on very well. It was great fun and suddenly I thought, "Blimey, this was meant to happen." We were looking for a singer and there he was, so I put it to him, and he agreed to join quite quickly. The guys in Mott knew him from way back, so no pushing was required. No one else was auditioned and it went very smoothly. As he was the singer and main songwriter, we all agreed that a new band was in order. John wouldn't be just another Mott member as his music was a big part of the new group.'

'In 1976 Peter Hope Evans decided to leave Medicine Head, again,' says Fiddler. 'The band was always breaking up and we never had any continuity. So I asked Morgan to finish some live dates with me and we had a great time. One night I invited Morgan round to dinner and the phone kept ringing for him, and it was Pete Watts who apparently was saying, "Have you asked him yet? Have you asked him?" So Morgan asked what I thought about going down to their rehearsals, which I did, and it was good. I hadn't been thinking about what I was going to do at all, which was probably a good thing. Suddenly, there was this great rock 'n' roll band around me, with guitars and basses and lots of noise.'

'Morgan asked me one day why hadn't we asked John to join us,' recalls Watts. 'I said he was a bit hippyish and a little overweight. After thinking about it, it occured to me that he had a good voice and he was a good writer, so I said why not ask him. He was delighted when the subject was broached. We had a couple of rehearsals and he came out with "Give Me One More Chance to Run", the first song he wrote with us. I thought "Bloody hell, that's good." We got the old feeling back.

'One day we had a rehearsal booked in the Kings Road and this bloke walked in with a guitar case. I didn't recognise him, but it was John. He'd changed his image overnight, had all his long hair cut off, his moustache and beard had gone and so were his glasses. He looked two stone thinner and was amazing. Mick Ronson's sister, Maggi, came down to the rehearsals. She was nice and said it sounded great. We were quite friendly with her and nothing was ever mentioned about Mick, although she obviously must have known what the situation was and read the articles where he'd had a go at us and we'd had a go back at him. So we did some demos and approached Colin Johnson, Status Quo's manager, and he was very interested.'

Whilst Fiddler was to become the main writer for the band, supported by Watts and Fisher, Major contributed 'Comin' Thru', taped at rehearsals but never recorded in the studio. Armed with demos of all new material, the group was named British Lions and signed to Phonogram Records' Vertigo label in the UK and RSO in America. They returned to The Manor Studios in Oxfordshire, previously used by Mott, to record and mix their first LP. The sessions, from 23 September to 8 October 1977, were produced and arranged by 'The Lions'.

'It was all done in two weeks,' explained Pete. 'We originally went there to do two singles and two B-sides. After four days we'd done all the backing tracks to the album, so we thought let's carry on and finish. It was a great album, so easy to do.'

The LP was released in February 1978 as *British Lions*, but didn't chart in the UK, even though DJ John Peel gave the band excellent airplay and a Radio One session appearance featuring three songs from the record. Dale Griffin believes that Peel didn't really like the British Lions, but rather felt some loyalty to Fiddler from his Medicine Head days.

Many of the Lions' tracks sounded 'current' and this had been encouraged to some extent by Morgan Fisher. 'I tried to make things happen musically and get the guys thinking more New Wave, which was what was happening at the time. I brought them records and asked them what they thought of this and that. I'd been going out to clubs regularly and listening to the punk bands which were appearing, and some of my ideas were picked up by The Lions.'

The first side of the album contained 'One More Chance to Run' and the stunning 'Fork Talking Man' written by John Fiddler and a Fiddler/Watts composition 'Break This Fool'. There were also two covers, Garland Jeffrey's 'Wild in the Streets', recently attempted with Hyams and 'International Heroes', written by Kim Fowley and Kerry Scott, and originally considered as a possible Mott The Hoople follow up to 'All the Young Dudes' in 1973. Fiddler had a hand in all of the songs on Side Two, 'Big Drift Away' and 'Eat the Rich', plus 'My Life's In Your Hands' written with Watts and Fisher, and 'Booster' composed with Overend.

Dale emphasised that the group were not Mott by any other name. 'This is a brand new band. We tried a mountain of names. One thing we didn't want was a name that sounded like we were cashing in on the New Wave. You know something like "The Nosebleeds".' Referring to the name 'British Lions', Griffin said, 'It's simple and direct, just the way we play.'

The other possible group names, largely Watts-inspired, included 'Electric Fires', 'The Dambusters,' 'Gretna Brown', 'The Stummer Cakes', 'The Chauvinist Pigs', 'Elegant Mess', 'Safety Last', 'Public Enemy No. 1', 'Mercury Wells', 'Landslide London' and 'British Lay Land'. Two other contenders were 'Brain Haulage' (a throwback to Mott the Hoople days) and 'Big Ben', which was adopted briefly. Pete even suggested 'Mott the Savage', 'Mott the King' or 'Mott the Lion', to try and connect with the former group name and reinforce their 'pedigree'. 'British Lions' was eventually chosen, largely for the American market.

In the UK, Vertigo issued two singles from the album, 'One More Chance to Run', backed with 'Booster', released in February 1978, followed by a 45rpm mix of 'International Heroes' with 'Eat the Rich' in April. RSO America opted for 'Wild in the Streets'.

British Lions made their live debut in Ireland and England supporting Status

Quo during November and December 1977. Colin Johnson, manager of both groups recalls the Lions first gig. 'I was sitting in the back of the hall and by the third number, they started sending shivers down my spine. It was a sense of togetherness with the crowd. You see some bands who don't give a damn – they play, take the money and go home. But they really worked to be a part of what was going on in the audience and the crowd loved them for it.'

The live set contained several tracks from their debut album plus a couple of covers, 'Come On' and 'Wild One'. At Aylesbury Friars, on 23 December, Ian Hunter joined Watts, Griffin and Fisher on stage for their encores. The Lions subsequently played a headlining tour in support of their debut album in February and March 1978 and in May toured again supporting AC/DC. In between these two tours Morgan Fisher recorded for Wayne County and the Electric Chairs' *Storm the Gates of Heaven* album.

During June, the Lions played a fifty-minute set on Musikladen TV in Germany. 'I put on make up to make me look unshaven,' recalls Morgan, 'and then smeared it all over my face in the last song, "Eat the Rich", which ended up with me throwing potted palms around. Those silly drunken times.'

The *British Lions* LP reached the Top 50 in the USA even before they commenced their August–September tour, supporting Blue Oyster Cult. Overend recalls, 'We thought if we pushed it, we'd get a Top 10 album, but we played all the wrong places and things got a bit grim.'

The first Lions tour of the USA was eventful from the moment their plane left England bound for New York. 'On the flight there was some kind of strike and we got free drinks all the way over,' recalls Fiddler. 'So we obviously obliged them and arrived pretty well wasted. Then, in the car from JFK Airport to West 57th Street, Morgan pulled a bottle of vodka from his bag which we drank. He was pleased to be taking the "new boy" on his first visit to New York, I'd never been there before. We checked into the hotel and RSO Records arrived and took us to Max's Kansas City where a punk band called The Rippers were performing, with a guitarist who sometimes played a huge stack of keyboards. So Morgan, with his Meerschaum pipe and "Our man in Havana" outfit, decides he's going to play and strolls on stage. The lead singer then starts pulling him about of course, saying, "Hey buddy, why don't you go fuck off!" while Morgan replies, "Away my man, away." He then announces to the audience, "Anybody who knows this guy better get him off the stage before I kill him." In the meantime, the singer had got an open cut throat razor out and sliced the bass player's arm. Suddenly this fight erupts on stage and the singer has Morgan on the floor, ripping his jacket, before Fisher gets up somehow, and throws the whole keyboard set up all over the place. We managed to rescue Morgan, but it was the one time Stan Tippins gave up on us I think. Enough was enough. All hell had broken loose and we hadn't even played a note in America, well Morgan had!'

Fiddler also recalls taking unprecedented action and dangerously discarding a guitar from the stage one evening during 'One More Chance to Run'. 'I'd never done that in my life before or since,' says John. 'I always started the song with crunching guitar, but this night it didn't work, nothing happened and I launched it. Suddenly, it was gone and I thought, "Why? What's going to happen? Who's it going to hit?" One of the roadies saved it, and me I think, from being taken off to jail, but it's the kind of simple thing that happens in bands, where you don't consider the consequences of your actions. On the same gig, I got really angry about the whole thing and started throwing microphone stands around. Silly, but the crowd really enjoyed it. I'd never been in a five piece rock 'n' roll band before, and it was tremendously exciting after Medicine Head.'

The Lions live set for the US tour now added a medley of 'So You Wanna Be a Rock 'n' Roll Star', 'It's Only Rock 'n' Roll' and 'Pretty Vacant', selected by Fisher.

'When we came back from America, we had to do the second album for which we hadn't got much material, because we'd been touring so heavily,' explains Watts. 'The second British Lions album, *Trouble with Women*, was perhaps the most difficult I'd ever done.' The LP was recorded and produced by the group at RAK Studios in London, during November and December 1978, but having completed eight tracks, RSO then passed on their option to release the record in America, closely followed by Phonogram who also refused to issue it in the UK.

'*Trouble with Women* was very understated,' says Ray Major. 'I was in hospital when a lot of that was made because I'd got hepatitis in San Antonio on the first Lions tour. When I got back to London, I started to go orange and my liver and kidneys closed down. Only out of sheer luck, a doctor friend of mine, who'd invited me dinner, asked me to see her the next day and stopped me from doing work on the album. I'd been playing well on it, but I was fighting this terrible illness so, I was hospitalised and Bruce Irvine came in and played on a couple of tracks.

'Again though, and I'm sorry to say it, when publishing and money comes into it, it all goes wrong. There's a pie with a slice for everybody, but Fiddler had his own publishing company, and Pete had April Music. As the pie gets smaller, the knives get sharper, and I thought, "I'm not into this game; I don't want to be involved." In any case, RSO pulled the plug because they didn't like "High Noon" and wanted two other tracks on the second album instead.'

Overend recalls, 'After the sessions came the decision about which way to go with the group. Buffin and I thought it was pointless carrying on as we had been. Colin, our manager, wanted to do the same with us as he had done with Status Quo, and build us up from nothing. He wanted us to do small gigs in England, but we were all over thirty and didn't want to spend five years doing that. Ray and John wanted to play, Morgan was unsure, but me and Buffin didn't like the idea. There were a lot of arguments over the policy of the group. The others wanted to do any gigs, but Buffin and I said the only way was to go to the States and get on a big tour. Colin was against it, saying it was difficult, though we couldn't see why. After that meeting, we never officially broke up, but there was a lot of disagreement in the band and with the management policy.

'Then they wanted us to do some extra tracks for the album. Some of the songs, like "Electric Chair", they didn't think were right. They felt they were a little way out for the US market that we were trying to hit. Ray was in hospital with hepatitis, so we had to leave holes for the solos and when he came out, he played stupendous guitar. We were all having personal troubles at home, so some days there was only one of us who turned up at the studio. It took about three months and was a drag, because we had a lot of difficulty getting the material together. When John wrote "Trouble with Women", that's the time we thought we'd got something really good, but things went downhill after that. The album was finished at the end of January and at subsequent meetings all the disagreements came out.'

Commitment and funds dried up and British Lions effectively disbanded in April 1979. Their second album lay in Phonogram's archives for eleven months, until a small and enthusiastic label, Cherry Red Records, led by vinyl mogul Iain McNay, released it under licence in May 1980. *Trouble with Women* contained another very fine set of songs. Side One was all composed by the group, 'Trouble with Women' and 'Any Port in a Storm' by Fiddler, 'Lady Don't Fall Backwards' by Watts and Fiddler and 'High Noon' by Fisher and Fiddler. The second side contained Overend and John's 'Lay Down Your Love' and 'Waves of Love', Fiddler's 'Electric Chair' and a cover of Martin/Scott's 'Won't You Give Him One (More Chance)'. As an 'historic' release from a defunct band, and with no promotion, the release of the record passed completely unnoticed.

'British Lions was potentially great, and Fiddler was good in lots of ways, but we felt a lot of pressure within the group,' says Watts. 'It was a bad time to start, during the punk craze. It wasn't good in the UK for us, and we were "old farts" according to most of the papers. Also, the management wasn't right and half the band wanted to go in one direction, while the other half wanted to go in the other. At that time I was thirty, and I wasn't prepared to slog it out on the circuit again for years and years, nor was Buffin. Colin Johnson had made Status Quo big by making them play everywhere, although they never cracked America, and it took seven or eight years to build them up. He wanted to do the same thing with us, because it was the only way he knew how to do it. We did all these horrible clubs to warm up and get British Lions tight, and it was fun. Then Colin wanted to do the same thing again.'

The problems of the second album and the continuing financial strain imposed on him by the music business was now the end of the line for Watts. There would be no future band involvement. 'I packed up playing in groups in 1979 because I thought I'd been a mug long enough. The Lions never officially split up. We'd done the American tour, come back and had to do the second album at RAK Studios. That was just absolute hell. We all had no money, not a penny. We hadn't got a lot of material, so it was quite difficult to do. John Fiddler was having personal problems with his wife, as was Buffin with Paula, and I'd just split up with Boo Boo (Carole Morley), which is why it's called *Trouble With Women*. Ray had hepatitis and was in isolation in hospital for most of the sessions. Morgan was off playing on other people's albums like Mike Harrison and John Otway mainly for money, because he couldn't pay his mortgage. So some days at RAK there was just one of us turning up and working on the tracks. It was no kind of atmosphere to be productive.

'After that we had a meeting with Colin Johnson to decide what we were going to do. The first thing he said was that Phonogram liked the album but there were four tracks they wanted us to leave off, including "Electric Chair". So

I got up and said, "Well, were not doing any more." Then Colin said, "I've got a gig list prepared. Were going to go back to PJ's Club in Harrogate to do that again, you went down very well there. Then we're going to go back to that little club in Plymouth." And Buffin and I said, "Oh no, no we're not, we are *not!*"

'I came out of that discussion knowing things were not looking good and then we all had a meeting with our accountant Tony Rose. Tony revealed that my tax liability was £85,000, but he'd reasoned with the tax people and pleaded poverty, so he'd managed to get it down to £15,000. I had nothing at all. My house was falling apart with dry rot and I had to borrow the money to fix it. If I'd sold it at that stage, I'd have got about £6,000 for it, and apparently I owed the Inland Revenue £15,000. Ray had a bill for about £2,000 and Buffin's was the same as mine.

'As we left the building, Colin Johnson was just falling about laughing. He said: "I can't believe it. How the hell did you get yourselves in that position?" And I recall walking down the street thinking, "I've done this for fifteen years, ended up with nothing and I owe fifteen thousand quid. That's it, I'm not playing in a group anymore. I don't know what I'm going to do but I've had enough." I felt I'd been a mug to the music industry long enough. I also felt out of control because I didn't really know what was going on on the business side of things. You had no control over money, you didn't know what was happening. So I packed it all in.' The early eighties were a time of real poverty for Watts after the glory of his former years, and he barely survived by virtue of a market stall on Portobello Road.

Hunter states that Stan Tippins and Dale Griffin made contact with him after the demise of British Lions, but he knew for sure that he wasn't going back to work with them any more. 'I like all of the boys very much, but I'd rather keep Mott The Hoople as a souvenir. A reunion would mean nothing. Roxy Music was a good example.'

After British Lions folded, John and Ray worked on new material at Fiddler's studio in Twickenham and formed Freeway with Status Quo's drummer John Coughlan. Muff Winwood then signed Major in a new band, Partners In Crime, who recorded one album, *Organised Crime,* which was keyboard orientated and a nightmare for Ray.

'I met my second wife during the *Partners in Crime* project, re-married and had two sons,' says Ray. 'I brought them through the first five years, but my second wife thought I should have a "proper" job everyday. I had this big house and it was in the eighties when Nigel Lawson put interest rates up, so with a millstone round my neck, we could hardly eat and live. I had to sign on the dole and went out and played in clubs with a little amp and guitar for fifty quid a night, but I was dying. My wife thought she had married a rock star and money. When it came to an abrupt halt three years later, she was off. I fought for my kids in the courts and then I thought, "Wait, what am I doing – they're going to New Zealand, a place I'd love to see." And I lost them.'

In recent years, Ray Major joined The Jim McCarty Band, and has worked with Steve Hyams, The Yardbirds, Art Wood and Sandy Dillon and put together a solo album, provisionally titled *Indian Summer.*

John Fiddler meanwhile joined Box of Frogs with former members of The Yardbirds and recorded two albums. He subsequently reformed Medicine Head and released a series of CDs including *Medicine Head Live, Return of the Buffalo* and *Acoustic Medicine Head* which contained 'unplugged' versions of his best known songs.

In 1980, Dale Griffin masterminded the compilation of a stunning LP of un-released Mott The Hoople Island material, titled *Two Miles from Heaven – New and Rare Tracks 1969–1972*. Many of the recordings were enhanced with Griffin, Watts, Major and Fisher overdubbing instrumental parts or backing vocals to improve and in some cases complete the original masters. 'That was good fun,' says Ray. 'Dale was in his element behind the desk producing and getting the sounds. He is good. It opened my eyes and I understand what a pressure it is in the studio.'

Two Miles from Heaven was issued briefly on Island Records in the UK and Ariola in Germany but an American release on the Antilles label, an Island/Atlantic offshoot, was shelved. With no press coverage or major retail stocks, the record was swiftly deleted and is one of Mott's rarest albums. The record had sides titled 'Dark Cargo' and 'Bald at the Station' rather than the con-ventional sides 1 and 2. 'Dark Cargo' was named after Watts' favourite poem by The Barrow Poets. 'Bald at the Station' was named courtesy of Mick Ralphs. Whilst auditioning bass players for Bad Company at their Berkshire rehearsal rooms, Ralphs went to pick up a potential candidate from a train. He and his aide fled when they saw the individual sporting a guitar case and a huge shiny bald head, quite inappropriate for Bad Co. They wrote in their audition book, 'reason for rejection – bald at the station', which Mott always thought would be an excellent title for a mournful blues song.

Dale subsequently explained his involvement in the Island rarities project. 'We tried very hard on the album to improve the originals. All the material was transferred to 24-track from 8- and 16-track sources and added to, in many cases. All were remixed.'

Sadly, the *Two Miles from Heaven* collection did not include 'The Debt', 'Downtown' or 'Ohio', which existed in live form, but it was nonetheless a stunning insight into Mott's Island archive and a credit to Griffin's production capabilities.

After the demise of British Lions in April 1979, Fisher set up Pipe Music, an independent studio in London, which he ran until 1980. 'When the Lions fold-ed, I exploded into activity and everything I'd been holding in came out in this chaotic blast. I met Iain McNay who had formed Cherry Red Records. They were mainly a punk label who got bands started, like Aztec Camera and Everything But the Girl. Rather than join another group, I wanted to build a home studio, and Iain agreed to release my material. I was asked by Zal Cleminson of the Sensational Alex Harvey Band to form a group, but I turned that down.'

Morgan's solo albums have been diverse, including *The Sleeper Wakes, Slow Music* (an ambient album) and *Miniatures* (a collection of 51 one-minute tracks by artists including Robert Fripp, Robert Wyatt and XTC). Two of Morgan's other releases were *A Collection of Classic Mutants,* and a Christmas album, *Claws,* both under the name 'The Hybrid Kids', which Fisher described as 'a pseudonym for an imaginary band playing punk remakes and art collages of pop songs.' Morgan also recorded a solo version of 'Roll Away the Stone' and taped tracks with Watts, Griffin and Major under the name 'The Paper Bags'. Fisher was asked to join The John Otway Band, touring and recording an album, *Where Did I Go Right.* The group were also featured in a new wave film called *Urgh! A Music War.* Morgan subsequently recorded and toured with Dead Kennedys, The Photos, Slaughter and the Dogs, and Neil Innes.

In 1981, Fisher decided to move abroad and planned to leave the music scene for two years. 'At the age of 30, after seeing too many friends die from drink and drugs, I started an inner-directed lifestyle and lived in spiritual communes in Belgium, India, England and America.'

Morgan's 'retirement' in Belgium was interrupted by an offer to play keyboards with Queen on their *Hot Space* European tour. 'I lived in Brussels from September 1981 to May 1982 just before the Queen tour, in a meditation commune. Then I fancied working again so I wrote to friends asking them, if you know of some work please tell me. I got a telegram from Brian May and he said, "Please come and play on the tour." It was a shock, because I had been living a quiet and simple life. Suddenly I was playing with Queen!'

After the concerts with Queen, Morgan returned to England in 1983 and recorded an album of sixties cover versions by artists like Argent, Jimi Hendrix and Traffic, entitled *Seasons.* Fisher's title was more apt, *Eighties Head, Sixties Heart,* but Cherry Red didn't like it. Morgan chose to move to Los Angeles for a couple of years and author Willard Manus recalls that Fisher made contact with him. 'I got a telephone call from Morgan one day. He said he had always wanted to meet me and he'd come from England to try and make it in the music world here. We became friendly for a time, though he was very involved in the cult run by Bagwan, the one with the twenty Rolls Royces and the commune up in Oregon. When that went bust, Morgan took off for Japan where he has remained ever since.'

'By 1985, I just wanted to see Japan,' explains Fisher. 'I had no plan to stay. I just came as a tourist. It was very exciting. For the first two years I did ordinary work which was not music related. Then I did some work for Yamaha and independent labels invited me to make records, so I stayed in Japan.'

Morgan built his own personal studio, and his musical output became far removed from his earlier work in the field of rock. He recorded the ambient albums *Look at Life, Water Music, Flow Overflow, Life under the Floor* and *Peace in the Heart of the City,* and moved into abstract photography using slides to accompany his live performances, directing his music towards relaxation. Fisher also recorded music for art videos and movies and worked on numerous television commercials including Maxell, Ricoh, Japan Air Lines and American Express. In 1990 Morgan released his *Echoes of Lennon* album with guest Yoko Ono, recorded in California and containing new age piano/synth versions of John Lennon songs, inspired by the *Imagine* movie. 1992 heralded the recording of *Relax, Refresh* and *Recharge,* in the *Re-* series of ambient/polyrhythmic music albums, and in 1994 Morgan added *Rebalance* and co-produced and played on *Far East Samba,* an album by Japanese rock band Boom.

Morgan's live concert appearances have included Expo 90 in Osaka, a 1993 tour of China plus concert tours with various Japanese bands including Dip In The Pool, Tensaw, The Yellow Monkey and Boom. He wrote a book, *The Boom Far East Tour Diary,* published in 1995, being his account of life on the road across Japan with the group between November 1994 and April 1995.

In September 1996, Morgan released a Japanese tribute album to Mott The Hoople entitled *Moth Poet Hotel.* Fisher's work with The Yellow Monkey on two Japanese Mick Ronson memorial concerts gave birth to the project and, backed by the Triad label, part of Nippon Columbia, Morgan produced the entire CD. The record was a showcase for Japanese rock talent and also featured Brian May on a re-recording of 'All the Way from Memphis' with drummer Cozy Powell. Other Mott covers included a stunning version of 'Honaloochie Boogie' and Morgan also accommodated less obvious tracks – 'Rock and Roll Queen', 'Death May Be Your Santa Claus' and 'Trudi's Song' – plus a message from the late Frank Zappa. Selling 50,000 copies in Japan alone, the disc was a successful and touching celebration of the group.

After British Lions, Overend Watts and Dale Griffin went on to form Grimtone Productions and produced the groups Slaughter and the Dogs, Department S and Hanoi Rocks. Dale recalls that Muff Winwood had promised to help them advance their production career once they actually produced a chart hit. 'We achieved this in 1981 with Department S and the Demon single "Is Vic There?" which reached number 22 in Britain. When we approached Muff again and told him of our success, we were effectively despatched with a mumbled, embarrassed response. That was really the straw that broke the camel's back for Watts.'

From January 1980 to February 1993, Dale Griffin worked for BBC Radio One as a freelance producer on a record number of sessions (almost 2,000), many of which were released on Strange Fruit Records, and some of which resulted in commercial record releases by Frankie Goes To Hollywood, The Housemartins, The Wedding Present, Happy Mondays and The Stranglers.

Pete Watts removed himself from the music industry, running an antique shop in West London and spending his spare time carp fishing. Richard Digby-Smith from Island Records met Watts by chance years later. 'When I came back from the States to London in 1984 I found a corner shop at the top of Southfield Road in W4. It had some lovely bric-a-brac and crazy stuff in there, including some rock and pop memorabilia. I wandered in one day quite by chance and there was Overend. The shop was *so* him. It actually looked a little off the wall, and had all sorts of cryptic little messages on the things in the window, like, "If you buy this, you must be stupid, but you can have it for four quid!"

Watts is now successful with a similar shop which he owns and runs in Hereford. He has always had little desire to return to the dizzy musical heights of the seventies, however, in 1989, he agreed to contribute to re-recordings with his former schoolboy group The Silence, organised by Dale Griffin. On 3 July 1989, Patrick Brooke, Paul Jeffery, Robert Fisher, Pete and Dale, met up for a jam session at Survival Studios and agreed to get together the following year to record material, 1990 being the 25th Anniversary since the original members last performed. From 8 to 12 October 1990, The Silence spent five days rehearsing, recording and mixing sixteen songs at Rockfield Studios in Monmouth. The album entitled *Shotgun Eyes* featured cover versions of old standards that the group used to perform – 'Shame, Shame, Shame', 'Dr Feelgood' and 'You Can't Judge a Book by Looking at the Cover' – plus two Silence originals, 'See You Tomorrow', written by Jeffery in 1963 and initially performed by The Anchors, Watts and Griffins' first group, and 'We'll Silence You', composed by Fisher in 1990 as an autobiographical account of Silence and its members. The tape was labelled Side A40 and Side B4233, after two roads in the Ross area regularly travelled by The Silence and The Soulents. *Shotgun Eyes* was finally released on CD in March 1998 by Angel Air Records, with the original 1967 Doc Thomas Group LP, re-named *The Italian Job*.

Dale Griffin said of the The Silence sessions, 'My memory of this recording, apart from the pleasure of being with old friends again, was the pain in my hands, wrists and arms. I needed six months of hard practice. I had none. We recorded everything as if for live performance, with the minimum of overdubs. Fisher, Jeffery and Brooke performed as if the 25 year break had been only 25 days. As much as I hate to admit it, the boy Watts played a blinder and was only just beginning to warm to his task when we had to pack up and go. Watts was amazing. He hadn't played lead guitar since 1965!'

1989 saw Griffin involved in another Island compilation of Mott The Hoople tracks, this time for compact disc. Released in April 1990, *Walking with a Mountain* was a fine retrospective with an excellent booklet of historical notes written by Dale. Some interesting edits were made to combine 'You Really Got Me' and 'Wrath 'n' Wroll' as one track ('Crossfades'), and to shorten the live version of 'Keep A-Knockin' ', but, sadly, the elusive 'Downtown' and 'The Debt' were once again excluded.

Dale's reflects on his involvement in the industry and the fact that he could never resist the pull of musicianship. 'There has to be something in you of the crazy man to be in a rock group, because before I became a professional musician, everything warned against doing anything like that. It's like hoping you're going to win the pools and that's going to get you through life. You're going to be a musician and you hope to God something wonderful will happen and that will see you through. Not that money comes in to it, but with music, it hypnotises you and perhaps against your will you must do it.

'I was certainly in that category. Having been in a semi-pro group with Watts when we were at school, he then went professional and the rest of us were left thinking, "Jesus, he's gone professional, he's a musician now, he's not a trainee architect." And of course, parents and teachers and all the people around you were saying, "No you musn't do that, you must get a proper job." But in the person that wants to do it, there's this crazy man saying, "No, you've got to do it, you've got to be wild, you've got to be free."

'I remember when I was still going to school, Watts was out being a pro-musician, and I was gnashing my teeth and thinking, "The bastard, that's what I want to do." And eventually that's what I did when the drummer in the group he was in left, or was caused to leave, and the place became available. As soon as they said, "Would you like ...?", before they'd finished the sentence, I said, "Yes, anything, yes please."

'Of all the groups that Watts and I had at school, only he and I became professional musicians. The singer in one of the bands went into accountancy and is incredibly successful, but he's still bitter that he never became a professional musician. It still eats him that Watts and I went off and did what he would have liked to do. He managed to subdue the crazy man, and stop himself doing it, but we couldn't. It is a drug.'

21
Noises

'Noises' – Ian Hunter

Having split with Corky Laing in 1978, Ian decided that his future recording plans lay with his old colleague and friend Mick Ronson. 'It's really good,' said Hunter. 'He sort of wanders in to my life now and again. We have a good time. I see him all the time when we don't work together and my wife and his wife get on very well.'

Since the duo parted in 1975, Ronson had worked on tours, albums, sessions and production for Roger McGuinn (*Cardiff Rose*), Kinky Friedman (*Lasso from El Passo*), Van Morrison (*A Period of Transition*), Rob Stoner (*Topaz*), Sparks (*Big Beat*), David Cassidy (*Gettin' It in the Street*), Roger Daltrey (*One of the Boys*), John Cougar (*Chestnut Street Incident*), Philip Rambow, Annette Peacock (*X-Dreams*), Slaughter and the Dogs (*Do It Dog Style*), Benny Mardones (*Thank God for Girls*) and Bob Dylan's Rolling Thunder Revue. He even recorded one track, 'She's a Roller', for a new Spiders From Mars album, fronted by Trevor Bolder.

Ronson first met Dylan during the summer of 1975 at 'The Bitter End', in Greenwich Village New York, where Dylan started playing with Patti Smith, Jack Elliott and Bobby Neuwirth, performing the songs 'Abandoned Love', 'Joey' and 'Isis' for the first time. Dylan's rekindled enthusiasm and interaction with other musicians brought about the idea of a travelling road show of performers and poets, playing small venues, unannounced, throughout the USA. The plan became reality with The Rolling Thunder Revue which hit the road in New England during October 1975.

Mick said of his link up with Bob Dylan, 'I met him in the Village one night. I got thrown out of a club which Ian took me down to and Dylan came up and said, "Come with us for a drink." And he said, "Well, why don't you come out on the road with me for a bit?" and I said, "Yeah, all right." And that was it. I never heard from him. Six months later, on a Friday afternoon or something, the phone rang and he said, "Are you ready to start rehearsals on Sunday?" So I said, "Yeah, I suppose so." A quick rehearsal – we never played the same song twice, and we were on the road.'

Hunter explains how Ronson's involvement with Dylan evolved. 'We all used to go to "Trudella's" in New York, where Defries held court, and one night, I said I didn't want to go there, so we went to "The Bitter End". This guy, Paul Colby, who ran it, knew us and sat us down and gave us beers. The place is empty and Bob Dylan walks in with Bobby Neuwirth and plays the whole of *Desire*. We're sitting a table away and Mick's not even interested, saying, "Fucking Yogi Bear," which is what Ronson called Dylan. Mick liked The Shadows, which shows you where he was at. Suzi, Mick's wife, is checking things out with Neuwirth and the place is mobbed now. Mick's drunk. They threw him out three times. He told Colby if he threw him out again, he'd come back in through the window. The upshot of it was that Mick was living downtown and I was living in Chappaqua, and three days later he calls me and says, " 'Ere, I'm in this band." "What fuckin' band?" "I'm in Bob Dylan's band. I can't figure it out, it's all C, F and G and he never sings the same one twice!"

'Ronson kept asking me to come down, but I felt somebody around Dylan had to ask me. Mick kept saying, "Nah, just come down," and that's exactly what it was. Anybody who went along was in. It was so haphazard but I never went because I never got the official invite. It really pissed me off, because I was sitting at home alone, while they're having a great time on the road. In *Rolling Stone* they did an article and said I was very good, and I wasn't even there!'

In October 1975, Ronson joined Dylan's successful and extensive US tour through to May 1976. Over 60 concerts were played and several were captured on bootleg albums, a television documentary filmed in Colorado, a four-hour movie entitled *Renaldo and Clara* and the official CBS live album, *Hard Rain*. Prior to Dylan's appearances, his 'band' performed for about one-third of each show. Ronson sang 'Is There Life on Mars?' and backed Roger McGuinn, Bobby Neuwirth and T-Bone Burnett on their solo performances. Mick often played solos on 'Maggie's Farm' and 'Chestnut Mare'.

'The whole set up with that tour was very loose, it was chaotic,' admitted Ronson. 'Arlo Guthrie came up and sang his songs, as did Leonard Cohen and Joni Mitchell. It was really laid back. You just strolled on and off and played. I never knew what I was doing from night to night, what songs or even what key they would be in. One night "Blowing in the Wind" would be in C, the next night it was in F! Not just that, he would play it twice as fast. Then he used to stop in the middle of a number suddenly, then start again suddenly, and you really had to watch him all the time.'

On 13 and 14 December 1975, Ronson recorded several solo tracks at Sundragon Studios in Manhattan, including 'I'd Rather Be Me', Bowie's 'Soul Love' (re-titled 'Stone Love'), 'Pain in the City', 'Dogs (French Girl)', '28 Days Jam' and 'Is There Life on Mars?'. The songs were all released posthumously on Ronson CDs between 1994 and 1998.

After the first Dylan tour, Mick worked in London with John Cougar, who was managed by Tony Defries, then completed the second part of The Rolling Thunder Revue and went to Europe to work with Dr John and Van Morrison, helping on the album, *A Period of Transition*. 'We spent a lot of time hanging out together and playing in hotel rooms and rehearsal halls. Dr John and myself started renting rehearsal rooms and inviting all the London scene down to play with us for fun. We had some great jams with different musicians.'

Mick was invited to produce and work on Roger McGuinn's *Cardiff Rose* LP released on CBS in 1976. Ronson played guitar, piano, recorder, accordion, organ, percussion, and autoharp on the record but was fairly unenthusiastic about the project, even though it was probably McGuinn's hardest hitting album ever. 'It was all right. He only had four songs. We were in the studio trying to scramble this stuff together and we were both going out partying. I think it could have been better. That period just flew by.'

Mick put together a short-lived group, Guam, with McGuinn and T-Bone Burnett. 'The band never really got off the ground, but we had some good laughs,' said Ronson years later. 'Drinking was a problem too. I've got to say I've done some stupid things in the past, like turning down Bob Seger and Rod Stewart!'

1976 saw an unexpected collaboration when RCA label-mate David Cassidy asked Ronson to join a permanent band. Instead, Mick played steely lead guitar for the gritty title track of Cassidy's album, *Gettin' It in the Street*, which also featured contributions from The Beach Boys and Richie Furey. Released as a single, the song reached number 12 in Germany.

In September and October of that year, Ronson worked on a series of tracks at Bearsville Studios in Woodstock with musicians from the Cassidy sessions and, after some live dates supporting Rush, more material was recorded in Bearsville in summer '77 with Ricky Fataar, Mick Baraken, John Holbrook and Jay Davis, who had played with Rod Stewart. The songs 'I've Had a Hard Life' (with 'Ziggy Stardust' refrain), 'Just Like This', 'Crazy Love', 'Taking a Train', I'd Give Anything to See You', 'Plane to England', 'Desert Star' and a Moby Grape cover, 'Hey Gran'ma', were astounding, but although an album release was discussed with Ahmet Ertegun and the Atlantic label, the recordings were never issued..

In 1976, Mick also performed with Roger McGuinn, Carmine Appice, Tim Bogert, Albert Lee, Bo Diddley, Mark Steiner and Barry Goldberg on a US television super-jam in Los Angeles. Ronson also featured on an album by Kinky Friedman, who had guested occasionally with Dylan and Mick was invited to play live with John Cale and Patti Smith in Manhattan.

During 1977, Ronson played for John Cougar on his album *Chestnut Street Incident* and did a British tour with The Philip Rambow Band, which brought Mick in touch with the new punk movement. One song from Rambow's set, 'Underground Romance', was included on a live compilation LP entitled *Hope & Anchor Front Row Festival.* The following year saw Mick recording with new wave band Slaughter and the Dogs and one of his favourite artists, Annette Peacock. He had covered some of her songs on his earlier solo records and was invited by Annette to play on her *X-Dreams* LP with guitarist Chris Spedding.

Ronson tried unsuccessfully to form another band, Rebel of Future, in the summer of 1978 and then met up with Ian to talk about joining forces again. Mick had just completed production duties on an album entitled *Ghosts Of Princes In Towers* by The Rich Kids, who featured guitarists Midge Ure and Steve New, drummer Rusty Egan and bass player Glen Matlock. 'It was great going into the studio with them,' said Ronson. 'It was great to watch Steve, 17 years old. He didn't care if the guitar was in tune or not. He'd just plug in, turn it up and crank it out. I'd kind of forgotten how to live with music that way. I'd tended to get very serious about music.' The Rich Kids now acknowledge that in their youthful exuberance and naivety, they failed to tap into Mick's considerable ability and experience. Matlock also opines that 'Ronno', uncredited, was largely responsible for The Sex Pistols' 'God Save the Queen' riff!

Mick still had some production work to fulfil with a band called Dead Fingers Talk, so Ian accepted an offer from Chrysalis Records to produce the second album for New Wave band Generation X, who had vocalist Billy Idol and bassist Tony James in their line up. Hunter produced sessions in London during August and September 1978 and the *Valley of the Dolls* LP and 'King Rocker' single were both UK chart hits. 'Their offer came at a time when I was willing to take anything,' said Ian. 'I looked in the papers and I saw they were getting a lot of press. So I stated my price which wasn't a problem. What impressed me was that they knew what they wanted. That and their love of rock and roll. But Gen X was difficult to do. I think I was a little too dominant, and I've spoken to Billy about it since. Anyway, we got the desired effect and had a hit single out of it, because Chrysalis was saying to me that they owed a lot of money and, if it didn't happen, they were out!'

'Around this time Ronson came to stay with me,' says Ian. 'He was telling me about The Rich Kids and Dead Fingers Talk and how much he'd been paid for producing them. I freaked, because he was up to his usual stupidity. One night I said, "You'd go and do anything for people that screw you, and the people that help you, you'd shit all over them." I think that was the first time I ever broke through. For a couple of months, I was on his case for his own sake, because he was a great artist. With the David Johansen album, he was offered a certain fee for that and I said, "Look, that's what they think you're worth, because you do it for these stupid fucking fees!" He got on the phone and told Blue Sky what he wanted and he got very near to it, which was infinitely better than what he had been getting.'

Hunter was soon to resist further production for other artists. 'People wanted us to produce their albums because of the first solo album I did. It didn't really teach us anything except the energy level. We always got lumbered with these people who couldn't play. It annoys me when people ask if I'd like to be a producer, because it means they don't understand me. What I'm doing is really good, but it doesn't catch on quick. It has always caught on to a certain extent, but it isn't Styx or Fleetwood Mac. I don't particularly want to be, though I wouldn't mind their sales!'

Following production of Generation X, Chrysalis Records offered Hunter a recording contract and Ian found new management in the form of Steve Popovitch and Sam Lederman at Cleveland International, Meatloaf's management company. Popovitch was a friend from Hunter's former Columbia days. 'Steve heard what I was doing at the same time as Chrysalis and, all of a sudden, I had management who I liked. That was a nice time, because I felt as though I was in with a shot and that people were really rooting for me, including Chrysalis.'

In October 1978, Ian started his next album with various 'New Wave' musicians, including Glen Matlock, at Bill Price's Wessex Studios in North London. Within a few days however, he felt the demos weren't right and the project was scrapped. 'After three or four days, I didn't think it was going to happen,' said Ian. In the interim, Popovitch had been playing tapes of Hunter's new material to some of Bruce Springsteen's Band, who were working on Meatloaf's LP, and they liked what they heard. By the end of 1978, Ian and Mick had returned to the US and began pre-production rehearsals for the record. Ian had got the basic ideas for most of the new songs from working with other musicians after *Overnight Angels*.

By January 1979, Ian and Mick were settled in New York's Power Station

Studio and had re-commenced the sessions for Hunter's album, provisionally titled *The Outsider*. Three members of Springsteen's E Street Band were brought in for the record; pianist Roy Bittan, bassist Gary Tallent and drummer Max Weinberg. Within two days, Ian had re-written seven songs and rehearsed them with Ronson and the band. Armed with another three songs they completed the album. He described a couple of the tracks as 'weird', but believed the record to be a step in the right direction. 'It's more commercial, much better than the other albums. I wanted to use a rhythm section who were used to each other and they were great. Max was super and the drum sound was amazing, the best I've ever heard.'

Hunter is still animated about the record years later. 'That album was people getting down to business and really working hard. Bob Clearmountain was just about to take off and we had Cale coming in for odd sorts of things like "Bastard". The E Streeters were all extremely nice people, nothing was too much trouble.'

The LP was re-named *You're Never Alone with a Schizophrenic*, taken from a slogan found on a wall by Ronson. Ian said of the title, 'Mick called it that and it kind of suited. So I said to him, "We'll use this for mine and when we do yours we'll call it *Bat out of Hull!*" '

The *Schizophrenic* title wasn't meant to be wholly serious; however on listening to the record it became clear that musically it was split. Side One featured five relatively commercial songs and Side Two, four longer, more introverted pieces that dwelt on past influences in Ian's life and showed the other side of his character. 'This isn't the person that writes the songs,' explains Ian. 'The individual who writes the songs is a totally different person. It's a whole different thing, like an *alter ego*. The person who writes the material is a lot more truthful.'

Hunter also agrees his best work is always written in the worst emotional times. 'Revenge is a great motivator. Anger. Total misery. Negative emotions. Especially when people think I ain't got a shot. That's when I'm great. That's when I can do it. I almost aim for non-shots to come back off them.'

With three months of pre-production, the record produced by Mick and Ian, arranged by Hunter, Ronson and Bittan and engineered by the notorious Bob Clearmountain, took only one week to record and a further three weeks to mix. Overall, the album was a hard hitting, surging rock record with superb studio sound and production techniques.

The LP opened with the punchy drum beat of 'Just Another Night', followed by a spoken introduction and piano before the song snapped into life. Immediately, the music fired and spat in stylish fashion. This Hunter-Ronson credited track, which had started life as 'The Other Side of Life', was inspired by Mott The Hoople's 1973 US touring exploits and the night that Ian spent in an Indianapolis city jail. The track swaggered to a halt but merged without any physical break into the bump and groove of 'Wild East'. A mildly energetic and melodic piece, with a sax-based riff, it concerned the crazed east side of New York City, and had an undoubted Springsteen and Dylan flavour.

First written as 'Cleveland Rocks', then changed to 'England Rocks' for the 1977 Overnight Angels single, Ian's ode to Cleveland, Ohio was re-recorded in its original form, but given added spice and zest for the album by Ronson's playing. It opened with a spoken section by Alan Freed, the infamous DJ who had originally coined the phrase 'rock 'n' roll' on his early fifties *Moondog's Rock 'n' Roll Party* radio show. Freed was exiled from the airwaves in 1959 after being charged with inciting a concert riot and was then made chief scapegoat in the 'payola' corruption scandals of the early 1960s, being fined on 26 counts of commercial bribery. Ian's idea for the Freed introduction was influenced by the group Devo.

Hunter included a touching, hymn-like ballad, 'Ships', concerning his relationship with his father, a song which he had started writing for Mott The Hoople. It took on an eerie and dreamlike perspective, courtesy of Procul Harum-style keyboards, as Ian bared his emotions and shared the transparency of his feelings. ' "Ships" was around for two or three years but it didn't have a hook. I was sitting with Max Weinberg one night and he happened to say "ships that pass in the night". That was two years of waiting. My mother was funny when she said, "Typical. I do all the work and he gets all the credit." I didn't know it was going to be about my Dad, it just turned out that way. I liked my Dad. We had a terrible time, but the older I got, the more I realised what he'd been up against and he was a character. He was a lot nicer than me in some ways, but a regular bastard in other ways.'

'Ships' was subsequently covered by Barry Manilow and charted as a hit single in America, a recording that prompted an interesting reaction from Ian. 'Clive Davis has always liked my material and Clive always keeps a bunch of stuff in his office. Manilow went into the office, Clive played 'Ships', Manilow loved it, and recorded it. Once it's in the public domain, anybody can do anybody's song. Financially, it's incredible, because it's not only in the top ten, it's on an album that's top ten, it's also on the greatest hits album, the live album, the thing goes on forever. For people who would be upset with me for letting him do it, I can't stop him. I listened to it and my mouth was open. I didn't know what to make of it. It's kind of like an ambivalent feeling. I can't think of anything that I really like that somebody else did. You like your own songs best, because that's the way you envisage them.'

'When the Daylight Comes' was a light and simple song, and a favourite of Ronson's, so Ian encouraged him to take joint lead vocal on the track. It was Chrysalis Records' choice for the first single to promote the album, but Hunter wasn't so sure of its hit potential. 'I used to make accessible singles. We had two straight years of hits. They were kind of acceptable to me. Then, I don't know what happened, but all of a sudden, I couldn't have a hit. If one comes along great, that's the way I look at it.'

Side Two opened with 'Life After Death', a track which allowed Ian to explore metaphysical issues. The atmosphere was reminiscent of Bowie's *Ziggy Stardust* period and Hunter appeared to have his tongue firmly in his cheek with this song. 'Standing in My Light' shifted moods and dynamics in gospel fashion, enhanced by shadowy keyboards. It built up slowly and compellingly in terms of musical anger, as Ian gave a stately account of a new beginning in his life. He could have been addressing his parents, his wife, a friend or a fellow musician as he sang "Move over, cos you're standing in my light". In fact, he seemed to be targetting himself, another counterpart to the album's title. Ian explained subsequently that Mott's former manager, Tony Defries, was a stimulus for the lyric and that the song triggered the whole album when he re-focused his life after *Overnight Angels*. 'It started with "Standing in My Light", right in the middle of when I was getting clean of everybody.'

> Well I finally found you out
> All through your mess of dreams
> You won't make it to the night
> And you're standing in my light
>
> You know you've been bad for me
> You ain't got the weight to hate
> But you ain't no pretty sight
> Any you're standing in my light

'Bastard' was a powerful piece of macho-funk with throbbing beat and percussion and recalled the Rolling Stones' *Black and Blue* era. Built on a relentless grinding slow burn, the track concerns some unfortunate who crossed Hunter and incurred his wrath. Asked to whom was he addressing the lyric, and assuming it was a male, Ian replied, 'It's a she actually!' It was a cluttered but exciting song of detached hostility and featured astounding keyboard playing from John Cale. 'I like working with John. There's something in the room when John's in a room. There is a musical aura about him. You can get together with some people and the creative spark goes automatically. He has problems because he's not as commercial as he should be, which kind of hampers his style somewhat, but he's an amazing musician.'

Hunter's vocals were stronger than ever on this album, and they were set off against the correct instrumentation too, his voice paired with echoey piano on 'The Outsider' to remarkable effect. A western-style ballad, it closed the record in dramatic fashion, employing arresting drum and vocal echoes, topped with more scorching Ronson lead guitar. 'Everybody types me as a guy that writes hard rock songs, but I've always liked to write ballads,' remarked Ian. 'The three slow songs on this album are the best ones I've ever written.'

You're Never Alone with a Schizophrenic was released in April 1979 by Chrysalis. It entered the UK charts on 5 May and stayed for a total of three weeks, reaching number 49, Ian's third highest British album chart placing. In The USA, the album reached number 35 on *Billboard*, where it stayed for a total of 24 weeks. The record received highly favourable press reviews on both sides of the Atlantic, *New Musical Express* excepted, who slated Ian for 'creative redundancy'. They were wrong, and in the minority, as the record was to be one of Hunter's most successful and popular solo releases.

In Britain, Chrysalis released an edited version of 'When the Daylight Comes', backed with 'Life after Death' as a limited edition single pressed on white vinyl. They followed this up with 'Ships' and 'Wild East' in July, while in America, 'Just Another Night' was chosen, with 'Cleveland Rocks' on the B-side.

The *Schizophrenic* album was a natural continuation of the *Ian Hunter* LP, and similarly it carried Ronson's unmistakable influence. Hunter remains satisfied with the project. 'That was the best experience. Bob Clearmountain, the E Streeters, everybody was serious about it. The only problem was that it didn't have a single, but it was a good record. In fact, Chrysalis told me at the time it was the best record they ever put out. I wanted to hold it back, because it didn't have a single, but Chrysalis were so gung-ho they released it. They were really proud of it. In retrospect I wish we had held it back. I just couldn't write a single. "Ships", as it is, is a little too bland. It would have needed more colour. When we were doing it, we thought it was just a ballad. Later on, it turns into a hit single for Barry Manilow, but we never thought of it like that. "When the Daylight Comes" sounds like a single. When a song sounds like a single it's the kiss of death. A single is basically something that gives you the chills. It's as simple as that.

'Recording the album was a good experience. Mick and I kept it simple, sometimes because that was just the way it happened. We put the tracks down and the songs would not accept a lot of things that we'd normally try,' said Ian. 'I was well prepared for the fact that it might not sell, but the way it went out of the box shocked everybody. It shocked me. It was a big turnabout.'

In the spring of 1979, Hunter and Ronson had agreed to produce *Nightout*, the debut album by Ellen Foley, who had been signed by Cleveland International and Epic Records after her work on Meatloaf's *Bat Out of Hell* LP. Ian had been impressed with her demo tape, which included a version of 'All the Way from Memphis', and asked Ronson to help him. Some pre-production work was done at Bearsville Studios in Woodstock, Mick's new-found home, and the final album sessions were recorded at Media Sound in New York with engineer Harvey Goldberg. Hunter gave Ellen a beautiful ballad for the record which he had written called 'Don't Let Go' and did some keyboards, guitar, percussion and backing vocals on *Nightout*. Ian was pleased with the Foley project. 'That sold a lot of records and was one of the biggest records Holland ever had. Foley was great and easy to work with, but she was Broadway based and so to get her organic, you had to get her completely plastered. But she was a great girl.'

Hunter Ronson also came close to producing an album for Joe Cocker. Ian admitted, 'At the moment, Mick and I are having talks with someone, a well-known person who has been making worthless LPs for years. I can't possibly give any names yet, because we're still in the middle of talks, but if it goes through it'll be recorded in August or September.'

Whilst working on Ellen Foley's record, Ian finished production on his own *Schizophrenic* album and agreed to assist Bob Clearmountain with David Werner's self-titled LP, which he was also recording at The Power Station. Hunter helped out on a couple of Werner's tracks and shared vocals on a song called 'High Class Blues'.

At New York's Media Sound Studios, Ronson also assisted Genya Ravan on a track entitled 'Junkman', for her LP *And I Mean It!* She had intended to make the song a dual vocal with Van Morrison but when he let her down, Mick suggested she duet with Ian and the result was special. Ronson also went on to produce and orchestrate ex-New York Doll, David Johansen's solo LP, *In Style*, playing guitar on 'She Knew She Was Falling in Love', 'Melody', 'Justine', 'In Style' and 'Flamingo Road', Ian guesting on piano for the latter track.

After the release of the *Schizophrenic* album, Ian and Mick were eager to tour using The E Street Band but had to form a group using musicians from Ellen Foley's sessions. The live band comprised mainly American musicians and included drummer Hilly Michaels (Ronson had done sessions with him for Sparks and John Cougar), guitarist Tommy Morrongiello (who had worked with David Byron), Georgie Meyer on keyboards and saxophone (ex-Randy Pie), keyboard player Tommy Mandel (soon to become best known for his work with Bryan Adams) and 'lone-Brit' Martin Briley on bass (formerly a member of UK progressive group Greenslade).

The Ian Hunter Band featuring Mick Ronson spent part of April and May touring the West Coast of America and Europe before embarking on a six-month US tour in June 1979. The concerts featured occasional guest appearances from Ellen Foley, Rory Dodd and Meatloaf. Several shows were broadcast on radio, concerts in Cleveland and Toronto were filmed for television and the band also appeared on *The Friday Show* and *Midnight Special.*

The selection of songs for the live set was lengthy and one of Ian's best, the material tracing the breadth of his Mott The Hoople and solo repertoire, as well as showcasing new songs from *Schizophrenic*. 'Once Bitten Twice Shy', 'Life After Death', 'Laugh at Me', 'When the Daylight Comes' / 'Ships', 'Letter to Britannia from the Union Jack', 'One of the Boys', 'All the Way from Memphis' / 'Jumpin' Jack Flash', 'Standin' in My Light', 'Bastard', 'Irene Wilde', 'Sweet Angeline', 'Just Another Night', 'Walking with a Mountain' / 'Rock and Roll Queen', 'Cleveland Rocks', and 'All the Young Dudes' were all performed live. Ronson was featured on The Shadows' instrumental 'FBI' and 'Slaughter on 10th Avenue'. Later in the tour, 'I Wish I Was Your Mother', 'The Golden Age of Rock 'n' Roll' and a new composition, 'Sons and Daughters', were added to the set.

By August, drummer Hilly Michaels left Hunter's band to pursue a solo career and was replaced by Eric Parker, formerly of The Fabulous Rhinestones and Little Feat. Plans were made to commence another Hunter studio album in October, but Cleveland International and Chrysalis were keen to maintain the momentum generated by live work and convinced Ian to continue touring and release a live LP instead. 'I didn't want to put it out in the first place, because I wanted another one like *Schizophrenic*, only better. I probably could have gone in the studio again around October, but they wanted to keep my name going.'

Hunter Ronson played and recorded six shows at the Roxy in Los Angeles from 5 to 11 November, breaking the club's record for most consecutive nights booked at the Sunset Boulevard venue. 'That was good fun,' offers Hunter. 'We had Billy Connolly there as support and he left on the first night because nobody would listen to him. He was headlining in Canada the following week, but they just couldn't get it in LA and kept talking and drinking throughout his act. It was sad, because I liked the guy and was looking forward to seeing him.'

Ian and his band came to London to play one night at the Hammersmith Odeon on 22 November, supported by Rachel Sweet. The show was sold out and was taped and broadcast by BBC Radio One. To coincide with this sole UK concert appearance, Chrysalis released a third single from the *Schizophrenic* album, 'Cleveland Rocks', backed with 'Bastard'. Whilst in London, Ian spoke of his renewed working relationship with Mick. 'We just seem to take it one stage at a time. Initially we were only going to tour for a month. That turned into five months, which turned into a live album and that'll turn into something else. I think it's better for us both if we don't know exactly what we're going to do. When we don't know what's happening we work harder.'

On 10 and 11 January 1980, Ian and Mick went into Media Sound in New York, to mix the American concert tapes with Harvey Goldberg, and to record four new songs. They had decided that the proposed LP would be a double set, with three sides taken from The Roxy shows and the fourth, comprising new material, in a live studio format. 'I never like live albums,' remarked Hunter. 'It's hard mixing them because you've heard it all before!'

During Hunter's sessions at Media Sound, another Cleveland International group, The Iron City Houserockers, were recording *Have a Good Time ... But Get Out Alive*. Ronson produced and arranged the LP and involved Mandel, Briley, Foley and Hunter on some tracks. Ian contributed guitar, piano and backing vocals and produced and arranged two songs. Mick would also take time out to guest on one track, 'Gotta Go Home', for The Johnny Average Band album *Some People,* and to produce Moda's LP, *Canto Pagana,* in Italy. Ian produced a single, 'Dangerous Eyes', for New York group Sam The Band.

Immediately prior to the issue of the new Hunter live album, Columbia, in their wisdom, decided to release a double compilation of Ian's work entitled *Shades of Ian Hunter – The Ballad of Ian Hunter and Mott The Hoople.* The set was issued in February 1990 in Britain, and featured two sides of Mott material, including all the rare CBS single B-sides plus a previously unreleased live version of 'Marionette' from Broadway, one side of Hunter solo material and a fourth side of Overnight Angels tracks, previously unissued in America. The gatefold sleeve included reasonable notes but, sadly, lacked photographs tracing Ian's career. Hunter was upset about the Columbia album. 'Fortunately, they're not spending a cent on promoting it. That's fine by me, because the idea of two double albums coming out within four or five months of each other, containing some of the same songs, is going to sound like a right rip off!'

Chrysalis Records' live LP was released on 4 April 1980 in a gatefold sleeve, distinctly lacking imagination in the 'outer covers department' but housing excellent live colour photographs of the band on the inner spread. The album entered the UK charts on 26th April and stayed for two weeks, peaking at number 61. The original title was the imaginative *From the Knees of My Heart,* but this was changed to *Welcome to the Club* by the time of release. The fourth side of the two record set included the 'anti-disco' 'We Gotta Get Out of Here' (featuring Ellen Foley dueting with Ian), 'Silver Needles '(reviewers assumed this was a song about recently deceased Sid Vicious of The Sex Pistols, but it had been rehearsed as a Mott The Hoople track back in 1973), a tongue-in-cheek Hunter-Ronson rocker 'Man O'War' and a live concert version of the autobiographical 'Sons And Daughters', which referred to Ian's divorce in the early seventies.

The album was promoted in Britain with a limited edition gatefold double single featuring 'We Gotta Get Out of Here' as the lead track. The package also contained 'Sons and Daughters', a special remixed live medley of 'Once Bitten Twice Shy' / 'Cleveland Rocks' / 'Bastard' plus an exclusive live version of 'One of the Boys'.

In the spring of 1980, Hunter played on two European television shows, at the Rockpalast at Essen in Germany on 19 April, where he shared the bill with ZZ Top and Joan Armatrading, and for Antenne 2 in Paris the following week, where he recorded a thirty-minute set. During this trip, they also filmed a three-track promotional video featuring 'Once Bitten Twice Shy', 'Irene Wilde' and 'We Gotta Get Out of Here'. Ian had pencilled-in a six-date UK tour at this time, but he returned to America and rehearsed a new live set instead. Before he left, he starred on Radio One's *Roundtable* review programme and *Star Special,* where he could indulge in playing all-time favourite records by Jerry Lee Lewis, Little Richard, The Rolling Stones and Roy Wood.

Hunter was considering moving away from New York at this time. 'I came out of the sticks to London and it was a big change for me. I went from London to New York and it was a big change for me. Now I'm looking at Mexico. It's dangerous to stay in one country all your life. I like moving around.'

Hunter Ronson presented a new live set during a further American tour in May 1980, which included a re-visit to the Los Angeles Roxy. 'Who Do You Love?', 'The Truth, The Whole Truth and Nothin' But The Truth' and 'Man O'War' had now been introduced to the show. Then, before the Dr Pepper Festival at Central Park, New York on 11 July, Mick announced that he wanted to leave Hunter's band. Twenty-five dates, plus an appearance at the Reading Festival in England on 23 August, were scrapped, the band folded and Hunter returned to New York to write new material throughout the latter half of 1980. During this period he offered a song entitled 'Lullaby' to Tommy Mandel, which he recorded for Cleveland International's charity album, *Children of the World,* released on Epic.

In October, Hunter decided to play a series of concerts with Todd Rundgren, who asked him to join two to three weeks of charity gigs in support of American congressman John Anderson. Ian decided to participate in the shows purely for fun. 'Todd's a lovely guy. He got Mick and me into a Stones rehearsal once, because he remembered we liked them. In 1980, I agreed to form a band with Todd because I had nothing better to do. We had Tommy Mandel and Michael Shreeve, the drummer from Santana. Todd's songs sound simple, but there are millions of chords in them. "Mr Busy", they call him. He's always up to something. Todd's mind is unbelievable and he gets terribly bored pretty quick.'

Rundgren described the liaison with Hunter as an interesting non-merging of two styles. The shows included solo material plus a combined set of covers including 'Cathy's Clown', 'Needles and Pins', 'Do Ya' and 'Eight Days a Week'. Mick Ronson joined Rundgren and Hunter for one concert in Cleveland and Ian also appeared briefly in a party scene for a Rundgren film, *The Ever Popular Tortured Artist Effect.* Todd called up everybody he knew for a section which recreated Max's Kansas City, particularly people who had been there. Rundgren's list included Rick Derringer, Hunter and Suzi Ronson.

Ian started recording his next album, tentatively titled *Theatre of the Absurd*, in December, using The Power Station, Wizard Sound and Electric Lady studios in the process. For the sessions he engaged Martin Briley, Tommy Mandel, Tommy Morrongiello, Eric Parker, Georgie Meyer and Ronson. The album was completed at Wessex Studios in London with Bill Price, and was re-titled *Short Back 'n' Sides*.

Ronson had started producing the LP but, by mutual agreement, Mick Jones of The Clash was invited to assist with the production of one song, the reggae-influenced 'Theatre of the Absurd'. Jones then played guitar on some tracks and invited drummer Topper Headon and violinist Tymon Dogg to the sessions, plus Ellen Foley who he was dating. 'It wasn't any major move,' said Ronson. 'We didn't really know how to deal with reggae stuff, so we thought we'd ask Mick to help us out.'

'I met Mick Jones around 1977 and he told me that he'd liked Mott a lot and I started messing around with him,' says Hunter. 'I'd heard what Jones had done on Ellen Foley's album, *Spirit of St. Louis,* and I'd liked the Clash's *Sandanista,* so I knew Mick was good with sound. I was doing "Theatre of the Absurd" and asked him to come down to the Power Station Studio, just before Christmas 1980, to play on the track and it developed from there. We liked him straight-away. He had all kinds of ideas and used the mixing board like a musician. I only asked him to overdub on one track and he kind of took over from there. He stayed for the rest, but did very well. Couldn't argue with him. Very strong personality in the studio, very very strong. Stronger than me. Most upsetting.'

The slight downside for Ian was Jones's apparent fanaticism with him and Mott The Hoople, which made Hunter increasingly cagey of people who cite Mott as a major influence. 'I'm continually wary now, because Mick thought I was God. He really did. I walked in to a Clash session and the whole place went still. Jones said to somebody, "Play him that track." So I listened to this song and he asked me what I thought, and I said, "Yeah, it's fine." And he turned round to the others and said, "It's the blessing." So from then on in, I was put on this God-like level by Mick and he was most upset when he found out I was a perfectly normal bloke. It was because of that, when Joe Elliott and Def Leppard wanted to meet me so bad, I didn't want to meet them, because I thought these people obviously think I'm something that I really am not. When I eventually met Joe though, he was a totally different kettle of fish. You see it is a different person who walks on stage and it is a different person who writes the songs just as it's a different person talking now. I can't walk round like fucking Job all my life, just to please kids!'

Hunter may not have liked the hero persona seen by other artists, but one of music's greatest heroes was sensationally assassinated causing enormous grief on the day Ian commenced the *Short Back* LP. 'Lennon died the night we started recording the album and I guess every session in the world stopped that night. There's an aura on the album on almost every track – "Keep on Burning", "Old Records Never Die", "Central Park 'n' West" and "Gun Control". They weren't about John Lennon so to speak, but they all assumed a different aura because of that incident. The difficulty was how to express the way you felt without being dumb or cliche about it.'

The ten tracks on the LP were all written by Hunter and were selected from a final shortlist of twelve, creating the most varied, diversified and experimental record that Ian had ever made. The record opened with 'Central Park 'n' West', originally a poem of Hunter's which Mick Jones suggested should be set to music. He had written the lyric in New York's Mayflower Hotel and Jones helped with some of the chords during the Wessex sessions. 'I like it,' says Ian. 'Lots of little sounds I'd never have thought of. A little off the norm.'

'Lisa Likes Rock 'n' Roll' saluted Mick Ronson's four-year-old daughter. 'I wanted to write a kids song for her,' said Ian. 'We had a hell of a job getting her to say, "Here's my Daddy," but she did it in the end. I can't remember what the deal was!' The track was described as having the 'radiator and tin can rattle of Bo Diddley.'

Hunter had become good friends with Todd Rundgren and they worked together on "I Need Your Love". Todd took care of the mixing, engineering, bass playing and backing vocals and used fellow Utopia musicians, Gary Windo on sax and Roger Powell on backing vocals. Ian felt unsure of the original recording and an alternative version was recorded with Mick Jones, but the album take was issued as an American single. 'This was done at the back end of the sessions,' says Hunter. 'It was a one off. There was a day where the song worked but we never got it back. It's my fault – I persisted with it.'

"Old Records Never Die" was also recorded in various forms and took on an entirely new perspective in the light of John Lennon's assassination. 'I wrote it originally for Elvis, then the night we recorded it, Lennon died. The atmosphere in the studio was really bad. It was crazy. We went outside in the street and people were running round all over the place going, "It's not true, it's not true." It was a really sad night. Two or three days later it hit us bad. It was so stupid, but then lots of things in life are. The song has a good hook and could have been a single for somebody.'

> Sometimes you realise, that there is an end to life
> Yesterday, I heard them say, a hero's blown away
> And it's so hard to lose, someone who's close to you
> Poor old me, I did not see, the danger every day.

Side One of the record closed with "Noises", another Hunter poem set to music at Jones' insistence. 'I don't think this would've ever got on vinyl if Mick Jones hadn't been around,' said Ian. 'He's responsible for the stop-start stuff at the beginning. I remember Guy Stevens, not in the best of shape, wanted us to lop the intro off – "too pretentious".' The song was credited to Hunter and Morrongiello.

'Rain' opened Side Two and was a peaceful, broody and hypnotic ballad recalling Hunter's youth and naming several of his friends from his early years. 'It's about all my mates in Northampton, a great town at the time. It's a pity you have to leave those years behind. I still think of them and they are very much part of me,' said Ian.

Hunter took a direct shot at the American government and its gun laws with the stunning 'Gun Control'. In the song, he adopted the persona of a gun-crazy psycho to emphasize the point, although one journalist missed the message and sadly called the song irresponsible. 'I feel very strongly about gun control, and always have done. It was written as a piss-take of all the gun freaks in the US,' explains Hunter. The track was a late substitute for 'Na Na Na', which was withdrawn from the record and was recorded in Woodstock with guitarist Mick Baraken, drummer Wells Kelly and bassist John Holbrook, who were effectively the 'house-band' at Bearsville Studios.

> Stick to your guns boys, stick to your guns
> We'll make a lot of money if we stick to the guns
> The president's with us boys, so join in the fun
> We can make a lot of money if we stick to our guns

'Theatre of the Absurd' was Hunter's first and only attempt at a reggae-flavoured piece, inspired, in part, by Ellen Foley's *Spirit of St Louis* album. 'Black kids listening to white kids' music, white kids listening to black kids' music. "Brixton Power" would have been a better title,' says Ian. 'It's a story about the Brixton section of London and the combination of rock and reggae that began to take shape there. The sound of The Clash was Brixton rock, exactly the kind of music I had seen coming as early as 1973. "Theatre of the Absurd" is about a conversation Mick Jones and I had concerning rock 'n' roll. "Theatre of the absurd" is *my* rock 'n' roll, and when I say "*your* theatre of the absurd", I'm talking about his rock 'n' roll.'

The album closed with two unusual love songs. 'Leave Me Alone' spoke soppily of new, young love and was a lyrical contrast to the final track on the album. On reflection, Ian disliked the song, remarking that it showed 'an alarming lack of taste' but he felt it could have originated as a 'mickey take', and it probably did. Conversely, 'Keep on Burning', initially called 'Burning Bridges', was about maintaining current love and, musically, there were signs of Hunter's Leon Russell influences and a distinct gospel flavour.

Short Back 'n' Sides, which Mick Jones christened 'Haircut' courtesy of Ian's new slicked and shorn hairstyle, had originally been scheduled for April 1981 release, but was eventually issued in August. The LP entered the UK chart on 29 August, where it spent two weeks rising to number 79, and eleven weeks reaching number 62 on *Billboard* in America.

Jones' influence on the sessions shone through in the record's trick fadeouts, percussion, odd sounds and liberal echo. Hunter also admits the LP was ambitious, unfocused and contained more styles than any album should. 'It's very different from a production point of view. Then again all my albums tend to change because I like to change a bit now and again. I don't like doing things that people expect. I didn't want to do another one like *Schizophrenic* because I'd done that, so I did something different. I tend to take my time. It takes me maybe two years to do an album and your tastes change. When I did *Schizophrenic,* I was very heavy on bass and drums. When I did *Short Back 'n' Sides* I didn't care. A lot of the songs were demos and they sounded okay so we put them on it. This was much more like a garage album. It wasn't like a studio album.

'It was an interesting record to do. We wrote a lot of stuff in the studio and I met a lot of interesting people. Trudi was pregnant at the time and I was extremely worried about that. Ronson and I were at a loose end and weren't too energetic. I don't know why we were in there, so it became more Mick Jones. That's why we've got peculiar noises on it. Everybody hated the result, but I thought it was quite interesting.'

According to Hunter, Ronson 'was there but he wasn't really there' for the *Short Back* sessions and, predictably, Mick soon departed to record 'More Than You Deserve' for Meatloaf's *Deadringer* LP, with Elton John's guitarist Davey Johnstone. Meanwhile, Ian's album received excellent press reviews including a five-star rating from *Sounds* who said, '*Short Back 'n' Sides* delivers against all the odds. It works. *Short Back* is irresistibly big and loud. Ian Hunter has made the best old rock album of the year thus far. It's a lovely, silly surprise'.

Several songs were omitted from the final LP, including the aforementioned 'Na Na Na', inspired by Little Richard, vocal and instrumental versions of a song called 'Detroit', 'an ode to the American car industry when it was losing out to Japan,' and a ballad, 'China', featuring Ronson on lead vocal. 'We got Mick to sing this because it's a trawler boat song and he was from Hull!' says Ian. John Waite had previously recorded 'Detroit' for his 1982 album *Ignition,* but it was not included on the final track listing.

Chrysalis released one UK single from the *Short Back 'n' Sides* LP, 'Lisa Likes Rock 'n' Roll', backed with 'Noises'. 'Central Park 'n' West'and 'I Need Your Love' were released variously as A-sides in Europe and America.

Ian spoke at the time of the 'new romantics' music which was popular in the UK and he was not impressed. 'I'm not particularly keen on what most of the popular English bands are doing at the moment. I was a little while ago. I just don't see much at the moment. I don't think the world is going to be changed by Adam and the Ants or Duran Duran. That's not to put down the new music, I don't really like it at the moment.'

Hunter decided to promote *Short Back 'n' Sides* by playing live concerts in England, Sweden, Belgium, Holland, Germany and America from August 1981 through to January 1982, including appearances at the Milton Keynes Festival, Cobo Arena in Detroit and Richfield Coliseum in Cleveland. Amazingly, Hunter's group did not include Ronson.

'Every three years Mick wants to be a star, so he was playing for me reluctantly and I wasn't happy with the way he was playing,' explained Ian. 'We argued for about two months. He was playing slow stuff great, but he wanted to go into a country thing. Mick is a very complex character. To explain my relationship with Mick Ronson would take 48 hours. We do play together now and again. Sometimes we do, sometimes we don't. So far we've played together twice and we've not played together twice. At the moment, we're not playing together.'

Ronson formed a new band in 1981, The New York Yanquis, using musicians from The Falcons, who were effectively Bearville Studio's 'house-band' in Woodstock. Mick, with Shane Fontaine (who was Mick Baraken), Frank Campbell (Bryan Briggs), Wells Kelly, Tommy Gun (John Holbrook) and girl singers Ann Lang and Dede Washburn (who also performed in The Falconettes), played seven concerts including Long Island, Massachusetts, Albany, The Agora in Hertford and the Savoy New York. Ronson also helped Lisa Bade on her 1982 album *Suspicion*.

Hunter sought to form a new group and hinted that, because the music on his new album marked a fresh approach, a change of personnel was probably overdue in any case. 'The old band got to know me too well. Some of the others came to me and wanted to do the tour, but three new people were around and were really keen. Somehow Mandel was still there – he was always around. We thought we'd go for a five-piece, instead of a seven-piece, because it had got a bit cumbersome on the faster stuff. This band is capable of thinking independently of me. Musicians like that are hard to find.'

The new group comprised 'old faithful' Tommy Mandel on keyboards, Mark Clarke on bass, drummer Mark Kaufman on drums and guitarist Robbie Altar. Kaufman and Altar had never played in groups of any note, but bassist Clarke had been with Tempest, Rainbow, Stephen Stills and Colosseum.

'I'm very proud of the new band. I know there will be people who say it's better when Mick's with me, but that's not the way of the world. The drummer's never played in front of people before. The bass player's pretty experienced, he was with Stephen Stills, but this is the first band with any kind of name that Robbie's been in. He gets very nervous and it's really difficult for him, because he's standing where Mick used to stand. I tend to go in and out of situations with bands because I tend to get bored with them really quickly. I'm very proud of them and I think in the future, when I look back, I'll still feel the same, because they really got it together quick, when I needed it.'

The Ian Hunter Band played second top of the bill at The Milton Keynes Concert Bowl on 8th August, with Thin Lizzy, Judie Tzuke and Paul Young's Q Tips. The following evening they played an impromptu gig at Clapham's 101 Club in London. Hunter's Rotterdam concert on 16 August was broadcast on radio and his US tour also included a televised appearance at The Dr.Pepper Festival in New York on 11 September which was eventually released as a Chrysalis video in 1990. The live set included several tracks off the new LP plus the usual classics – 'Once Bitten Twice Shy', 'Just Another Night', 'Central Park 'n' West', 'Bastard', 'I Need Your Love' / 'Honky Tonk Women', 'Gun Control', 'Noises', 'Cleveland Rocks', Bob Dylan's 'Is Your Love in Vain?', 'All the Way from Memphis', 'Lisa Likes Rock 'n' Roll', 'Irene Wilde' and a medley of 'All the Young Dudes', 'Roll Away the Stone', 'Honaloochie Boogie' and 'Ships'.

During September, Ian played with Rick Derringer, Todd Rundgren, Ellen Foley, Southside Johnny, Hall and Oates and Edgar Winter at the Hollywood Palladium. The show was a charity concert, put together for Derringer. Back with a ground-breaking album and actively touring with a new band, Hunter's activities were suddenly interupted with tragic news.

22
God bless you, Guy

'Guy Stevens' Poem' – Ian Hunter

On 29 August 1981, Guy Stevens died. When his involvement with Mott The Hoople ended after the *Brain Capers* album sessions, back in the Autumn of 1971, Stevens' career with Island became increasingly destructive and tempestuous. In hindsight, Guy had actually entered a twilight period with Mott, that would send him veering from amazing perceptiveness and creativity to total madness. Had he been able to maintain a modicum of control, he could have secured his rightful status as one of the most important 'producers' in British rock music.

In the early days of Mott The Hoople, Ian Hunter felt Stevens had been at his best. 'He'd just come out of jail, he was clean, he really had a lot of energy. Guy would talk and talk and run round the studio. That was his game, because when you actually got to play, it would come bursting out from his annoying you. Ultimately, that's what he did with The Clash too. He wasn't a producer in the sense that you think. He would get you on the edge. He would have a lot of energy from time to time and, as soon as he did something that was really good, it would slip away again. He couldn't handle success. He always had problems.'

Richard Digby-Smith was a young engineer from Birmingham who joined Island Records in January 1970 and assisted on various albums with Free, Mott The Hoople, Spooky Tooth, John Martyn and Sparks, amongst others. He worked with Stevens on several sessions and rated his ability to draw the best out of the artists he worked with, even if some of Guy's methods were a little unorthodox.

'Guy was very fast, very speedy, and invariably chemically assisted, like a lot of musicians and engineers at that time. But I rated him as a producer. One knew he had a track record, but as a collector and a fan, to be in that stable as a young engineer was hard to believe. Guy had his own special technique. I always feel that you learn a little bit from each engineer or producer that you might have worked with. What I learned from Guy was that, perhaps in the absence of any musical knowledge or musical ability, he could get the best out of a band in the studio, just by his excitement.

'I remember one evening in Island Studio One upstairs. It was the big room, with a large control room, very much like a spaceship, and you used to look out across the whole studio. It was terrific working in there and Mott used to like it. On this particular evening, during the Mott The Hoople session that I was assisting on with Guy, the band had their chins down and nothing sounded good. They couldn't get any drive and they didn't really feel particularly inspired, but they kept plugging away and eventually they were doing a take and it was starting to come together. They were actually getting a good backing track down. Suddenly, Guy leapt onto the desk, actually on the console, and started jumping up and down and started shaking his hands and his fists. Of course, the guys in the studio could see into the control room and could see this maniac shaking his fists and shouting "Yeah", and that was all it took. All you need is just that chemistry between you and the band, and Guy had that, even if it was in a less intellectual, barbaric way at times.

'Guy always seemed to be in a little bit of a mess. I remember seeing him once when he had his whole jaw in a frame. He was all wired up and was black and blue and could hardly talk. The story was that he was leaving a club or a pub, and happened to walk in between two people who were engaged in a fight, and as he walked past, there was Guy's head on the receiving end of a blow that was being thrown. He met it full on.'

Hunter still marvels at Island's patience with Guy. 'Nobody else could have run a company and have Guy Stevens within that organisation; Blackwell was the only one who could have ever done that. Chris was amazing. No matter what Guy did, no matter what Guy got up to, somehow Blackwell could understand him, and that in a record company is hard to find. I don't think Mott The Hoople was Chris Blackwell's favourite band by any means, he liked Free and Traffic and great natural singers and musicians. Mott was a band that wasn't great natural anything, it was just the sum total of what it was, our faults making up the Mott The Hoople sound.'

In spite of Chris Blackwell's understanding, after the recording of *Brain Capers,* increased binges over the next three years and increasing rows between Stevens and Island Records, Guy was forced to part company with the label. The arrangement became impossible. Trevor Wyatt, still part of Island, remembers joining the organisation in 1974, just prior to Guy's departure and witnessing his heavy drinking, particularly the 'Special Brew lunches' which were consumed most days with people like saxophonist Chris Wood and percussionist Reebop Kwaku-Baah both of Traffic, and like Stevens, now both deceased.

Guy's persona had become erratic and his acute alcoholism affected his abilities, with the result that fewer artists considered using him. Having left Island Records, Stevens then worked in A&R with Warner Brothers for a time but frustrated, fought to return to production. 'Mo Ostin wanted him to be an A&R man, and sacked him because he couldn't find anybody,' says Hunter. 'But Guy couldn't find anybody. What's the point of laying half-assed bands on people?'

Stevens chanced on Mick Ralphs again in 1974 while he was recording with Bad Company, after leaving Mott in 1973. Ralphs recalls, 'I was working with Paul Rodgers to get Bad Company together and Guy came round to hear what we'd being doing. We'd just done a version of "Can't Get Enough", a demo or something, but as soon as he heard it, he was jumping up shouting, "Yes that's it! That's going to be a smash hit!" I couldn't really see it. I thought it was alright, not that great, but he said, "Oh yes, that's the one; that's going to be big." And he was right!'

In 1975, Guy produced the only album by Chrysalis band The Winkies, who were fronted by Canadian vocalist Phil Rambow. Stevens took Mick Ronson down to the sessions at one point and Ronson would later do live work with Rambow. Guy also tried to instigate a project at AIR Studios in August of that year with singer Kelvin Blacklock and Mick Jones who had previously played together in groups called The Delinquents and Little Queenie. Mick and Kelvin had both been avid fans of Mott and had travelled widely to watch them in concert, but Jones was considered superfluous by Stevens for the Warner Records showcase.

Guy wanted to create a new Mott The Hoople for Warner Brothers, so he invited Verden Allen to guest on keyboards and also brought in Leo Sayer's drummer, Theodore Thunder. With Bill Price as engineer, Stevens recorded three tracks; a Blacklock composition 'That's Why My Baby (Let Me Go)', a Ramones' cover, 'Slow Death' and a re-make of Mott's 'No Wheels to Ride'. Verden recalls Guy, as eccentric as ever, bringing toy money into the studio to pay for the session.

Guitarist Brady remembered the AIR sessions with Stevens. 'He christened us 'Violent Luck' which was more than apt, Guy being paid £100 per week by Warners just to stay away from their office. Frantic alcohol-fuelled calls to Mo Ostin in the States failed to get us a deal. Wrecked studios, outraged landlords, sulphate binges and unbridled glee were the order of the day. I became his drinking buddy. His Swiss Cottage flat was a *Hello* magazine feature from hell. Thick dust everywhere, fridge full of empty beer cans and a fully inflated life raft in the bedroom, courtesy of Spooky Tooth's Mike Harrison. Mad, bad and dangerous to know, Guy could veer from hysterical laughter to manic depression in one sentence, but by August everything had fizzled out and Guy sought refuge in a river of booze.'

The 'Violent Luck' project aborted, but Mick Jones re-surfaced with Stevens shortly afterwards in The Clash, one of the New Wave's most popular bands. Guy originally worked on some demos for The Clash's debut album in 1977, thanks to their manager Bernie Rhodes, a former Scene attendee, but he didn't produce *The Clash* LP. A 1994 retrospective, *Clash on Broadway,* did feature two previously unreleased demo tracks from the early Guy Stevens sessions, 'Janie Jones' and 'Career Opportunities', which sounded very close to the eventual versions taped for the first album. The CD also included the rare 'Midnight to Stevens', regarded by many as a downbeat and lyrically lacklustre tribute to Guy.

Out of work, Guy went back to Island Records, Blackwell asking director Tim Clark to take Stevens on as a roving A&R man. Clark says, 'Chris was always ready to give it another shot. Guy sat and said, "Look, I've been working in Woolworths – my talent is going to waste. I've got to get back into the business." And we welcomed him back. We knew that he wasn't taking drugs particularly; what we hadn't realised was that alcohol was now the bugbear. He kept disappearing – you wouldn't see him for two or three days. He was just being too unreliable. In the end he disappeared to America and told Chris about how awful the company was and then broke up his hotel room in New York. He was, in the end, a rather desperate figure. He lasted less than a year.'

David Betteridge recalls, 'It was an uncomfortable period, because Island had moved on and there wasn't a place for him anymore. He brought the company up as a baby and now it was a youth, and he didn't like some of the things that youth was doing.'

Hunter confirms that Stevens would oscillate between drugs and alcohol, using one to supress the other in turn, during a slow downward spiral. 'Guy felt his mother didn't like him, too, which gave him a tremendous inferiority complex. He really had great difficulty simply living.'

Stevens was given another chance in 1979 to produce a Clash album. Originally titled *The New Testament,* the double LP, re-named *London Calling,* became one of the most revered records of the eighties and marked a major comeback for Guy. CBS Records had demanded a name producer to take charge of the third Clash album and the band opted for Stevens, partly for his inspiration and influence, but also because they could do what they wanted while Guy passed out under the mixing desk. Stevens was still drinking heavily and guitarist Joe Strummer had to track Guy down in a London pub to ask him to produce the record. During the sessions Stevens would often telephone Ian Hunter in America for pep talks, claiming that he couldn't continue. Hunter continually told him to 'stop pissing about' but allegedly, engineer Bill Price ended up making many of the production decisions. Mick Jones still spoke highly of Stevens' input describing Guy as a driving force and catalyst.

Drummer Topper Headon recalled the sessions. ' "Brand New Cadillac" was the first track we did. We were just running it through and didn't know it was being recorded and at the end, Guy said, "That's it!" I said, "Guy, you can't keep that one, it speeds up." And he said, "Great. All rock 'n' roll speeds up. Take!" '

The Clash sessions at Wessex in North London were littered with incident, reminiscent of Guy's studio smashing routines with Mott The Hoople. Mick Jones recalled various episodes including the time Guy lay in front of the head of CBS Records' Rolls Royce and his fights with Bill Price. According to Jones and Strummer, Guy also trashed a pile of chairs, poured beer into the piano and television, blew up the desk, and threw ladders at Jones. Guy would also come into the studio yelling and put on a recording of an Arsenal Cup Final, stand in front of the speakers with outstretched arms, waving a scarf and joining in with the chants. Strummer felt Guy's contribution was to give a crazed edge to proceedings and, like Digby-Smith, he learned that Stevens' *modus operandi* was to get a performance out of the band using any method he could, at full throttle if necessary.

London Calling is considered Stevens' great finale however, and by some, one of the finest albums of that period. Once described as 'a glorious rewriting of pop history, mashed up and spat out by a band at the peak of its powers, or perhaps the work of a group that was all over the place like a lunatic's breakfast, with an alcoholic at the helm,' the double LP became a top-ten UK album and hit the top thirty in the USA. The success of the album should have heralded a renewed career for Guy, but resistance to work with him remained. Jones was regretful that *London Calling* was voted best album of the eighties by *Rolling Stone* magazine, and Guy didn't live to see it.

In December 1979, Guy reflected on his work with Charles Shaar Murray and claimed that he never really recovered from working with Mott The Hoople. 'The real trouble with Ian is that he takes himself so seriously,' said Guy. However in contradictory tone, Stevens went on to say, 'Making a record is an event. Big letters; AN EVENT. It's not just 'another session'. I hate people with that attitude. I could quite well die while making a record. It's that important. That's why – if it came to it – I could produce anybody.' Guy explained, 'There are only two Phil Spectors in the world, and I am one of them!'

RIGHT Ian's parents, Walter and Freda
Patterson *(Trudi Hunter)*

OVE Freddie Lee & The Shriekers, March 1964.
ft to right: Lee, Tony Marriott, Ian Patterson, Julian
ulter *(Fred Cheeseman)*

RIGHT Ian and daughter Tracey at Hornsey Open Air Pool
in North London, 1967 *(Fred Cheeseman)*

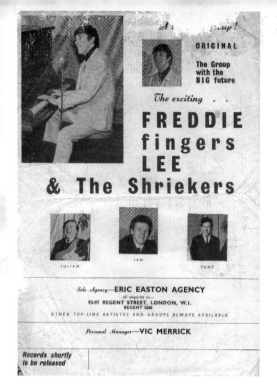

ABOVE LEFT Freddie Fingers Lee & The Shriekers: 1964 unpublished handbill featuring Fred,
Ian, Julian Coulter and Tony Marriott (*Fred Cheeseman*)

ABOVE RIGHT At Last the 1958 Rock & Roll Show, 1968. Top down: Pete Phillips, Ian Patterson,
Freddie Fingers Lee, Miller Anderson (*Fred Cheeseman*)

BELOW Charlie Woolfe, 1968. Left to right: Anderson, Lee, Phillips, Patterson (*Fred Cheeseman*

The Buddies,
September 1965

Left to right:
Stan Tippins,
Mick Ralphs,
Bob Hall,
Cyril Townsend
(*Stan Tippins*)

Promotional card for
The Buddies, 1965

Mick Ralphs in The Buddies, January 1966
Bat Cave Club, Cortina d'Ampezzo, Italy
(*Mick Ralphs*)

ABOVE The Soulents at Walford Fete, Ross-on-Wye, Herefordshire, 18 May 1964 (*Dale Griffin*)

BELOW Doc Thomas Group in 1966. Left to right: Mick Ralphs, Dave Tedstone, Stan Tippins, Bob Hall, Peter Watts (*Mick Ralphs*)

ABOVE The Inmates, Hereford, 1964. Left to right: Gerry Broad, Brian Pilling, Dave Scudder, Tony Breen, Terry Allen *(Verden Allen)*

LEFT Lee Starr and the Astrals, 1966.
Rear: Dave Tedstone, Terry Allen.
Front: Rob Harris, Percy Francis, Lee Starr (Jon Best) *(Verden Allen)*

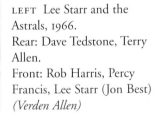

LEFT Terry Allen with Jimmy Cliff and The Shakedown Sound, Voom Voom Club, St Tropez, France, July 1967 *(Verden Allen)*

Silence poster, 1969
(Dale Griffin)

Overend Watts in his 'room' at
20b Lower Sloane Street, Chelsea, London,
May 1969 *(Dale Griffin)*

ABOVE Guy Stevens and Buffin at Hampstead Country Club, London, 1971 *(Dale Griffin)*

LEFT Mott The Hoople on their second US Tour, Eastown Theatre, Detroit, Michigan, 18 June 1971. Left to right: Ralphs, Watts, Hunter, Buffin, Allen *(Dale Griffin)*

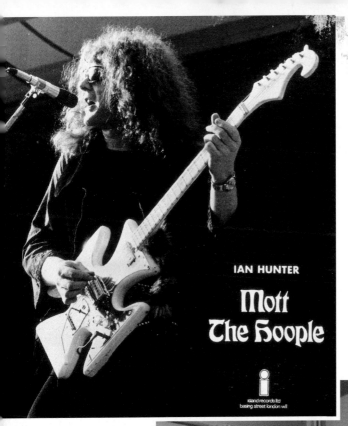

IAN HUNTER

Mott
The Hoople

island records ltd
basing street london w11

LEFT Hunter with infamous Maltese Cross at the Oval Festival, London, 18 September 1971 *(Sony Music / Island Records)*

RIGHT Ian Hunter, Verden Allen and promoter Mel Bush, backstage at the Rainbow Theatre, North London, 14 November 1971 *(Dale Griffin)*

LEFT Mott The Hoople 'front line'. Left to right: Hunter, Ralphs (with white Gibson Firebird), Watts, at the Rainbow, London, 14 November 1971 *(Dale Griffin)*

I am lonely for you all! I miss the 'SOUND'. I wish I could adopt you - Can't afford it - I wish you all - collectively and individually - BEST of luck, plus a HIT single. I loved the tour and the emotional cacophony. I hope you were NOT sending me up?? LOVE. WALL.

Mott the Hoople
c/o Island Artistes.
10. Basing St.
LONDON. W. 11.

MOUNTED SENTRY, HORSE GUARDS, LONDON   PT1015

ABOVE Max Wall postcard to
'his boys', 1972 (Dale Griffin)

RIGHT Max Wall and
Ian Hunter, Basing Street, London,
April 1972 (Ian Hunter)

BELOW Verden Allen with group
Ford Zodiac, Stonor Road,
London, 1972 (Dale Griffin)

LEFT Original *All the Young Dudes* album sleeve photograph, 1972 *(Mick Rock / Sony Music)*

BELOW David and Angie Bowie during *All the Young Dudes* album sessions at Trident Studios, Soho, London, June 1972 *(Dale Griffin)*

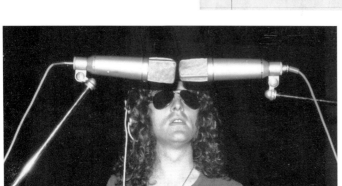

VIOLENCE

VIOLENCE – VIOLENCE, AIN'T NOTHING ELSE
GONNA MAKE YOU SEE SENSE.

MISSING LINK, POOLROOM STINK, I CAN'T TALK
WHAT'S GOIN ON, SOMETHIN'S WRONG, I CAN'T WORK
CAN'T GO TO SCHOOL TEACHER'S A FOOL, PREACHER'S A JE
NOTHIN TO DO, STREET CORNER BLUES, NOWHERE TO WALK

GOTTA FIGHT, NOTHIN RIGHT, LIVIN NOWHERE
WATCH OUT FOR THE GUN, SNAKE ON RUN, HIDE IN MY HAIR
KEEP YOUR MOUTH SHUT, OR YOU'LL GET CUT, I LIKE TO SCA
I'M A BATTERY LOUSE, SUPERSTAR MOUSE, N' I DON'T CARE
GET OFF MY BACK OR I'll ATTACK I DON'T OWE YOU NOTHIN
HEAD FOR YOUR HOLE, YOU'RE SICK N' YOU'RE OLD N' I'm HERE
TO TELL YOU SOMETH

LEFT Hunter during 'Mot
album session at AIR No.
Studio, London, March 19
(*Dale Griffin*)

RIGHT Ian with newly-weds
Mr & Mrs T. D. Griffin at
Brent Registry Office,
London, 13 December 1973
(*Dale Griffin*)

LEFT Watts in a spin with
white Gibson Thunderbird, 1973
(*Dale Griffin / Sony Music*)

OPPOSITE Presentation of gold discs
Soho Square, London, 19
Left to right: Grosvenor, Watts, Hun
Richard M. Asher (CBS Managing Directo
Griffin, Fisher (*Sony Mu*

ABOVE LEFT Mott The Hoople Mark III: Watts, Griffin, Grosvenor, Hunter.
Los Angeles 1974 *(Sony Music)*
ABOVE RIGHT Ian and Trudi Hunter, Long Island, New York, 1973 *(Ian Hunter)*

ABOVE LEFT Overend, Ian and Trudi with Irwin Siegelstein of CBS, backstage at the Uris Theatre, Broadway, New York, May 1974 *(Sony Music)*

ABOVE RIGHT Mott at Earl's Court, London, 1975. Rear: Nigel Benjamin, Overend Watts, Ray Major. Front: Buffin, Morgan Fisher *(Sony Music)*

LEFT Eric Bloom of Blue Oyster Cult (disguised as Morgan Fisher) with Morgan Fisher at the Old Waldorf Club, San Francisco, September 1978 *(Morgan Fisher)*

BELOW 'If only!' – Mott The Hoople Mark IV. Left to right: Watts, Hunter, Ronson, Griffin, Fisher, at Mick Ronson's flat, Kensington, London, September 1974 *(Sony Music)*

ABOVE Dale Griffin, with Mike Robinson, at BBC Langham Studio, London W1, February 1981 *(Dale Griffin)*

LEFT Lord Peter Overend Watts with Joan Sims (18lb Carp), Woodchester Lake, 18 June 1997 *(Pete Watts)*

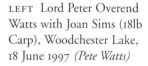

LEFT The Cheeks in Kensington Gardens, London (opposite Royal Albert Hall), 1975. Rear: Kelvin Wilson, Martin Chambers. Front: James Honeyman Scott, Verden Allen *(Verden Allen)*

ABOVE LEFT Ian Hunter at California's, Windsor, Ontario, Canada,
16 November 1987 *(Alan Smith)*
ABOVE RIGHT Mick Ronson at Rock 'n' Roll Heaven, Toronto, Canada,
11 May 1988 *(Alan Smith)*

LEFT Ian Hunter with Bob
Dylan, New York, 1985
(Ian Hunter)

Although clear of drugs at this stage, Guy was suffering from serious drink problems and would disappear for days at a time, or often end up fighting or passing out in the studio. On 29 August 1981, at 38 years of age, Guy Stevens died at his mother's home in South London, when he overdosed on prescription drugs he was using to reduce his alcohol dependency and suffered a heart attack.

At the time of his death, Guy had been working on a possible comeback album by Twinkle, Lynn Annette Ripley, who had recorded six singles for Decca Records in the mid-sixties, most notably 'Terry', a number-four chart hit. Stevens produced a re-working of The Left Banke's 'Walk Away Renee' for Twinkle, but this was rejected in favour of another cover version, The Monkees' 'I'm a Believer', released by EMI in April 1982.

Guy's funeral in South London was attended by Dale Griffin, Pete Watts and Verden Allen together with members of The Clash and various Island Records personnel. 'Guy was such a big figure and yet the funeral was a small affair,' says Watts. 'They played "A Whiter Shade of Pale" and "Visions of Johanna" at such a low volume, and I could visualize Guy screaming, "Turn it up!" It was a sad occasion. There were absurdities too, Guy's mother saying to Twinkle, "So you were working on a record with Guy? Well, he can't finish it now, he's dead." The Clash were distraught and white, and had to go out at one point to smoke a joint.'

Of all his work, Stevens' involvement with Mott The Hoople is most widely known and remembered, and although his remaining musical output was not of the very highest profile, Guy's technique remains unique and his influence incalculable.

Ian Hunter had seen Guy Stevens a few weeks before his death and knew the end was near. 'You just knew he was going to go. You couldn't understand what he was saying and you just knew. A lot of people shed a tear when Guy went. It wasn't totally unexpected, but we felt shattered because he was never happy. By any normal standard he was a fool, but he wasn't. He knew about rock 'n' roll. Guy was one of those fascinating people you only meet once in a lifetime.

'The fondest memories of Guy are invisible, and that was his whole problem, Guy's talent was invisible. It frustrated the shit out of him, too. When he sang it was like a horse in trouble, it was awful, trying to get his point across at times. Guy, like me, did not have any apparent talent on the surface. You had to dig down and Guy dug down into me, which was an amazing compliment. You know, a lot of people in England don't even know they're living, they just exist. There's the football on a Saturday, there's work, there's the moaning, there's the mates, they don't actually know they're here. Until Guy actually paid me that enormous compliment of talking to me, about me, I never really knew I existed, I just sort of went on. That was Guy's genius, finding things in people that weren't really there. It wasn't only me, he found it in other people too, where the talent wasn't immediately apparent. Somebody like me would have no chance nowadays, absolutely no chance at all.

'Guy could be a total maniac, too. He always drove his car slow if the song was slow, and he always drove the car fast if the song was fast. We were in a pub in Hampstead Heath one night, and I made the mistake of getting in the car with him when we were listening to this track that went slow and fast, "Half Moon Bay". Now Guy never had much regard for roads, he just drove. So we were on the Heath in the middle of the night and it was misty, and we could have hit somebody quite easily as he's driving all over the park screaming about this track. He was so madly enthused and all of a sudden, the quick bit came and you were off at high speed, and then it would go slow and he'd screech on the brakes. And this is what life with Guy would be like.

'You'd go round to his house and you'd have to ask, "Where's the toilet Guy?" because there was a hole in the floor. He more than once broke into Basing Street because he felt it was getting too big and that Island was going corporate and losing its originality. Guy would smash the place up and Chris would come down the following day and simply say, "Clear it up, put the furniture back." '

Hunter does question the label of 'producer' for Guy Stevens and emphasises that his methods were completely unorthodox and strange to say the least. 'Guy wasn't the slightest bit interested in production. He was called a 'producer', but people found that out to their cost, when they tried to emulate us later on. Guy believed complete lunacy was the answer. We would sit in the control room and he would start on a train of thought and take it through the roof, through the clouds, through the ozone and it was amazing to listen to this stream of consciousness. Then, five minutes later, you'd be playing and this stuff was coming out. "When My Mind's Gone" is a case in point. There was a telepathic thing going on. He couldn't do it, but I was supposed to do it for him. I was his channel. Things got very intense around the time of *Mad Shadows*.'

Ian would write 'Guy Stevens' Poem' for inclusion on his next solo album and Patrick Campbell-Lyons, of former Island group Nirvana, who knew Guy in the late sixties, would similarly record a spoken tribute, 'The Indiscreet Harlequin'. He described Guy during his Island days as 'A&R man, talent scout, art director, producer, image maker and provider of joints – an amalgamation of mushroom hair, sheepskin coat and rainbow scarf.' Campbell-Lyons told of his invitation to the launch party for *London Calling*, where he discovered Guy's former smile had frighteningly become a manic grin, and his final sighting of Stevens, slumped on a bench near Swiss Cottage, which was a sad and shocking experience for him. He knew the end of Guy's story was near.

Jeff Dexter, who had been a 'rival' disc jockey at the Lyceum while Stevens worked The Scene Club, remembers his final meeting with Guy, just before his death. Stevens had hurled verbal abuse at an acoustic group in Dingwalls club on that particular evening, but wanted to fight Jeff when he tried to calm Guy down. 'The end was very sad,' recalls Dexter.

Tony Brainsby, Mott's publicist, describes Guy as an erratic figure but recalls Steven's undying passion for music, right until the end of his life. 'He was a mentor, manager and producer for Mott The Hoople, but he would always flit off on to other projects. He was really a will o'the wisp character and was never a true manager anymore that he was ever a true producer. He was an instigator. I hadn't heard of Guy for years, and I'd been helping Paul McCartney for a long time. The night that Lennon got shot, Guy phoned me up at four o'clock in the morning when it had been confirmed, and he was in tears.'

Richard Digby-Smith remembers Stevens with affection. 'There was a certain genre of producers who weren't particularly musical per se, they probably couldn't play a musical instrument or wouldn't know an E Flat if one landed in their lap, but they had an ear for being able to fashion a good record. Guy was one of those. He wasn't particularly interested in the chord shapes on the guitar or the notes on the piano, he used to leave the music to the musicians, but he had an ear for a hook. He sometimes appeared sad and pathetic, but music seemed like everything to him, almost to the exclusion of everything else. He liked to laugh and he had a great laugh. He was a lovely, warm, wild man with a nice sense of humour. I'm so glad I had the pleasure of working with him.'

Dale particularly recalls Guy's enthusiasm for Mott and his motivation of the group. 'During the difficulties of the early days, Guy Stevens would tell us over and over, 'You *are* The Rolling Stones. You *are* Bob Dylan. You are up there with them. You are better than them.' We believed him after a while – there was no alternative. Guy was beyond normality and everybody was so affected by what Guy did. He was brutal with material selection and his instinct was good.'

Mick Ralphs had been the first of the group to meet Stevens. 'I loved Guy. He was a genius, but of course like all geniuses, he was wracked with pain and was a tortured soul. He was a wonderful man, though and very passionate about what he did. If he believed in something he would do anything for it. Like Pete Watts, he had great ideas and he was the catalyst for Mott The Hoople. He instigated our wildness, although it was probably in there I think, and he encouraged it.'

Pete Watts says of Stevens, 'Guy was tone deaf, totally unmusical, couldn't sing in tune or hear a mistake on tape and really had no sense of rhythm but, God, did he make up for it in other departments. He used to motivate the group by screaming things at us. Lots of people have got something special buried in them, but they haven't got the courage to let it out. Guy gave us that courage. We were timid tigers in a cage, and Guy opened the door and let us out at everybody's throats.'

Diane Stevens, separated but not divorced from Guy in the late seventies, remembers her final discussion with Guy one Friday evening. It was optimistic and buoyant. He was trying to avoid drink and drugs, intended to move out of his mother's flat and was going to re-launch the Sue label. The Sunday telephone call from Guy's mother was all the more surprising and devastating.

Diane believes Mott The Hoople's music was real rock 'n' roll, warts and all, and that that was an essential ingredient for Guy, who was unique and ahead of his time. 'That was what was sad about it. All those records that he imported, all the things he tried to do with Mott The Hoople, they all live on. But at the time, people don't really appreciate that.'

* * *

Guy Stevens' Poem

Guy – what am I supposed to say about you
Crazy – restless – on the move
You found a me I never knew
And you loved me and I loved you

So off we went – the beginning of me
Wrote a few songs into history
Most never knew the gift you sent
But then most people ain't one hundred percent

I had to do something just for you
I wasn't lazy and I've tried to be true
You were my father – you were my son
Maybe you felt your work was done

For you dealt in beginnings – never in ends
You dealt in magic so you had few friends
I watched your vivid colours fade
As you had to face the corporate jade

To you the best was all that matters
You screamed, you cried, put down 'n' flattered
And they never did give you much respect
Your talent was too indirect

Don't rest in peace – insult me on!
Or nothing will change because you're gone
Thanks a lot for believing in me
You know how I feel privately

Some tears were shed in the world tonight
For the man who never got living right
A friend got off the phone just now
I gotta get to sleep somehow

I'll be rehearsing tomorrow at SIR
Still trying to be your superstar
'N if I don't make it – when we're through
Don't worry 'bout me – I'll be blaming you

I remember the guy with the electric hair
At that first rehearsal standing there
You gave your heart – you gave your soul
God bless you Guy – rock 'n' roll!

– Ian Hunter, 1983

23
Take another roller coaster ride

After Guy's death, rumours circulated that Mott The Hoople might re-unite to pay tribute to the man who originally founded, managed and produced the band, but it was not to be.

'Four of us have been talking about it,' admitted Ian at the time. 'Mick Ralphs, Pete Watts, Buffin and myself. Whether it'll happen or not I don't know. We're talking about doing an album and I'd like to do it. Apart from Ralphs, I haven't played with them for years. It would be interesting to see where they're at now. The music would probably be totally different. My suggestion was that we left two months out of our schedules to do that, and then no one would go in with any pre-conceived ideas. It would just be Mott The Hoople now, rather than trying to do something that we did a long time ago.'

During one of his visits to England, Ian met up with his former Mott colleagues in London. The plan was for Hunter, Ralphs, Watts, Griffin, Fisher and Scorpions' guitarist Michael Schenker to commence recording at Wessex Studios. 'There was talk of finding a studio, but this was at 11 at night after a huge amount of champagne,' says Dale. 'Nothing came of it, but it was a great convivial evening. It went from 8 in the evening until dawn, and was great fun. There was no pressure, no fighting. Just five people having a chat about old times.

'The problems involved overcame the initial enthusiasm. There was an agreement while the group was going, that having stopped, we would at some point get back together again. In 1981 we all agreed to do a special re-union on the B.A. Robertson television show. It was going to be a really big thing. What it actually came down to was a three-minute slot. The producer said, "Can you do a medley of three of your hits?" at which point I told her to "Fuck off". The show turned out to be so piss-poor anyway, and their plans for us so small time, that I was very relieved to have pulled us out.

'I think the perception of Mott's success is much greater than the reality,' remarks Griffin. 'We had fantastic publicity. People thought we were much more successful than we actually were. The only problem with getting Mott The Hoople back together again is the possibility of ruining the rosy memories people have of those days, not least of all our own.'

After completion of the *Short Back 'n' Sides* tour, Ian split his band and left Chrysalis Records, Cleveland International and his manager Steve Popovitch. His musical activities started to take a lower profile for the next five or six years as he moved out of Manhattan and took Trudi and his baby son, Jess, to a new house in upstate New York.

Ronson in the meantime, kept busy on several fronts. He helped John Cougar Mellencamp on his album *American Fool* and, completely uncredited, transformed one of John's discarded songs in to a number-one US hit single, as Mellencamp acknowledges. 'I owe Mick Ronson the song "Jack and Diane". Mick was very instrumental in helping me arrange that. As a matter of fact I'd thrown that song on the junk heap and we were down in Miami making that record, and Ronson came down and played on three or four tracks and worked on *American Fool* for about four or five weeks. With "Jack and Diane", he came in and suggested putting percussion on there and then he sang the part, "let it rock, let it roll," as a choirish-type thing, which never occured to me. It was Mick's idea and I reckon that's the part everybody remembered on the song any-way. All of a sudden the song worked.'

Early in 1982, during a visit to A&M Records in Toronto, Mick agreed to work with Canadian group, The Payola$, and produced their second album, *No Stranger to Danger*, in Vancouver, contributing keyboards and backing vocals. The LP was affectionately dedicated to Alex Harvey who had collapsed on stage during a European tour and died while the album was being recorded. Ronson would later work with Canadian artist Rick Rose including his bands Lennex, Perfect Affair and as a solo artist.

Ronson appeared on stage at a Sunday Peace Rally concert in the Rose Bowl Pasadena, California during June, Bob Dylan, The Band, Linda Ronstadt, Jackson Browne, Tom Petty and the Heartbreakers, Crosby Stills and Nash and Donovan all performing at the event. Mick also worked on The Who's 1982 US Tour, playing with supporting artist T-Bone Burnett, and turning down a much more 'profitable' offer. Hunter admired the fact that Ronson always stood up for what he believed in. 'Mick played with T-Bone for $100 a week. His wife was having kittens because Bob Seger wanted him for $2,500 a week, but he liked T-Bone and didn't want to play just basic chords.'

In 1982, Hunter accepted The Musical Syndrome Award from the students of Ohio State University in appreciation of his long and creative career in rock. During this period, Ian also wrote a song called 'You're Messing with the King of Rock 'n' Roll', in furious response to Albert Goldman's controversial biography on Elvis Presley. The track has never been released. 'It was a good song, in Rockabilly style, like Queen's "Crazy Little Thing Called Love",' says Hunter. 'I hated that book and I think people like Goldman should be shot.'

The early eighties saw the release of more Mott The Hoople compilations. Budget label Pickwick issued *All the Way from Memphis* in 1981, containing a good selection of tracks and 1982 saw a Mott reissue in the German CBS *Rock Giants* series. The usual hits were included but for once the selection of album tracks on the German release was wider than most, including 'Sea Diver', 'Alice', 'Pearl 'n' Roy' and live versons of 'Sucker' and 'Rest In Peace'.

By the winter of 1982 Ian was working in Wizard Sound Studios, New York State on his next LP, *All of the Good Ones are Taken*, having re-signed with Columbia Records. He decided to collaborate with producer Max Norman and for the sessions used Tommy Mandel, Mark Clarke, Robbie Altar and Hilly Michaels. Various guest musicians featured on the record including Dan Hartman, Clarence Clemmons, Bob Mayo and Mick Ronson on one track. Norman was credited as producing the album in association with Hunter. 'Max was just great,' says Ian. 'He really hangs in there, 24 hours a day, to get the job done. He produced Ozzy Osbourne and Bad Company, more hard rock stuff than me really, but he did a great job on my record.'

All of the tracks were Hunter compositions except two songs which he had co-written with Clarke and Michaels and, in similar vein to *All American Alien Boy*, Ian made lyrical assaults on several controversial topics including US television, government nuclear policy and the recent Falklands War between Britain and Argentina.

'All of the Good Ones are Taken' was recorded both as a fast and slow version, in pointedly different moods, to open and close the album. The first track was the up-tempo song, and Ian explained why he had recorded two versions. 'I originally did the slow version for the album and that was the one I wanted to release. They would not have it as a single though. So they asked me to record a fast version of "Good Ones", which I did, like a fucking idiot. Even my wife was saying to me. You see, it was written fast, but then I lost the tape of the session and I could never get the groove back. I never found it again, so it only worked as a ballad for me after that. The video was good though. My first proper video.'

'Every Step of the Way' was described by Ian as 'a smutty, dumb, love song.' 'I mean good dumb, like "Woolly Bully", that's the rhythmic feel I wanted. I usually have one song like this on all of my albums.' Composed by Hunter and Clarke, the track was subsequently covered by The Monkees on their 1987 album *Pool It!* 'Fun' was also co-written by Hunter, Clarke and Michaels. 'There's a sort of desperation about this one, like "we have to have fun, whether it's really fun or not, we're gonna have it." I was just thinking that in general, fun doesn't seem to be what it used to be!'

'Speechless' was the first of two songs on the album about the absurdity of television:

> Everytime I watch you
> Gotta switch you off
> You surely can't be serious
> Everytime I see you
> I just can't believe
> You go below ridiculous

'It's written as though it's sung to a person you're fed up with,' remarked Ian. 'There's a nice sort of ambiguity in there, which I like, so it could go either way. But I was thinking of the TV when I wrote it and when I sang it. It came from noticing how much time people, kids included, spend just sitting there passive in front of the television.' 'Speechless' was covered by Status Quo on their 1986 LP *In the Army Now.*

Mick Ronson played his usual shattering lead guitar on 'Death 'n' Glory Boys', a comment on the Falklands War. Britain felt obliged to defend the Islands in 1982 after an invasion by Argentina, at a time when British Prime Minister Margaret Thatcher's mid-term popularity was waning slightly.

> When your head is on the scaffold
> And your ass is on the line

You gotta give it that ole religion one mo' time
Bring out the death 'n' glory boys

'This was inspired by the Falklands,' admits Ian. 'It wasn't particularly about The Falklands, it was just the idea of 18-year-olds getting topped, or in Argentina's case, 15-year-olds. Just the thought that old men could get together and fuck around with people getting killed. It's not a political thing, I wouldn't want to put my nose in that. But I have a 17-year-old daughter and it's frightening that a kid can be killed that young.'

Side Two of the record kicked off with the basic and self-explanatory 'That Girl is Rock and Roll', but 'Somethin's Goin' On' was a more serious commentary referring to nuclear warfare. The lines 'The world is a subway, all the leaders are muggers', 'Just do what we say, then we'll blow you all away' and 'We'll watch you die in vain, from the safety of our plane' demonstrated distrust and dislike of political leaders. 'It's just what the average guy on the street, meaning me, thinks after reading the papers and trying to figure out why things happen the way they do, and then giving up and getting disgusted by it all. It may be cynical, but I really think it's the way some people feel,' explained Hunter.

Ian addressed the absurdity of television once more in 'Captain Void 'n' the Video Jets', but this time in comical mood. 'It was just another comment on the power TV has over people,' said Hunter, 'only here it's a funny sort of fantasy. The aliens land and take us over through our TV screens. I guess I must have been playing a video game and losing before I came up with this one!'

'Seeing Double' displayed desperation, as Hunter explains. 'It's a bit like "All of the Good Ones", a sad little song about when you feel you're at the end of your rope. It was written and improvised live in the studio and we recorded it live in the studio as well. I really liked Bob Mayo, the keyboard player. He was very organic and "Seeing Double" was the same.'

Doctor, Doctor, am I alright?
I keep on stayin' up, all through the night
Smokin', drinkin', watchin' TV 'til the light
It's been a long time since I last slept
All I seem to think about is what I ain't yet
I'm seeing double

The album closed with a slower version of the title track. 'The title was just a sort of cliche, something people say at odd moments. Lines like that often spark a song for me like "once bitten twice shy". Anyway, the feeling of it is bittersweet, lost love, the feeling you get at the end of a romance, that that's just it!'

All of the Good Ones are Taken was released by Columbia Records in July 1983 and failed to chart in the UK aided by an appalling lack of promotion. In America the album reached number 125 on the *Billboard* chart where it spent a total of eleven weeks. The cover featured a photo of Ian minus shades and the inner sleeve to the record contained Hunter's touching 'Guy Stevens' Poem'. Columbia also issued two singles from the album. The first had the faster version of the title track as the A-side, backed with 'Death 'n' Glory Boys', but a limited edition twelve-inch disc was also released in the UK containing a rare bonus track, 'Traitor'. Written by Ian, in 'Bastard' vein, this up-tempo song was superb lyrically and featured stupendous piano playing from Tommy Mandel. Ian also filmed a video to promote the 'All of the Good Ones are Taken' single, the storyline being a humorous play on Dudley Moore's comedy movie *Arthur*. The second UK single release was 'Somethin's Goin' On' while America opted for 'That Girl is Rock 'n' Roll'.

Press reviews for the singles and album were virtually non-existent and, in one case, even inaccurate, stating that the record was issued on Chrysalis, Ian's former label. By Hunter's own admission, he was now out in a musical wilderness and he left Columbia Records a short time later, after considerable upheaval at the label.

'I went back to Columbia again because Dick Asher, Mott's old boss at CBS, was president. Then, four weeks after I signed, he got fired. It was one of the worst days of my life. The record came out and they didn't do anything to push it. They shoved it out the back door like they were embarrassed or something. Then they asked me to do another one, which I wasn't signed to do, and I couldn't understand why they'd want me to do that quite honestly, because I had no good songs and the ones I'd just given them they hadn't done anything with. So rather than do another record, I got my manager to try and get me a situation where I could experiment, and Columbia gave me a sixteen-track studio.' Ian would use this for demos and film soundtrack work, but he left the label and renewed management links with Steve Popovitch and Sam Lederman at Cleveland International.

In the autumn of 1983, it was announced in the press that Ian was to make his acting debut in a movie. 'Ian Hunter, known for his hell raising days fronting Mott The Hoople, is to become wheelchair bound. But it's not for reasons of health. Hunter has landed his first film role. He is to play two parts, in a horror tale called *The Graduation*, as a 53-year-old paralysed professor, with a nasty habit of doing away with people, and a rock and roll musician. The film, his first stab at acting, is a small scale affair by Hollywood standards, with a budget of £1,600,000.'

'I get offered film parts and scores all the time,' says Ian, 'but it's always some dumb movie about groupies and cocaine. I remember one movie opportunity after *All of the Good Ones are Taken*. A guy wanted me to do it but I said, "I can't act, well maybe I can, but you're taking a chance here." They said, "No, we just want you to do what you did in that video." It was all looking good, until it came to the financing.'

Ian received a further film opportunity when Sam Lederman introduced a director from Chicago. 'He had some amazing ideas and then he died, so if I'm ever going to be in a movie it's not yet,' says Hunter. Ironically, Ian's son Jess would make an appearance in a 1996 US film, *Sleepers*. Based on a famous sixties book, the movie was filmed in Newtown, Connecticut near the Hunter's home. 'Jess phoned one day and told me he was in this movie. I said, "Who's in it?" thinking it was a school movie. He says, "Kevin Bacon, some guy DeNiro, and who's the bloke in *The Graduate*?" I said, "Dustin Hoffman. What the hell are you talking about?" So Jess was in this film set in a reform school.'

During 1983 in Canada, Hunter worked on a track called 'I'll Find Another (Who Can Do It Right)', for The Payola$' third LP, *Hammer on a Drum* which was being produced by Ronson. Mick contributed keyboards and backing vocals again, as on their previous album. The track featuring Ian was originally entitled 'Dancing with Another' but this changed by virtue of Hunter's involvement. The Payola$ went on to win four honours at the 1983 Canadian Juno Awards.

In Canada, Mick also recorded an album entitled *Whomanforsays*, with Lisa Dalbello, and toured in support of the record. His work in Toronto led to a brief Bowie–Ronson re-union, when Mick joined David on stage at one of his concerts to play 'Jean Genie'. Perfect Affair and The Visible Targets were two more bands to receive Ronson's production and recording contributions.

By autumn 1983, Ronson was approached to produce a new album for Tina Turner, which was to include versions of David Bowie's '1984', 'Let's Stay Together' and The Beatles' 'Help'. 'Capitol Records asked me to work with Tina Turner,' said Mick. 'We met and talked a lot, then I booked the studio, but it all fell through.' The eventual album, *Private Dancer*, was a significant hit record and rejuvenated Turner's career.

Around this time, Ian wrote with Eric Bloom and Donald Roeser of Blue Oyster Cult, 'Let Go' being included on their *Revolution by Night* LP. Hunter had previously collaborated with Bloom co-writing 'Going through the Motions', issued on their 1977 album *Spectres* and subsequently covered by Bonnie Tyler on her 1983 LP, *Faster than the Speed of Light*.

Ronson worked with T-Bone Burnett on *Proof through the Night* in 1984, featuring on three tracks, 'The Murder Weapon', 'Pressure' and 'The Sixties', the last with Pete Townshend. Mick also played with an early version of The Power Station in New York, including Tommy Price, John Taylor from Duran Duran, Bernard Edwards from Chic and Billy Idol's guitarist, Steve Stevens. When the recording sessions eventually began for their LP, Ronson was 'unavailable'. Hunter subsequently held *The Power Station* album in high regard and this would influence his selection of Edwards as producer for a Hunter Ronson album in 1989.

Ian co-wrote four songs for Hanoi Rocks' *Two Steps from the Move* LP in 1984 – 'I Can't Get It', 'Boulevard of Broken Dreams', 'Underwater World' and 'Shakes' – and four tracks for Urgent's 1985 *Cast The First Stone* album – 'Love Can Make You Cry', 'Pay Up', 'Dedicated to Love' and 'So This is Paradise', which he co-produced with Mick in New Jersey. The Urgent sessions were a soulless experience for Hunter. He had become jaded by the eighties in many respects, Prince excepted, who he regarded as a viable artist. He certainly felt that record companies and radio had become closed books.

Over a four year period, 1984–87, Hunter still continued to compose and record a large amount of material. Some of this was retained for his next album, some was covered by other artists, some songs appeared in movie soundtracks and several never received commercial release – 'Don't Throw Your Life Away', 'Mad at the World', 'You Got What It Takes', 'I Can't Find You', 'Boys 'R' Us',

'More to Love', 'Mean Streets', 'Read Me Like a Book', 'Bluebirds' and 'Responsible'. Ian started to use his home studio for this work and admits that musically, he was frustrated and didn't know what to do in the eighties. Neither did Ronson, who put his guitar down and started learning keyboards. Using the studio became a learning process for Hunter, even though he wasn't releasing material.

'I didn't know what I wanted to do in mid-eighties, battling here, there and everywhere, so I started writing songs for movies, which wasn't much fun, but paid the bills. It's more like being a writer than a performer. This girl in LA rang me up and said, "Would you be interested in doing this soundtrack for a movie?" I'd never thought of it. It's a fluky business. It was great because it's lucrative. I really was lost and was writing a lot of country music, so I did short sessions. The soundtracks happened just at the right time. I've got a lot of material from that period which will never see the light of day. I would work in my home studio from 2 pm until 5 pm to be with Jess. I missed my first two kids and I was determined to be with Jess until he was five. It wasn't until 1986 that I really got back into being Ian Hunter again.'

The first song for a movie soundtrack was a collaboration with Mick Ronson, '(I'm the) Teacher', for the film *Teachers,* released in 1984. Bobby Colomby was involved with the project and Hunter was asked by Sandy Gibson, the music supervisor for the film, if he would write one track. The song, recorded at New York's Power Station Studio, was co-written by Ian and Mick, produced by Ronson, arranged by Hunter and mixed by Bob Clearmountain. '(I'm the) Teacher' appeared on Capitol Records' soundtrack album alongwith contributions from Joe Cocker, Freddie Mercury, ZZ Top and Bob Seger. It was also released by Capitol as a promotional twelve inch single featuring two versions of the track.

'That's one of my best lyrics,' says Ian. 'Somebody rang me up from Orion Movies. The producer was a fan. I had this lyric – "The question's arisen, is this a prison, some say it is, some say it isn't." I liked that first line. It was all over in five minutes. It was about 1 mph, real slow, a ballad. The producer came back and said, "I love the lyric, but the song's so slow, like a death march." So we revved it up. I got a gold record for that!'

> They can snap your soul, blow it away
> Like a fragile leaf on a windy day
> Can you read, can you write, say couldn't care less
> You can graduate on American Express

In the same year Hunter worked with producer Spencer Proffer, at The Pasha Music House in Hollywood, on a song for the movie *Up the Creek.* The track was recorded with a band called Shooting Star who were also featured on Epic's soundtrack LP with Cheap Trick, The Beach Boys and Heart, but Hunter substituted this with his original demo of the song. 'I sent a home demo and Proffer's band were no use, so it was the demo we used in the end. When I went over, they had this heavy metal band who couldn't play it. Like all my stuff, it sounds simple, but it's a little more sophisticated than that, when you actually get down to playing it.' Inspired by his daughter Tracey, 'Great Expectations (You Never Know what to Expect)', was tinged with humour.

Well, my little girl's a cute little thing
But she ain't grown up much yet
She plays with her toys, then she plays with the boys
And you never know what to expect

She does what she wants, she says what she wants
'Cause she knows what she wants, she gets
And she tells me lies, she makes me worry a lot
And I never know what to expect

Hunter went on to cover Tanner and Reede's 'Good Man in a Bad Time' for the 1985 Epic Records soundtrack, *Fright Night,* recorded and produced with Ronson. Ian was always happy to tackle one song commissions for movies but not full soundtrack albums, and, in 1986, he recorded 'Wake Up Call' written by Arthur Baker, Tina B and Tommy Mandel for *The Wraith* movie and Scotti Brothers album. 'I knew Arthur and he rang me up out of the blue and asked if I would do a vocal. We did the song in a day in New York. It started about six in the evening and finished about four in the morning. I worked with Arthur for a week and got on well. We did three or four things including a song called "Professional Lover", which is great, but nothing's happened with it yet. I liked the sound he got. The one track film is great for me. You put all your energies into one song and you're in and out in two days.'

Three other Hunter songs featured on film soundtrack albums, 'We Gotta Get Out of Here' in *Up the Academy* and a live version of 'Cleveland Rocks' in *Light of Day,* both taken from *Welcome to the Club,* and 'Standing in my Light', recorded by Sam Brown and Tom Van Landuyt for the film *Ad Fundum.* Mott's 'All the Way from Memphis' also featured in *Alice Doesn't Live Here Anymore* and 'Overnight Angels' in *Asphaltnacht.* More recently 'All the Young Dudes' has appeared in *The Last of the High Kings* and *Amongst Friends.*

Speaking some time later, about the period following his departure from Columbia Records, Hunter reflected, 'I started to write again and the writing was pretty poor. I realized it was probably something to do with the fact that I lived in upstate New York, so I moved back into New York City and the writing started to improve. We moved into this rabbit hutch on 23rd Street in Manhattan around 1985. I think I'd slipped a long way from 1979 to 1984, and a lot further than I thought I had. I know, because coming back was a long haul. I was doing occasional gigs and getting an average reaction to things I thought were great, so I had to make even more of an effort. I set up my 16-track studio in our Manhattan apartment, all in my bedroom, ten by six area, overlooking the river and I liked writing there.'

In November 1985, Bob Dylan was honoured for his contribution to rock music at New York's Whitney Museum and the guest list included Ian Hunter,

David Bowie and Billy Joel. 1985 also saw Ronson producing an album, *Some Strange Fashion*, for One The Juggler and recording an unreleased LP with Sandy Dillon, *Dancing on the Freeway*. Dillon and Ronson played concerts together, which sometimes featured Mick on two solo numbers, *All Night Long* and *Impossible Dream*. In the Autumn, Mick rehearsed for two weeks with Midge Ure and his band for a proposed tour. He had previously produced Ure in the Rich Kids, but there were disagreements before the concerts began and Mick departed. Ronson appeared on a single B-side, 'Fade to Grey', and on some rehearsal film of a song called 'Wastelands', shot for *The Old Grey Whistle Test*.

Two new Hunter compositions were released by other artists during 1986. Karla DeVito recorded Hunter/Mandel's 'Money Can't Buy Love' for her *Wake 'Em Up In Tokyo* LP and Billy Cross co-wrote 'Crazy Glue' with Ian for his first self-titled album. In 1987 Scott Fulsom also recorded 'Red Letter Day', and 'White on White', co-written with Hunter for *Simple Talk*. Around this period Willie Nelson taped two versions of Hunter's 'The Other Man', but neither were released.

Ronson spent part of the summer in 1986 recording four tracks, including *Voices*, with singer-songwriter Cody Melville at Proving Ground Studios in Detriot. Ian and Mick then assisted Urgent on their second album, *Thinking Out Loud*, for which they co-wrote 'If This Is Love', 'Inch by Inch' and 'Pain (Love is a Victim)', the latter to appear on a future Hunter Ronson LP. Mick subsequently produced an album, *Kiss And Tell*, for Kiss That, worked on three tracks for Lisa Dominique and produced four songs for French duo, Marie Laure et Lui in Geneva during January 1987.

The abundance of writing and production projects for other artists started to cease however, as Ian developed renewed interest in live work, and this soon marked the beginning of Hunter Ronson's final collaboration.

Hunter performed in Canada and America in 1986, backed by The Roy Young Band. Ian had known Roy from his time in Hamburg in the sixties, where Young had originally started as a band leader and booker for the Star Club in 1961. Roy had played with Tony Sheridan and Ringo Starr in The Beat Brothers at the Top Ten Club, and also recorded 'My Bonnie' and 'What'd I Say' with Sheridan. Over the years, Roy had played with Howie Casey, Chuck Berry, Ray Charles, Fats Domino, Jeff Beck, Nicol Williamson and David Bowie.

Originally born in England, Roy Young subsequently became a resident of Toronto and Florida. He had brought together an impressive group of Canadian musicians and, through liaison with Dennis Elliott, agreed to support Ian on live work. 'We met in New York up at Dennis' house,' says Roy. 'We were all having dinner and we got talking down in his basement, in the studio, and just said we'd like to play together. For me it was a big thing to go out and work with Ian. I'm very proud of being able to do that.'

Ian admired Roy's track record and explains his reasons for wanting to tour with him. 'In the early sixties, Roy was on TV shows called *Drumbeat* and *Oh, Boy!*, and he was like England's Little Richard. He had these bands like The Original Upsetters and it was my dream to have a band like that. There was always three horns and Roy had this great voice that came down in tune. Not many people can do that. I particularly wanted to get better as a singer and, with Roy, I learnt about what made my vocal work. Roy sung like Little Richard and to me he was the greatest. Roy was telling me to go up instead of down and, using his band in Canada, I found that certain songs I was writing weren't going to cross over to record. I had to knock a lot of material on the head.'

Young's group comprised nine musicians, including three horn players and an extremely talented 21-year-old bass player from Dartmouth, Nova Scotia, Pat Kilbride. The Roy Young Band prefaced Ian's set with various rock 'n' roll standards including 'Great Balls of Fire' and 'Dizzy Miss Lizzy', plus a Young composition 'Country Wine'. They toured the east and west coasts of North America with Hunter for several weeks. 'It's just that I liked the band so much,' said Ian. 'I originally signed up for a month, but it just sort of carried on from there. We were only going to do Canada, but then I thought the band was so good, maybe we should do some American dates.'

Ian used the US and Canadian gigs to try out material for the new album he was already planning. 'I'm about half way through at the moment,' he commented at the time. 'I've got five that match. They're eclectic, they're all over the place. I keep on writing all these weird things. Willie Nelson's done one, a real simple song called "The Other Man".'

On the topic of songwriting Hunter explains rather modestly, 'There's no talent involved at all. You have an aerial and waves come in. I don't go looking for it, it just comes in. You're just blessed. Everybody has a gift of some kind. I've never sat down and passed examinations, I'm just fluky. Perhaps if I'd been a little more conscientious, I probably would have written a lot more and maybe been a lot more prolific.'

When asked if he was going to work again with Mick Ronson on the new record Ian replied, 'Oh I don't know about that. Me and Mick get on better when we're not working together. I'm spending Christmas with him.'

By early 1987, Ian was working with John Jansen who had produced Lou Reed but, more pertinently, was the producer behind Cutting Crew's American success. 'John's just one of those guys I get on with really well,' said Hunter. 'We never actually made a record together. It's not that I chose him; he just came round one day, and he wasn't destroying my stuff like a lot of them have. John doesn't really want to spend too much time overdoing it. I've been through all that. I've had enough material for an album for a long time but not the way I want it. Now I'm in a much better position than I've been in the last three or four years. I went through a lot of different changes and alleyways.'

Ian was working on various new songs, including 'Sign of Affection', 'Angel', 'Cool Jerk', 'National Holiday', 'Pain', 'Wings', 'Red Letter Day', 'The Other Man', 'My Love'and 'Someone Else's Girl'. Guitarist Robbie Altar returned to help Ian with his demo recordings for the proposed album and in the summer of 1987 Hunter was offered two solo deals which he declined, preferring to wait for a label which he considered 'more appropriate'. Ian bought a second home in Worthing, on the south coast of England, around this time, although he was uncertain about moving back to the UK permanently.

In December 1987, Greendow Productions of Manchester, run by record

producer Martin Hannett, lined up various artists to participate in a major television documentary on Ian Hunter. The musicians approached to take part included Bryan Ferry, Queen, Big Audio Dynamite, Status Quo, Noddy Holder of
Slade and Morrissey, who it transpired had been a member of Mott The Hoople's
Sea Divers Fan Club in the early seventies. Material had been researched for the
documentary and part of the plan was to record Hunter live with an 'all-star'
band in April 1988, supporting Def Leppard in Ireland. The final fifteen minutes
of the film was to feature parts of the Dublin concert; however, the plan collapsed.

'That was Martin Hannett's project. He was the underground producer who
worked with Joy Division, and I agreed to do it because it was him,' said Ian. 'But
they'd got a movie to do before that, so they spent their money doing this programme about independent producers, which I think is a pretty boring subject,
and they couldn't flog it. Then they couldn't get the money together to get mine
going and it was sad, because they'd already got one backer, MTV Europe, who
were willing to go in. They rang me up and asked if I'd do it and I said, "Yeah."
I was completely off the roll, I didn't know what to do.'

Castle Records released a UK compilation, *Mott The Hoople featuring Ian
Hunter – The Collection* in February 1988, issued as a 24-track double record set
and 16-track CD. The album was particularly noteable as it contained a previously unavailable, full-length version of 'Walking with a Mountain', which had
originally been edited for *Mott The Hoople Live*. Chrysalis USA also issued *Shades
of Ian Hunter*, a collection of previously released solo material from 1979 to 1981,
including a previously unissued version of 'We Gotta Get Out of Here'.

In early 1988, Mick Ronson returned from Nashville where he had been living for eight months. 'Steve Popovitch called me up and said, "What are you
doing in London? You need to come to Nashville," ' said Mick. 'London is pretty depressing. Nashville was just a whole lot better.'

Ronson had spent time in Nashville in 1987 producing country singer David
Lynn Jones on his hit album, *Hard Times on Easy Street,* and then commencing
work on David's second LP. Mick recorded with The Phantoms and produced
The Price of Progression by The Toll, *Johnny D Is Back* for Dutch band The Fatal
Flowers, *Arco Valley* for Andi Sexgang and collaborated with Steve Harley on a
proposed EMI album, *El Grande Senor*. 'I did play on two songs that Mickie
Most produced,' said Ronson, 'but I don't know what happened to the project.
There was talk of Steve getting together with Ian and myself, playing dates to-
gether and writing songs, but that is as far as it went.'

Mick then gave serious consideration to leaving the music business and becoming a chef; he regularly cooked at Hunter's house and was affectionately
known as 'The Great Marinator'. 'I thought about going to college and becoming a chef,' said Ronson. 'I didn't want to be known just as a guitar player for the
rest of my life. For a while I lost myself. People do, and when that happens, it
can last for years. I'd been doing quite a bit of production and travelling a lot,
spending time in Italy, then France, then the UK for a while, but I wasn't having
a very good time. There were a lot of things going on in my life that weren't right.

'I'd given up playing the guitar for a long while and then I started wanting to play again. I rang up Ian, who I always talk to whether we're working together or not, and said, 'Look, I've got to do something. I want to play the guitar again and get out there.' The Hunter–Ronson partnership was about to be renewed for the third and last time.

Never too small to hit the big time

'Big Time' – Ian Hunter

Mick had spoken to Ian about a joint return to live performance in May 1988 and the following month they were back together on stage for the first time since 1981, when they undertook a short tour of Canadian clubs backed by The Roy Young Band.

Ian now had a demo tape ready of various new tracks including 'American Music', 'The Loner', 'Look Before You Leap' and 'Ill Wind'. The first two of these songs were played on the Canadian tour togetherwith '(I'm the) Teacher', a stunning cover of The Beatles' 'Day Tripper' and Don Gibson's 'Sweet Dreams', which Ronson had moulded into an emotional instrumental. The remainder of the set comprised 'Once Bitten Twice Shy', 'Just Another Night', 'FBI', 'Standing in my Light', 'Bastard', 'All the Way from Memphis', 'Cleveland Rocks' and a medley of 'All the Young Dudes',' I Wish I Was Your Mother', 'Roll Away the Stone' and 'Ships'.

Hunter Ronson also played a live version of 'While You Were Looking at Me', eventually recorded by ex-Hanoi Rocks vocalist Michael Monroe on his second solo LP, *Not Fakin' It*. Ian contributed piano to a track called 'She's No Angel', having previously worked on Monroe's first album. 'He played piano on "Nights Are So Long" and said just buy me a dinner!' remarked Michael.

'I did three songs in a day once for Hanoi Rocks,' said Ian. 'They wanted lyrics. The kid sang garbage, but it sounded good, and I just put words to it. I know Michael Monroe well now. His second album is pretty good. He came round to me one day and said, "Cop this," and it was "While You Were Looking at Me". Little Steven wrote it. Great song. I love it. We just do it live bacause it's such a good song.'

Monroe recalls Hunter's input on Hanoi Rocks' *Two Steps from the Move* album, produced by Bob Ezrin. 'We were doing the backing tracks at The Record Plant for two weeks in New York, and there were a few songs where the lyrics weren't happening. We needed some help, so Ezrin knew Ian and called him. We were big fans of Mott the Hoople, one of the greatest bands ever. I love Ian as well. His first solo album is still my favourite. Great songwriter. When I was a kid I always thought, "Yeah that's a rock 'n' roll star." We played Ian "Boulevard of Broken Dreams", and he worked on the chorus and put it together. What a genius. It was great to meet him and find out he was a great guy. It's a tough business and it's easy to lose it, but Ian is really down to earth.'

With Hunter ready to embark on live performance, he explained why he believed Ronson was tempted back into his company again. 'I think it was the songs. Mick was in Nashville and he'd had some success there as a producer. I happened to mention that I was going off to Canada on a two week tour of strip clubs and he said, "I want to play, I want to come too." The timing was great. I had songs ready and he turned up to play guitar.'

Hunter Ronson toured for two weeks in Canada, mainly around Ontario, culminating in a packed show at a Toronto club, where Joe Elliott of Def Leppard joined them on stage. 'We were playing the Blue Jays baseball stadium the same evening that Hunter Ronson played Rock 'n' Roll Heaven,' recalls Elliott. 'They didn't go on stage until about midnight, which gave me time to get off stage and get down there to see them. After their set, Ian asked if I want-ed to join him on an encore of "Cleveland Rocks". So we did it, but there was a power cut halfway through the song and we did it again. I did "Cleveland Rocks" one and half times that night, and we started to keep in touch after that and were even talking about writing a song together.'

Elliott's and Leppard's admiration for Mott, Ian and Mick was well known and this joint live appearance was the first of several. Joe has since included *Mott, Wildlife, Overnight Angels, Slaughter on 10th Avenue*, 'All the Young Dudes' and 'Angel No. 9' on his list of all time favourite albums and songs.

Ian spoke of the Canadian comeback concerts and new management. 'It was weird for about the first two or three days. I don't know what it is, what we have between us, but it wasn't there at first. Then, all of a sudden, it started clicking in. When it was still there, we both got quite excited about it. Then, Bob Ringe phoned us up from LA and said, "I want to manage you two, how do you feel about that?" Mick knew him because he was the guy who signed Bowie to RCA Records. He said he wanted to do a tour. I couldn't believe it, nine weeks. I figured two weeks at most!'

A major tour of the US and Canada was lined up from late September through to early December. Ronson explained, 'Ian was back in England at the time, so I called him up and said, "Remember those dates that are being set up? Well we've booked 61!" He just said, "Fine".'

Hunter admitted that part of the motivation for touring again came from Ronson. 'Mick wanted to play guitar again so much, and the new material is a lot better than the songs I've been composing since 1979. I moved back to Manhattan, into the filth, where I write best. This tour is to convince people of that.' The new songs met with Ronson's considerable approval as he believed they were similar to the *Schizophrenic* material.

The band for the autumn tour included drummer Shawn Isenber, Howard Helms on keyboards and the amazing Pat Kilbride on bass, whom Hunter rightly likened to the late Jaco Pastorius. Ronson said, 'I think it's your basic kind of rock 'n' roll band, without all your horn sections and backing singers and all that business. Back to basics. Straight rock 'n' roll. I've kind of missed that. I always enjoyed playing with a three-piece band. You can feel the power more. I think you can express yourself more with less.'

Looking back on the concerts Ian says, 'We toured America for two and a half months and it got really good. It really was great. It was one of the few times in my career when everything worked out the way I hoped it would.'

The live shows were so impressive that several record companies were eager to sign Hunter. 'I got the first offer for a deal in Scandinavia. It was pretty good but not on the level of a worldwide American. The next offer I got was from CBS, but I had to move back to England to do it. Over the last two weeks of the tour, RCA, Polygram and Epic started turning up.'

Polygram eventually signed Hunter and Ronson after witnessing gigs in New York and Indianapolis.

In February 1989, Ian and Mick were in London for two concerts and were also looking for a producer for their new album. 'At the moment we're trying to sort out a producer and it's really hard,' explained Ian. 'The ones we like are few and far between, and they tend to be rather busy. We don't want to produce it ourselves. In a way we know too much and in a way we don't know enough. We would like to bring in a third person with another dimension, but the songs are finished and we're ready to go. We want to do it as soon as possible, but for the kind of people we want, we might have to wait.'

Hunter Ronson's concert at London's Dominion Theatre on 15 February 1989 quickly sold out, so an extra show was added on the following evening. Kilbride and Helms remained in the line up but drumming duties were now fulfilled by Steve Holly formerly of Wings. The concerts were warmly received and the press reviews carried the headlines: 'Night of the Hunter', 'Old rock heroes never die' and 'Still in the hunt.' One journalist said, 'The truculent manner and magnificent moodiness of Hunter's stage persona is evidently more than skin deep, and what is more, has not been diminished one jot by the passage of time. If he can harness the new material and a show as good as this to the emergent trend in favour of adult rock 'n' roll, the Ian Hunter story is far from finished.'

The shows included a sprinkling of older Mott and Hunter classics such as 'Once Bitten Twice Shy', 'Just Another Night', 'Standing in My Light', 'Bastard', 'All the Way from Memphis', 'Irene Wilde', a medley of 'All the Young Dudes', 'I Wish I Was Your Mother', 'Roll Away the Stone' and 'Ships' and Ronson's 'Slaughter on 10th Avenue'. Several new songs were obviously featured including '(Give Me Back My) Wings', 'How Much More Can I Take?', '(You're Never Too Small to Hit the) Big Time', 'Beg a Little Love', '(Following in Your) Footsteps', 'The Loner' and 'Sweet Dreamer'. Joe Elliott made a further appearance at the Dominion and Ian closed both concerts with the triumphant message, 'For those who came to witness the end, this is the beginning.' Hunter Ronson also played dates in Europe including a packed show in Amsterdam's largest music club.

The first of the Dominion concerts was filmed, recorded and subsequently broadcast on radio. In September 1995, Windsong International issued *The Hunter Ronson Band in Concert* on CD, including the only commercially available release of 'Wings'. One magazine review for the disc remarked on, 'Hunter's redoubtable songwriting skills and idiosyncratic vocals, and the snap, crackle and flash of Ronson's guitar playing. A timely reminder of the talents of two pop mavericks, whose extensive influence is still recognised by many of today's young buckeroos.'

Ian and Mick's plan for the summer was to commence recording of their new album as soon as a decision could be made on a producer. Ronson said, 'I don't want to be babysitting this project. I just want to go in, play the guitar and, when I get tired, I want to be able to leave. I'm looking past the album, but this thing will last as long as it lasts. I'm enjoying playing again. I'm not very good at conversation on stage, I'd rather talk through the guitar. I can say a lot through that.'

By May, it was confirmed that Hunter Ronson were about to commence recording at New York's Power Station Studio with Bernard Edwards, who was completing production duties for Hall and Oates. Edwards was formerly the bass player with Chic and had worked with Bowie on *Let's Dance*, Rod Stewart and The Power Station. 'I love *The Power Station*,' said Ian. 'I think that record was the only eighties rock 'n' roll that made any ground sound-wise. Anybody who's capable of that is what I want to get into.'

While Hunter Ronson recorded their new album during the summer, American rockers Great White had a top-five US hit single with a cover of Ian's 'Once Bitten Twice Shy'. Hunter also assisted Mick Jones of Foreigner with a track for his self-titled solo LP, revamping the song 'Just Wanna Hold' and re-ceiving a co-writing credit with Jones and Mick Jagger, who had helped on the demo tape. Ian also appeared in Jones' video for the song which was released as a single.

'I've known Mick Jones since Island and Spooky Tooth,' said Ian. 'Mick has always been wanting to write with me. He's a really nice man. He didn't write the song with Jagger. Mick Jagger was warbling on a cassette over the main riff. Mick Jones had various bits and the riff on the tape and Jagger ignored the bits and concentrated, quite correctly in my view, on the riff. Mick played it to me, so I said, "What you should do is forget about all the other stuff and use the riff." We had to do a lot of editing and the drums are out. I put a new middle to it and wrote the words around Jagger's phrasing. We did it in one night with me pro-ducing. Mick said "What is it like?" I said, "Terrible." I did the video too. I like Mick. I took a day off and we shot it up on Long Island.'

The sessions for the Hunter Ronson record, provisionally titled *American Music*, were held during June and July and the album was completed in only forty-five days. Ian's other working titles for the record were *Balance* and *Wish*. Bass player Pat Kilbride continued to work with Ian and Mick in the studio but old diehard, Tommy Mandel, was brought in to play keyboards again, alongwith Bryan Adams' drummer Micky Curry. Adams had recently joined Hunter Ronson on stage, as did Ian Astbury of the Cult, and Slash and Axl Rose of Guns and Roses.

The spirit and momentum built up from almost six months of touring meant that Hunter Ronson were firing on all cylinders when they entered the Power Station. 'In the studio, the whole thing jelled like a band,' remarked Mick, 'and that was why we felt we had to do that tour. Playing the songs on the road first was absolutely essential to their success on this record.'

'In total I'd say I've been devoted to this album for over three years,' said Hunter. 'It's been a long searching process, but we were in and out of the studio in forty days, six hours a day. We could have done twelve hours a day for twen-ty days, so you can see the speed that we did the record in. And I'm glad we did, because we demo'd them first and it's fatal when you go in and you've already de-mo'd songs. It's something that happens all the time now, because in order to get a deal you've got to have these 36-track demos perfected, then you try and make a record and the record sounds about half as good as the demos. Records take such a long time these days. It used to be you put them out and it died or it went. Now it's nine months before records kick off. It's such a long process. I guess it's progress!'

The album opened with 'American Music', a track that Ian had tried unsuccessfully to amend and adapt, and a song he now disowns. 'That song came complete and I couldn't change it. For a start I didn't want to call it "American Music", because it would sound like an Exxon commercial. But it just came that way and, any time I tried to change it, it wouldn't have it. I wrote another verse, I put that in. I messed around with that song for three months. In the end I just gave up.'

The song, with references to the American musical nerve centres of Nashville, Memphis, New Orleans, Chicago and Harlem, was inspired by Ian's early influences, which he first heard on the radio as a youth in England.

> I love American music – I play it all night long
> Just me and my records and – a vivid imagination
> I love to dance in the mirror – I practise every single word
> And it seems to me – American music is all I've ever heard

'We were listening to the Light Programme on the BBC and it had light music on it. Then twice a week they'd play "Whole Lotta Shakin' Goin' On" or "Hound Dog". You never knew when these songs were going to come on, so you had to listen to all of this crap, all week long, just to hear these odd songs. It was almost like getting a letter from a friend. What it did to me was amazing.'

'The Loner' also successfully conveyed the image of Ian Patterson's early years, this time as an isolated and troubled individual.

> I was born – on the third of June
> Hard labour – Gemini moon
> I was raised in a – country town
> The living dead were all putting me down
> Flesh and blood – my flesh and blood
> They kicked me out – they never understood
> That it's alright – it's alright – it's alright to be a loner

Hunter regarded 'The Loner' as a strange but very simple song. 'It's like something Free would have done in the sixties. I couldn't believe it when I wrote that. I thought "You've still got it." It put the chills in me for a long time. I just got up one morning and I wrote it on an acoustic guitar and thought, "You better get this thing down quick," because I actually have a great deal of difficulty with rockers, they don't come that often. I'm still knocked out by it. I was originally living in Shrewsbury. I had no friends where I lived. You couldn't get much in the way of rock 'n' roll, but they were my friends, those rock 'n' roll songs.

'I like "The Loner". I think it's one of the best songs I ever wrote, being a culmination of all my early days. The demo with Robbie Alter is a killer, because it's a semi-tone lower and I sung it so much better. For some reason, when we did that album, everything was going so quick that we forgot to de-tune a semi and I prefer Alter's playing to Ronson's on that particular track. Robbie played a blinder. I clouded him with echo so he didn't know what he was doing, and he flashed about a bit, then we took the echo off afterwards. It was a great solo.'

One of the last tracks to be written for the album was Ian and Mick's 'Women's Intuition', featuring Bernard Edwards on bass. It was a six-minute epic played in open G tuning with Hunter prepared to lay bare his Rolling Stones influence. As one reviewer commented, 'If only The Stones could still sound this good in the studio.' The song was vengeful, concerning the theme of injured love. 'It's to do with fighting to be happy,' said Ian. 'It's men and women. Aggression versus possession.'

'Tell It Like It Is' was also written by Hunter and Ronson and opened with Mick adapting a T. Rex 'Get It On' style riff, while 'Livin' in a Heart' (originally titled 'Angel'), was a classic Hunter ballad, with Ian's voice set against warm keyboards and rich Ronson harmonies. The song referred to Ian's separation from his first wife and two children, in 'Waterlow' vein, and was tinged with guilt and regret. 'Your own family is more important than anything else. I've been guilty in the past of putting music before everything which has caused a lot of grief in some circles. "Livin' in a Heart" is basically an apology for a mistake I made many years ago. It's about atonement.'

> How could I turn my back on you
> I wanted to be a success but success never leaves you alone
> Maybe I tried a little too hard
> Maybe I pushed you away too far

One of the oldest songs on the LP was 'Big Time', written by Ian just after he returned to Manhattan in 1985 to reinvigorate his writing, but now reinforcing the possibility of renewed commercial success for Hunter Ronson. 'The minute I moved back there I just started working again. I wrote "Big Time" after only a couple of months and thought, "Well that's good fun. If I can get a few more like that, then it'll be a good record." That was the first song that made sense in a long time. It deals with hope. You should play this in the morning on your way to work if you're not doing much with your career. It's about what happens when you get very single minded. If you will things to go your way, anything can happen.'

'Cool' (originally 'Cool Jerk') was a direct shot at people who think they are cool but aren't. Ian aims it at 'the person who comes in with a preconceived idea and won't change their mind. It's about the herd mentality, the hipster in us.' The song was essentially heavy funk and featured a massive kicking drum beat, wah wah guitar and synthesised brass.

Hunter and Altar co-wrote the most dramatic track on the album, 'Beg a Little Love', which Ian also described as the most personal of all the songs on the record. 'That isn't about me to anybody else, that's about me to me. I really liked the lyric a lot. It's the diary of a guy floundering in the middle of his life.' Over a thundering crescendo Hunter poured out passionate and colourful lines:

Life takes a little piece of you away
Everyday of your life
You learn to get wise, you learn to compromise –
You learn to criticize yourself
I guess we all grow up 'cos one day everything –
Seems further from the truth
And you try find yourself – in this endless youth
You try find yourself – and you
Beg a little love

Ian even echoed lyrics that he had written for 'Mad Shadows':

When my mind had gone
When both of my minds had gone
When all of my minds had gone

'Following in Your Footsteps' was another moving ballad concerning gen-
etics, in particular Ian's troubled relationship with his father, who had died
in 1981. 'It's to do with not wanting to be like your father, but being like him,
and the older you get the more you realise the inevitability of the genes. I love
the way the lyric turned out. I had an intense dislike for my father and he had
an intense dislike for me. I couldn't do anything right the way he wanted it.
It was later on I realised what he'd been through, including a couple of wars
and the Depression. He was a brainy guy but got stuck in a job he couldn't
get out of. I'm very glad my Dad heard "Ships", extremely glad. He died soon
after that. He's more important to me now than perhaps when it should have
been.'

I'm following in your footsteps – tryin' to make some sense of it all
Maybe it's a sign of weakness – but that's where your footsteps fall
I'm following in your footsteps – tryin' to hang on to your dreams
You never got what you wanted
So I never got what I need
I'm following in your footsteps – 'cos that's where the footsteps lead

'Sons 'n' Lovers', like 'Livin' in a Heart' and 'Footsteps', continued the relationships theme. Ian remarked, 'I have an eight-year-old, and watching the relationship between the mother and the son, I think about myself with my mother,
and the jealousies kids have at eight. They want to marry their mothers. There's
nobody as beautiful and then it all changes and the mother gets left behind. It's
almost like she loses the guy she loves.'
     One of the most forceful tracks on the LP was 'Pain', a jagged, relentless song
concerning betrayal which Ian had originally co-written in 1987 as 'Pain (Love is
a Victim)', with Don Kehr of Urgent. Hunter Ronson's version was superior,
with fine piano by Tommy Mandel and determined chords and feedback from

Ronson.

> Oh, I believe in magic – ain't it kinda tragic – when you find out
> Angels can be devils – you were never on the level with me babe – at all
> Beggars can't be choosers – winners can't be losers – I'll get over you some-
>   how
> It's gonna take a little time – to put you to the back of my mind – forever

'How Much More Can I Take?' was the fourth relationships lyric on the LP, this time with a Beatlesque approach, which would have made an interesting single release. Hunter at first is unable to tolerate love and rejects it.

> You're breaking my heart – stealing my thunder
> How much more can I take?
> You're dragging me down – holding me under
> How much more can I take?
>
> How much more can I take? – won't somebody break
> The news to you gently ...
> You fill my eyes – but you don't fill the hunger
> How much more can I take?

He then yearns for unattainable love.

> I see your face – everywhere, everyplace
> How much more can I take?
> You're here in the night, you're here in the morning sunlight
> How much more can I take?
>
> How much more can I take – I wish that I could make
> Your mind up for you ...
> You fill my eyes – but you don't fill the hunger
> How much more can I take?

The closing track on the album, 'Sweet Dreamer', was a showcase instrumental version of Don Gibson's song, adapted by Ronson. It illustrated, yet again, why Mick remained a huge influence on so many guitarists as he injected the music with considerable emotion and expression. The original song had been recorded by Patsy Cline and subsequently played as an instrumental piece by Roy Buchanan. 'Only a small portion of my version is from the original tune, but from a publishing point of view, it remains a Patsy Cline song, with my arrangement,' said Ronson.

The Hunter Ronson album, now titled *YUI Orta*, was issued by Mercury Records on 22 January 1990 in the UK, having been given an earlier US release to tie in with another large American tour. The title came from a famous catch phrase used by The Three Stooges – 'Why you, I ought to ...' The album was released with ten songs on vinyl format and thirteen on CD, the 'bonus tracks' being 'Footsteps', 'Pain' and 'How Much More Can I Take?', arguably three of the strongest numbers on the collection.

'Give Me Back My Wings' was not included on the final album. 'It got to the point where we had fifteen tracks, and there didn't seem any point in pursuing all this, because there were others that we didn't want to lose. We got to "Wings", which ironically enough was the first song I played to Bernard. We didn't really want to knock it on the head, but there just didn't seem any point.'

Mercury issued 'American Music' as a single in the UK and the US, with 'Tell It Like It Is' and 'Sweet Dreamer' included, depending on the format, and Ian and Mick shot a black-and-white promotional video, filmed in a disused mental institution at Teddington in Middlesex. A second single was released in America, 'Women's Intuition (Edit)' backed with 'Following in Your Footsteps', which appeared commercially on cassette. Ian explained that 'American Music' had been the record company's choice for a first single. 'Now they're going with "Women's Intuition", which was our choice. They're not stopping there. They want to put out two more after that. They really believe in it.'

In hindsight, Ian has some reservations about *YUI Orta*. 'I put a lot of songs on there at the last minute because of Bernard Edwards and the kind of vibe we thought it would be. "Following in Your Footsteps" I really like and "Sweet Dreamer" is beautiful. I thought Mick did it better live than in the studio. Some nights I just wanted to walk off and cry.'

Hunter Ronson played a series of American concerts in November and December, including a special show at Cleveland Music Hall on 4 November, to benefit the Cleveland Rock 'n' Roll Hall of Fame and Museum. Former Sex Pistols' guitarist Steve Jones and Joe Elliott made an appearance on stage during a cover of Bowie's 'Suffragette City'.

In January 1990, Atlantic Records re-issued all of Mott The Hoople's early albums in America on compact disc for the first time. *Mott The Hoople, Mad Shadows, Wildlife, Brain Capers* and *Rock and Roll Queen* came with their original artwork and, although there were no bonus tracks or rare material, they were welcome releases nonetheless.

Commencing a European tour in January and February 1990 supported by Shy, Hunter Ronson played concerts in Holland, Sweden and Norway and seven dates in England including London's Hammersmith Odeon. The response from crowds and press was superb, one journalist saying, 'These old guys looked and sounded good. Ian Hunter sang better than on the latest album and Mick Ronson was stunning.' The live set comprised 'Once Bitten Twice Shy', 'While You Were Looking at Me', 'Tell It Like It Is', 'Central Park 'n' West', 'Standing in My Light', 'Pain', 'Beg a Little Love', 'American Music', 'Just Another Night', 'All the Way from Memphis', 'Irene Wilde', 'The Loner', 'Women's Intuition', 'Cleveland Rocks' and the 'All the Young Dudes' medley. Ronson was featured on 'White Light White Heat', and an extended version of 'Slaughter on 10th Avenue'. He also performed 'Darling (Let's Have Another Baby)', one of punk's most charismatic DIY love songs, originally recorded by Johnny Moped and later covered by Kirsty MacColl.

Brian May of Queen appeared on stage at Hammersmith during a barnstorming version of 'All the Way from Memphis'. He had played with Hunter before but not Ronson. 'I thought it would be great to play that number, so when Ian said, "Would you like to come along?" I said, "Yeah, and I'd like to play that if we can." It's a great memory because it's very expectant. They play it a little differently now, it's more kind of sophisticated I suppose. That was the first time I'd gone on stage with Mick and I think he's great. I'm quite an admirer of his and I think he has good ideas. He's one of those people who doesn't just play, he originates.'

Following the success of the tour, Ian and Mick made tentative plans for their next album which was to be recorded at Joe Elliott's studio in Ireland once Def Leppard had completed work on a new LP. Ronson commented that the record would be a harder rock album and 'Give Me Back My Wings' would probably be included. Then, inexplicably, Phonogram made the astounding decision to drop Hunter Ronson from their label, a spokesman saying that sales of the album had been 'below expectations'. Several other popular acts were being dropped around this period. The mood and structure of the industry was already changing.

YUI Orta had been overlooked in some quarters, and the lack of commercial success was all the more tragic, as it stood alongside Hunter's best work, being one of his more lyrically ambitious and mature records.

25
Michael Picasso, Goodnight

'Michael Picasso' – Ian Hunter

With the *YUI Orta* tour completed and no record label, Mick Ronson returned to Stockholm where he was now living with his girlfriend, Carola Westerlund. He had set up home in Sweden some time before and he and Carola had his third child, a baby son, Kym. For most of his life, Mick had seldom found a stable base where he lived for any length of time. He was often on the move, helping on assignments, invariably those of other artists.

Westerlund was a member of EC2 and although Mick produced an album for them, mixing the tapes at Wessex Studios in London with Ian, Polygram issued only three singles. To coincide with the release of the third, Mick appeared on Swedish television with EC2 playing 'Passion', 'Once Bitten Twice Shy' and 'FBI'. He also worked for two months at Sigma Studios in Bergen, Norway, at the end of 1990, producing and playing on Secret Mission's *Strange Afternoon* LP and performing some live dates with the band.

By spring 1991, Ronson was asked by Scandinavian musician, Johan Wahlstrom, if he would join him on a tour of small venues called 'Klubb Rock'. The show consisted largely of cover versions, but Mick previewed two new songs that would ultimately appear on his third solo album, 'Take A Long Line' and 'Trouble With You, Trouble With Me'. In May and June 1991 Hunter Ronson joined Wahlstrom, Dan Hylander, Tove Naess and Magnus Lindberg, playing around twenty concerts throughout Norway and Sweden under the banner 'Park Rock', their set including '(I'm the) Teacher', 'FBI' and 'Sweet Dreamer'.

After the tour, Mick produced and played with The Leather Nun on their album *Permanent Nun,* and guested on an LP by Dag Finn entitled *The Wonderful World of D. Finn*. Ronson was also writing more new material for a solo record and planned further live work with Lisa Dalbello, Dan Reed and Graham Parker. He also recorded an album with Norwegian, Casino Steel, released as *Casino Steel and The Bandits featuring Mick Ronson*. Ronson had met Steel at a gig in Oslo on the Klubb Rock tour.

Then, in August 1991, tragedy struck. During recording sessions in New York, with Randy Van Warmer, Ronson started suffering back pains and felt weak. He thought at first that he had flu and, although eager to rest, returned to Britain to assist a friend with a TV appearance. In London, he was persuaded to visit a doctor. Within two days it was confirmed that Mick was suffering from cancer which had spread to his liver.

Maggi Ronson, Mick's younger sister, spoke of his return to London. 'I could tell he wasn't well. He had a lot of pain in his back, neck and the right side of his body. I wondered if he had a gall bladder problem. One doctor diagnosed pleurisy and gave him antibiotics. Then Michael noticed a lump on his right side. After a liver biopsy, they found an inoperable tumour. The consultant told me at once that nothing could be done, and that Michael had three months to live.'

Maggi kept her secret for twenty-four hours. 'It was the longest day of my life.

I just couldn't tell him. As we drove to his hospital appointment the next day, he was so cheerful I couldn't bear it. When they told him, I think he was angry at first. Then he started to take a really positive attitude. He fought it all the way. He had some chemotherapy and also changed to a super healthy diet. He kept making plans and never talked about not getting better.'

Although shattered, Mick was absolutely determined to beat his illness. 'I'm going to get rid of this,' he said defiantly. 'The doctors say it's incurable but I don't believe anything is. People do go into remission and are still here ten years later. I feel really positive. I don't feel bad about it. I'm looking forward to fighting it and getting on with my life again. Cancer is something that everyone has inside them. You get it through stress, emotions, food or whatever. There comes a point where you have to change your life and now is as good a time as any. I wish I didn't have it, but I don't think of it as a serious illness.'

Ronson moved back from Stockholm to London in order that he could obtain the best specialist treatment, but still worked on his solo LP and material for other artists. As Mick explained in one of his last interviews, he had to be in London for medical reasons. 'It all depends on who you know. It's a personal thing. I mean hospitals are hospitals. They'll tell you anything, but if you haven't got the right guy, you haven't got the right guy. You know, you're not dealing with a broken knee cap or something. It becomes a very personal project.'

Ian Hunter pledged support and cash to help Mick with his treatment and Def Leppard decided to cover one of Ronson's songs in order to help him financially. Opting for the guitar laden 'Only After Dark', as the B-side of their triple-platinum 'Let's Get Rocked' single, the CD notes said, 'Check out ONLY AFTER DARK, a Mick Ronson song we've always liked. Mick's been ill and this track is our acknowledgement of his importance.'

Joe Elliott explained, 'When we were recording the *Adrenalize* album, the whole band was very aware that Mick had this cancer thing to deal with. And he wasn't overly fussy about a lot of things, he just got on with life, but we knew that he didn't really have much money and we wanted to be able to help him out. We wanted to be able to say, 'This is towards your chemotherapy,' and so we decided to cover one of his songs and chose the most Leppard-like thing, rather than trying to get one of us to work out the piano on "Growing Up and I'm Fine", which would have been nice, but would have taken us about a month. We opted for "Only After Dark", gave it a whirl and recorded it in a few hours. Mick actually heard it, and really liked it, which was kind and quite flattering for us. He rang me up and said, in his Yorkshire tones, "Oh aye, bloody great!" '

Ronson had agreed to produce an album for Swedish group Sonic Walthers, but his illness meant he was only able to complete two tracks. In addition, a proposed twenty date Norwegian tour with Casino Steel in September 1991 and concerts with Lisa Dalbello in November and Dan Reed in early 1992 had to be cancelled. The only planned Scandinavian dates that Mick could fulfil subsequently were with Graham Parker. Playing live on stage was not good for Ronson's health, but he went ahead, featuring two more new songs in his set, 'Take Me Away' and 'Don't Look Down', before backing Parker each night. Mick also performed 'FBI', 'Take a Long Line', 'Trouble With You' (with Parker on harmonica) and 'Sweet Dreamer'. David Bowie and Tin Machine attended their show at Stockholm, in what was to be Mick Ronson's last ever tour.

Packing as much work into the last year of his life as his failing health would allow, Mick moved back to London and in January and February 1992 produced Morrissey's album, *Your Arsenal,* which received much critical acclaim. Many regarded the record as Ronson's updated Spiders From Mars sound for the nineties, and this was certainly demonstrated in the powerful guitar-laden tracks, 'You're Gonna Need Someone on Your Side', 'Glamorous Glue', 'The National Front Disco' and 'Tomorrow'. Speaking of his work with Morrissey, Mick said, 'Oh it's great. I mean it was real easy. I think maybe it's because he's from Manchester and I'm from Hull. I think we have a bit of an easier time together from that end, because he's very English. He's very northern too and I'm pretty northern, so in that way, and also musically, it was good.' Plans for Ronson to record a second LP with Morrissey were aborted.

Mick still had time however, to work once more with David Bowie, on 'I Feel Free' for his number-one album, *Black Tie White Noise.* Bowie explained why he chose to do this. 'It was a stage favourite and Ronson's tour-de-force in the Ziggy Stardust days. I thought, "Well, if Mick and I are going to work together, let's try and make it mean something, give it some depth." I just picked that track because it was an old encore that we used to do. The first time The Spiders ever did that was at The Fox in Croydon. Roxy Music was our support act.' David said later of Mick's studio contribution to 'I Feel Free', 'He turned up and played his usual breathtaking solo. Extraordinary man. Extraordinary guitar player.'

Mick Ronson made his last live appearance at The Freddie Mercury Tribute at Wembley Stadium on 20 April 1992, an event which received worldwide television coverage to raise money for Aids charities, following Mercury's death from the disease. 'There's a lot of people I know who's playing, so it'll be nice to be able to see them all together,' said Mick before the concert.

The list of artists appearing at the Mercury Tribute was a 'who's who of rock 'n' roll' – Def Leppard, Extreme, Metallica, U2, Guns & Roses, George Michael, Elton John, Robert Plant, Annie Lennox, David Bowie, Queen and Ian Hunter. For most of the 70,000 crowd and millions of television viewers, one high point was 'All the Young Dudes', performed brilliantly by Hunter and Ronson, joined by Bowie on saxophone and backed by members of Queen and Def Leppard. Mick also remained on stage to play a robust version of 'Heroes' with David. One reviewer commented, 'The highlight? Ian Hunter doing "All the Young Dudes" with such gusto, he's clearly at a different event to everyone else.'

Joe Elliott and Phil Collen helped out on backing vocals on 'Dudes' and Joe was full of enthusiasm. 'It was the ultimate thing for us. We were like a couple of kids who had won the pools that day. You've got Queen as the backing band and you've got Bowie, Ronson and Ian Hunter all on stage in front of a billion and a half people. It was just like the ultimate three minutes of your life.'

Ronson said of the event, 'It was pretty hectic. I mean there were so many people. Wondering which amp you were going to plug into and everything. Anyway it was good. The whole event was wonderful. It was a magical sort of day. Everybody was smiling and that made me very happy. I didn't know Freddie

Mercury, but I know he brought a lot of happiness into people's lives. There's so much going wrong in the world. You can't watch the news, it's all so bad, and to bring happiness in to people's lives is a great thing.'

'If somebody has cancer, a gig like that was tremendous for him,' says Hunter. 'Mick was thrilled to bits to be there. The event was well organised with 4,000 crew and people were so nervous. Me and Mick were fine, thinking, "Big stage, show off up here no problem!" There is of course a lot of cameraderie at a gig like that. The rehearsals lasted a week and that was fabulous. I saw all sorts of people I hadn't seen for years. Roxy Music were there, Nick Faldo, footballers – Britain – in this room at Shepperton!' As a result of Ian's performance at the Mercury Tribute, and the reaction to it, Elton John's manager, John Reid, considered signing Hunter to Rocket Records.

Ian had planned to tour Scandinavia again in May and June with Johan Wahlstrom. Ronson wanted to join them but was advised not to on medical grounds. Hunter played around twenty concerts in Sweden and Norway, guesting on four shows with The Mats Ronander Band and backed by The Few on the other dates. Ian included 'Speechless' in his set, an up-tempo version of 'I Wish I Was Your Mother' (in the style of 'Brown Sugar'!), plus a new song, 'Now is the Time', which Ian wrote with Freddie Mercury in mind, following the Wembley Tribute Concert.

Throughout the remainder of 1992 and the beginning of 1993, Mick continued working on his solo album in London. The tentative title for the LP, chosen by Mick, was *Heaven and Hull*. At one stage, Ronson's cancer appeared to have gone into remission, but his decline in health soon became marked again and he would tire easily. Suzi Ronson said, 'The only time he forgot about it was when he was playing. He was fine if I could get him in the car and to the studio and sit him in front of a keyboard.'

In February 1993, Mick was admitted to hospital and given forty-eight hours to live. Amazingly, he rallied and went back to work in the studio. One of Ronson's last recording sessions, weeks before his death, was a track for The Wildhearts' LP *Earth versus the Wildhearts,* where he played astounding slide guitar.

Mick's solo album and his driving ambition to complete it became his final lifeblood, and he and Suzi spent part of April 1993, the last month of his life, at Joe Elliott's studio in Dublin. 'Once Mick was diagnosed as having cancer, I got a phone call from Ian to say he was making an album and that he wanted me to sing on it. It was a childhood dream of mine to do anything like that, so I was in there straightaway. Mick and Suzi stayed with me for two days and I sang on "Don't Look Down" and "Take a Long Line". My wife cooked him Yorkshire food that he hadn't eaten for fifteen years and we went down to the studio and worked our butts off to get this thing finished. He was painfully thin, but in great spirits, although we did have a couple of moments in the studio when he was in agony. He was taking all the prescription drugs that he was being given, and they were basically bearing him out as best they could.'

Hunter heard from Ronson regularly and was amazed to find Mick's spirits higher than those around him. 'The only calls I ever loved was when he rang me, because this was Mick. If Mick was sick twenty-three hours a day, the other hour he'd be on the phone telling everybody how wonderful he felt. So when I would talk to him it would be like, "What are all these people telling me? He's fine, he sounds great." But then, when I moved in with him towards the end, I saw what he was doing. I mean the morphine would come down to a point where he would be totally sane, and then he would pick up the phone and tell everybody how wonderful he felt. He had a real strange way. He wanted everybody not to worry about him. The first thing out of his mouth would be, "How are you?" '

The original plan had been to release *Heaven and Hull* in Autumn 1992, but that was postponed. Ronson had recorded most of the new songs that he previewed on his recent Scandinavian concerts and collaborated with David Bowie, Chrissie Hynde and John Mellencamp in addition to Elliott and Hunter. Projected tracks with Morrissey and Bryan Adams were not completed.

Mick spent his final days living in Hasker Street in Knightsbridge, London and worked on his solo album until two days before his death. Maggi recalls, 'On 26 April, he came to see me and somehow I just knew he had reached the end of the road. Even then he was making lists of people to call and things to do. Next day, the doctor said we should get him to hospital, but when we did, there was nothing they could do. It was heartbreaking taking him home in the ambulance, knowing he was going home to die. Even then, he kept waking up and smiling and asking if I was all right.'

Tragically, Mick Ronson lost his fight against cancer and passed away on 29 April 1993, one month short of his 47th birthday. He was survived by his wife, Suzi Fussey, and his 15-year-old daughter Lisa. A memorial service was held for Mick in Kensington on 6 May and he was buried the following day in his home town of Hull. Ian Hunter addressed the congregation at the memorial service and remarked of his long time friend, 'Mick didn't make a fortune, but he died rich in the knowledge that he was an innovator and a kind and gifted man'. Chrissie Hynde, Martin Chambers and Trevor Bolder were all present at the service, which closed with a tape of Mick playing 'Sweet Dreamer'. During the week of Mick's death, a tree-planting ceremony was held at Wilson State Park in Woodstock where Ronson had lived on and off for nearly twenty years. The music world mourned and the tributes flowed.

A spokesman for Hunter commented, 'Ian and Mick were as close as you can get without being brothers. Mick was a special person. He didn't bother with rock star trappings. He was just a guy with this incredible talent. He could play any musical instrument that existed.'

Hunter does not find it difficult to talk about Ronson and his passing. 'You have to understand that Mick died from 1991 to 1993. It took him two years and throughout that two years, Trudi and I were dealing with that. Mick was *really* dealing with it. I was with him when it happened and, when he died, it was a big relief, because you live with the dying and grieve for two years. Plus, we didn't want to show him, so one of the most horrible things was having to lie, because I'm not a good liar. I remember he was coming back to our house in the States on the day he died, and we had to go through the moves of booking the seats and everything else, because one false move and he'd know. Mick would not acknowledge the fact that anything was going to happen. He was brilliant and didn't lay down until three days before he died – he was in Ireland, he produced Morrisey, he did his album for Epic. What a way to deal with it. He was always an optimist. I couldn't have done it.'

Ian had flown in to London from America on the Sunday before Mick's death to record a song for his album, but suddenly Ronson's health deteriorated the day before the recording was due to happen and the session was cancelled. 'There was one particular track that Ronson wanted to do, in a "Once Bitten" kind of groove. Then he changed his mind. Those kind of songs are not easy to do, contrary to what people think, and I think Mick was looking for something simpler and he mentioned he had one song. He said to me the night he died, "I love to tour, because you just get better as a musician." Mick's thing was always about working and improving, not about making lots of money. His work was of great quality and will stand up long after a lot of people who are flashier players will be forgotten. On a personal level he was so kind and full of life. It's like a lot of people, when they die, you realise how good they were.'

Hunter relates passionately how Ronson would play solos in the studio, but to him they were actually songs within songs. 'It was always funny to see Mick on somebody else's sessions, because they wouldn't figure him out. Mick was creative, he came from the song, he didn't come from, "I'm a guitar player, I'm now going to put my solo on this," which so many of them do, flashing up and down the fretboard, impressing the front three rows. He came from the song. He would listen to the track for about an hour, over and over. Then he'd listen for another forty-five minutes and a solo would be forming in his head, which went down really well on sessions for other people. Then, when he started to play, there would be this horrible mess for half an hour and, just when you were ready to go home, this pure Ronson thing would start to happen. Mick was absolutely unique because he came from the song.'

Def Leppard learned of Ronson's death just before a concert in Stockholm and played 'Ziggy Stardust' and 'Slaughter on 10th Avenue' as a tribute during their show. Joe Elliott is full of praise for Ronson the man, and the musician. 'I don't think I ever saw every member of this band taking a liking to one guy like they did to Mick Ronson. He was just a nice guy. He had such emotion and power and his playing had personality. You knew it was him straightaway. To me it was a sound as distinctive as Jagger's vocals. When you die at the age of forty-six it sounds so tragically young. He must have known in his heart of hearts that he was dying, but he just wouldn't admit it and he wouldn't accept it, and he was going to fight on to the very end. He was making plans about a tour and they weren't pathetic or sad. He meant it. He was going to really try to beat this thing.

'Ronson was a big, big influence on me. When you hear the solos on "Life on Mars" and "Moonage Daydream", and some of the stuff he did on Ian Hunter's first solo album, his guitar playing was great. He was also a fantastic arranger and a very good producer as well. When he joined Mott The Hoople briefly, in 1974, it was a major coup for me – Ronson joining Mott should have been perfect – it was a great pity the band were winding down at the time. Mick was a diamond guy and a really sweet person. It was a tragic loss.'

Mike Garson, the piano player from The Spiders said of Mick, 'I've played with hundreds of guitar players since then, and there's no one who had a better sense for melody in rock than him. I really appreciated him also, after not playing with him, and seeing all these other people who were imitators. He was very musical, a very warm guy and a lot of fun to play with.'

David Bowie looked back on his career with Ronson saying, 'I think it was the general optimism and, "Don't worry we'll get through," kind of attitude in everything Mick did. Even if I would get depressed, he was a very, very buoyant figure and was able to keep the morale within the band at a very high point all the time. He just did his own type of performance which was very strong indeed. He was a natural performer, a very good lead guitar front man and, I think, an extremely great foil for the Ziggy character. He was really good because where he was rooted in a very solid kind of thing, and Ziggy was very ephemeral, I think the two worked off each other very well.'

Bowie continued, 'He lived at the end on very much a day-to-day basis, but each day was a fresh experience for him and he seemed to embrace that wholeheartedly. It was a real lesson in dignity, I thought, and the perseverance of the human spirit.'

Photographer Mick Rock wrote, 'Ronno was Ziggy Stardust's anchor. His guitar gave the music its rock 'n' roll edge. In performance, he played the perfect robust foil to Ziggy's ambiguous persona. He also did all the live and studio arrangements. It's impossible to imagine Ziggy's magical rise without him. All the years I knew him, he remained very unspoiled and he never showed any interest in stardom. I don't think he understood the depth of his own talent; he was too busy being in awe of the talent of others.'

John Mellencamp lavished praise on Ronson. 'I don't mean to diminish anything David Bowie has done, but in my mind, the best records he ever made was when Ronson was involved with him. *Ziggy, Hunky Dory,* all those records Bowie made, Mick was a very big part of those records. You see Ronson was just a good guy. He didn't really care about credit, he didn't really care if he got paid, and that's the truth about Mick. It just wasn't on his agenda. If Ronson had money, everybody had money.

'The thing about Ronson's guitar playing was, and the reason it was so good is, that I never saw him plan out anything,' said Mellencamp. 'Everything just came from him and the way he was feeling, and the way the music fed into him. I never knew Mick to plan out anything in his life – personal, private, public, nothing. Ronson was absolutely a force of nature.'

Trevor Bolder, Ronson's former colleague from The Spiders, said: 'Mick could play two notes, and those notes meant more than the millions of notes that guitar players are playing today.'

Benny Marshall admired Ronson's human touch as well as his musical ability. 'Mick was a man who cared about other people. He was never malicious to anyone as far as I knew. I've never seen any interviews with him where he talks about his time with the Rats, and I think that's because we spent a lot of time together and were really close. When Mick decided to go to London, it was heartbreaking for me. A significant part of my life had finished and I couldn't see it getting together again.'

Reeves Gabrels, Bowie's guitarist in Tin Machine also praised Mick's technique. 'Ronson had almost the same thing as B.B. King, where he could play one note because of his tone and the type of vibrato. He defined the guitar sound for a whole period of time. He had this tone that was really broad, but it was just him plugged into an amp.'

Morrissey thought highly of Ronson as an individual. 'Mick spoke to me a few days before he died. He was very happy, very enthusiastic about writing songs with me and getting back in the studio. He was positive about his health and positive about his future. And it was astonishing, because a few days later his wife telephoned me and said, "My baby's gone." It was so painful and so sad, because I had become so attached to him that I couldn't attend the funeral. Mick Ronson was one of the most astonishingly human and attractive people that I've ever met. A very, very uplifting person.'

Ronson was hugely influential on dozens of younger bands such as Suede, The Wildhearts and Gene Loves Jezebel. Wildhearts' frontman Ginger remarked, 'Without doubt, Mick is the nicest bloke I've ever or will ever meet. He was an influence to anyone who met him, as well as an amazing, emotional player.'

Gene Loves Jezebel's guitarist James Stevenson said, 'There are two reasons I picked up an electric guitar. One was my best friend in high school buying one and insisting I did too, so we could form a band. The other was Mick Ronson. I met Mick many times over the last decade and he was the nicest and most unassumimg of men. Down to earth, modest, almost unaware of his own brilliance and huge sphere of influence among my generation of guitarists.'

In spite of his obvious influence and creativity, Mick was always low key about his contribution as demonstrated in an interview included in an MTV tribute, broadcast just after his death. He was, for example, slow to claim credit for his work with Bowie, describing it in very modest tones. 'I just used to take care of the band things that were going on. When David had finished a song or whatever he was writing, we'd just play it acoustically and then I used to do a lot of the orchestration and arrangements and things.'

At the time of his death, Mick's proposed solo album was approximately 80 per cent complete. Suzi Ronson decided that she would take the master tapes to Los Angeles in order that it could be mixed and finished for release by Epic Records in Autumn 1993. As it transpired, the record was held back to coincide with a planned memorial event.

The Mick Ronson Memorial Concert was held on 29 April 1994, the first anniversary of Mick's death, at London's Labbatts Appollo (Hammersmith Odeon). The stars paying tribute included The Rats with Tony Visconti, Dana Gillespie, Glen Matlock and The Mavericks, Big Audio Dynamite, Willy and the Poor Boys featuring Gary Brooker and Bill Wyman, The Spiders comprising Trevor Bolder, Mick Woodmansey, Billy Rankin of Nazareth, Bill Nelson, and Joe Elliott and Phil Collen of Def Leppard, Steve Harley, Roger Taylor of Queen, Roger Daltrey, and heading the bill, Ian Hunter. Bob Harris acted as compère for the evening.

Many of the audience were surprised by the non-appearance of Ronson's former associate David Bowie, and late rumours of a Morrissey guest spot were likewise unfounded. Bowie denied reports that he snubbed the concert, saying, 'I loved Mick, but want to remember him privately. His family know that, and there is absolutely no ill-feeling.'

The event had been organised by Maggi Ronson and Kevin Cann, author of several books on Bowie and former *Starzone* contributing editor, who had, in latter years, become close friends with Mick. Before the concert and between sets, video screens portrayed vintage film of Ronson, including live footage and interviews. Maggi explained why she chose to organise the memorial. 'One of the reasons I decided to do a concert was so other people, artists who knew Michael or had worked with him, and fans of his, could take part and celebrate Michael's life, and get to see him as he really was. I felt it was important to let others outside of the family say goodbye to him.'

The Rats played a fine opening set including 'It Ain't Easy' from the *Ziggy Stardust* album and Cream's 'I Feel Free'. The Spiders were one of the highlights, Joe Elliott taking Bowie's place on lead vocals as they spilled out stunning, heavyweight versions of 'Width of a Circle', 'Ziggy Stardust', 'Angel No. 9', 'Don't Look Down', 'Moonage Daydream', 'White Light White Heat' and 'Suffragette City'. The climax of the evening, and the finest moment, was rightly reserved for Ian Hunter. Backed by Roger Taylor and his band The Cross, and with his former guitarist Robbie Altar and Mott keyboard player Morgan Fisher, Hunter opened with 'Once Bitten Twice Shy' and then played two new songs, 'Resurrection Mary' ('because Mick always liked new songs') and a beautiful ballad and poignant tribute to his old partner entitled 'Michael Picasso' which he dedicated to 'Suzi, Maggi and Minnie Ronson, Mick's Mum'. The finale was the timeless 'All the Young Dudes', featuring the entire cast including a wheelchair-bound Geoff Appleby. Geoff, former bass player with The Rats and The Hunter Ronson Band, had tragically contracted multiple sclerosis and suffered two brain haemorrhages which caused severe disability. It was difficult to find a dry eye in the house. As one journalist remarked, 'The show went straight for the heart and hit a bullseye.'

The proceeds from the concert were eventually used to build a covered memorial stage in the middle of Queen's Gardens where Mick used to work as a gardener in Hull, the remainder of the proceeds going to a children's cancer charity to fund a holiday home. 'Music was such a powerful force in Michael's life and he was a very kind, loving and generous person, with a child-like innocent character, so I thought that would pertain to him well,' said Maggi Ronson.

A Japanese memorial event took place on 15 May 1994 at the Nissan Power Station in Tokyo when The Yellow Monkey held a concert entitled, *Ronson, 'Play Don't Worry' in Heaven*. Morgan Fisher guested in part of the show which featured 'Love Me Tender', 'Billy Porter', 'Moonage Daydream', 'The Prettiest Star', 'Watch That Man', 'The Girl Can't Help It', 'All the Way from Memphis', 'Saturday Gigs', 'All the Young Dudes' and 'This Is For You'. The Yellow Monkey also released an LP *Jaguar Hard Pain* featuring Fisher and dedicated it to Ronson.

They repeated the memorial concert at a larger venue on 29 April 1995, the second anniversary of his death.

Ronson's *Heaven and Hull* LP was eventually issued on 3 May 1994. There had been proposals at one stage to change the title to *From Heaven to Hull* or *To Hull and Back,* but thankfully, Epic Records stayed with Mick's choice. The album's opening track, 'Don't Look Down', co-written by Mick and featuring Joe Elliott on lead vocals, was released as a single. 'It was amazing fun putting the whole thing together, despite the fact that Mick was obviously ill for some of it,' said Joe. 'But he never liked to see long faces around him and we did our best to make sure there weren't many. He was great to work with. He knew exactly what he wanted. I just did it the way Mick had sung the demo.'

The second track was a storming 'Ziggyesque' cover version of the Dylan classic 'Like a Rolling Stone', with David Bowie on lead vocal. Guitarist Keith Scott and drummer Micky Curry also helped out on this track, one of four recorded by Bowie with Bryan Adams' band in Los Angeles during 1990. It was one of the first songs given to Mick for the album, David sending the tapes over to England when Ronson was working on Morrissey's *Your Arsenal* LP, Mick overdubbing guitar parts in London and Bowie adding further vocals after that.

The next three tracks were all written by Ronson and Sham Morris; the warm and atmospheric 'When the World Falls Down', 'Trouble With Me' – with Pretenders' singer and Ronson 'fan' Chrissie Hynde on lead vocals, and 'Life's a River', which had originally featured Ian Hunter, before he handed that honour to John Mellencamp. Mick delivered some fine guitar and Mellencamp was reminiscent of Daltrey in his vocal treatment.

'You and Me', composed by Suzi Ronson, was originally titled 'Maria', a beautiful and delicate acoustic instrumental and one of the most emotional tracks on the LP. Mick had wanted to develop this song using Mick Woodmansey and Trevor Bolder.

The fourth Ronson/Morris composition on the album, 'Colour Me', had a moving lyric, inspired by colour healing, an alternative, holistic cure that Mick had tried to help ease his physical pain from the cancer. Ironically, the track was completed by Mick a mere five days before his death. Ronson took lead vocal on this song with Bowie helping out on backing vocals.

'Take a Long Line' was a cover of a song originally written and performed by Australian group, The Angels. Ronson's version careered along at breakneck pace with Joe Elliott and Ian sharing, and clearly enjoying, vocal duties, while Mick spilled out aggressive and abrasive chords. Ronson also included a beautiful cover of the Georgio Moroder track, 'Midnight Love', from the film *Midnight Express,* featuring piano and guitar. This was the second piece that Mick had planned to use for a Bolder–Woodmansey collaboration and, like 'You and Me', the painfulness seeped through on this touching instrumental.

The LP closed with Ian and Mick's live version of 'All the Young Dudes', taken from the Freddie Mercury Tribute Concert recorded at Wembley Stadium, Ronson's final live performance and the last track on his final album.

Heaven and Hull entered the *Melody Maker* Top 50 chart and received highly complimentary press reviews – 'A timely reminder that Ronson had touch and grace as well as power and flash,' said *Q* magazine.

There were two other songs that Mick had wanted to include on his album – 'Indian Summer' and 'Just Like This' – but these were dropped. He also worked on a song called 'Get a Grip on the Arm of Love'. 'A lot more people were lined up to do tracks but time ran out,' confirmed Suzi Ronson.

Frankie LaRocka, A&R Director of Epic Records, explained how the un-finished project was concluded. 'The album was almost completed. There were a couple more songs that Mick was supposed to do, one by himself, one with Morrissey and one with Bryan Adams, but he never got around to them. All the other stuff was practically finished, it just needed to be mixed. Mick did my sec-ond record when I was in The David Johansen Group back in 1979. I knew how Mick worked, just from watching him back then, so it was an honour to work on this record after all these years. It was like trying to figure out what would Mick want. He left a rough mix of the album, so we took that and enhanced it a bit.'

Ian Hunter remarked, 'Putting Mick's album out is great, because to be able to make music, especially his own album, just filled his whole head. To a large extent he managed to minimise the discomfort from the cancer, which was really bad at times, and it probably put six months on his life. That record's a success before it even starts.'

In November 1994, Mick's first two solo albums were posthumously released on compact disc by Trident International Records in conjunction with Mainman. *Slaughter on 10th Avenue* and *Play Don't Worry* were issued as a double-CD set entitled *Only After Dark,* with six bonus tracks. including two single B-sides, two 1974 live tracks and two previously unreleased songs, 'Stone Love (Soul Love)' and 'I'd Rather Be Me', from sessions held in 1975. One mag-azine remarked that 'Ronson's outstanding guitar work, exemplified in the plain-tive arrangement of *Slaughter on 10th Avenue's* title track or the grinding 'White Light White Heat', underlines how sadly his talent as a player was undervalued during his lifetime.' The album reached number 73 in *Record Collector's* 1994 Top 100 chart. Subsequent individual re-issues of both solo albums, and a double-CD compilation *Main Man* in 1998, included further unreleased Ronson material and alternate takes.

An historic Ronson release also saw the light of day in February 1995 when Tenth Planet Records issued a limited edition Rats compilation entitled *The Rise and Fall of Bernie Gripplestone and the Rats from Hull.* This 12-track LP came in a gatefold sleeve with a 24-page booklet and included both Columbia singles, six previously unreleased songs and the two numbers performed by The Rats at the Ronson memorial concert. The albums were issued as 1,000 individually num-bered vinyl copies and a 1998 CD release by Angel Air has added new recordings of 'The Hunter', 'Colour Me' and 'Life's A River'.

The story of Mick Ronson, one of rock music's greatest and most innovative talents, was virtually at an end although, as Ian Hunter reminds us, he will con-tinue to influence generations of guitarists over many years. 'There will always be guitar players out there copying Ronson, because someone will tell them to check it out. I remember Andy Taylor from Duran Duran talking about him. Now it's Phil from Def Leppard and Bernard from Suede. They're all fanatics. They put it through their little condenser and it comes out somewhere else. To be perfectly honest with you, at times, it kept Mick and me alive, because we'd never been big artists and yet we survived twenty odd years.'

Perhaps one of the most poignant remarks came from DJ and presenter Bob Harris, famous for his *Sounds of the Seventies* radio programmes and *The Old Grey Whistle Test* television shows. Reflecting on his first meeting with David Bowie in 1968 and his involvement on the early Ziggy Stardust concerts as compere, Harris remarked of David in New Millenium CD notes for a Bowie BBC session sampler, 'It's an odd thing. At no time did I remotely get to know him. Soon the public schoolboy was wearing dresses and shocking Texans. He had his direction. These days we would call him "focused". I don't begrudge David his self-obsession. It is the pre-requisite of superstardom. He has been endlessly able to re-invent himself, to become the definitive musical chameleon. I just wish he'd given Mick Ronson the credit he deserved.'

Mick shone in his own right as a musician, but also as a human being, bringing out the very best in those around him, in a modest, unaffected, low-key manner. When 'experts' talk about a resurgence in the seventies guitar sound, they refer largely to the fullness, spontaneity, power and grace of Ronson's firebrand playing, although they might not realise it. Mick transformed David Bowie's acoustic material and even prefaced nineties 'noise pop' by twenty years with his burning technique and creativity, on tracks like 'Panic in Detroit'. It was Ronson's classical tuition that enabled him to write entire solos and arrangements, mentally, before touching any instrument; that training, fused with his innovation and emotion, produced a unique, creative and irreplaceable musician.

* * *

Michael Picasso

Once upon a time – not so long ago
People used to stand and stare
At the Spider with the platinum hair
They thought you were immortal

We had our ups and downs – like brothers often do
But he was there for me
I was always there for him
And we were there for you

How can I put into words what my heart feels
It's the deepest thing – when somebody you love dies
I just wanted – to give something back to you – gift to gift
Michael – Michael Picasso – Goodnight

You used to love our house – you said it was relaxing
Now I walk in the places you walked
I talk in all the spaces you talked – it still hasn't sunk in

Are the words real – that come into my head on a morning walk
Do the shadows – play tricks with my mind
For it feels like – nothing has changed – but I know it has
Michael – Michael Picasso – Goodnight

Heal me – won't you heal me – nothing lasts forever – let it be
Heal me – won't you heal me – I'm the one who's left here
Heal me

You turned into a ghost – surrounded by your pain
And the thing that I liked the least – was sittin' round Hasker Street
Lying about the future

And we all cry – in a room full of flowers on a windy day
And I look down – but none of these words seem right
I just wanted to give something back to you – gift to gift
Michael – Michael Picasso – Goodnight

– Ian Hunter, 1993

26
Something to believe in

Hunter's outlook on music and performing changed with Ronson's death. 'Mick called me in 1991 to tell me he had incurable cancer, and that went on for two years and it was a terrible time. When he died, it dawned on me that we were both lazy. We could sit around all day and not touch a guitar. When people had called with ideas, I liked staying at home and became a bit reclusive actually, so I just thought, "Fuck it, from now on, if anybody rings, I'm going." And that's what I did.'

Ian embarked on a further Scandinavian tour in the summer of 1993 followed by three British concerts. He was accompanied once again by Johan Wahlstrom and his band The Yobs but introduced Ricky Scott Byrd on lead guitar, formerly of Joan Jett And The Blackhearts and, more recently, Roger Daltrey's band. It was subsequently mentioned that former Suede guitarist Bernard Butler was to join Hunter.

The original concept of the Scandinavian Hamn Rock (Harbour Rock) tour was to play from a boat called Rockvagen, which was taken around various Swedish ports. However, the first show in Visby was cancelled due to technical problems and all of the other Rockvagen dates were scrapped. A club tour was re-scheduled, opening in Gothenburg on 2 July, with a show in Stockholm on 8 August, where Ian dedicated 'Michael Picasso' to Carola Westerlund, Ronson's girlfriend, who was present in the audience. Hunter said of his musical tribute to Mick, 'I was there when he died. The hardest part was not when he died, but when we learned he was ill. "Michael Picasso" was very hard to write. I did the best I could to make sure it didn't sound pathetic.'

Hunter played live on Swedish television from the Stockholm Water Festival performing 'Once Bitten Twice Shy' and 'All the Young Dudes', backed by The Mats Ronander Band, and played three UK shows in Leeds, London and Dudley during August. Johan Wahlstrom and The Yobs prefaced Ian's set, playing two excellent new songs, 'No One Ever Said' and 'I Don't Care,' which was reminiscent of 'Laugh at Me'. Ian's set list for the shows was virtually a 'greatest hits' package – 'Once Bitten Twice Shy', 'Women's Intuition', 'Central Park 'n' West', 'Roll Away the Stone', 'Michael Picasso', 'Bastard,' 'The Loner', 'The Golden Age of Rock 'n' Roll', 'Cleveland Rocks', 'All the Way from Memphis', 'Just Another Night', 'Big Time' and 'All the Young Dudes'. After the London Forum gig, Maggi Ronson, who had been in the audience, decided to organise a memorial concert for Mick. Ian was the first to support the initiative.

In 1993, Def Leppard released a compilation CD of rare tracks entitled *Retroactive*. This contained a re-mixed version of Ronson's 'Only After Dark', 'Desert Song', inspired by Mick's battle against cancer, and a re-recording of 'Ride into the Sun' featuring Ian Hunter – 'Honky Tonk Messiah' – on piano.

During a visit to Europe in August, Ian started discussing a new project with Casino Steel who had previously recorded with Ronson. They planned an album,

The Gringo Starrs, on which Hunter would contribute songs, lead vocals and arrangements. The sessions, originally scheduled for March 1994, were held in August. Meanwhile, Ian joined Michael Monroe on stage at one of his gigs in New York in September 1993, playing 'Roll Away the Stone' and, during early 1994, he demo'd new material for the next Ian Hunter album with guitarist Robbie Altar.

The early nineties saw a further flurry of Mott and Hunter compilations and continued references to their importance and musical influence. Columbia's *The Very Best of Ian Hunter,* Castle's *Ian Hunter – The Collection* (a selection of solo Chrysalis tracks from 1979–81), Mott The Hoople's *London to Memphis* and *The Ballad of Mott: a Retrospective* (which included unreleased and alternate takes including 'Lounge Lizard', 'Through the Looking Glass', 'American Pie', 'Henry and the H Bombs' and 'Saturday Gigs') were all issued. Chrysalis Records celebrated their 25th Anniversary in 1994 by releasing 25 of their greatest albums in limited-edition CD box sets including Hunter's *You're Never Alone with a Schizophrenic.* A welcome release was Chrysalis's *Welcome to the Club* and *Short Back 'n' Sides,* featuring bonus tracks and previously unissued songs, including a bonus disc, *Long Odds and Out-takes* with 'Detroit', 'China', 'Na Na Na', 'Venus in the Bathtub', 'You Stepped into My Dreams' and 'I Believe in You' all issued for the first time. Rhino Records of the US also compiled Mott The Hoople's *Backsliding Fearlessly – The Early Years,* which reached number 76 in *Record Collector*'s 1994 Top 100 Chart.

Having headlined at The Mick Ronson Memorial Concert in April 1994, Ian returned to London again in late July, to start recording *The Gringo Starrs* album at Abbey Road Studios. 'I was working on my own album when Casino rang me up and said he wanted me to sing some songs on this project, and did I want to record at Abbey Road. The fee was agreed, but when I got there, it all changed and it just took off on its own, in a completely different direction. It switched into this raucous album, *Dirty Laundry,* which sounds like '62-era Stones. The musicians were a right bunch of unsavoury characters, and I loved every minute of it. It was great fun. We recorded lots of Rolling Stones and Dylan references, something I've always enjoyed doing. It was a pleasant surprise.'

The sessions commenced on 28 July and Ian was supported in the studio by two guitarists, Honest John Plain of The Boys and The Cry Babies and Darrell Bath of UK Subs, Dogs D'Amour and The Godfathers. Vom, ex Doctor and The Medics, played drums, Glen Matlock, ex Sex Pistols and Rich Kids, handled bass, and Casino Steel and Blue Weaver alternated on keyboards. They recorded eighteen songs in eleven days, with fourteen originally scheduled for the LP, later reduced to twelve tracks; 'Big Kid', for example, was omitted from the final running order. Seven of the songs were penned by Ian including two of his older compositions, 'The Other Man' and 'Red Letter Day'. The other recordings were new tracks including 'Dancing on the Moon', 'Invisible Strings', 'Scars', 'My Revolution' and 'Another Fine Mess', a humorous ode to Hunter Ronson and their touring exploits:

> Well you say I'm kicking up too much fuss

> But twenty-four hours is too long on the bus
> The band's all moaning, the driver's slow
> There's not enough people, too many shows
> Down in the dumps with the birthday blues
> Another fine mess you've gotten me into

The backing tracks and guide vocals were taped at Abbey Road and the vocals at Nidaros Studios, Trondheim in Norway. Over-dubbing was completed at Right Track Studios and The Power Station, New York and Ambience Studios, Oslo. The project was recorded with the assistance of Norwegian producer Bjorn Nessjo.

'Bjorn helped an awful lot,' says Hunter. 'I have never written so much in the studio. I reckon it is always a good sign writing in there. It's a great way to do it. Neil Young does it that way. "Dancing on the Moon" was written in the studio and the band didn't know what they were doing at all. The drummer just sorts of keeps time, because he doesn't know where to roll, as I keep on changing the chords. They're just following me. It wasn't a song. It was just something that happened when we were in there.

'By the end of the sessions, I really rated Bjorn and liked the way he did the album, which assisted me, because I didn't have anybody else. When Mick went, I lost my friend, producer and arranger. I didn't have that any more but I really started to put music first again, which I hadn't done in about fifteen years. I never really thought of it in terms of a career. I thought of it in terms of a life. I'd hate to look back at sixty and have had no freedom, throughout. When you get big, the freedom goes, the very thing that you actually set out to join bands for!

'The couple of years that I was really big with Mott The Hoople, I didn't enjoy it one little bit. It's not much fun. Money doesn't mean anything, nor does being known. I always wanted to be famous and, when I was famous, I loved it for a fortnight and then it became a pain in the arse. Girls outside the door morning, noon and night. You've got to have a bath before you go and get the paper in the morning. Ronson had it really bad because he looked like God. I prefer to come and go as I please, but it's shorter to fall and it's not easy. I've slipped a lot but I like it.'

Initially regarded as a 'fun' project, the resultant Abbey Road recordings were far better than original expectations and the album was soon re-named *Ian Hunter's Dirty Laundry*, at the record label's request. 'Red Letter Day' was issued as a promotional CD single in October 1994 and the LP, originally scheduled for November release, was held back to March 1995 and issued with a different track sequence by Norwegian label Norsk Platproduksjon. The album was preceeded by a Scandinavian single, 'My Revolution', released in February and Hunter visited Norway to promote the record with a Rondo NRK television appearance on 10 March 1995. Steve Popovich's Cleveland International label issued the *Dirty Laundry* CD in America, and a single version of 'Good Girls' scored highly on several radio charts in Ohio.

Dirty Laundry received highly positive comment by one British reviewer. 'In a perfect world, we would hear more from pros like Hunter and less from too many younger, lesser talents with too little to say. Ian Hunter's Dirty Laundry, his first band project since leaving Mott The Hoople in 1974, finds the leather-lunged rocker in fine form, in a set boasting unusually strong songs. You get 45 minutes of first rate rock and roll delivered with considerable panache and savvily produced by Bjorn Nessjo.'

March 1995 saw the CD re-release of the *Mott* album on Sony Rewind, and the music journals praised it highly – 'Hunter left behind the most truthful insights we have into the life of a 24-carat '70's pop idol. And of course some of the finest hobnail stomping rock 'n' roll of his time. All your fave bands rip off this LP.'

In 1996, K-Tel Records issued a *Best of Mott The Hoople* CD, the inference being that the disc contained new re-recordings of their classic hits involving Hunter and Ronson who contributed to the sessions shortly before Mick's demise. 'The sleeve notes would have the buyer believe that in 1993 Ian Hunter and Mick Ronson re-formed Mott The Hoople and re-recorded the biggest hit songs alongwith a clutch of "originals", written by Danny McCulloch and Gerry Chapman,' says Dale Griffin. 'Total bullshit. Neither Ian, Ronno or any other Mott personnel had any part in this farce. It sinks even lower, with the sleeve notes claiming that the recordings on the disc are the last work of the ailing Ronson, who died shortly afterwards. In a business where chicanery and reprehensible behaviour are commonplace, they even have the gall to dedicate the project to Mick Ronson's memory.' In a subsequent court case, held in March 1998, K-Tel were fined £8,000 plus £1,488 costs by Hampshire magistrates.

Autumn 1996 also saw the re-issue of *Diary of a Rock 'n' Roll Star* by Independent Music Press amidst glowing reviews. Ian could never understand why the book was withdrawn in the first place. 'I couldn't figure it out. Originally it sold out two editions at the time and they just stopped publishing it. We never heard from anybody about that book for twenty years and then I get two offers in a row. The first edition of the re-issue has sold out already. But it's still difficult to get in certain places. I wanted it in airports and places like that, but it seems to me, if you're not sucking somebody's toes in a book, or it's not Danielle Steele, they won't have it. The tabloid mentality.'

'I only wrote the diary originally because I'd just got married and didn't want to get involved on the road. It was venereal disease; now Aids has reared its ugly head, so we were lucky. So much has changed. Touring's better because PAs and sound are better these days. Travel and hotels have improved too. We used to get the tour manager saying, "How many more telephone calls are you going to make?", stuck in a single bed with a winceyette sheet and a radio.

'On the corporate end of things, I think they've disappeared up their own arses. Trying to go forwards, they've gone backwards. They're over-pressuring bands, putting too much money into too few baskets and they're fucking up the golden goose, because something's going to happen. There's also too many people in it, that don't know enough about it. It used to be you were mad on records and you'd work in a shop, then become a teaboy at a record company and work your way up. Now, you have to come out of business school and speak the corporate language, because they're the people you have to pacify.

'They over-market bands too, until people get bored with them and the life of groups is shorter. They don't allow bands to develop like they used to. Mott The Hoople had four stiff albums at Island. You can't do that now – you're out of there – one and you're gone. We had that time to grow, but now it all costs too much. Kids realise they've only got one shot and, if it doesn't happen, they're out. Fans also have shorter concentration spans and go berserk on one fad and then another fad. The whole marketing thing puts too much pressure on youngsters now and I don't like that. Then they start acting up and the tabloids start killing them. They're not blessed with wonderful intelligence, they just happen to play music. If you had any brains you wouldn't do it. I know a band who sold 1·3 million records, and had a top-five single in America, and they were in debt.'

Ian commenced sessions for his next solo LP in May 1995 at Time Machine Studios, Vermont, and Nidaros Studios, Trondheim in Norway, where the bulk of the recording and mixing were done. The album, originally titled *Life!... Get One,* then *Pilgrim's Progress* and finally *The Artful Dodger,* was to have been recorded originally at Abbey Road. Hunter worked with producer Bjorn Nessjo again, various Scandinavian musicians, Dennis Elliott, Pat Kilbride, Darrell Bath and Robbie Alter. Sixteen tracks were taped, 'Fuck It Up', 'A Little Rock 'n' Roll', 'Ain't No Way to Treat a Lady', 'Worthing' and 'Testosterone' failing to make the album.

'Bjorn had a lot of heavy rock hits in the eighties and owns a studio which is state of the art,' says Hunter. 'Nobody else is allowed to use it and if he's not there it's locked. Norway is a great country. People ask why I recorded it there and I say, "You should nip out and look at it." Bjorn does things for the soul and things for money. He did rock and he's also recorded a violinist and trumpet player, things he loved. He liked The Stones so he wanted to do *Dirty Laundry.* The money and the clock are totally irrelevant. When we went to Vermont and it didn't work, it cost about fifty grand of Bjorn's money. I felt embarrassed but he said, "Look, if we didn't do that, we wouldn't be here." He has a great attitude. The sessions were good. It took four guitar players though to replace Ronson!'

Hunter decided to structure a leasing arrangement for his new release after previous experiences with major labels. The record was first issued on Polydor Norway in September 1996, preceeded by a promotional single, *Too Much,* a beautiful, low-key, love song which opened the album with startling lyrics.

> Maybe you don't want me – I'm so scared of losing you
> I never miss an opportunity to miss an opportunity
> Watch me screw up this one too
> It's so hard to talk about love
> I'm leaving now – it's just
> All I ever wanted – was you
> Is that too much?

The Artful Dodger album was lyrically reminiscent of *All American Alien Boy* as Ian tackled personal and serious subject matter; his parents, parenthood and youth, New York, the tabloid press, the afterlife and religion. There were also songs concerning friends departed, 'Michael Picasso', 'Walk on Water' and 'Now is the Time', three of the strongest tracks on the record and examples of Hunter's best ever work.

'Now is the Time' was inspired by the Mercury Tribute at Wembley Stadium, Ian referring to his friend as 'the killer with the kiss.' 'Freddie was a wonderful man and crazy as a loon, the archetypal rock star – shy really, but when you knew him, you could see that people aspired to be what Fred naturally was. People show off and pretend in front of media, but Fred was the real thing. He was out-rageous – morning, noon and night. Queen opened for Mott The Hoople and were lovely blokes and it really upset me when Fred died, even though I hadn't seen him for a while, so I wrote "Now is the Time".'

The pseudo-intellectual and philosophical 'Something to Believe In', express-es some resistance to religion, whilst acknowledging that 'one man's God's just as good as another' and that we all need to place faith in something. In many re-spects the song is a companion to 'God (Take One)' as Ian speaks of the shal-lowness of faith.

'Resurrection Mary' was inspired by a television documentary. 'The pro-gramme was about a ghost who haunts Resurrection Cemetery in Justice, a dis-trict of Chicago,' says Ian. 'She was killed in a car crash and she's since been picked up by several taxi drivers. The words just kept coming to me – Resurrection, Justice, Cicero, Big Jim Sullivan, Mickey Finn – I loved all that. I rang the cemetery and they admitted she's buried there, but they weren't allowed to comment. The song's all factually correct. It's a proper story.'

The Caledonian swing on the introduction to 'Walk on Water' gives way to a heavy drum beat and robust guitar, Ian describing a 'little flame, tormented soul' who gets 'lost' in rock 'n' roll and does not come out alive. The victim tries to turn his 'savage sound' upside down and Hunter understands his thinking, but goes on to express regret about his demise with the line, 'I'm just so sorry that your flame went out.' Savage Rose and Fixable? Guy Stevens? Sadly not, but Hunter will not disclose the subject of the song. 'Anonymity is part of the fun,' says Ian.

'23A Swan Hill' was originally the residence that Hunter knew as a youth, above Shrewsbury Police Station, and again, the up-tempo music is tangential to the lyrical tale of resistance from his father, parental discord and the unwanted restraint of his hometown. 'My parents had a tough time,' remarks Ian. 'Born in 1911, First World War, the depression, Second World War and then me! It was hell at home and 23A Swan Hill was where it came to a head. I left home when I was sixteen and went to Butlins.'

The earlier live treatment of 'Michael Picasso' was downgraded for this album to an emotional arrangement featuring only Hunter on acoustic guitar and a string quartet, a sparse compliment to the highly personal lyrics. The song was not difficult to write as Hunter explains. 'You simply approach it as a song, and you know what you're dealing with, and you know how corny it could be. I always get this vision of Mickey Rooney going, "Judy. Judy. Where are you Judy?" So, you've got to be very careful, because you know all his folks. What you come up with is simplicity and truth, and, when you sing it, you don't think about it, otherwise it's impossible to do. It took me three and half days to get a studio take that we liked. It's easier on stage. In the studio, it's like a doctor's waiting room.'

Hunter's involvement with the musicians he encountered on the *Dirty Laundry* project had clearly motivated and influenced the title track and 'Skeletons (in your Closet)', the latter a cunning and sarcastic address to invasive television and journalism, lightened only by an almost Vaudeville-style accompaniment. Co-written and sung with Darrell Bath and Honest John Plain, the trio speak of 'conversations full of filth', mud-raking, lurid tales and intrusive photography, virtually every topic and tactic regularly pursued by the tabloid press in their relentless, journalistic, feeding frenzy. 'In America every morning, there are sick, mindless shows – people snooping into other people's lives. Britain has it with tabloid journalism. Over there they get headlines like "Lesbo Weirdos" and "I Shot My Mother's Sister". The lyric to Skeletons is quite serious, if you get past the fun of it.'

Wrapped around these two songs were 'Open My Eyes', where Ian describes the light and dark of New York City, and 'Still the Same', in which he ponders over past love, but, there is no question that 'The Artful Dodger' and 'Skeletons (in your Closet)', were at variance with the remainder of the record, and interrupted the flow of the album, as Hunter acknowledges. 'Those two tracks were the back end of *Dirty Laundry*, and sneaked on to this record, and they're kind of at odds, which pisses me off a bit. I think the album's flawed, but I am pleased with it. It was different because, for some reason, I kept going, but I've found a way I think to place the fast songs in context with the slow songs. "Something to Believe In" is a step in the right direction and the next one will be a complete unit. Dylan's *Oh Mercy* album was like that. That's what I want to do, a complete record, where you sit down and you're never taken out of the mood. I just missed it with *The Artful Dodger*.

'Writing is difficult and there are no set rules for me. I had two huge hits in America; one took six years to write ("Ships") and the other took ten hours ("Once Bitten Twice Shy"). I'm envious of people who can write lyrics and music at the same time. Usually, for Ian Hunter, it's the music first, because he has a terrible job with lyrics. I'm a big one for the first line, and you can wait forever. Since Mick died, I'm very in focus and the antenna's up. I've had a problem writing for fifteen years so you have to enjoy it when it comes. There's been times when I've done an album and it's sold a lot of records, and obviously they want you to go straight back in. I find when I tour, it takes a year to get the muscle back and then you need a year to write. When I worked with the E Streeters, they said Springsteen carries five new songs in his head all the time, which astonished me. But now I know it's possible because at the moment I've got seven.'

The Artful Dodger contained some of Ian's finest and most consistent songs and as it was completed, he briefly came under the new management of David Spero, who has represented Joe Walsh, Glen Frey and The Eagles. Hunter then switched to Out Of Time Management, owned by old friend, Kris Gray, and April 1997 saw a UK release for *The Artful Dodger* album, with Gray's label, Citadel Records. 'Michael Picasso' and the title track were also issued as singles, the latter featuring the unreleased, PJ Proby-inspired 'Fuck It Up'. 'I read Proby's living in a semi-detached in North London with garden gnomes on his lawn,' remarked Ian. 'What a wonderful character!'

Hunter's career seemed to be rejuvenated with high profile appearances on MTV's VH1, where he performed 'Michael Picasso' and 'Irene Wilde' and a slot on *My Top 10*, Ian introducing some of his favourite videos. This collection, un-like previous radio appearances, focused on more recent material all spanning the eighties, with the exception of one track. Prefaced by Mott The Hoople's 'Golden Age of Rock 'n' Roll' video, Hunter's selection comprised Run DMC / Aerosmith's 'Walk This Way', Robert Palmer's 'Addicted to Love', Cyndi Lauper's 'Money Changes Everything', Bob Dylan's 'Dignity', The Waterboys' 'The Whole of the Moon', Prince's 'Kiss', Keith Richards' 'Take It So Hard', The Police 'Every Breath You Take' and Chuck Berry's 'Sweet Little Sixteen'.

With former Mott publicist Tony Brainsby in tow again after more than twenty years, a month-long British tour was set up throughout May to promote *The Artful Dodger* including London's Shepherd's Bush Empire. Hunter's band comprised Paul Francis, ex-Paul Weller and Chris Farlowe on bass, Alvin Lee drummer Alan Young, Kinks, Sweet, Roger Chapman and ex-English Assassin Ian Gibbons on keyboards and guitarists Paul Cuddiford and Darrell Bath. The set contained seven songs from the new album, standard Mott and Hunter clas-sics plus the surprise inclusion of 'Who Do You Love?' and sensationally, 'The Moon Upstairs'.

Ian confesses that live performance remains enjoyable but apart from the stage, the road can still be desperate. 'If a hall is full of people who love you, and I have a fair few loyal fans over the years, you can have some great times. Touring varies. I never liked the 20,000-seater syndrome, it didn't make any sense. You hear 20,000 people roaring the group's name when you come on, but then it's so isolated it's just like you're playing on your own. I much prefer clubs. I like 500-seaters now because you can see people.'

Hunter worked briefly with Joe Elliott in a demo studio after a live date in Dublin on his summer 1997 tour. 'Ian said he had two new songs and wanted to try and record them. Bow Lane Studios is a tiny place and I knew the guys there from doing parts of Def Leppard's *Retroactive* and *Slang* albums. So we arranged for Ian and his group to set up, and from 2 until 6 in the morning they tried two new songs. His band didn't really know the material, but to see Ian operate and guide them all by eye contact was fantastic to watch.'

The Mick Ronson Memorial II at Hull Arena, and the opening of the Ronson memorial stage in Queen's Gardens, took place on 9 and 10 August 1997, Hunter headlining at both events. The jetting to and from America continued with a further UK tour in September and October, Ian using the same band, but pulling further rabbits from the hat with his first ever live performances of 'Waterlow', '3,000 Miles from Here', 'Red Letter Day', 'The Saturday Gigs', plus the occa-sional preview of a new song entitled 'Salvation'.

Mott The Hoople material does not present too much of a problem for Hunter live. 'I don't mind doing a couple of the old songs, apart from "Dudes". I like most of the other hits that we had. "Dudes" isn't a problem because it's a great song, but I have to do it live, or I'll piss people off. I went to see Procul Harum once and laboured my way through their entire set waiting for "A Whiter Shade of Pale" and they didn't do it. Assholes!'

Optimism had been high for Ian's album and tours, but with no coordinated worldwide release for the CD, like *Dirty Laundry*, sales dissipated over many months. Hunter confessed that whereas record companies were clamouring for his signature in the eighties when he was musically dry and 'busking it' with compositions for movie soundtracks, now he had songs-a-plenty, but no world-wide deal. He also admitted that a new Mott The Hoople project would easily tempt several international record companies, so what of the other Mott members and could the future conceivably hold anything in terms of a possible re-union?

Verden Allen lives near Neath and continues to play in occasional bands around Herefordshire and South Wales. Following his solo album release he recorded five tracks, 'Two Miles from Heaven', 'The Weather Report', 'It's Too Late Now', 'All Over You' and 'Channel Train', for a mini-album, but his group Thunderbuck Ram has since folded. More recently he has formed Flat Out, play-ing original songs including 'New Way', 'Backdoors', 'All the Young Dudes' and covers such as 'Wishing Well' and 'Feel Like Makin' Love'.

Morgan Fisher and his Japanese wife remain based in Tokyo, and he contin-ues to play with a number of local groups. In 1993, Morgan released a self-com-posed single entitled 'Humtone 4' with one of the versions sub-titled 'Sea Diver Mix'. More recently Morgan put together a Mott The Hoople covers album fea-turing various Japanese musicians and a guest appearance by Brian May on 'All the Way from Memphis'. 'Some famous Japanese friends wanted to play on the Mott The Hoople tribute album,' says Fisher. 'There's a lot of musicians here who love Mott. The album was very effortless and a pleasant recording experi-ence.'

Released by Sony Japan under the title *Moth Poet Hotel*, the CD contained new recordings of Mott's most famous hits, most notably a stunning re-working of 'Honaloochie Boogie' by The Yellow Monkey, covers of two older songs, 'Death May Be Your Santa Claus' and 'Rock and Roll Queen', plus a new Fisher composition about Mott's members and their exploits, *Moth Poet Hotel*, which cleverly utilised original tapes of Ian introducing live tracks in the mix. Fisher's memories of Mott are good ones.

'Mott The Hoople gave me some of the most fun-filled years of my music career but also a lot of heart and a lot of humanity. When I look at Ian's lyrics now I see that he likes to write about the common people – the ordinary people – the whore on 42nd Street. He also writes about himself very honestly and very frankly and I wish I'd realised that at the time. I wish we all had, because I think we might still be together if we had. Somehow he couldn't communicate it to us directly, he just did it through his songs, which was quite enough, why should we expect anymore? He ought to write another book, a story based on all his ex-periences, make it fictional and turn it into a movie.'

Dale Griffin no longer works for BBC Radio One but holds the record for producing more rock sessions than any other producer on the station. He still lives in London and remains loosely involved with the music industry. Dale's energies have more recently been channelled into the re-mixing and mastering of the long-awaited Mott The Hoople CD Anthology for Sony Music. Originally titled *Mott's the Story* ...(and almost *The Game of Life* after REM's lyric), commercial marketing considerations won the day and, after nearly four years of preparation, the 3 CD box-set, *All the Young Dudes – the Anthology*, has finally seen the light of day. The package features 63 tracks, over 30 being unreleased or alternate versions, including 'Moonbus', 'Ohio', 'Downtown', 'The Debt', 'The Hunchback Fish' and 'All the Young Dudes' with David Bowie vocal.

Pete Watts sold his London antiques store and returned to Herefordshire to open and run a second-hand records, instruments and clothes outlet with 'business partner and best friend' Roberta Griffiths (Berto). He remains a keen carp fisherman and has no desire whatsoever to renew his association with the music industry, being unwilling to participate in any Mott The Hoople reunion.

Mick Ralphs still lives in Oxfordshire and virtually severed links with Bad Company after their acoustic CD, *Stories Told & Untold*. His current musical plans are 'uncertain' although he has been 'talking' with Paul Rodgers and a Bad Company boxed set may be compiled.

Stan Tippins has worked as tour manager for The Pretenders, Simple Minds, Sade and King Crimson and is still involved and highly regarded in the industry, even turning down significant offers, such as the Sex Pistols re-union tour. Tippins still resides near Leominster and continues to visit Edgar Street to watch his beloved Hereford United.

1990 saw renewed speculation about a possible Mott The Hoople reunion with several companies interested in signing the band, most significantly an American label in a five million dollar deal. Lengthy dialogue took place between Hunter, Ralphs, Watts and Griffin at Ian's Worthing home but Mick Ralphs, whilst prepared to consider some recording work, was unwilling to re-unite in a more active capacity due to continuing commitments with Bad Company at that time. Watts and Griffin offered to reform with Ronson in the line-up but the plan failed. Undoubtedly, the last chance of Mott The Hoople's resurrection had gone forever.

Whilst a group re-union is unlikely, it is possible that the original story of Norman Mott may yet be captured on film, as Willard Manus explains. 'Mott the novel has been optioned six or seven different times by Hollywood producers, but to date the film version has obviously not been made. Recently, one of the guys who had formerly optioned it called to ask if the rights were still available. He has actually written a screen adaptation of the book. I read it a few years ago – it wasn't bad, though he envisaged cutting down my Rabelasian, bigger-than-life character of Norman Mott to Dustin Hoffman size! I have my doubts about the book ever being turned into a movie; it's such a sixties novel, but you never know. As with just about everything else in life, I have hope but no faith.'

Dale Griffin recently had what sounded like the final say on any prospect of a re-united Mott The Hoople. 'The main thing missing from everything I've ever read about Mott The Hoople is the fun and good times we all had. Of course it wasn't 100 per cent fun, nothing that's worthwhile ever is, but a good time was had by all. There was a great team spirit. On 5 June 1969, Ian Hunter joined a Herefordshire four-piece called, at that time, Savage Rose and Fixable. On 27 June 1969, Mott The Hoople was adopted as the name of Hunter, Watts, Ralphs, Allen and Griffin. Today, more than twenty-five years later, I can see no possibility of, or good reason for, re-forming Mott. It would not truly be fun any more. So, if you do hear of a new Mott The Hoople album or gig, it'll either be for a very good cause or an enormous sum of money. Be honest, what's the point of All the Old Dudes?'

Dale subsequently confessed that he would at least like to see some Mott The Hoople re-activity, particularly one final attempt to set their recorded work straight. 'When we talked with Ian in 1990, Watts and I suggested a Mott The Hoople reformation with Mick Ronson,' says Griffin. 'But Ian was adamant that it had to be Mick Ralphs or nobody, because he felt that the competition would have helped the songwriting, whereas Mick Ronson didn't really do anything in the way of songwriting, which may or may not be true. Whether we needed the songwriting or not, I don't know.

'The reason that I wanted a Mott The Hoople re-union was the same reason that I wanted to record a final single after "Foxy Foxy", which is why I went through all the hoops to get "The Saturday Gigs" recorded. The idea of a Mott The Hoople re-union with Ronson was probably slightly last ditch. I don't mean that as any offence to Ronson, but I don't think he ever considered himself to be a part of Mott The Hoople. We still respected him as a guitarist; how could you not? Certainly, my wish was that somehow we could put the story of Mott as a recording group straight because live, you could never get that back. Once Verden Allen and Mick Ralphs had left, the original Mott The Hoople was gone forever and that was the real essence of the group. After that, it was a slightly different thing and when Mick Ronson joined it was different again.

'We could never get back to where we were as a live group and, probably at our advanced ages, it would be a bad idea to go on stage. I've seen all these bands who come back, trotting themselves around and it's appalling, absolutely appalling. I'd hate to be a part of that, these old farts who just come back and croak out their old hits and some disastrous new song they've written.

'I never kidded myself about anything Mott The Hoople did because it was never right, and I knew it was never right. It wasn't popular to say that a particular record wasn't very good, whether it be *Wildlife* or *Brain Capers,* because there were good things about it, but there were also ineptitudes about all of our records that were just unforgiveable. Some of them were not our own. Some were to do with the production and recording engineering, and the advice that we were given by professional people like producers and engineers was wrong. I now know it to be wrong and I'm quite appalled that these people who we trusted, gave us such wrong information. I assume that they did it in good faith, but it doesn't really say much for their knowledge that they were saying these things.'

'A classic case to me was "Sweet Angeline", which we did one night at Island Studios with Guy Stevens, totally pissed. Mick Ralphs had got a Sunn guitar amp and it was incredible, it was the best guitar sound I ever heard him get. So we did "Sweet Angeline" and Guy Stevens was leaping about raving, and we came in after doing the take that he said was "the one" and listened to it and we were thinking, "Fantastic, this is great." We all went home happy and came back to the studio the next day sober, and listened to it again and it was diabolical, which shows you how bad the influence of alcohol can be. There's one point in the song where it almost collapses, because we all make a similar mistake at the same time, and the song all but stops, and then re-starts and carries on. And we said to Guy, "We can't use that, that's awful, let's try it again," but he refused point blank to let us try again and so that's the take on record that we have to live with. There's things like the whole of the *Dudes* album. It's nothing like we heard it when we were recording it. Things like "Sucker" were as heavy as Led Zeppelin.

'I think the most inept album we did was *Wildlife*, in terms of the engineer getting it totally wrong and insisting that we did it that way. I don't know what's worse, that he insisted we did it that way or that we just let him get on with it. I think we thought this guy had done so many good things that he must be right and we must be wrong, and when it comes out it's going to sound great, really, because he said it would. Unfortunately, it sounded just as crap when it was on record as it did in the studio to us. Things like "Whiskey Women", which was supposed to be a heavy rocker, just came out with what I call the "flubadubba" sound, very prominent in the seventies; no attack, no depth, no power to the drums or the track in general. Very, very disappointing. If there was ever a Mott The Hoople reunion, what I would want to do is to re-record some of the songs that we ruined, and maybe to do some new songs, if new songs came up that we felt were good enough to include.'

Watts is also saddened in hindsight with some of the group's recorded work and, in spite of the technological restrictions and the group's innocence at the time, unduly scathing of Mott The Hoople's recorded output. 'We hardly made a decent record in the history of the band. Most of our recordings were crap! "All the Way from Memphis" was a great song, but our take is insipid and the production is awful. It should have sounded like Brian May's version on *Moth Poet Hotel*. "The Golden Age of Rock 'n' Roll" was another classic! It was a great idea for a lyric, but we didn't really know what we were doing musically when we learnt and recorded it. We were just lopping along. Ian would say, "F here, C there," and I'd just be playing one-note bass to it. We were probably thinking we'd do it properly one day, but what happened was that we put it down as we'd got it, and added millions and millions of things on later, to try and make it sound better, but if the foundation isn't right, how can it work? Because we were working all the time, most of our material was recorded too quickly, so the bass and drum parts were never worked out properly. They were thrown down and things added to it, which to me isn't how you do it. Ian would come along with a song and we'd go in to record without planning it, and before you'd know what had happened, a three or four minute track was taped, instead of us going away and developing good parts for it.

'In the later period, Hunter tended to like brass and saxes, harping back to old rock 'n' roll. He liked Leon Russell and *Mad Dogs and Englishmen*, and I couldn't stand any of that stuff, I couldn't stick it. Ian always wanted to get girl singers in and sax players and trombonists and I kept thinking, "why can't we just be fucking Mott The Hoople!" The strength was the five of us together. He also wanted us to sound like The Stones, and have Buff and me playing like Charlie Watts and Keith Richards, because Keith played bass on a lot of their tracks. The difference was that Keith Richards was totally out of his brains and was a laid-back guy, playing laid-back bass. I wasn't, and I didn't want to be. I was more in tune with what came later, which the punks did. That was my personality.

'There were many wrangles in the group about our direction. Travelling to gigs, the car often got stopped in a lay-by for a fight, but someone would hold two of us apart in the end. There would be lots of shouting, like on "Violence", but never quite a punch-up. The arguments could be over a song, or someone's playing, or politics, which was always a group favourite. We often had arguments and yet, when we played, we were totally together and focused.

'On the *Anthology* set, there are one or two demos that have got the electricity that none of our original releases ever had, like "Moonbus", where we were just jamming. That is great, because it has got the electric tension that we used to get live, rather than on record. Maybe "Moonbus" is an example of what we really had?'

When asked if Mott might still reunite or whether the legend should be left to sleep on, Hunter is as frank as ever. 'I think the words "let the legend sleep" sound nice to me. I think if somebody made it extremely easy, something might be done, but I can't see us getting together, not without somebody in between us to sort it out. Mott was a democratic band and I've been a solo artist for a long, long time, plus Bad Company was basically Ralph's band, so Mick's full of Bad Co and I'm full of me. I don't know if there could be a Mott The Hoople now, especially with Guy no longer around. Maybe it is better to let sleeping dogs lie. I don't think it's a big deal. I think there's a few people who would like to see it and I know a couple of record companies have approached us over the years, one as recently as 1994. But to reform Mott The Hoople would mean taking the personalities into account all over again, and I don't know if I could do that. I'm too set in my ways.

'I would find a band very hard now. I'm naturally dominant and aggressive, and I'm also nervous. I don't like aggravation, so it's very hard for me to be a part of something. In Mott The Hoople, everything seemed to be very intense and very dramatic. People look back with rose-tinted glasses and the reality might not be quite what they think. It's like Gary Glitter's Christmas Shows that he does – that means absolutely nothing to me. I like to do something with my life, and that's not doing anything, so I don't really see the point.'

Pete Watts is particularly lukewarm about the prospects of any re-union. 'I run a very successful shop and it has taken some time and a lot of very hard work to make it profitable and worthwhile. I wouldn't give that away, because I'm also my own boss now, which you're not in a major group, contrary to what people think. Technically, you're in charge in a band, but really they're in charge, the management and the label. That's what "Marionette" is all about. I've always hated everyone from record companies, agencies, management and music business accountants, who are all full of shit. The only person I loved was Guy Stevens, but then Guy was different. I'm in charge of my own destiny now with my business, and I'm content with doing some painting, guitar collecting and fishing too. I may write and record some material soon, including an album of ambient music, just for my own pleasure, but I am finished with the industry. I'm a loner, who will always have a wild streak, but I just keep out of people's way, free of clubs and pubs. I pay my taxes and that's it. If I sat down with a record label now, I'd end up laughing and walking out, or they would, because the starting point for me would be £3 million, tax-free, or forget it! It really wouldn't be worthwhile.'

Reluctance was confirmed during finalisation of the Sony *Anthology* in 1997. With Dale Griffin as the catalyst, all five original members of Mott The Hoople agreed in principle to spend 2 November 1997 in a London studio to record 'Like A Rolling Stone', as a special bonus track for the CD set. However the final act was to fail, days before the session, and Mott's re-union has now gone forever.

'It was unfortunate for the *Anthology* and Mott's fans,' says Griffin. 'We always agreed in the band that we would do something as Mott The Hoople again one day. Hunter used to say right at the beginning, "If ever the group breaks up, we'll always have the family jewels. We can always do something, even as our pension." But it wasn't to be. The absence of one member devalued the planned *Anthology* session, even though we'd recorded that way before with "Road to Birmingham", which didn't have Pete on bass, although no one really knew.'

Reformation or not, the ballad of Mott The Hoople and Ian Hunter is still being sung almost thirty years after Mott's genesis, in terms of the latest *Anthology* project and continuing solo records and live performances from Hunter, which is a gratifying scenario when one looks at the decaying and insipid music scene. Mott The Hoople made some of the most glamorous and exciting music of the early seventies, but were also more innovative and percipient than most. Today, Ian Hunter remains one of rock's finest practitioners; single minded, valid and remote from the manufactured, musical wilderness of formula-ridden, trend-driven groups whose unimaginative appearance mirrors their followers.

The common denominator throughout Mott's trials and tribulations was the anarchic honesty of their performances and Ian's potent writing, which is still uncompromising today. Watts feels that Hunter's ability, observations and his experience of life were key factors. 'Ian had lived a life before he was in Mott The Hoople. I don't like to say he was older than the rest of us, but because he was, he had experience and understood things I didn't care about – injustice, hardship, politics. He'd seen poverty, whereas I'd always had a reasonably easy life, and all I was interested in was playing music and meeting girls. I didn't really care who was Prime Minister. I didn't matter to me then, and it doesn't now. They were all useless then and, whilst I understand more about it now, they're still useless. Ian cared much more about things and took them to heart. He was a level-headed guy and very down to earth. He was never seduced by people saying, "Ah, you're much better than the rest of them," like Freddie Mercury used to get in Queen.'

Watts agrees that Hunter had great foresight and that 'Marionette' prefaced *Stardust* and 'Bohemian Rhapsody' just as 'The Moon Upstairs' and 'Crash Street Kids' were uncanny forerunners to punk. 'That was typical Mott The Hoople

SOMETHING TO BELIEVE IN

really. Always do it first and never get the recognition. That's why the group was so good. Everything we did then, and do now, is so fucking difficult.'

Ian is candid in his thoughts on his contribution to the group and accepts that he was in effect Mott The Hoople, but not without caveats and acknowledgement of the other members. 'To be honest, throughout Mott The Hoople, I considered myself a songwriter. I didn't really take much notice of the songs that Mott did that I didn't write. It sounds terrible I know, but I was just totally into what I did and so, when I left, I was writing just the same as I always wrote. In a way, Ian Hunter was Mott The Hoople. But that was a fucking great band, and they were all there one hundred per cent at the point where we were great, and they all had a part to play.

'When it split, Guy Stevens came up to Wembley and sat with me for hours saying, "You are Mott The Hoople. You are Mott The Hoople. You must stay Mott The Hoople." But, to be honest, I was sick of Mott The Hoople by that time and I just wanted to be Ian Hunter. I also knew what was going to happen with the rest of the guys. What would the rhythm section do? Nobody was going to book them unless they used the name Mott. I was okay, I was writing and getting a few bob, but they had only ever made wages. Guy really went at me and I wouldn't do it. But that was when I realised in one way I was Mott The Hoople, and Guy wanted me to be that. He wanted me to be the character in the book.'

The music and lyrics of Mott The Hoople have inspired and influenced some of the world's greatest bands – Queen, Kiss, The Clash, Motley Crue, Primal Scream, Blur and Oasis to name but a few. Joe Elliott is one of the biggest fans within the industry. As well as the music, it was the visual aspect of the group that caught Elliott's attention and inspired him.

'When I was growing up and took an interest in music, I was very much into watching *Top of the Pops* and seeing a band like Sweet – the way they looked almost meant as much as the way they sounded. Bolan had this very effeminate image and Bowie was similar, so to see this guy, Ian Hunter, who had long curly hair and sunglasses, was refreshing. It was almost like you could never get to see him. It was like a mask, but not really. Visually, Mott influenced me a lot and I can honestly say if it hadn't been for Ian Hunter, I probably wouldn't have been in a band. He was as responsible for me doing what I do as Bolan ever was.

'Musically Mott are a million miles from what Def Leppard does, but they're always there in the background. There's always little influences that you can steal from, and the way Ian writes songs that you can take note of. He is a constant reference to me, especially his early work. He has the ability to write words for a song that aren't as banal as your average rock lyric. Hunter never pandered to that mundane approach and wrote more from the Dylan side of things but, in my opinion, much better than Dylan.

'Personally, I'd place Mott The Hoople at the top in terms of popular music history. Obviously that would go against the grain of a lot of people who would say, "How can they be better than Led Zeppelin or The Beatles?" Maybe they're not, but in my eyes, The Beatles are such a big institution and Zep are loved so much, that's already taken care of, so I'm allowed my own little indulgence as an underdog. Mott are the one band I could play all day and every day and never get bored. I still discover things in their records that I missed having played them for twenty years. For me, Mott The Hoople are tops without a shadow of a doubt.'

Recorded covers of Mott The Hoople and Ian Hunter material, and musical collaborations, have been widespread – 'Thunderbuck Ram', 'Waterlow', 'Moving On', 'Sweet Angeline', 'The Moon Upstairs', 'Death May Be Your Santa Claus', 'Ready for Love', 'All the Young Dudes', 'One of the Boys', 'Honaloochie Boogie', 'All the Way from Memphis', 'I Wish I Was Your Mother', 'Violence', 'The Golden Age of Rock 'n' Roll', 'Foxy Foxy', 'Once Bitten Twice Shy', 'Who Do You Love?', 'Irene Wilde', 'England Rocks', 'Ships', 'Standin' in My Light', 'Cleveland Rocks', 'Detroit', 'Every Step of the Way', 'Speechless', 'Big Time', 'Pain', 'Red Letter Day', 'The Other Man' – by artists including Joe Walsh, The Dictators, The Skids, The Damned, Ellen Foley, Blue Oyster Cult, Generation X, Barry Manilow, Shaun Cassidy, John Waite, Bonnie Tyler, Hanoi Rocks, Mountain, Status Quo, The Monkees, Little Angels, Willie Nelson, Great White, Andy Taylor, Bruce Dickinson, Contraband, The Angels, Maria McKee, Thunder and The Presidents of the United States of America.

Pete Watts is amazed at the praise given by artists and contemporary groups over the years. 'God knows why we influenced all these people. Sometimes I can't see what all the fuss is about to be honest although, I think in the early days, Ian's lyrics were very pointed and that was a big part of it. Before Mott started, Ian had lived quite a full life whereas most kids in a band, when they start at twenty or twenty one, haven't really got anything to write about at all. I think Hunter had had a difficult time and he was able to express things well lyrically – like "The Moon Upstairs" – you can see the anger in it. He'd been through horrible, hard times. He'd lived it, but also had unmatched ability to express it, in a cutting kind of way.'

Nevertheless, Watts believes it was right for Mott The Hoople to split when they did. 'There is a school of thought that says pop artists should pack it in when they're over thirty, and it might be right. I can't say I like what David Bowie does now, although you have to admire him for chopping and changing and not sticking to one formula. Bowie, Dylan, The Stones – they're not breaking any new ground anymore. There's no point in The Rolling Stones carrying on, really, because they're just becoming caricatures of themselves. It may be unfair to say that, because they've clearly got something and influenced lots of bands. Maybe it's that bit of magic. Maybe Mott The Hoople had that, I don't know if it did or not. If people say they love Mott, I just can't see it, I don't know why. I do think our strong point was our live show, but none of that remains – there's no video, no film, none of the records sound any good. If we were good live, there's no evidence, and all you can really go by is the testimony of people like Pete Frame, who seemed to be quite impressed by us. It felt good on stage at the time, but was there really something there or not? It's easy to see the group through rose-tinted glasses, but it's nice to think people really liked what we did. It's also funny to think that people are probably as mad on Mott The Hoople as I am on The Monks and The West Coast Pop Art Experimental Band. Poor devils!'

Without question, Mott The Hoople were hugely innovative and ahead of their time – clothes and boots, classic guitars and dramatic custom guitar shapes, the idea of a covers album way before Bowie and Ferry. The music was potent and varied, the lyrics always carried a message and visually they were powerful. With modern-day aggressive marketing, management and the medium of video and Music Television, they could have been commercially successful from the start. Sadly, the relatively amateurish and inexperienced music world of 1969 worked to their disadvantage, and Mott shambled along in their own inimitable way, unconsciously leaving hugely influential recordings in their wake.

Hunter firmly believes that Mott The Hoople has died once and for all. 'We did it, but it's gone. I know it may be a duff attitude, but that's the way I feel. I find it hard to listen to anything I've done, with the band or solo. I always re-member what went on. I can't enjoy it for itself. Hopefully I will eventually. I look back with absolutely nothing and I don't feel a thing. To look back and do all that bullshit is all right when you're 75 or something, but I'm not the slight-est bit interested. Neither was Ronson. We never sat around listening to old records like people seem to think you do. I still feel I'm a viable proposition and I'm still happening. Mick, like me, never particularly wanted to be huge. He just wanted to have a good time, which we did, on a daily basis. He did what he wanted to do and I've always done what I wanted to do. If a situation went a bit funny, then I've left that situation. That's how we both felt. We left each other very often for that reason, but somehow we survived.'

Ian is also settled and content in Connecticut. 'It's the longest I've ever lived anywhere. Culturally it's better in Britain but there's a lot of things that are bet-ter in America, like the size of house you can have and education I think. I read the English papers everyday and I watch English TV every night and I still love coming to Britain, but I came up at a time when Harold Wilson came to power. I knew nothing about money and then when money started falling through the letterbox, I found out the government took it all back. I'd been labouring for eight years and didn't want to go back to it, so I was one of the guys who left. Then Maggie wanted us to come back but really it's about the same still, with VAT, hidden taxes and fuel. It's better in America. The difference is that in England the people are scared off the government, while in the States the gov-ernment are scared of the people. In America people admire it if you want to get ahead, but here they don't like it – "Get back down here, with me!" '

In May 1998, Hunter is writing for a further album. 'At the moment, I'm try-ing to write pop songs, as a kickback to *The Artful Dodger* which had no hits on it. I've got songs like "Salvation" and I'm working on a great one called "It's Alright With Me". I've also done another book in draft, a tour diary written in the UK, with the working title, *The Life and Times of the Essex Man*, a reference to my tour manager Kris Gray. I've set the complete diary aside for a while though. The book I want to write is almost like a textbook or a handbook. It's an improvement on a rhyming dictionary strictly for writers, so it's pretty boring for your average person, but it would be a valuable tool for composers. I'll probably do a novel at one point, but again, it would be qualified like the diary.'

During the eighties, Pete Watts attended an after-gig party with Queen at Legend's Club in London's West End, during which Freddie Mercury asked him persistently why Hunter had left Mott The Hoople, and never reformed the group, a situation which Mercury perceived as 'commercial suicide'. It remains testament to Ian's single-mindedness and self-belief in his material however that he has continuously shunned this option and pursued a stylistically varied and eclectic solo career in an uncompromising fashion. *Ian Hunter, All American Alien Boy, Short Back 'n' Sides* and *YUI Orta* display an invigorating musical diversity and illustrate Hunter's artistic integrity.

Ian remains absolutely uncompromising in the songs that he writes and regards commercial success and money as secondary. 'Success is doing what you want to do. My Grandma always said it's a terrible thing if people can't do what they want to do. Sometimes it might not be too fashionable and it might not be what other people think you ought to do, and sometimes you suffer for it, but life is doing what you want to do. If you want to have a career and be huge and monstrous more power to you, but money's bullshit. It's convenient and you get what you want, but it's not the be-all and end-all, and more and more people think that's what success is and they're making a big mistake. Like when Ronson went on the road with T-Bone Burnett for $100 a week, sleeping on people's floors. The alternative was $2,500 a week with Bob Seger but he didn't like the music. I really admired him for that.

'Americans have a difficult time with people like me because they really think in terms of the appearance of success, rather than actual success. They learn to be successful, you have to have a lot of money, a nice house and all the appliances. That to them is success. A lot of them find out that when they actually wind up in the big house full of things, there's nothing there. You can't get away from yourself. A lot of that may not gel with what everybody thinks you should do, but I don't have to live with these people. I have to live with me. I'm sorry if that's not a fan's delight but I always resort to what Jerry Lee Lewis said, "They can kiss my ass."

'I consider myself a rock 'n' roll artist. I'm not in it for the *Billboard*. I'm in it for something much bigger than that. Having a complete life and looking back on it knowing I did it according to me. According to me, my life has been a total success, so far. I've had to work really hard to keep it that way. Everything I've wanted to do I did. There are times when you're trying to get a record deal and it's precarious, so you have to fight a bit harder. But it comes. I will not sit around for ten years writing the same songs and playing in the same band. I won't do it. That's not my idea of success. Anyway, it's nice to be always on the way up!'

Appendix 1

Chronology

1963
Hunter joins The Apex Rhythm & Blues All Stars in Northampton, recording first EP for John Lever Records, and forms his own band, Hurricane Henry and The Shriekers
Watts and Griffin meet at Ross Grammar School and co-found The Anchors, then Wild Dog's Hell Hounds
Stan Tippins forms The Stormraisers

1964
Hunter's group becomes Freddie Fingers Lee and The Shriekers who undertake several tours of Germany
Watts and Griffin form The Soulents
Verden Allen joins The Inmates then The Astrals
Ralphs joins The Buddies with Stan Tippins becoming the vocalist soon after

1965
Hunter joins The Homelanders and plays bass on one Freddie Fingers Lee single, 'The Friendly Undertaker', for Fontana Records
Watts and Griffin form The Silence
Watts joins Stan Tippins and Mick Ralphs in The Buddies

1966
The Buddies become The Problem and then The Doc Thomas Group, touring Italy
Hunter moves to London and auditions as bass player for Miller Anderson's Scenary, who also act as backing band for The Young Idea, David McWilliams and Mike Berry
Dale Griffin makes major label recording debut on singles by The Interns and Bryn Yemm and the Yemen

1967
Doc Thomas Group LP and single released on Dischi Interrecord
Griffin is invited to join Watts, Ralphs and Tippins in The Doc Thomas Group who are featured on Italian television
Verden Allen joins The Shakedown Sound backing Jimmy Cliff and playing on *Hard Road to Travel* LP
Mick Ralphs follows Allen into The Shakedown Sound

1968

JANUARY
Griffin declines offer to play drums with Dave Edmunds Love Sculpture, opting to join Ralphs and Allen in Jimmy Cliff's Shakedown Sound
Ralphs rejoins Watts, Griffin and Tippins and the Doc Thomas quartet invite Allen to join them and gig as The Shakedown Sound

MARCH
Hunter joins Freddie Lee with Miller Anderson in At Last The 1958 Rock & Roll Show who release 'I Can't Drive' single on CBS Records

AUGUST
With a name change to Charlie Woolfe, the same line up records 'Dance, Dance, Dance' single, released by NEMS

Ian backs Billy Fury on bass, and works for music publishers Francis Day and Hunter with compositions recorded by Nicol Williamson and Dave Berry

SEPTEMBER
Shakedowns/Doc Thomas become Silence

1969
Hunter joins The New Yardbirds under direction of Mickie Most
Watts auditions for Free and Island A&R man Guy Stevens

MAY
Silence audition for Guy

JUNE
Ian Hunter Patterson auditions for Silence
Named 'Savage Rose and Fixable' by Guy, sessions begin for the first album

JULY
Album concluded as Mott The Hoople

AUGUST / SEPTEMBER
Mott play their first gigs at The Bat Cavern Club, Riccione, Italy and make their live British debut at Romford supporting King Crimson

OCTOBER
'Rock and Roll Queen' single issued

NOVEMBER
Mott The Hoople debut album released on Island

1970

FEBRUARY
Mott make UK Radio and TV debuts on *Top Gear* and *Disco 2*

APRIL
Mott record first BBC *In Concert*

JUNE–AUGUST
9 week Mott The Hoople US tour

SEPTEMBER
Mott record a live album at Croydon supporting Free
Mad Shadows album is released

NOVEMBER–DECEMBER
Mott record third studio album

1971

MARCH
Wildlife album released

APRIL
Second US tour

MAY
Recording session with George Shadow Morton in New York

JUNE
'Midnight Lady' single issued

JULY
Mott sell out The Royal Albert Hall, London causing scenes compared to Beatlemania. Damage leads to a ban on all rock events at the venue.
Top of the Pops TV debut

AUGUST
Mott commence sessions for their fourth studio album

SEPTEMBER
'Downtown' single issued and Guy Stevens returns for *Brain Capers* album sessions

OCTOBER
Mott UK tour with Paul Rodgers' Peace as support
Luther Grosvenor solo album *Under Open Skies* released

NOVEMBER
Brain Capers, Mott's final Island album, issued

DECEMBER
European tour
Final *In Concert* for BBC Radio One

1972

JANUARY
Mott record new Island single

MARCH
Mott split after uninspired gigs in Switzerland

APRIL
Mott The Hoople's Rock 'n' Roll Circus UK tour

MAY
David Bowie rescues Mott, writing and producing a new single, 'All the Young Dudes'

JUNE
Mott The Hoople sign with CBS Records and record a Bowie produced album

JULY
'All the Young Dudes' single issued

SEPTEMBER
All the Young Dudes album released

OCTOBER
Island Records attempt to cash-in on Mott's new chart success with release of *Rock and Roll Queen* compilation album.
UK tour with Home as support plus demo recordings

NOVEMBER–DECEMBER
Mott commence their third tour of the USA and play their first headlining American concert
Hunter writes his book, *Diary of a Rock 'n' Roll Star*

1973

JANUARY
Organist Verden Allen leaves Mott The Hoople to pursue a solo career

FEBRUARY
Mott tour Scotland and Northern England as a quartet and commence recording sessions for their next album at AIR Studios in London

APRIL
Mott album sessions completed

MAY
'Honaloochie Boogie' single issued

JULY
Mott album released
Ex-Love Affair keyboard player Morgan Fisher joins the group on piano with Mick Bolton on organ

JULY–AUGUST
First headlining US tour

AUGUST
'All the Way from Memphis' single released
Lead guitarist Mick Ralphs quits Mott and forms Bad Company with Paul Rodgers

SEPTEMBER
Ex-Spooky Tooth guitarist Luther Grosvenor joins Mott The Hoople as Ariel Bender

SEPTEMBER – OCTOBER
Mott's second headlining US tour

NOVEMBER
'Roll Away the Stone' single released

NOVEMBER–DECEMBER
Mott play headlining sell out UK tour with Queen as support
Two concerts in one evening at London's Hammersmith Odeon culminate in a crowd riot. Mott record both shows for a live album and prepare for their next studio LP. Mick Bolton leaves Mott – Morgan Fisher stays as permanent keyboard player

1974

JANUARY
Mott record *The Hoople* at London's Advision Studios

FEBRUARY
Hoople sessions completed with mixing at AIR London
Ian's book, *Diary of a Rock 'n' Roll Star* is published by Panther books

MARCH
'The Golden Age of Rock 'n' Roll' single and *The Hoople* album are released by CBS
Mott play 6 English dates in preparation for a major US Spring tour. Blue Weaver joins Mott as organist for live work
Mick Ronson's solo album *Slaughter on 10th Avenue* released on RCA

APRIL
Mott commence another headlining American tour with Queen as support

MAY
Mott sell out a week of concerts in New York's theatreland – the first rock band to play on Broadway. Concerts taped for live LP

JUNE
'Foxy Foxy' single released

SEPTEMBER
Guitarist Luther Grosvenor leaves Mott and forms Widowmaker
Former Spider From Mars, Mick Ronson, overdubs on 'The Saturday Gigs' single and records 'Lounge Lizzard', his first and only Mott track

OCTOBER
'The Saturday Gigs' single issued
Mott commence an extensive European tour with Ronson

NOVEMBER
Mott The Hoople Live LP released
Mott plan new recording sessions for next LP
Hunter collapses in New York
Mott's sell out UK Winter tour is re-scheduled and then scrapped

DECEMBER
Ian Hunter and Mick Ronson quit Mott the Hoople
Watts, Griffin and Fisher regroup as Mott, joined by ex-Hackensack guitarist Ray Major and Royce vocalist Nigel Benjamin

1975

JANUARY
Ian Hunter commences recording sessions with Mick Ronson for a new solo LP

FEBRUARY
Ronson's second solo LP *Play Don't Worry* released

MARCH
Ian Hunter album released and The Hunter Ronson Band play a sell-out UK tour

APRIL
'Once Bitten Twice Shy' single issued while Hunter emigrates to the USA and settles in New York state

APRIL AND MAY
Mott record debut LP at Clearwell Castle, Gloucestershire

MAY AND JUNE
Hunter Ronson play US live dates but cut short the original tour schedule. Ian and Mick work on demo tracks for a new Ronson LP but this is never recorded

AUGUST
Mott debut single 'Monte Carlo' released

SEPTEMBER
Mott's *Drive On* album is released, promoted with European and UK tour

OCTOBER
Mott embark on 40-date US tour supporting Aerosmith, Rush and Kiss

NOVEMBER
'By Tonight' single issued from *Drive On*
Mick Ronson joins Bob Dylan's Rolling Thunder Revue and tours the USA through to May 1976
Pop Chronik and *The Golden Age of Mott The Hoople* compilations are released in Germany

1976

JANUARY
Ian Hunter records his second solo album at Electric Lady Studios in New York City, working with Chris Stainton, David Sanborn, Jaco Pastorius and Queen

FEBRUARY
Mott record their second album at The Manor Studios, Oxfordshire
'It Takes One To Know One' issued as third *Drive On* single

MARCH
CBS release *Mott The Hoople's Greatest Hits*

APRIL
'All American Alien Boy' single and LP released. Hunter chooses not to promote the album with any concerts

JUNE
Shouting & Pointing issued, the second and final Mott LP

JUNE, JULY AND AUGUST
Mott's second US tour

JULY
'You Nearly Did Me In' single issued from *All American Alien Boy*
Hunter plays with The Fabulous Rhinestones
Mick Ronson produces Roger McGuinn album and forms band with him – Guam

OCTOBER
Mott tour Britain, appear on BBC Radio One *In Concert* and record 'Get Rich Quick' for single release

DECEMBER
Nigel Benjamin quits Mott

1977

JANUARY
Mott record with vocalist Steve Hyams. The tracks are shelved and Mott split

FEBRUARY
Hunter records a new album at Morin Heights near Montreal with producer Roy Thomas Baker.

The band's temporary residence is destroyed one night in an explosion

MAY
Overnight Angels LP released preceeded by a single, 'Justice of the Peace'

JUNE
Ian Hunter's Overnight Angels play UK and European live dates

JULY
Hunter's 'England Rocks' single issued
Mick Ronson works with John Cougar and Philip Rambow

SEPTEMBER
Watts, Griffin, Fisher, Major and new vocalist John Fiddler form British Lions and record debut album at The Manor

NOVEMBER AND DECEMBER
British Lions UK tour supporting Status Quo. Hunter joins The Lions on stage at Aylesbury Friars

1978

FEBRUARY
British Lions album and 'One More Chance to Run' single released on Vertigo records

APRIL AND MAY
Lions' release 'International Heroes' as a single, play UK tour supporting AC/DC and record session for John Peel on Radio One

JUNE
British Lions appear live on *Musikladen* on German TV
Ronson works with Annette Peacock, The Rich Kids and forms Rebel of Future
Hunter teams up with Corky Laing, Felix Pappalardi and Ronson and records an album

AUGUST
Ian produces Generation X

OCTOBER
Hunter signs with Chrysalis Records and commences album sessions in London with British 'New Wave' musicians

NOVEMBER AND DECEMBER
British Lions record second album, *Trouble With Women*, at RAK Studios

1979

JANUARY
Hunter reunites with Mick Ronson for recording sessions at New York's Power Station Studios with Bruce Springsteen's E Street Band

APRIL
British Lions split – Watts and Griffin form Grimtone Productions, Fisher Pipe Studios and Fiddler and Major play in Freeway and Box of Frogs
Hunter Ronson produce Ellen Foley's *Nightout* LP and work with David Werner and Genya Ravan.

MAY
You're Never Alone With A Schizophrenic album released

JUNE, OCTOBER AND NOVEMBER
Ian Hunter Band featuring Mick Ronson tour USA playing unprecedented week at The Roxy Los Angeles and one London concert
Guy Stevens resurfaces as producer of critically acclaimed *London Calling* LP by The Clash

1980

JANUARY
Hunter Ronson record at Media Sound Studios, NY.

Dale Griffin joins BBC Radio One as a session producer and compiles Mott The Hoople rarities album
Two Miles From Heaven, released by Island

FEBRUARY
Shades of Ian Hunter double LP issued by CBS,
containing Mott The Hoople and solo material
Griffin produces 'Slaughter and the Dogs'

APRIL
Welcome to the Club live double album issued on
Chrysalis

MAY
Hunter Ronson US tour
British Lions' *Trouble With Women* LP issued by Cherry
Red Records

OCTOBER
Hunter and Todd Rundgren play US live dates

DECEMBER
Hunter commences album sessions in New York

1981

MARCH
All the Way from Memphis compilation LP issued

AUGUST
Hunter releases *Short Back 'n' Sides* album, 'Lisa Likes
Rock 'n' Roll' single, and plays Milton Keynes
Festival plus European dates
Guy Stevens dies on 29 August in London

SEPTEMBER
Hunter US tour including Central Park concert
Watts and Griffin produce hit single for Department S
Hunter, Ralphs, Watts, Griffin and Fisher meet in
London to discuss Mott The Hoople reunion

1982
Morgan Fisher tours with Queen
Ian Hunter receives Musical Syndrome Award from
Ohio State University
Rock Giants compilation released by CBS Germany
Watts and Griffin produce Hanoi Rocks
Hunter re-joins CBS Records and commences album
sessions at Wizard Sound New York

1983

JULY
Ian Hunter's *All of the Good Ones are Taken* LP issued,
promoted with two singles – the title track and
'Somethin's Goin' On'

1984
Hunter records '(I'm the) Teacher', with Ronson, and
'Great Expectations' for *Teachers* and *Up the Creek*
movie soundtracks
History of Rock Mott The Hoople LP issued

1985
Hunter records 'Good Man in a Bad Time' with
Ronson for *Frightnight* film
Morgan Fisher moves to Japan

1986
Ian records 'Wake-Up Call' with Arthur Baker for *The
Wraith* movie soundtrack

1987

JANUARY
Ian demos new album with John Jansen ex-Cutting
Crew / Lou Reed producer
Hunter undertakes Autumn tour of Canada backed by
The Roy Young Band

DECEMBER
Greendow Productions announce proposed UK TV
documentary on Hunter

1988

FEBRUARY
Castle Communications release *Mott The Hoople – The
Collection* on double album and CD

JUNE
Ian and Mick reunite for Canadian concert tour. Joe
Elliott of Def Leppard joins Hunter Ronson on stage
in Toronto

NOVEMBER AND DECEMBER
Hunter Ronson US tour

1989

FEBRUARY
Hunter Ronson play two nights at London's Dominion
Theatre

JUNE AND JULY
Hunter Ronson commence album sessions at New
York's Power Station with producer Bernard
Edwards

JULY
Dale Griffin organises re-union of The Silence and
compiles *Walking with a Mountain*, Island compilation CD

NOVEMBER AND DECEMBER
Hunter Ronson US tour including Benefit Concert for
Cleveland Rock & Roll Hall of Fame

1990

JANUARY AND FEBRUARY
YUI Orta album issued on Mercury Records and
Hunter Ronson tour the UK and Europe
Hunter, Ralphs, Watts and Griffin meet to discuss Mott
The Hoople reunion

APRIL
Walking with a Mountain Island CD compilation released

OCTOBER
The Silence record at Rockfield Studios
Italian magazine releases *Mott* LP as *Mott The Hoople*

1991

JANUARY
Atlantic Records release US CD's of *Mott The Hoople*,
Mad Shadows, *Wildlife*, *Brain Capers* and *Rock and
Roll Queen*

MAY AND JUNE
Hunter Ronson Parkrock Scandinavian tour

AUGUST
Mick Ronson diagnosed as having liver cancer

1992

JANUARY AND FEBRUARY
Ronson produces album for Morrisey

APRIL
Ian and Mick play at The Freddie Mercury Tribute concert at Wembley, televised worldwide, Ronson's last
concert appearance

MAY AND JUNE
Hunter Scandinavian tour
Ronson continues to work on a solo album

JUNE
Sony release *London to Memphis* compilation CD

1993

JANUARY
Edsel issue *Mott The Hoople / Mad Shadows 2* on 1 CD in the UK

FEBRUARY
Dale Griffin leaves BBC Radio One, having produced nearly 2, 000 sessions

APRIL
Mick Ronson dies on 29 April in London

JUNE AND JULY
Hunter Scandinavian tour

JUNE
Mott featuring Steve Hyams CD issued on See For Miles

AUGUST
Ian plays three UK live dates

NOVEMBER
Columbia release *The Ballad of Mott The Hoople* double CD compilation

1994

APRIL
Backsliding Fearlessly, compilation CD of Mott The Hoople Island/Atlantic tracks, is released by Rhino
Hunter headlines the Mick Ronson Memorial Concert at London's Hammersmith Odeon

MAY
Ronson's album *Heaven and Hull* released

JULY AND AUGUST
Gringo Starrs album sessions at Abbey Road featuring Ian Hunter
Verden Allen's *Long Time No See* album issued on Spinit

1995

MARCH
Gringo Starrs sessions released as *Ian Hunter's Dirty Laundry* CD featuring Glen Matlock and Blue Weaver

MAY
Hunter commences sessions in Vermont for a new solo album

SEPTEMBER
Hunter Ronson 1989 *In Concert* CD released by Windsong
Mott The Hoople Sony CD Anthology planned
Luther Grosvenor makes musical comeback on Peter Green tribute album *Rattlesnake Guitar*
Research on Mott The Hoople tapes for *Anthology* box set begins

1996

JULY
Mott The Hoople BBC Sessions CD released by Windsong
Diary of a Rock 'n' Roll Star re-published

AUGUST
Luther Grosvenor releases second solo album *Floodgates*

SEPTEMBER
Ian Hunter's *The Artful Dodger* CD released in Norway

1997

FEBRUARY
Sony *Anthology* mixed by Martin Colley and Dale Griffin

APRIL
Hunter's *Artful Dodger* album released in UK

MAY
Ian plays 23-date British tour. 'Artful Dodger' single released

AUGUST
Hunter headlines at Mick Ronson Memorial II in Hull
Mott The Hoople Super Hits CD issued in USA

SEPTEMBER AND OCTOBER
Hunter plays second UK tour

1998

MARCH
'Michael Picasso' single released
Doc Thomas Group *The Italian Job* and The Silence *Shotgun Eyes* 2-on-1 CD issued by Angel Air

SEPTEMBER
Mott The Hoople – All the Young Dudes – The Anthology released by Sony Music

Appendix 2

Discography

Mott The Hoople

UK Singles

'Rock and Roll Queen' / 'Road to Birmingham'
November 1969 – Island WIP 6072

'Midnight Lady' / 'The Debt'
June 1971 – Island WIP 6105
initial copies in picture sleeve

'Downtown' / 'Home'
September 1971 – Island WIP 6112

'All the Young Dudes' / 'One of the Boys'
July 1972 – CBS 8271 – No. 3

'Honaloochie Boogie' / 'Rose'
May 1973 – CBS 1530 – No. 12

'All the Way from Memphis' / 'The Ballad of Mott the
Hoople'
August 1973: CBS 1764 – No. 10

'Roll Away the Stone' / 'Where Do You All Come
From?'
November 1973 – CBS 1895 – No. 8

'The Golden Age of Rock 'n' Roll' / 'Rest In Peace'
March 1974 – CBS 2177 – No. 16

'Foxy Foxy' / 'Trudi's Song'
June 1974 – CBS 2439 – No. 33

'Saturday Gigs' / Live Medley – 'Jerkin' Crocus' /
'Sucker' / 'Violence'
October 1974 – CBS 2754 – No. 41

Re-issued UK Singles

'All the Young Dudes' / 'Roll Away the Stone'
1976 – CBS 3936
Hall of Fame Hits – picture sleeve

'All the Young Dudes' / 'One of the Boys'
1977 – CBS 8271

'Roll Away the Stone' / 'All the Way from Memphis'
1979 – CBS Golden Decade 7065

'All the Young Dudes' / 'Roll Away the Stone'
1983 – Old Gold OG 9312

'All the Young Dudes' / 'Honaloochie Boogie'
1984 – CBS Backtracks A4581

'All the Young Dudes' / 'All the Way from Memphis' /
'Roll Away the Stone' / 'The Golden Age of Rock
'n' Roll'
1989 – CBS Solid Gold CD: CBS 654853 3

'All the Young Dudes' / 'Roll Away the Stone'
1990 – Old Gold OG 9312 – picture sleeve

'All the Young Dudes' / 'Once Bitten Twice Shy' / 'Roll
Away the Stone'
1992 – Sony Columbia EP
7-in. single: 658177 – picture sleeve
CD single: 658177 2

Import Singles

'Rock and Roll Queen' / 'Backsliding Fearlessly'
Atlantic – USA

'Midnight Lady' / 'It Must Be Love'
Island – Europe – picture sleeve

'Lay Down' / 'Whiskey Women'
Island – Holland – picture sleeve

'All the Young Dudes' / 'One of the Boys'
Columbia – USA – picture sleeve

'One of the Boys' / 'Sucker'
Columbia – USA, Holland

'Sweet Jane' / 'Jerkin' Crocus'
Columbia – USA, Spain, Holland and Portugal –
picture sleeve

'Roll Away the Stone' / 'Through the Looking Glass'
Columbia – USA

'All the Young Dudes' / 'Honaloochie Boogie'
Columbia Hall of Fame
plus stock Columbia single with rare miss-spelt
'Mott The *Hopple*' label

'All the Young Dudes' / 'Ten Years After' – 'I'd Love to
Change the World' – 'Goldmine'

Albums

Mott The Hoople
Island ILPS 9108 – November 1969 – No. 66

Mad Shadows
Island ILPS 9119 – September 1970 – No. 48

Wildlife
March 1971 – Island ILPS 9144 – No. 44

Brain Capers
Island ILPS 9178 – November 1971

All the Young Dudes
CBS 65184 – September 1972 – No. 21

Mott
CBS 69038 – UK – July 1973 – No. 7

The Hoople
CBS 69062 – March 1974 – No. 11

Mott The Hoople Live
CBS 69093 – November 1974 – No. 32

Compilations

Rock and Roll Queen
Island ILPS 9215 – October 1972

Pop Chronik
2-LP set – Island 88 292 XCT – Germany – 1975

The Golden Age of Mott The Hoople
GOVI CBS LSP 13128 – Germany – 1975

Greatest Hits
CBS 81225 – March 1976

Shades of Ian Hunter: The Ballad of Ian Hunter & Mott The Hoople
2-LP set – CBS 88476 – February 1980

Two Miles from Heaven
New and Rare Tracks 1969-1972
Island 202 429-270 – Germany – 1980

All the Way from Memphis
Pickwick SHM 3055 – March 1981

Rock Giants
CBS 54 440 – Germany – 1982

The History of Rock Volume 27
Double LP – Orbis HRL 027 – 1984

The Collection
2-LP set – Castle CCSLP 174 – February 1988

Mott The Hoople
CBS Il Rock IGDA 1131/132 – Italy – 1990

Compact Discs

Greatest Hits
CBS 81225 UK 1986
Columbia CK 34368 – US – 1986

The Collection
Castle CCSCD 174 – UK – 1988

Mott
Castle CLACD138X – UK – April 1988
Columbia CK 32425 – US – November 1988
Sony Rewind COL 467 402 2 – UK – March 1995

All the Young Dudes
Columbia CK 31750 – US – November 1988
Sony Rewind COL491691 2 – August 1998

Mott The Hoople Live
Columbia CK 33282 – US – November 1989

Walkin' with a Mountain
Island Masters IMCD 87 – UK – April 1990

The Hoople
Columbia CK 32871 – US – July 1990

Mott The Hoople
Atlantic 8258-2 – US – January 1991

Mad Shadows
Atlantic 8272-2 – US – January 1991

Wildlife
Atlantic 8284-2 – US – January 1991

Brain Capers
Atlantic 8304-2 – US – January 1991

Rock and Roll Queen
Atlantic 7297-2 – US – January 1991

London to Memphis
Sony A 22677 – US – June 1992

Mott The Hoople / Mad Shadows
Edsel Records EDCD361– UK – January 1993 – Limited-edition picture disc

The Ballad of Mott: A Retrospective
2-CD set: Columbia Legacy C2K 46973– US– June 1993
UK – November 1993

Mott featuring Steve Hyams
See For Miles SEACD 7 – UK –June 1993

Backsliding Fearlessly: The Early Years
Rhino Records R2 71639 – US – April 1994

Original Mixed-up Kids: The BBC Recordings
Windsong WINCD 084 – UK – July 1996

Super Hits
Columbia Legacy CK 65273 – USA – August 1997

Doc Thomas Group / The Silence:
The Italian Job / Shotgun Eyes
Angel Air SLPCD020 – UK – March 1998

All the Young Dudes – The Anthology
3-CD Boxed Set: Columbia 491400 2 – UK – September 1998
Disc 1: The Twilight of Pain Through Doubt
Disc 2: Temptations of the Flash
Disc 3: Blistered Psalms

Bootlegs

Hoopling Furiously
Guy Stevens' Testament of Rock and Roll Part 1
CD: HiWatt MTH 001:
BBC Session tracks and *In Concert* December 1971

Sticky Fingers
Vinyl: Brigand BRIG 025 – 1993:
BBC Session tracks and *In Concert* December 1971

Long Red
CD: Oh Boy 1-9036
Vinyl: Oh Boy Records PD006– Picture Disc: 500 copies:
Stockholm, February 1971 and New York, May 1974

Island Farewell
CD: Rock 'n' Roll Circus #2:
Wolverhampton Civic Hall, 6.4.72

Mott The Hoople Live With David Bowie
Vinyl: LTD 1973 – Germany:
Tower Theatre Philadelphia, 29.11.72

Behind Enemy Lines – The Whizz Kidz Meet The Concrete: The 1974 American Tour
Vinyl: TAKRL 1918:
Santa Monica Civic, 13.4.74

Rest In Peace
Vinyl: The Impossible Recordworks USA IMP 2.08:
CD: Rock 'n' Roll Circus #1:
Santa Monica Civic, 13.4.74

Flash and Crash
CD: Colosseum 96-C-003:
Santa Monica 13.4.74

The Golden Age of Mott The Hoople
Vinyl: ALAGA 1009:
Expo, Portland ME 28.4.74

European Ending
CD: Rock 'n' Roll Circus #4
October 1974

Ian Hunter

UK Singles

'Once Bitten Twice Shy' / '3000 Miles From Here'
April 1975 – CBS 3194 – No. 14

'Who Do You Love' / 'Boy'
July 1975 – CBS 3486

'All American Alien Boy' / 'Rape'
April 1976 – CBS 4268

'You Nearly Did Me In' / 'Letter to Britannia from the
Union Jack'
July 1976 – CBS 4479

'Justice of the Peace' / 'The Ballad of Little Star'
(as Ian Hunter's Overnight Angels)
May 1977 – CBS 5229

'England Rocks' / 'Wild 'n' Free'
(as Ian Hunter's Overnight Angels)
July 1977 – CBS 5497

'When the Daylight Comes' / 'Life After Death'
April 1979 – Chrysalis CHS 2324 –
picture sleeve, white vinyl

'Ships' / 'Wild East'
July 1979 – Chrysalis CHS 2346 –
picture sleeve

'Cleveland Rocks' / 'Bastard'
November 1979 – Chrysalis CHS 2390 –
picture sleeve

'We Gotta Get Out Of Here' / Live Medley: 'Once
Bitten Twice Shy' – 'Bastard' – 'Cleveland Rocks' /
'Sons and Daughters' –/'One of the Boys'
April 1980 – Chrysalis CHS 2434 –
limited-edition double single with gatefold picture
sleeve

'Lisa Likes Rock 'n' Roll' / 'Noises'
August 1981 – Chrysalis CHS 2542 –
picture sleeve, clear vinyl

'All of the Good Ones are Taken' / 'Death 'n' Glory
Boys'
August 1983 – CBS A3541 – picture sleeve

'All of the Good Ones are Taken' / 'Death 'n' Glory
Boys' / 'Traitor'
August 1983 – CBS TA3541 –
limited-edition 12-in. picture sleeve

'Somethin's Goin' On' / 'All of the Good Ones are
Taken' (Slow version)
October 1983 – CBS A3855

'American Music' / 'Tell It Like It Is'
February 1990
7-in. single: Mercury MER 315 – picture sleeve
Cassette: MERMC 315

'American Music' / 'Tell It Like It Is' /
'Sweet Dreamer'
12-in. single: MERX 315
CD single: MERCD 315

'The Artful Dodger' / 'Now Is The Time' /
'Fuck It Up'
April 1997 – Citadel CIT101CDS

'Michael Picasso' (Live) / 'Michael Picasso' (Studio) /
'23a Swan Hill'
March 1998 – Citadel CIT102CDS

Import Singles

'Just Another Night' / 'Ships'
Chrysalis 100712-A – Spain – picture sleeve

'Just Another Night' / 'Cleveland Rock'
Chrysalis 2352 – USA

'Standing in My Light' / 'Wild East'
Chrysalis 100.583 – Holland – picture sleeve

'We Gotta Get Out of Here' / 'All the Young Dudes'
(Live)
Chrysalis 101 762 – Holland – picture sleeve

'We Gotta Get Out of Here' / 'All the Young Dudes '/
'All the Way from Memphis'
Chrysalis CHS 2426 – Canada

'Central Park 'n' West' / 'Rain'
Chrysalis CHS-2587 – Spain – picture sleeve

'Central Park 'n' West' / 'Noises'
Chrysalis 103.580 – Holland – picture sleeve

'Central Park 'n' West' / 'Keep On Burning'
Chrysalis CHS 2558 – Canada

'I Need Your Love'
Promo 7-in.: Chrysalis CHS 2542 – USA

'(I'm the) Teacher' / '(I'm the) Teacher'
Promo 12-in.: Capitol SPRO-9244 – USA

'All of the Good Ones are Taken' / 'All of the Good
Ones are Taken'
Promo 12-in.: Columbia AS 1683 – USA – picture
sleeve
7-in.: CBS A-3668 – Holland – picture sleeve

'That Girl Is Rock 'n' Roll' / 'Every Step of the Way'
Promo 12-in.: Columbia AS 1756 – USA

'Women's Intuition' (Remix) / 'Following In Your
Footsteps'
Cassette: Mercury 876 478-4 – USA

'Red Letter Day' / 'Red Letter Day'
(as Ian Hunter's Dirty Laundry)
Promo CD: Norsk Plateproduksjon IDCDPR 44 –
October 1994 – card sleeve

'My Revolution' / 'Dancing on the Moon'
(as Ian Hunter's Dirty Laundry)
CD: Norsk Plateproduksjon IDS44 – February
1995

'Too Much (Hunter)'
Promo CD: Mercury ProHunt 921 – September
1996

Albums

Ian Hunter
CBS 80710 – March 1975 – No. 21

All American Alien Boy
CBS 81310 – April 1976 – No. 29

Overnight Angels
CBS 81993 – May 1977

You're Never Alone with a Schizophrenic
Chrysalis CHR 1214 – April 1979 – No. 49

Shades of Ian Hunter:
The Ballad of Ian Hunter & Mott The Hoople
CBS 88476 – February 1980 – 2 LP set

Welcome to the Club
Chrysalis CJT6 – April 1980 – No. 61

Short Back 'n' Sides
Chrysalis CHR 1326 – August 1981 – No. 79

All of the Good Ones are Taken
  CBS 25379 – July 1983

YUI Orta
  Mercury 838 973-2 – January

The Very Best of Ian Hunter
  CBS 467508 1 Germany – December 1990

The Artful Dodger
  Citadel CIT1Box April 1998
  Special Limited Edition Vinyl with hard back
  Diary of a Rock 'n' Roll Star and signed photograph
  – 1, 000 copies

Compact Discs

Shades of Ian Hunter
  Chrysalis VK 41670 – USA – November 1988

YUI Orta
  Mercury 838 973-2
  Picture Disc CD: October 1989 – USA
  February 1990 – UK

All American Alien Boy
  Columbia CK 34142 – USA – January 1990
  Sony Rewind COL 491695 2 – UK – August 1998

Ian Hunter
  Columbia CK 33480 – USA – July 1990
  Sony Rewind COL 477359 2 – UK – August 1994

The Very Best of Ian Hunter
  CBS 467508-2 – Germany – December 1990

The Collection
  Castle CCSCD 290 – UK – August 1991

You're Never Alone with a Schizophrenic
  Razor & Tie RE 2011 – USA –April 1993 –
  picture disc
  Chrysalis CD25CR03 – UK – 25th Anniversary
  Special Edition, March 1994 – boxed set, limited
  edition of 1500 copies

All of the Good Ones are Taken
  Columbia 474780 2 – Germany – December 1993

Overnight Angels
  Columbia 474781 2 – Germany – December 1993

*Shades of Ian Hunter: The Ballad of Ian Hunter & Mott
  The Hoople*
  2-CD set: Columbia 474782 2 – Germany –
  December 1993

Short Back 'n' Sides / Long Odds and Out-takes
  2-CD set: Chrysalis CDCHR 6074 – May 1994

Welcome to the Club
  2-CD set: Chrysalis CDCHR 6075 – May 1994

Ian Hunter's Dirty Laundry
  Norsk Plateproduksjon IDCD 44 – Norway –
  March 1995
  Cleveland International – USA – October 1995

The Hunter Ronson Band: BBC Live In Concert
  Windsong WINCD078 – September 1995
  Strange Fruit SFRS CD057 – February 1998

The Artful Dodger
  Polydor 531 794-2 – Norway – September 1996
  Citadel CD1 – April 1997

Film Soundtracks

'We Gotta Get Out of Here' from *Up The Academy*
  Capitol E-ST 12091 – 1980

'Great Expectations (You Never Know What To
  Expect)' from *Up The Creek*
  Epic EPC 70251 – 1984

'(I'm the) Teacher' from *Teachers*
  Capitol EJ 24 02471 – 1984 and
  CDP 7 46062 2 – Japanese CD

'Good Man in a Bad Time' from *Frightnight*
  Epic EPC 70270 – 1985

'Wake-Up Call' from *The Wraith*
  Scotti Bros. Records 4503731 – 1986

'Cleveland Rocks' (Live) from *Light of Day*
  Epic EPC 450501 1 plus CD – 1987

Bootlegs

Drunk on Wisdom and Wine
  Vinyl: The Excitable Recordworks USA 4516.1:
  Berkeley, California, 7.7.79

Parkwest Party
  CD: Rock 'n' Roll Circus #3:
  Park West Theatre, Chicago, Illinois, 22.6.79

Collaborations/Productions

Bronco
  Ace of Sunlight
  Island LP: ILPS 9191 – 1971
  'Amber Moon': Ian Hunter *piano*

Mick Ronson
  Play Don't Worry
  RCA LP: APL1 0681 – 1975
  'The Girl Can't Help It':
  Ian Hunter & The Microns *backing vocals*

Johnny Clarke
  Rocker Time Now
  Virgin LP: L10258 – 1976
  Ian Hunter *keyboards*

Mr Big
  Single A-side: EMI 2819 – 1978
  'Senora' (Dicken/Carter/Hunter)

Tuff Darts
  Tuff Darts
  Sire LP: SRK 6048 – USA – 1978
  'Love' / 'Trouble & Slash': Ian Hunter *electric
  piano*

David Johansen
  In Style
  Blue Sky PZ 36082 – 1979
  'Flamingo Road': Ian Hunter *acoustic piano*

Ellen Foley
  Nightout
  Epic LP: EPC 83718 – 1979
  'Don't Let Go' (Ian Hunter):
  Produced/arranged by Hunter Ronson;
  Ian Hunter *keyboards / guitars / percussion*

Generation X
  Valley of the Dolls
  Chrysalis LP: CHR 1193 – 1979
  Produced by Ian Hunter

Genya Ravan
And I Mean It
20th Century Fox LP: T 595 – 1979
'Junkman': Ian Hunter *duet vocal*

David Werner
David Werner
Epic LP: EPC 83862 – 1979
'High Class Blues': Ian Hunter *guest vocal*
'Every New Romance': mixed by Ian Hunter

Iron City Houserockers
Have a Good Time … But Get Out Alive
MCA LP: MCA-5111 – 1980
'We're Not Dead Yet': arranged by Ian Hunter
'Hypnotized': Ian Hunter *guitar / background vocal*

Payola$
Hammer On A Drum
A&M LP: SP 64958 – 1983
'I'll Find Another (Who Can Do It Right)':
Ian Hunter *backing vocals*

Hanoi Rocks
Two Steps From the Move
Epic LP: CD – 1984
'I Can't Get It' (A. McCoy / R. Ezrin / I. Hunter)
'Underwater World' (A.McCoy / I.Hunter)
'Boulevard of Broken Dreams' (A. McCoy /
R. Ezrin / I. Hunter)
'Shakes' (McCoy / Ezrin / Hunter): B-side of
'Underwater World' single (non LP)

Urgent
Cast the First Stone
Manhattan LP: ST 53004 – USA – 1984
'Love Can Make You Cry' (Kehr/Kehr/Hunter)
'Pay Up' (Kehr/Hunter/Pickett/Kissel)
'Dedicated to Love' (Kehr/Vaz/Black/Hunter)
'So This Is Paradise' (Kehr/Vaz/Black/Hunter)
Produced by Hunter & Ronson

Mountain
Go For Your Life
Scotti Bros LP: SCT 26379 – 1985
'Hard Times' / 'Shimmy In The Footlights':
Ian Hunter *sequencer/keyboards*

Michael Monroe
Nights Are So Long
Yahoo Records LP: 105 – 1987
Ian Hunter *piano*

Urgent
Thinking Out Loud
Manhattan LP: MLT 46680 – USA – 1987
'Pain' (Love Is A Victim) (Kehr/Hunter)
'If This Is Love' (Kehr/Kehr/Ronson)
'Inch By Inch' (Kehr/Kehr/Ronson/Hunter)

Mick Jones
Mick Jones
Atlantic CD Single: 789 991 2 – 1989
'Just Wanna Hold' (M. Jones / I. Hunter /
M. Jagger):
Ian Hunter *piano / background vocals*

Michael Monroe
Not Fakin' It
Mercury CD: 838 627-1: 1989
'She's No Angel': Ian Hunter *piano*

Def Leppard
Retroactive
Bludgeon Riffola 518 305-2: 1993
'Ride into the Sun' (Ian Hunter)
'Honky Tonk Messiah': Ian Hunter *piano*

Mick Ronson
Heaven and Hull
Epic CD: 474742 2: 1994
'Take a Long Line': Ian Hunter *backing vocals*
'All the Young Dudes' (live):
Ian Hunter *lead vocal / guitar*

Mick Ronson

The Rats

The Rise and Fall of Bernie Gripplestone and the Rats from Hull
Tenth Planet Records TP012 – February 1995 –
1, 000 numbered vinyl copies
Angel Air SJPCD 022 – May 1998

Ronno

'Fourth Hour of My Sleep' / 'Powers of Darkness'
Vertigo 6059 029 – January 1971

Vertigo Classics and Rarities 1969–1973: Volume One
Vertigo 846522-1 –
Compilation LP/CD with 'Powers of Darkness'

Mick Ronson

Singles

'Love Me Tender' / 'Only After Dark'
RCA APBO 212 – January 1974

'Slaughter on 10th Avenue' / 'Leave My Heart Alone'
RCA LPBO 5022 – April 1974

'Billy Porter' / 'Seven Days'
RCA 2482 – January 1975

'Billy Porter' / 'Slaughter on 10th Avenue'
RCA Golden Grooves Gold 54 –
May 1982 – picture sleeve

'Don't Look Down' / 'Slaughter on 10th Avenue' /
'Billy Porter' / 'Love Me Tender'
Epic 660358 2/4/6 – April 1994
Digipac CD / Cassette / 12-in. Picture Disc

Albums

Slaughter on 10th Avenue
RCA APL1 0353 – March 1974

Play Don't Worry
RCA APL1 0681 – February 1975

Compact Discs

Slaughter on 10th Avenue
MIDI Inc. CD: MDCP 4067 – Japan – October 1995
Snapper UK SMMCD 503 – September 1997 –
bonus tracks

Play Don't Worry
  MIDI Inc. CD: MDCP 4068 – Japan – October
  1995
  Snapper SMMCD 504 – UK –
  September 1997 – bonus tracks

Heaven and Hull
  Epic 474742 2: May 1994

Only After Dark
  2-CD set: Golden Years CD GY003
  also issued as Griffin Music GCD-344-2 – USA –
  November 1994 –
  contains *Slaughter on 10th Avenue* and *Play Don't
  Worry* plus bonus tracks; picture disc set

Main Man
  Snapper SMDCD 119 – April 1998 –
  2 CD compilation

David Bowie recordings featuring
Mick Ronson

Albums

The Man who Sold the World
  Mercury 6338 041 – April 1971
  re-released on RCA LSP 4816 – 1972

Hunky Dory
  RCA SF 8244 – December 1971

*The Rise and Fall of Ziggy Stardust and the Spiders from
  Mars*
  RCA SF 8287 – June 1972

Aladdin Sane
  RCA RS 1001 – April 1973

Pin Ups
  RCA RS 1003 – October 1973

Changes One Bowie
  RCA RS 1055 – 1976

Ziggy Stardust – The Motion Picture (Live 1973)
  RCA PL 84862 – October 1983

Bowie: The Singles Collection
  EMI 7243 28099 2 0 – 1993 – 2CD

Black Tie White Noise
  BMG 74321 13697 – 1993
  'I Feel Free' (featuring Ronson)

Santa Monica 1972
  Trident Music CD GY002 – April 1994
  Griffin USA GCD-392-2
  Recorded live at Santa Monica Civic Auditorium
  CA, 20.10.72

Rarestonebowie
  Trident Music CD GY014 – May 1995

Singles

'Memory of a Free Festival' (Parts 1 & 2)
  Mercury 6052 026 – June 1970

'Holy Holy' / 'Black Country Rock'
  Mercury 6052 049 – January 1971

'Moonage Daydream' / 'Hang on to Yourself'
  B&C CB149 – April 1971

'Hang on to Yourself' / 'Man in the Middle'
  B&C CB189 – September 1971
  both as Arnold Corns

'Changes' / 'Andy Warhol'
  RCA 2160 – January 1972

'Starman' / 'Suffragette City'
  RCA 2199 – April 1972

'John, I'm Only Dancing' / 'Hang on to Yourself'
  RCA 2263 – September 1972

'The Jean Genie' / 'Ziggy Stardust'
  RCA 2302 – November 1972

'Life on Mars?' / 'The Man who Sold the World'
  RCA 2316 – April 1973

'Drive In Saturday' / 'Round and Round'
  RCA 2352 – June 1973

'Sorrow' / 'Amsterdam'
  RCA 2424 – November 1973

'Rebel Rebel' / 'Lady Grinning Soul'
  RCA APBO 0287 – 1974

'Rock 'n' Roll Suicide' / 'Quicksand'
  RCA LPBO 5021 – April 1974

'Diamond Dogs' / 'Holy Holy'
  RCA APBO 0293 – June 1974

'Suffragette City' / 'Stay'
  RCA 2726 – July 1976

'Ziggy Stardust' / 'Changes' / 'Velvet Goldmine'
  RCA 2593 – 1975

'White Light White Heat' / 'Cracked Actor' (live)
  RCA 372 – November 1983

Mick Ronson Sessions and Productions

Michael Chapman
  Fully Qualified Survivor
  Harvest SHVL 764 – 1970

Elton John
  Madman Across the Water (demo) – 1970
  Rare Masters DJM 1993

Dana Gillespie
  Weren't Born a Man
  RCA APLI 0354 – 1972

Mott The Hoople
  'Sea Diver' (*All the Young Dudes* LP)
  CBS 65184 – 1972

Lou Reed
  Transformer
  RCA LSP 4807 – 1972

Pure Prairie League
  Bustin' Out
  RCA SF 8417 – 1972

The Fallen Angels
  unreleased studio sessions – 1973

The New Seekers
  'Milkwood' / 'Split'
  unreleased 1973

Al Stewart
  unreleased studio sessions – 1973

Lulu
  'The Man who Sold the World' /
  'Watch That Man'
  Polydor 2001 490 – 1974

Bob Sargeant
First Starring Role
RCA LPLI 5076 – 1974

Bob Dylan
Hard Rain
CBS 86016 – 1975
Biograph
CBS 66509 – 1985
Bootleg Series
CBS 4680862 – 1991
'Dignity' / 'Dignity' / 'It Ain't Me Babe'
Sony 662076 5 – 1995

Sparks
unreleased Big Beat demos – 1975

Solo Sessions
Sundragon Studios, Manhattan
December 1975 – unreleased

The Spiders From Mars
unreleased studio sessions
unreleased single – 'She's a Roller'

Roger McGuinn
Cardiff Rose
CBS 81369 – 1976

Guam
unreleased studio sessions – 1976

Mary Hogan
unreleased sessions – 1976

David Cassidy
Gettin' It in the Streets
RCA RVP 6108 – US – 1976

Kinky Friedman
Lasso From El Paso
EPIC EPC 81640 – 1976

Van Morrison
A Period of Transition
Warner Brothers K56322 – 1977

Roger Daltrey
One of the Boys
Polydor 2441 146 – 1977

Topaz
Topaz
Columbia 34934 – 1977

Michael Chapman
Michael Chapman Lived Here 1968–72
Cube – 1977
The Man Who Hated Mornings
Decca – 1977

Dr John
Unreleased album sessions – 1977

John Cougar Mellencamp
Chestnut Street Incident
Mainman MML 602 – 1977
American Fool
Riva 7501 – 1982

Hope and Anchor Front Row Festival
Philip Rambow Band
Underground Romance (double LP) – 1977
plus unreleased studio sessions – 1977

Rich Kids
Ghosts of Princes in Towers
EMI EMC 3263 – 1978

Slaughter and the Dogs
Do It Dog Style
Decca SKL 5292 – 1978

Dead Fingers Talk
Storm the Reality Studios
PYE NSPH 24 – 1978

Annette Peacock
X Dreams
Aura AUL 702 – 1978

Benny Mardones
Thank God For Girls
Private Stock PS 7007 – US – 1978

Careless Talk
Unreleased sessions – 1978

John Cale / Corky Laing / Ian Hunter / Mick Ronson
unreleased Album sessions – 1978

David Johansen
In Style
Blue Sky SKY 83745 – 1979

Ellen Foley
Nightout
EPIC EPC 83718 – 1979

Genya Ravan
And I Mean It
20th Century Fox T 595 – 1979

Iron City Houserockers
Have a Good Time ... But Get Out Alive
MCA 5111 – US – 1980

Johnny Average Band
Some People
Bearsville BRK 3514 – US – 1980

Lennex
Struggle
Evatone 81382XS – 1980

Rubber City Rebels
Possible album production – 1980

Meat Loaf
Dead Ringer
EPIC EPC 32692 – 1981

Album sessions
Bearsville Studio, Woodstock 1981
with Falcons / New York Yanquis

Payola$
No Stranger to Danger
A&M AMLH 64908 – 1982
Hammer on a Drum
A&M AMLH 64958 – 1983
Between a Rock and a Hyde Place (Best of)
A&M CD 9134 – 1987

Lisa Bade
Suspicion
A&M LP SP 6-4897 US – 1982

T-Bone Burnett
Proof Through the Night
Demon Fiend 14 – 1983

Los Illegals
Internal Exile
A&M SP 4925 – US – 1983

Perfect Affair
Perfect Affair
Attic LAT 1182 – US – 1983

Visible Targets
Autistic Savant
Park Avenue PA 82803 – 1983

Ian Thomas
Strange Brew – Soundtrack
Anthem ANR11042 – 1983
Riders on Dark Horses – Soundtrack
Mercury 822 319-1 – 1984

Girls Next Door
Unreleased studio sessions – 1984

Charlie Sexton
Studio sessions unreleased – 1984

Dalbello
Whomanforsays
Capitol 2401 381 – 1984

Urgent
Cast the First Stone
Manhattan ST 53004 – US – 1985
Thinking Out Loud
Manhattan 74 6680 – 1987
Iron Eagle – Soundtrack
Capitol 24 04981 – 1987

One The Juggler
Some Strange Fashion
RCA PL 70606 – 1985

Midge Ure
'That Certain Smile' / 'The Gift' / 'Fade to Grey'
Chrysalis 602125 – 1985

Kiss That
Kiss and Tell
Chrysalis CHR 1513 – 1986

Lisa Dominique
'Act Tuff'/ 'The Big Kiss' / 'Dreammaker'
Scorpio cassette – 1986

Moda
Canto Pagano
IRA 508 009 – 1986

Andi Sexgang
Love & Danger
IRA 508005-1 – 1986
Western Songs for Children
Triple X 51186-2 – 1995

David Lynn Jones
Hard Times on Easy Street
Mercury 832 518 – 1987
1988 Album sessions not released

Rick Rose
'Gypsy Jewelry' / 'Under the Sky, Under the Moon'
97.7FM 7CDN-49 – 1987

The Phantoms
Woodstock Sampler Vol. 2
Wildlife Records 410 Cassette – 1987

Marie Laurie
'This Is Not Peru' / 'Same Me Freeze'
WEA 248107-7 – 1987

The Fatal Flowers
Johnny D Is Back
WEA 242 333 – 1988
Pleasure Sound
Mercury 842 581 Holland – 1990

The Toll
The Price of Progression
Geffen 924 201 – 1988

Steve Harley
El Grande Senor
Unreleased album – 1988

The Fatal Flowers
Pleasure Ground – 1990

EC2
'You're My Man' / 'Communication'
Mercury 875560-7 – 1990
'I'm So Sorry' / 'Kiss Me'
Mercury 876922-7 – 1990
'Passion' / 'I'm Forever Blowing Bubbles'
Mercury 878500-7 – 1990
Album unreleased

Secret Mission
Strange Afternoon
EMI 777-7961122 – 1991

Leather Nun
Nun Permanent
Wire WRCD 018 – 1991

Dag Finn
The Wonderful World of D. Finn
Mercury 848-494-2 – 1991

Randy Vanwarmer
The Vital Spark
Alias M22851 – 1991

Sonic Walthers
Medication
Radium RA 91782 – 1992

Casino Steel
Casino Steel & The Bandits (featuring Mick Ronson)
Revolution Records REXCD 03 – 1991

Morrissey
Your Arsenal
EMI CDCSD3790 - 1992

David Bowie
Black Tie White Noise
EMI – 1993 –
Ronson on 'I Feel Free'

The Wildhearts
Earth versus The Wildhearts
Bronze/East West – 1993

Dana Gillespie
Andy Warhol: The Best of the Mainman Years
Trident CD GY001 – 1994

Sandy Dillon
Dancing on the Freeway
Griffin GCD 423-2 – 1995
(Recorded in 1985)

Ava Cherry and the Astronettes
People From Bad Homes
Griffin GCD 424-2 – 1995
(Recorded in 1973)

Mott

Singles

'Monte Carlo' / 'Shout It All Out'
  CBS 3528 – August 1975

'By Tonight' / 'I Can Show You How It Is'
  CBS 3741 – November 1975

'It Takes One to Know One' / 'I'll Tell You Something'
  CBS 4005 – February 1976

Albums

Drive On
  CBS 69154 – 12 September 1975 – No. 54

Shouting and Pointing
  CBS 81289 – 4 June 1976

Compact Discs

Drive On
  Sony SRCS 9022 – Japan – August 1996
  Columbia Rewind CD 487237 2 – March 1997

Shouting and Pointing
  Sony SRCS 9023 – Japan – August 1996
  Columbia Rewind CD 489492 2 – March 1998

British Lions

Singles

'One More Chance To Run' / 'Booster'
  Vertigo 6059 192 – February 1978 – Picture sleeve

'International Heroes' / 'Eat The Rich'
  Vertigo 6059 201 – April 1978

Albums

British Lions
  Vertigo 9102 019 – February 1978

Trouble with Women
  Cherry Red Records ARED 7 – May 1980

Appendix 3

Sessionography

Mott The Hoople

Mott The Hoople
(Working titles: *The Twilight of Pain Through Doubt / Talking Bear Mountain Picnic Massacre Disaster Dylan Blues*)

11.4.69	The Rebel (C. Ward) (Ralphs vocal)
11.4.69	Find Your Way (Ralphs) (no vocal)
20.6.69	Half Moon Bay Part 1 (Hunter/Ralphs)
20.6.69	Rabbit Foot and Toby Time (Ralphs)
24.6.69	Backsliding Fearlessly (Hunter)
24.6.69	Laugh at Me (Bono)
24.6.69	At the Crossroads (Sahm)
24.6.69	The Rebel (Hunter vocal)
27.6.69	Little Christine (Ralphs)
27.6.69	You Really Got Me (Davies)
27.6.69	Wrath and Wroll (Stevens)
7.7.69	Road to Birmingham (Hunter)
2.9.69	Rock and Roll Queen (Ralphs)
2.9.69	Rock and Roll Queen: Alternate version with Stevens piano

Backtracks with no vocal ;
Back in the States Again (Hunter/Ralphs)
Can You Please Crawl Out Your Window (Dylan)
Just Like Tom Thumb Blues (Dylan)
Little Queenie (Berry)
Desolation Row (Dylan)

Ian Hunter – Vocals and Piano
Mick Ralphs – Lead Guitar and Vocals
Verden Allen – Organ
Overend Watts – Bass and Backing Vocals
Buffin – Drums
Recorded at Morgan Studio 2, London
Producer – Guy Stevens
Engineer – Andy Johns

Mad Shadows
(Working title: *Sticky Fingers*)

15.11.69	Thunderbuck Ram (Ralphs)
15.11.69	Moonbus (Hunter/Ralphs/Watts/Allen/Griffin)
29.11.69	The Hunchback Fish (Hunter)
16.1.70	Going Home (Ralphs)
10.2.70	Wrong Side of the River (Ralphs)
15.2.70	It Would Be a Pleasure (Ralphs)
17.2.70	Coalminer's Dilemma (Hunter)
18.2.70	Keep A-Knockin' (Penniman)
16.3.70	No Wheels to Ride (Hunter)
16.3.70	You Are One of Us (Hunter)
31.3.70	Can You Sing a Song Like I Sing? (Hunter)
6.4.70	Walking With A Mountain (Hunter)
	I Can Feel (Hunter)
	Threads of Iron (Ralphs)
	When My Mind's Gone (Hunter)
	The Wreck of the *Liberty Belle* (Hunter/Ralphs)

The Ballad of Billy Joe (backtrack)
Enough Is Enough (Hunter)
The Chosen Road (Hunter)
In The Presence of Your Mind (Hunter)

Ian Hunter – Vocals and Piano
Mick Ralphs – Guitar, Vocals and Recorder
Verden Allen – Organ
Overend Watts – Bass
Buffin – Drums
Guy Stevens – Spiritual percussion, psychic piano
Recorded discontinuously at Olympic Studio 1, London – February to April 1970
Producer – Guy Stevens
Engineer – Andy Johns

Wildlife
(Working title: *Original Mixed-Up Mott*)

10.9.70	Lay Down (Safka)
13.9.70	Keep A-Knockin' (Live) (Penniman)
13.9.70	Ohio (Live) (Young)
13.9.70	No Wheels to Ride (Live)
13.9.70	You Really Got Me (Live)
13.9.70	Rock 'n' Roll Queen (Live)
13.9.70	Thunderbuck Ram (Live)
17.10.70	Black Hills (Ralphs)
16.11.70	Growing Man Blues (Hunter)
16.11.70	Home Is Where I Want To Be (Ralphs)
23.11.70	Angel of Eighth Avenue (Hunter)
24.11.70	Waterlow (Hunter)
24.11.70	Whiskey Women (Ralphs)
14.12.70	Surfin' UK (Ralphs)
28.12.70	The Original Mixed-Up Kid (Hunter)
30.12.70	Like a Rolling Stone (impromptu jam) (Dylan)
	It Must Be Love (Ralphs)
	Round and Around (backtrack)

Ian Hunter – Piano and Vocals
Mick Ralphs – Guitar and Vocals
Verden Allen – Organ
Overend Watts – Bass
Buffin – Drums
Recorded at Island Studios 1 and 2, London, November & December 1970
Produced by Mott The Hoople
Engineer – Brian Humphries assisted by Richard Digby-Smith and Howard Kilgour
Strings arranged and conducted by Michael Gray
Solo Violin – James Archer
Pedal Steel – Jerry Hogan
Backing Vocals – Jess Roden and Stan Tippins

Brain Capers
(Working titles: *AC/DC, Bizarre Capers & Brain Damage*)

11.4.71	One of the Boys (Hunter/Ralphs)
11.4.71	Till I'm Gone (Ralphs)
12.4.71	Long Red (West/ Pappalardi / Ventura / Landsberg)

12.4.71   It'll Be Me (Clement)
12.4.71   Where Do You All Come From?
          (Backtrack) (Hunter)
14.4.71   Ill Wind Blowing (Hunter)
21.4.71   Downtown (Whitten/Young)
21.4.71   The Debt (Hunter)
12.5.71   Midnight Lady* (Hunter/Ralphs)
4.8.71   The Journey (Hunter)
4.8.71   A Year Ago Today (Hunter)
4.8.71   Mental Train (Hunter/Ralphs)
4.8.71   How Long? (Hunter/Allen)
          Darkness Darkness (Young)
          Your Own Backyard (Dimucci)
          Second Love (Allen): Hunter & Allen vocal
20.9.71   Sweet Angeline (Hunter)
20.9.71   Death May Be Your Santa Claus
          (Hunter /Allen)
20.9.71   The Moon Upstairs (Hunter/Ralphs)
20.9.71   The Journey (Hunter)
20.9.71   The Wheel of the Quivering Meat
          Conception (Hunter/Stevens)
          Show Me the Bottle (Ralphs)
          I Don't Know (Ralphs)

Ian Hunter – Vocals and Piano
Mick Ralphs – Guitar and Vocals
Verden Allen – Organ
Overend Watts – Bass and Backing Vocals
Buffin – Drums
Trumpet on Second Love – Jim Price
Producer – Guy Stevens
Engineer – Andy Johns
Recorded at Island Basing Street Studios 1 and 2 1971

Midnight Lady* – Recorded at Ultra Sonic Studios, H
empstead, Long Island, New York – Produced by S
hadow Morton – Backing vocals on 'Midnight
Lady' – Steve Marriott, Mott and Stan Tippins

Island Single session

24.1.72   Black Scorpio (Hunter/Watts)
24.1.72   Ride On The Sun (Hunter)
24.1.72   Moving On (Ralphs)

Produced by Mott The Hoople
Executive Producer – Muff Winwood
Recorded at Basing Street Studios, London

All the Young Dudes

14.5.72   All the Young Dudes* (David Bowie)
14.5.72   One of the Boys* (Hunter/Ralphs)
June/July   Sweet Jane (Lou Reed)
            Momma's Little Jewel (Hunter/Watts)
            Sucker (Hunter/Ralphs/Watts)
            Jerkin' Crocus (Hunter)
            Soft Ground (Allen)
            Ready For Love / After Lights (Ralphs)
            Sea Diver (Hunter)
5.7.72   Shakin' All Over (Heath)
5.7.72   Please Don't Touch (Heath/Robinson)
5.7.72   So Sad (Everly)
            Henry & The H-Bombs (Hunter)
            The First Third (Hunter)

Ian Hunter – Vocals and Piano
Mick Ralphs – Guitar and Vocals
Verden Allen – Organ

Overend Watts – Bass
Buffin – Drums
Recorded at Olympic 2* & Trident Studios, London
May/June/July 1972
Produced by David Bowie for Mainman
Arranged by Mott The Hoople and David Bowie
Engineers Ted Sharp and Dave Hentschel
Engineer on 'All the Young Dudes' /
    'One of the Boys' – Keith Harwood
Saxes/Acoustic guitar – David Bowie
Strings and brass on 'Sea Diver' arranged and
    conducted by Mick Ronson

Mott

CBS Studios:
18.10.72   Hymn for the Dudes (Hunter/Allen)
           Honaloochie Boogie (Hunter)
           Nightmare (Allen)

AIR/Abbey Road Studios:
           Honaloochie Boogie (Hunter)
           Hymn for the Dudes (Hunter/Allen)
           Rose (Hunter/Ralphs/Watts/Buffin)
           Drivin' Sister (Hunter/Ralphs)
           Ballad of Mott the Hoople (26th March
           1972 Zurich) (Hunter/Ralphs/
           Watts/Buffin/Allen)
           All the Way from Memphis (Hunter)
           Whizz Kid (Hunter)
           I'm A Cadillac /
           El Camino Doloroso (Ralphs)
11.4.73   I Wish I Was Your Mother (Hunter)
11.4.73   Violence (Hunter/Ralphs)
           Where Do You All Come From?
           (Hunter/Ralphs/Watts/Buffin)
June   Roll Away the Stone (Hunter)

Ian Hunter – Vocals, Piano and Guitar
Mick Ralphs – Guitar, Organ and Vocals
Overend Watts – Bass
Buffin – Drums and Backing Vocals
'Recorded at AIR London Studio 2 and EMI Studio 2
    Abbey Road – February to April 1973'
Produced by Mott The Hoople
Arranged by Ian Hunter
Engineers – Bill Price, Alan Harris (AIR), John Leckie
    (EMI)
Saxophones – Andy Mackay
Electric Cello – Paul Buckmaster
Violin – Graham Preskett
Backing Vocals – Thunderthighs

The Hoople
(Working titles: Weekend / The Bash Street Kidds)

The Advision Jam – Whole Lotta Shakin/Your
    Cheating Heart / What'd I Say
The Golden Age of Rock 'n' Roll (Hunter)
Rest In Peace (Hunter/Watts/Griffin)
Marionette (Hunter)
Alice (Hunter)
Crash Street Kidds (Hunter)
Born Late '58 (Watts)
Trudi's Song (Hunter)
Pearl 'n' Roy (England) (Hunter)
Through the Looking Glass (Hunter)
Foxy Foxy (Hunter)

Ian Hunter – Vocals and Rhythm guitar
Overend Watts – Bass and Vocals
Dale Griffin – Drums
Ariel Bender – Lead Guitar
Morgan Fisher – Keyboards
Recorded at Advision Studios, London W1, January 1974
Engineers – Alan Harris, Mike Dunne and Paul Hardiman
Re-mixed and dubbed at AIR London Studios 2 and 3, January 1974
Engineers – Bill Price with Sean Milligan, Gary Edwards, Peter Swettenham
Produced by Hunter, Watts & Griffin
Production Supervisor – Dan Loggins
Saxophones – Howie Casey and Rocking Jock McPherson, (Andy Mackay)
Violin on 'Marionette' – Graham Preskett
Cello on 'Golden Age' – Mike Hurwitz
Orchestral arrangement and conductor on 'Looking Glass' – Graham Preskett
Guest appearances – Mick Ralphs, Blue Weaver, Lynsey de Paul
Backing Vocals – Barry St John, Sue and Sunny

August/September 1974: AIR London Studios:
Sunset Summer Nights (Griffin)
The Saturday Kids (Hunter)
The Saturday Gigs (Hunter) (with Ariel Bender and Mick Ronson solos)
Lounge Lizard (Hunter), with Mick Ronson

Other sessions

The following songs were rehearsed or demoed:
The Parrot & the Cat (Hunter) 1969
Jekyll & Hyde (Hunter) 1969
The Wreck (Watts) 1969
Yma Sumac (Mott The Hoople) 1969
Lavender Days (Hunter) 1969
Black Staff (Son of the Wise Ones) (Allen) 1972
Beside The B-side 1972
Electric Robot 1972
I Don't Dig It (Hunter) 1972
I Can't Get No Breakfast In Texas (Hunter/Ralphs) 1972
Tell Your Brother (Hunter) 1973
Slow Song (Hunter) 1973
Silver Needles (Hunter) 1973
Symphony In O Minor (Watts) 1973
Ships (Hunter) 1973
Golden Opportunity (Hunter) 1974
Did You See Them Run (Hunter) 1974
3000 Miles From Here (Hunter) 1974
One Fine Day (Hunter) 1974
Colwater High (Hunter) 1974
Three Blind Mice (Hunter) 1974

Radio Sessions

Top Gear – John Peel
    Recorded 3 February 1970
    BBC Maida Vale Studio 4

Sunday Concert – John Peel
    Recorded 23 April 1970
    BBC Paris Theatre, London

Sunday Concert – John Peel
    Reecorded 15 October 1970
    BBC Paris Theatre, London

Sounds of the Seventies – Mike Harding
    Recorded 8 March 1971
    BBC Maida Vale Studio 5

Top Gear – John Peel
    Recorded 6 July 1971
    BBC Maida Vale Studio 4

Rosko Show
    Recorded 17 July 1971
    BBC Paris Theatre, London

Sounds of the Seventies – Pete Drummond
    Recorded 25 October 1971
    BBC Maida Vale Studio 5

In Concert – Andy Dunkley
    Recorded 30 December 1971
    BBC Paris Theatre, London

Sounds of the Seventies – Bob Harris
    Aired 16 October 1972: Songs were not BBC session recordings but *All the Young Dudes* album tracks, re-mixed (minus David Bowie's saxophone)

Ian Hunter

Ian Hunter

One Fine Day (Hunter)*
Colwater High (Hunter)*
3000 Miles From Here (Hunter)
Lounge Lizard (Hunter)
Boy (Hunter/Ronson)
It Ain't Easy When You Fall (Hunter)
Shades Off (Hunter)
The Truth, The Whole Truth, And Nuthin' But The Truth (Hunter)
I Get So Excited (Hunter)
Who Do You Love (Hunter)
Once Bitten Twice Shy (Hunter)
*unreleased

Ian Hunter – Vocals, Rhythm Guitar, Piano, Percussion, Harmony Vocals
Mick Ronson – Lead Guitar, Organ, Mellotron, Mouth Organ, Bass Guitar
Geoff Appleby – Bass Guitar, Harmony Vocals
Dennis Elliott – Drums, Percussion
Pete Arnesen – Piano
John Gustafson – Bass on Lounge Lizard
Recorded at Air Studios, London
January to March 1975
Produced by Ian Hunter and Mick Ronson
Arranged by Mick Ronson
Engineered by Bill Price

All American Alien Boy

Letter to Britannia from the Union Jack (Hunter)
All American Alien Boy (Album & Single versions) (Hunter)
Irene Wilde (Hunter)
Restless Youth (Hunter)

Rape (Hunter)
You Nearly Did Me In (Hunter)
Apathy '83 (Hunter)
God (Take 1) (Hunter)
Common Disease (Hunter)*
3 tracks – titles unknown*

Ian Hunter – Lead Vocals, Guitar and Piano on 'Alien Boy'
Chris Stainton – Piano, Organ, Mellotron and Bass on 'Restless Youth'
Jaco Pastorius – Bass and guitar on 'God (Take 1)'
Aynsley Dunbar – Drums
Gerry Weems – Lead Guitar
David Sanborn – Alto Saxophone
Dominic Cortese – Accordion
Cornell Dupree – Guitar on 'Britannia'
Don Alias – Congas
Arnie Lawrence – Clarinet
Dave Bargeron – Trombone
Lewis Soloff – Trumpet
Backing Vocals – Ann E. Sutton, Gail Kantor, Erin Dickens, Bob Segarini and Ian Hunter
Freddie Mercury, Brian May and Roger Meadows Taylor – Backing vocals on 'You Nearly Did Me In'
Recorded at Electric Lady Studios, New York during the first three weeks of January 1976
Engineers – David Palmer, David Wittman
Mastered and Mixed at A&M Studios, Los Angeles by David Palmer, Chris Stainton and Ian Hunter during the last week of January 1976
Produced and Arranged by Ian Hunter

Overnight Angels

Golden Opportunity (Hunter)
Shallow Crystals (Hunter)
Overnight Angels (Hunter)
Broadway (Hunter)
Justice of the Peace (Hunter)
(Miss) Silver Dime (Hunter/Slick)
Wild 'n' Free (Hunter)
The Ballad of Little Star (Hunter)
To Love a Woman (Hunter)
England Rocks (Hunter)

Ian Hunter – Lead and Harmony Vocals, Piano, Rhythm Guitar
Earl Slick – Lead, Slide & Rhythm Guitars
Peter Oxendale – Keyboards
Rob Rawlinson – Bass and Harmony Vocals
Dennis Elliott – Drums
Miller Anderson & Lem Lubin – Harmony Vocals on Broadway
Roy Thomas Baker – Percussion
Recorded at Le Studio, Morin Heights, Quebec, Canada, and Utopia and Olympic Studios, London – Winter 1976/7
Mixed at Sarm Studio, London
Mastered at Sterling Sound New York
Produced by Roy Thomas Baker
Engineered by Gary Lyons

You're Never Alone with a Schizophrenic
(Working title: *The Outsider*)

Don't Let Go (Hunter)
Just Another Night (Hunter/Ronson)
Wild East (Hunter)

Cleveland Rocks (Hunter)
Ships (Hunter)
When The Daylight Comes (Hunter)
Life After Death (Hunter)
Standin' In My Light (Hunter)
Bastard (Hunter)
The Outsider (Hunter)

Ian Hunter – Lead and Harmony Vocals, Piano, Guitars, Moog, ARP, Organ, Percussion
Mick Ronson – Guitars, Dual Vocal on 'Daylight', Harmony Vocals, Percussion
Roy Bittan – ARP, Moog, Organ, Piano, Harmony Vocals
Max Weinberg – Drums
Gary Tallent – Bass
John Cale – Piano, ARP on 'Bastard'
George Young – Tenor Sax
Lew Delgatto – Baritone Sax
Ellen Foley, Rory Dodd, Eric Bloome – Harmony Vocals
Recorded at The Power Station, New York 1979
Producers – Mick Ronson and Ian Hunter
Arrangements – Mick Ronson, Ian Hunter and Roy Bittan
Engineer – Bob Clearmountain

Welcome to the Club
(Working title: *From the Knees of My Heart*)

Live:
FBI
Once Bitten Twice Shy
Angeline
Laugh At Me
All the Way from Memphis
I Wish I Was Your Mother
Irene Wilde
Just Another Night
Cleveland Rocks
Standin' In My Light
Bastard
Walking with a Mountain / Rock and Roll Queen
All the Young Dudes
Slaughter on 10th Avenue
The Golden Age of Rock 'n' Roll
When the Daylight Comes
Life After Death

Studio:
We Gotta Get Out Of Here (Hunter)
Silver Needles (Hunter)
Man O'War (Hunter/Ronson)
Sons & Daughters (Hunter)

Ian Hunter – Vocals, Guitar, Piano
Mick Ronson – Lead Guitar, Vocals
Eric Parker – Drums
Martin Briley – Bass, Vocals
Tommy (Mad Dog) Morrongiello – Guitar, Vocals
Tommy (Moondog) Mandel – Keyboards, Vocals
Georgie Meyer – Keyboards, Vocals
Suzi Ronson & Ellen Foley – Vocals on 'We Gotta Get Out of Here'
Live tracks recorded 5–11 November 1979 at The Roxy, Los Angeles
Studio tracks recorded live at Media Sound, New York on 10 & 11 January 1980
Produced and Arranged by Mick Ronson and Ian

Hunter

Short Back 'n' Sides
(Working title: *Theatre of the Absurd*)

Wessex mixes:
    Theatre of the Absurd
    Leave Me Alone
    Burning Bridges
    Central Park 'n' West

New York Mixes:
10.12.80 NaNaNa
10.12.80 The Prisoner
12.12.80 A Song About You
14.12.80 Detroit (Vocal & Instrumental)
16.12.80 Venus in the Bathtub
16.12.80 I Believe In You
4.1.81   Burning Bridges (Keep on Burning)
    China
    Lisa Here's My Daddy
    Something Simple
    You Stepped in to My Dreams
    Listen to the Eight Track
    Theatre of the Absurd
    I Need Your Love
    Old Records Never Die
    Central Park 'n' West
    Lisa Likes Rock 'n' Roll
    Leave Me Alone
    Noises
    Rain
    Gun Gontrol

Ian Hunter – Lead Vocals, Guitar, Piano
Mick Ronson – Lead Guitars, Keyboards, Vocals
Eric Parker – Drums
Martin Briley – Bass
George Meyer – Keyboards
Tom Mandel – Keyboards
Tommy Morrongiello – Bass and Vocals
Mick Jones – Guitars, Vocals
Topper Headon – Drums, Percussion
Tymon Dogg – Violin
Ellen Foley/Miller Anderson – Vocals
'Gun Control' – Mick Baraken – Guitar, Wells Kelly
    – Drums, John Holbrook – Bass
'I Need Your Love' – Gary Windo – Sax,
Roger Powell – Backing vocals,
Todd Rundgren – Bass/Vocals
Mixed and Engineered by Todd Rundgren
Recorded at Wessex Studios, London and The Power
    Station, Electric Lady and Wizard Sound Studios,
    New York, Winter 1980 – 1981
Produced by Mick Ronson and Mick Jones

All of the Good Ones are Taken

All of the Good Ones are Taken (Fast Version)
    (Hunter)
Every Step Of The Way (Hunter/Clarke)
Fun (Hunter/Clarke/Michaels)
Speechless (Hunter)
Death 'n' Glory Boys (Hunter)
That Girl Is Rock 'n' Roll (Hunter)
Somethin's Goin' On (Hunter)
Captain Void 'n' The Video Jets (Hunter)
Seeing Double (Hunter)

All of the Good Ones are Taken (Slow Version)
    (Hunter)
Traitor (Hunter)
Ian Hunter – Vocals
Mark Clarke – Bass, Vocals
Robbie Alter – Guitar, Vocals
Tommy Mandel – Keyboards
Bob Mayo – Keyboards
Hilly Michaels – Drums
Clarence Clemmons – Tenor Sax on 'Good Ones' and
    'Seeing Double'
Lou Cortlezzi – Alto Sax
Dan Hartman – Bass on 'Speechless'
Jeff Bova – Keyboards on 'Speechless'
Jimmy Rip – Guitars on 'Good Ones' and 'That Girl'
Mick Ronson – Lead Guitar on 'Death 'n' Glory
    Boys'
Rory Dodd and Eric Troyer – Backing vocals on
    'Good Ones'
Recorded at Wizard Sound Studio in New York State
    during Winter 1982/3
Produced by Max Norman in association with Ian
    Hunter

Sessions and Demos 1979–88

You're Messing with the King of Rock 'n' Roll
Don't Let Go
The Lady with the Lamp
Professional Lover
Wake Up Call
(I'm the) Teacher
Good Man in a Bad Time
Great Expectations (You Never Know What to
    Expect)
Look Before You Leap
More to Love
Read Me Like a Book
Ill Wind
Junkman
Waiting Game
Boys 'R Us
Mean Streets
Bluebirds
Responsible
The Other Man
Hell
Man with the Perfect Hands
Gimme Another
Enough to Make Me Cry
Crazy Glue
Money Can't Buy Love
Favourite Dreams
Angel
Sign of Affection
Cool Jerk
National Holiday
My Love
Someone Else's Girl
Don't Throw Your Life Away
Mad at the World
You Got What It Takes
I Can't Find You
Slave

YUI Orta
(Working titles: *Balance / Wish / American Music*)

American Music (Hunter)
The Loner (Hunter)
Women's Intuition (Hunter/Ronson)
Cool (Hunter/Ronson)
Big Time (Hunter)
Livin' in a Heart (Hunter)
Sons 'n' Lovers (Hunter)
Beg a Little Love (Hunter/McNasty)
Tell It Like It Is (Hunter/Ronson)
Sweet Dreamer (Gibson/Ronson)
Following in Your Footsteps (Hunter/Ronson)*
Pain (Hunter/Kehr)*
How Much More Can I Take (Hunter)*
Give Me Back My Wings (Hunter)**
Day Tripper (Lennon & McCartney)**
While You Were Looking At Me (Little Steven)**

*Bonus tracks on CD
**unreleased/unfinished

Ian Hunter – Vocals
Mick Ronson – Guitars
Micky Curry – Drums
Tommy Mandel – Keyboards
Pat Kilbride – Bass
Backing Vocalists – Joey Cirecano, Carmela Long, Donnie Kehr, Robbie Alter, Mick Ronson, Ian Hunter
Bass on Women's Intuition – Bernard Edwards
Piano on 'Sweet Dreamer' – Ian Hunter
Recorded at The Power Station, New York City, June and July 1989
Produced by Bernard Edwards

Ian Hunter's Dirty Laundry
(Working title: *The Gringo Starrs*)

Another Fine Mess (Hunter/Bath/Plain)
The Other Man (Hunter)
Red Letter Day (Hunter)
Scars (Hunter/Bath/Plain)
Dancing on the Moon (Hunter/Bath/Plain)
Invisible Strings (Hunter)
My Revolution (Steel/Hunter/Dangerfield)
Good Girls (Plain)
Psycho Girl (Plain)
Never Trust a Blonde (Bath)
Everyone's a Fool (Bath/Roig)
Junkee Love (Matheson/Steel)

Ian Hunter – Guitar, Vocals
Casino Steel – Keyboards, Vocals, Percussion
Honest John Plain – Guitar, Vocals
Darrell Bath – Guitar, Vocals
Glen Matlock – Bass
Vom – Drums
Mitt Gorman – Harmonica
Blue Weaver – Keyboards
Torstein Flakne – Additional Guitar on ;Invisible Strings;
Lasse Hafreager – Piano, Organ
Backing Vocals – Vanesse Thomas, Angela Clemmons Patrick, James Williams, Bard Svendsen, Torstein Flakne
Recorded at Abbey Road, London – August 1994
Nidaros Studio, Trondheim, Norway,
Right Track Studios and The Power Station, New York,
Ambience Studio, Oslo, Norway
Produced and Recorded by Bjorn Nessjo

The Artful Dodger
(Working titles: *Life … Get One! / Pilgrim's Progress*)

Too Much
Now Is the Time
Something to Believe In
Ressurection Mary
Walk on Water
23a Snow Hill
Michael Picasso
Open My Eyes
The Artful Dodger
Skeletons (in Your Closet)
Still the Same
Fuck It Up
A Little Rock 'n' Roll
Testosterone
Worthing
Treat Her Like a Lady

Ian Hunter – Lead Vocals, Guitars, Harp
Robbie Alter, Darrell Bath, Frode Alves, Torstein Flakne – Guitars
Per Lindvall, Dennis Elliott – Drums
Sven Lindvall, Pat Kilbride – Bass
Kjetil Bjerkestrand – Keyboards
Honest John Plain – Vocals
Recorded and mixed at Nidaros Studios, Trondheim, Norway, with additional recording at The Time Machine, Vermont, USA
Produced by Bjorn Nessjo

Appendix 4

Live Dates

Mott The Hoople
(Support acts in brackets)

1969

AUGUST
6 Bat Caverna Club, Riccione, Italy
   (7-day residency)

SEPTEMBER
5 Romford Market Hall, Essex (King Crimson, MTH (1st UK gig))
17 Fillmore North, Sunderland (Free, MTH)
   The Roundhouse, London
   Hartlepool Grammar School for Boys
   Aylesbury Grammar School for Girls

OCTOBER
7 Speakeasy, London
19 Harwell AEA, Oxfordshire
20 Letchworth Youth Club, Herts.
23 Van Dyke Club, Plymouth
25 Van Dyke Club, Plymouth

NOVEMBER
9 Peterlee Jazz Club, Durham
12 Speakeasy, London
13 Country Club, Hampstead, London
16 Georges Club, Manchester
17 Letchworth Youth Club, Herts
21 Wake Arms, Epping or Freakeasy, Wood Green
24 Old Granary, Bristol (MTH, Phineas Fogg)

DECEMBER
5 CLCE (Colosseum)
7 Lyceum, London (Taste, MTH, One, Forevermore)
8 Aylesbury Friars, Bucks
11 The Country Club, Hampstead (Kelly James)
13 Barking College, Essex (Wildmouth, Castle Farm)
14 Greyhound, Croydon (Liverpool Scene, MTH)
21 The Roundhouse, Chalk Farm, London (Quintessence, MTH, Village)
24 Van Dyke Club, Plymouth
28 Northcote Arms, Southall
31 Northcote Arms, Southall (My Cake)

1970

JANUARY
1 Friars Addison Centre, Kempston, Bedford
3 Mother's, Birmingham (Taste, MTH)
4 Cloud 9, Peterborough
8 Westfields College, Hampstead
9 The Temple, Wardour Street, London (Daddy Longlegs, MTH, Skin Alley)
11 Cheeses, Chapel Hill, Stansted
12 Cleethorpes Wintergarden, Yorks
15 Scarborough Penthouse, Yorks
16 University of East Anglia, Norwich
17 University of Surrey, Guildford (Champion Jack Dupree)
18 Barn Club, Pied Bull, Islington (Music) or Croydon Greyhound(?)
21 Joints, Wimbledon (Stone The Crows, Black)
23 Drifter's Escape, Beaumont, South Wales
24 Victoria Ballroom, Chesterfield
25 Barn Club, Pied Bull, Islington (Gin)

26 Leys Youth Club, Letchworth, Herts
29 The Old Granary, Bristol
30 Lanchester College of Technology, Coventry (King Crimson, Free, MTH)
31 Loughborough University, Leics

FEBRUARY
1 Bletchley Youth Centre, Bucks (Daddy Longlegs)
2 Aylesbury Friars
3 Maida Vale Studio 4, London: *Top Gear*
4 Leicester Top Rank (Bonzo's, Joe Cocker, Spirit, MTH)
5 Stonehenge Club, Oxford
6 University of Exeter
7 Chelsea College, London (Skin Alley)
12 Eden Park Hotel, Beckenham, Kent
13 Leicester College, Leicester
14 Alma Road Youth Club, St Albans
19 New Penny Club, Watford (College)
20 The Temple, London (Rat, Hackensack)
21 University of Nottingham
22 Northcote Arms, Southall
25 Bristol University
27 Warwick University, Coventry
28 London School of Economics (Quintessence, MTH) or The Temple, London

MARCH
1 Northcote Arms, Southall (Genesis)
2 Keele University, Stoke
3 Nickelodeon, Wood Green, London
4 Aylesbury Friars
6 The Factory, Birmingham
7 Imperial College, London (Gypsy)
8 Mr.Smith's, Manchester (Raging Storm)
12 Jimmy's Club, Brighton
13 Newcastle Polytechnic
14 Leeds University
15 Angel Hotel, Godalming, Surrey
17 Dacorum College, Hemel Hempstead (Hard Meat)
19 Bingley College, Bingley (Bridget St John)
20 Hartlepool Grammar School
21 Kirklevington Country Club
22 Oswald Hotel, Scunthorpe, Yorks
24 *Beat Club*, Bremen, Germany – TV
25 Electric Circus, Lausanne, Switzerland
26 Electric Circus, Lausanne
28 Electric Circus, Lausanne

APRIL
1 Victoria Road Hall, Chelmsford
3 Bluesville, High Wycombe
4 Eel Pie Island, London (White Lightning)
8 The Castle, Tooting (Status Quo)
9 Lafayette Club, Wolverhampton
11 Van Dyke Club, Plymouth
14 Watford Town Hall (Keef Hartley, MTH, East of Eden)
16 Winter Gardens, Weston super Mare
18 Barn Club, Thaxted, Essex (Gin)
19 Farx, Northcote Arms, Southall,
20 The Roundhouse, London (Traffic, MTH, Bronco, If)
22 Guildford Civic Hall (Spooky Tooth or Humble Pie, If)

23 Paris Theatre, London: *John Peel In Concert*
24 Hospital Medical School, Cleveland, Middlesex
25 Newmans Technical College, Birmingham
26 Croydon Greyhound
27 Kingston Hotel, Kingston, Surrey
28 Cambridge Corn Exchange (Wild Oats, Principal Edwards)

MAY

1 Maryland Club, Glasgow
2 C. F. Mott Technical College, Liverpool
4 Aylesbury Friars
6 Fox on the Hill, Dulwich Hall, Denmark Hill, London
8 The Country Club, Hampstead
9 Watford College of Technology (Warm Dust)
10 Cooksferry Inn, Edmonton, London
16 Dagenham Roundhouse

First Mott The Hoople US Tour
29 East Town Theatre, Detroit
30 East Town Theatre, Detroit

JUNE

4 State University, New York
5 Electric Factory, Philadelphia (Kinks, MTH)
6 Electric Factory, Philadelphia (Kinks, MTH)
10 Fillmore East, New York – 2 shows (Traffic, Fairport Convention, MTH)
11 Fillmore East, New York – 2 shows (Traffic, Fairport Convention, MTH)
13 Crosley Fields, Cincinatti (Traffic, Ten Years After, Mountain, MTH, Stooges)
15 Boston Tea Party, Boston
16 Boston Tea Party, Boston
17 Boston Tea Party, Boston
19 Capitol Theatre, Porchester, NY
20 Capitol Theatre, Porchester, NY
23 Tarant County Convention Centre Arena, Forth Worth, Texas (Traffic, Mountain, MTH)
24 Hemisphere Arena, San Antonio, Texas (Traffic, Mountain, MTH)
25 Hofheinz Pavilion, Houston, Texas (Traffic, Mountain, MTH)
26 Aragon Ballroom, Chicago (B. B. King, MTH)
27 Aragon Ballroom, Chicago

JULY

1 Harvard Stadium, Cambridge, Massachusetts (Ten Years After, MTH)
4 Convention Centre, Asbury Park, New Jersey
5 Atlanta Pop Festival, Macon, Georgia
6 Whiskey A Go Go, Los Angeles (Toe Fat)
7 Whiskey A Go Go, Los Angeles
9 Fillmore West, San Francisco (Quicksilver Messenger Service, MTH, Silver Metre, Brotherhood of Light)
10 Fillmore West, San Francisco (Albert King, MTH, Freddie King)
11 Fillmore West, San Francisco (Albert King, MTH, Freddie King)
12 Fillmore West, San Francisco (Albert King, MTH, F reddie King)
16 Spectrum, Philadelphia (Jethro Tull, MTH)
18 The Warehouse, New Orleans (Jethro Tull, MTH)
19 Houston, Texas (Jethro Tull, MTH)

AUGUST

21 Mayfair Ballroom, Newcastle (Quintessence, MTH, Supertramp)
22 Barn Club, Bishops Stortford, Herts (High Broom)

23 Redcar Jazz Club, Coatham Arms, Redcar, County Durham
31 Canterbury, Kent (Grateful Dead, Caravan, MTH, Faces, Pink Floyd, Edgar Broughton) Filmed for Warner Bros *The Great Medicine Ball*

SEPTEMBER

4 Flamingo Redhill Ballroom, Hereford
5 Elm Court Youth Centre, Potters Bar, Herts (Spiro Gyra)
10 Paradisio Club, Amsterdam
11 Paradisio Club, Amsterdam
13 Fairfield Hall, Croydon (Free, MTH): Live recording – 2 shows, 6.00 & 8.45
18 The Country Club, Hampstead, London (Sun)
19 Liverpool Stadium (Free, MTH, Fotheringay, If)
21 Cooksferry Inn, Edmonton, London
24 Manchester Polytechnic
25 Bristol Polytechnic (Pete Brown)
26 Van Dyke Club, Plymouth
27 Farx, Northcote Arms, Southall
28 Leys Youth Club, Letchworth, Herts
29 High Wycombe Town Hall (Stack Waddy)
30 The Marquee, London (Bronco)
30 BBC TV *Disco 2*

OCTOBER

1 McIlroy's Ballroom, Swindon
3 Lancaster University (Stonefeather)
4 Wormwood Scrubs Prison, London – Cancelled
5 Dunstable Civic Hall, Herts
6 Birmingham Town Hall (Free, MTH)
7 The Castle, Tooting (Status Quo)
9 Brunel University, Uxbridge (Boris & Friends)
10 Liverpool Stadium (Traffic, MTH, Quintessence, If): Filmed by Granada TV?
10 Kirklevington Country Club
11 Wake Arms, Epping
15 Paris Theatre, London: *John Peel In Concert*
16 Eel Pie Island, London (Garnet Wolseley)
17 Dagenham Roundhouse (Nosher Brown)
18 The Fox, Croydon
19 The Old Granary, Bristol – Cancelled
20 Resurrection Club, Barnet, Herts – Cancelled
22 Windrush Club, Reading – Cancelled
23 Northern Polytechnic, London Cancelled
24 Crewe College – Cancelled
25 Lyceum, London – Cancelled

NOVEMBER

Second US Tour – Cancelled
6 Sisters, London – Cancelled
8 Lyceum, London – Cancelled
10 Resurrection Club, Barnet – Cancelled
11 Resurrection, Hitchin – Cancelled
13 Poperama, Devizes – Cancelled
14 Bromley Technical College – Cancelled
15 Bournemouth Pavilion – Cancelled
21 Reading University (John Martyn, John Morgan)
22 The Roundhouse, London (Curved Air, Stoneground, Quiver)
25 Dartford College of Technology (Renaissance II)
26 Friars, Bedford
27 Westfield College, Hampstead, London (Supertramp, Cochise)

DECEMBER

3 Blow Up, Munich, Germany
4 Zoom Club, Frankfurt, Germany
5 High School, Frankfurt, Germany
6 Schorndorf TV Hall, Stuttgart, Germany
9 York University, Heslington – Cancelled
10 Scarborough Penthouse

11 Bedford College, London – Cancelled
12 Elm Court Youth Centre, Potters Bar, Herts (Knocker Jungle)
15 South Parade Pier, Portsmouth (Alan Bown)
16 Hermitage Ballroom, Hitchin, Herts (Sin)
18 Redcar Jazz Club, Coatham Arms, Redcar
19 Liverpool Stadium (Bronco, If)
21 Dudley Town Hall, Worcs
22 Resurrection Club, Salisbury Hotel, Barnet, Herts
26 Birmingham Town Hall (Bronco)
27 Croydon Greyhound (Mike Maran)

1971

JANUARY
3 Starlight Club
8 Knufflesplunk Club, Community Centre, Welwyn Garden City, Herts (Sin)
9 Kirklevington Country Club, Yorks
12 Starlight Club, Crawley
15 Edinburgh University
16 Strathclyde University, Glasgow
17 Kinema Ballroom, Dunfermline
19 The Marquee, London (Blondel)
20 Big Brother Club, Oldfield Tavern, Greenford, Middlesex – filmed for Australian TV
21 Van Dyke Club, Plymouth
22 Exeter University
23 Big Apple, Brighton
25 Swansea Top Rank

Mini tour (MTH, Wishbone Ash, Red Dirt)
27 Nottingham Albert Hall
28 Newcastle City Hall
29 Sheffield City Hall
30 Hull City Hall
31 Bradford St George's Hall

FEBRUARY
2 Wolverhampton Civic Hall
4 High Wycombe Town Hall – Cancelled
5 West Bromwich Town Hall
6 Manchester University
7 The Lyceum, London (Bronco, Karakorum)
12 Trent Polytechnic, Nottingham
16 Konserthuset, Stockholm, Sweden – Radio broadcast
17 Stockholm University, Sweden
18 Vaxjo University, Vaxjo, Sweden
19 Ljungskille, Sweden
20 Uppsala University, Uppsala, Sweden
21 Cue Club, Gothenburg, S weden – Cancelled
26 Sister's Club, Tottenham (Brewer's Droop)
27 Bromley Technical College (Renaissance)

MARCH
2 Civic Hall, Tunbridge Wells, Kent
4 McIlroy's Ballroom, Swindon, Wilts
5 Parr Hall, Warrington – Cancelled
6 South Parade Pier, Portsmouth (Satisfaction, Galliard)
7 Cheltenham Town Hall, Gloucester (Man)
8 Maida Vale Studio 5, London: *Sounds of the 70s'* session
12 Southampton University (Brinsley Schwarz)
13 Imperial College, Kensington (Crushed Butler)
14 Black Prince, Bexley, Kent
17 Westfield College, Hampstead – Cancelled
19 Blackpool Winter Gardens (Marmalade, Colosseum, MTH, Gentle Giant)
20 Leeds University (Curved Air,)
21 Coatham Arms, Redcar (Bronco)
23 Mayfair Club, Newcastle

25 Locarno Ballroom, Sunderland
26 Mayfair Ballroom, Newcastle
27 Lanchester College of Technology, Coventry
28 Fairfield Hall, Croydon (Bronco)
30 The Marquee, London

APRIL
3 Liverpool Stadium (Greasy Bear, Stoned Rose)
4 Palace Theatre, Westcliff on Sea, Essex (Bronco)
9 Mistrale Club, Beckenham, Kent
10 Village Roundhouse, Dagenham (Collusion)
13 BBC TV *Disco 2* session
14 Watford Top Rank (Arthur Brown's Kingdom Come)
15 Plymouth Guildhall (John Martyn)
16 Bournemouth Winter Gardens
17 Malvern Winter Gardens, Worcs (Karakorum)
18 Victoria Hall, Stoke (John Martyn)
19 Cooksferry Inn, Edmonton, London
22 Birmingham Town Hall (Bronco)
23 Lowestoft College, Lowestoft
24 Kingston Polytechnic, Kingston upon Thames (Flying Fortress)

Second US Tour
28 Maryland (Jethro Tull, MTH)

MAY
Free withdraw from US tour and all Mott's supporting dates are cancelled
11 Guthrie Theatre, Milwaukee (ELP, MTH)
14 Fillmore East, New York (MTH, Mandrill, Delaney & Bonnie)
19 Kiel Opera House, Kiel (ELP, MTH) Gateway Regional High School Philadelphia Spectrum (John Mayall, MTH, Alice Cooper)
28 Rockpile, Long Island (Mandrill)
29 Rockpile, Long Island (Hog Heaven)

JUNE
1 Blackwood College, Blackwood (Edgar Winter, MTH)
3 Fillmore West, San Francisco
4 Fillmore West, San Francisco
5 Fillmore West, San Francisco
6 Fillmore West, San Francisco (Freddie & Albert King, MTH)
11 Civic Auditorium, Albequerque (Jethro Tull, MTH)
12 Warehouse, New Orleans (MTH, Brownsville Station)
13 Allentown – Cancelled
17 Atlanta (Edgar Winter, MTH, J. Geils)
18 East Town Theatre, Detroit (Edgar Winter, MTH, Sweathog)
19 East Town Theatre, Detroit (Edgar Winter, MTH, Sweathog)
20 *Mott return to London via New York*
25 Durham University
26 Leicester Polytechnic
29 Rehearse, Hammersmith Town Hall
30 Rehearse, Hammersmith Town Hall

JULY
1 Rehearse, Hammersmith Town Hall
3 Pier Pavilion, Felixstowe
6 Maida Vale Studio, London: BBC *Top Gear*
8 Royal Albert Hall, London (MTH, Heads, Hands & Feet)
9 Kinetic Circus, Birmingham
10 Spa Royal Hall, Bridlington, Yorks
11 Floral Hall, Southport, Lancs

17 Paris Theatre, London: Radio One *Rosko Show*
21 *Top of the Pops* – 'Midnight Lady'
24 Truro Town Hall, Cornwall (Sutherland Brothers)
25 Plymouth Guildhall (Sutherland Brothers)
30 Cheltenham Town Hall (Hookfoot)
31 The Dome, Brighton (Sutherland Brothers)

AUGUST
7 Torquay Town Hall (Sutherland Brothers)
8 Caravari Theatre, Southsea Common, Portsmouth
13 Mayfair Ballroom, Newcastle
14 Lads Club, Norwich (Pete Brown's Piblokto)
28 Weeley Festival, Clacton, Essex (T Rex, Faces,
    King Crimson, MTH, Colosseum, Rory
    Gallagher, Groundhogs, Mungo Jerry)
29 Lyceum, London (Warm Dust, Frumpy)
30 Hereford United Football Stadium (MTH,
    Heads, Hands & Feet, Amazing Blondel,
    Karakorum, Frumpy)

SEPTEMBER
2 Royal Ballroom, Bournemouth (Marble Orchard)
4 Friars, Aylesbury Town Hall
8 The Winning Post, Twickenham
12 Kinetic Cellar, Kenilworth
18 Oval Cricket Ground, London (The Who, Faces,
    MTH, Lindisfarne)
25 Dagenham Roundhouse (Titanic)
29 TV Show, Paris

OCTOBER
1 Casino Club, Bolton (Medicine Head)
2 Manchester University
5 Refectory, Leeds University
7 Sheffield Civic Hall (Peace)
8 Victoria Hall, Stoke on Trent (Peace)
9 Liverpool Stadium (Peace)
10 Bradford St George's Hall (Peace)
13 Top Rank Suite, Cardiff (Slade)
15 Lancaster University (Graphite)
16 University College, London (Medium)
18 Surrey Rooms, The Oval, Kennington
    (Sunshine)
22 Doncaster Top Rank (Peace, Sutherland Brothers)
23 Portsmouth Guildhall (Peace)
25 Maida Vale Studio 5, London: BBC session
27 Oxford Town Hall (Peace)
30 Nottingham Albert Hall (Peace)

NOVEMBER
1 Birmingham Town Hall (Peace)
4 Green's Playhouse, Glasgow (Peace)
5 Newcastle City Hall (Peace)
6 Hull City Hall (Peace)
13 Leicester University
14 The Rainbow, London (Peace, Stoneground)
19 London Goldsmiths College – Cancelled
20 Twickenham St Mary's College – Cancelled
21 Guildford Civic Hall (Peace)
22 Colston Hall, Bristol (Peace)
25 Southampton Guildhall (Peace)
26 Kings Hall, Derby
28 Plymouth Guildhall (Peace)
29 Wolverhampton Civic Hall (Peace)

DECEMBER
European Tour (Grand Funk Railroad, MTH):
Germany, France, Denmark, Holland
3 Copenhagen, Denmark
9 Deutschland Halle, Berlin, Germany
    Hamburg, Germany
19 The Roundhouse, London
20 Wolverhampton Civic Hall
30 Paris Theatre, London: Radio One *In Concert*

1972

JANUARY
2 Redcar Jazz Club, Coatham Arms, Redcar
7 High Wycombe Town Hall (Carole Grimes,
    Uncle Dog)
8 Great Malvern Winter Gardens (Sutherland
    Brothers)
15 The Village, Roundhouse, Dagenham
20 Warwick University, Coventry
21 Chelsea Village, Bournemouth
22 University of Essex, Colchester
29 Watford College of Technology

FEBRUARY
2 Swansea Top Rank
4 Waltham Forest Technical College, London
    (Hookfoot)
5 Rock Street Youth Centre, Wellingborough –
    Cancelled
10 Kelvin Hall, Glasgow (Nazareth)
11 Beach Ballroom, Aberdeen
12 Edinburgh University
13 Up The Junction, Crewe
14 Manchester Free Trade Hall – Cancelled
18 Newcastle City Hall
19 Liverpool Stadium
20 Fairfield Hall, Croydon (Bronco)
25 Locarno Ballroom, Sunderland

MARCH
1 Aberystwyth University – Cancelled
3 Central Hall, York University
4 Belfry Hotel, Sutton Coldfield
10 Bath University
14 Main Hall, Aberystwyth University
17 Preston Public Hall
18 Rock Street Centre, Wellingborough, Northants
24 Volkshaus, Zurich, Switzerland
25 Youth Centre, Berne, Switzerland

APRIL
1 Marquee Festival, Middlewick, Essex (Stray,
    Fruup, Snake Eye)

Rock and Roll Circus UK Tour (Max Wall and
Hackensack support on all dates)
5 Plymouth Guildhall
6 Wolverhampton Civic Hall
8 Liverpool Stadium
9 Guildford Civic Hall
11 Empire Theatre, Edinburgh
12 Green's Playhouse, Glasgow
13 Newcastle City Hall
14 Empress Ballroom Blackpool
15 Carlisle Market Hall
16 Victoria Hall Stoke
17 Sheffield City Hall
18 Bradford St.George's Hall
19 Lyceum London
20 Portsmouth Guildhall
21 Luton College of Education
22 Starlight Rooms Boston – Cancelled
22 Norwich East Anglia University
27 Glen Ballroom Llanelli
29 Bracknell Sports Centre – Cancelled
29 High Wycombe Town Hall (Skin Alley, Junkyard
    Angel)

MAY
4 Warwick University
5 Aston University, Birmingham
6 Imperial College, London (Junkyard Angel)
7 Redcar Jazz Club, Coatham Arms, Redcar

8 Cleethorpes Winter Gardens
11 Malcolm's Disco, Hull
13 Loughborough University
17 Grona Lund, Stockholm, Sweden
18 Liseberg, Gothenburg, Sweden
19 Olympen, Lund, Sweden
20 Wamohallen, Karlskrona, Sweden
21 W-Dala Nation, Uppsala, Sweden
23 Culture House, Helsinki, Finland
24 Concert House, Abo, Finland

JUNE
3 King's Cross Cinema, London
4 Croydon Greyhound (Shamelady)
24 Croydon Greyhound

JULY
8 Royal Festival Hall, London (David Bowie,
  MTH, Marmalade, JSD Band): Mott withdraw
16 Chelsea Village, Bournemouth (Inside Out)
20 Watford Top Rank
21 Doncaster Top Rank (Budgie, Mam Machine)
22 Bridlington Spa
28 Newcastle City Hall

AUGUST
9 Worthing Assembly Hall
12 Kings Cross Cinema, London
13 Guildford Civic Hall (Bowie on encore, Frupp)
  Top of The Pops: 'All the Young Dudes'
  Slough Community Centre
  Barry Memorial Hall (Frupp, Quicksand)
  Barnstaple Queen's Hall
26 Plymouth Guildhall

SEPTEMBER
'All the Young Dudes' UK Tour (*Home as support)
15 Dunstable Civic Hall* (Sunshine)
16 Manchester Free Trade Hall*
17 Hanley Victoria Hall*
19 Middlesborough Town Hall*
20 Newcastle City Hall
21 Sheffield Top Rank
22 Mayfair Entertainment Centre, Doncaster
  (Vinegar Joe) – Cancelled
23 Liverpool Stadium
24 Carlisle Market Hall
25 Wolverhampton Civic Hall
26 Leeds City Hall
27 Birmingham Top Rank
28 Coventry Locarno
29 Bristol Top Rank
30 Malvern Winter Gardens

OCTOBER
2 Chatham Central Hall
4 Brighton Top Rank
6 Dreamland Ballroom, Margate*
7 Southampton University*
8 Chelsea Bowl, Bournemouth
14 Rainbow, London
15 Rainbow, London*
22 *Three week US tour commencing in Atlanta
  cancelled*
27 College of Printing, London (Ro Ro)

NOVEMBER
18 Northampton Town Hall

'All the Young Dudes' US Tour
24 Hollywood Palladium, Los Angeles (West Bruce
  & Laing, MTH)
25 Hollywood Colliseum, Los Angeles (Sly Stone,
  MTH) – Cancelled

29 Tower Theatre, Philadelphia (Brownsville
  Station): Radio broadcast

DECEMBER
2 Porchester Palace, New York (John McLaughlin,
  MTH)
3 Music Fair, Valley Forge (Savoy Brown)
4 Springfield
6 Convention Hall, St Louis (Fleetwood Mac,
  MTH, Bloodrock)
11 Fort Wayne, Embassy (Flash Cadillac)
13 Detroit Metropolitan
14 Dallas – Cancelled
15 Houston – Cancelled
16 Chicago Auditorium (Eric Anderson, New Riders
  of the Purple Sage)
17 Cleveland, Ohio (Dr Hook)
20 Scranton, New Jersey (Edgar Winter)
22 Ellis Auditorium, Memphis (Joe Walsh &
  Barnstorm)

1973

JANUARY
16 Glen Ballroom, Llanelli (Good Habit, Thank
  You)
19 Sheffield University (Nazareth) (Final Verden
  Allen gig)

FEBRUARY
10 Aylesbury Friars (Darien Spirit) – Cancelled
17 Bradford University – Cancelled
18 Cheltenham Town Hall

UK Mini Tour (Sensational Alex Harvey Band support)
19 Birmingham Town Hall
21 Falkirk Town Hall
22 Green's Playhouse, Glasgow
24 Empire Theatre, Edinburgh
25 Newcastle City Hall

MARCH
Five-week US Tour – Cancelled
2 Leeds Polytechnic (Maldoon)

JUNE
  Top of the Pops: 'Honaloochie Boogie'
21 Seeheim, Germany (film *Hits a Go Go*): with
  Lynsey de Paul – "Ariel Bender" coined
22 Seeheim, Germany (2nd day filming)

JULY
*'Mott' US Tour: T. Rex pull out as support to Mott The
Hoople!*
27 Aragon Ballroom, Chicago (Joe Walsh)
28 Cloverleaf Speedway or Mussillon Stadium,
  Cleveland (New York Dolls)
29 Detroit

AUGUST
1 Virginia Beach
3 Felt Forum, New York
4 Boston
7 Pittsburg
8 Spectrum, Philadelphia
10 Portland
11 Providence
12 Asbury Park, New Jersey
14 Milwaukee
17 Memphis
18 Fayetteville – Cancelled
19 Washington (Final Mick Ralphs gig)
25 Santa Monica Civic, Los Angeles – Cancelled

SEPTEMBER

3   *Top of the Pops*: 'All the Way from Memphis' with Ariel Bender
11 Aquarius Theatre, Los Angeles – Rehearsal
12 Aquarius Theatre, Los Angeles – Rehearsal
13 Los Angeles: NBC TV *Midnight Special*
14 Hollywood Palladium, Los Angeles (first Ariel Bender gig)
15 Celebrity Theatre, Phoenix (Joe Walsh & Barnstorm)
16 San Diego – Cancelled
20 Commandor Ballroom, Vancouver – Cancelled
22 Paramount Theatre, Portland
23 Paramount Theatre, Seattle
25 Denver, Colorado – Cancelled
28 Winterland, San Francisco (Joe Walsh & Barnstorm)
29 Winterland, San Francisco (Bachmann Turner Overdrive): Pioneer radio 'Concert'

OCTOBER

3   Municipal Auditorium, Chattanooga – Cancelled
4   Municipal Auditorium, Atlanta
5   WPB Auditorium, West Palm Beach
6   Coliseum, Jacksonville
7   Birmingham, Mississippi – Cancelled
10 Music Hall, Cincinatti
11 Auditorium Theatre, Chicago (Aerosmith, New York Dolls)
12 Masonic Temple, Detroit
13 John Carroll University, Cleveland
14 Massey Hall, Toronto, Canada
16 Auditorium Theatre, Rochester
17 Kleinhans Music Hall, Buffalo
18 Syria Mosque, Pittsburg
19 Ohio State University, Columbus
20 Shubert Theatre, Philadelphia
21 Seaton Hall, South Orange
24 Palace Theatre, Providence
26 Radio City Music Hall, New York
27 Orpheum Theatre, Boston
28 Hartford, Connecticut
29 Bethlehem
31 Indianapolis Theatre, Indianapolis

NOVEMBER

1   Civic Centre, St Paul
2   Kansas City
3   St Louis
4   Massey Hall, Toronto
    Top of the Pops: 'Roll Away The Stone'

Mott' UK Tour (Queen support on all dates)
12 Leeds Town Hall
13 Blackburn St George's Hall
15 Worcester Gaumont
16 Lancaster University
17 Liverpool Stadium
18 Hanley Victoria Hall
19 Wolverhampton Civic Hall
20 Oxford New Theatre
21 Preston Guildhall
22 Newcastle City Hall
23 Glasgow Apollo
25 Caley Cinema, Edinburgh
26 Manchester Opera House
27 Birmingham Town Hall
28 Swansea Branglyn Hall
29 Bristol Colston Hall
30 Bournemouth Winter Gardens

DECEMBER

1   Southend Kursaal
2   Chatham Central Hall
14 Hammersmith Odeon, London: 2 shows, both recorded for *Live* LP

1974

MARCH

20 *Top of the Pops*: 'The Golden Age of Rock 'n' Roll'
21 Bradford St George's Hall (Judi Pulver)
22 Leicester De Montfort Hall
24 Bristol Colston Hall (Judi Pulver)
25 Sheffield City Hall (Judi Pulver)
26 Paignton Festival Hall (Judi Pulver)
27 Bournemouth Winter Gardens (Judi Pulver)

'The Hoople' US Tour (Queen support)

APRIL

7   *Mott fly to Los Angeles*
11 Celebrity Theatre, Phoenix
12 Santa Monica Civic Auditorium
13 Santa Monica Civic Auditorium: 2 shows – Radio broadcast
14 Warner Theatre, Fresno, California
16 Reiges College Fieldhouse, Denver
17 Memorial Hall, Kansas City
18 Keil Auditorium, St Louis
19 International Building, Oklahoma City
20 Mid South Coliseum, Memphis
21 St Bernard Civic, New Orleans
25 R. P. I. Troy, New York
26 Orpheum Theatre, Boston
27 Orpheum Theatre, Boston
28 Exposition Hall, Portland, Maine

MAY

1   State Farm Arena, Harrisburg
2   Agricultural Hall, Allentown
3   Kings College, Wilkes-Barre
4   Palace Theatre, Waterbury, Connecticut
5   Rehearsal – New York, Fillmore East or Capitol
6   Rehearsal, New York

One-week residency on Broadway
7   Uris Theatre, Broadway, New York
8   Uris Theatre, Broadway, New York – Recorded for King Biscuit Radio
9   Uris Theatre, Broadway, New York – Recorded for King Biscuit Radio
10 Uris Theatre, Broadway, New York – 2 shows
11 Uris Theatre, Broadway, New York – 2 shows
12 Uris Theatre, Broadway, New York – Optional date – Cancelled
Queen withdraw from Mott tour
14 Syria Mosque, Pittsburg
15 Constitution Hall, Washington
16 Municipal Auditorium, Charleston
17 Fox Theatre, Atlanta
18 Knoxville Coliseum, Knoxville
20 Masonic Temple, Detroit
21 Auditorium Theatre, Chicago
22 Bruce Hall, Milwaukee Auditorium
23 Morris Civic Auditorium, South Bend, Illinois
24 Toledo Sports Arena, Toledo, Ohio
25 Allen Theatre, Cleveland, Ohio
26 Mershon Auditorium, Columbus
27 Massey Hall, Toronto, Canada
28 London Gardens, London, Ontario, Canada
30 The Mosque, Richmond

31 Shubert Theatre, Philadelphia – 2 shows (REO Speedwagon)

JUNE
1 Shubert Theatre, Philadelphia
3 *Mott return to the UK via New York*

Various support groups opened for Mott on their 1973 & 1974 US tours, including: Aerosmith, Joe Walsh, Kansas, REO Speedwagon, Styx, New York Dolls, Blue Oyster Cult, The Pointer Sisters

19 *Top of the Pops*: 'Foxy Foxy'

JULY
3 *Top of the Pops*: 'Foxy Foxy'
5 Buxton Festival, Derbyshire (Lindisfarne, Man, JSD Band)
6 Palace Lido, Douglas, Isle of Man (final Ariel Bender gig)
31 London Music Festival, Alexandra Palace, London – Cancelled

OCTOBER
Top of the Pops: 'Saturday Gigs'

European Tour (Titanic support)
10 Olympen, Lund, Sweden (first Mick Ronson gig)
11 Scandinavium, Gothenburg, S weden
12 Konserthuset, Stockholm, Sweden
14 Falkon, Copenhagen, Denmark
16 ATSV-Halle, Saarbrucken, Germany
17 Austellungshalle, Stuttgart, Germany
18 Volkhaus, Zurich, Switzerland
19 Vaduzersaal, Vaduz, Lichtenstein
20 Congress House, Berne, Switzerland
21 Brienner Theatre, Munich, Germany – Cancelled
23 Roma, Antwerp, Belgium
24 Forest National, Brussels, Belgium
25 Offenbach Stadthalle, Frankfurt, Germany
26 Stadthalle, Heidelburg, Germany
28 Niedersachsenhalle, Hanover, Germany
29 Nordmarkhalle, Rendsburg, Germany
30 Musikhalle, Hamburg, Germany

NOVEMBER
2 Olympia, Paris, France
3 Concertgebouw, Amsterdam, Holland (final Mott The Hoople gig)

Ian Hunter suffered a physical breakdown in the USA between Mott's European and planned US tours. The initial four dates in Scotland* were re-scheduled but the complete itinerary (with Sailor as support) was subse-quently scrapped. A major US tour (April–June 1975), including several dates at Madison Square Gardens, New York and the Spectrum, Philadelphia were also cancelled. The planned UK winter tour dates which were never played were:

NOVEMBER
10 Glasgow Apollo*
11 Leith Hall, Edinburgh*
12 Caird Hall, Dundee*
13 Aberdeen Music Hall*
15 Leeds Town Hall
16 Liverpool Empire
17 Manchester Palace
18 Portsmouth Guildhall
19 Malvern Winter Gardens
21 Swansea Brangwyn Hall
22 Cardiff Capitol
23 Taunton Odeon
24 Bournemouth Winter Gardens

26 Birmingham Town Hall
27 Preston Guildhall
28 Stockton Globe Theatre
30 Lancaster University

DECEMBER
1 Bristol Hippodrome
4 Ipswich Gaumont
6 Hammersmith Odeon, London
7 Hammersmith Odeon, London
8 Newcastle City Hall
10 Southampton Gaumont
11 Oxford New Theatre
12 Wolverhampton Civic Hall
16 Leith Hall, Edinburgh
17 Caird Hall, Dundee
19 Aberdeen Music Hall
20 Glasgow Apollo

'Dates are vague for 1969. If only we could raid "The Stan Tippins Diaries". He's kept diaries since before he was born.' – Dale Griffin

Ian Hunter

1975

MARCH
'Ian Hunter' UK Tour (Jet supporting on all dates)
18 Exeter University
19 Friars Aylesbury – Cancelled
20 Sheffield City Hall
21 Manchester Free Trade Hall
22 Liverpool Empire
23 Glasgow Apollo
24 Aberdeen Music Hall
26 Newcastle City Hall
27 Leeds City Hall
29 Birmingham Town Hall – Cancelled
29 Aylesbury Friars
30 Croydon Fairfield Halls – Cancelled
31 Hammersmith Odeon

APRIL
1 Bristol Colston Hall – Cancelled
2 East Ham Granada – Cancelled
3 Birmingham Town Hall
4 Bristol Colston Hall
5 East Ham Granada
6 Croydon Fairfield Halls

MAY
'Ian Hunter' US Tour
8 Felt Forum, New York
Grand Rapids, Ohio
Toledo, Ohio
Philadelphia, Spectrum

1977

JUNE
'Overnight Angels' UK Tour (Vibrators supporting on all dates)
3 Newcastle Mayfair
4 Doncaster Gaumont
7 Birmingham Town Hall
8 Manchester Free Trade Hall
9 Leicester De Montfort Hall
10 Uxbridge Brunel University
11 Aylesbury Vale Hall
12 London New Victoria – Cancelled
12 Hammersmith Odeon London
Grona Lund, Stockholm, Sweden

Orebro, Sweden

1979

JUNE

'You're Never Alone with a Schizophrenic' Tour
12 My Father's Place, Roslyn, NY
    Toad's Place, New Haven, Connecticut
    Pine Crest Country Club, Connecticut
18 Agora Ballroom, Cleveland
22 Park West Theatre, Chicago
28 The Palladium, New York

JULY
    Fort Wayne Colisseum, Indiana
7   Community Theatre, Berkeley, CA
11 Celebrity Theatre, Phoenix
27 Nassau Coliseum, Uniondale, NY
28 Philadelphia Spectrum
29 New Haven Court Colliseum

AUGUST
2   Glens Falls New York
3   Portland Civic Centre
5   Music Inn, Lenox, MI
7   Kleinhaus Music Hall, Buffalo, NY
10 Cobo Hall, Detroit
    Rhyerson Theatre, Toronto, Canada

SEPTEMBER
1   Bontwell Auditorium, Birmingham

NOVEMBER
3   Old Waldorf, San Francisco
5   The Roxy, Los Angeles (Billy Connolly)
6   The Roxy, Los Angeles
7   The Roxy, Los Angeles
8   The Roxy, Los Angeles
9   The Roxy, Los Angeles
10 The Roxy, Los Angeles
11 The Roxy, Los Angeles
22 Hammersmith Odeon London (Rachel Sweet)

1980

APRIL
20 Rockpalast, Grugahalle, Essen, Germany
22 Empire Theatre, Paris

MAY
20 The Roxy, Los Angeles

JUNE
8   Cobo Arena, Detroit (Heart)

JULY
11 Dr Pepper Festival, Central Park, New York

AUGUST
23 Reading Festival – Cancelled)

OCTOBER
15 Orpheus Theatre, Boston, MA (Todd Rundgren)

1981

AUGUST
'Short Back 'N' Sides Tour
8   Milton Keynes Concert Bowl (Thin Lizzy, Judie
    Tzuke, Q Tips)
9   101 Club, London
10 Gota Lejon, Stockholm
16 Rotterdam

SEPTEMBER
6   Fastlane, Asbury Park, NJ
11 Doctor Pepper Festival, Central Park, New York
    (filmed)

OCTOBER
2   Le Club, Montreal
3   Alumni Hall

4   O'Keefe Centre
5   Michigan State University
6   Vets Memorial Auditorium
8   Richfield College
9   Cahn Auditorium
10 Cobo Hall, Detroit
11 Youngstown Agora
12 Ole Man River
13 Cardi's
14 Cardi's
16 Club Foot
18 Dooley's
19 University of San Diego
20 Aquarius Theatre (filmed for *Don Kirshner's TV Rock Concert*)
21 Country Club
22 Perkin's Palace
23 Perkin's Palace
25 Old Waldorf, San Francisco

1982

APRIL
23 Royal Oak Theatre, Michigan

JULY
30 Pier 84, New York

1986

Ian Hunter & The Roy Young Band

OCTOBER
1   Rock 'n' Roll Heaven, Toronto, Canada
5   California's, Windsor, Canada
6   California's, Windsor, Canada
14 The Diamond, Toronto, Canada

DECEMBER
6   Coach House, San Juan Capistrano
10 One Step Beyond, Santa Clara, CA
11 One Step Beyond, Santa Clara, CA
    Stone, San Francisco
    The Ritz, New York

1987

NOVEMBER
11 Rock 'n' Roll Heaven, Toronto, Canada
16 California's, Windsor, Canada

1988

Ian Hunter, Mick Ronson & The Roy Young Band Canadian Tour

MAY
30 Kitchener, Ontario

JUNE
2   Entex, Mississauga
7   California's, Windsor
10 Oshawa, Ontario
11 Rock 'n' Roll Heaven, Toronto

Hunter Ronson 1988 US Tour

SEPTEMBER
27 Entex, Mississauga
29 The Forge, Victoria
30 86th Street, Vancouver

OCTOBER
1   99 Club, Seattle
2   Starry Nights, Portland
4   Oasis, San Jose, California
5   Oasis, San Francisco, California
6   New George's, San Rafael, California
7   The Palace, Hollywood, California
8   Deanza Theatre, Riverside, California

9   Terrace Theatre, Ventura, California
10 Bogart's, Long Beach, California
11 Coach House, San Juan Capistrano
12 Bacchanal, San Diego
13 San Juan Capistrano, California
14 Tucson Gardens, Tucson, Phoenix
16 Tommie's, Dallas
17 The Backdoor, Austin
18 Vogue Theatre, Indiana
19 Rockefeller's, Houston
20 Tipitina's, New Orleans
21 W C Don's, Jackson
22 Metroplex, Atlanta
23 Old Post Office, Hilton Head, SC
25 Sweeney's, Orlando
27 Summers, Fort Lauderdale
28 The Pier, Tampa
29 The Moon, Tallahassee
30 Gulf Shores, Margaritaville
31 Gainsville University, Memphis (Screaming Blue
    Messiahs)

NOVEMBER
1   The Cannery, Nashville
2   Winston Salem
3   Goldsboro, NC
4   Peppermint Beach Club, Virginia
5   The Chance, Poughkeepsie, NY
6   Baltimore, MD
8   Bayou, Washington
9   Chestnut Cabaret, Philadelphia
10 Morgan, New Jersey
11 Sundance, Bayshore, Long Island (Eddie Havoc
    Group)
12 The Channel, Boston
13 The Living Room, Providence, RI
14 City Gardens, Trenton, New Jersey (Aviator)
15 Albany, New York
16 The Ritz, New York
17 Rochester, New York
18 Asbury Park, New Jersey
19 Graffiti, Oakland, Pittsburgh
20 Bogart's, Cincinnati, Ohio
21 Kent, Ohio
22 Newport Music Hall, Columbus
23 Royal Oak Music Theatre, Detroit (The Jack
    Bruce Band)
25 Agora Metropolitan Theatre, Cleveland (The Jack
    Bruce Band)
26 Riviera Theatre, Chicago
27 Westport Playhouse, St Louis
28 First Avenue, Minneapolis
30 Indianapolis

DECEMBER
1   Club Soda, Kalamazoo
2   Uptown Theatre, Kansas City
3   Hartford, Connecticut
4   Phoenix Hill, Louisville, KY

1989

Hunter Ronson European Tour
JANUARY
26 Maxime, Bergen, Norway
29 Sardines, Oslo

FEBRUARY
2   Melody, Stockholm
7   Frankfurt Music Hall
8   Hamburg Grosse Freiheit
9   Cologne Alter Wartesaal
15 Dominion Theatre London (Dogs D'Amour)

16 Dominion Theatre London (Dogs D'Amour)
    Amsterdam (Dogs D'Amour)

Hunter Ronson 'American Music' US Tour
NOVEMBER
1   The Cannery, Nashville (The Bulletboys)
2   The Ritz, Roseville
3   The Ritz, Indianapolis
4   Music Hall, Cleveland
5   Newport Music Hall, Columbus
7   Grafitti's, Pittsburg
8   Chestnut Cabaret, Philadelphia
11 The Channel, Boston
12 The Ritz, New York
17 Living Room, Providence, RI
21 Club Soda, Montreal
27 Greenstreets, South Carolina
29 Mississippi Nights, St Louis

DECEMBER
5   Jimmy's, New Orleans
10 Anderson's Fifth Estate, Scottsdale, Arizona
13 Hollywood Palace, Los Angeles
15 San Jose, California
16 Cabaret, San Jose, California
17 Forge, Victoria
18 Vancouver

1990

Hunter Ronson 'American Music' European Tour
JANUARY
18 Maxime, Bergen
19 Student Centre, Trondheim
20 Rockefeller, Oslo
21 Rockefeller, Oslo
22 Melody, Stockholm
23 Melody, Stockholm
24 Tavastia, Helsinki
25 Tavastia, Helsinki
26 Nya Vagen, Gothenburg
27 Majeriet, Lund
29 Stakladen, Arhus
30 Pumpehuset, Copenhagen

FEBRUARY
1   Watesaal, Cologne
2   Schlachthuf, Bremen
4   Ghent
5   Elysees Montmartre, Paris
7   Nachtwerk, Munich
8   Music Hall, Frankfurt
9   Grosse Freiheit, Hamburg

13 Nottingham Rock City (Shy)
14 Manchester International 2 (Shy)
15 Sheffield Octagon (Shy)
16 Hammersmith Odeon London (Shy)
18 Norwich UEA (Shy)
19 Folkestone Leas Cliff Hall (Shy)
20 Worthing Assembly Halls (Shy)

1991

Hunter Ronson 'Parkrock' Swedish Tour
MAY
18 Laholm
19 Olofstrom
23 Sundsvall
24 Umea
25 Lulea
28 Stromsborg Park, Stockholm

29 Stockholm Galaxy
31 Grangesberg

JUNE
1 Avesta
5 Vasteras
7 Rockefellers, Oslo
8 Stromstad
12 Eskilstuna
14 Sandviken
15 Hultsfred
16 Vanersborg
20 Smogen
21 Ahus
22 Marstrand

1992

APRIL
20 Freddie Mercury Memorial Concert, Wembley
    Stadium, London

*Ian Hunter Swedish Tour (3, 4, 5 & 6 July, with Mats
Ronander Band – all other dates Hunter backed by The
Few)*

JUNE
23 Tylosand
24 Tylosand
25 Tylosand
26 Tylosand
27 Tylosand

JULY
3 Mariehamn
4 Skara
5 Stockholm
6 Borgholm
7 Visby
10 Vaxjo
14 Sveg
15 Pitea
16 Ornskoldsvik
17 Skelleftea
18 Ostersund
22 Eskilstuna
23 Kungshamn
24 Helsingborg
25 Akersberga (with Mats Ronander)
27 Stromstad
28 Gothenburg
29 Vanersborg
31 Stenungsund

AUGUST
1 Sandviken

1993

AUGUST
Ian Hunter European Tour (Ian Hunter & The Yobs)
8 Melody, Stockholm
12 Leeds Irish Centre (Sarajevo)
13 The Forum London (Sarajevo)
14 Robin Hood Club, Dudley (Sarajevo)

1994

APRIL
29 Mick Ronson Memorial Concert, Hammersmith
    Apollo, London

1997

APRIL
29 Amsterdam Milky Way, Holland

30 Nidrum Twilight Cafe, Belgium

MAY
3 Burnley Mechanics
4 Buxton Opera House – Alexis Korner Memorial
6 Cambridge Junction
7 Norwich Waterfront
8 Felixstowe Spa Pavilion
9 Folkestone Lees Cliff Halls
10 Market Harboro Willbaston Hall
13 Southampton The Brook
14 London Shepherd's Bush Empire
15 Leeds Irish Centre
16 South Shields Cellar Club
17 Dudley Robin Hood
18 Swindon Wyvern Theatre
20 Bristol Beirkellar
21 Liverpool Irish Centre
22 Barry Powerhouse
23 Oxford Zodiac Club
24 Plymouth Cooperage
25 Brighton Paradox – Cancelled
26 Reading Alley Cat
28 Manchester Jillys
29 South Shields Cellar Club
30 Glasgow Cat House
31 Edinburgh Venue

JUNE
1 Stoke Wheatsheaf
2 Kenmare, Ireland – Cancelled
2 Kerry, Ireland
3 Roisin Dubh, Galway, Ireland
4 Gothenburg, Sweden – Cancelled
4 Whelan's, Dublin, Ireland
5 Malmo, Sweden – Cancelled
5 The Old Oak, Cork, Ireland
6 TBC, Sweden – Cancelled
7 Skara, Sweden – Cancelled
7 Belfast, Ireland – Cancelled

AUGUST
9 The Hull Arena: Mick Ronson Memorial II
10 Queens Gardens, Hull: Mick Ronson Memorial
    Stage

SEPTEMBER
6 Nottingham Running Horse
7 Glasgow Pavilion
8 Alexanders, Chester
9 Rhyl New Pavilion
10 Martell, Falkirk
12 Salisbury Arts Centre
17 South Shields Customs House
18 Tunbridge Wells Assembly Hall
24 The Room, Hull
25 Sheffield Boardwalk
26 Cannock Prince of Wales Theatre
28 Hastings White Rock Theatre
30 Haslingden Public Hall

OCTOBER
1 Fibbers, York
2 Cleethorpes Winter Garden
3 Lucky Break, Bury St Edmunds
4 Liscombe Park Complex, Soulbury – Cancelled
5 Croydon Fairfield Halls
6 Dartford Orchard Theatre – Cancelled
9 Rayners Lane Cine Centre, London
10 Dudley Robin Hood
11 Liverpool – Cancelled
12 Stoke Wheatsheaf
16 Galway – Cancelled
17 Mean Fiddler, Dublin – Cancelled

19 Derry Rialto Centre – Cancelled

NOVEMBER
 7 Fabrik, Hamburg, Germany
 9 Hirsch, Nuremburg, Germany
10 Fernverkehr, Hoff, Germany
11 Rock Haus, Vienna, Austria
13 Frederica Theater, Frederica, Denmark

14 Pumpehuset, Copenhagen, Denmark
15 Henrik's Bar, Gothenburg, Sweden
16 Fredmans, Uppsala, Sweden
18 Colos Saal, Aschaffenburg, Germany
19 Mors, Norrkoping, Sweden
20 K B Club, Malmo, Sweden
21 Quasimodo, Berlin, Germany

Also available from

CHERRY RED BOOKS / THE RED OAK PRESS

Indie Hits 1980–1989
The Complete UK Independent Charts
(Singles & Albums)
Compiled by Barry Lazell

Indie Hits is the ultimate reference book for alternative music enthusiasts. Indie Hits is the first and only complete guide to the first decade of Britain's Independent records chart, and to the acts, the music and the labels which made up the Indie scene of the 1980s. The book is set out in a similar format to the *Guinness Hit Singles* and *Albums* books, with every artist, single and album to have shown in the indie charts over the 10-year period being detailed. The first Independent charts were published by the trade paper *Record Business* in January 1980, by which time they were well overdue. By that time, Mute Graduate, Factory, Crass, Safari and Rough Trade were just a few of the new breed of rapidly expanding labels already scoring hit records. They were producing acts like Depeche Mode, UB40, Toyah, The Cult, Joy Division and Stiff Little Fingers, all to become major international sellers. Later years brought the likes of the Smiths, New Order, Erasure, The Stone Roses, James, The Fall and Happy Mondays (not to mention Kylie and Jason!) – all successful and influential independently distributed hitmakers. The A–Z section details every chartmaking 1980s indie act and all hit records in a detailed but easy-to-reference format. Also included are complete indexes of single and album titles, an authoritative history of the origin and development of the Indie charts during the 1980's, listings of all No 1 singles and albums with illustrations of rare original sleeves, print ads and other memorabilia of the period plus a fax 'n' trivia section including the artists and labels with the most chart records, the most No. 1s and the longest chart stays. If it was in the indie charts of the 1980s, it's in here!

Paper covers, 314 pages, £14.95 in UK

Also available from

CHERRY RED BOOKS / THE RED OAK PRESS

Cor Baby, That's Really Me!
(New Millennium Hardback Edition)
John Otway

Time was when John Otway looked forward to platinum albums, stadium gigs and a squad of bodyguards to see him safely aboard his private jet. Unfortunately it didn't happen that way. A series of dreadful career decisions, financial blunders and bad records left Otway down but not out. This is his true story in his own words. It is the story of a man who ...

- has never repaid a record company advance in his life
- once put on a benefit concert for his record company after they had cancelled his contract
- signed himself to the mighty Warner Bros label simply by pressing his own records with the WB logo
- broke up with Paula Yates telling her it was the last chance she would get to go out with a rock star

This book is Otway's hilarious yet moving account of his insane assault on the music industry, a tale of blind ambition and rank incompetence, and a salutary lesson for aspiring musicians on how not to achieve greatness. But if the John Otway story is one of failure, it is failure on a grand scale. And it makes compulsive reading too!

Hardback, 192 pages and 16 pages of photographs: £11.99 in UK

CHERRY RED BOOKS / THE RED OAK PRESS

We are always looking for any interesting book projects
to get involved in. If you have any good ideas, or indeed manuscripts,
for books that you feel deserve publication, then please
get in touch with us.

CHERRY RED BOOKS
a division of Cherry Red Records Ltd
Unit 17, Elysium Gate West,
126–8 New King's Road
London sw6 3jh

E-mail: infonet@cred.demon.co.uk
Web: http://www.cherryred.co.uk

The companion CD

Mott The Hoople:
All the Young Dudes –The Anthology
3-CD Boxed Set on Columbia records, catalogue No. 4914002

The definitive 3-CD retrospective of one of the most important
bands of the late 60s and early 70s. This DigiPak 'longbox' set is a
collectors' dream. It features 62 superb songs, including 37 previously
unreleased tracks or versions, and all the UK hits. The band's career on
Columbia and Island is covered, plus earlier and later incarnations of
Mott The Hoople.

Amongst the gems that have been unearthed from the vaults are a
David Bowie vocal version of '**All the Young Dudes**' and the sought-
after rarities 'Like a Rolling Stone', 'The Hunchback Fish' and 'Ohio'.

Every track has been remastered by Dale Griffin and Ray Staff, creating
a sound quality that is simply astounding.

The 56-page colour booklet features numerous previously unseen
photos, track-by-track notes, a discography and chronology, and quotes
from and about the band.

This is the *ultimate* Mott The Hoople collection,
the perfect companion to this book.

TRACK LISTING

CD1: The Twilight of Pain through Doubt
1   Like a Rolling Stone (impromptu jam)
2   Rock and Roll Queen
3   You Really Got Me (original mix)
4   Wrath 'n' Wroll
5   Find Your Way
6   Moonbus (1998 mix)
7   It Would Be a Pleasure (demo)
8   Ohio (live) (1998 mix)
9   Midnight Lady
10 The Debt
11 Downtown (1998 mix)
12 Long Red (1998 mix)
13 It'll Be Me (1998 mix)
14 Until I'm Gone (1998 mix)
15 One of the Boys (1998 mix)
16 The Journey (alternative version, 1998 mix)
17 Mental Train (1998 mix)
18 How Long? (1998 mix)
19 Ride on the Sun (1998 mix)
20 Movin' On (1998 mix)
21 The Hunchback Fish

continued overleaf

CD2: Temptations of the Flash

1 All the Young Dudes
2 One of the Boys
3 Sweet Jane
4 Ready For Love
5 Honaloochie Boogie
6 The Ballad of Mott The Hoople
7 I Wish I Was Your Mother (1998 mix)
8 I'm a Cadillac
9 All the Way from Memphis
10 Hymn for the Dudes
11 Violence
12 Roll Away The Stone
13 Crash Street Kidds
14 Marionette
15 The Golden Age of Rock 'n' Roll
16 Rest in Peace
17 Born Late '58
18 Foxy Foxy
19 (Do You Remember) The Saturday Gigs?

CD3: Blistered Psalms

1 All the Young Dudes (David Bowie Vocal)
2 It's Goodbye
3 Just Can't Go to Sleep
4 Transparent Day
5 Shakin' All Over
6 Please Don't Touch
7 So Sad
8 Honaloochie Boogie (demo)
9 Hymn for the Dudes (demo)
10 Nightmare (demo, 1998 mix)
11 The Saturday Kids
12 Lounge Lizard
13 Shout It All Out
14 It Don't Come Easy
15 Barking Up the Wrong Tree (1998 mix)
16 Too Short Arms (I Don't Care)
17 Get Rich Quick
18 International Heroes
19 American Pie / The Golden Age of Rock and Roll
20 Roll Away the Stone / Sweet Jane (live, 1998 mix)
21 Rock and Roll Queen (live, 1998 mix)
22 Blowing in the Wind (live, 1998 mix)

Sony Music Entertainment (UK) Ltd

are the exclusive licensees for this compilation